THE AMERICAN REVOLUTION

THE AMERICAN REVOLUTION

Writings from the War of Independence

THE LIBRARY OF AMERICA

Distributed to the trade
in the United States by Penguin Putnam Inc.
and in Canada by Penguin Books Canada Ltd.

Library of Congress Catalog Number: 00—045373
For cataloging information, see end of Index.
ISBN 1–883011–91–4

First Printing
The Library of America—123

Manufactured in the United States of America

JOHN RHODEHAMEL
SELECTED THE CONTENTS AND WROTE THE NOTES
FOR THIS VOLUME

Contents

THE AMERICAN REVOLUTION

Paul Revere: Memorandum on Events of April 18, 1775

PAUL REVERE of Boston, in the Colony of Massachusetts Bay in New England; of Lawfull Age, doth testify and say, that I was sent for by Docr Joseph Warren, of said Boston, on the evening of the 18th of April, about 10 oClock; when he desired me "to go to Lexington, and inform Mr Samuel Adams, and the Honle John Hancock Esqr that there was a number of Soldiers, composed of Light troops, & Grenadiers, marching to the bottom of the Common, where was a number of Boats to receive them; it was supposed, that they were going to Lexington, by the way of Cambridge River, to take *them* or go to Concord, to distroy the Colony Stores." I proceeded immediately, and was put across Charles River, and landed near Charlestown Battery, went in town, and there got a Horse. while in Charlestown, I was informed by Richd Devens Esqr that he mett that evening, after Sun sett, Nine Officers of the Ministeral Army, mounted on good Horses, & Armed, going towards Concord; I set off, it was then about 11 oClock, the Moon shone bright. I had got almost over Charlestown Common, towards Cambridge, when I saw two Officers on Horseback, standing under the shade of a Tree, in a narrow part of the roade. I was near enough to see their Holsters, & cockades. One of them Started his horse towards me, the other up the road, as I supposed, to head me should I escape the first. I turned my horse short about, and rid upon a full Gallop for Mistick Road, he followed me about 300 yardes, and finding he could not catch me, returned. I proceeded to Lexington, thro Mistick, and alarmed Mr Adams & Col. Hancock. After I had been there about half an hour Mr Daws arrived, who came from Boston, over the neck; we set off for Concord, & were overtaken by a young Gentn named Prescot, who belonged to Concord, & was going home; when we had got about half way from Lexington to Concord, the other two, stopped at a House to awake the man, I kept

along. When I had got about 200 Yards ahead of them, I saw
two officers as before. I called to my company to come up,
saying here was two of them, (for I had told them what Mr
Devens told me, and of my being stoped) in an instant, I saw
four of them, who rode up to me, with their pistols in their
hands, said G—d d—n you stop, if you go an Inch further,
you are a dead Man. immeditly Mr. Prescot came up we attempted to git thro them, but they kept before us, and swore
if we did not turn in to that pasture, they would blow our
brains out, (they had placed themselves opposite to a pair of
Barrs, and had taken the Barrs down) they forced us in, when
we had got in, Mr Prescot said put on. He took to the left, I
to the right, towards a Wood, at the bottom of the Pasture,
intending, when I gained that, to jump my Horse & run
afoot; just as I reached it, out started six officers, siesed my
bridle, put their pistols to my Breast, ordered me to dismount, which I did. One of them, who appeared to have the
command there, and much of a Gentleman, asked me where
I came from; I told him, he asked what time I left it; I told
him, he seemed surprised, said Sr, may I crave your name. I
answered my name is Revere, what said he, Paul Revere; I answered yes; the others abused me much; but he told me not
to be afraid, no one should hurt me. I told him they would
miss their Aim. He said they should not, they were only waiting for some Deserters they expected down the Road. I told
him I knew better, I knew what they were after; that I had
alarmed the country all the way up, that their Boats were
catch'd aground, and I should have 500 men there soon; one
of them said they had 1500 coming; he seemed surprised and
rode off into the road, and informed them who took me, they
came down immeditly on a full gallop, one of them (whom I
since learned, was Major Mitchel of the 5th Regt) clapd his
Pistol to my head, and said he was going to ask me some
questions, if I did not tell the truth, he would blow my brains
out. I told him I esteemed myself a man of truth, that he had
stopped me on the highway, & made me a prisoner, I knew
not by what right; I would tell him the truth; I was not afraid.
He then asked me the same questions that the other did, and
many more, but was more particular; I gave him much the
same answers; he then ordered me to mount my horse, they

first searched me for pistols. When I was mounted, the Major took the reins out of my hand, and said, by G—d Sr, you are not to ride with reins I assure you; and gave them to an officer on my right to lead me. he then Ordered 4 men out of the Bushes, and to mount their horses; they were country men which they had stopped who were going home; then ordered us to march. He said to me "We are now going towards your friends, and if you attempt to run, or we are insulted, we will blow your Brains out." When we had got into the road they formed a circle and ordered the prisoners in the centre & to lead me in the front.

We rid towards Lexington, a quick pace; they very often insulted me calling me Rebel, &c &c. after we had got about a mile, I was given to the Sergant to lead, he was Ordered to take out his pistol (he rode with a hanger) and if I run, to execute the Major's sentence; When we got within about half a Mile of the Meeting house, we heard a gun fired; the Major asked me what it was for, I told him to alarm the country; he Ordered the four prisoners to dismount, they did, then one of the officers dismounted and cutt the Bridles, and Saddels, off the Horses, & drove them away, and told the men they might go about their business; I asked the Major to dismiss me, he said he would carry me, lett the consequence be what it will; He then Orderd us to march; when we got within sight of the Meeting House, we heard a Volley of guns fired, as I supposed at the tavern, as an Alarm; the Major ordered us to halt. he asked me how far it was to Cambridge, and many more questions, which I answered; he then asked the Sergant, if his horse was tired, he said yes; he Ordered him to take my horse; I dismounted, the Sarjant mounted my horse; they cutt the Bridle & saddle off the Sarjant's horse & rode off down the road. I then went to the house where I left Mess Adams & Hancock, and told them what had happined; their friends advised them to go out of the way: I went with them, about two miles a cross road; after resting myself, I sett off with another man to go back to the Tavern, to enquire the News; when we got there, we were told the troops were within two miles. We went into the Tavern to git a Trunk of papers belonging to Col. Hancock, before we left the House, I saw the Ministeral Troops from the Chamber window. We made haste

& had to pass thro' our Militia, who were on a green behind the Meeting house, to the number as I supposed, about 50 or 60. I went thro' them; as I passed I heard the commanding officer speake to his men to this purpose. "Lett the troops pass by, & don't molest them, without they begin first" I had to go a cross Road, but had not got half Gun shot off when the Ministeral Troops appeared in sight behinde the Meeting House; they made a short halt, when a gun was fired. I heard the report, turned my head, and saw the smoake in front of the Troops, they imeaditly gave a great shout, ran a few paces, and then the whole fired. I could first distinguish Iregular fireing, which I suppose was the advance Guard, and then platoons. At the time I could not see our Militia, for they were covered from me, by a house at the bottom of the Street. and further saith not.

Frederick MacKenzie:
Diary, April 18–21, 1775

18th April 1775.   An order was received this afternoon before 6 o'Clock, signifying the Commander in Chief's pleasure that the suspension ordered Lt Colo Walcott of the 5th Regt shall be taken off, from this day inclusive. — It also stated, that it has appeared throughout the course of the trial of Lt Colo Walcott, and Ensign Patrick, that the said Ensign Patrick did behave disrespectfully to his Commanding Officer, but it not being inserted in his Crime, the Court did not proceed upon it, and Lt Colo Walcott now excuses it, and will not bring it to a trial; but the Comr in Chief thinks proper to warn Ensign Patrick, that he behaves with more respect for the future to his Commanding Officer.

   At 8 this night the Commanding Officers of Regiments were sent for to Headquarters, and ordered to have their respective Grenadier and Light Infantry Companies on the beach near the Magazine Guard exactly at 10 oClock this night, with one day's provisions in their Havresacks, and without knapsacks. — They were directed to order their Companies to parade quietly at their respective Barracks, and to march to the place of Rendezvous in small parties, and if Challenged to answer *"Patrole."* — The Companies of our Regiment (the 23rd) marched accordingly, and were the first, complete, at the place of parade; Here we found a number of the Men of War's and Transports boats in waiting. — As there was no public Officer attending to superintend the Embarkation, which it was evident would take up a good deal of time, our two Companies, with the approbation of the Officers of the Navy, embarked in the nearest boats, and pushed off a little way from the shore. As the other Companies arrived soon after, as many men embarked as the boats would contain. By this time Lieut Colo Smith of the 10th, who was to have the Command, arrived, and with him Major Pitcairn of the Marines. The boats then put off, and rowed towards Phipps's farm, where having landed the troops they returned for the remainder and landed them at the same place. This was not completed untill 12 o'Clock.

The Companies embarked are,

Grenadiers — 4th, 5th, 10th, 18th, 23rd, 38th, 43rd,
    47th, 59th Regts. 1st & 2ed Marines.
Light Infantry — 4th, 5th, 10th, 23rd, 38th, 43rd, 47th,
    59th, & 1st & 2ed Marines.

Lt Colo Smith, & Major Pitcairn are the two Field Officers first for duty, and the Senior of each rank.

The town was a good deal agitated and alarmed at this Movement, as it was pretty generally known, by means of the Seamen who came on shore from the Ships, about 2 o'Clock, that the boats were ordered to be in readiness.

19th April.   At 7 o'Clock this morning a Brigade order was received by our Regiment, dated at 6 o'Clock, for the 1st Brigade to assemble at 1/2 past 7 on the Grand parade. We accordingly assembled the Regiment with the utmost expedition, and with the 4th, and 47th were on the parade at the hour appointed, with one days provisions. By some mistake the Marines did not receive the order until the other Regiments of the Brigade were assembled, by which means it was half past 8 o'Clock before the brigade was ready to march. Here we understood that we were to march out of town to support the troops that went out last night. A quarter before 9, we marched in the following order, Advanced Guard, of a Captain and 50 men; 2 Six pounders, 4th Regt, 47th Regiment, 1st Battn of Marines, 23ed Regt, or Royal Welch Fusiliers, Rear Guard, of a Captain & 50 men. The whole under the Command of Brigadier General Earl Percy. We went out of Boston by the Neck, and marched thro' Roxbury, Cambridge and Menotomy, towards Lexington. In all the places we marched through, and in the houses on the road, few or no people were to be seen; and the houses were in general shut up. When we arrived near Lexington, some persons who came from Concord, informed that the Grenadiers & Light Infantry were at that place, and that some persons had been killed and wounded by them early in the morning at Lexington. As we pursued our march, about 2 o'Clock we heard some straggling shots fired about a mile in our front: — As we advanced we heard the firing plainer and more frequent, and at half after 2, being near the Church at Lexington, and the fire encreasing, we were ordered to form the Line, which was immediately done by extending on each side of the road, but by reason of the Stone walls and other obstructions, it was not formed in so regular a manner as it should have been. The Grenadiers & Light Infantry were at this time retiring towards Lexington, fired upon by the Rebels, who took every advantage the face of the Country afforded them. As soon as The Grenadiers & Light Infantry perceived the 1st Brigade drawn up for their support, they shouted repeatedly, and the firing ceased for a short time.

The ground we first formed upon was something elevated, and commanded a view of that before us for about a mile, where it was terminated by some pretty high grounds covered with wood. The Village of Lexington lay between both parties. We could observe a Considerable number of the Rebels, but they were much scattered, and not above 50 of them to be seen in a body in any place. Many lay concealed behind the Stone walls and fences. They appeared most numerous in the road near the Church, and in a wood in the front, and on the left flank of the line where our Regiment was posted. A few Cannon Shot were fired at those on, and near the road, which dispersed them. The flank Companies now retired and formed behind the brigade, which was soon fired upon by the Rebels most advanced. A brisk fire was returned, but without much effect. As there was a piece of open Morassy ground in front of the left of our Regiment, it would have been difficult to have passed it under the fire of the Rebels from behind the trees and walls on the other side. Indeed no part of the brigade was ordered to advance; we therefore drew up near the Morass, in expectation of orders how to act, sending an Officer for one of the 6 pounders. During this time the Rebels endeavored to gain our flanks, and crept into the covered ground on either side, and as close as they could in front, firing now and then in perfect security. We also advanced a few of our best marksmen who fired at those who shewed themselves. About 1/4 past 3, Earl Percy having come to a resolution of returning to Boston, and having made his

disposition for that purpose, our Regiment received orders to
form the Rear Guard. We immediately lined the Walls and
other Cover in our front with some Marksmen, and retired
from the right of Companies by files to the high ground a
Small distance in our rear, where we again formed in line, and
remained in that position for near half an hour, during which
time the flank Companies, and the other Regiments of the
Brigade, began their march in one Column on the road towards Cambridge. As the Country for many miles round
Boston and in the Neighbourhood of Lexington & Concord,
had by this time had notice of what was doing, as well by the
firing, as from expresses which had been from Boston and the
adjacent places in all directions, numbers of armed men on
foot and on horseback, were continually coming from all
parts guided by the fire, and before the Column had advanced a mile on the road, we were fired at from all quarters,
but particularly from the houses on the roadside, and the
Adjacent Stone walls. Several of the Troops were killed and
wounded in this way, and the Soldiers were so enraged at suffering from an unseen Enemy, that they forced open many of
the houses from which the fire proceeded, and put to death
all those found in them. Those houses would certainly have
been burnt had any fire been found in them, or had there
been time to kindle any; but only three or four near where we
first formed suffered in this way. As the Troops drew nearer to
Cambridge the number and fire of the Rebels encreased, and
altho they did not shew themselves openly in a body in any
part, except on the road in our rear, our men threw away
their fire very inconsiderately, and without being certain of its
effect: this emboldened them, and induced them to draw
nearer, but whenever a Cannon shot was fired at any considerable number, they instantly dispersed. Our Regiment having
formed the Rear Guard for near 7 miles, and expended a great
part of its ammunition, was then relieved by the Marines
which was the next Battalion in the Column.

Lord Percy, judging that the returning to Boston by way of
Cambridge, (where there was a bridge over Charles river,
which might either be broken down, or required to be
forced) and Roxbury, might be attended with some difficulties and many inconveniences, took the resolution of re-

turning by way of Charlestown, which was the shortest road, and which could be defended against any number of the Rebels. Accordingly where the roads separate, the Column took that to the left, and passing over Charlestown Neck, drew up on the heights just above, and which Command it. This was about 7 oClock in the Evening. During the March, the Marines had been relieved in the duty of forming the rear guard by the 47th Regiment, and that Corps by the 4th. The Grenadiers and Light Infantry being exceedingly fatigued by their long march, kept at the head of the Column, where indeed, latterly, the fire was nearly as severe as in the rear. During the whole of the march from Lexington the Rebels kept an incessant irregular fire from all points at the Column, which was the more galling as our flanking parties, which at first were placed at sufficient distances to cover the march of it, were at last, from the different obstructions they occasionally met with, obliged to keep almost close to it. Our men had very few opportunities of getting good shots at the Rebels, as they hardly ever fired but under cover of a Stone wall, from behind a tree, or out of a house; and the moment they had fired they lay down out of sight until they had loaded again, or the Column had passed. In the road indeed in our rear, they were most numerous, and came on pretty close, frequently calling out, *"King Hancock forever."* Many of them were killed in the houses on the road side from whence they fired; in some of them 7 or 8 men were destroyed. Some houses were forced open in which no person could be discovered, but when the Column had passed, numbers sallied out from some place in which they had lain concealed, fired at the rear Guard, and augmented the numbers which followed us. If we had had time to set fire to those houses many Rebels must have perished in them, but as night drew on Lord Percy thought it best to continue the march. Many houses were plundered by the Soldiers, notwithstanding the efforts of the Officers to prevent it. I have no doubt this inflamed the Rebels, and made many of them follow us farther than they would otherwise have done. By all accounts some Soldiers who staid too long in the houses, were killed in the very act of plundering by those who lay concealed in them. We brought in about ten prisoners, some of whom were taken in arms. One or two more were killed on the march while prisoners by the fire of their own people.

Few or no Women or Children were to be seen throughout the day. As the Country had undoubted intelligence that some troops were to march out, and the Rebels were probably determined to attack them, it is generally supposed they had previously removed their families from the Neighbourhood.

As soon as the troops had passed Charlestown Neck the Rebels ceased firing. A Negro (the only one who was observed to fire at the Kings troops) was wounded near the houses close to the Neck, out of which the Rebels fired to the last.

When the troops had drawn up on the heights above Charlestown neck, and had remained there about half an hour, Lord Percy ordered the Grenadiers and Light Infantry to march down into Charlestown, they were followed by the brigade, which marched off by the right, the 4th Regiment leading, and the 23rd being in the rear. Boats being ready to receive them, the wounded men were first embarked, then the flank Companies, the 4th & 47th. The boats returned with the Picquets of the 2nd, & 3rd brigades, the 10th Regiment, and 200 of the 64th who had been brought up from Castle William. Those troops were under the Command of Brigadier General Pigot, and were ordered to take possession of Charlestown, and the heights Commanding the Neck. As these movements took up a considerable time, the 23rd, and Marines were ordered into the Town house. Here we remained for two hours, when the boats being ready, we marched out and embarked; but it was past 12 at night before the whole of our Regiment was landed at the North end, Boston, from whence we marched to our Barracks.

Lieut Rooke of the 4th Regiment, Aide-de-Camp to Genl Gage, marched out in the Morning with the first Brigade, and just as the firing began he was sent back by Lord Percy to inform the General of the situation of affairs; but as he was obliged to cross the Country and keep out of the road, in order to avoid the numerous parties of Rebels who were coming from all parts to join those who attacked us, he did not arrive in Boston, by way of Charlestown, 'till past 4 o'Clock.

*Return of the Killed, Wounded, & Missing
in the Action of the 19th April 1775.*

Corps.	Killed.	Wd.	Missing
4th	7 –	25 –	8
5th	5 –	15 –	1
10th	1 –	13 –	1
18th	1 –	4 –	1
23rd	4 –	26 –	6
38th	4 –	12 –	.
43rd	4 –	5 –	2
47th	5 –	22 –	.
52nd	3 –	2 –	1
59th	3 –	3 –	.
Marines	31 –	38 –	2
Artillery	. –	2 –	.
Total	68 –	167 –	22

Officers Not Included.

Regt	Names of Officers Wounded.	
4th	Lieut Knight	Died 20th Apl
–	Lieut Gould	In the Foot
5th	Lieut Tho: Baker	Hand
–	Lt Hawkshaw	Cheek
–	Lt Cox	Arm
10th	Lt Colo Smith	Leg
–	Capt Parsons	Arm.—Contusion
–	Lt Kelly	Arm
–	Ens. Lister	Arm
23rd	Lieut Colo Bernard	Thigh
38th	Lieut Sutherland	Breast. Slight
43rd	Lieut Hull	{ Body } Died { & 2 other places } 2d May
47th	Lt McLeod	Breast
–	Lt Baldwin	Throat
Marines.	Capt Souter	Leg
–	Lt McDonald	Slight
–	Lt Potter	Slight

*Return of the Rank & file of the Royal Welch Fusiliers under arms in
the Action at Lexington. 19th Apl. 1775.*

	Rank & file.
Grenadier Company	29
Light Infantry Company	35
Eight Battalion Companies	218
Total	282

Lord Percy behaved with great spirit throughout this affair, and at the same time with great coolness. His determination to return by way of Charlestown prevented the loss of many men.

The loss of The King's Troops is stated on the opposite page. It is almost impossible to ascertain the loss of the Rebels, but in the opinion of most persons, they must have lost above 300 men, most of whom were killed. It is extremely difficult to say what number of men they had opposed to us, as their numbers were continually encreasing; but I imagine there was not less than 4000 actually assembled towards the latter part of the day.

The whole of The Kings troops did not exceed 1500 men.

The following is another Account of the Action of the 19th of April, by an Officer of one of the Flank Companies.

The Grenadier & Light Companies of the Regiments in Boston were ordered to assemble on the Beach near the Magazine at 10 o'Clock last night. The whole was not assembled 'till near 11; and as there were not boats enough to embark them at once, as many as they could contain were embarked, and landed at Phipps's farm. The boats then returned for the remainder, and it was near One oClock in the Morning before the whole were landed on the opposite shore. Two days provisions which had been dressed on board the Transports, were distributed to the troops, at Phipps's farm, which detained them near an hour; so that it was 2 oClock before they marched off. Their march across the marshes into the high road, was hasty and fatiguing, and they were obliged to wade, halfway up their thighs, through two Inlets, the tide being by that time, up. This should have been avoided if possible, as the troops had a long march to perform. In order to make up for the time they had lost, the Commanding Officer marched at a great rate, 'till they reached Lexington, where, about daybreak, they found a body of Rebels, amounting to about 100 men, drawn up, under arms. They were hastily called to, to disperse. Shots were immediately fired; but from which side could not be ascertained, each party imputing it to the other. Our troops immediately rushed forward, and the Rebels were dispersed, 8 of them killed, and several wounded.

One Soldier was wounded, and Major Pitcairn's horse was wounded.

Colo Smith was not then in front, owing to the troops marching so fast, and his being a heavy man.

When the firing had ceased, and the troops were put in order, several of the Officers advised Colo Smith to give up the idea of prosecuting his march, and to return to Boston, as from what they had seen, and the certainty of the Country being alarmed and assembling, they imagined it would be impracticable to advance to Concord and execute their orders. But Colo Smith determined to obey the orders he had received, and accordingly pursued his march, and arrived at Concord without further interruption. Soon after leaving Lexington, he was met by Major Mitchel of the 5th Regt, and some other Officers, who had been sent out from Boston on Horseback the Evening before towards Concord, with directions to stop all persons going that way in the night with intelligence. These Officers had been informed that Colo Smith would meet them within a few miles of Concord at day break. From the place where Major Mitchel met the troops, an Officer was dispatched to inform Genl Gage of the situation of affairs. It was 10 o'Clock before the troops arrived at Concord. Colo Smith was here informed that at some distance from the town there were two bridges, which it was necessary to secure, in order to prevent the Rebels from interrupting the troops while they were destroying those Military Stores at Concord, which it was the object of the Expedition to effect; Accordingly three Companies of Light Infantry were detached to the bridge on the right, which proved to be 3 miles distant; and 3 Companies to that on the left. The houses at Concord were now searched, and some pieces of Cannon, Carriage-wheels, Ammunition, & flour, found. The Trunnions of the Guns were knocked off, the wheels broken, & the ammunition destroyed. During this time the Rebels were assembling in considerable numbers opposite the bridges, and at other places, but did not attempt to fire on the detached Companies, altho they drew up within shot of them. As soon as the Stores were destroyed, orders were sent to the detached Companies to return; at one of the bridges they retired in a confused manner, and some shots were exchanged by which two of the Light Infantry were wounded. The whole being re-assembled at Concord about 12 oClock, they began their march back towards Lexington. The Rebels now appeared in considerable numbers, drawn up in a regular manner, keeping principally on the high grounds, firing occasionally on the troops, but never attempting to make any regular or serious attack. As soon as they found the troops had got into a Column of march, they grew bolder, extended themselves on the flanks and rear of the Column, and fired briskly from behind any thing which afforded them shelter. The Troops returned their fire, but with too much eagerness, so that at first most of it was thrown away for want of that coolness and Steadiness which distinguishes troops who have been inured to service. The contempt in which they held the Rebels, and perhaps their opinion that they would be sufficiently intimidated by a brisk fire, occasioned this improper conduct; which the Officers did not prevent as they should have done. A good deal of this unsteady conduct may be attributed to the sudden and unexpected commencement of hostilities, and the too great eagerness of the Soldiers in the first Action of a War. Most of them were young Soldiers who had never been in Action, and had been taught that every thing was to be effected by a quick firing. This ineffectual fire gave the Rebels more confidence, as they soon found that notwithstanding there was so much, they suffered but little from it. During the march to Lexington the numbers of the Rebels encreased, and the fire became more serious; several men were killed, and some Officers, and many men wounded. Colo Smith was wounded in the leg, but walked on to Lexington. The arrival of Lord Percy, with the 1st brigade and 2 6-pounders, who joined Colo Smith's detachment about 1/2 past 2 oClock at Lexington, checked the Rebels, who remained on the eminences near, and were a good deal alarmed at some Cannonshot which were fired at them.

The troops now drew up on the high grounds on the Boston side of Lexington; and the Grenadiers and Light Infantry assembled in the rear of the brigade and were put in order. Soon after which, Lord Percy gave orders for the whole to begin their march towards Boston. Colo Smith's detachment marched in front, as they were a good deal fatigued, and had expended most of their ammunition. Flanking parties were sent out, and the Welch Fusiliers ordered to form the rear Guard. As soon as the rear Guard began to move, the Rebels commenced their fire, having previously crept round under cover, and gained the walls and hedges on both flanks. The firing continued without intermission, from Lexington, until the troops passed over Charlestown Neck. Those Rebels who came in from the flanks during the march, always posted themselves in the houses and behind the walls by the road-side, and there waited the approach of the Column, when they fired at it. Numbers of them were mounted, and when they had fastened their horses at some little distance from the road, they crept down near enough to have a Shot; as soon as the Column had passed, they mounted again, and rode round until they got ahead of the Column, and found some convenient place from whence they might fire again. These fellows were generally good marksmen, and many of them used long guns made for Duck-Shooting.

The troops drew up on Charlestown heights about dusk; soon after which some of the Corps began to embark and passed over to Boston. The last Regiment did not get to their Barracks 'till past 12 at night. The 10th Regiment, and the Picquets of the 2ed & 3rd brigades, with a Detachment of the 64th Regiment, came over to Charlestown, took post on the heights, and placed their advanced posts at Charlestown Neck.

We brought off most of our Wounded men.

20th April.   During the absence of the troops yesterday, orders were given for all those in Boston to remain in their Barracks, ready to turn out with arms, ammunition, and provisions, the moment they are ordered. General Gage was not without some apprehensions that the Rebels might make some attempt upon the town while so considerable a part of the troops were in the Country.

As soon as the troops from Boston took post on Charlestown heights last night, they began to throw up a redoubt to command the Neck; it was in a good state of forwardness this morning, when Genl Gage, having determined to abandon Charlestown, gave orders for its being demolished, and the Troops to be withdrawn into Boston; which was done by 4 oClock in the afternoon.

Great numbers of the Rebels are in arms at Roxbury, and there has been no free communication with the Country this day.

It is conceived by many, that the expedition to Concord for the destruction of the Military Stores, which it was said were deposited there in considerable quantities, might have been conducted with greater secrecy, and been effected without the loss which ensued and, the consequences which must now inevitably follow. It had been usual for some of the troops, whenever the weather was favorable, to march several miles into the Country, and return in the Afternoon. The 38th & 52ed Regiments marched once to Watertown, which indeed occasioned some alarm, and Cannon were fired, bells rung, and expresses sent off, to give the alarm; but as they returned again the same Evening after refreshing their men, the people were eased of their fears, and there was no assemblage of any consequence. This mode might have been continued, still encreasing the number of troops, and going different roads, until the time intended for putting the design in execution; when the troops destined for that service, might have marched as far as Watertown, which is near 11 Miles on one of the roads to Concord, whence, after remaining 'till towards Evening to rest the men, instead of returning to Boston, they might have pursued their march to Concord, where they would have arrived & effected their purpose before the Country could possibly have been sufficiently alarmed to have assembled in any numbers, either to prevent them, or molest them in their return to Boston. For greater security a brigade might have marched by different roads from Boston at daybreak, which would have prevented the Rebels assembling in one point, and have secured the return of the troops without any material loss. But as it was, it was known early in the day, the 18th, that provisions were dressing on board the transports for a body of troops, that the boats were ordered to be on the beach near the Common at night, and that several Officers had gone out towards Concord in the afternoon. As the people in Boston were constantly on the watch, these indications of some enterprize, were sufficient; accordingly expresses were sent out early in the Evening, and the whole Country was soon alarmed. It was not until 10 at night that orders were sent to The Lines to prevent any person from going out there. There is no doubt but the Country had information of the movement of the troops, as a Company was found under arms at Lexington at daybreak.

There was a general Muster of all the Neighbouring Militia only the day before, (whether by accident, or in consequence of information of the General's intention is not certain; but most probable the latter) so that every man was in a state of preparation and equipment. This should have been known, because, if their meeting was not on purpose to oppose the troops, there was hardly time for them to disperse and return to their several homes. I believe the fact is, that General Gage was not only much deceived with respect to the quantity of the Military Stores said to be collected at Concord, but had no conception the Rebels would have opposed The King's troops in the manner they did. But the temper of the people, the preparations they had been making all the winter to oppose the troops should they move out of Boston with hostile intentions, and above all their declared resolution to do so, made it evident to most persons, that opposition would be made, on any attempt to destroy Stores and Ammunition which they had avowedly collected for the defence of the Province.

An Officer of more activity than Colo Smith, should have been selected for the Command of the troops destined for this service.

Orders were given this day for the Officers to lay in their men's barracks 'till further orders.

From the want of proper accomodations for Officers in most of the Barracks, they have been under the necessity of hiring lodgings as near as they could to them. It is conceived that in case of an alarm, or sudden insurrection, the Officers might be prevented from repairing to their posts. Every Regiment is now ordered, in case of alarm, to assemble at their respective Barracks, and not march to the Alarm posts which had been assigned them.

The troops ordered to lay dressed in their Barracks this night.

21st Apl 1775. The town is now surrounded by armed Rebels, who have intercepted all communication with the Country.

The Guards ordered to mount at 4 o'Clock in the afternoon 'till further orders.

The Orderly hour fixed at 5 in the Afternoon.

Lieut Knight of the 4th Regiment, who died yesterday of a wound received in the action of the 19th, was buried this afternoon with the usual Military honors. He was an Excellent Officer, and a good man, and is universally regretted.

Thomas Gage to the Earl of Dartmouth

BOSTON April 1775.

(No 28)

MY LORD,

Two Vessels arrived from Falmouth at Marblehead on the 2d Inst, and brought Papers which contained the Address of both Houses to His Majesty with other Articles of News relating to this Country to the 11th of February. I can't learn whether she brought Letters to any of the Faction here, but the News threw them into a Consternation, and the most active left the Town before Night.

The Nautilus arrived on the 14th and the Faulcon on the 16th by which opportunitys I received your Lordship's Letters to the 22d of February.

I am to acquaint your Lordship that having received Intelligence of a large Quantity of Military Stores being collected at Concord, for the avowed Purpose of Supplying a Body of Troops to act in opposition to His Majesty's Government, I got the Grenadiers and Light Infantry out of Town under the Command of Lieut Colo Smith of the 10th Regt and Major Pitcairne of the Marines with as much Secrecy as possible, on the 18th at Night and with Orders to destroy the said Military Stores; and Supported them the next Morning by Eight Companys of the 4th the same Number of the 23d, 47th and Marines, under the Command of Lord Percy. It appears from the Firing of Alarm Guns and Ringing of Bells that the March of Lieutenant Colonel Smith was discovered, and he was opposed by a Body of Men within Six Miles of Concord; Some few of whom first began to fire upon his advanced Companys which brought on a Fire from the Troops that dispersed the Body opposed to them; and they proceeded to Concord where they destroyed all the Military Stores they could find, on the Return of the Troops they were attacked from all Quarters where any Cover was to be found, from whence it was practicable to annoy them, and they were

19

so fatigued with their March that it was with Difficulty they could keep out their Flanking Partys to remove the Enemy to a Distance, so that they were at length a good deal pressed. Lord Percy then Arrived opportunely to their Assisstance with his Brigade and two Pieces of Cannon, and Notwithstanding a continual Skirmish for the Space of Fifteen Miles, receiving Fire from every Hill, Fence, House, Barn, &ca. His Lordship kept the Enemy off, and brought the troops to Charles-Town, from whence they were ferryed over to Boston. Too much Praise cannot be given Lord Percy for his remarkable Activity and Conduct during the whole Day, Lieutenant Colonel Smith and Major Pitcairn did every thing Men could do, as did all the Officers in general, and the Men behaved with their usual Intrepidity. I send your Lordship Lord Percy's and Lieutenant Colonel Smiths Letters to me on this Affair to which I beg Leave to referr your Lordship for a more Circumstantial Account of it. I have likewise the honour to transmit your Lordship a Return of the killed, wounded and Missing. The Loss sustained by those who attacked is said to be great.

The whole Country was assembled in Arms with Surprizing Expedition, and Several Thousand are now Assembled about this Town threatning an Attack, and getting up Artillery. And we are very busy in making Preparations to oppose them.

I have the honour to be with the greatest Regard, Respect, and Esteem, My Lord Your Lordship's Most obedient, and most humble Servant,

April 22, 1775

John Dickinson to Arthur Lee

April 29th, 1775.

Dear Sir, — The *'immedicabile vulnus'* is at length struck. The rescript to our petition is written in blood. The impious war of tyranny against innocence, has commenced in the neighbourhood of Boston.

We have not yet received any authentic accounts, but I will briefly mention the most material parts of the relations that have reached us.

Gen. Gage having lately received despatches from England, gave orders on Saturday the 15th of this month, that the grenadiers and light-infantry should be excused from duty until further orders. Some of the inhabitants of the town being alarmed by this circumstance, observed between 10 and 11 o'clock on Tuesday night following, those bodies to be moving with great silence towards that water which is usually crossed in going to Cambridge. Notice of this movement was immediately conveyed into the country. The troops mentioned embarked in boats, and landed at Cambridge about four or five miles from Boston. From thence they marched on Wednesday the 19th in the morning, to Lexington, about twelve miles from Boston. At this place they found some provincials exercising. The commander of the party ordered them to disperse. They did not. One of them said he was on his own ground; that they injured no person, and could not hurt any one, for they had no ammunition with them. The word was given, and the brave Britons, emulating no doubt the glorious achievements of their ancestors, gallantly gave fire upon those who were exercising, killed some, and put the rest to flight. This victory was gained by the grenadiers and light-infantry, without the assistance of any other corps, though their numbers it is said did not exceed a thousand, and the provincials amounted to at least, as it is reported, twenty-five or thirty men!

From Lexington the victors pursued their march to Concord, about twenty miles from Boston, where they destroyed a small magazine, and set fire to the court house. By this time two or three hundred of the inhabitants were collected, and an engagement began. The troops soon retreated, and lost two pieces of cannon which they had seized.

General Gage receiving intelligence of this engagement, or of the murder at Lexington, between eight and nine o'clock on Wednesday morning sent out a brigade under the command of Lord Percy, consisting of the marines, the Welsh fusiliers, the 4th, 38th, and 47th regiments, with two field-pieces. The grenadiers and light infantry, still retreating, met his lordship advancing to their relief; but the place of meeting is uncertain, supposed to be about five or six miles from Boston. The numbers of the country people being also now increased, a very warm contest ensued. The provincials fought as desperate men. The regulars bore the attack awhile, still retreating, but at length broke, and retired in the utmost confusion to a hill called Bunker's hill, not far from Charlestown, which place is situated opposite Boston, on the other side of Charles River. About a mile from the hill, one vessel of war, if not more, was stationed to cover the retreat into Charlestown down to the water side, in order to pass over to Boston. In the retreat of this one mile, it is said the regulars lost twelve officers and 200 privates. The provincials, afraid of the shipping's firing on Charlestown, and of hurting the town's people, stopped the pursuit.

On the whole, the accounts say, the regulars had about 500 men killed, and many are wounded and prisoners. The advices by several expresses are positive that Lord Percy is killed, which gives great and general grief here, and also General Haldimand, the two first in command; that a wagon loaded with powder and ball, another with provisions, and the field pieces attending the reinforcement are taken. It is added that a party of 300 sent out to Marshfield, are cut off and taken to a man. Several letters from Boston mention that the officers returned there, several of whom are wounded, declare they never were in hotter service. The whole of the fight lasted about seven hours. Part of it was seen from the hill in Boston.

I cannot say I am convinced of the truth of all the particulars above-mentioned, though some of them are supported by many probabilities. But these facts I believe you may depend on, — That this most unnatural and inexpressibly cruel war began with the butchery of the unarmed Americans at Lexington; that the provincials, incredible as it may be at St. James or St. Stephens, fought bravely; that the regulars have been defeated with considerable slaughter, though they behaved resolutely; that a tory dare not open his mouth against the cause of America, even at New-York; that the continent is preparing most assiduously for a vigorous resistance; and that freedom or an honourable death are the only objects on which their souls are at present employed.

What human policy can divine the prudence of precipitating us into these shocking scenes? Why have we rashly been declared rebels? Why have directions been sent to disarm us? Why orders to commence hostilities? Why was not Gen. Gage at least restrained from hostilities until the sense of another congress could be collected? It was the determined resolution of some, already appointed delegates for it, to have strained every nerve at that meeting to attempt bringing the unhappy dispute to terms of accommodation, safe for the colonies, and honourable and advantageous for our mother country, in whose prosperity and glory our hearts take as large a share as any minister's of state, and from as just and as generous motives, to say no more of them.

But what topics of reconciliation are now left for men who think as I do, to address our countrymen? To recommend reverence for the monarch, or affection for the mother country? Will the distinctions between the prince and his ministers, between the people and their representatives, wipe out the stain of blood? Or have we the slightest reason to hope that those ministers and representatives will not be supported throughout the tragedy, as they have been through the first act? No. While we revere and love our mother country, her sword is opening our veins. The same delusions will still prevail, till France and Spain, if not other powers, long jealous of Britain's force and fame, will fall upon her, embarrassed with an exhausting civil war, and crush or at least depress her; then turn their arms on these provinces, which must submit to wear their chains or wade through seas of blood to a dear-bought and at best a frequently convulsed and precarious independence.

All the ministerial intelligence concerning us is false. We are a united, resolved people; are, or quickly shall be, well armed and disciplined; our smith's and powder-mills are at work day and night; our supplies from foreign parts continually arriving. Good officers, that is, well-experienced ones, we shall soon have, and the navy of Great Britain cannot stop our whole trade. Our towns are but brick and stone, and mortar and wood. They, perhaps, may be destroyed. They are only the hairs of our heads. If sheared ever so close, they will grow again. We compare them not with our rights and liberties. We worship as our fathers worshipped, not idols which our hands have made.

I am, dear sir, your sincerely affectionate friend,

Peter Oliver: from "The Origin & Progress of the American Rebellion"

In the Spring of 1775, the War began to redden. Genl. *Gage* having Intelligence, that a Quantity of Warlike Stores were collected at *Concord*, about 20 Miles from *Boston*, judged it most prudent to seize them. Accordingly, just about Midnight of the 18th. of *April*, he privately dispatched about 800 Men for that Purpose: they executed Part of their Orders, but to no important Effect. This Party was attacked by a Number, who had previously Notice of their March. Much Stress hath been laid upon, who fired the first Gun. This was immaterial, for as the civil Government had been resolved by the *Suffolk* Resolves, the military Power had a right to suppress all hostile Appearances. But in the present Case, the commanding Officer ordered the armed Rabble to disperse, upon which some of the armed Rabble returned an Answer from their loaded Muskets. The King's Troops then returned the fire — the Alarm spread, & 10 or 12000 Men, some say more, flanked them & kept in the rear, at turns. The Battle continued for the whole Day. After this first Corps had fought, on their Return, for many Miles, they had expended most of their Ammunition, & must have submitted as Prisoners, had not Ld. *Percy* met them with a fresh Brigade, with two Pieces of Artillery. This fortunate Circumstance saved them from a total Ruin. When united, they still fought, but the Cannon checked the Progress of the Rebels; who kept at a greater Distance, & chiefly fired from Houses, & from behind Hedges, Trees, and Stone Walls. As the King's Troops approached their Head Quarters, ye. Battle thickened upon them; for every Town, which they passed through, increased the numbers of their Enemys; so that they had not less than 10 or 12000 to combat with in the Course of the Day.

At last they arrived at a Hill, on the same Range with that of *Bunker's* Hill: here Lord *Percy* took Post, in so defensible a

Place, that there was no danger of being annoyed by the
Enemy; but unhappily this Post was quitted in a few Days; for
the principal Men of *Charlestown*, in which this Hill was situated, interceeded with Genl. *Gage* not to fix any Troops
there, lest it should injure the Town; & they gave their Words
& Honor, and some of them were men of Honor, & Friends
to Government, that if there should be any Attempts to
throw up Works to annoy the town of *Boston*, they would give
timely Intelligence of them. But neither Genl. *Gage* or they
calculated the Probability of the Rebels guarding the River in
such a Manner as to prevent any Intelligence across it to the
Town of *Boston*—and this Mistake was the Occasion of the
Battle of *Bunkers Hill*, two months after. This was a Battle of
Chevy Chase, & many have had, & others will have Reason *to
rue the hunting of that Day*. This was called the Battle of
Lexington, because it was at that Town, abt. 15 Miles from
Boston, where it first began.

Many were the Exploits of that Day, variegated wth.
Courage, Generosity, & Barbarity. Lord *Percy* was distin-
guished by Conduct & Gallantry; & the other Officers &
Soldiers by great Bravery. Some of each Rank travelled 50
Miles that Day, wthout. a Morsel of Food.

Many were the Instances of the british Soldiers great
Humanity, in protecting the aged, the Women & the
Children from Injury; notwithstanding the great Provocation
they had to a general Slaughter. One among the many was
this, vizt. A Soldier seeing an old Man, with a Musket, who
had been in the Battle, much wounded & leaning against a
Wall; he went up to him, tore off the Lining of his own Coat
& bound up his Wounds, with it, desiring him to go out of
Harm's Way. The Soldier had scarcely turned from him, when
the old Man fired at his deliverer: human Passion could not
bear such Ingratitude, & the Man lost his Life by it. Another
Instance was this: from one particular House the Troops were
much annoyed; a Capt. *Evelyn* rush'd in; but finding no Body
below, he ran up Stairs, & a Woman in Bed begged her Life:
he told her she was safe, & asked where her Husband was?
She said that he was just gone out of the Room; upon which
Capt. *Evelyn* returning to the Door, the Man, who was under
the Bed, fired at him: Capt. *Evelyn* then put the Man to death.

There was a remarkable Heroine, who stood at an House Door firing at the Kings Troops; there being Men within who loaded Guns for her to fire. She was desired to withdraw, but she answered, only by Insults from her own Mouth, & by Balls from the Mouths of her Muskets. This brought on her own Death, & the Deaths of those who were within Doors.

Many Lives were lost this Day; the King lost about 90 Men, & the Rebels at least as many. Many were wounded on each side. Two of the British Troops, at fewest, were scalped, & one of them before he was dead. Let Patriots roar as loud as they please, about the Barbarity of an Indian scalping Knife; but let them know, that an Indian Savage strikes the deadly Blow before he takes off the Scalp. It was reserved for a *New England* Savage, only, to take it off while his Brother was alive.

Messrs. *Hancock* & *Saml. Adams* happened to be at *Lexington*, on the Night before the Battle. They heared, the Kings Troops were coming out; & their Guilt whispering in their Ears, that the Design was to take them into Custody, they fled. Their Flight confirmed that observation made by *Solomon*, viz. *the wicked fleeth when no Man pursueth.* There was also a Colo. *Lee* of *Marblehead*, a weak but violent Partizan of Rebellion, who was there; & he imagining the same Design of seizing him, fled also, ran into Distraction & died miserably; this Man had great Influence, as he was supposed to be a Man of a large Estate. Several Men of Estates, from Ambition & a mistaken private Interest, as well as from Resentment, engaged in this Rebellion; but upon settling their Books found the Ballances against them. Others who were firmly Attached to Government fared no better; for what with Sequestrations & enormous Taxes & an illegal Prevention of receiving the Debts due to them, they were mowed down to a Level with the others. Never did the World exhibit a greater Raree Show, of Beggars riding on Horse back & in Coaches, & Princes walking on Foot. One Instance is Striking, of a Sand Man who carried Sand to the Doors of the Inhabitants in *Boston*, & is now riding in a Coach. This material World is turned topsey turvey every Day; & doubtless, it is necessary that the System of the political World should under & overgo too, a similar Rotation —

> Variety alone doth Joy,
> The sweetest Meats do soonest cloy.

After the Battle of *Lexington*, there was a general Uproar through the Neighbouring Colonies; the Echo of which soon extended throughout the Continent. *Adams*, with his Rabble Rout, & his Clergy sounding the Trumpet of Rebellion to inspire them, had blown the Bellows so long, that the Iron was quite hot enough to be hammered. The News of the Battle flew with Rapidity; one Post met another to tell the dolefull Tale, of the Kings Troops burning Houses & putting to Death the Inhabitants of Towns. Industry never labored harder, than the Faction did, in propagating the most atrocious Falshoods, to inspirit the People to the grossest Acts of Violence; & they had a great Advantage in doing it, by engrossing the tale almost to theirselves, & by suppressing the true State of Facts. At last, indeed, Genl. *Gage*, by great Assiduity, found Means to undeceive those who had preserved any Coolness of Temper. As for the *qui vult decipi decipiatur*, he there could make no Impression — thus the Rupture could not be closed.

Amidst this general Confusion, the famous Mr. *Putnam*, now a Brigadier General in the Rebel Service, went to *Boston*, & offered his Service to Genl. *Gage*, & proposed for himself a Birth in the royal Artillery; but Mr. *Gage* having no Vacancy above 3/6 p. Day, he did not incline to accept, saying at the same Time, that 10/p. Day was the utmost of his Ambition. It hath been wished by many, that Genl. *Gage* had secured him to the royal Interest. It possibly might have turned out *well*, had he have done so, but I imagine it hath turned out *better*, by not engaging him; for Mr. *Putnam* hath not only been the least obnoxious Man in their Service, but he hath really exercised great Humanity to Prisoners taken by the Rebels; & had there been no worse Men to conduct their Opposition than he is, I have no Doubt that the Rebellion would have ceased long since.

As Mr. *Putnam* hath been a Subject for News Paper Paragraphs, & as his Picture hath been exposed in the Windows of Print Shops, both of Town & Country, although very unlike him, it may not be amiss to give you some Traits

of a Semblance. I am pretty sure, that they will be less dis-
gustfull than some others I feel myself obliged to give you
very soon. Know then, that he was a Person who commanded
a ranging Party when General *Amherst* reduced *Canada* to
British Subjection. In that Service he distinguished his self
with Fidelity, Intrepidity & Success. After the Campaign was
over, he returned to his small Farm in *Connecticut*, & to his
old Business, as a Retailer of Cider & Spirits, in which he
gained something to the Support of his Family. He was well
esteemed by those who knew him, according to the provincial
Phrase, as an *honest, good Sort of Man* — his Parts are not brilliant, but he is hardy, bold, & daring in Execution. His
Courage is of that Sort which hath sometimes been deemed,
fool hardiness. An Anecdote or two, which have been cur-
rently believed in *New England*, may be explanatory of the
latter. It is said, that some Years ago he had a few Sheep upon
his Farm, which a Wolf had destroyed; he was determined to
avenge his loss by the Death of ye. Robber. He accordingly
took a Companion, & repaired to his Den, then tied a Rope
around his Waist, & with his Gun crawled on his Hands &
Knees into the Den; when he soon percieved the Wolf with
his Eyes glaring, at the further End of it; he fired his Gun &
killed him; & seizing him by the Ears, gave the Signal to his
Comrade, who pulled them both out. This rash Action was
bruited about, & his Minister under took to expostulate with
him upon it; but he closed the Dispute by saying, "that if the
Devil himself had stolen as many of his Sheep as the Wolf had,
he would have gone into his Dominions & pulled *him* out by
the Ears." Another Story they tell of him, is; that he was
taken by the Indians in the last War & having destroyed many
of their Tribe, they were determined to destroy him; & accordingly bound him to a Tree, & retreated to a Distance, to
fling their Hatchets into him; when he, just as the fatal Stroke
was to be given, laughed in their full View. The Indians, being always pleased with a brave Action, immediately released
him. These Instances are Characteristick of some Sort of bravery, which though it may not be justified upon the Principles
of true Courage, yet often meets with Success: & as far as it
coincides with true Courage, it will confirm that part of Mr.
Putnams Character which I at first mentioned, agreeable to

that Maxim, vizt. "a Man of true Courage is always a Man of Humanity": & I make not the least Doubt, that when a List of the Barbarities which have been committed by *Washington* & his Savages may be published, *Putnam's* Name will be in vain searched for as one of the Perpetrators.

George Washington: Address to the Continental Congress, June 16, 1775

THE President informed Colo. Washington that the Congress had yesterday, Unanimously made choice of him to be General & Commander in Chief of the American Forces, and requested he would accept of that Appointment; whereupon Colo. Washington, standing in his place, Spake as follows.

"Mr. President, Tho' I am truly sensible of the high Honour done me in this Appointment, yet I feel great distress, from a consciousness that my abilities & Military experience may not be equal to the extensive & important Trust: However, as the Congress desire it I will enter upon the momentous duty, & exert every power I Possess In their service & for the Support of the glorious Cause: I beg they will accept my most cordial thanks for this distinguished testimony of their Approbation.

"But lest some unlucky event should happen unfavourable to my reputation, I beg it may be remembered by every Gentn in the room, that I this day declare with the utmost sincerity, I do not think my self equal to the Command I am honoured with.

"As to pay, Sir, I beg leave to Assure the Congress that as no pecuniary consideration could have tempted me to have accepted this Arduous emploiment at the expence of my domestk ease & happiness I do not wish to make any proffit from it: I will keep an exact Account of my expences; those I doubt not they will discharge & that is all I desire."

John Adams to Abigail Adams

June 17

I can now inform you that the Congress have made Choice of the modest and virtuous, the amiable, generous and brave George Washington Esqr., to be the General of the American Army, and that he is to repair as soon as possible to the Camp before Boston. This Appointment will have a great Effect, in cementing and securing the Union of these Colonies. — The Continent is really in earnest in defending the Country. They have voted Ten Companies of Rifle Men to be sent from Pensylvania, Maryland and Virginia, to join the Army before Boston. These are an excellent Species of Light Infantry. They use a peculiar Kind of [   ] call'd a Rifle — it has circular or [   ] Grooves within the Barrell, and carries a Ball, with great Exactness to great Distances. They are the most accurate Marksmen in the World.

I begin to hope We shall not sit all Summer.

I hope the People of our Province, will treat the General with all that Confidence and Affection, that Politeness and Respect, which is due to one of the most important Characters in the World. The Liberties of America, depend upon him, in a great Degree.

I have never been able to obtain from our Province, any regular and particular Intelligence since I left it. Kent, Swift, Tudor, Dr. Cooper, Dr. Winthrop, and others wrote me often, last Fall — not a Line from them this Time.

I have found this Congress like the last. When We first came together, I found a strong Jealousy of Us, from New England, and the Massachusetts in Particular. Suspicions were entertained of Designs of Independency — an American Republic — Presbyterian Principles — and twenty other Things. Our Sentiments were heard in Congress, with great Caution — and seemed to make but little Impression: but the longer We sat, the more clearly they saw the Necessity of pursuing vigorous Measures. It has been so now. Every Day We sit, the more We are convinced that the Designs against Us, are hostile and sanguinary, and that nothing but Fortitude, Vigour, and Perseverance can save Us.

But America is a great, unwieldy Body. Its Progress must be slow. It is like a large Fleet sailing under Convoy. The fleetest Sailors must wait for the dullest and slowest. Like a Coach and six — the swiftest Horses must be slackened and the slowest quickened, that all may keep an even Pace.

It is long since I heard from you. I fear you have been kept in continual Alarms. My Duty and Love to all. My dear Nabby, Johnny, Charly and Tommy come here and kiss me.

We have appointed a continental Fast. Millions will be upon their Knees at once before their great Creator, imploring his Forgiveness and Blessing, his Smiles on American Councils and Arms.

My Duty to your Uncle Quincy — your Papa, Mama and mine — my Brothers and sisters and yours.

Adieu.

Eliphalet Dyer to Joseph Trumbull

Dear Sir   Philadelphia June 17th 1775

I have wrote you 2 or 3 letters since I receivd any from you. My last was by Doctor Church. I yesterday wrote to Genll Spencer which he will shew you. This is only private. You will hear that Coll Washington is Appointed Genll or Commander in Chief over the Continental Army by I dont know but the Universal Voice of the Congress. I believe he will be Very Agreable to our officers & Soldiery. He is a Gent. highly Esteemed by those acquainted with him, tho I dont believe as to his Military, & for real service he knows more than some of ours, but so it removes all jealousies, more firmly Cements the Southern to the Northern, and takes away the fear of the former lest an Enterprising eastern New England Genll proving Successfull, might with his Victorious Army give law to the Southern & Western Gentry. This made it absolutely Necessary in point of prudence, but he is Clever, & if any thing too modest. He seems discret & Virtuous, no harum Starum ranting Swearing fellow but Sober, steady, & Calm. His modesty will Induce him I dare say to take & order every step with the best advice possible to be obtained in the Army. His allowance for Wages expences & every thing is we think very high, not less than £150 lawll per month, but it was urged that the largeness of his family, Aide Camps, Secretary Servts &c, beside a Constant table for more or less of his officers, daily expresses, dispatches &c Must be very expensive. There is an allowance of 63 dollars per month for his Secretary who is to be Considered as one of his (the Genlls) family, every way provided for by the Genll so as to have no expence for the Secretary. I have so without your knowledge or Consent been laying in for that birth for you. I first mentioned it to Mr Dean. He appeared ready & Chearfull to give all his assistance. Mr Jno Adams & some others of Massachusetts I think they will favor it. Genll. Washington has been spoke to on the occasion, as I thot it would be a Clever genteel Birth, the Wages tollerable considering no expence for living. I believe you will much esteem him & believe he will be pleased with you. I dare say you may live Very happy with him. It is not Certain as yet it can be accomplished but if I knew it would be agreable I should leave no stone unturned to Accomplish it. A line from you as soon as possible would be very agreable tho cannot expect it before he will set out. In the mean time shall use our best Indeavers & tis but to refuse if you do not choose it if offerd. We hope to supply the Army with Six or 8 hundred fine Paxten boys & other riflers from the back of this Province some from Virginia. I hope they will arrive before Genlls How & Burgoyne Attempt to give you a Confounded flogging & which they will do if you are not well on your Guard & manage them right when they do come. Regards respects Compliments &c as usual from your most sincere friend &c.

Samuel Blachley Webb to Joseph Webb

CAMBRIDGE, June 19th, 1775, Monday Morn, 9 o'Clock.
MY DEAR BROTHER:

The Horrors and Devastations of War now begin to appear
with us in Earnest. The Generals of the late engagement and
present manuvres you will Doubtless hear before this can possibly reach you. However, as you may be in some Doubt I
shall endeavour to give you some particulars which I hope
will not be disagreeable, tho' it may be repeating. Know then
that last Friday afternoon orders were issued for about 1800 of
the province men and 200 of Connecticut men to parade
themselves at 6 o'clock with one day's provisions, Blankets,
etc., and there receive their Order. (Nearly the same orders in
Roxbury Camp also.) Near 9 o'Clock they marched (with
Intrenching tools in Carts by their side) over Winter's Hill
in Charlestown and passed the intrenchments the Regulars
began when they retreated from Concord and went to
Intrenching on Bunker's hill which is nearer the water &
Castle & Shiping. Here they worked most notably and had a
very fine fortification which the enemy never knew till morn.
They then began a most heavy fire from the Cop's Hill near
Dr. Cutler's Church & from all the ships that could play, continued till near night. About one o'Clock P. M. we that were
at Cambridge heard that the regulars were Landing from their
Floating Batterys, & the alarm was sounded & we ordered to
march directly down to the Fort at Charlestown. Before our
Company could possibly get there the battle had begun in
earnest, and Cannon and Musket Balls were flying about our
Ears like hail, and a hotter fire you can have no Idea of. Our
men were in fine spirits. Your Bror. and I Led them & they
kept their Order very finely 2 & 2.

My Dear Brother, You'll see by this the amazeing hurry we
are in, — Capt. Chester is call'd of and begs me to go on with
this letter, which I'll endeavor to do, — tho if it appears in-
correct and unconnected you must make proper allowance. —

After the Alarm, on our March down we met many of our
worthy friends wounded sweltering in their Blood, — carried
on the Shoulders of their fellow Soldiers — judge you what
must be our feelings at this shocking Spectacle, — the orders
were, *press on, press on,* — our Bretheren are suffering and will
soon be cut of. — We push'd on, and came in to the field of
Battle. Thro the Cannonadeing of the Ships, Bombs, — Chain
Shot, Ring Shot & Double headed Shot flew as thick as Hail
Stones, — but thank Heaven, few of our Men suffered, by
them, but when we mounted the Summit, where the
Engagement was, — good God how the Balls flew. — I freely
Acknowledge I never had such a tremor come over me before. — We descended the Hill into the field of Battle, — and
began our fire very Briskly, — the Regulars fell in great plenty,
but to do them Justice they keep a front and stood their
ground nobly, — twice before this time they gave way, — but
not long before we saw numbers mounting the Walls of our
Fort, — on which our Men in the Fort were ordered to fire
and make a swift Retreat. — we covered their Retreat till they
came up with us by a Brisk fire from our small Arms, — the
Dead and wounded lay on every side of me, — their Groans
were pierceing indeed, tho long before this time I believe the
fear of Death had quited almost every Breast, — they now had
possession of our Fort & four field pieces, — and by much the
Advantage of the Ground, — and to tell you the truth, — our
Reinforcements belonging to this Province very few of them
came into the field — but lay sculking the opposite side of the
Hill. — Our orders then came to make the best Retreat we
could, — we set of almost gone with fatague, — and Ran very
fast up the Hill, leaving some of our Dead and Wounded in
the field — we Retreated over Charlestown Neck, thro the
thickest of the Ships fire, — here some principle Officers fell
by Cannon & Bombs, — after we had got out of the Ships fire
under the Covert of a Hill — near another Intrenchment of
ours, we again Rallied and line'd every part of the Road and
fields — here we were Determined to Die or Conquer if they
ventured over the Neck, — but it grew dark — and we saw
them pitching Tents, — we retired to our Intrenchment & lay
on our Arms all Night, — keeping vast Numbers of our
Troops out on Scouting Parties, — they keep up a constant

fire from the Ships and floating Batteries all Night, — but few of them Reach'd us. — But alas how Dismal was the Sight to see the Beautiful & Valuable town of Charlestown all in Flames — and now behold it a heap of Ruins — with nothing Standing but a heap of Chimneys, — which by the by remains an Everlasting Monument of British Cruelty and Barbarity — this Battle — tho: we lost it, — cannot but do Honor to Us — for we fought with less Numbers — and tho they once or twice almost surrounded the Fort, we secured their Retreat, — but alas in the Fort fell some Brave Fellows — among the unhappy Number, was our worthy friend Dr. Warren, alas he is no more, — he fell in his Countrys Cause, — and fought with the Bravery of an Ancient Roman, they are in possession of his Body and no doubt will rejoice greatly over it. — After they entered our Fort they mangled the wounded in a Most horrid Manner, — by running their Bayonets thro them, — and beating their Heads to pieces with the Britch's of their Guns.

In this Bloody Engagement, we have lost, Wilson Rowlanson, Roger Fox, Gershom Smith, and Lawrence Sullivan, — who we suppose fell (at least their Bodys) into the hands of our Enemy — their souls we hope in the happy Regions of Bliss. — Wounded Daniel Deming, Samuel Delling, Epaphras Stevens, & Constant Griswould, — none of them Mortally, — are in a fair way, and likely to Recover, — to give you the exact number of the whole of our kill'd and wounded is Impossible, — Opinions are various — and no returns yet made to the Council of Warr — but the best I can find out is about 120 of our Men kill'd and wounded, perhaps there may be double that number, — I cannot say, — a few days & we shall know exactly, — of the Regulars I doubt not their are many more lost than of ours — the truth of their numbers 'tis not probable we shall know, — The kings troop to the number of 2 or 3,000 are now encamped on the same Hill they were after the Battle of Lexington, — have twenty field pieces with them, and lie under the Protection of the ships — our grand Fortification is on prospect Hill — within a mile and a half of theirs — we have about three thousand Men in it, & 2–12 Pounders, 2–9 Do, 2 24 pr. & 6 6 pounders — here we mean to make a stand, — should they prove victori-

ous (which Heaven forbid) and get possession of this Hill, —
we must retire before them & leave Cambridge to the
Destruction of those merciless Dogs — but Heaven we trust
will appear on our side, — and sure I am many thousands of
Us must fall, before we flee from them. — Gage has said that
the 19th of June should be made as memorable as the 19th of
April is — this is the day, and I assure you we are properly on
our Guard.

MONDAY, 11 o'Clock.

I have one moments Leisure again to Continue my Scrawl.
Yesterday we had another Alarm, & I wish it had not been a
false one as it prov'd. Our men were Marching Down in
much Better Order & better Spirits, for Prospect (alias
Spectacle) Hill. We heard all the Light horse with a Reinforcement enough to make 4000 in all, were on their
March from Bunkers Hill to our entrenchments. But before
we had got half way Down there we were Order'd back again.
Gen! Putnam wrote back from our fort that the Regulars had
made no Movement since Last Night.

Our Retreat on Saturday was Shameful & Scandalous, &
owing to the Cowardice Misconduct & want of Regularity of
the Province troops. Tho to Do them Justice there was a
Number of their Officers & men that were in the fort & a
very few others that did honor to themselves by a most noble
manly & spirited Effort in the heat of the engagement & 'tis
said Many of them the flower of the Province have sacrificed
their Lives in the Cause. Some say they have lost more
Officers than men. Good Doctr. Warren, "God rest his
Soul," I hope is Safe in Heaven! Had many of their Officers
the Spirit & Courage in their Whole Constitution that he had
in his little finger, we had never retreated. Many considerable
Companies of their men I saw that said there was not so
much as a Corporal with them, one in Particular fell in the
rear of my Company, & march'd with us. The Capt. had
mustered & Orderd. them to March & told them he would
overtake them directly, but they never saw him till next Day.
A vast number were Retreating as we Marchd. up & within a
quarter of a mile of the Scene of Action. If a man was
wounded 20 more were glad of an Opportunity to Carry him

away when not more than three could take hold of him to advantage. One cluster would be sneaking down on their Bellies behind a Rock & others behind Hay cocks & apple trees. At last I got pretty near the Action & I met a considerable Company with their Officer at their Head retreating. I spoke to Lt. Webb & told him it would not do to see so many going Back & that we must stop them, by all means says he. I then enquired of the Officer why he went back. He made no answer. I told him to proceed if he Dare, he still went on. I ordered my men to make Ready very Loud, & told him if he went another step he should have the fire of my whole Company. My men Declared they would fire if I ordered them. But the Poor Dogs were forced to Come back like Dogs that had been stealing sheep. But after the Retreat when we came to rally & attempt to form again, we found it impossible, for they all most all said they had no Officers to head them. In short the most of the Companies of this Province are commanded by a most Despicable set of Officers, & the whole success of the Battle with them depends on their virtue; for almost all from the Capt. General to a Corporal are afraid to set up proper Martial authority, & say, as affairs are situated, they think their people will not bear it. But in my humble oppinion they are very much in the wrong. Publick Business here goes on very Dull — if any thing of importance heaves up it must go thro a long dispute in the Congress of near 200 Members & then thro a Committee of Safety & then a Committee of War & a Committee of Supplies & by that means they are forever doing Nothing.

George Washington to Burwell Bassett

Dear Sir,   Philadelphia, June 19th 1775.

I am now Imbarkd on a tempestuous Ocean from whence, perhaps, no friendly harbour is to be found. I have been called upon by the unanimous Voice of the Colonies to the Command of the Continental Army — It is an honour I by no means aspired to — It is an honour I wished to avoid, as well from an unwillingness to quit the peaceful enjoyment of my Family as from a thorough conviction of my own Incapacity & want of experience in the conduct of so momentous a concern — but the partiallity of the Congress added to some political motives, left me without a choice — May God grant therefore that my acceptance of it may be attended with some good to the common cause & without Injury (from want of knowledge) to my own reputation — I can answer but for three things, a firm belief of the justice of our Cause — close attention in the prosecution of it — and the strictest Integrety — If these cannot supply the places of Ability & Experience, the cause will suffer, & more than probable my character along with it, as reputation derives its principal support from success — but it will be rememberd I hope that no desire, or insinuation of mine, placed me in this situation. I shall not be deprivd therefore of a comfort in the worst event if I retain a consciousness of having acted to the best of my judgment.

I am at liberty to tell you that the Congress in Committee (which will, I daresay, be agreed to when reported) have consented to a Continental Currency, and have ordered two Million of Dollars to be struck for payment of the Troops, and other expences arising from our defence — as also that 15,000 Men are voted as a Continental Army, which will I daresay be augmented as more Troops are Imbark'd & Imbarking for America than was expected at the time of passing that Vote. As to other Articles of Intelligence I must refer you to the Gazettes as the Printers pick up every thing that is

stirring in that way. The other Officers in the higher departments are not yet fixed — therefore I cannot give you their
names. I set out to morrow for Boston where I shall always
be glad to hear from you; my best wishes attend Mrs
Bassett — Mrs Dandridge & all our Relations and friends —
In great haste, as I have many Letters to write and other business to do I remain with the sincerest regard Dr Sir Yr Most
Obedt & Affecte Hble Servt

P.S. I must Intreat you & Mrs Bassett, if possible, to visit at
Mt Vernon as also my Wife's other friends — I could wish you
to take her down, as I have no expectations of returning till
Winter & feel great uneasiness at her lonesome Situation — I
have sent my Chariot & Horses back.

John Adams to Abigail Adams

My Dear   Philadelphia June 23. 1775

I have this Morning been out of Town to accompany our Generals Washington, Lee, and Schuyler, a little Way, on their Journey to the American Camp before Boston.

The Three Generals were all mounted, on Horse back, accompanied by Major Mifflin who is gone in the Character of Aid de Camp. All the Delegates from the Massachusetts with their Servants, and Carriages attended. Many others of the Delegates, from the Congress—a large Troop of Light Horse, in their Uniforms. Many Officers of Militia besides in theirs. Musick playing &c. &c. Such is the Pride and Pomp of War. I, poor Creature, worn out with scribbling, for my Bread and my Liberty, low in Spirits and weak in Health, must leave others to wear the Lawrells which I have sown; others, to eat the Bread which I have earned.—A Common Case.

We had Yesterday, by the Way of N. York and N. London, a Report, which distresses us, almost as much as that We had last fall, of the Cannonade of Boston. A Battle at Bunkers Hill and Dorchester Point—three Colonels wounded, Gardiner mortally. We wait to hear more particulars. Our Hopes and our Fears are alternately very strong. If there is any Truth in this Account, you must be in great Confusion. God Almightys Providence preserve, sustain, and comfort you.

June 27

This Moment received two Letters from you. Courage, my dear! We shall be supported in Life, or comforted in Death. I rejoice that my Countrymen behaved so bravely, tho not so skillfully conducted as I could wish. I hope this defect will be remedied by the new modelling of the Army.

My Love every where.

Peter Oliver: from "The Origin & Progress of the American Rebellion"

I NOW return to the disagreeable Situation, after the Battle of *Lexington*. The old Bickerings continued, & new ones increased. Genl. *Gage* was obliged to fortifie the Town, to secure his Troops & those who had resorted to them for Protection. The People, on their Parts, complained of his so doing; pretending that the Inhabitants could not be supplied with Provisions from the Country. This they knew to be false, but used it as a Pretence to keep the Town exposed to the inroads of the Numbers they designed to bring in, to take Possession: & had not the General taken those Precautions, it is probable that the Loyalists, who had fled to the Town, would many of them have been massacred; & others of them have fared but little better. The Faction, who were out of the Town were constantly urging the Inhabitants to quit the Town, & threatning to destroy it. Many went out, & it was with great Hardships & Difficulties that they could find where to lay their Heads; insomuch, that of 10 or 12,000, who left it after that Battle, 1200 died by *November* following. The Operation of that Battle occasioned so great an Evacuation, that the Town was reduced to a perfect Skeleton.

In May Generals Howe, Clinton, & Burgoyne, arrived from *England*; but, little else was done but fortifying, untill the Battle of *Bunker's Hill*, on the 17th. June, cut out Work enough for the Troops, not only for that Day but for nine Months after. That memorable Day exhibited a Scene, which crowned british Valor with Laurels of unfading Honor; but it was much to be lamented, that the Laurels were not to be obtained without the Sacrifice of a greater Disproportion of heroick Officers than perhaps ever fell in one Battle; owing to that savage Way of fighting, not in open Field, but by aiming at their Objects from Houses & behind Walls & Hedges. The Battle came on thus. It hath been already said, that the principal Inhabitants of *Charlestown* had told Genl. *Gage*, that he should have Intelligence of any Designs against him from that Town; but they were either disinclined, or not able to give the Information; so that, on the Night of the 16th. June, about 3 or 4000 Men were busied in throwing up a Redoubt, to contain 500 fighting Men; in fixing down 13 Rail Fences in the Front of it; & in making an impenetrable Hedge, which ran from the Redoubt to the Water's Edge, several hundred Feet. The other Part of the Redoubt was flanked by Dwelling Houses, from whence they fired with great Security; by which Means they could take Aim at the Officers of the british Troops, whom they made the particular Objects to be fired at. Thus prepared, & never was a more advantageous Defence prepared, they began early in the Morning of *17th. June* to fire upon the Town of *Boston*, from their Redoubt of 3 pieces of Artillery, of 3 Pounds Shot; & they might have fired untill this Time, without doing little other Damage than by keeping the Town in constant Alarm, & keeping up their own Spirits.

Charlestown is a Peninsula made by an artificial Isthmus about 2 Rods wide. On one Side a Gondalo with Cannon could pass almost to the Neck of Land, at high Water, & on the other Side, a Vessell of considerable Force could approach very near, to meet the opposite Gondalo. *Charles River* is the Boundary between *Boston* & *Charlestown*. At the Ferry it is not 1/2 a Mile in Width — at the North Part of *Boston* is an Hill, called *Copp's* Hill, which was well fortified with heavy Cannon. This Hill is opposite to *Bunker's* Hill, about 3/4 of a mile Distant. From this Hill the Redoubt of the Rebels was battered; & it did some Execution, by damaging the Redoubt, & by killing about 40 Men in it; & this Battery plaid untill the Kings Troops were in Action, about 2 or 3 o'clock in the Afternoon. The Fatalities of War, attending this Days Action were singular in their Quality, but not so in their Number; as may be observed in the following Relation, & the Day was remarkably hot, as well as the Action.

Genl. *Gage* found it necessary to dislodge the Rebels; a further Indulgence to them would have been irremediable. He accordingly proposed to the Admiral, to send an armed Vessell on that side of the Enemy's Encampment, where they could have been effectually annoyed. The aforesaid Hedge which concealed great Numbers, who afterwards galled the

King's Troops, would have been so flanked, that not a Rebel could have stood his Ground. Besides which, there could have been no Retreat for them, as such a Vessell would have lain near to the Isthmus & prevented it. This Manæuvre would have made Prisoners of near 4000 Rebels, & perhaps put an End to the Rebellion. But it seems, that, at this Time, & during a great Part of this american Contest, the King's Ships were looked upon in too sacred a Light to be destroyed by any Thing, except by Storms, Rocks & Worms. In this Case, a Vessell of £200 Value, would have been as effectual as one of £20,000. This I term the Fatality of Fatalities of this memorable Day.

It was high Water about one o'clock after noon. About 1700 of the Kings Troops then embarked, & landed without any Opposition. They formed, & marched towards the Redoubt on their March. They were fired upon, through the aforementioned Hedge by two pieces of Cannon peeping through it: upon which Genl. *Howe*, who commanded, called for his 6 Pound Artillery; but when they began to load them, they had only 12 Pound Shot for 6 Pound Cannon. Here was a second Fatality. Genl. *Howe* then, with true british Courage, said that "they must do as well as they could with their Muskets," & marched on. When the Soldiery came to the Fences, they attempted to break them down; but they were so well fixed, that the Ardor of the Troops could not wait to level them, but climbed them. This Sort of Attack was fatal to them; for they were now Objects of Aim, from the Houses as well as the Redoubt.

At this Time, the Encampment, upon *Copp's* Hill, seeing the Troops so much distressed from the Houses, flung a Shell, which fell upon a very large Meeting House built with Wood, which instantaneously kindled; & the wind blowing in the Course of the Buildings, the whole Town became one general Conflagration. The british Troops by repeated Efforts had made a Passage through the Fences, & were marching to the Redoubt; but in great Disorder. Mr. *Howe*, observing it, ordered a Retreat, he was obeyed. He soon formed them, & they marched on again in good Order; & immediately, upon one or two having mounted the Parapet, the Rebels fled from the Redoubt. Major General *Warren*, who commanded in the

Redoubt, exerted himself to prevent their rushing out at the Passage, but all in vain. He was the last Man who quitted it; & while his Men were running off, he very slowly walked away; & at about 20 or 30 Yards distant from the Redoubt he dropped; a Bullet having entered the back Part of his Head, & gone through it so far as to occasion a Prominence on his Forehead.

Thus the Battle ended. And why there was no Pursuit is an Arcanum that must reside in those Breasts where many other Mysteries have been locked; but, of which, a Key hath been found to open many of them to publick View. The Gondalo, which came at no great Distance from the Isthmus, did some Damage, & served *in terrorem* to those who were going to assist at the Redoubt. Had it gone nigher, as it might have done, there would have been great Slaughter of the Rebels — a Remarkable Circumstance attended the firing from the Gondalo. A Colo. *Mc. Clary* was leading on a strong Party of Succours, across the Isthmus. Some of his Men flinched, through fear of the Canonade from this armed Boat; the Colo. seeing it, cryed out, "Come on brave Boys! that Shot is not yet cast that is to kill me." The Words were scarcely spoke, before a Cannon Ball cut him almost to Pieces.

Colo. *Putnam* was at the Redoubt, when the british Troops were marching up to it. He knew their Bravery, & the Rawness of the Rebel Army. He said to the commanding Officer of the rebel Army; "I know the british Troops, I have acted with them; We must retreat, for they will defeat us;" upon which he was sent off to *Cambridge*, about 3 Miles Distance, for more Men; but the Battle was over before his return.

The Kings Troops had about 1000 killed & wounded, & of the latter many died of their Wounds, through the excessive Heat of the Season. The Rebels did not lose one half that Number: about thirty of them, who were wounded; were lodged in Prison, at *Boston*, & were as well tended as the Kings wounded Troops. Among the rest was a Colo. *Parker*, who died with his Wounds not long after the Battle. This un-happy Man lamented the Ambition that led him into this Mistake, & sent Word, to some of his active Friends, to quit the Cause, as he now too late found himself in the wrong.

This Day was distinguished by as many Acts of Heroism as
so short a Time could be well be crowded with. One of which
was relative to the above Colo. *Parker*; who being wounded,
sat upon a Stone in great Anguish begging for a little Water.
A Soldier seeing him was going to run him through with his
Bayonet, to ease him of his Pain. A Grenadier, at that instant,
interposed & prevented the fatal Stab, saying to the Soldier,
"Go fetch him some Water; let him live to know that a British
Soldier is humane as well as brave." After the Battle, the
Kings wounded Troops were carried to *Boston*; & it was truly
a Shocking Sight and Sound, to see the Carts loaded with
those unfortunate Men, & to hear the piercing Groans of the
dying & of those whose painfull Wounds extorted the Sigh
from the firmest Mind. As I was a Witness to one Instance, in
particular, of Stoicism, I will relate it. I was walking in one of
the Streets of *Boston*, & saw a Man advancing towards me, his
white Waistcoat, Breeches & Stockings being very much dyed
of a Scarlet Hue. I thus spake to him; "My friend, are you
wounded?" He replied, "Yes Sir! I have 3 Bullets through
me." He then told me the Places where; one of them being a
mortal Wound; he then with a philosophick Calmness began
to relate the History of the Battle; & in all Probability would
have talked 'till he died, had I not begged him to walk off to
the Hospital; which he did, in as sedate a Manner as if he had
been walking for his Pleasure. I forbear to mention others lest
you should complain of Tediousness.

As I have mentioned Major Genl. *Warren*, it may not be
amiss to give you a short Sketch of his Character. He was
born near to *Boston*; & when young, was a bare legged milk
Boy to furnish the *Boston* Market. He was a proper Successor
to the bare legged Fisher Boy *Massianello*, & his Fate was almost as rapid. Being possessed of a Genius which promised
Distinction, either in Virtue or Vice, his Friends educated him
at the College in *Cambridge*, to take his Chance of being a
Curse or a Blessing to his Country. After he had been graduated, he studied Physick under a Capital Physician in *Boston*.
But in that Town, a Man must look one Way & row another
to get any Way a head; & that will not always do; if it would,
Mr. *Warren* had a Mind susceptible of all Duplicity — and in
his Profession, his Practice was not very rapid. He therefore

look'd out for other Means of Subsistance. He married a tolerable Sum of Mony: he also took Administration on Part of a Gentlemans Estate which he appropriated to his own Use. Being of a very ambitious Cast, he listed under the Banner of the Faction, & urged on the boldest of their Schemes; untill his close Attendance, at the Altar of Sedition, had reduced his Finances to a very low Ebb. He was now forced to strike any bold Stroke that offered. Conquer or die were the only alternatives with him, & he publickly declared, that "he would mount the last Round of the Ladder or die in the Attempt." The Prophecy was ambiguous, he met his Fate in the latter. Had he conquered, *Washington* had remained in Obscurity; at least, he would not have been honored with the Eclat of a Coffee house, or of any other Assembly of Politicians, as the american *Fabius*. That Honor would have been reserved for those celebrated Heroes, who retard every Operation that tends to the Salvation of their Country.

An Engineer, who served at this Battle, & was wounded in it, was a Mr. *Richard Gridley*. At the taking of *Cape Breton*, in 1745, he acted in the same Capacity, & executed his Office with great Applause. Being a Man of Ingenuity, he, since that Time, had turned Projector, & met with the common Fate of Projectors, who, by attempting a Transmutation of other Substances into Gold, generally find a *Caput Mortuum* at the Bottom of their Crucibles. Thus being reduced, & swelled with great Self Importance, he deviated into the Road of Rebellion, in order to acquire Fame & a Subsistance. His Wound hath immortalized his Fame, as a Rebel. But as to increasing his Hoards, it is not probable that Congress Paper Dollars will increase them, except in Bulk; for they are too like the *New-England* Parson's Description of Self righteousness, vizt. "that the more a Man hath of it, the poorer he is."

A Mr. *Henry Knox*, who now fills the chief Departments in *Washington's* Artillery, is another high Partizan in the Rebellion. He was a Bookseller in the Town of *Boston*, but he was too Deep in Debt, for his Stock, to hesitate a Moment at any Scheme to extricate himself. Rebellion first offered her Services, & he accepted them. Some of the late intercepted Letters are descriptive of his present Situation, & it appears by them that he can not expect to make a Fortune by the

Congress Paper Dollars. It takes so great a Quantity of them to crowd into a Man's Stomach for one Dinner, that an hard Mexican Dollar is much easier of Digestion. In Short, if we review the List of those Heroes who compose Congresses, Committees, mock Government, & the chief army Departments, we shall find it filled up with Men, desperate in Ambition or in Fortune. As for those who follow their Leaders, they stand upon ye. compassionate List, for they know not what they do. The Foundation & Progress of this Rebellion may be epitomized in the Moral of the following Story.

Among the Prisoners who were wounded, & confined in the Jail at *Boston*, was a Lieutenant, by the Name of *Scott*, a Person of a good natural Understanding. A Gentleman of Humanity went to the Jail to visit & converse with the wounded, & to offer the *Samaritan* Service, of pouring Oil & Wine into their Wounds. Among the rest, he found this *Scott* to be a sensible, conversible Man; he offered to send him some Refreshment, to alleviate his Distress. *Scott* seemed surprized at the humane Offer, & said to him, "are you in earnest Sir?" The Gentleman replied, "that he was; & if a Bottle or two of Wine, or any other Thing would be acceptable, that he'd send it to him." Such a kind Offer did *Scott's* Heart good equal to the Medicine itself; & he accepted the Offer. The Gentleman then addressed him in this Manner: "*Scott!* I see you are a sensible Man; pray tell me how you came into this Rebellion?"

He returned this Answer: "the case was this Sir! I lived in a Country Town; I was a Shoemaker, & got my Living by my Labor. When this Rebellion came on, I saw some of my Neighbors get into Commission, who were no better than my self. I was very ambitious, & did not like to see those Men above me. I was asked to enlist, as a private Soldier. My Ambition was too great for so low a Rank; I offered to enlist upon having a Lieutenants Commission; which was granted. I imagined my self now in a Way of Promotion: if I was killed in Battle, there would be an end of me, but if my Captain was killed, I should rise in Rank, & should still have a Chance to rise higher. These Sir! were the only Motives of my entering into the Service; for as to the Dispute between *great Britain*

& the *Colonies*, I know nothing of it; neither am I capable of judging whether it is right or wrong." This Instance will solve many Conjectures, relative to the Unanimity of the Colonists in this Rebellion; & separate such Instances from the Numbers collected in carrying it on, the Justice of their Cause, when weighed in the Balance, will be found wanting.

After the Battle of *Bunker's Hill*, Genl. *Howe*, took Post on an Hill, of the same Range of Hills, near to the Isthmus, where there could be no Approaches to discommode him. Had this Post been maintained after the Battle of *Lexington*, it is now evident, that all the Carnage of the 17th. June would have been prevented — all that was to be done, now, was to endeavor to do better next Time — *felix quem faciunt*, was a Lesson to be well learned, but there are some Persons, who grow so callous upon a severe Flogging, that they seem unsusceptible of future Instruction; similar to the Discipline of the celebrated *Dr. Busby*, who, it was said, had whipped more Understanding *out* of his Pupils, than he had ever whipped *into* them.

The Rebels took Possession of some very strong Posts, opposite to those of Mr. *Howe*, at about a Mile's Distance; & they very rapidly extended them for 13 Miles, untill they had surrounded the Town of *Boston*, except where the Tide flowed to intercept them; & thus was the Town changed into a Prison. Mr. *Washington* was now fixed upon, by the Congress, to take upon him the Command of the continental Army. He had the greatest Reputation, as a Soldier, among the Southern Colonies. He was polite, humane, & popular. He soon came to the *Massachusetts*, & encamped in & about *Cambridge*, in View of the King's Troops. He had been promised, by the *Massachusetts*, a Body of 20,000 Men, well cloathed & armed; but when he came, he was much disappointed. However, as he had engaged in the Service, he was resolved to make the best of it, & discipline his Men to the most Advantage. Ammunition & Artillery he much wanted; otherwise he might have done more than was done; for it seemed to be the principal Employment, of both Armies, to look at each other with Spy Glasses. The Rebel Army was so destitute of Artillery, that they sent to *Ticonderoga*, 200 Miles distant, to bring down a single Mortar, by Land; but luckily for them, tho' unfortunately for the british Troops, they had a Supply of War Stores, by taking an Ordnance Ship loaded for *Boston*. This gave them another Mortar. Powder also had been much wanted untill the Winter, when they were supplied with that also.

In the mean Time, both Armies kept squibbing at each other, but to little Purpose; at one Time a Horse would be knocked in the Head, & at another Time a Man would be killed, or lose a Leg or an Arm; it seemed to be rather in Jest than in Earnest. At some Times, a Shell would play in the Air like a Sky Rocket, rather in Diversion, & there burst without Damage; & now & then, another would fall in the Town, & there burst, to the Terror or breaking of a few Panes of Glass; and during the whole Blockade, little else was done but keeping both Armies out of the Way of Idleness, or rather the whole Scene was an idle Business. But as little as the red Regiments performed, the black Regiment played its Artillery to some purpose, and

> The Pulpit, Drum ecclesiastick
> Was beat with Fist, instead of a Stick

to such Purpose, that their Cushions contained scarce Feathers, sufficient for the Operation of tarring & feathering one poor Tory. The Name of the Lord was invoked to sanctifie any Villainy that was committed for the good old Cause. If a Man was buried alive, in Order to make him say their Creed, it was done in the Name of the Lord. Or if a Loyalist was tyed to an Horses Heels, & dragged through the Mire, it was only to convert him to the Faith of these Saints. It was now, that Hypocrisy, Falsehood & Prevarication with Heaven, had their full Swing, & mouthed it uncontrold. Mr. *Washington* was provided with a Chaplain, who, with a Stentorian Voice & an Enthusiastick Mania, could incite his Army to greater Ardor than all the Drums of his Regiments; but he, unhappy Man! not long after, retired to his Home & *made himself away*, from future Service.*

*By cutting his throat.

Benjamin Franklin to William Strahan

Mr. Strahan,   Philada. July 5. 1775

    You are a Member of Parliament, and one of that Majority which has doomed my Country to Destruction. You have begun to burn our Towns, and murder our People. Look upon your Hands! They are stained with the Blood of your Relations! You and I were long Friends: You are now my Enemy, and I am, Yours,

The Continental Congress: Address to the Six Nations

July 13, 1775

A Speech to the Six Confederate Nations, Mohawks,
Oneidas, Tuscaroras, Onondagas, Cayugas, Senekas,
from the Twelve United Colonies, convened in Council
at Philadelphia.

BROTHERS, SACHEMS, AND WARRIORS,

We, the Delegates from the Twelve United Provinces, viz. New Hampshire, Massachusetts Bay, Rhode Island, Connecticut, New York, New Jersey, Pennsylvania, the three lower counties of New Castle, Kent, and Sussex, on Delaware, Maryland, Virginia, North Carolina, and South Carolina, now sitting in general Congress at Philadelphia, send this talk to you our brothers. We are sixty-five in number, chosen and appointed by the people throughout all these provinces and colonies, to meet and sit together in one great council, to consult together for the common good of the land, and speak and act for them.

Brothers, in our consultation we have judged it proper and necessary to send you this talk, as we are upon the same island, that you may be informed of the reasons of this great council, the situation of our civil constitution, and our disposition towards you our Indian brothers of the Six Nations and their allies.

(*Three Strings, or a small Belt.*)

BROTHERS AND FRIENDS, NOW ATTEND,

When our fathers crossed the great water and came over to this land, the king of England gave them a talk: assuring them that they and their children should be his children, and that if they would leave their native country and make settlements, and live here, and buy, and sell, and trade with their brethren beyond the water, they should still keep hold of the same

54

covenant chain and enjoy peace. — And it was covenanted, that the fields, houses, goods and possessions which our fathers should acquire, should remain to them as their own, and be their children's forever, and at their sole disposal.

Trusting that this covenant should never be broken, our fathers came a great distance beyond the great water, laid out their money here, built houses, cleared fields, raised crops, and through their own labour and industry grew tall and strong.

They have bought, sold and traded with England according to agreement, sending to them such things as they wanted, and taking in exchange such things as were wanted here.

The king of England and his people kept the way open for more than one hundred years, and by our trade became richer, and by a union with us, greater and stronger than the other kings and people who live beyond the water.

All this time they lived in great friendship with us, and we with them; for we are brothers — one blood.

Whenever they were struck, we instantly felt as though the blow had been given to us — their enemies were our enemies.

Whenever they went to war, we sent our men to stand by their side and fight for them, and our money to help them and make them strong.

They thanked us for our love, and sent us good talks, and renewed their promise to be one people forever.

BROTHERS AND FRIENDS, OPEN A KIND EAR!

We will now tell you of the quarrel betwixt the counsellors of king George and the inhabitants and colonies of America.

Many of his counsellors are proud and wicked men. — They persuade the king to break the covenant chain, and not to send us any more good talks. A considerable number have prevailed upon him to enter into a new covenant against us, and have torn asunder and cast behind their backs the good old covenant which their ancestors and ours entered into, and took strong hold of.

They now tell us they will slip their hand into our pocket without asking, as though it were their own; and at their pleasure they will take from us our charters or written civil constitution, which we love as our lives — also our plantations, our houses and goods whenever they please, without asking our leave. — That our vessels may go to this island in the sea, but to this or that particular island we shall not trade any more. — And in case of our non-compliance with these new orders, they shut up our harbours.

Brothers, this is our present situation — thus have many of the king's counsellors and servants dealt with us. — If we submit, or comply with their demands, you can easily perceive to what state we will be reduced. — If our people labour on the field, they will not know who shall enjoy the crop. — If they hunt in the woods, it will be uncertain who shall taste of the meat or have the skins. — If they build houses, they will not know whether they may sit round the fire, with their wives and children. They cannot be sure whether they shall be permitted to eat, drink, and wear the fruits of their own labour and industry.

BROTHERS AND FRIENDS OF THE SIX NATIONS, ATTEND,

We upon this island have often spoke and intreated the king and his servants the counsellors, that peace and harmony might still continue between us — that we cannot part with or lose our hold of the old covenant chain which united our fathers and theirs — that we want to brighten this chain — and keep the way open as our fathers did; that we want to live with them as brothers, labour, trade, travel abroad, eat and drink in peace. We have often asked them to love us and live in such friendship with us as their fathers did with ours.

We told them again that we judged we were exceedingly injured, that they might as well kill us, as take away our property and the necessaries of life. — We have asked why they treat us thus? — What has become of our repeated addresses and supplications to them? Who hath shut the ears of the king to the cries of his children in America? No soft answer — no pleasant voice from beyond the water has yet sounded in our ears.

Brothers, thus stands the matter betwixt old England and America. You Indians know how things are proportioned in a family — between the father and the son — the child carries a little pack — England we regard as the father — this island may be compared to the son.

The father has a numerous family — both at home and upon this island. — He appoints a great number of servants to assist him in the government of his family. In process of time, some of his servants grow proud and ill-natured — they were displeased to see the boy so alert and walk so nimbly with his pack. They tell the father, and advise him to enlarge the child's pack — they prevail — the pack is increased — the child takes it up again — as he thought it might be the father's pleasure — speaks but few words — those very small — for he was loth to offend the father. Those proud and wicked servants finding they had prevailed, laughed to see the boy sweat and stagger under his increased load. By and by, they apply to the father to double the boy's pack, because they heard him complain — and without any reason said they — he is a cross child — correct him if he complains any more. — The boy intreats the father — addresses the great servants in a decent manner, that the pack might be lightened — he could not go any farther — humbly asks, if the old fathers, in any of their records, had described such a pack for the child — after all the tears and entreaties of the child, the pack is redoubled — the child stands a little, while staggering under the weight — ready to fall every moment. However he entreats the father once more, though so faint he could only lisp out his last humble supplication — waits a while — no voice returns. The child concludes the father could not hear — those proud servants had intercepted his supplications, or stopped the ears of the father. He therefore gives one struggle and throws off the pack, and says he cannot take it up again — such a weight would crush him down and kill him — and he can but die if he refuses.

Upon this, those servants are very wroth — and tell the father many false stories respecting the child — they bring a great cudgel to the father, asking him to take it in his hand and strike the child.

This may serve to illustrate the present condition of the king's American subjects or children.

Amidst these oppressions we now and then hear a mollifying and reviving voice from some of the king's wise counsellors, who are our friends and feel for our distresses, when they heard our complaints and our cries, they applied to the king, also told those wicked servants, that this child in America was not a cross boy, it had sufficient reason for crying, and if the cause of its complaint was neglected, it would soon assume the voice of a man, plead for justice like a man, and defend its rights and support the old covenant chain of the fathers.

BROTHERS, LISTEN!

Notwithstanding all our entreaties, we have but little hope the king will send us any more good talks, by reason of his evil counsellors; they have persuaded him to send an army of soldiers and many ships of war, to rob and destroy us. They have shut up many of our harbours, seized and taken into possession many of our vessels: the soldiers have struck the blow, killed some of our people, the blood now runs of the American children: They have also burned our houses and towns, and taken much of our goods.

Brothers! We are now necessitated to rise, and forced to fight, or give up our civil constitution, run away and leave our farms and houses behind us. This must not be. Since the king's wicked counsellors will not open their ears, and consider our just complaints, and the cause of our weeping, and hath given the blow, we are determined to drive away the king's soldiers, and to kill and destroy all those wicked men we find in arms against the peace of the twelve United Colonies upon this island. We think our cause is just; therefore hope God will be on our side. We do not take up the hatchet and struggle for honor and conquest; but to maintain our civil constitution and religious privileges, the very same for which our forefathers left their native land and came to this country.

BROTHERS AND FRIENDS!

We desire you will hear and receive what we have now told you, and that you will open a good ear and listen to what we are now going to say. This is a family quarrel between us and Old England. You Indians are not concerned in it. We don't wish you to take up the hatchet against the king's troops. We desire you to remain at home, and not join on either side, but keep the hatchet buried deep. In the name and in behalf of all our people, we ask and desire you to love peace and maintain it, and to love and sympathise with us in our troubles; that the path may be kept open with all our people and yours, to pass and repass, without molestation.

Brothers! we live upon the same ground with you. The same island is our common birth-place. We desire to sit down under the same tree of peace with you: let us water its roots and cherish its growth, till the large leaves and flourishing branches shall extend to the setting sun, and reach the skies.

BROTHERS, OBSERVE WELL!

What is it we have asked of you? Nothing but peace, notwithstanding our present disturbed situation — and if application should be made to you by any of the king's unwise and wicked ministers to join on their side, we only advise you to deliberate, with great caution, and in your wisdom look forward to the consequences of a compliance. For, if the king's troops take away our property, and destroy us who are of the same blood with themselves, what can you, who are Indians, expect from them afterwards?

Therefore, we say, brothers, take care — hold fast to your covenant chain. You now know our disposition towards you, the Six Nations of Indians, and your allies. Let this our good talk remain at Onondaga, your central council house. We depend upon you to send and acquaint your allies to the northward, the seven tribes on the river St. Lawrence, that you have this talk of ours at the great council fire of the Six Nations. And when they return, we invite your great men to come and converse farther with us at Albany, where we intend to re-kindle the council fire, which your and our ancestors sat round in great friendship.

Brothers and Friends!

We greet you all farewell.

(*The large belt of intelligence and declaration.*)

BROTHERS!

We have said we wish you Indians may continue in peace with one another, and with us the white people. Let us both be cautious in our behaviour towards each other at this critical state of affairs. This island now trembles, the wind whistles from almost every quarter — let us fortify our minds and shut our ears against false rumors — let us be cautious what we receive for truth, unless spoken by wise and good men. If any thing disagreeable should ever fall out between us, the twelve United Colonies, and you, the Six Nations, to wound our peace, let us immediately seek measures for healing the breach. From the present situation of our affairs, we judge it wise and expedient to kindle up a small council fire at Albany, where we may hear each other's voice, and disclose our minds more fully to each other.

(*A small belt.*)

Abigail Adams to John Adams

Dearest Friend   Braintree July 16 1775
   I have this afternoon had the pleasure of receiving your
Letter by your Friends Mr. Collins and Kaighn and an English
Gentle man his Name I do not remember. It was next to seeing my dearest Friend. Mr. Collins could tell me more perti-
culiarly about you and your Health than I have been able to
hear since you left me. I rejoice in his account of your better
Health, and of your spirits, tho he says I must not expect to
see you till next spring. I hope he does not speak the truth. I
know (I think I do, for am not I your Bosome Friend?) your
feelings, your anxieties, your exertions, &c. more than those
before whom you are obliged to wear the face of chearfulness.
   I have seen your Letters to Col. Palmer and Warren. I pity
your Embaresments. How difficult the task to quench out the
fire and the pride of private ambition, and to sacrifice ourselfs
and all our hopes and expectations to the publick weal. How
few have souls capable of so noble an undertaking — how often are the lawrels worn by those who have had no share in
earning them, but there is a future recompence of reward to
which the upright man looks, and which he will most assuredly obtain provided he perseveres unto the end. — The
appointment of the Generals Washington and Lee, gives universal satisfaction. The people have the highest opinion of
Lees abilities, but you know the continuation of the popular
Breath, depends much upon favorable events.
   I had the pleasure of seeing both the Generals and their Aid
de camps soon after their arrival and of being personally made
known to them. They very politely express their regard for
you. Major Miflin said he had orders from you to visit me at
Braintree. I told him I should be very happy to see him there,
and accordingly sent Mr. Thaxter to Cambridge with a card
to him and Mr. Read to dine with me. Mrs. Warren and her
Son were to be with me. They very politely received the
Message and lamented that they were not able to upon

account of Expresses which they were that day to get in readiness to send of.

I was struck with General Washington. You had prepaired me to entertain a favorable opinion of him, but I thought the one half was not told me. Dignity with ease, and complacency, the Gentleman and Soldier look agreably blended in him. Modesty marks every line and feture of his face. Those lines of Dryden instantly occurd to me

> "Mark his Majestick fabrick! he's a temple
> Sacred by birth, and built by hands divine
> His Souls the Deity that lodges there.
> Nor is the pile unworthy of the God."

General Lee looks like a careless hardy Veteran and from his appearence brought to my mind his namesake Charls the 12, king of Sweeden. The Elegance of his pen far exceeds that of his person. I was much pleased with your Friend Collins. I persuaded them to stay coffe with me, and he was as unreserved and social as if we had been old acquaintances, and said he was very loth to leave the house. I would have detaind them till morning, but they were very desirous of reaching Cambridge.

You have made often and frequent complaints that your Friends do not write to you. I have stired up some of them. Dr. Tufts, Col. Quincy, Mr. Tudor, Mr. Thaxter all have wrote you now, and a Lady whom I am willing you should value preferable to all others save one. May not I in my turn make complaints? All the Letters I receive from you seem to be wrote in so much haste, that they scarcely leave room for a social feeling. They let me know that you exist, but some of them contain scarcely six lines. I want some sentimental Effusions of the Heart. I am sure you are not destitute of them or are they all absorbed in the great publick. Much is due to that I know, but being part of the whole I lay claim to a Larger Share than I have had. You used to be more communicative a Sundays. I always loved a Sabeth days letter, for then you had a greater command of your time — but hush to all complaints.

I am much surprized that you have not been more accurately informd of what passes in the camps. As to intelegance from Boston, tis but very seldom we are able to collect any thing that may be relied upon, and to report the vague flying rumours would be endless. I heard yesterday by one Mr. Rolestone a Goldsmith who got out in a fishing Schooner, that there distress encreased upon them fast, their Beaf is all spent, their Malt and Sider all gone, all the fresh provisions they can procure they are obliged to give to the sick and wounded. 19 of our Men who were in Jail and were wounded at the Battle of Charlstown were Dead. No Man dared now to be seen talking to his Friend in the Street, they were obliged to be within every evening at ten o clock according to Martial Law, nor could any inhabitant walk any Street in Town after that time without a pass from Gage. He has ordered all the melasses to be stilld up into rum for the Soldiers, taken away all Licences, and given out others obligeing to a forfeiture of ten pounds L M if any rum is sold without written orders from the General. He give much the same account of the kill'd and wounded we have had from others. The Spirit he says which prevails among the Soldiers is a Spirit of Malice and revenge, there is no true courage and bravery to be observed among them, their Duty is hard allways mounting guard with their packs at their back ready for an alarm which they live in continual hazard of. Doctor Eliot is not on bord a man of war, as has been reported, but perhaps was left in Town as the comfort and support of those who cannot escape, he was constantly with our prisoners. Mr. Lovel and Leach with others are certainly in Jail. A poor Milch cow was last week kill'd in Town and sold for a shilling stearling per pound. The transports arrived last week from York, but every additional Man adds to their distress. — There has been a little Expidition this week to Long Island. There has been before several attempts to go on but 3 men of war lay near, and cutters all round the Island that they could not succeed. A number of whale boats lay at Germantown; 300 volenters commanded by one Capt. Tupper came on monday evening and took the boats, went on and brought of 70 odd Sheep, 15 head of cattle, and 16 prisoners 13 of whom were sent by Simple Sapling to mow the Hay which they had very badly executed. They were all a sleep in the house and barn when they were taken. There were 3 women with them. Our Heroes came of in triumph not being observed by their Enimies. This spiritted up others. They

could not endure the thought that the House and barn
should afford them any shelter. They did not distroy them the
night before for fear of being discoverd. Capt. Wild of this
Town with about 25 of his company, Capt. Gold of Weymouth
with as many of his, and some other volenters to the amount
of an 100, obtain leave to go on and distroy the Hay together with the House and barn and in open day in full view
of the men of war they set of from the Moon so call'd coverd
by a number of men who were placed there, went on, set fire
to the Buildings and Hay. A number of armed cutters immediately Surrounded the Island, fired upon our Men. They
came of with a hot and continued fire upon them, the Bullets
flying in every direction and the Men of Wars boats plying
them with small arms. Many in this Town who were spectators expected every moment our Men would all be sacrificed,
for sometimes they were so near as to be calld to and damnd
by their Enimies and orderd to surrender yet they all returnd
in safty, not one Man even wounded. Upon the Moon we lost
one Man from the cannon on board the Man of War. On the
Evening of the same day a Man of War came and anchord
near Great Hill, and two cutters came to Pig Rocks. It occa-
siond an alarm in this Town and we were up all Night. They
remain there yet, but have not ventured to land any men.

This Town have chosen their Representative. Col. Palmer is
the Man. There was a considerable musture upon Thayers
side, and Vintons company marched up in order to assist, but
got sadly dissapointed. Newcomb insisted upon it that no
man should vote who was in the army — he had no notion of
being under the Military power — said we might be so situated as to have the greater part of the people engaged in the
Military, and then all power would be wrested out of the
hands of the civil Majestrate. He insisted upon its being put
to vote, and carried his point immediately. It brought Thayer
to his Speach who said all he could against it. — As to the
Situation of the camps, our Men are in general Healthy, much
more so at Roxbury than Cambridge, and the Camp in vastly
better order. General Thomas has the character of an Excelent
officer. His Merit has certainly been overlook'd, as modest
merit generally is. I hear General Washington is much
pleased with his conduct.

Every article here in the West india way is very scarce and dear. In six weeks we shall not be able to purchase any article of the kind. I wish you would let Bass get me one pound of peper, and 2 yd. of black caliminco for Shooes. I cannot wear leather if I go bare foot the reason I need not mention. Bass may make a fine profit if he layes in a stock for himself. You can hardly immagine how much we want many common small articles which are not manufactured amongst ourselves, but we will have them in time. Not one pin is to be purchased for love nor money. I wish you could convey me a thousand by any Friend travelling this way. Tis very provoking to have such a plenty so near us, but tantulus like not able to touch. I should have been glad to have laid in a small stock of the West India articles, but I cannot get one copper. No person thinks of paying any thing, and I do not chuse to run in debt. I endeavour to live in the most frugal manner posible, but I am many times distressed. — Mr. Trot I have accommodated by removeing the office into my own chamber, and after being very angry and sometimes persuaideding I obtaind the mighty concession of the Bed room, but I am now so crouded as not to have a Lodging for a Friend that calls to see me. I must beg you would give them warning to seek a place before Winter. Had that house been empty I could have had an 100 a year for it. Many persons had applied before Mr. Trot, but I wanted some part of it my self, and the other part it seems I have no command of. — We have since I wrote you had many fine showers, and altho the crops of grass have been cut short, we have a fine prospect of Indian corn and English grain. Be not afraid, ye beasts of the field, for the pastures of the Wilderness do spring, the Tree beareth her fruit, the vine and the olive yeald their increase.

We have not yet been much distressed for grain. Every thing at present looks blooming. O that peace would once more extend her olive Branch.

> "This Day be Bread and peace my lot
> All Else beneath the Sun
> Thou knowst if best bestowed or not
> And let thy will be done."

> But is the Almighty ever bound to please
> Ruild by my wish or studious of my ease.
> Shall I determine where his frowns shall fall
> And fence my Grotto from the Lot of all?
> Prostrate his Sovereign Wisdom I adore
> Intreat his Mercy, but I dare no more.

Our little ones send Duty to pappa. You would smile to see them all gather round mamma upon the reception of a letter to hear from pappa, and Charls with open mouth, What does par say — did not he write no more. And little Tom says I wish I could see par. Upon Mr. Rice's going into the army he asked Charls if he should get him a place, he catchd at it with great eagerness and insisted upon going. We could not put him of, he cryed and beged, no obstical we could raise was sufficent to satisfy him, till I told him he must first obtain your consent. Then he insisted that I must write about it, and has been every day these 3 weeks insisting upon my asking your consent. At last I have promised to write to you, and am obliged to be as good as my word. — I have now wrote you all I can collect from every quarter. Tis fit for no eye but yours, because you can make all necessary allowances. I cannot coppy.

There are yet in Town 4 of the Selectmen and some thousands of inhabitants tis said. — I hope to hear from you soon. Do let me know if there is any prospect of seeing you? Next Wedensday is 13 weeks since you went away.

I must bid you adieu. You have many Friends tho they have not noticed you by writing. I am sorry they have been so neglegent. I hope no share of that blame lays upon your most affectionate

Portia

Lord Rawdon to the Earl of Huntingdon

CAMP on the heights of Charlestown. As I am certain that every letter from America will be opened at the post office, I cannot in general give you my thoughts freely upon the situation of our affairs. At present, however, I may write with a little more freedom. You will have found by my former letters that the skirmish on the 19th of April was, as you predicted, a very foolish affair. Our men were even unprovided with sufficient ammunition, and the two pieces of cannon which were sent out with the brigade under Lord Percy were only supplied with four and twenty rounds, when they had to fight every yard of their way for almost as many miles. Immediately after this affair, the town was surrounded by the rebels, all communication with the country cut off, and all supplies of fresh provision entirely put a stop to. Notwithstanding this general appearance of hostility, as many of the inhabitants of Boston as chose to quit the town were permitted to remove with all their valuable effects, and what was very extraordinary, each man was permitted to carry out his arms with him. In this manner some thousand stand of arms were carried out, though every officer that saw it knew well that they were to be used against us. I believe General Gage to be a very worthy man; I really do not doubt but his want of activity proceeded from a fear of hurrying these Americans into rebellion by harsh measures. The people about him, I believe, blinded him to the true state of affairs, and buoyed him up with hopes that the hostile declarations of the Bostonians were only the clamour of a small wrong-headed party, whose rage would quickly subside if left to itself, whereas any exertion of military force might only make the affair become serious. With what views these representations were made, I cannot pretend to say. Many have asserted that the emoluments of office made these counsellors wish to protract the war, but for my own part I do not readily believe any man a rascal without having good proofs of it. I rather think that they feared the consequences of a civil war, and flattered themselves that the storm would blow over. Many little skirmishes on the islands in the harbour succeeded the action of the 19th, but at length the rebels having thrown up works on the heights of Charlestown with a manifest intention to cannonade the town of Boston, we were forced to make an effort. I have in former letters given you an account of this action; it will be sufficient to say that we found it a much more difficult piece of work to dislodge them than any of us imagined. Although from the advantage of their situation, and the strength of their works, they should have repelled a much greater force than ours was, yet there are few instances of regular troops defending a redoubt till the enemy were in the very ditch of it, and I can assure you that I myself saw several pop their heads up and fire even after some of our men were upon the berm. As to fighting us in open ground, I believe no advantage of number will ever tempt them to do that, but while they have a wall to lie behind be assured they will fight. Our confidence in our own troops is much lessened since the 17th of June. Some of them did, indeed, behave with infinite courage, but others behaved as remarkably ill. We have great want of discipline both amongst officers and men. We should, however, be happy in any reinforcement whatsoever, disciplined or undisciplined. We are at present lying behind lines of great strength, so that we are sure of maintaining our post, but we can do nothing towards suppressing the rebellion. Their lines are much stronger than ours, within sight of us, and almost within cannon shot. Their army in this neighbourhood consists, by what I can learn, of considerably above twenty thousand men. General Washington commands in chief, and under him, in this quarter, Lee. The latter, by what some deserters say, has resolved to attempt our lines. I wish he may. It would be putting the finishing stroke to the madness of his past behaviour. Ten thousand of the best troops in Europe would scarcely force our entrenchments at present, so strong is our situation by nature. In order to attack us, they must advance over an open common exposed to all the fire of our cannon, as well as the fire of two officers' parties, placed in small redoubts about four hundred yards in front of our lines. When they have forced these, they have a neck of land, not a hundred yards wide, to cross, with part of Boston Harbour on one side, and the Mistick River on the other. This neck, besides the fire from the lines, is flanked by a sloop of war on one side, and on the other by a floating battery. When they have surpassed all these difficulties, they have the lines to force, which as I told you above are very strong, and if they force them, there still remains three very formidable redoubts, under the cover of which they would find our little army drawn up in a most advantageous situation. By this description of our post, I believe you will be under no apprehensions for us. Notwithstanding all this, a deserter assures us that General Lee had determined to attack us on Sunday night last, but his design was frustrated by a sortie, which was made from the lines at Boston. The detachment which made this sally advanced to the village of Roxbury, just above which the rebels are encamped, drove back the advanced guards of the enemy, and burnt down part of the town. Imagining this to be a serious attack the general who commanded in that quarter immediately recalled the troops which he had furnished to Lee for his purposed expedition, so that he was obliged to give it up for that time. As to taking us by surprise, they know perfectly well that they must not expect it, as both officers and men at the lines stand to their arms all night and in all weathers, there being no shelter whatsoever for them to retire to. What with sick and wounded, we have not above 1,600 men upon this ground fit to do duty, but it is sufficient for the defence of the post. The most shameful accidents that have befallen us have been by sea. Notwithstanding the powerful fleet we have in this harbour, the rebels have made several expeditions to the islands in boats with impunity. It is but four days ago that they cut off an officer and forty men who were stationed to protect the lighthouse, and entirely destroyed that building, yet the lighthouse was upon an island a considerable distance from the mainland, and it must have required a great many boats to have transported men sufficient for that enterprise. Everybody exclaims against the admiral (Graves) not only on account of this remissness, but also for many unjust things he has done towards the army. A ship or two came in from the West Indies with turtle and pineapples in order to sell them to the officers, but they were all immediately secured by the admiral, as well as some sheep which came aboard other vessels. Now when men have been feeding for two or three months upon salt pork, the loss of such refreshments becomes of consequence, more especially as we have no vegetables to accompany our salt meat. Miserable lean mutton may now and then be bought in Boston at eighteen-pence a pound, and slander does not scruple to hint at the admiral as the seller. If one wishes to live at all comfortable here at present, you must go to as great an expence as if you lived in the best tavern in London. Every article of life is now charged about ten times the usual price. Send us out a proper number of troops, and matters will soon change, but with six thousand men we cannot pretend to attack twenty thousand behind strong entrenchments, and at the same time keep the town of Boston. Had we been defeated on the 17th of June, it was over with the British empire in America, and I can assure you at one time the chance was against us

August 3, 1775

Ethan Allen: from "A narrative of Col. Ethan Allen's captivity"

Ever since I arrived to a state of manhood, and acquainted myself with the general history of mankind, I have felt a sincere passion for liberty. The history of nations doomed to perpetual slavery, in consequence of yielding up to tyrants their natural-born liberties, I read with a sort of philosophical horror; so that the first systematical and bloody attempt at Lexington, to enslave America, thoroughly electrified my mind, and fully determined me to take part with my country: And while I was wishing for an opportunity to signalize myself in its behalf, directions were privately sent to me from the then colony (now state) of Connecticut, to raise the Green Mountain Boys; (and if possible) with them to surprize and take the fortress Ticonderoga. This enterprize I chearfully undertook; and, after first guarding all the several passes that led thither, to cut off all intelligence between the garrison and the country, made a forced march from Bennington, and arrived at the lake opposite to Ticonderoga, on the evening of the ninth day of May, 1775, with two hundred and thirty valiant Green Mountain Boys; and it was with the utmost difficulty that I procured boats to cross the lake: However, I landed eighty three men near the garrison, and sent the boats back for the rear guard commanded by Col. Seth Warner; but the day began to dawn, and I found myself under a necessity to attack the fort, before the rear could cross the lake; and, as it was viewed hazardous, I harangued the officers and soldiers in the manner following; "Friends and fellow soldiers, you have, for a number of years past, been a scourge and terror to arbitrary power. Your valour has been famed abroad, and acknowledged, as appears by the advice and orders to me (from the General Assembly of Connecticut) to surprize and take the garrison now before us. I now propose to advance before you, and in person conduct you through the wicket-gate; for we must this morning either quit our pretensions to valor, or possess ourselves of this fortress in a few minutes; and, in as much as it is a desperate attempt, (which none but the bravest of men dare undertake) I do not urge it on any contrary to his will. You that will undertake voluntarily, poise your fire-locks."

The men being (at this time) drawn up in three ranks, each poised his firelock. I ordered them to face to the right; and, at the head of the center-file, marched them immediately to the wicket gate aforesaid, where I found a centry posted, who instantly snapped his fusee at me: I run immediately toward him, and he retreated through the covered way into the parade within the garrison, gave a halloo, and ran under a bomb-proof. My party who followed me into the fort, I formed on the parade in such manner as to face the two barracks which faced each other. The garrison being asleep, (except the centries) we gave three huzzas which greatly surprised them. One of the centries made a pass at one of my officers with a charged bayonet, and slightly wounded him: My first thought was to kill him with my sword; but, in an instant, altered the design and fury of the blow to a slight cut on the side of the head; upon which he dropped his gun, and asked quarter, which I readily granted him, and demanded of him the place where the commanding officer slept; he shewed me a pair of Stairs in the front of a barrack, on the west part of the garrison, which led up to a second Story in said barrack, to which I immediately repaired, and ordered the commander (Capt. Delaplace) to come forth instantly, or I would sacrifice the whole garrison; at which the Capt. came immediately to the door with his breeches in his hand, when I ordered him to deliver to me the fort instantly, who asked me by what authority I demanded it: I answered him, "In the name of the great Jehovah, and the Continental Congress." (The authority of the Congress being very little known at that time) he began to speak again; but I interrupted him, and with my drawn sword over his head, again demanded an immediate surrender of the garrison; to which he then complied, and ordered his men to be forthwith paraded without arms, as he had given up the garrison; In the mean time some of my officers had given orders, and in consequence thereof, sundry of the barrack doors were beat down, and about one third of the garrison imprisoned, which consisted of the said commander, a Lieut. Feltham, a conductor of artillery, a gunner, two serjeants, and forty four rank and file; about one hundred pieces of cannon, one 13 inch mortar, and a number of swivels. This surprize was carried into execution in the gray of the Morning of the 10th day of May, 1775. The sun seemed to rise that morning with a superior lustre; and Ticonderoga and its dependencies smiled on its conquerors, who tossed about the flowing bowl, and wished success to Congress, and the liberty and freedom of America. Happy it was for me, (at that time) that the then future pages of the Book of fate, which afterwards unfolded a miserable scene of two years and eight months imprisonment, was hid from my view: But to return to my narration; Col. Warner, with the rear guard, crossed the lake, and joined me early in the morning, whom I sent off, without loss of time, with about one hundred men, to take possession of Crown Point, which was garrisoned with a serjeant and twelve men; which he took possession of the same day, as also upwards of one hundred peices of cannon. But one thing now remained to be done, to make ourselves complete masters of lake Champlain: This was to possess ourselves of a sloop of war, which was then laying at St. John's; to effect which, it was agreed in a council of war, to arm and man out a certain schooner, which lay at South Bay, and that Capt. (now general) Arnold should command her, and that I should command the batteaux. The necessary preparations being made, we set sail from Ticonderoga, in quest of the sloop, which was much larger, and carried more guns and heavier metal than the schooner. General Arnold, with the schooner sailing faster than the batteaux, arrived at St. John's; and by surprize, possessed himself of the sloop, before I could arrive with the batteaux: He also made prisoners of a sergeant and twelve men, who were garrisoned at that place. It is worthy remark, that as soon as General Arnold had secured the prisoners on board, and had made preparation for sailing, the wind, which but a few hours before was fresh in the south, and well served to carry us to St. John's, now shifted, and came fresh from the north; and in about one hours time, Gen. Arnold sailed with the prize and schooner for Ticonderoga: When I met him with my party, within a few miles of St. John's, he saluted me with a discharge of cannon, which I returned with a volley of small arms: This being repeated three times, I went on board the sloop with my party, where several loyal Congress healths were drank. We were now masters of lake Champlain, and the garrisons depending thereon. This success I viewed of consequence in the scale of American politics; for if a settlement between the then colonies and Great-Britain, had soon taken place, it would have been easy to have restored these acquisitions; but viewing the then future consequences of a cruel war, (as it has really proved to be) and the command of that lake, garrisons, artillery, &c. must be viewed to be of signal importance to the American cause, and it is marvellous to me, that we ever lost the command of it. Nothing but the taking a Burgoyne, with a whole British army, could (in my opinion) atone for it; and notwithstanding such an extraordinary victory, we must be obliged to regain the command of that lake again, be the cost what it will: By doing this, Canada will easily be brought into union & confederacy with the United States of America. Such an event would put it out of the power of the western tribes of Indians to carry on a war with us, and be a solid and durable bar against any further inhuman barbarities committed on our frontier inhabitants, by cruel and blood-thirsty savages; for it is impossible for them to carry on a war, except they are supported by the trade and commerce of some civilized nation; which to them would be impracticable, did Canada compose a part of the American empire.

Early in the fall of the year, the little army, under the command of the Generals Schuyler and Montgomery, were ordered to advance into Canada. I was at Ticonderoga, when this order arrived; and the Gen. with most of the field officers, requested me to attend them in the expedition; and tho' at that time, I had no commission from Congress, yet they engaged me, that I should be considered as an officer the same as tho' I had a commission; and should, as occasion might require, command certain detachments of the army — This I considered as an honorable offer, and did not hesitate to comply with it, and advanced with the army to the isle Auix Noix; from whence I was ordered (by the general) to go in company with Major Brown, and certain interpreters, through the woods into Canada, with letters to the Canadians, and to let them know, that the design of the army was only against the English garrisons, and not the country, their liberties, or religion: And having, through much danger negociated this business, I returned to the isle Auix Noix the fore part of September, when Gen. Schuyler returned to Albany; and in consequence the command devolved upon general Montgomery, whom I assisted in laying a line of circumvallation round the fortress St. John's: After which I was ordered by the general, to make a second tour into Canada, upon nearly the same design as before; and withal to observe the disposition, designs and movements of the inhabitants of the country: This reconnoitre I undertook with reluctance, chusing rather to assist at the siege of St. John's, which was then closely invested; but my esteem for the general's person, and opinion of him as a politician and brave officer, induced me to proceed.

I passed thro' all the parishes on the river Sorrel, to a parish at the mouth of the same, which is called by the same name, preaching politics; and went from thence across the Sorrel to the river St. Lawrance, and up the river through the parishes to Longale, and so far met with good success as an itinent. In this round, my guard was Canadians, (my interpreter and some few attendants excepted.) On the morning of the 24th day of September, I set out with my guard of about eighty men, from Longale, to go to Lapraire; from whence I determined to go to Gen. Montgomery's camp; but had not advanced two miles before I met with Major Brown, (who has since been advanced to the rank of a Col.) who desired me to halt, saying that he had something of importance to communicate to me and my confidents; upon which I halted the party, and went into an house, and took a private room with him and several of my associates, where Col. Brown proposed, that "Provided I would return to Longale, and procure some canoes, so as to cross the river St. Lawrance a little north of Montreal, he would cross it a little to the south of the town, with near two hundred men, as he had boats sufficient; and that we would make ourselves masters of Montreal." — This plan was readily approved by me and those in

Council; and in consequence of which I returned to Longale collected a few canoes, and added about thirty English Americans to my party, and crossed the river in the night of the 24th, agreeable to the before proposed plan. My whole party, at this time, consisted of about one hundred and ten men, near eighty of whom were Canadians. We were the most of the night crossing the river, as we had so few canoes that they had to pass and re-pass three times, to carry my party across. Soon after day break, I set a guard between me and the town, with special orders to let no person whatever pass or re-pass them, and another guard on the other end of the road, with like directions; in the mean time, I reconnoitred the best ground to make a defence, expecting Col. Brown's party was landed on the other side of the town, he having (the day before) agreed to give three huzzas with his men early in the morning, which signal I was to return, that we might each know that both parties were landed; but the sun, by this time being near two hours high, and the sign failing, I began to conclude myself to be in a premunite, and would have crossed the river back again, but I knew the enemy would have discovered such an attempt; and as there could not more than one third part of my troops cross at one time, the other two thirds would of course fall into their hands. This I could not reconcile to my own feelings as a man, much less as an officer: I therefore concluded to maintain the ground, (if possible) and all to fare alike. In consequence of this resolution, I dispatched two messengers, one to Lapraire, (to Col. Brown) and the other to Lasumptiou, (a French settlement) to Mr. Walker, who was in our interest, requesting their speedy assistance; giving them at the same time, to understand my critical situation: In the mean time, sundry persons came to my guards, pretending to be friends, but were by them taken prisoners and brought to me. —These I ordered to confinement, 'till their friendship could be further confirmed; for I was jealous they were spies, as they proved to be afterwards: One of the principal of them making his escape, exposed the weakness of my party, which was the final cause of my misfortune; for I have been since informed that Mr. Walker, agreeable to my desire, exerted himself, and had raised a considerable number of men for my assistance, which brought him into difficulty afterwards; but upon hearing of my misfortune, disbanded them again.

The town of Montreal was in a great tumult. Gen. Carlton and the royal party made every preparation to go on board their vessels of force, (as I was afterwards informed) but the spy escaping from my guard to the town, occasioned an alteration in their policy, and emboldened Gen. Carlton to send the force, which he had there collected, out against me. I had previously chosen my ground, but when I saw the number of the enemy, as they sallied out of the town, I perceived it would be a day of trouble, if not of rebuke; but I had no chance to flee, as Montreal was situated on an island, and the river St. Lawrance cut off my communication to Gen. Montgomery's camp. I encouraged my soldiery to bravely defend themselves, that we should soon have help, and that we should be able to keep the ground, if no more. This, and much more I affirmed with the greatest seeming assurance, and which in reality I thought to be in some degree probable.

The enemy consisted of not more than forty regular troops, together with a mixed multitude, chiefly Canadians, with a number of English who lived in the town, and some Indians; in all to the number of near 500.

The reader will notice that most of my party were Canadians; indeed it was a motley parcel of soldiery which composed both parties. However, the enemy began the attack from wood-piles, ditches, buildings, and such like places, at a considerable distance, and I returned the fire from a situation more than equally advantageous. The attack began between two and three of the clock in the afternoon, just before which I ordered a volunteer, by the name of Richard Young, with a detachment of nine men as a flank guard, which, under the cover of the bank of the river, could not only annoy the enemy, but at the same time, serve as a flank guard to the left of the main body.

The fire continued for some time on both sides; and I was confident that such a remote method of attack, could not carry the ground, (provided it should be continued 'till night:) But near half the body of the enemy began to flank round to my right; upon which I ordered a volunteer, by the name of John Dugan, who had lived many years in Canada, and understood the French Language, to detach about fifty of the Canadians, and post himself at an advantageous ditch, which was on my right to prevent my being surrounded: He advanced with the detachment, but instead of occupying the post, made his escape, as did likewise Mr. Young upon the left, with their detachments. I soon perceived that the enemy was in possession of the ground, which Dugan should have occupied. At this time I had but about forty five men with me; some of whom were wounded: The enemy kept closing round me, nor was it in my power to prevent it, by which means, my situation which was advantageous in the first part of the attack, ceased to be so in the last; and being almost entirely surrounded with such vast unequal numbers, I ordered a retreat, but found that those of the enemy, who were of the country, and their Indians, could run as fast as my men, tho' the regulars could not: Thus I retreated near a mile, and some of the enemy, with the savages, kept flanking me, and others crowded hard in the rear: In fine I expected in a very short time, to try the world of spirits: for I was apprehensive that no quarter would be given to me, and therefore had determined to sell my life as dear as I could: One of the enemy's officers boldly pressing in the rear, discharged his fusee at me; the ball whistled near me, as did many others that day. I returned the salute, and missed him, as running had put us both out of breath; for I conclude we were not frighted: I then saluted him with my tongue in a harsh manner, and told him that inasmuch as his numbers were so far superior to mine, I would surrender, provided I could be treated with honor, and be assured of good quarter for myself and the men who were with me; and he answered I should; another officer coming up directly after, confirmed the treaty; upon which I agreed to surrender with my party, which then consisted of thirty-one effective men, and seven wounded. I ordered them to ground their arms, which they did.

The officer I capitulated with, then directed me and my party to advance towards him, which was done; I handed him my sword, and in half a minute after a savage, part of whose head was shaved, being almost naked and painted, with feathers intermixed with the hair of the other side of his head, came running to me with an incredible swiftness; he seemed to advance with more than mortal speed; (as he approached near me, his hellish visage was beyond all description; snakes eyes appear innocent in comparison of his; his features extorted; malice, death, murder, and the wrath of devils and damned spirits are the emblems of his countenance) and in less than twelve feet of me, presented his firelock; at the instant, of his present, I twitched the officer to whom I gave my sword, between me and the savage; but he flew round with great fury, trying to single me out to shoot me without killing the officer; but by this time I was near as nimble as he, keeping the officer in such a position that his danger was my defence; but in less than half a minute, I was attacked by just such an another imp of hell: Then I made the officer fly around with incredible velocity, for a few seconds of time, when I perceived a Canadian (who had lost one eye, as appeared afterwards) taking my part against the savages; and in an instant an Irishman came to my assistance with a fixed bayonet, and drove away the fiends, swearing by Jasus he would kill them. This tragic scene composed my mind. The escaping from so awful a death, made even imprisonment happy; the more so as my conquerors on the field treated me with great civility and politeness.

The regular officers said that they were very happy to see Col. Allen: I answered them, that I should rather chose to have seen them at Gen. Montgomery's camp. The gentlemen replied, that they gave full credit to what I said, and as I walked to the town, which was (as I should guess) more than two miles, a British officer walking at my right hand, and one of the French noblesse at my left; the latter of which in the action, had his eyebrow carried away by a glancing shot, but was nevertheless very merry and facetious, and no abuse was offered me 'till I came to the barrack-yard at Montreal, where I met general Prescott, who asked me my name, which I told him: He then asked me, whether I was that Col. Allen, who took Ticonderoga. I told him I was the very man: Than he shook his cane over my head, calling many hard names, among which he frequently used the word rebel, and put himself in a great rage. I told him he would do well not to cane me, for I was not accustomed to it, and shook my fist at him, telling him that that was the bane of mortality for him, if he offered to strike; upon which Capt. McCloud of the

British, pulled him by the skirt, and whispered to him (as he afterwards told me) to this import; that it was inconsistent with his honor to strike a prisoner. He then ordered a sergeant's command with fixed bayonets to come forward, and kill 13 Canadians, which were included in the treaty aforesaid.

It cut me to the heart to see the Canadians in so hard a case, in consequence of their having been true to me; they were wringing their hands saying their prayers, (as I concluded) and expected immediate death. I therefore stepped between the executioners and the Canadians, opened my cloaths, and told Gen. Prescott to thrust his bayonets into my breast, for I was the sole cause of the Canadians taking up arms.

The guard in the mean time, rolling their eye-balls from the General to me, as tho' impatient waiting his dread commands to sheath their bayonets in my heart; I could however plainly discern, that he was in a suspence and quandary about the matter: This gave me additional hopes of succeeding; for my design was not to die, but save the Canadians by a finesse. The General stood a minute, when he made me the following reply: "I will not execute you now; but you shall grace a halter at Tyburn, God damn ye."

To the Virginia Gazette

November 24, 1775

Mr. PURDIE,

Here you have a proclamation that will at once show the *baseness* of lord Dunmore's heart, his *malice* and *treachery* against the people who were *once* under his government, and his *officious* violation of all law, justice, and humanity; not to mention his *arrogating* to himself a power which neither he can assume, nor any power upon earth invest him with.

> —— *Not in the legions*
> *Of horrid hell, can come a devil more damn'd*
> *In evils, to top* D****e.

By his EXCELLENCY, & c.
A PROCLAMATION.

As I have ever entertained hopes that an accommodation might have taken place between *Great Britain* and this colony, without being compelled, *by my duty*, to this most disagreeable, but now absolutely necessary step, rendered so by a body of armed men, unlawfully assembled, firing on his majesty's tenders, and the formation of an army, and that army now on their march to attack his majesty's troops, and destroy the well-disposed subjects of this colony: To defeat such treasonable purposes, and that all such traitors, and their abetters, may be brought to justice, and that the peace and good order of this colony may be again restored, which the ordinary course of the civil law is unable to effect, I have thought fit to issue this my proclamation, hereby declaring, that until the aforesaid good purposes can be obtained, I do, in virtue of the power and authority to me given, *by his majesty*, determine to execute martial law, and cause the same to be executed throughout this colony; and to the end that *peace* and *good order* may the sooner be restored, I do require every person capable of bearing arms to resort to his majesty's STANDARD, or be looked upon as traitors to his majesty's crown and government, and thereby become liable to the penalty the law inflicts upon such offences, such as *forfeiture of life, confiscation of lands*, &c. &c. And I do hereby farther declare all *indented servants, negroes*, or others (appertaining to rebels) *free*, that are able and willing to bear arms, they *joining his majesty's troops*, as soon as may be, for the more speedily reducing this colony to a *proper sense* of their duty, to his majesty's crown and dignity. I do farther order, and require, all his majesty's liege subjects to retain their quitrents, or any other taxes due, or that may become due, in their own custody, till such time as peace may be again restored to this at present most unhappy country, or demanded of them for their former salutary purposes, by officers properly authorised to receive the same.

Given on board the ship William, *off Norfolk, the 7th day of* November.

Mr. PURDIE,

A copy of the above proclamation having fallen into my hands, I thought it was necessary, for the welfare of two sorts of people, that its publick appearance should be attended with comments of the following nature. Such as have mixed much in society, and have had opportunities of hearing the subject of the present unnatural contest discussed, will be but little startled at the appellation of *rebel*, because they will know that it is not merited; but others there may be whose circumstances may, in a great measure, have excluded them from the knowledge of publick matters, who may be sincerely attached to the interests of their country, and who may yet be frightened to act against it from the dread of incurring a guilt which, by all good men, is justly abhorred. To these, it may be proper to address a few remarks upon this proclamation; and as part of the proclamation respects the negroes, and seems to offer something very flattering and desirable to them, it may be doing them, as well as the country, a service, to give them a just view of what they are to expect, should they be so weak and wicked as to comply with what lord *Dunmore* requires.

Those, then, who are afraid of being styled rebels, I would beg to consider, that although lord *Dunmore*, in this proclamation, insidiously mentions his having till now entertained hopes of an accommodation, yet the whole tenour of his conduct, for many months past, has had the most direct and strongest tendency to widen the unhappy breach, and render a reconciliation more difficult. For what other purpose did he write his false and inflammatory letters to the ministers of state? Why did he, under cover of the night, take from us our powder, and render useless the arms of our publick magazine? Why did he secretly and treacherously lay snares for the lives of our unwary brethren, snares that had likely to have proved but too effectual? Why did he, under idle pretences, withdraw himself from the seat of government, where alone he could, had he been willing, have done essential service to our country? Why, by his authority, have continual depredations been since made upon such of our countrymen as were situated within the reach of ships of war and tenders? Why have our towns been attacked, and houses destroyed? Why have the persons of many of our most respectable brethren been seized upon, torn from all their connections, and confined on board of ships? Was all this to bring about a reconciliation? Judge for yourselves, whether the injuring of our persons and properties be the readiest way to regain our affections. After insulting our persons, he now presumes to insult our understandings also. Do not believe his words, when his actions so directly contradict them. If he wished for an accommodation, if he had a desire to restore peace and order, as he professes, it was to be upon terms which would have been disgraceful, and in the end destructive of every thing dear and valuable. Consider again the many attempts which have been made to enslave us. Nature gave us equal privileges with the people of Great Britain; we are equally, with them, entitled to the disposal of our own property; and we have never resigned to them these rights, which we derived from nature. But they have endeavoured, unjustly, to rob us of them: They have made acts of parliament, in which we in no manner concurred, which dispose of our property; acts which abridge us of liberties we once enjoyed, and which impose burthens and restraints upon us too heavy to be born. Had we immediately taken up arms to assert our rights, and to prevent the exercise of unlawful power, though our cause would have been just, yet our conduct would have been precipitate, and so far blameable. We might then, with some shadow of justice, have been charged with *rebellion*, or a disposition to rebel. But this was not the way we behaved: We petitioned once and again, in the most dutiful manner; we hoped that the righteousness of our cause would appear, that our complaints would be heard and attended to; we wished to avoid the horrours of a civil war, and so long proceeded in this fruitless track that our not adopting a more vigorous opposition seemed rather to proceed from a spirit of meanness and fear than of peace and loyalty, and all that we gained was to be more grievously oppressed. At length, we resolved to with-hold our commerce from Britain; and, by thus affecting her interest, oblige her to redress our grievances. But in this also we have been disappointed: Our associations have been deemed unlawful combinations, and opposition to government; we have been entirely deprived of our trade to foreign countries, and even amongst ourselves, and fleets and armies have been sent to reduce us to a compliance with the unjust and arbitrary demands of the British minister, and corrupt parliament. Reduced to such circumstances, to what could we have recourse but to arms? Every other expedient having been tried, and found ineffectual, this alone was left; and this we have, at last, unwillingly adopted. If it be *rebellion* to take up arms in such a cause as this, rebellion then is not only a justifiable, but an honourable thing. But, let us not be deceived with empty sounds. They who call us rebels cannot make us so. Rebellion is open, and avows opposition to lawful authority; but it is usurped and arbitrary power which we have determined to oppose. Societies are formed, and magistrates appointed, that men may the better enjoy the blessings of life. Some of the rights which they have derived from nature they part with, that they may the more peaceably and safely possess the rest. To preserve the rights they have reserved is the duty of every member of society, and to deprive a people of these is *treason*, is *rebellion against the state*. If this doctrine then be right, which no one,

I believe, will venture to deny, we, my countrymen, are dutiful members of society; and the persons who endeavour to rob us of our rights, *they are the rebels, rebels to their country, and to the rights of human nature*. I repeat it again, let us not be deceived with empty sounds. We are acting the part of loyal subjects, of faithful members of the community, when we stand forth in opposition to the arbitrary and oppressive acts of any man, or set of men. Resort not then to the *standard* which lord *Dunmore* has set up; and if any of you have been so far mistaken in your duty as to join him, fly from his camp, as an infected place, and speedily rejoin your virtuous suffering countrymen; for, be ye well assured, that the time will come when these invaders of the rights of human kind will suffer the punishment due to their crimes; and when the insulted and oppressed Americans will, if they preserve their virtue, triumph over all their enemies.

The second class of people, for whose sake a few remarks upon this proclamation seem necessary, is the *negroes*. They have been flattered with their freedom, if they be able to bear arms, and will speedily join lord *Dunmore*'s troops. To none then is freedom promised but to such as are able to do lord *Dunmore* service. The aged, the infirm, the women and children, are still to remain the property of their masters, of masters who will be provoked to severity, should part of their slaves desert them. Lord *Dunmore*'s declaration, therefore, is a cruel declaration to the negroes. He does not even pretend to make it out of any tenderness to them, but solely upon his own account; and should it meet with success, it leaves by far the greater number at the mercy of an enraged and injured people. But should there be any amongst the negroes weak enough to believe that lord *Dunmore* intends to do them a kindness, and wicked enough to provoke the fury of the Americans against their defenceless fathers and mothers, their wives, their women and children, let them only consider the difficulty of effecting their escape, and what they must expect to suffer if they fall into the hands of the Americans. Let them farther consider what must be their fate, should the English prove conquerors in this dispute. If we can judge of the future from the past, it will not be much mended. Long have the Americans, moved by compassion, and actuated by sound policy, endeavoured to stop the progress of slavery. Our Assemblies have repeatedly passed acts, laying heavy duties upon imported negroes, by which they meant altogether to prevent the horrid traffick; but their humane intentions have been as often frustrated by the cruelty and covetousness of a set of English merchants, who prevailed upon the king to repeal our kind and merciful acts, little indeed to the credit of his humanity. Can it then be supposed that the negroes will be better used by the English, who have always encouraged and upheld this slavery, than by their present masters, who pity their condition, who wish in general to make it as easy and comfortable as possible, and who would willingly, were it in their power, or were they permitted, not only prevent any more negroes from losing their freedom, but restore it to such as have already unhappily lost it? No, the ends of lord *Dunmore* and his party being answered, they will either give up the offending negroes to the rigour of the laws they have broken, or sell them in the West Indies, where every year they sell many thousands of their miserable brethren, to perish either by the inclemency of weather, or the cruelty of barbarous masters. Be not then, ye negroes, tempted by this proclamation to ruin yourselves. I have given you a faithful view of what you are to expect; and I declare before GOD, in doing it, I have considered your welfare, as well as that of the country. Whether you will profit by my advice, I cannot tell; but this I know, that whether we suffer or not, if you desert us, you most certainly will.

William Woodford to Edmund Pendleton

Great Bridge 5th Decr. 1775

Sir,

After my Letter of yesterday, I recd. an Acct. from Capt. Taliaferro, that the Boat intended for him to cross in could not be got off till day light, & desired my further Instructions I had sent Capt. Nicholas with 42 men to reinforce Taliaferro & on Rect. of his letter, order'd Colo. Stevens to take the command of the whole, they crossed about midd night, & got to the Enemys centinals without being discover'd, one of them challenged & not being answer'd, Fired at our party, the fire was returnd by our men, & an over Eagerness at first, & rather a backwardness afterwards, occation'd some confusion, & prevented the Colos. plan from being so well executed as he intended, however, he Fired their Fortification & House, in which one negro perished, killed one dead upon the spott, & took two others prisoners (who's Examination I now enclose you, this party (consisting of 26 Blacks & 9 Whites) escaped under cover of the night, he allso took four new Muskets. my Instructions mention proceding against Slaves taken in arms, according to the rules of War, I believe the Unanimous opinion of the officers would have been to make an Immediate Example of them, but considering you inform me in yours of the 1st Inst. that a counter proclamation to that of Ld Dunmore would be out in a few Days, & wishing to have the express commands of your Honble. Boddy, now sitting, in a matter of so much importance as Life & Death, I thought proper to postpone any step of the sort, 'till I am further Instructed. These instructions, I would likewise wish, might point out my conduct in many other things, that could be fix'd by the wisdom of your councills, much better then left wholly to my discretion — we have likewise confined here negro Tom belonging to a man in Carolina, has been Run away two years, I have inform'd his master, that

upon proving his property, & paying all charges his slave shall
be deliver'd —

Charles, belonging to —— Montgomery of Portsmouth,
taken by our scouts, a very suspicious Fellow, & from what
appear'd upon his examination, upon no good in this neighbourhood, he continues under Gaurd in Irons — Will who
says he belongs to George Corby of black Water (Norfolk
County) remains confined till further orders — Capt. Wm.
Hodges (who's instructions from Ld Dunmore I enclosed to
the Honble Mr. Page), his character as to political princables,
is very bad, & if I am rightly inform'd, deserves to be punished, except his insignificancy should excuse him, he is confined till further orders — John Ryal, a Baker taken in a Boat
with 400 lbs. Flour & 12 1/2 Bushs. Salt coming up this River,
is said to be an Enemy to our cause, & has Baked & assisted
the ministerial Troops since they took part here, these articles
being much wanted by us, & supposing they were intended
for the Enemy, are made use of & the person confined 'till
further orders — Colo Wells is this moment return'd from
Carolina & brings a Letter from Colo Vail (a coppy inclosed)
likewise informs that the cannon are not mounted, no powder with the party but 300ls. on this side, in possession of a
Mr. Lamb, who will deliver it to Vail upon his march, the
mens arms but Indifferent, no kind of Furniture to the
Cannon, he says they have Accts from Genln, from Philada.
that our Troops are in possession of Bunker Hill, but with a
considerable loss, that a Vessell informs, 50 or 60 sail was seen
within these few Days off Newbern, supposed to be Transports with Troops. Colo. Jarvis with 12 men arrived here last
night from the above party

I am just inform'd that Batchellers Mill Dam upon Deep
creek is gone, so that our Waggons cannot pass without a
Bridge, this is 10 miles from here on the Road to Suffolk, &
wheather it was destroy'd by the Tories, or went by accident
is uncertain, the people inform my messenger that Ld
Dunmore has promised to send a party there in a few Days to
take post. I have dispatch'd two Horse men to inquire into
the Truth of this matter, & reconnoitre the Water Courses &c
& an officer & 25 men march Immediately to repair the
Damages, & take post there, this Country between this &

Suffolk is so exposed to several Water courses, that there will
be an absolute necessity to Establish two or three posts upon
the Road, as the Inhabitants are all Tories & when the Fort
over the Bridge is reduced, a strong party must gaurd this
Important pass. all these reasons induce me to advise what I
recommended yesterday. some 4 lb. shott with 3 or 4 the best
mounted cannon of that size (with swabbers, Ram Rods &c)
I would likewise advise to follow with the Greatest Expedition. The want of that necessary article for the Soldiery, Shoes, begins to be sevearly felt by some, & will
shortly be so by the whole, unless a speedy supply arrives. I
mention'd this to Mr Page upon my first crossing James
River. The bearer brings you one of the Balls taken out of the
cartirages found upon the negro Prisoners, as they were extremely well made, & no doubt by some of the non comd officers of the Regulars, will submitt it to the Convention, by
who's orders this Horrid preparation was made for the Flesh
of our Country men, the others is prepared in the same manner, likewise all that have been found in the Houses &c — I
have never suffer'd a soldier of mine to do a thing of this
kind — nor will I allow it to be done for the future, notwithstanding this provocation, we are much at a loss for a good
Glass. I'm told there is very fine ones at the College, which
would be of great service. This part of the country affording
no such thing. I am with much Respect

     Sir Your obedt humble servt

Examination of negroes George and Ned taken prisoners
by Colo Stephen's detachment December 5th 1775 before the
field officers. —

Negro George belonging to Mr Donaldson at Suffolk informs that he left Norfolk yesterday with 55 Black and 2 white
men; that he thinks there are 400 Blacks in that town, besides
Soldiers and Tories; That a tender went down the river to
meet a ship & a snow which the soldiers told him were expected from St Augustine with troops to the amount of 4 or
500; That the intrenchment at Norfolk was nearly compleated, and that they were to begin to mount their Cannon
yesterday on the works, twelve peices. — That there are in the

fort at the bridge about 30 Whites & 90 blacks; The fort is commanded by one Cunningham; They have six peices of Cannon on Carriages in the fort, and he believes plenty of amunition and provision. That last saturday there were about 30 head of Cattle & 50 sheep driven into Norfolk by the country people and put into an inclosure. That in general they are plentifully supplied with fresh provisions from the market in Norfolk. — That all the blacks who are sent to the fort at the great Bridge, are supplied with muskets, Cartridges &c and strictly ordered to use them defensively & offensively. — That the officer who commanded the party from which he was taken last night, is named Wodross. — That negro Ned taken Prisoner with him the said George, entered as a Volunteer into the service. —

Examination of Negro Ned taken prisoner by Lieut Colo. Stephens's Detachment December 5th 1775

Negro Ned, belonging to Mr. Newton of Kemps Landing, upon his Examination, informs that a Ship & a snow arrived at Norfolk on friday last with soldiers. That he came from Norfolk yesterday with twenty odd Blacks & three whites. — That all the Blacks who are at any time sent up to the fort at the Great Bridge are supplied with Muskets Ammunition &c. and ordered to use them against us.

Martha Washington to Elizabeth Ramsay

Dear Miss   Cambridge December the 30th 1775
    I now sit down to tell you that I arrived hear safe, and our
party all well — we were fortunate in our time of setting out
as the weather proved fine all the time we were on the road —
I did not reach Philad till the tuesday after I left home, we
were so attended and the gentlemen so kind, that I am lade
under obligations to them that I shall not for get soon. I dont
doubt but you have see the Figuer our arrival made in the
Philadelphia paper — and I left it in as great pomp as if I had
been a very great somebody

    I have waited some days to collect something to tell, but
allas there is nothing but what you will find in the papers —
every person seems to be cheerfull and happy hear, — some
days we have a number of cannon and shells from Boston and
Bunkers Hill, but it does not seem to surprise any one but
me; I confess I shudder every time I hear the sound of a
gun — I have been to dinner with two of the Generals, Lee
and Putnam and I just took a look at pore Boston &
Charlstown — from prospect Hill Charlestown has only a few
chimneys standing in it, thare seems to be a number of very
fine Buildings in Boston but god knows how long they will
stand; they are pulling up all the warfs for firewood — to me
that never see any thing of war, the preparations, are very ter-
able indeed, but I endever to keep my fears to myself as well
as I can.

    Your Friends Mr Harrison & Henly are boath very well and
I think they are fatter than they were when they came to the
Camp — and Capt Baylor is as lusty man to what he was when
you see him — the girls may rest sattisfied on Mr Harrisons
account for he seems two fond of his country to give his heart
to any but one of his virginia Friends, thare are but two
young Laides in Cambridge, and a very great number of
Gentlemen so you may gess how much is made of them —
but neither of them is pretty I think,

This is a beautyfull country, and we had a very plasant journey through New england, and had the plasure to find the
General very well we came within the month from home to
the Camp

I see your Brother at Princeton he was very well but did
not talk of comeing home soon

Please to give my love and good wishes to your Mamma &
grandmamma, Mr Ramsay and Family, my compliments to all
enquiring Friends, the good gentlemen that came with me up
to Baltimore, and Mrs. Herbert — in which the General and
Mr & Mrs Custis' joins, please to remember me to Mr & Mrs
McCarty and Family

> I am Dear Miss your most affectionate
> Friend and Servt

Isaac Senter: Journal, November 1–December 31, 1775

Wednesday, Nov. 1st. Our greatest luxuries now consisted in a little water, stiffened with flour, in imitation of shoemakers' paste, which was christened with the name of Lillipu. Instead of the diarrhœa, which tried our men most shockingly in the former part of our march, the reverse was now the complaint, which continued for many days. We had now arrived as we thought to almost the zenith of distress. Several had been entirely destitute of either meat or bread for many days. These chiefly consisted of those who devoured their provision immediately, and a number who were in the boats. The voracious disposition many of us had now arrived at, rendered almost any thing admissible. Clean and unclean were forms now little in use. In company was a poor dog, who had hitherto lived through all the tribulations, became a prey for the sustenance of the assassinators. This poor animal was instantly devoured, without leaving any vestige of the sacrifice. Nor did the shaving soap, pomatum, and even the lip salve, leather of their shoes, cartridge boxes, &c., share any better fate; passed several poor fellows, truly commisserating them.

Thursday, 2d. Long ere this necessity had obliged us to dismiss all our encamping equipage, excepting a small light tin kettle among a number; but nothing to cut our wood, &c. According to our strength and spirits, we were scattered up and down the river at the distance of perhaps twenty miles. Not more than eight miles had we marched, when a vision of horned cattle, four footed beasts, &c. rode and drove by animals resembling Plato's two footed featherless ones. Upon a nigher approach our vision proved real! Exclamations of joy. — Echoes of gladness resounded from front to rear! with a te deum. Three horned cattle, two horses, eighteen Canadians and one American. A heifer was chosen as victim to our wants; slain and divided accordingly. Each man was

restricted to one pound of beef. Soon arrived two more
Canadians in B. Canoes, ladened with a coarse kind of meal,
mutton, tobacco, &c. Each man drew likewise a pint of this
provender. The mutton was destined for the sick. They proceeded up the river in order to the rear's partaking of the
same benediction. We sat down, eat our rations, blessed our
stars, and thought it luxury. Upon a general computation we
marched from 20 to 30 miles per day. Twenty miles only from
this to the settlements. Lodged at the great falls this night.

Friday, 3d. Last night's lodging was nature's bed without
any covering. Every moment expecting to bring the inhabitants in view. Forded a very considerable river, emptying itself
into the Chaudiere upon the S. W. side. Half after 10 o'clock,
A. M. we arrived at the first town, principally inhabited by the
Aborigines. Just ere we entered the town we came to another
river much larger than any we'd crossed, which emptied into
the Chaudiere in the first settlements. Here was an old native
stationed under a hut built with blankets, in wait for us with
his boiled potatoes, bread, &c., offering them for sale, he was
also ferryman. We trafficked to some small amount with him,
and hired his assistance with his little bark over the river, and
bid him adieu. The politeness and civility with which the poor
Canadian peasants received us, added to our joy when we
were conducted to the place of rendezvous, and served out
firkin butter and hot bread, which we attacked with great
spirit. This place is called Sartigan, naturally excellent soil,
beautifully situated. Inhabited with part Canadian French, the
other natives. Proceeded five miles.

Sartigan, Saturday, 4th. The five miles march last evening
brought us to the Colonel's quarters, and this morning the
savages assembled in *statu quo*, and waited on the Colonel to
know our reasons for coming among them in a hostile manner, pretending they were unacquainted with our intentions,
among which was the two expresses despatched from Nor-
rigewalk with letters to Quebec. In the assembly the savages
were prepared with an interpreter. They addressed the
colonel in great pomp, and one of their chiefs delivered an
oration with all the air and gesture of an accomplished ora-
tor. After this being explained or translated, the colonel returned the following answer. Friends and brethren: — "I feel

myself very happy in meeting with so many of my brethren from the different quarters of the great country, and more so as I find we meet as friends, and that we are equally concerned in this expedition. Brethren, we are the children of those people who have now taken up the hatchet against us. More than one hundred years ago, we were all as one family. We then differed in our religion, and came over to this great country by consent of the king. Our fathers bought lands of the savages, and have grown a great people. Even as the stars in the sky. We have planted the ground, and by our labour grown rich. Now a new king and his wicked great men want to take our lands and money without our consent. This we think unjust, and all our great men from the river St. Lawrence to the Mississippi, met together at Philadelphia, where they all talked together, and sent a prayer to the king, that they would be brothers and fight for him, but would not give up their lands and money. The king would not hear our prayer, but sent a great army to Boston and endeavoured to set our brethren against us in Canada. The king's army at Boston came out into the fields and houses, killed a great many women and children, while they were peaceably at work. The Bostonians sent to their brethren in the country, and they came in unto their relief, and in six days raised an army of fifty thousand men and drove the king's troops on board their ships, killed and wounded fifteen hundred of their men. Since that they durst not come out of Boston. Now we hear the French and Indians in Canada have sent to us, that the king's troops oppress them and make them pay a great price for their rum, &c.; press them to take up arms against the Bostonians, their brethren, who have done them no hurt. By the desire of the French and Indians, our brothers, we have come to their assistance, with an intent to drive out the king's soldiers; when drove off we will return to our own country, and leave this to the peaceable enjoyment of its proper inhabitants. Now if the Indians, our brethren, will join us, we will be very much obliged to them, and will give them one Portuguese per month, two dollars bounty, and find them their provisions, and they liberty to *chuse* their own officers."

This declaration had the desired effect, about fifty of them embodied according to agreement, took their canoes and proceeded. From our last lodgings hired a peasant, and proceeded down the river in a canoe five miles to a victualling house or other place of rendezvous. This village, St. Josephs, made a further agreement, and continued down the river about four miles further, as we found nothing agreeable since our arrival, except one quart of New England rum, (if that was to be allowed so) for which I paid one hard dollar. We were making enquiry at every likely stage, for this purpose visited an old peasant's house, where was a merry old woman at her loom, and two or three fine young girls. They were exceedingly rejoiced with our company. Bought some eggs, rum, sugar, sweetmeats, &c., where we made ourselves very happy. Upon the old woman being acquainted from whence we came, immediately fell singing and dancing "Yankee Doodle" with the greatest air of good humour. After making the old woman satisfied for her kickshaws, saluted her for her civilities, &c., marched. The distance computed from the Chaudiere Lake to the inhabitants, one hundred miles. From thence to Quebec, ninety.

Sunday, 5th. Our army was in a very scattered condition, expresses were sent to hurry them on as fast as possible. The colonel had an express arrived this day, informing of Mr. Robbisho's being taken prisoner, an express sent by colonel from Sartigan. This put the people in a great panic, as they heard the English were determined to burn and destroy all the inhabitants in the vicinity of Quebec, unless they came in and took up arms in defence of the garrison. Arrived at St. Mary's Chapel, where we had very good entertainment. Good roast turkey, Spanish wine, &c.

Monday, 6th. This morning orders were given for every captain to get his company on as fast as possible, and not to leave a man behind unless unfit for duty. Had thirty computed miles yet to go ere we came to Point Levi.

Tuesday, 7th. Water carriage now failing, was either obliged to foot pad it, or hire a horse — chose the latter. Chaplain Spring hired another in the same village, for which we were to pay three hard dollars. After being equipped in the Hudibrastic taste, (except a spur.) In lieu of a saddle, we had an old piece or cushion, across which was a rope, which served as stirrups. Arrived within four leagues of Quebec. Terrible road, mud and mire to the horses' belly.

Wednesday, 8th. Were within four leagues of Quebec this morning, all possible despatch was used to arrive ere the enemy got any reinforcements of either men or provisions. Arrived at Point Levi 11 o'clock A. M. Snow over shoes. In open sight of the enemy nought but the river divided us. Few of the army arrived this day. Provisions buying up. Canadian mechanicks at work making scaling ladders, lannuts, &c., as many of the men being destitute of shoes, as fast as the beefs were killed, the hides were made into savage shoes. Nothing of great moment while we lay here. We were daily preparing to cross the river St. Lawrence. The enemy had destroyed all the boats canoes, &c., for many miles up and down the river, upon the side we were ere our arrival. The confusion in Quebec was very great. But if we had been in a situation to have crossed the river immediately upon our arrival, they would have fallen an easy prey. Our army daily coming up, our preparations for crossing, the enemy's for repelling us, were the chief occurrences for this four days past.

Saturday, 11th. Two of the enemy's vessels quit the harbour and went down the river this morning, imagined with valuable effects. I had forgot to mention the arrival of one Mr. Haulstead, into our camp the 9th inst. He was formerly from the Jerseys, followed merchandize in Quebec, had been suspected by the enemy of holding a correspondence with the Bostonians, and previous to our arrival sent down the river about fourteen miles to the Isle d' Orleans. This gentleman could give us no fresh intelligence from the city, not having been there for several days. Our situation was in view of the enemy, who were exerting all their power in furnishing their magazines for their support in the seige. Arrived to their relief this evening Colonel McClean and crew from Montreal in a vessel. We captured Mr. McKenzie, one of their midshipmen, who came ashore on the Point Levi side. This was acted in sight of two of their ships of war, which occasioned heavy fire from one of them upon the party, but no damage. Log and bark canoes were daily carrying down the river Chaudiere, which emptied into the St. Lawrence but four miles above Point Levi.

Sunday, 12th. On the chapel door at Point Levi, I found the following pompous proclamation to ensnare the ignorant:

"Conditions to be given to such soldiers as shall engage in the Royal Highland Emigrants. They are to engage during the present troubles in America only. Each soldier is to have 200 acres of land in any province in North America he shall think proper. The king to pay the patent fees, secretary's fees and surveyor general, besides twenty years free of quit rent. Each married man gets fifty acres for his wife, and fifty for each child, on the same terms, and as a gratuity besides the above great terms, one guinea levy money.

ALLEN MCLEAN, Lt. Col.

Quebec, Aug. 3, 1775.   Commandt."

Monday, 13th. The report from the lower guard mentions three vessels passing down the river from Quebec, this morning early, supposed to be laden with more valuable effects. Two savages from the suburbs of Montreal, arrived with an express from General Montgomery, that he was on the point of entering the city. This gave us new spirits, being in hopes to have as good intelligence to communicate to the General. Things were now hurried with all possible speed. The enemy had advantageously posted two vessels of war in the river, in order to obstruct our passing the river to the Plains of Abraham. The mechanicks had now finished their works. Ladders, lannuts, &c., were in readiness for crossing, when we had orders to be ready at a minute's warning. 2 o'clock at night, assembled at a certain place, where we had for shelter some mills, when the boats were to be drawn from the cave of the Chaudiere to receive us. Mr. Haulstead, the gentleman before mentioned, served as Pilot. The canoes were but few in number; therefore were obliged to cross and return three times ere the army got over. The night being exceeding dark, every thing was conducted with the utmost secrecy, no lights, no noise. Captain Hatchett and company were left as a guard at Point Levi, to some effects left behind there. It was proposed to cross immediately into Wolfe's Cove, the distance a league. I went in the first division, and in the Pilot boat, in which was General Arnold, Captain Morgan with some riflemen, and one boat load of savages, with others to the amount of six boats. Crossed between the two vessels, notwithstanding the armed barges were plying every hour from ship to ship. We had nigh come in contact with one of them in the midst of the stream, but luckily passed her undiscovered. Landed above the Cove, without being discovered, and contrary to our expectation where there were no sentinels. Guards were detached immediately up and down the river as security, while the canoes returned for the remainder, till all completely made their landing, though in a very scattered condition, by reason of the darkness of the night, distance and rapid ebb tide, &c. However at daylight we were all in the Cove, without any accident except one of the birch canoes bursting asunder in the midst of the St. Lawrence, but happily saved them all, by dragging them ashore, lost all their guns, &c.

The enemy were not yet seen — a large fire was built in a house in Wolfe's Cove, where were the castaways a drying themselves, &c. Spies were sent down the river, on the Plains, &c., to discover the movements of the enemy (if any.) The fire was spied by one of the patrolling barges, who came towards the shore, when fired upon by the riflemen, though contrary to orders. Wounded some of them, when they thought proper to put off. They did not yet believe that we had crossed, imagining it impossible on account of their destroying the boats &c., nor were they alarmed in the city, as we could hear the watch very often. Captain Smith with a detachment were ordered to reconnoitre the enemies lines, but could discover no movements. The idea of storming the city was now inadmissible, our plight being so bad, and the enemy's much better after the arrival of Colonel McLean. The city gates were all closed, cannon in order, &c. We marched upon the Plains, took possession of Major Caldwell's house at St. Foys, where we detected some teams loaded with beef, vegetables, &c., going into the city, we surrounded the house and took a servant of the Major's.

Tuesday, 14th. Had a general alarm at 12 o'clock, by reason of their taking one of our advanced sentinels, with the report of their coming out to give us battle. The army turned out, marched within fifty yards of the walls, gave them three cheers, upon which they gave us as many cannon shot. Took several loads of provisions going into the enemy. Attempted to send in a flag of truce by Major Ogden, but they would not receive it.

Wednesday, 15th. Nothing of consequence transpired this day. Attempted sending by flag again, but was fired upon. Had a false alarm.

Thursday, 16th. A brisk cannonade the most of the day upon a party of Captain Morgan's riflemen, who were stationed upon St. Charles River by the Nunnery. Wounded one Sergeant Dixon, that his leg was amputated. No other harm.

Friday, 17th. No extraordinary occurrence this day. A Canadian in McLean's regiment came from the enemy, brought intelligence advantageous.

Saturday, 18th. Another deserter from the city, by which we were informed they were preparing their field pieces in order to pay us a visit. A council was called, an examination of our arms, ammunition, &c. The former were found much deficient in numbers, much in disorder. No bayonets, no field pieces and upon an average of the ammunition there amounted only to about four rounds per man. Under these circumstances it was thought proper to raise the siege, and proceed up the river St. Lawrence, 8 leagues to "Point Aux Tremble." In the mean time dispatched an express to General Montgomery, informing him of our situation, &c. Orders were given accordingly, and at eight in the morn we decamped, leaving the old Abraham Plains to the Britons. Orders were likewise dispatched over the river to Point Levi, informing of our determination, and they marched upon the south side. Arrived there the night ensuing.

Sunday, 19th. The main of this day's occurrences under yesterday's head. Met with a large brig coming down from Montreal, in which was General Carleton, as we afterwards heard.

Monday, 20th. The post arrived in our camp this morning, brings certain news of the City of Montreal being in the hands of General Montgomery, and that he was on his march down to our assistance. An express was sent back again to the General.

Tuesday, 21st. Intelligence from Montreal informs of the capture of 11 sail, 800 barrels of pork, a large quantity of flour,

&c. Till now our army had been tolerably healthy since our arrival over the river, but free eating, more than usually cold weather, &c., produced inflammations, &c. Nothing material from this to the 25th. Some severe "Peripneumias," "Anginas," &c. Upon the 25th three up of the enemies ships of war came up the river, and lay off opposite us. Undoubtedly to intercept our shipping, as we every day expected them from Montreal.

Sunday, 26th. A proclamation came to hand issued by General Carleton, commanding all the citizens of Quebec, that would not take arms to defend the city, to disappear within four days; that it found after that they would be treated as spies. In consequence of this order several came out to our army.

Monday, 27th. As the General now approached, a detachment of 60 men were sent to escort him, while Captain Morgan and company was ordered down the river to the suburbs of Quebec to blockade the enemy. From this to the 1st of December no occurrences of note. The ministerial ships returned to the city.

Friday, Dec. 1st. Still at Point Aux Tremble. Arrived some of the ammunition from General Montgomery's army. At 12 o'clock two of our ships appeared from Montreal with soldiers on board. Anchored off Point Le Chapple. On board the top sail schooner was the General. A division from our little army was ordered out to receive him.

Saturday, 2d. Weather very rainy. This day and Sunday we were busily employed in making ready to proceed down the river to Quebec. A division of men, cannon, &c., were sent down the river.

Monday, 4th. General orders for all to decamp, and I hired a Frenchman with his charrioll, and proceeded to St. Foys, from thence to St. Charles, and took lodgings at Mr. Burrough's.

Tuesday, 5th. I had now orders to take possession of the General Hospital for the reception of our sick and wounded. This was an elegant building situate upon St. Charles river, half a mile from St. Roque's gate. A chapel, nunnery, and hospital, were all under one roof. This building was every way fit for the purpose, a fine spacious ward, capable of containing fifty patients, with one fire place, stoves, &c. The number of sick were not very considerable at this time, however they soon grew more numerous. The Hospital being in an advanced part of the army, I did not think it expedient to assume a residence therein as yet. In consequence of which I was obliged to visit it daily in open view of the enemy's walls, who seldom failed to give me a few shots every time.

Wednesday, 6th. The disposition of our army was such now, as to environ the enemy as much as possible, thereby to prevent any further supplies arriving to them, with other necessary preparations as facines, gabions, &c. Nothing extraordinary from this to the 9th, except two prisoners being caught and brought into camp from St. L. R., purchasing up provisions for the enemy. They had 300 dollars in specie.

Saturday, 9th. General order for a number of fatigue men for erecting a battery on the heights of the plain, distant from the walls of the city 200 yards. This was all done in the night time when the enemy were not apprised of it. In the mean time Captain Wool of the artillery was ordered to proceed into St. Roques in an advantageous place to heave bombs in the city. This was complied with, and I attended the affair. The enemy immediately gave us a fire from the ramparts, whenever they could bring their cannons to bear upon us. What effect our fire had we were never able exactly to ascertain, but I believe nothing considerable, as the bombs were very small. The enemy's fire did us no harm, except killing an old Frenchwoman in her *brodel* administering a spirituous potion to one of our lads.

Sunday, 10th. The enemy spying our battery, opened a brisk cannonade of their heavy cannon, in order to demolish it, likewise rushed out of St. John's gate in the cover of their cannons, burnt a number of houses, in one of which was a sick woman consumed. This was a distressing circumstance to the poor inhabitants, who were obliged to abandon their houses, notwithstanding the dire inclement season, and seek a shelter in the different parts of the country, where the humanity of the people would admit them. The view of the enemy in this *incineration* was to prevent our troops making a lodgment in them, and facilitating the operation of a general storm upon the city, which they had too much reason to apprehend.

Monday, 11th. Agreeable to prescription, fifty-five more of the fire pills were given to the Carletonians last evening. Operated with manifest perturbation, as they were (as usual) alarmed. Bells beating, dogs barking, &c. Their cannonade still continued on the battery but to no advantage. Forty-five more pills as cathartic last night.

Thursday, 14th. The snow or ice battery was finished last night, it chiefly consisted of first, a laying of fascines, then snow, to fill the interstices. The gabions were filled with earth and snow, little, however, of the former, as it was almost impossible to procure any, as the ground was very hard frozen. After the fabric was sufficient in magnificence to cement firm, large quantities of water were poured thereon. This freezing, soon formed into a heterogeneous body, not, however, sufficient to repel the monstrous force of their 32s and 42s, as sad experience soon proved. While mounting the cannon this morn, a shot came through the battery, killed and wounded five of the train. In all killed and wounded ten this day. Four of whom were Frenchmen.

Friday, 15th. At the dawn of day our battery opened upon them, in which was mounted five guns, none larger than 12s. The enemy soon followed suit, and the fire and refire was almost incessant for several hours. In the afternoon a flag of truce attempted to go in, but was ordered back immediately, or be fired upon.

Saturday, 16th. Quit my old lodgings at Monsieur Dorrough's and took a room in the nunnery by consent of the Lady Superior, Monks, &c. The sacredness by which this place was esteemed even by Milion's heterogeneous banditti, seemed to put me out of the power of their shot much more than when I visited every day. However, I seldom failed to have a shot every time I went from this to any of the officers quarters. Cannonade from both sides, not so severe as yesterday. A brave soldier by the name of Morgan received a grape shot under the lower edge of the left scapula close to the uxila, and went obliquely through both lobes of the lungs. Walked more than a mile, with the assistance of a messmate, into the Hospital. A superficial dressing was all that could be done, as violent henoptoi ensued; concluded his residence was not long.

Sunday, 17th. Had a very heavy snow storm. Cannonade not very heavy. From this to the 23d no occurrences of consequence, except the small pox broke out in the army, and on the 18th five were brought into the hospital.

Saturday, 23d. Not only the small pox, but the pleurisy, peripneumonia, with the other species of pulmonic complaints, were now very prevalent in the army. However, the issue of in all general favourable.

Sunday, 24th. By this time the artillery were pretty generally sick of their ice battery, which they fatally experienced to be too feeble for the purpose for which it was erected. The enemy's cannon being very heavy as well as numerous, and as nigh as necessary, our soldiers were obliged to quit the battery. From this time the enemy began their bombarding our barracks, mostly under the shelving precipices of St. Roque, out of the range of most of their cannon, but no considerable damage was done.

Monday, 25th. The enemy's bombardment still continuing day and night, that the glass of the Hospital was much damaged, but nothing considerable to the soldiery. Had the variloid matter transfused into my arm this day.

Wednesday, 26th. Nothing extraordinary transpired this day. The enemy continuing their discharge of bombs, &c.

Thursday, 27th. Preparations were made in a manner as secret as possible for the storming the city in the night. After all things were arranged accordingly, the weather cleared away serene and bright, which foiled our undertaking. For a mark of distinction each soldier was ordered to procure a fir sprig, and fix it in the front of their caps, whereby they might be discriminated. Of this the enemy were advised by some unaccountable *incident*. At this assemblage there were three captains of companies who were averse to storming, though urged by the general. Their men were willing, but they obstinately determined. Their names I have omitted in consequence of their better behaviour. Upon their declining, the general said he would not compel them, that he wanted no persons with him who went with reluctance. Several of the men signifying their earnest desire of going with the rest of their fellows who went through the woods. Upon which I wrote a billit to Colonel Arnold, desiring his permission to

head one of the companies which we then thought would
tarry behind in consequence of the absence of their commander. Upon which I received this upon the opposite side,
which I have preserved in "perpetuam rei memoriam" for future posterity:

> "DEAR SIR: — I am much obliged to you for your
> offer, and glad to see you so spirited, but cannot con-
> sent you should take up arms, as you will be wanted in
> the way of your profession. You will please to prepare
> dressings, &c., and repair to the main guard house
> at 2 o'clock in the morning with an assistant.
>
> I am in haste, yours,
>
> DOCT. CENTER.   B. ARNOLD, Col.
> 27 Dec. 1775."

The undertaking was postponed in hopes of a night by it's
darkness more favourable. The enemy were daily cleaning out
their ditch round the city walls, in order to obstruct our ascending the fortification. From intelligence the enemy undoubtedly expected us every night, especially if thick and
cloudy, for which we were now waiting. In this situation we
held ourselves in readiness 'till Saturday the 31st, which was
stormy, and increased towards evening. The troops from the
advanced post were ordered to Head-Quarters in the night.
The storm increased most violently, wind northeast, what fell
mostly consisted of hail in the night though it snowed the
preceeding day. The disposition of the army being made, they
were ordered to proceed at four in the morning.

Sunday, 31st. Head-Quarters was at St. Foys. Here General
Montgomery kept Colonel Arnold, with several more of the
field officers. The arrangements of the army was as follows,
viz., General Montgomery on the right wing, with the majority of the troops from Montreal, &c. Colonel Arnold on the
left, with his division of "Famine proof Veterans." Colonel
Livingston's Canadian Regiment, to assault the walls at St.
John's gate, with combustibles for firing the gate, and thereby
to draw the attention of the enemy that way, and at the same
time attempt the walls a little distance with scaling ladders,
&c. The place where the General was to assault, was on the
bank of the St. Lawrence, at the termination of the city walls,

and where large piquets were substituted. For this purpose instruments were carried to make the breach. Arnold was to attack at the other extremity of the town, where he first
expected to be opposed by some small batteries before he arrived in the lower town, where the two extremes were to
form a junction. To discriminate our troops from the enemy
in action, they were ordered each officer and soldier to make
fast a piece of white paper across their caps from the front to
the acmé of them. Thus matters being arranged in the
evening, upon their arms they lay 'till 4 o'clock in the morn,
during which time the General was noticed to be extremely
anxious, as if anticipating the fatal catastrophe.

Ruminating in this despondency, back and forth he traversed his room 'till the limited time bade him go forth!

> "The dawn is overcast, the morning lowr's
> And heavily in clouds brings on the day,
> The great, the important day big with the fate
> Of Montgomery, and his host."

The decree being fixed, and the assailants determined,
though gloomy the prospect in this tremendous storm —
snow not less than six feet deep, while yet a heavy darkness
pervaded the earth almost to be felt. Thus went they on,

> "Through winds and storms, and mountains of snow,
> Impatient for the battle. But, alas!
> Think what anxious moments pass between
> The birth of enterprises, and their last fatal periods,
> Oh! 'tis a dreadful interval of time,
> Filled up with honor all, and big with death."

No sooner had they crossed that bloody plain, American
Pharsalia, than the fiery signal was given for the attack.
Montgomery at the front of his division forced his way
through the strong piquets upon the precipice of the river
bank.

> "Greatly unfortunate, he fought the cause,
> Of honor, virtue, liberty and his Country."

But a little way had they entered ere a dire display from the
whole extent of their lines illuminated the air, and shocked

the environs of the city by the tremendous explosion. The discharge was kept up from the whole extent of the city walls incessantly. While fire balls where kept out beyond where they supposed our troops were, thereby to discover them between the walls and their ball, which burnt notwithstanding the depth of snow with amazing advantage to the enemy. Not more than an hour had the action continued before the wounded came tumbling in, that the grand ward was directly filled. They continued coming until the enemy rushed out at St. John's Gate and St. Roque's suburbs, and captured the horses and carriages, the men escaping which were employed in that service. Few of the wounded escaping from their hands, after the capture of the horses, &c., except those wounded slightly. Daylight had scarce made its appearance ere Colonel Arnold was brought in, supported by two soldiers, wounded in the leg, with a piece of a musket ball. The ball had probable come in contact with a cannon, rock, stone or the like, ere it entered the leg which had cleft off nigh a third. The other two-thirds entered the outer side of the leg, about midway, and in an oblique course passed between the tibia and fibula, lodged in the gastrœnnemea muscle at the rise of the tendon achilles, where upon examination I easily discovered and extracted it. Before the Colonel was done with, Major Ogden came in wounded through the left shoulder, which proved only a flesh wound. The Major gave it as his opinion that we should not be successful. The fire and re-fire continued incessant. No news from the General and his party yet, which gave us doubtful apprehensions of their success. Not long had we remained in an anxious suspense ere an express came down from the plain informing of the fatal news of the death, and that the remainder of his division had retreated precipitately back to Head-Quarters. We were also immediately advised of the fall of Captain Cheesman, and Mr. McPherson, two gallant young officers, the former commanding one of the New York Companies, the latter his Aid-de-Camp. To this melancholy news was immediately added the capture of Captain Darby and company, by a sortie of the enemy from St. Roque's Gate, and that the enemy were still without the walls advancing towards the Hospital. We soon perceived this to be true, in consequence of which all the invalids, stragglers and some few of the artillery that were left behind were ordered to march immediately into St. Roque street with a couple of field pieces under command of Lieut. Captain Wool, who much distinguished himself on this occasion. He took the advantage of a turn in the street and gave the enemy so well directed a fire, as put them to flight immediately. Notwithstanding this, we were momentarily expecting them out upon us, as we concluded Arnold's division, then under the command of Lieut. Col. Greene, were all killed, captured, &c. Under these circumstances we entreated Colonel Arnold for his own safety to be carried back into the country where they would not readily find him when out, but to no purpose. He would neither be removed, nor suffer a man from the Hospital to retreat. He ordered his pistols loaded, with a sword on his bed, &c., adding that he was determined to kill as many as possible if they came into the room. We were now all soldiers, even to the wounded in their beds were ordered a gun by their side. That if they did attack the Hospital to make the most vigorous defence possible. Orders were sent out into the villages round the city, to the Captains of the militia to immediately assemble to our assistance. The peasants, however friendly disposed, thought it too precarious a juncture to shew themselves in that capacity, and those nigh rather retreated back into the country, than give any assistance. The storm still continued tremendously. Colonel Livingston's Regiment who were employed in firing St. John's Gate made the best of their way off soon after the heavy fire began. Orders were dispatched up to St. Foy's for assistance from the party who were retreated, who assisted but little. An express was sent off to Congress informing of our situation, and requesting immediate assistance. No news from Greene's division to be depended on. The prospect was gloomy on every side. The loss of the bravest of Generals, with other amiable officers smote the breasts of all around with inexpressible grief. "Oh, Liberty! Oh, virtue! Oh, my country!" seemed the language of all.

Sarah Hodgkins and Joseph Hodgkins

Ipswich Febry ye 1 1776
Loveing Husband these lines come with my most afectionate
regards to you hoping they will find you in as good health as
they Leave me & rest of the family I received your Letter of
the 29 instant Mr Coldwel brought me a gun and Some peas
a Sater day night your Letters are Something of a rearity I
wish you would write oftener if you can this day was the turn
for Mr Danas Lecture he thought the times calld for fasting
and acordingly he tirnd it into a day of fasting & prayer and
desird our parrish to join with them I have been to meeting
all day & heard two as find Sermons as amost ever I heard Mr
Frisby preachd in the forenoon and mr Dana in the afternoon
next wensday is our ordanation it is apointed a day of fasting
I Should be very glad if you could be at home but I dont ex-
pec [   ] deprivd of it god only knows I must jest you inform that your brotr John Webber has been here he desires to
be rembered to you he Says he wants very much to See you
So no more at present but I remain your Loving wife till
Death   Sarah Hodgkins

PS give regards to Capt Wade and tell I have wanted his bed
fellow prety much these cold nights that we have had Father
and mother Sends their Love to you

In Camp att Prospect Hill Feby 3 1776
My Dear I take this oppertunity to inform you that I am will
att Presant & I hope these lines will find you Posest of the
same Blesings I Received yours of ye 28 of January and I
Rejoice to hear that you & our Children are will and as it
gives me grate satisfacton to Receive Letters from you so you
may Depend on my imbrasing Every opportunnity to write to
you I have no News to write we Live in our tent yet only
when we are smoked out and then we git shealter some whare
Else we live Pretty well and our Duty is not hard we go on

guard only once in tin Day but we spend a grate Part of our time in Exersising the Regiment I must Conclude give my Duty to my Parence and Respects all my frinds so no more at Presant But Remain your loving Husband

Joseph Hodgkins

My Dear I whant a little shothread & I should Be glad to have you send my shirts as soon as you Can Till Brother he must write to Mr Hall Before he will send the papper

———

In Camp att Prospect Hill Feby ye 5 1776

Loveing wife I take this oppertunity to write a line or two to Let you know that I am well & I hope thase Lines will find you and our Children Persest of the same Blessings that I Enjoy I Received yours of the first instant & I Rejoyce to hear that you whare all well You informed me that Mr Frisby is to ordaned next Wensday I wish I could Be at home But I cannot you are Pleased to say that Letters from me are somthing of a rearaty I wish I could send offender But we have not so many oppertunitys as we ust to have But you may Depend on my Chearfulness to Embrace Every oppertunity that Presents for my Part I take grate Pleasure in writing to you & likewise in Receiving Letter from you But I must Be short I have no News to write Capt Wade has Ben something unwell But he is Better now give my Regards to all Enquiring frinds so no more att Presant But Remain your Loving Husband till Death

Joseph Hodgkins

PS I gave your Regards to Capt Wade But he Did not wish that you had his Bed fellow But I wish you had with all my heart

———

In Camp at Prospect Hill Feby ye 6 1776

My Dear having an oppertunity this morning to write a line By Capt Wade I would inform you that I am well & I hope these lines will find you the same I should Ben Very glad to Come home to ordanation and upon my making applycation to Capt he whent to the Colol & when he found that one officer out of the Company might go home insted of speaking a word for me he spok two for himself But if you should have the oppertunity to see him Due ask him to supper with you though I Due not Expect you will see him soon enough So I must Conclude att this Time By subscribing my self your Loving Husband till Death   Joseph Hodgkins

give my Duty to all Parence & Love to all friends

———

                              Ipswich Febry ye 11 1776
Loveing Husband haveing an oppertunity this evening to write a line or two to you I gladly embrace it to Let you know that we are well hopeing they will find you posest of the Same Blessing I received two Letters from you on ordanation day after meeting which was a greate comfort to me to hear that were well I received one by the hand of Capt Wade but not till after Supper I have been glad to have invited to Supper if I had Seen him Soon enough we had a comfortable ordana-tion but there Seems to me to be Something wanting I wanted you at home & that would have crownd all it is very cold to night I hope you will be provided for with a Comfortable Lodging I think a great deal about you both by night & by day but I desire to commite you to God who has hitherto preserved you & he is able Still to preserve you at all times O my Dear Let me beg of you to pute your trust in him att all times who alone is able to deliver us out of all our tro-bles will doo it if we trust in him aright but I must conclude I remain your most afectionate companion till Death
                              Sarah Hodgkins

PS farther & mother Sends their Love to you wensday I wrote the above Letter on Sabbath day night I did not know but Capt Wade would go down the next day but I hear he is not gone yet & I dont know as I shall See him but I hoped. [   ]

———

                    In Camp Prospect Feby ye 12 1776
My Dear these Lines Comes with my most afectniate Regards to you hoping thay will find you and our Children in as good health as thay Leave me at this Time through the goodness of

god I enjoy a good state of health But we under go a good Deal of Defielty for whant of a Better house But I Expect to move in a Day or two to our Barrak whare we have got a Prety Room as I must Be shor for the weather is Very Cold & our tent smoks so that it is with Defelty that I can stay in it My Dear as for News we have not much But it is sayed that the Generals are Determaned to do something very soon But What the event will be god only knows But I hope god will Direct them in there Counsels & order Every thing for his Glory & our good so I must Conclude at this time By subscribing my self your Loveing Husband Till Death

Joseph Hodgkins

PS Give my Duty to farther & mother and Love to all frinds tel Brother I sent his Letter to Mr Hall But I have not had oppertunity to go to him since I am Prity much tied at home

————

Ipswich Febry ye 20 1776

My Dear I take this oppertunity to write aline or two to inform you that we are all in a Comfortable State of Health through the goodness of God & I hope these lines will find you posest of the Same Blessing I received yours by Mr Smith & I rejoice to hear that you are well I want to See you very much I think you told me that you intended to See me once a mounth & it is now amonth & I think a very long one Since you left home & I dont hear as you talk of comeing but I must confess I dont think it is for want of a good will that you dont come home it is generaly thoght that there will be Something done amongst you very Soon but what will be the event of it God only knows o that we may be prepared for all events I am destressd about you my Dear but I desire to commit you to God who alone is able to preserve us through all the deficulty we have to pass through may he Strenghten your hands & incorage your heart to carry you through all you may be called in the way of your duty & that you may be enabled to put your trust in him at all times but I must conclude att this time by Subscribing myself your most afectionate Companion till Death   Sarah Hodkins

PS Joanna Sends her duty to you

John Bowater to the Earl of Denbigh

Centurion: King's Road, Boston March 25th. 1776
My Lord

I wrote to your Lordship by the *Preston*, Admiral Graves, which was the only Ship that has Saild from hence since my Arrival in America. Neither has Any ship Arrived here since she saild nor have I Received a line from any one since I left England. The Violence of the Winds at this Season of the Year with the extream Coldness of the Weather has prevented any ship Approaching the Coast. By a Sloop that came in Yesterday from Antigua we have an account of three men of War & Seventy sail of Transports Victualers & store Ships being drove in there & was Refitting in order to join us as soon as possable. And we are now all looking with the utmost anxiety for Vessels to Appear in sight as no one here is free from the dreadfull Thought of famine as I am inform'd we have not a months provisions Remaining for either Army or Navy. Tho we have been for this week past put upon two thirds of Allowance, and I believe this was the principal Reason for our Evacuating Boston, tho many others are Assign'd. The Rebels taking Possession of Dorchester Heights, & at last made their Approaches within a Thousand Yards of the Town, it was said to be no longer Tenable. Indeed at last they Amused us with both shot and shells in every part of the Town, but did no damage to the Shiping. An other Reason Assign'd was, that by our being Embarked must puzzle the Enemy exceedingly as they wou'd not Know where to guard most — And we might go to any place that wou'd Joyn us heartily. The present orders says Halifax but that Cannot be for any time as we have exausted that Country during the Winter. Meat was rose to 10*d.* per pound all over the province two months ago. We have three & twenty Battalions embarkt with us yet we have not seven Thousand fighting men. But with Women & Children civil Officers, followers of the Army, and many of the principal Inhabitants of Boston, (who if they did not accompany us would be either hung or sent to the mines) we are above twenty Thousand people to Receive Victuals & drink. The Transports are very much Crowded & a great many Children was Sufficated the first night and if the Weather turns Warm I am afraid the Troops will be sickly. It wou'd be a pitty to loose any of them, as I never saw a more spirited sett of fellows — and they have the greatest Confidence in their Generalls, if they Lament any thing it is that they can die but once in the service of their Country. The Cruelty Committed daily by the Rebels makes them keen for Revenge.

Mr. Feilding writes to your Lordship by this Oppertunity and will give you an Exact Account of all the millitary motions previous to the Retreat — as Every precaution was taken the same as if the Enemy meant to anoy us. But they chose to save the Town as the principal seat of their Rebellion, and we wou'd not destroy it as the principal part of it belongs to the Friends of Government, also it might be Nessisary for us to retake it again for the next Winter Quarters. Tho I now think we shall go either to New York or Virginia, we have still a Regiment of light Horse with us which takes up as much Room as six Regiments of Foot and they never could be of the least service in any one of the Colonies, this with a Thousand other Absurdities which the wise heads at home have transmitted to us has laid us under the most dreadful misfortunes. Coals Porter & Potatoes have been brought out to us in great Plenty and in large Ships with twenty Guns & a hundred men. Brass Cannon, Mortars, Shells, Balls, flints, Powder &c. &c., have been sent out in small Briggs, with two & four Guns & ten or twelve men. And they have been taken by the Enemy who have beat us Very severely with our own Weapons. (The Board of Ordinance is in great disrepute with us at present.) If we are Expected to do any thing considerable we must have very great Reinforcements as the Rebels are so Numerous, they have above five & twenty Thousand Round us now & they take the utmost pains in Disciplining them, & they have got a great many Foreigners amongst them Runegadoes & partisans from all Countrys which are Very great Rascals but are generally Very Clever fellows. We have not had any late Accounts of Genl. Carleton but we are in hopes he will be Able to hold out at Quebec untill we can send him a Reinforcement he has perform'd Wonders already.

My best Respects attends Lady Denbigh & family. The packett going in haste obliges me to Conclude. Major Charles Stewart is well we often Converse and he desires to be Remember'd to your Lordship.

You must not Expect to hear from me often as we are so often sent out of the way when any thing is going home & it is at least a Thousand to one you do not Receive this.

Abigail Adams to John Adams

Braintree March 31 1776

I wish you would ever write me a Letter half as long as I write you; and tell me if you may where your Fleet are gone? What sort of Defence Virginia can make against our common Enemy? Whether it is so situated as to make an able Defence? Are not the Gentery Lords and the common people vassals, are they not like the uncivilized Natives Brittain represents us to be? I hope their Riffel Men who have shewen themselves very savage and even Blood thirsty; are not a specimen of the Generality of the people.

I am willing to allow the Colony great merrit for having produced a Washington but they have been shamefully duped by a Dunmore.

I have sometimes been ready to think that the passion for Liberty cannot be Eaquelly Strong in the Breasts of those who have been accustomed to deprive their fellow Creatures of theirs. Of this I am certain that it is not founded upon that generous and christian principal of doing to others as we would that others should do unto us.

Do not you want to see Boston; I am fearfull of the small pox, or I should have been in before this time. I got Mr. Crane to go to our House and see what state it was in. I find it has been occupied by one of the Doctors of a Regiment, very dirty, but no other damage has been done to it. The few things which were left in it are all gone. Cranch has the key which he never deliverd up. I have wrote to him for it and am determined to get it cleand as soon as possible and shut it up. I look upon it a new acquisition of property, a property which one month ago I did not value at a single Shilling, and could with pleasure have seen it in flames.

The Town in General is left in a better state than we expected, more oweing to a percipitate flight than any Regard to the inhabitants, tho some individuals discoverd a sense of honour and justice and have left the rent of the Houses in which they were, for the owners and the furniture unhurt, or if damaged sufficent to make it good.

Others have committed abominable Ravages. The Mansion House of your President is safe and the furniture unhurt whilst both the House and Furniture of the Solisiter General have fallen a prey to their own merciless party. Surely the very Fiends feel a Reverential awe for Virtue and patriotism, whilst they Detest the paricide and traitor.

I feel very differently at the approach of spring to what I did a month ago. We knew not then whether we could plant or sow with safety, whether when we had toild we could reap the fruits of our own industery, whether we could rest in our own Cottages, or whether we should not be driven from the sea coasts to seek shelter in the wilderness, but now we feel as if we might sit under our own vine and eat the good of the land.

I feel a gaieti de Coar to which before I was a stranger. I think the Sun looks brighter, the Birds sing more melodiously, and Nature puts on a more chearfull countanance. We feel a temporary peace, and the poor fugitives are returning to their deserted habitations.

Tho we felicitate ourselves, we sympathize with those who are trembling least the Lot of Boston should be theirs. But they cannot be in similar circumstances unless pusilanimity and cowardise should take possession of them. They have time and warning given them to see the Evil and shun it. — I long to hear that you have declared an independancy — and by the way in the new Code of Laws which I suppose it will be necessary for you to make I desire you would Remember the Ladies, and be more generous and favourable to them than your ancestors. Do not put such unlimited power into the hands of the Husbands. Remember all Men would be tyrants if they could. If perticuliar care and attention is not paid to the Laidies we are determined to foment a Rebelion, and will not hold ourselves bound by any Laws in which we have no voice, or Representation.

That your Sex are Naturally Tyrannical is a Truth so thoroughly established as to admit of no dispute, but such of you as wish to be happy willingly give up the harsh title of Master for the more tender and endearing one of Friend. Why then, not put it out of the power of the vicious and the Lawless to use us with cruelty and indignity with impunity. Men of Sense in all Ages abhor those customs which treat us only as the vassals of your Sex. Regard us then as Beings placed by providence under your protection and in immitation of the Supreem Being make use of that power only for our happiness.

Peter Oliver: from "The Origin & Progress of American Rebellion"

I SHALL now leave the Congress at *Philadelphia*, & return to *Boston*, if I can get a Passport through the Rebel Army, which every day blockades the Town closer than the preceeding. I must leave all the Delicacies that so important a Body of men are epicurizing upon, & return to my former Fare of coarse Salt Beef on one day, & upon nothing the next; but which to give the Preference to, I am at a loss. If I can be excused from Shells & Shot, I shall be content with the latter, for they are much harder of Digestion, than nothing at all.

In the Autumn of *1775*, difficulties increased upon the British Troops & the Inhabitants, in *Boston*, whilst the rebel Army increased in Resources of Men & Stores, of which they had a full supply. Many Vessells, which were coming from *England* & *Ireland*, with Provisions & Stores for the Army & for the Inhabitants, were captured within a few Leagues of *Boston*; and the Rebels Vessells arrived safe with Supplies for *them*. Genl. *Gage* embarqued for *England* in October, & left the Command of the Civil, or rather no Government, to the Care of Lieut. Governor *Oliver*; & of the Army to General *Howe*.

It was rather Astonishing, that so many Vessells should be captured, & so near to so many King's Ships; when a great Part of them might have been saved. For, at a Place called *Salem*, within 3 or 4 hours Sail from *Boston*, & another Place, vizt. *Newbury*, at abt 7 or 8 Hours Sail from *Boston*, were hauled up 7 or 800 Vessells of various Sorts, which might have been easily taken or destroyed. Had this been done, their privateering Resources of rigging & Sails would have been destroyed, for some Time at least. Besides, those two Towns of *Salem* & *Newbury* were deep in Rebellion, & if they too had been destroyed, such Destruction might have been justified on the common Principles of War, & of Humanity also; for had such Measures been taken at first, there is the highest Probability that thousands of Lives would have been saved, as well as enormous Expences of Treasure, to both *England* & *America*. But the Plea then was; that if such Measures were pursued, it would irritate the Americans & make them desperate. Those who have made this Plea have lived to see the Erroneousness of their Calculations; & that ill-judged Lenity & a Forbearance to irritate have thrown Rebellion into the utmost Desperation. In short, it seemed to be the Business, of Navy & Army, to help each other in doing nothing, except parrying of the Knife which was held to their Throats; without disabling the Hand, which held it, from Execution.

In the Winter of *1775*, the severe cold Northwest Winds blew off the Coasts several Vessells with Troops & Provisions, that were transporting Relief for the Garrison at *Boston*; and the Rebels had received such Supplies of Ammunition, so as to be ready for an Attack on the Opening of the Spring. It was expected that they would have made an Attack, upon the Ice, which surrounded the Town in the Depth of Winter. The Soldiers of their Army expected it, & the chief Men of their civil Government expressed their Uneasiness to Mr. *Washington* that he did not suffer it; when he told them that he had scarce a Round of Powder to a Man; but they soon had a Supply after the Severity of Winter was over, & then they began upon Exertions to drive off the Kings Troops from their strong Holds.

There was an Hill, called *Foster's Hill* on *Dorchester's* Neck, to the South East of *Boston*, across an Arm of the Sea, & within point blank Shot of the Town; from whence only, it seemed that the Town could be greatly annoyed. It had often been wished that this Hill had had proper Attention paid to it; & it had been repeatedly mentioned, that it was of the last Necessity to secure such a Position; but the general Answers were, that there was no Danger from it, & that it was to be wished that the Rebels would attempt to take Possession of it, as they could soon be dislodged — We shall presently see how wise those military Calculations were.

There was another Hill, a little to the Southward of *Foster's Hill*, still higher; a Redoubt upon which, with a small Force, would have been tenable against a very large Army of so undisciplined Troops as surrounded the Town: but perhaps it was against the Rules of War to have fortified either of those Hills. We are now to see the Consequences of such Conduct.

The Weather now opening, to begin military Operations, the Rebels mustered between 20 & 30,000 Men: about 10 or 11,000 of whom began to throw up Works on the last mentioned Hill. This being observed from *Boston*, Genl. *Howe* determined to attack them. Accordingly he ordered a Corps of about 1700 Men to embark in large Vessells & Boats, to cross the Water, to attack them; he himself designing to march by Land to flank them, with another Corps. The first Corps were embarqued & sailed; but a most severe Storm arising at South, some of these Vessells grounded, & a Retreat was ordered. It was an happy Disappointment, for had the Attack been made, this steep Hill must have been climbed with Musquetry only; & the Rebels had placed Rocks & large Stones on the Top of it, to roll down & break the Ranks of the Kings Troops, whilst they theirselves were discharging their Balls at them. I have no doubt but the Kings Troops would have defeated the Rebels; but it would have been another *Bunker's Hill* affair; the Carnage would have been great, & Men could not have been so well spared as then; & after so many of them had been used up, there were no Resources for a Recruit. Thus this Expedition failed.

The Month of March 1776 opened with a new Scene. The Rebels had waited long enough for the King's Troops to fortifie *Foster's Hill*; & since they would not do it, the Rebels thought it a Pity so fine a Situation should not be occupied, and so fortified it theirselves. It was done thus! They had prepared a large Timber Battery, in separate Pieces, as also a large Quantity of screwed Hay to fill between the Timbers when they were put together. There was no Suspicion of such a Battery being in Preparation, untill after a long dark Night it arose in full View, & began to play upon the Town. It was now Time for the Troops in Town to make the best Terms for theirselves, & to get off as fast as they could; for in vain would they have fired to destroy this Battery, made of Wood & Hay; they might have fired at it 'till this Day & would have made but little Impression. Although the Weather was cool, yet the Town was hot enough; for the Rebels kept up an incessant Fire with Shells & Shot into it, for 6 successive Nights; but, to the astonishment of all, with scarcely any Damage.

Affairs being in this Situation, & Genl. *Howe* having had Orders from Home to evacuate *Boston*, he gave Notice to Genl. *Washington* of such his Purpose; informing him, that if he would suffer him to embark unmolested that he would not injure the Town; otherwise, that he would lay it in Ashes. Some of the Rebels were for suffering the Town to be demolished; but there being so many good Buildings & so much Treasure in it, the major Part prevailed, & his Proposal was complied with. Immediately all Hands were at Work for evacuation; & the Cathartick was of so drastick a Nature, that by the 17th. of the Month, *Boston* was emptied of it's late Inhabitants, & a new Generation supplied their Places. Notwithstanding of the great Assiduty in embarking, Genl. *Howe* was obliged to leave many valuable Stores behind him.

The Destruction of that fine Fortress, *Castle William*, took up about a Week; & on the 20th. of March it was finished. On the 27th. the last Division of the Fleet of Troops & Inhabitants sailed from *Nantasket* road, about 9 Miles from *Boston*, & on the 2nd. of April arrived at *Hallifax*.

There were Vast Numbers of the Inhabitants of *Boston* & of those who had fled thither, as to an Asylum, from the Cruelties of Rebellion. Many Loyalists were left behind, who had nothing to support them from their Homes; & many, who had Families which they were loth should be separated, as there was not Transports for all who would have been willing to have embarked. These were obliged to take their Chances of ill Usage, & some of them felt it severely; particularly six Gentlemen of good Reputation. One of these six, in particular, was used in a strictly diabolical Manner; he was a Loyalist, but an inoffensive one in his Behavior; he had an amiable Wife & several amiable Children; the Rebel Cart, in Imitation of the Inquisition Coach, called at his Door in the Morning, & they ordered him into the Cart, not suffering him to take his Hat with him; his Wife, at the same Time, begging on her Knees, to spare her Husband; & his Daughters crying, with Intreaties. This infernal Crew were deaf to the Cries of Distress, & drove on, untill they had got the six into the Cart; whom they carried to the Kings Lines, at the extreme Part of the Town, & there tipped up the Cart, & tumbled them into a Ditch; & not content with this diabolical Barbarity, they forbad their entring the Town again; & at the same Time, also, forbad the People in the Country to give them Food or to shelter them. Step forward thou *Iroquois* Savage! & drop *your* Tear of Humanity over this horrid Scene of Barbarity, perpetrated in a Town which for many, very many Years past, hath boasted of the Sanctity of Christianity!

It is in vain to plead Excuse, that this & many other like Diabolical Cruelties were acted by Mohawks, or the Rabble: they, & this also, were transacted in open Day, that the Sun & the civil Government might be Witnesses to the horrid Deeds, but Heaven, in this Instance, interposed, & inspired into the Hearts of some People in the Country so much Humanity, as to save these unhappy Sufferers from meeting the cruel Deaths assigned to them by their Persecutors, and even a Colo. of a rebel Regiment, who was quartered near the Town, was so roused wth. a compassionate Resentment, that he succoured them; & declared to his Employers, that if such Inhumanity was suffered, he would resign his Commission & quit their cause.

John Adams to Abigail Adams

Philadelphia July 3. 1776

Your Favour of June 17. dated at Plymouth, was handed me, by Yesterdays Post. I was much pleased to find that you had taken a Journey to Plymouth, to see your Friends in the long Absence of one whom you may wish to see. The Excursion will be an Amusement, and will serve your Health. How happy would it have made me to have taken this Journey with you?

I was informed, a day or two before the Receipt of your Letter, that you was gone to Plymouth, by Mrs. Polly Palmer, who was obliging enough in your Absence, to inform me, of the Particulars of the Expedition to the lower Harbour against the Men of War. Her Narration is executed, with a Precision and Perspicuity, which would have become the Pen of an accomplished Historian.

I am very glad you had so good an opportunity of seeing one of our little American Men of War. Many Ideas, new to you, must have presented themselves in such a Scene; and you will in future, better understand the Relations of Sea Engagements.

I rejoice extreamly at Dr. Bulfinches Petition to open an Hospital. But I hope, the Business will be done upon a larger Scale. I hope, that one Hospital will be licensed in every County, if not in every Town. I am happy to find you resolved, to be with the Children, in the first Class. Mr. Whitney and Mrs. Katy Quincy, are cleverly through Innoculation, in this City.

I have one favour to ask, and that is, that in your future Letters, you would acknowledge the Receipt of all those you may receive from me, and mention their Dates. By this Means I shall know if any of mine miscarry.

The Information you give me of our Friends refusing his Appointment, has given me much Pain, Grief and Anxiety. I believe I shall be obliged to follow his Example. I have not

Fortune enough to support my Family, and what is of more Importance, to support the Dignity of that exalted Station. It is too high and lifted up, for me; who delight in nothing so much as Retreat, Solitude, Silence, and Obscurity. In private Life, no one has a Right to censure me for following my own Inclinations, in Retirement, Simplicity, and Frugality: in public Life, every Man has a Right to remark as he pleases, at least he thinks so.

Yesterday the greatest Question was decided, which ever was debated in America, and a greater perhaps, never was or will be decided among Men. A Resolution was passed without one dissenting Colony "that these united Colonies, are, and of right ought to be free and independent States, and as such, they have, and of Right ought to have full Power to make War, conclude Peace, establish Commerce, and to do all the other Acts and Things, which other States may rightfully do." You will see in a few days a Declaration setting forth the Causes, which have impell'd Us to this mighty Revolution, and the Reasons which will justify it, in the Sight of God and Man. A Plan of Confederation will be taken up in a few days.

When I look back to the Year 1761, and recollect the Argument concerning Writs of Assistance, in the Superiour Court, which I have hitherto considered as the Commencement of the Controversy, between Great Britain and America, and run through the whole Period from that Time to this, and recollect the series of political Events, the Chain of Causes and Effects, I am surprized at the Suddenness, as well as Greatness of this Revolution. Britain has been fill'd with Folly, and America with Wisdom, at least this is my Judgment. — Time must determine. It is the Will of Heaven, that the two Countries should be sundered forever. It may be the Will of Heaven that America shall suffer Calamities still more wasting and Distresses yet more dreadfull. If this is to be the Case, it will have this good Effect, at least: it will inspire Us with many Virtues, which We have not, and correct many Errors, Follies, and Vices, which threaten to disturb, dishonour, and destroy Us. — The Furnace of Affliction produces Refinement, in States as well as Individuals. And the new Governments we are assuming, in every Part, will require a Purification from our Vices, and an Augmentation of our

Virtues or they will be no Blessings. The People will have unbounded Power. And the People are extreamly addicted to
Corruption and Venality, as well as the Great. — I am not
without Apprehensions from this Quarter. But I must submit
all my Hopes and Fears, to an overruling Providence, in
which, unfashionable as the Faith may be, I firmly believe.

Philadelphia July 3d. 1776

Had a Declaration of Independency been made seven
Months ago, it would have been attended with many great
and glorious Effects. . . . We might before this Hour, have
formed Alliances with foreign States. — We should have mas-
tered Quebec and been in Possession of Canada. . . . You
will perhaps wonder, how such a Declaration would have influenced our Affairs, in Canada, but if I could write with
Freedom I could easily convince you, that it would, and explain to you the manner how. — Many Gentlemen in high
Stations and of great Influence have been duped, by the ministerial Bubble of Commissioners to treat. . . . And in real,
sincere Expectation of this Event, which they so fondly
wished, they have been slow and languid, in promoting
Measures for the Reduction of that Province. Others there are
in the Colonies who really wished that our Enterprise in
Canada would be defeated, that the Colonies might be
brought into Danger and Distress between two Fires, and be
thus induced to submit. Others really wished to defeat the
Expedition to Canada, lest the Conquest of it, should elevate
the Minds of the People too much to hearken to those Terms
of Reconciliation which they believed would be offered Us.
These jarring Views, Wishes and Designs, occasioned an opposition to many salutary Measures, which were proposed for
the Support of that Expedition, and caused Obstructions,
Embarrassments and studied Delays, which have finally, lost
Us the Province.

All these Causes however in Conjunction would not have
disappointed Us, if it had not been for a Misfortune, which
could not be foreseen, and perhaps could not have been prevented, I mean the Prevalence of the small Pox among our
Troops. . . . This fatal Pestilence compleated our Destruc-

tion. — It is a Frown of Providence upon Us, which We ought to lay to heart.

But on the other Hand, the Delay of this Declaration to this Time, has many great Advantages attending it. — The Hopes of Reconciliation, which were fondly entertained by Multitudes of honest and well meaning tho weak and mistaken People, have been gradually and at last totally extinguished. — Time has been given for the whole People, maturely to consider the great Question of Independence and to ripen their Judgments, dissipate their Fears, and allure their Hopes, by discussing it in News Papers and Pamphletts, by debating it, in Assemblies, Conventions, Committees of Safety and Inspection, in Town and County Meetings, as well as in private Conversations, so that the whole People in every Colony of the 13, have now adopted it, as their own Act. — This will cement the Union, and avoid those Heats and perhaps Convulsions which might have been occasioned, by such a Declaration Six Months ago.

But the Day is past. The Second Day of July 1776, will be the most memorable Epocha, in the History of America. — I am apt to believe that it will be celebrated, by succeeding Generations, as the great anniversary Festival. It ought to be commemorated, as the Day of Deliverance by solemn Acts of Devotion to God Almighty. It ought to be solemnized with Pomp and Parade, with Shews, Games, Sports, Guns, Bells, Bonfires and Illuminations from one End of this Continent to the other from this Time forward forever more.

You will think me transported with Enthusiasm but I am not. — I am well aware of the Toil and Blood and Treasure, that it will cost Us to maintain this Declaration, and support and defend these States. — Yet through all the Gloom I can see the Rays of ravishing Light and Glory. I can see that the End is more than worth all the Means. And that Posterity will tryumph in that Days Transaction, even altho We should rue it, which I trust in God We shall not.

The Declaration of Independence

IN CONGRESS, JULY 4, 1776.
THE UNANIMOUS DECLARATION
OF THE THIRTEEN UNITED STATES
OF AMERICA,

WHEN in the Course of human events, it becomes necessary for one people to dissolve the political bands which have connected them with another, and to assume among the powers of the earth, the separate and equal station to which the Laws of Nature and of Nature's God entitle them, a decent respect to the opinions of mankind requires that they should declare the causes which impel them to the separation. We hold these truths to be self-evident, that all men are created equal, that they are endowed by their Creator with certain unalienable Rights, that among these are Life, Liberty and the pursuit of Happiness. That to secure these rights, Governments are instituted among Men, deriving their just powers from the consent of the governed, That whenever any Form of Government becomes destructive of these ends, it is the Right of the People to alter or to abolish it, and to institute new Government, laying its foundation on such principles and organizing its powers in such form, as to them shall seem most likely to effect their Safety and Happiness. Prudence, indeed, will dictate that Governments long established should not be changed for light and transient causes; and accordingly all experience hath shewn, that mankind are more disposed to suffer, while evils are sufferable, than to right themselves by abolishing the forms to which they are accustomed. But when a long train of abuses and usurpations, pursuing invariably the same Object evinces a design to reduce them under absolute Despotism, it is their right, it is their duty, to throw off such Government, and to provide new Guards for their future security. Such has been the patient sufferance of these Colonies; and such is now the necessity which constrains them to alter their former Systems of Government. The history of the present King of Great Britain is a history of repeated injuries and usurpations, all having in direct object the establishment of an absolute Tyranny over these States. To prove this, let Facts be submitted to a candid world. He has refused his Assent to Laws, the most wholesome and necessary for the public good. He has forbidden his Governors to pass Laws of immediate and pressing importance, unless suspended in their operation till his Assent should be obtained; and when so suspended, he has utterly neglected to attend to them. He has refused to pass other Laws for the accommodation of large districts of people, unless those people would relinquish the right of Representation in the Legislature, a right inestimable to them and formidable to tyrants only. He has called together legislative bodies at places unusual, uncomfortable, and distant from the depository of their public Records, for the sole purpose of fatiguing them into compliance with his measures. He has dissolved Representative Houses repeatedly, for opposing with manly firmness his invasions on the rights of the people. He has refused for a long time, after such dissolutions, to cause others to be elected; whereby the Legislative powers, incapable of Annihilation, have returned to the People at large for their exercise; the State remaining in the mean time exposed to all the dangers of invasion from without, and convulsions within. He has endeavoured to prevent the population of these States; for that purpose obstructing the Laws for Naturalization of Foreigners; refusing to pass others to encourage their migrations hither, and raising the conditions of new Appropriations of Lands. He has obstructed the Administration of Justice, by refusing his Assent to Laws for establishing Judiciary powers. He has made Judges dependent on his Will alone, for the tenure of their offices, and the amount and payment of their salaries. He has erected a multitude of New Offices, and sent hither swarms of Officers to harrass our people, and eat out their substance. He has kept among us, in times of peace, standing Armies without the Consent of our legislatures. He has affected to render the Military independent of and superior to the Civil power. He has combined with others to subject us to a jurisdiction foreign to our constitution, and unacknowledged by our laws; giving his Assent to their Acts of pretended Legislation: For Quartering large bodies of armed troops among us: For protecting them, by a mock Trial, from punishment for any Murders which they should commit on the Inhabitants of these States: For cutting off our Trade with all parts of the world: For imposing Taxes on us without our Consent: For depriving us in many cases of the benefits of Trial by Jury: For transporting us beyond Seas to be tried for pretended offences: For abolishing the free System of English Laws in a neighbouring Province, establishing therein an Arbitrary government, and enlarging its Boundaries so as to render it at once an example and fit instrument for introducing the same absolute rule into these Colonies: For taking away our Charters, abolishing our most valuable Laws, and altering fundamentally the Forms of our Governments: For suspending our own Legislatures, and declaring themselves invested with power to legislate for us in all cases whatsoever. He has abdicated Government here, by declaring us out of his Protection and waging War against us. He has plundered our seas, ravaged our Coasts, burnt our towns, and destroyed the Lives of our people. He is at this time transporting large Armies of foreign Mercenaries to compleat the works of death, desolation and tyranny, already begun with circumstances of Cruelty & perfidy scarcely paralleled in the most barbarous ages, and totally unworthy the Head of a civilized nation. He has constrained our fellow Citizens taken Captive on the high Seas to bear Arms against their Country, to become the executioners of their friends and Brethren, or to fall themselves by their Hands. He has excited domestic insurrections amongst us, and has endeavoured to bring on the inhabitants of our frontiers, the merciless Indian Savages, whose known rule of warfare, is an undistinguished destruction of all ages, sexes and conditions. In every stage of these Oppressions We have Petitioned for Redress in the most humble terms: Our repeated Petitions have been answered only by repeated injury. A Prince, whose character is thus marked by every act which may define a Tyrant, is unfit to be the ruler of a free people. Nor have We been wanting in attentions to our Brittish brethren. We have warned them from time to time of attempts by their legislature to extend an unwarrantable jurisdiction over us. We have reminded them of the circumstances of our emigration and settlement here. We have appealed to their native justice and magnanimity, and we have conjured them by the ties of our common kindred to disavow these usurpations, which, would inevitably interrupt our connections and correspondence. They too have been deaf to the voice of justice and of consanguinity. We must, therefore, acquiesce in the necessity, which denounces our Separation, and hold them, as we hold the rest of mankind, Enemies in War, in Peace Friends.

We, therefore, the Representatives of the united States of America, in General Congress, Assembled, appealing to the Supreme Judge of the world for the rectitude of our intentions, do, in the Name, and by Authority of the good People of these Colonies, solemnly publish and declare, That these United Colonies are, and of Right ought to be Free and Independent States; that they are Absolved from all Allegiance to the British Crown, and that all political connection between them and the State of Great Britain, is and ought to be totally dissolved; and that as Free and Independent States, they have full Power to levy War, conclude Peace, contract Alliances, establish Commerce, and to do all other Acts and Things which Independent States may of right do. And for the support of this Declaration, with a firm reliance on the protection of divine Providence, we mutually pledge to each other our Lives, our Fortunes and our sacred Honor.

John Hancock

Button Gwinnett	Thos. Nelson jr.	Richd. Stockton
Lyman Hall	Francis Lightfoot Lee	Jno Witherspoon
Geo Walton.	Carter Braxton	Fras. Hopkinson
Wm. Hooper	Robt. Morris	John Hart
Joseph Hewes,	Benjamin Rush	Abra Clark
John Penn	Benja. Franklin	Josiah Bartlett
Edward Rutledge.	John Morton	Wm: Whipple
Thos. Heyward Junr.	Geo Clymer	Saml. Adams
Thomas Lynch Junr.	Jas. Smith.	John Adams
Arthur Middleton	Geo. Taylor	Robt. Treat Paine
Samuel Chase	James Wilson	Elbridge Gerry
Wm. Paca	Geo. Ross	Step. Hopkins
Thos. Stone	Cæsar Rodney	William Ellery
Charles Carroll of	Geo Read	Roger Sherman
Carrollton	Tho M:Kean	Saml. Huntington
George Wythe	Wm. Floyd	Wm. Williams
Richard Henry Lee	Phil. Livingston	Oliver Wolcott
Th: Jefferson	Frans. Lewis	Matthew Thornton
Benja. Harrison	Lewis Morris	

Isaac Bangs: Journal, July 10, 1776

July 10, 1776. Orders were issued for one Brigade to be in readiness at 4 o'clock tomorrow Morning for a March. We all imagined that we were designed to make an Attack upon the Enemy on Staten Island, but on farther consideration we had reason to doubt of it as no perticular Orders were Issued with Respect to our Baggage which would be Necessary to take with us if this was the Intention of the General. Last Night the Statue on the Bowling Green representing George Ghwelps alias George Rex was pulled down by the Populace. In it were 4000 Pounds of Lead & a Man undertook to take 10 oz. of Gold from the Superfices, as both Man & Horse were covered with Gold Leaf; the Lead we hear is to be run up into Musquet Balls for the use of the Yankies, when it is hoped than the Emanations from the Leaden George will make as deep impressions in the Bodies of some of his red-Coated and Torie Subjects, and that they will do the same execution in poisoning and destroying, them as the Super-abundant Emanations of the Folley and pretended Goodness of the real George, have made upon their Minds, which have, effectually poisoned and destroyed their Souls, that they are not worthy to be ranked with any Beings who have any Pretensions to the Principles of Virtue & Justice, but would to God that the unhappy contest might be ended, without puting us to the disagreeable necessity of sending them to dwell with those beings, for the Company of whom alone their Tempers and dispositions are now suitable.

Landon Carter: Diary, June 26–July 16, 1776

26. Wednesday.

Last night after going to bed, Moses, my son's man, Joe, Billy, Postillion John, Mulatto Peter, Tom, Panticove, Manuel and Lancaster Sam, ran away, to be sure, to Ld. Dunmore, for they got privately into Beale's room before dark and took out my son's gun and one I had there, took out of his drawer in my passage all his ammunition furniture, Landon's bag of bullets and all the Powder, and went off in my Petty Auger new trimmed, and it is supposed that Mr. Robinson's People are gone with them, for a skow they came down in is, it seems, at my Landing. These accursed villains have stolen Landon's silver buckles, George's shirts, Tom Parker's new waistcoat and breeches; and yet have not touched one thing of mine, though my door was open, my line filled with stockings and my buckles in my shoes at the door. {Col. Carter attributed this to his keeping the slaves in their places. This fellow Moses, who belonged to his son, was the occasion of Col. Carter's receiving once an affront from his son (Robert Wormeley Carter) who because Col. Carter reproved him for cutting off victuals at table to give Moses, called Col. Carter} an inhuman creature to his slaves. {Col. Carter had retorted with much indignation at the time, because he had never used an angry word to Moses or the deluded fellow slaves} these 6 or 7 years.

29. Saturday.

{Col. Carter tells of the fugitive slaves.} At 7 in the morning after their departure some minute men at Mousquito Point saw the Petty Auger with ten stout men in her going very fast on the Middlesex shore. They pursued and fired at them, whereupon the negroes left the boat and took to the shore where they were followed by the minute men. By their firing they alarmed 100 King and Queen minute men who were waiting for the *Roebuck's* men, should any of them come

ashore there. It is supposed that Moses and many of the negroes were killed.

Joseph Harwood in treaty about my horse Nimrod brought
down from Rippon Agreed to buy him at 30 £ but must try
him at first for about 5 miles. Never sent me the money,
Pretending the danger of the times. {Col. Carter says that
Harwood who lived at Tappahannock told an untrue report
of the fugitive slaves.}

3. Wednesday.

Monday at Court we heard the King and Queen men below had killed a mulatto and two of the blacks out of the 8 of
my people who ran away and the remaining 5 surrendered;
how true it is I don't know.

Mr. Page there gave me an account that Pat. Henry was
chosen Governor in convention, a great majority over
President Nelson, who though he had 45 votes was in the
Election of a Council of State but the 7th man and Charles
Carter of Corotoman the 8th man. We shall now see what we
shall see. Bat Dandridge, a most insignificant lawyer, also chosen one; this a creature of his Excellency's. Electible only 3
years successively, and must be out 4 years before reeligible. I
see and condemn, but as the Multitude of my city has done it
I say nothing, but can't admire the choice. I rather mourn its
destructive tendency in secret against.

Our parson is a comical man. He said he imagined I should
now be for independancy at last. Yes! I replied because
the People of [   ] had compelled me to it. His answer was
[   ] even against it without any reserve as to compulsion. I
declared to the contrary. He said I forgot. I answered he
could invent, and I am now resolved never to speak to him on
the subject.

4. Thursday.

Yesterday brought me from Jos. Harwood £30 for my
horse Nimrod; one 12 pound one 10 pound and one 8 pound
note, James River bank.

I hope I am not deceived when I say that this Mr. Bruce
seems to be an honest and, in this instance of the American
struggle, not what the diagnosis of Toryism would call a
moderate man: for he seems to be quite hearty in the cause

although a Scotchman; I have had much conversation with him detesting the behaviour of his countryman, in particular a late runegado to Govr. Eden and Dunmore, who carried off all the slaves and servants almost out of Maryland.

{Col. Carter will probably have to sell his sorrell horse and Rippon black and keep Mundungus to supply their place, for free money is only to be got that way.

Sends to Col. Tayloe for Duck grass seed, who sowed it on his poorest land and obtained a vast crop.}

Stiff land on this side of the swamp now twice done hoeing and twice plowing.

In our this day's ride to my Fork, Bruce took notice of the corn being very fine and clean. He asked me how many barrels I ever made to a thousand. I told him not above 3 barrels. He said, he saw Ruffin's corn, to be sure very fine, but he had seen as good, that did not yield above 5 barrels; and Ruffin asserted that his had yielded 10 barrels. He said he even counted the stalks, and the ears on a hill, and he could not see above 10 ears at most and on many much less. I said that was a great deal but I believe that Arithmetic would not make that 10 barrels; for 10 barrels were one with another 8,000 — ten ears though 10,000, the thousand, must be excessive to be every hill alike. I said many people deceived others so often that at last they deceived themselves. He said that a tenant of a certain gent. up with him, was said to make 10 barrels, when the man swore that let his landlord say what he would, he never turned out above 3 barrels. I observed the same in others.

5. Friday.

Hearing so many contradictory stories about Moses and his gang, I sent Beale off this morning to get fully informed either in Lancaster, Middlesex, or Gloster. I gave him 10s to bear his expenses. The Gent. made a demur about his breeches being dirty. I told him dirty breeches are as certainly good to ride in as to stay at home in. He is to bring an account of Mr. J. Beale about Bluff Point and also from Norris and carry letters to both.

Yesterday another hand bill seen going by to [   ] Bridge to tell us that Gen. Thomas and 150 men were killed and taken prisoners at the cedars near Quebeck. This I suppose to balance the former letters from N. York, which gave an account that Thomas had taken the whole of that party and that Carleton had sent him word if he did not exchange them he would put his prisoners to death. N. Y. can write anything and 'tis as likely the last hand bill was false as the other was. I can't believe others.

This express confirms the report which J. Howe brought of the N. Y. conspiracy against Washington, the Magazine, and a signal to the Enemy to land there; and says that it was discovered by a Centinel who took all the bribes given him and then informed the Genl. what was doing on which he made close prisoners of above 500, Mr. Mayor, and kept the rest under strong guard. I wish it was true, if it was a conspiracy. It is also said some Highlanders are got to Dunmore. Our privateers have taken 5 more transports with Highlanders. It seems that Burgoyne has got to Canada with 10,000 men and that he brought them in 70 transports, which are better than 148 in a vessel, and yet Howe took 130 sail to remove 7,000 and these officers are all come on there. Believe it who will, I can't. If it is true, these 10,000 have had great good luck to come 3,000 miles so cooped up. But what if they come? Are not 12,000 on land already a good match for them? Depend upon it they will never come down Hudson River to do any harm unless this 100,000£ has got vastly multiplyed and has flown about.

6. Saturday.

The first real summer heat—for it obliges me to wear but one pair of thin stockings.

Much is said of the slavery of negroes, but how will servants be provided in these times? Those few servants that we have don't do as much as the poorest slaves we have. If you free the slaves, you must send them out of the country or they must steal for their support.

The story of Dunmore's reinforcement turns out a lie, a vessel only brought home some prisoners from Ireland.

8. Monday.

A warm day. On Saturday last sowed turnips in my drilled Timothy grass field.

Pulled all my flax on Saturday by 12; we are getting it in this day.

9. Tuesday.

Beale returned but brought no account of Moses and his gang. He went to the King and Queen camp on the point between Rappahannock and Pianketank and talked with the commander. They had catched other people's negroes but not mine. Beale reported that the men who followed my people in the Petty Auger when they were driven ashore was the Towles Point guard in a boat of Burgess Ball. {Col. Carter thinks they could readily have overtaken the Petty Auger if they tried.}

Another report from Guthrie, who I have a long time known to be an egregious liar, that some runaways told him that they saw some slaves who had run away from Dunmore, who told him that they saw Moses on the Island; who swore to them if he could get back he would return to his master; for Dunmore had deceived all the Poor Slaves and he never met so barbarous or so vile a fellow in all his life.

Beale owns the Captain of that guard told him the slaves were returning daily, most miserably and barbecued, and did aver the whole gang of slaves must leave the Island as soon as they could get off.

Beale tells me that when he went to ask for the Petty Auger which the minute men had taken from my People, Captain Berryman with an oath refused to give it up. {Col. Carter thinks that he may find himself mistaken.}

12. Friday.

{Col. Carter has some comments on his cucumbers which have thousands of blossoms but no fruit. To make them bear he topped them but it did no good. He thinks, therefore, that the plants are all male plants and that he has been mistaken in supposing that each cucumber plant was both male and female.}

13. Saturday.

Nat tells us that he heard Capt. Wmson. Ball write an order to Capt. Sallard of the minute men from Colo. P. Thornton, his Colo. requiring his Company instantly to march to Potowmack river, for all the fleet had left Gwyns Island and were against the mouth of Potowmack, as our battery had drove them all from that Island. It is imagined that they are gone to take possession of Sharpe's Island above on the Eastern Shoar.

I fancy Maryland will now begin to see their folly in not confining Eden, as the Congress directed them. {Colo. Carter thinks that the going to Sharpe's Island is by his advice.}

The report from our Courthouse is, that Genl. Lee has beat Clinton in So. Carolina, a prodigious battle, drove the army all away and killed Genl. Clinton. That our Gloster battery and forces drove Dunmore and all his fleet from Gwin's Island, sunk 6 ships, took two, and disabled the men of war so much, they were obliged to go away. That two days ago 90 of the fleet were seen against Smith's Point in the Bay; but that yesterday all were gone to 9 vessels but where not said. God send this may be true.

By Ned Purcell from his yesterday's message we hear there is a great foundation for the report from the courthouse; for Jno. Beale writes that on Tuesday last our battery sunk one ship, quickly disabled another which they burnt, and obliged the rest to tow out of harbor; and our men the Thursday following drove off Dunmore and made those that could escape fly to the ships for protection, leaving their cannon, etc., to the amount of some thousand pounds value. John Selden met Purcell coming up and bid tell me that Dunmore last week sent off a load of negroes to one of the Islands which so alarmed the rest that the county of Gloster was disturbed with their howlings. Possibly Capt. Moses, the freeman, may be one of them to glut his genius for liberty which he was not born to.

News just come John Self at Rings Neck turned a Baptist, and only waits to convert my People. He had two brethren Preachers and two others with him; and says he cannot serve God and Mammon, has just been made a Christian by dipping, and would not continue in my business but to convert my people.

This a strange year about my overseers; some, horrid hellish rogues and others religious villains. Came here after dinner Mr. John Selden, who told us Capt. Burgess Ball wrote from Hampton that Patrick Henry, the late elected Governor, died last tuesday evening, So that being the day of our battery's beginning to Play on Dunmore's gang and they being routed we ought to look on those two joined as two glorious events. Particularly favourable by the hand of Providence.

14. Sunday.

It is not many days past I heard that in the lobby of the late convention it was urged the late dignified person was the first who opened the breath of liberty to America. But it was with truth replied, and Proved that that breath was first breathed and supported by a person not then taken notice of. I know this merit is claimed also by another, But I only say I never courted Public applause; and if any endeavour assists my country, I care not who enjoys the merit of it. This I am certain of, that nothing renders a man more suspected than his schemes for Popularity, and I will forever be like the Prophet, who is only without honour in his own country, rather than be conscious of anything so base as deceiving the people, let the success be what it will. In this sense, Virtue will ever carry its own reward; and he is a Villain that aims at any thing by a lie that his conscience cannot support.

15. Monday.

{A report coming through Mr. Colston, Colo. Peachy and Dr. Robinson, that five of his runaways were in Middlesex jail.}

Last night John Beale came up. I intend to agree with him, if I can, to take Norris' plantation under his care. He says that two French, who deserted from Dunmore's camp on the Island after our people had drove them off, declared we killed abundance of their men; and that no negroes were kept by Dunmore but were fine active fellows, but were all sent away to some of the West India Islands, and out of the strong and active scarce one in ten escaped death by distempers or ill usage except when a man was wanted in his vessels. These men, who are said to be great engineers and sensible, further told the officers of our camp our batteries had destroyed and injured abundance of their vessels both big and small, and others were taken.

This night at 9 all Tappahannock illuminated and as low down the river as Clement's house, where Ritchie lives. What can be the Joy? There is no day particular set down in the Almanac. Certainly some great victory is obtained. Possibly Clinton's defeat is true or it may be Dunmore killed in the late engagement at the Island by way of distraction; or it may be George 3d is dead.

16. Tuesday.

I sent last night to Mt. Airy after 9 last night to know the occasion of the illumination, and received a paper containing an extract from a Paper going Express to the Congress, giving an account of an engagement with 9 men of war mounting 268 guns, which no doubt attempted to force a battery in Charles Town, Carolina, prepared to resist the landing of an army. The ships had 103 men killed besides 2 captains and 38 wounded besides one captain who lost an arm. One ship abandoned and burnt by the enemy about 10 shattered as not to be repared in this Part of America; all the ships lost all their anchors being in a hurry obliged to cut and run. One vessel lost her bowsprit. They had but 2/3 allowance in fresh Provisions and in want of water.

This account brought by some Americans on board taken at different times by the men of war who deserted during the engagement, and made oath before one John Cullock to the above particulars. Note: 5,000£ was offered for Genl. Lee's head, who commanded the whole. The enemy's engineer had been in the tavern at Charles Town and visited all the fortifications. We had only 20 men killed and 22 wounded. More Particulars will be more satisfactory and we may say from this account that God was on our side, a thought worth rejoicing for. We must have good Engineers on our side at Charles Town.

John Beale told me last night that at Gwyns Island 18 pound shot went between Dunmore's thighs and cut a boatswain in two behind him. I don't doubt this shot cooled his latitudinous virility for that night at least, and I will hope that some wound of this sort has disabled him if not killed him. I wonder who feels the water hot now, himself, or the Virginians!

Cool still, and no rain. Nothing certainly can grow, under this Northerly dominion of this element the air. But it is enough barely to Exist when such barbarous enemies are defeated in their expectations to destroy us. Providence who directs all things will not forsake the cause of justice.

My people mowing my wheat at the Fork and elsewhere are now cutting down the spelt and after that the oats.

John Beale gone home. Colston and the devil, my son, gone to Capt. Beale's to dinner.

I understand by J. Beale the wench Peg, who died here, last was in his time subject to gross ulcers and was cured often by me. She had a brother and a sister which all died then from a mere family disorder, indeed, presumptively the yaws or hereditary pox.

Rode out. Light grounds may make corn and tobacco with a very little rain; but it seems as if stiff grounds cannot without more than it seems that we are likely to have. As to cotton I see drilling stands the only chance, because near 3 feet rows shade each other.

Ambrose Serle: Journal, July 12–23, 1776

FRIDAY, 12th.

This Morning, the Sun shining bright, we had a beautiful Prospect of the Coast of New Jersey at about 5 or 6 Miles Distance. The Land was cleared in many Places, and the Woods were interspersed with Houses, which being covered with white Shingles appeared very plainly all along the Shore. We passed Sandy Hook in the Afternoon, and about 6 o'Clock arrived safe off the East Side of Staten Island. The Country on both Sides was highly picturesque and agreeable. Nothing could exceed the Joy, that appeared throughout the Fleet and Army upon our Arrival. We were saluted by all the Ships of War in the Harbour, by the Cheers of the Sailors all along the Ships, and by those of the Soldiers on the Shore. A finer Scene could not be exhibited, both of Country, Ships, and men, all heightened by one of the brightest Days that can be imagined. What added to their Pleasure was, that this very Day about Noon the Phoenix of 40 Guns & the Rose of 20, with three Tenders forced their Passage up the River in Defiance of all their vaunted Batteries, and got safe above the Town, which will much intercept the Provisions of the Rebels. We heard the Canonade, and saw the Smoke at a Distance. As soon as we came to Anchor, Admiral Shuldham came on board, and soon after Genl. Howe, with several officers of their respective Departments. By them we learnt the deplorable Situation of His majesty's faithful Subjects; that they were hunted after & shot at in the Woods & Swamps, to which they had fled for these four months to avoid the savage Fury of the Rebels; that many of them were forced to take up Arms & join their Forces; and that Deserters & others flocked to the King's Army continually. We also heard, that the Congress had now announced the Colonies to be INDEPENDENT STATES, with several other Articles of Intelligence, that proclaim the Villainy & the Madness of these deluded People. Where we anchored was in full View of

New York, and of the Rebels' Head Quarters under Washington, who is now made their Generalissimo with full Powers.

SATURDAY 13th. JULY.

This Morning the Captains of the Fleet waited on the Admiral, and received his Lordship's Orders. They acquainted us, that General Burgoyne is coming down to Albany with the Army under his Command, together with 1000 Indians; and that they had overtaken the Rebels, who had penetrated into Canada, driven them into a Swamp, and put above 500 of them to the Sword. The Troops hold them very cheap, and long for an opportunity of revenging the Cause of their Countrymen, who fell at Bunker's Hill.

The Congress have at length thought it convenient to throw off the Mask. Their Declaration of the 4th. of July, while it avows their Right to Independence, is founded upon such Reasons only, as prove *that* Independence to have been their Object from the Beginning. A more impudent, false and atrocious Proclamation was never fabricated by the Hands of Man. Hitherto, they had thrown all the Blame and Insult upon the Parliament and ministry: Now, they have the Audacity to calumniate the King and People of Great Britain. 'Tis impossible to read this Paper, without Horror at the daring Hypocrisy of these Men, who call GOD to witness the uprightness of their Proceedings, nor without Indignation at the low and scurrilous Pretences by wch they attempt to justify themselves. Surely, Providence will honor its own Truth and Justice upon this Occasion, and, as they have made an appeal to it for Success, reward them after their own Deservings.

I heard likewise, that Lieut. Stanhope has run from his Parole of Honor, wch he had given to the Rebels on being taken Prisoner, and that they have advertised him in the New York Papers.

Genl. Howe and three of his Aides de Camp dined with the Admiral on board the Eagle, and continued on board till late in the Evening. The Discourse chiefly turned upon military Affairs, upon the Country, and upon the Rebels. The Army seem to be actuated by one Spirit, and impatiently wait for the Arrival of the Hessians & other Troops.

Govr. Tryon also came on board, to whom I delivered a Packet I had in Charge for him, who recd. it & the Bearer with his usual Politeness.

By a perspective Glass, we have a distinct View of the Rebels' Encampments, of the Town of New York, and of Hudson's River for a considerable Space beyond the Town. The Rebels appeared very numerous, & are supposed to be near 30,000; but from the Mode of raising them, no great matters are to be expected, especially when their loose Discipline is considered.

SUNDAY, 14th. JULY.

An excessive hard Rain, prevented going on Shore this Day, and we had no divine Service on board. Mr. Reeve, our first Lieutenant, returned from Amboy this Afternoon, whither he had been sent yesterday by the Admiral with Dispatches, addressed to the several Governors in North America, notifying his Arrival and the Objects of his Commission, and inclosing a Declaration to be published by them in their respective Colonies. This was a prudent and decent Way of acquainting the People of America, that the Door was yet open for Reconciliation; for it was expected, they would have the Curiosity to read the Inclosures, which were dispatched under a flying Seal, being their Interest & Concern more than that of the Governors. Mr. Reeve breakfasted with *Mercer*,* the American Commander, who behaved civilly, yet rather dryly. They had very coarse Fare, which the American noticed, but added, they had Plenty of Necessaries, and did not wish for Luxuries. The Lieutenant very properly replied, that it was very happy for those who had not them not to wish for them.

Mr. Brown, another Lieutenant, was dispatched with a Flag of Truce to Washington at New York. He was stopped by three Boats at a little Distance from the Town, demanding his Business. Upon being told that he had a Letter from Lord Howe to their Commander, they ordered him to lay to, while one of the Boats went to the Shore for Directions. In a short time, three officers came off, and desired to know to whom the Letter was addressed. They would not touch it, but

*This Man was mortally wounded by our Soldiers in the Skirmish at or near Princeton, in Jan. 1777.

begged the Lieutenant to read it. As the Address was, *To George Washington Esq. &c. &c. &c.* they said, there was no such Person among them, and therefore would not receive it. Upon being asked what Address they required, it was answered, that "all the World knew who Genl. Washington was since the Transactions of last Summer." So high is the Vanity and the Insolence of these Men! The Truth is, the Punctilio of an Address would never have retarded the Reception of a Letter from a Person, with whose high Rank & Commission they were well acquainted, and whose Bravery & Honor are so well known every where; if their Minds had been in the least disposed to the Duties of Humanity, Law, and Allegiance. They have uniformly blocked up every Avenue to Peace, and whenever they have pretended to make Advances of that kind, they have always done it in a mode, that they well knew (and, because they knew, designed) was inadmissible, upon every Principle of Honor and Decency. There now seems no Alternative but War and Bloodshed, which must lay at the Door of these unhappy People: They pretend (or rather have pretended) to seek Peace, and yet renounce it. The Faction have thrown aside all Appearances at length, and declare openly for Independence & War.

This Evening a Gentleman came on board from New Jersey for Protection.

The Ships, we heard, are safe about 7 or 8 Miles above the Town.

MONDAY, 15th. JULY.

I went on Shore upon Staten Island this Morning for the first Time, and walked up to a Redoubt, which our People were making on a Hill. The Prospect was very fine and extensive; the Country in several Parts tolerably cleared, and beautifully diversified into Hill and Dale. How happy might the People live, if they knew their own Blessings, or were properly sensible of the Advantages of that mild and just Government, which they are endeavoring to extirpate among them, and under which they so long have lived happy and safe.

By a Deserter we learn, that the Rebels are much disheartened upon the two Ships passing by in Defiance of all their Batteries, and that they lost six men, though we have not heard that we have lost so much as one. He gave us a State of their Fortifications, which are pretty numerous, of the Jealousies that prevail among themselves, of the Intentions of some to burn the Town, & of the Resolution of others (if possible) to preserve it. The Inhabitants (the male, for the Female & Children are removed) are particularly anxious for its Preservation. The mad multitude who have no Interest or Property in the Town, which appears a very fine one, are alone intent upon its Destruction. The hearty Wish of our People is to save it, if it be consistent with any Degree of Safety, upon the Attack.

Govr. Wentworth & Son dined on board this Day. Govr. Grant (late of East Florida) waited on Ld. Howe in the morning: and so did the General, & others.

A Flag of Truce was sent by Washington, to which an Answer was promised to be given, when the Admiral shall have conferred with the Genl.

It was observed, that a Sailor sate in a Bravado upon the Top Gallant Yard of the Phoenix during the Fire of all the Batteries upon the Ships, as they passed along. To such a Pitch does the Courage, or perhaps the Insensibility of some Men arise!

The Loss of Col. Campbell, and a Part of the Highlanders, who attempted to get into Boston, not knowing of Genl. Howe's Departure, is too fully confirmed. Here is a great Fault somewhere, which will merit Inquiry. The Number is said to amount to 600 Men.

TUESDAY, 16th. JULY.

Adml. Shuldham, and several of the Captains of the Navy, dined with us this Day. Their Discourse turned upon the Capture of the Highlanders, and the Blame was attempted to be thrown upon their Commanders: How justly, Time will shew. I walked with the Chaplain on Shore this Afternoon. The Soil is for the most part a light sandy Loam, and barren. The People of the Island, like their Soil, are thin and meagre; the Voices faint, and their whole Frame of a loose languid Texture. Very few stout men could I see among them.

Another Flag of Truce was sent to-day with a Letter to

Washington from the General, wch was refused for the same idle and insolent Reasons as were given before. Their Leaders seem determined to risque every thing, rather than abate of their new Power & Consequence; so that Blows & War seem inevitable. There is this Reflection on our Side, that we strove as far as Decency and Honor could permit, or Humanity itself demand, to avert all Bloodshed & to promote an Accommodation. And yet, it seems, to be beneath a little paltry Colonel of Militia at the Head of a Banditti or Rebels to treat with the Representative of His lawful Sovereign, because 'tis impossible for him to give all the Titles which the poor Creature requires. Rebellion is indeed as the Sin of Witchcraft, blinds the Eyes, and hardens the Heart against every sound Principle of Religion and Duty. If such men in such a Cause can prosper, it is only the Prosperity of a Night, which the morning Cloud shall chase away.

An American News Paper was put into my Hands, full of Bitterness and Malignancy. The following Sentence may serve for a Specimen. "Be assured, the Sun, moon & Stars shall fall, the Ocean cease to roll, and all nature change its Course, before a few English, Scotch & German *Slaves* shall conquer this vast Country." There are several other Paragraphs in the Paper equally full of Nonsense, Madness & Fury.

We have Intelligence that since the Ships had passed the Town, the Connecticut People have moved to relieve the New Yorkers, who are stationed in the Town. The Wish of the former is to destroy the Place, both as a Rival to themselves, and a Station for the British Army: The Desire of the latter is to preserve it, because it is their Property. The Eastern Rebels have so little Confidence in the New Yorkers, that they declare openly that they may consider themselves as in an Enemy's Country.

A young officer in the Army, Mr. Blennerhasset, was shot at by a large Party of the Rebels concealed on the opposite Shore, & mortally wounded. They are fond of carrying on this unmanly and infamous kind of War, which no civilized Nation will allow. An uncommon Spirit of Murder & Cruelty seems to actuate them in all their Proceedings.

WEDNESDAY, 17th. JULY.

Nothing very material occurred this Day. Govr. Tryon, Col. Oliver Delancey, Mr. Kemp, Attorney General, Mr. Apthorpe, Major Bayard, Col. Clarke, & Mr. Fanning, dined with us. The Discourse turned principally upon the Distresses of the Inhabitants, and of themselves who had not seen their Wives and Families for the Space of nine Months, upon the general Inhumanity of the Rebels, their Jealousies of each other, and the Probability of reducing them to Order. The People begin to be weary of their new masters the mob, & to think that British Govt. is rather more lenient & less arbitrary than that of a Congress. Their Practices & their Revolt are alike inexcusable and unexampled.

In the Evening, Lord H. carried Mr. Strachey & myself on Shore for a Walk into the Country. The Soil is mostly poor, and receives a very inferior Cultivation than our Lands in G. Britain. Their Corn is full of Weeds, and no Pains seem to be taken for clearing them. The Residence of the Army enriches the Island, and gives it a good Reward for its Loyalty. I saw many Fire-flies this Evening, and heard the hideous Noise of the Bull-frogs.

THURSDAY, 18th. JULY.

Waited on Govr. Tryon this Morning to settle the Means of printing the Declaration; and found that we can command every thing necessary but the Types. Saw the famous Major Rogers at the Governor's, who it seems has been very active for His Majesty's Service, and may be usefully employed. The Govr. was so obliging as to furnish me with Papers of Information, respecting the State of the Province, for my Perusal. The Gentlemen with him have a despicable opinion of the Rebels and their opposition, and are earnest for the Commencement of our operations. A little Time, however, will be usefully passed in Preparations, &c. and till the Arrival of our Reinforcements.

Walked in the Evening upon Staten Island. There is something romantic in the wild unbroken Country, which though it does not enchant, gives the Sense a kind of pleasing Melancholy. The Soil is very light & poor, & the Strength of it soon exhausted. It very much resembles the Land on the

Edge of Windsor Forest. From the Hills we have a distant View of the Jerseys, New York, Long Island, &c. all pleasing to the Eye, and for the most part fine & fruitful.

FRIDAY, 19th. JULY.

Lord Howe, the Captains of the Fleet, the Chaplain, myself, &c, dined on board the Chatham with Admiral Shuldham.

A Flag of Truce was sent this Afternoon to the Town, and recd. for Answer, that Washington would see a General officer, if the Admiral & General pleased, on the morrow.

Walked on Shore in the Evening; but the Heat and Dust made the Excursion rather unpleasant.

SATURDAY, 20th.

Another Flag of Truce went this Morning from the General, which met with a better Reception than any of the preceding.

Walked this Evening into the Woods, which were tolerably pleasant. The Herbage of Staten Island is very indifferent, and consequently the Cattle small.

Wrote Letters, in Readiness for the first Conveyance, to my dear Friends in England.

I could perceive, several Times in the Day, the Rebels watching the opposite Coast of Long Island, lest any of their People should come over to us. Poor unhappy Men! how are they led astray from the Blessings of a lawful & settled Government, into the worst Sort of Tyranny, into Anarchy and Tumult?

Read over Adams's Pamphlet, entitled "Common Sense." A most flagitious Performance, replete with Sophistry, Impudence & Falshood; but unhappily calculated to work upon the Fury of the Times, and to induce the full avowal of the Spirit of Independence in the warm & inconsiderate. His Attempt to justify Rebellion by the Bible is infamous beyond Expression. That Religion, which renders Men bad Subjects and bad Citizens, can never be of GOD, who instituted Civil Government that all things might be done decently, and in order. He is not the author of Confusion, but of Peace.

SUNDAY, 21st.

No divine Service this Morning, because of watering the Ship. I first espied the Signal Flag at the Light-house for more than

5 Ships; and, in a few Hours, 7 Transports laden with
Highlanders came into the Harbor. About 900 were on
board. The Flora Frigate, wch should have convoyed them,
and another Transport, parted Company from them off
Boston about a Fortnight since. A Lieutenant, on board one
of the Transports, had great Merit in bringing them in. They
had a Passage of 12 Weeks from Greenock.

The Rebels fired upon one of our Boats, wch approached
too near the Jersey Shore, but did no Damage.

MONDAY, 22d. JULY.

A poor Black deserted to us early this Morning, and came
down paddling in a Canoe from the Town. Three or four
Whites had agreed to come off with him; but, staying beyond
the Time agreed on, the poor Fellow ventured down alone.
By him we learnt, that the Rebels were much disconcerted on
the Passage of the Ships, and that they had six Men killed;
and that Genl. Burgoyne was arrived at Albany, as the Rebels
had heard on Saturday. This last Article we wish to be confirmed.

A very hot and sultry Day, which rendered the Ship our
best Retreat. On the Shore, which is near a Mile distant, I
heard that the Weather was extremely close and uncomfortable.

The Rebels have a large blazing Light set up every Evening,
near the Town.

TUESDAY, 23d. JULY.

Govr. Tryon called upon us this Morning. Adml. Shuldham
and the Captains of the Fleet dined with us. In the Evening
the Chaplain and myself took a Walk upon Staten Island for a
considerable Way. The Scenes were romantic to the Eye,
though barren for the most part in the Soil. We met several
People who had just escaped out of Long Island from the
Tyranny of those insolent Demagogues, who, under pretences
of superior Liberty, are imposing upon all about them the
worst of Bondage. It excited one's Sympathy to see their poor
meagre Faces, and to hear their Complaints of being hunted
for their Lives like Game into the Woods and Swamps, only
because they would not renounce their allegiance to their

King and affection for their Country. These are some of the
choicest Blessings of the Faction, which pretends to Religion,
Patriotism, and a hundred other Virtues, but knows nothing
of any of them but by their Name.

Joseph Reed: Memorandum on Meeting Between George Washington and James Paterson, July 20, 1776

AFTER usual Compliments in which as well as through the whole Conversation Col. P. addressd Gen. Washington by the Title of Excelly: Col: Patterson entered upon the Business by saying That Gen. Howe much regretted the Difficulties which had arisen respecting the Address of the Letters to Genl W. — that it was deemed consistent with Propriety & founded upon Precedents of the like Nature by Embassadors & Plenipotentiaries where Disputes or Difficulties of Rank had arisen — That Gen. W. might recollect he had last Summer address'd a Letter to Gen. Howe to the Hon: William Howe Esqe — That Ld Howe & General H. did not mean to derogate from the Respect or Rank of Genl W. — that they held his Person & Character in the highest Esteem — That the Direction with the Addition of &c. &c. &c. — implied every thing that ought to follow. He then produced a Letter which he did not directly offer to Gen. W. but observed that it was the same Letter which had been sent & laid it on the Table with a Superscription to Geo. Washington &c. &c. &c. — The General declined the Letter & said that a Letter directed to a person in a publick Character should have some Description or Indication of it otherwise it would appear a mere private Letter — That it was true the &c. &c. &c. implied every thing & they also implied any thing. That the Letter to Gen. Howe alluded to was an Answer to one received under a like Address from him — which the Officer on Duty having taken he did not think proper to return, but answered it in the same Mode of Address. That he should absolutely decline any Letter directed to him as a private Person when it related to his publick Station. Col. P. then said that Genl Howe would not urge his Delicacy farther & repeated his Assertions that no

Failure of Respect was intended. He then said that he would
endeavour as well as he could, to recollect Gen. Howes
Sentiments on the Letter & Resolves of Congress sent him a
few Days before respecting the Treatment of our Prisoners in
Canada — "That the Affairs of Canada were in another
Department not subject to the Controul of Genl Howe —
but that he & Ld Howe utterly disapproved of every In-
fringement of the Rights of Humanity." Col. P. then took a
Paper out of his Pocket & after looking it over said he had
expressd nearly the words — Gen. W. then said that he had
also forwarded a Copy of the Resolves to Gen. Burgoyne. To
which Col. P. replied he did not doubt a proper Attention
would be paid to them, & that he (Gen. W.) was sensible
that Cruelty was not the Characteristick of the British
Nation.

Col. P. then proceeded to say he had it in Charge to mention the Case of Genl Prescott who they were informd was
treated with such Rigour that under his Age & Infirmities
fatal Consequences might be apprehended. Gen. Washington
replied that Genl Prescotts Treatment had not fallen under his
Notice — That all Prisoners under his particular Direction he
had treated with Kindness & made their Situation as easy &
comfortable as possible. That he did not know where General
Prescott was, but believed his Treatment very different from
their Information. Gen. W. then mentioned the Case of Col.
Allen & the Officers who had been confined in Boston
Gaol — As to the first Col. P. answered that Gen. Howe
had no Knowledge of it but by Information from Gen.
Washington & that the Canada Department was not under
his Direction or Controul. That as to the other Prisoners at
Boston whenever the State of the Army at Boston admitted it
they were treated with Humanity & even Indulgence — that
he asserted this upon his Honour & should be happy in an
Oppy to prove it.

Gen: W. then observed that the Conduct of several of the
Officers would well have warranted a different Treatment
from what they had received — some having refused to give
any Parole, & others having broke it when given by escaping
or endeavouring so to do. Col. P. answered that as to the
first they misunderstood the Matter very much & seemed to

have mistook the Line of Propriety exceedinly — and as to the latter Gen. Howe utterly disapproved & condemned their Conduct — that if a Remonstrance was made such Violations of good Faith would be severely punished — but that he hoped Gen. W. was too just to draw publick Inferences from the Misbehaviour of some private Individuals that bad Men were to be found in every class & Society — that such Behaviour was considered as a dishonour to the British Army.

Col. Patterson then proceeded to say that the Goodness and Benevolence of the King had induced him to appoint Ld Howe & Gen. H. his Commissioners to accomodate this unhappy Dispute — that they had great Powers & would derive the greatest Pleasure from effecting an Accomodation — & that he (Col. P.) wish'd to have this Visit considered as making the first Advances to this desirable Object. Gen. W. replied he was not vested with any Powers on this Subject by those from whom he derived his Authority & Power. But from what had appeared or transpired on this Head Ld Howe & Gen. Howe were only to grant Pardons — that those who had committed no Fault wanted no Pardon: that we were only defending what we deemed our indisputable Rights — Col. P. said that that would open a very wide Field for Argument. He then expressed his Apprehensions that an Adherence to Forms was likely to obstruct Business of the greatest Moment & Concern. He then observed that a Proposal had been formerly made of exchanging Govr Skene for Mr Lovel, that he now had Authority to accede to that Proposal. Gen. W. replied that the Proposition had been made by the Direction of Congress, and having been then rejected he could not now renew the Business or give any Answer till he had previously communicated it to them.

Col: Patterson behaved with the greatest Politeness & Attention during the whole Business — express'd strong Acknowledgments that the usual Ceremony of blinding his Eyes had been dispensed with — At the breaking up of the Conference General Washington strongly invited him to partake of a small Collation provided for him — which he politely declined, alledging his late Breakfast — & an Impatience to return to Gen. Howe tho he had not executed his Commission so amply as he wish'd — Finding he did not propose staying he was introduced to the General Officers, after which he took his Leave & was safely conducted to his own Boat which waited for him about 4 Miles distant from the City.

Benjamin Franklin to Lord Howe

My Lord,   Philada. July 20th. 1776.

I received safe the Letters your Lordship so kindly forwarded to me, and beg you to accept my Thanks.

The Official Dispatches to which you refer me, contain nothing more than what we had seen in the Act of Parliament, viz. Offers of Pardon upon Submission; which I was sorry to find, as it must give your Lordship Pain to be sent so far on so hopeless a Business.

Directing Pardons to be offered the Colonies, who are the very Parties injured, expresses indeed that Opinion of our Ignorance, Baseness, and Insensibility which your uninform'd and proud Nation has long been pleased to entertain of us; but it can have no other Effect than that of increasing our Resentment. It is impossible we should think of Submission to a Government, that has with the most wanton Barbarity and Cruelty, burnt our defenceless Towns in the midst of Winter, excited the Savages to massacre our Farmers, and our Slaves to murder their Masters, and is even now bringing foreign Mercenaries to deluge our Settlements with Blood. These atrocious Injuries have extinguished every remaining Spark of Affection for that Parent Country we once held so dear: But were it possible for *us* to forget and forgive them, it is not possible for *you* (I mean the British Nation) to forgive the People you have so heavily injured; you can never confide again in those as Fellow Subjects, and permit them to enjoy equal Freedom, to whom you know you have given such just Cause of lasting Enmity. And this must impel you, were we again under your Government, to endeavour the breaking our Sprit by the severest Tyranny, and obstructing by every means in your Power our growing Strength and Prosperity.

But your Lordship mentions "the Kings paternal Solicitude for promoting the Establishment of lasting *Peace* and Union with the Colonies." If by *Peace* is here meant, a Peace to be entered into between Britain and America as distinct States now at War, and his Majesty has given your Lordship Powers to treat with us of such a Peace, I may venture to say, tho' without Authority, that I think a Treaty for that purpose not yet quite impracticable, before we enter into Foreign Alliances. But I am persuaded you have no such Powers. Your Nation, tho' by punishing those American Governors who have created and fomented the Discord, rebuilding our burnt Towns, and repairing as far as possible the Mischiefs done us, She might yet recover a great Share of our Regard and the greatest part of our growing Commerce, with all the Advantage of that additional Strength to be derived from a Friendship with us; I know too well her abounding Pride and deficient Wisdom, to believe she will ever take such Salutary Measures. Her Fondness for Conquest as a Warlike Nation, her Lust of Dominion as an Ambitious one, and her Thirst for a gainful Monopoly as a Commercial one, (none of them legitimate Causes of War) will all join to hide from her Eyes every View of her true Interests; and continually goad her on in these ruinous distant Expeditions, so destructive both of Lives and Treasure, that must prove as perrnicious to her in the End as the Croisades formerly were to most of the Nations of Europe.

I have not the Vanity, my Lord, to think of intimidating by thus predicting the Effects of this War; for I know it will in England have the Fate of all my former Predictions, not to be believed till the Event shall verify it.

Long did I endeavour with unfeigned and unwearied Zeal, to preserve from breaking, that fine and noble China Vase the British Empire: for I knew that being once broken, the separate Parts could not retain even their Share of the Strength or Value that existed in the Whole, and that a perfect Re-Union of those Parts could scarce even be hoped for. Your Lordship may possibly remember the Tears of Joy that wet my Cheek, when, at your good Sister's in London, you once gave me Expectations that a Reconciliation might soon take place. I had the Misfortune to find those Expectations disappointed, and to be treated as the Cause of the Mischief I was labouring to prevent. My Consolation under that groundless and malevolent Treatment was, that I retained the Friendship of many Wise and Good Men in that Country, and among the rest some Share in the Regard of Lord Howe.

The well founded Esteem, and permit me to say Affection, which I shall always have for your Lordship, makes it painful to me to see you engag'd in conducting a War, the great Ground of which, as expressed in your Letter, is, "the Necessity of preventing the American Trade from passing into foreign Channels." To me it seems that neither the obtaining or retaining of any Trade, how valuable soever, is an Object for which Men may justly Spill each others Blood; that the true and sure means of extending and securing Commerce is the goodness and cheapness of Commodities; and that the profits of no Trade can ever be equal to the Expence of compelling it, and of holding it, by Fleets and Armies. I consider this War against us therefore, as both unjust, and unwise; and I am persuaded cool dispassionate Posterity will condemn to Infamy those who advised it; and that even Success will not save from some degree of Dishonour, those who voluntarily engag'd to conduct it. I know your great Motive in coming hither was the Hope of being instrumental in a Reconciliation; and I believe when you find *that* impossible on any Terms given you to propose, you will relinquish so odious a Command, and return to a more honourable private Station. With the greatest and most sincere Respect I have the honour to be, My Lord your Lordships most obedient humble Servant

Henry Laurens to John Laurens

Charles Town, August 14, 1776

Uncommon & exceedingly mortifying my Dear Son has been the late long interruption in our correspondence, I find that I have not put pen to Paper in any address to you since the 29th. April & unless certain Letters referred to in the subjoined list have reached you, I have no ground to hope that you have learned any thing concerning me since November last. — in the mean time, after long & anxious waiting I have had the pleasure of receiving your Letters of the 5th. Decem. from St. Augustine & of 20th. March by the hand of Mr. Read, but that which you say was sent Viâ Virginia franked by the Post Master came no nearer to me than Cockspur where it was either destroyed or returned in the Packet, if Govr — Wright who was there had been possessed of my feelings he would have sent a Son's Letter to a Father notwithstanding the opposition of their Political tenets.

Once more I will attempt to present my Love to you by the hands of Monsr. Rilliet who poor Gentleman is making another effort after many disappointments to regain a footing on his native soil. you will see in the schedule of Letters, he is already the bearer of several to you, which are now perhaps not worth Carriage I have not time to review them & since they are written & Packetted let them go.

I told you in my last that I was going to Georgia. I began my Journey the 1st. May & at Wright's Savanna Broton Island & New Hope found Crops of Rice amounting to about 1300. Barrels which I caused to be removed to places less exposed to the threatned depredations of Picaroons from St. Augustine, in such places that great value still remains — I have lately learned that each Plantation is again well covered — the best Crop they say that ever was borne at Broton Island — but what of that? the whole will either be destroyed stolen or lye with the former to perish by time & Vermin — no small sacrifice at the shrine of Liberty, & yet very small compared with that which I am willing to make — not only Crops, but Land

Life & All must follow, in preference to sacrificing Liberty to Mammon. in such sentiments I found the People of Georgia with a few exceptions, but none more hearty than our Highland friends the McIntoshes, Lachlan is Colonel of a Battalion upon Continental establishment, two of his Sons Lach — & William are sūbs. — his Brother William Commands a Troop of Rangers in Pay of the Colony or as I should now say the State, Jo. Habersham is Major & John a Captain in the Battalion, in a word the Country is Military.

My Negroes there all to a Man are strongly attached to me, so are all of mine in this Country, hitherto not one of them has attempted to desert on the contrary those who are more exposed hold themselves always ready to fly from the Enemy in case of a sudden descent — many hundreds of that Colour have been stolen & decoyed by the Servants of King George the third — Captains of British Ships of War & Noble Lords have busied themselves in such inglorious pilferage to the disgrace of their Master & disgrace of their Cause. — these Negroes were first enslaved by the English — Acts of Parliament have established the Slave Trade in favour of the home residing English & almost totally prohibited the Americans from reaping any share of it — Men of War Forts Castles Governors Companies & Committees are employed & authorized by the English Parliament to protect regulate & extend the Slave Trade — Negroes are brought by English Men & sold as Slaves to Americans — Bristol Liverpoole Manchester Birmingham &ca. &ca. live upon the Slave Trade — the British Parliament now employ their Men of War to steal those Negroes from the Americans to whom they had sold them, pretending to set the poor wretches free but basely trepan & sell them into ten fold worse Slavery in the West Indies, where probably they will become the property of EnglishMen again & of some who sit in Parliament; what meanness! what complicated wickedness appears in this scene! O England, how changed! how fallen!

You know my Dear Sir, I abhor Slavery, I was born in a Country where Slavery had been established by British Kings & Parliaments as well as by the Laws of that Country Ages before my existence. I found the Christian Religion & Slavery growing under the same authority & cultivation — I never-theless disliked it — in former days there was no combatting the prejudices of Men supported by Interest, the day I hope is approaching when from principles of gratitude as well as justice every Man will strive to be foremost in shewing his readiness to comply with the Golden Rule; not less than £20000. Stg. would all my Negroes produce if sold at public Auction tomorrow. I am not the Man who enslaved them, they are indebted to English Men for that favour, nevertheless I am devising means for manumitting many of them & for cutting off the entail of Slavery — great powers oppose me, the Laws & Customs of my Country, my own & the avarice of my Country Men — What will my Children say if I deprive them of so much Estate? These are difficulties but not insu-perable I will do as much as I can in my time & leave the rest to a better hand, I am not one of those who arrogate the pe-culiar care of Providence in each fortunate event, nor one of those who dare trust in Providence for defence & security of their own Liberty while they enslave & wish to continue in Slavery, thousands who are as well intitled to freedom as themselves. — I perceive the work before me is great. I shall appear to many as a promoter not only of strange but of dan-gerous doctrines, it will therefore be necessary to proceed with caution, you are apparently deeply Interested in this af-fair but as I have no doubts concerning your concurrence & approbation I most sincerely wish for your advice & assistance & hope to receive both in good time.

I finished my Journey, going round by Mepkin, & returned to CharlesTown the 1st June half an hour after I had entered my House Intelligence was brought of a ffleet at Anchor a lit-tle to the Northward of Charles Town Bar for the history of this Fleet I refer you to Jack Wells's Paper of the 2d Inst. & to certain Notes which I have added. his account although true in general substance is the most bungling & inaccurate of any thing I have seen from him, it would be easier to build a true & proper narrative at full length than to mend the botchery which he took a full Month to compose, I wish you or somebody else would publish a fair & honest compilation from his Gazette & my Papers — You know me too well to suppose I would in a tittle exagerate or suppress. you may add as much of what follows as may appear to be necessary, but let the whole be cleverly done & introduced by such declaration of Candor as these accounts are well entitled to — nothing more abhorrent to me than publications of falsehood for Truth.

Upon the tremendous range of 55 Sail of Hostile Ships before our doors & in full view, after wishing they had rather come as seekers for ffreights of Rice, I thought it my Duty to add to the dignity of Vice President of the Colony (now State observe) the several Offices of Engineer, Super Intendent of Works, Aid de Camp. & occasionally any other which could in the least contribute to the service of my Country then seeming to verge on a precipice & to require the support of every Man in it — I, who you know had resolved never again to Mount a Horse, I, who thought it impossible for me to Gallop five Miles in a day, was seen for a Month & more every day on the back of a Lively Nag at 1/2 past 4 in the Morning sometimes Galloping 20 Miles before Breakfast & sometimes sitting the Horse 14 Hours in 18 — & what you will say was more extraordinary I never got a tumble, but mark he was a trotting Horse I will never cross a Pacer again if I can avoid it — I have spoken so particularly of myself, not meaning to claim any singular or extraordinary merit, but because I know you will draw pleasing inferences of my state of health from an Account of such exertions — the President was as diligent as active as a Man could be & so much more useful than myself as his authority superior abilities & advantages of Youth enabled him. every Man except a few unhappy misled whom the People call Tories & a few of a worse stamp whom I call property Men, was animated, discovered a Love of Country & a boldness arising from an assurance of being engaged in a just Cause; Charles Town was in a very short time inclosed by Lines Trenches & Redoutes — Wharves were cleared of all incumbrances. Streets strongly barracadoed — retrenchments within — Batteries erected for defence at practicable Landings above the Town — Thousands of Men came in from the Country from North Carolina & Virginia & all this with a degree of Celerity as amazing as our former neglect had been. much indeed are we indebted to Gen Lee as well as to his seconds the Brigadiers Armstrong & Howe, these arrived at a Critical time & we were favoured by weather which fortunately witheld the Enemy from striking a sudden blow & every moment of the Interval was improved to advantage on our side.

Gen Lee at first sight was exceedingly displeased with the Fort at Sullivant's wished we could save our Stores & abandon it although he acknowledged the exterior work was impregnable. however as that could not be done, he recommended some amendments gave advice Orders & his presence in the beginning of the action to which if we do not altogether owe the honour of the 28 June we are certainly greatly indebted. but from the General's better knowledge of the Harbour & the vast Importance of that Post he must now be of a different opinion.

At the approach of the Ships of War towards Sullivant's the Ramparts & Parapets of Fort Johnson where Colonel Gadsden had chosen his Command were seen covered by Officers & Soldiers, every one Interesting himself in the fate of the Sister Fortress & standing ready in case of need to second her efforts. all the Batteries round this Town were at the same time Manned, Guns loaded every article in readiness for acting in turn, Troops of Regulars & Militia properly stationed for repelling all attempts to Land, Engines & Men at proper stands for extinguishing Fires in the Town — there was every appearance of an universal determination to give General James Grant the flat Lie. it was the fortune of his old freind Will Moultrie to speak first & he Monopolized the Glory of the Day.

The Country Militia as well as the Town continued chearfully to do duty on this frontier as long as one of the Enemy's ffleet remained in sight — the Active was the last, she with a Tender went about ten days ago to Bull's Island the property of Capt Shubrick landed 40 White & 20 black Men killed by Platoon firing a few head of Cattle, augmented their black Guard by stealing Six more Negroes & then sailed off the Coast or perhaps only a little out of sight. to hear Shubrick's Overseer relate the manner of their firing on the Cattle & the very few of their shot which hit the Mark, is droll enough, & serves to raise the contempt of those, who with single Ball at 150 Yards distance will hit the Circle of an English Crown.

After the attack upon Sullivant's Island seconded by Ravages & Murders by the Cherokee Indians on our Western frontier who probably acted in a concerted Plan with the Ships & Troops, I beleive there were few Men here who had not lost all inclination for renewing our former connexion with your King & his Ministers, however that might have been. the great point is now settled — On the 2d Inst — a Courier arrived from Philadelphia & brought a Declaration of the 4th July by the Representatives of the 13 United Colonies in Congress met, that from thenceforward those Colonies should be "Free & Independent States." You have no doubt seen the Paper or will in a few days see a Copy often repeated at full length. therefore I need not mark the particular Contents — this Declaration was proclaimed in Charles Town with great Solemnity on Monday the 5th Inst. attended by a Procession of President, Councils, Generals Members of Assembly Officers Civil & Military &ca. &ca. amidst loud acclamations of Thousands who always huzza when a Proclamation is Read. — to many, who from the Rashness Impolicy & Cruelty of the British Administration had foreseen this Event — the scene was Serious Important & Awful. — even at this Moment I feel a Tear of affection for the good old Country & for the People in it whom in general I dearly Love. — there I saw that Sword of State which I had before seen four several Times unsheathed in Declarations of War against France & Spain by the Georges now unsheathed & borne in a Declaration of War against George the third — I say even at this Moment my heart is full of the lively sensations of a dutiful Son, thrust by the hand of violence out of a Father's House into the wide World, what I have often with truth averred in London & Westminster I dare still aver, not a sober Man & scarcely a single Man in America wished for seperation from Great Britain. Your King too, I feel for, he has been greatly deceived & abused.

Soon after the Men of War had Anchored within our Bar alarming Accounts were brought of new attempts by John

Stuart Henry Stuart Alexr. Cameron & other Ministerial Agents to stir up the Savage Indians to attack our Western frontier, several Intercepted Letters from them confirmed the Reports — the Indians & particularly the Cherokees had amused us by the most flattering Talks, full of assurances of friendship & promises to follow our advice which always had been that they should observe a strict neutrality — but very suddenly, without any pretence to Provocation those treacherous Devils in various Parties headed by White Men & pushed on by those who are in employment for this cruel purpose, made an Inroad upon our settlements burned several Houses & Murdered about sixty Persons chiefly Women & Children Colol. Aw. Williamson in South, Brigadier Rutherford in North Carolina were immediately in Arms & a large Command marched from Virginia what Rutherford & the Virginia Troops have done we are not yet informed but Colonel Williamson & his parties have driven back the Savages of the lower Towns killed as many as could be come at in fight & taken some Prisoners among whom are no less than 15 White Men, they have also destroyed Sennecca, Keowee, Warrachy, Estatohee, Toxawa & Sugar Town together with the Crops of Corn & other grain found in fields & Barns, the only possible way of reducing the Barbarians, this Intelligence comes from Colo. Williamson in late Letters, If the Virginians act their part well the Cherokees will soon be reduced to the utmost distress & may possibly turn their vengeance against those hellish Instigators to this hellish War. at the Entrance of Senneca a new Town which I am told was very extensive on the Banks of Keowee, Colonel Williamson suffered from an ambuscade, his Horse by two Shot was killed under him. Mr. Salvador a Gentleman whose Death is universally regretted was killed by his Side, eight Men wounded, two of whom are since dead. — he nevertheless rallied his Troops, attacked the Savages beat them out & after destroying a Town of near four Miles long Marched forward — he is undoubtedly a brave Man & not a bad General — you know his deficiency in Education, what heights might he have reached if he could have improved his Genius by Reading. — If we succeed against the Cherokees the Creeks & other Indians may continue to be simple

Spectators of our contest with British Ships & Soldiers, otherwise we shall be attacked on all sides & greatly distressed, but Men here are fearless of distress & determined to maintain their Rights, trusting in a Righteous God for a happy Issue.

I told you in a former Letter of the dangerous Insurrections by thousands of the back Country People, these were suppressed by the vigilance & activity of Colo. Williamson in a first Instance & in a second & more formidable by Col? Richardson & Troops from North Carolina — hundreds or more properly thousands were taken Prisoners, informed truly of the nature of the dispute between Great Britain & the Colonies converted & sent to their habitations, about an hundred of their Colonels Captains & other Officers (from whence it appears the whole body was very large) were brought to Charles Town, these except 13 or 14 of the most tenacious soon confessed their errors united in the American Cause & also returned home — of the 13 or 14, were some sensible Men particularly their chief Colonel Robert Cunningham a Man of great honour, whose Conscience as he said fettered him in the Oath of allegiance although he admitted the injustice of Taxing Americans without their own Consent, & censured the British Administration; he often moved me while I was President of the Council of Safety & often since the President of the Colony to accept from him & his Companions an Oath of Neutrality, he would not at first believe that the British Administration were so wicked as to Instigate the Savages to War against us — as soon therefore as he was convinced of the truth his Conscience freed him from old obligations & he most heartily desired to take the Oath of fidelity to the United Colonies & to have an opportunity of giving proofs of his sincerity, his fellow Prisoners joined him in a Petition to the President & Council, who ordered the whole to be released — they immediately repaired to Colonel Williamson's Camp & offered their service but he considering their long absence from their several homes recommended to them the care of their families — Not all however whom we have enlarged have continued faithful, some of the Common fellows have quoted the example of Sir James & broke their Parol — most of these are now among the Indians some of them have again been taken Prisoners & must suffer the Penalty of an old Law—

Kirkland you may have heard made his Escape where he left his Son a Child of 10 or 12 Years old in Gaol—we know nothing of him since his flight, possibly this ignorant fellow may have found his way to St. James's, he was confident of a hearty welcome there, & of much free conversation with the Master of that House—If he were honest he might make a tolerable Serjeant but any thing less than a Regiment will fall short of his own Mark.

the Reverend Mr. Cooper from time to time gave offence to his Parishoners & they have dismissed him.

the King's Officers that is to say the Atty. General, Chief & Assistt. Judges, Postmaster & Mr. Outerbridge are confined to the Post Master's House—the late Commander of Fort Johnson & the Collector are at large on their Parol. W Wragg remains at his Plantation & lately James Brisbane & some seven or eight others of our Neighbours who had signed the Association & acknowledged the Justice of the American Cause but refused to do any thing which might endanger their property in case of Conquest by the other side (these & some who play still a more cunning Game are <u>Property Men</u>) were sent to Cheraw Gaol—the success of the 28 June made some Converts & those Gentlemen in particular, advanced so far as to consent to bear Arms take the Test Oath &ca but still under the Air of obedience to avail themselves of the Plea of compulsion & to save property—such Men deserve no station of honour on either side; I can have no pity for these while I sincerely commiserate the circumstances of the King's Officers & of every suffering Candid Man, although he may be mine Enemy.

Mrs. Stuart the Wife of the cruel Superintendent had been long confined to her House & hindred from leaving the Colony, the People had hoped that Stuart would in the Case of his own have had some tender feelings for the Wives & Innocent Children of our friends on the Indian frontier, but when we found that he had struck the blow, instead of retaliating as his friends ever do. the President & Privy Council ordered Mrs. Stuart to be enlarged; no valuable end could be obtained by a continuance of her suffering.

America is now well supplied with Gun Powder & Arms & every Day will probably increase our commerce by slow steps.

The General Assembly is to meet on the 17th. September when the Declaration of Independence will be recorded among our Acts & every salutary measure pursued for the Welfare of the State — to tell you the Virginians had routed Lord Dunmore, that North Carolina is very quiet, Mary Land & Philadelphia as yet unmolested, New York likely to become the Seat of War for this Summer, that Boston is now secured to us by strong Fortifications, that the New England Privateers had made prizes of several Transport Ships & Prisoners of many hundred Highland Soldiers would probably be to relate what you will know before this can reach you — but it may be new to you, that Gen Lee & Gen Howe went last Week to Georgia, whence some expedition is intended to the Southward — the Season of the Year & some other circumstances are not so favorable as to give me sanguine hopes of success; & you will feel some concern when I tell you, we expect another visit by the British Ships & Troops in the Winter Months.

I have now gone through with much Intelligence such as it is, don't wonder if I tell you I write in haste, I had determined to take time by the forelock & to have saved four or five days for writing to my friends in England, but through some unexpected Public Calls & the long sickness of my good Man James I am reduced to one, & I must Copy for different conveyances, however I have a few words more to add. — I am now by the Will of God brought into a new World & God only knows what sort of a World it will be — what may be your particular opinion of this change I know not — You have done well to avoid writing on Politics, Remember you are of full Age entitled to judge for your self, Pin not your faith upon my sleeve, but act the part which an honest Heart after mature deliberation shall dictate & your services on the side which you may take, because you think it the right side, will be the more valuable

I need not tell you whatever may be your determinations to avoid all party disputes & to act inoffensively & circumspectly in the State where you are — I cannot rejoice in the downfall of an old friend of a Parent from whose nurturing Breasts I have drawn my support & strength, every Evil which befalls old England grieves me, would to God she had listned in time to the Cries of her Children & had checked the Insidious slanders of those who call themselves the King's Servants & the King's friends especially such of them as had been transported to America in the Character of Civil Officers — If my own Interests if my own Rights alone had been concerned I would most freely have given the whole to the demands & disposal of her Ministers in preference to a Seperation, but the Rights of Posterity were Involved in the Question I happened to stand as one of their Representatives & dared not betray my Trust —

I am now more than ever anxious to see you, to see my Dear Harry & your Sisters, to see your Uncle & Aunt — but when & where? God direct you for the best — but pay particular attention to those friends especially to your eldest Sister & to Harry, your other Sister is at an Age & has qualities to make her Foster Mother happy. I could add very much on this head — but Clouds & Darkness are before me. —

Remember me respectfully to each of my old friends tell them that as an Individual I have a right to acknowledge my obligations to them & that I will take every opportunity of shewing my Regard & although I hold my Life by a most precarious tenure yet I trust in God we shall meet again as friends particularly inform both the Mr. Cowles's that I will when it is possible look into our Accounts & adjust them, it has not been in my power to do so since my arrival from England. Mr. William Cowles will do me the justice to own that tis not my fault those Accounts were left unsettled I had often wrote to him for them, I made one journey to Bristol for the sole purpose of settling them & when I was leaving the Kingdom I again took Bristol in my way to Falmouth for the same purpose, I waited there to the very last hour for saving my Passage in the Packet & did not receive the Papers from him till I had kept the Post Chais long in waiting at my door & in despair was just stepping into it — My friend is to blame on this score.

I am glad you continue with Mr. Bicknel & your Brother with Mr. Henderson frugality is essential to you both, consider I cannot supply you while the Sword of Britain remains unsheathed. Improve every moment of your time my Dear Son & continue your guidance & protection to your Brother & your Sisters, your respect & Duty to your distressed Uncle & Aunt. I feel much for them. may God protect & guide you all & may he still give Peace & mutual friendship to the divided family of Britain & promote the happiness equally of the ancient Root & of the transplanted branches — If you do not come enquire for opportunities in Holland & in France & write as oft as you can — & Harry too. —

　　　　　　　　　　Adieu My Dear Dear Son —
Why do you never say a word of MB.

Philip Vickers Fithian:
Journal, August 11–30, 1776

AUGUST 11

The Lords Day is come once more. But the Sabbath is scarcely known in the Army. Profaned is all religious Exercise. Dreadful is the thought that Man who expect an Engagement every Day with a obstinate, wise, & powerful Enemy, should dare be so ungodly. But the God of this World has blinded the Mind.

With Col: Newcomb I went in the Morning to Dr. Rogers's Church — Afternoon to Mr. Masons. Before the Afternoon Sermon was finished the Town was alarmed by the firing of Cannon below. All the places of worship instantly thrown into Disorder. But the whole was no more than a Ship or two arrived, & the Guns were a Salutation.

At 5 o Clock our Battalion met; I preached to them & hope we were all improved.

AUGUST 12

No Movement yet of the Enemy. They expect a strong Reinforcement no Doubt.

4 o Clock Afternoon firing below at the Fleet. — The Tops of the Houses are covered with Gazers; All the Wharves where there is any View lined with Spectators — It is an Addition to the Fleet: Ship after Ship came floating up, til we counted forty one, & many of them large.

An Express just now arrived from Gen: Green on Long-Island, that the Fleet which entered within Sandy Hook yesterday consists of fifty Sail. Be on our Side, O Lord, & we fear them not! —

AUGUST 13

Last Evening, with the Remainder of Capt: Debois's Company; came Thos: B. Greenman, in the Character of a private; Good young Man, he will find other Usage than round his Father's Board.

Changeable World! Orders are out for us to move tomorrow Morning — the whole Brigade is to move over on Long-Island.

We were down at the Battery this Morning to view the Shipping; they lie in a long, thick Cluster; we had a good Glass, but could not precisely tell their Numbers, we think there is near two hundred Sail, probably more! —

Four Funerals, all Citizens, went past our Door this Evening! The Town I believe is sickly, as the Army.

AUGUST 14

Our Regiment object to going over to the Island, but military Orders are strong. It is determined & must this very Day away.

It is said by a Deserter who left the Fleet this morning that the Army had Orders to cook three Days Provision, from which it was conjectured that we may soon be attacked.

We were not over the Ferry til near sunset; & when over, our Battalion had Orders to march on near to Red-Hook, & lie on their Arms. I marched with them to Quarters; Gave them a short Address on the Expectation of an Attack in the Morning, prayed, & retired to Mrs. Borums, at whose House I lodged when on the Island before.

AUGUST 15

A very rainy Morning. Our hard-fated Men were at the Alarm Post between three & four o Clock — stood there more than two Hours under Arms, some without Blankets, or even a Coat it raining hard all the Time. — The whole Regiment was quartered in a House & Barn, so that many chose rather to sleep in their Blankets on the Ground, than with the Throng — At any Rate it is all hard.

This morning poor I am again sick. Unable to go about. My good Landlady consents to my stay with her til I am better.

No Signs of an Attack, but it is said to be prevented only by the very rainy Morning.

Dr. Freeman of Col: Furman's Battalion, a friendly Soul, waits on me, Dr. Ewing at the Ferry.

Hard indeed it will be, if I am confined on a Bed of Sickness, & unable to retreat, when the Enemy makes a Descent on the Island, if they shall prove Victors! — No; they will never be so blest. Curses must follow the Executors of such ill Designs. Heaven will not pass them by unpunished. This healing Thought distends my Heart; tho sick I am yet strong. I fear not *George's Tory Fleet* & *Army*; Let them ride yonder before our Town, & Fortifications, in their highest Grandieur, we dread them not. Timidity belongs to them. May the God of Peace fill them all with Confusion because they came from their Homes to rob us of our *Peace* & *Freedom*. Do it, good Lord. Amen. Amen.

Press Warrants are issued to draught three Men out of every five of the Militia, till the several Brigades be filled.

August 16

Mr. Hunter & I took Lodgings at Mrs. *Coburn's*.

I stop drawing my Rations.

Our Situation, & Living now are most fine. A genteel, sober, patriotic Family, of which, in order to be agreeable, I need say no more. We have a small neat Room, free of Noise, well furnished, & with a good Bed — But our Situation —! From the Door of our Room, we have a good View of the Fleet — A perfect View of New-York; Governors Island; Powles-Hook; & Red-Hook — We live on the very Bank of the Water opposite to Governors Island.

Some say our Situation is dangerous; but all places in the Neighberhood of York are, I think, equally dangerous — We fear not Tory *George*, & his War-worn Army! — We fear them not. I prefer my Situation here, where I can discover the first Motions of his Fleet, & trace them along to their Place of Action, or out of the Harbour — To any Situation whatever of *Eligance*, *Safety*, or *Ease*.

Another Chevaux de Frize went up the North River to Day, to help in compleating the Security of the two Ships already up.

Nothing, but a proper Wind, is wanting to the Fireships — Send it soon, & be propitious, kind Heaven!

I find myself in Body to Day by God's Goodness much better — but in Mind I am quite elated; never yet so full of Certainty that we shall prevail; never had I so few Reasons why we should not.

AUGUST 17

My Fever is quite gone, I am now only weak.

The Fleet lies quiet below. Each Night we expect them, & yet each Night we have been disappointed. By Express we are informed that last Night an Attempt was made with two Fire-Vessels to burn one or both the Ships up the North-River — They sail'd up well; grappled, & set fire to a Brig fastened to the Phoenix; but such was the Alertness, & Spirit of the Seamen, that by cutting away instantly their own Rigging, She was disintangled & towed off! — One of the Tenders, a ten Gun Sloop, was set on Fire, & consumed. The Capt: of one of the Fire-Vessels is yet missing, we hope not lost.

The Ships are not destroyed, but we cannot learn Particulars.

Before Evening the Galleys came down & anchored — We hope yet to chastise those pilfering Plunderers who have gone up to distress our Market! —

Since Thursday we have damp, lowering Weather threatening a Storm.

AUGUST 18

A Flag from the Fleet came up yesterday Evening we know not yet the Contents.

By Mr. Peck, in the Evening, I received a third Letter from my ever-dear Betsey; my faithful Wife — O preserve us both, Good Providence, to possess the Wish of both our Souls, the Comfort of enjoying each other's Society, after these stormy Days are blown quite over — O grant it; Amen.

Whew — ! What means this roaring above us? — Crack! Crack! Crack! What can this cracking mean! — It is the upper Battery contending with the Ships coming down the River.

Just a Quarter of an hour before seven in the morning the firing begun. At seven precisely they were abreast of the grand Battery at New-York. They kept over as near Powles Hook as they could, in Order to be as far as possible from the York Batteries. Before they were down so low as the grand Battery at New-York, & then quite down to the Fleet, as they passed by the Fire from Governors Island, & Red-Hook, we had them in perfect View. The Morning is rainy, the Wind at North East & Violent, so that they passed briskly, tho' the

Ebb was quite expended before they were past Red-Hook. For about four Minutes the firing was really tremendous! This was the Time while the Ships were passing between the grand Battery & Governors-Island; they were then sailing in the midst of a perpetual Blaze! — The lower Batteries at New-York; the Batteries over at Powles-Hook; the Gallies which lay between New-York & Governors Island; & all the Cannon on Governors Island, were all, like incessant Thunders, rattling on them! The *Phoenix* was ahead of the *Rose* a Mile & a half, or more; & the two Tenders were a Mile behind the *Rose*; Both the Ships fired briskly, on the Town & Batteries, but without much Effect, as their Pass was so transient. Our Lodging is on the Shore in Range with Governors-Island, at which the Ships fired bitterly, but we saw no Balls come quite ashore, tho' great Numbers struck the Water between the Island & us. When they were past Red-Hook they clued up their Sails & scudded away proudly to the Fleet under only a Main Top Sail each! Thus the British Navy triumphs: And that Daemon *Wallace*, is, no Doubt, elated with his present Security.

But let the Traitors dare to tread the Land! Let us stand on equal Ground, & we defy even British Prowess.

All Day rainy we had neither Prayers nor Sermon. — Orders are given that all the Women & Children remove out of New-York forthwith. This confirms the common Belief that the *General* expects soon an Action.

AUGUST 19

Still very rainy. The General is sinking Vessels between the Town & Governors Island to prevent the Fleet from going up East River. Orders are repeated for Women, & all the Infirm, to remove out of N. York.

It is said that the Fellow who was principal in sinking the Vessels up the River, was the infernal Traitor who piloted the Men of War down! —

Towards Evening I walked down to the Hook the Fleet appear numerous.

AUGUST 20

Much Talk yet of the Enemy's landing, but we know not where. The General is sinking old Vessels in the Stream between the Town & Governors Island. Since yesterday evening very many have been sunk.

General Sullivan came over to Day to take the command of the Force on this Island.

Great Numbers are engaged to Day in throwing up Breastworks along the Shore to prevent a Landing with small Arms.

All Day a heavy Firing is heard below, but chiefly towards Evening most frequent & large Platoons, it is thought to be the Hessians training.

Yesterday five Tories were taken at Rockway, below the Narrows; it is said they were driving Cattle for the Use of the Fleet. A Detatchment of 226 Men was immediately sent down to prevent any plundering by the disappointed Crews of the Tenders.

Seven very heavy Cannon were fired this Evening between seven & eight on the Jersey Shore supposed to be at Elizabeth Town Point.

AUGUST 21

Large Additions are made to those who are working on Fatigue. Col: Cortlandt's Regiment, to a Man, is taken: General Sullivan was out early & is very busy: Our Works are extending from Fort Sterling almost to Red-Hook, near three Miles.

Before Dinner Mr. Shepherd & Wetherington from Cohansie called to see us; they came up Sunday Evening, & are now returning — How sweet to see Old Acquaintances — I sent a Line to my lonely Betsey.

Yesterday Evening a Flag came to Town, we know not yet the Contents.

AUGUST 22

We had last Night a most terrible Storm of Wind, Thunder, & Lightening! So violent as I have not seen since about this time in August 1773. We expect it must have damaged the Shipping. It has done a little Injury in the Harbour tho not so much as from a most furious sudden Wind, lasting an hour & a half, might be expected! These two Days past many of the Ships have gone out. And this morning, before seven, thirteen weigh'd & went out: It is said by express those which went yesterday were fitted with troops.

Several Hundred Men are making a Breastwork still along the River only as a Defence from Musquetry. It runs close by our Lodging so that we shall have only to step into the Trench, load, Fire &c!

Crack: Crack! An Alarm from Red-Hook. Crack! Crack! Crack! the Alarm repeated from Cobble-Hill. Orders are given for the Drums to beat *To Arms*. The Enemy have been landing for some time down at the Narrows, &, it is said, have now ashore several thousand. — The Battalion of Riffle-Men stationed there, on the Enemy's landing, left their Camp, & came up the Island, setting on Fire, all the Way, the Stacks of Grain; this is the first Degree of Ravage occasioned by this unworthy & unchristian Assault of our Enemies, that I have been Witness to.

Every Battalion, for the present, was ordered to repair to its proper Alarm-Post.

Ours, however, soon had Orders to enter Fort-Box. I equipt myself for an Action. With my Gun, Canteen, Knap-sack, Blanket, & with the Regiment entered the Fort & waited for further Orders.

Three Battalions were ordered off immediately to intercept them, & annoy their March.

The Alarm Guns were fired a little before twelve o Clock.

Before four two Brigades were over from New-York, the greater Number of which marched on to meet the Enemy. Generals Sullivan & Green rode on to gain some Intelligence of their Place & Numbers. Word soon came back that they are within a few Miles.

Our Battalion all turned out & made a formidable Piquet round our little Fortification, in Order to retard the Approach of the Enemy, & hinder their surrounding us, especially their Horse. The Men work with Vigor, a Sense of Necessity, & the Security of Life, are strong Springs to Industry.

About eight in the Evening the Generals returned into Camp, & inform that the Enemy have made a halt at Flat-Bush, about four Miles Distance — that the several Battalions advanced are in Ambush & otherways arranged to annoy them — & that our Battalions, after the Guards are taken out, may repair to Quarters til two in the Morning, when all without fail are to be at their Post. No Officer or Soldier is to take off his Clothes; & all are to lye on their Arms.

AUGUST 23

All at Alarm-Posts by two. No Approach of the Enemy. About eight we hear heavy firing. We hear the Riffle-Men are distressing them with loose firing. The Hessians, on the other hand, single themselves out & skirmish our Riffle-Men — At twelve we have none yet killed; two wounded, one in the Groyne, the other is shot through the Knee, we hope neither is mortal.

At two o Clock the Alarm Guns were again fired from Cobble Hill — To Arms, to arms, thro' all the Regiments! It is said they gain Ground, & the Officer there has desired a Reinforcement — Col:s Martin's, & Littles Regiments immediately march off with two Field-Pieces. Our People about twelve o Clock with Howitzers set fire to a large elegant House, & a Barn on the hither End of Flat-Bush, said to belong to a Tory, in which many Officers of the Regulars were quartered; one of which, we have Reason to believe, was killed — Thus they have been already compelled to give Way, tho' it is but little yet. Towards Evening we hear one of our Riffle-Men was killed.

Our Battalion is ordered, for the first Time, to take Post in a Wood, by Red-Hook there to stay all Night "sub-jove." Some of our Lads may think it hard but Hardships are always the Attendants of War.

AUGUST 24

Firing very early this morning. — Webster of Philad: breakfasted with us; he belongs to the third Battalion of Philad: Volunteers, two Companies of which Batt: are on this Island.

Before Noon I walked to the Place of Action, two Miles & a half. Like all earthly things, the Scenes of War are diverse & mixed. Some of our Men were in Companies sitting under the shady Trees and conversing about the Occurrences of the Day: who were killed, or wounded, or taken Prisoners; & which Army, on the Whole, gained Ground or lost; — Others were preparing their Victuals, & eating; — Many were lying on the sides of the Hills opposite to the Enemy, & securely sleeping — While others, as it comes in turn, were standing among whistling Bullets, on the other Side of the Hills, taking Trees for their Security & shooting when they can.

The Fire while I staid was nearly constant, & sometimes a Cluster would Rattle off together! two Field-pieces industrously playing also, sometimes with Balls, & sometimes with Canister Shot. But the Enemy are stopped, we hope, in their progress, & we pray that they may lose their Strength & Courage & return to their Ships with Shame.

Col: Martin to Day was wounded in the Breast, the Bullet is not extracted, but the Wound is not thought mortal.

A private had his Leg shot to pieces by a six-pounder, the Limb has been taken off & he is hopefully mending.

AUGUST 25

Another holy Sabbath presents to our View. No social Worship to be performed this Day — Carts & Horses driving every Way among the Army — Men marching out & coming in to & from the front Camp — Small Arms & Field Pieces continually firing; all in Tumult.

Mr. Noble at ten in the Dutch Church gave us a Sermon; about forty straggling Hearers were present.

Afternoon I visited our Battalion — one was fined by a Court-Martial for spend his Amunition, one Dollar — We had Prayers & the Battalion went to the Wood destined for them to guard. I to my Quarters with my kind Family.

AUGUST 26

Much unwell I find myself to Day. Mr. Ludlam & Hudson are here from Cohansie by them I write to my absent Betsey. No very important movement of the Enemy to Day. Our People in Parties annoy them.

Col: Ramsons Battalion is degraded. Fryday night last they left their Post before the Enemy & retreated with the utmost Confusion & Fear! The General gave it out in this Days Order that they shall stay within the Lines & do Fatigue from Day to Day: that they shall not even be allowed to mount a Guard of more than twelve! An Admonition indeed very humbling —

AUGUST 27

O doleful! doleful! doleful! — Blood! Carnage! Fire! Our People drove this Morning within their Lines! The Alarm Guns were fired a little before Day. Many Battalions, of excellent Men, went out into the Woods on the right & left Wing of the Enemy; — Alas! numbers went never to return! — The Enemy surrounded them. Those who could, retreated within the Lines. Those who could not were obliged to fight their Way thro the Enemy at every Hazard — But many, many we fear are Lost. General Lord Sterling's Brigade, in special, excited our tenderest Pity; A Savage would have pitied them — They stood formed in a large Body, on a good Eminence, in our plain View, but where we could give them no Relief! — On three Sides of them were the Enemy — on the other Side was a broad Marsh, & a Creek. There the brave Men stood more than four Hours — they found their Enemies surrounding them more, at last they divided placed a Body to attack the Enemy while a Part crossed over the Water — Here was a desperate Fire. But it was the best they could do. The Officers swam their Horses over, the Men some swam & some passed in Boats, but many stood behind; among these is Lord Sterling. Gen: Sullivan also is yet missing! The daring Britains came up boldly to our Works twice, & twice they were beat off — But such a dreadful Din my Ears never before heard! — And the distressed wounded, came crying into the Lines! We have taken upward of thirty of them.

Towards Evening the Riffle-Men, without Orders stole away & set fire to Houses, Barns &c. which presented a most dismal Scene.

AUGUST 28

Our Enemies enlarge their Appearance; show us more Tents & begin a Breastwork — The Riffle-Men went out in Parties & are perpetually firing; the Balls come buzzing over our Lines. Yet no Execution as we hear of done. Afternoon, at three, a Alarm in the midst of a violent Rain. Drums heavily calling to Arms. Men running promiscuously, & in Columns to the Lines. All the Time the Rain falling with an uncommon Torrent. The Guns of the whole Army are wetted. And after the Alarm was over, which was occasioned by the Regulars coming in a greater Body than usual to drive our Riffle-Men, our Troops fired off their Guns quite till Evening so that it seemed indeed dangerous to walk within our own Lines—for we could from every Part hear perpetually Firing, & continually hear the Balls pass over us.

We cannot yet learn our Loss by our Retreat; the Generals Sullivan & Sterling are either killed or taken.

THURSDAY AUG: 29

Orders are given that there shall be no firing either out or in the Lines: Last Night the Enemy threw up a Breast-work opposite Fort Putnam at about a half a miles Distance. Our People are a little Alarmed. But yet we fear them not; even in Death we despise them. The weather is most unfavourable, very rainy; yesterday & to day, so much that the Trenches, Forts, Tents, & Camp are overflowed with water, & yet our Men must stand exposed themselves & Firelocks to it all. Twenty four hours at least the Lines are manned by the same Persons, & some Regiments have been on Duty since Monday! Sickness must follow.

Yesterday our Family except one to keep the House together, moved over to New-York, & from thence up the North-River to some Place of greater Security.

Towards Evening our Brigade has Orders to parade this Evening at seven o clock with all the Baggage. Many Conjectures are made of the Cause, none however can be clearly given. Mr. Hunter & I concluding that no Rest can be had if we pass over so late, & that it will be as well to go over in the Morning, & having a good Room & Bed here, agreed & stay the Night on Long-Island.

FRYDAY AUG: 30

As soon as it was well light we were up & preparing to go over. Between twelve & one the Woman who keeps our house, being informed by one from the Camp, came into our Room & told us she had packed up most of her remaining Effects, & wanted the Bed on which we were lying; & at the same time advised us to consult immediately for our own Safety as the Army is leaving the Island! —As an idle Tale we considered what She said, & unfolded our Blankets & again laid ourselves down, & slept quietly til Day! —

We got down to the Ferry, & happily came over, among the last Boats — those which came next were fired at, & in one of them five were badly wounded!

We brought all off with Deliberation, except two Bottles, one of which with Bitters, an useful Article now.

Once more our Army is in New-York, having fled before our Enemies are full of Anxiety — the prevailing Opinion is we cannot keep this Capital more than two or three Days. The Winds are northerly & have been since they came on Shore but the huge Ships beat up a little nearer every Tide, & we hourly expect them before the Town.

Jabez Fitch: Diary, August 27–28, 1776

Tuesd: the 27th: We were alarm'd very Early in the Morning by a Rept: of an Action at the Post from whence we were Reliev'd the Night before, upon which we Emediately March'd to support the Party there; We first March'd up into the Edg of the Wood, for a Flank Guard, & then Retreated back some way Reconitring the Wood, while Ld: Sterling at the head of a Considrable party Maintain'd an unsteady fire with the Enimy on their Left Wing; at about 7 oClock we were Reinforc'd by several partys from our Left, when we again Advanc'd & Extended a Line on the Left of Ld: Sterlings Party, where we had two or three sevear Attacts, in which a Lt: Col: of ours was Kil'd, & also Col Grant of the Regulars; While we were thus Engaged here, we heard a Smart Fire Toward our Left Wing, which gave us to Apprehend that we were in Danger of having our Retreet cut off, on which our Regt: were Order'd to March toward the Fire, & on our Approaching in Sight of the Enimy (to our Surprise) we found our Apprehensions but too well grounded; After this we met with several small Attacts, in which we Generally Fought on Retreet, without much Loss, untill we found ourselves Surrounded by the Enmy, when we Attempted to Join Lord Sterlings party, but found our Selves Likewise cut off from them. we then Collected our Scatter'd Force in the best manner possable, & took our March over Eastward, with Intention to brake through the Enimy & Secure a Retreet that way, but after croosing a thick Swamp, we came onto a Plain partly cover'd with Wood, where we soon found our selves between two sevear Fires from the Hessian Troops: on which we again Retreeted into the Swamp, & Repared to the Ground that we had Occupied before, where we were again Attacted by a Small party who soon Retreeted; we had now lost Col: Clark & Genll: Person, on which a Number of our Officers Assembled & concluded it best, as we were Intirely Surrounded by the Enimy, to Resign our selves up to them in small Partys, & Each one

Take care for himself, accordingly, I went alone Down to the Northward, where I lit of Sargt: Wright, who had his Leg Broak, I carried him some way Down the Hill, & Lay'd him in a Shade where I Left him; I then Went up the hill to the Eastward, where I see at a small Distance a party of Regulars, on which I Emediately Advanc'd to them, & gave up my Arms; They Treated me with Humanity &c

Kings County on Long Island
Tuesd: Augt: 27th: 1776
Having Surrendered myself to the 57th: Regt: I was kept under the care of a Guard for some Time, while some others Likewise came in & Surrendered; & at about 5 oClock, I was guarded by sd: Regt: over on to the Edge of Flat Bush Plain, where I see a Large Body of Hessian Troops on a Hill at our Left; We then took a Turn to the Right, & was March'd by the Front of several Batallions of the Hessians, where I Recd: many Insults from those Formidable Europeans; We then March'd through a Considrable Wood, & came onto the Hill, where I first Discovered the Enimy in the Morning; here we found the greater part of two Brigaids under Arms & Genll: Agnue at their Head, I was then Conducted down to a Barn near the Road where I March'd homeward the Night before, & Confin'd with a great number of Prisoners of Different Regts: here I found Capt: Trowbredge Capt Percivel Lt: Fanning & Ensn: Gillit, & soon after Capt: Jewett was Brot: in who was Wounded with the Stab of a Bayonet in the Breast, & also another in the Belly, the Latter of which was sopos'd to be the Occasion of his Death, for he Languish'd & suffered great Pain for about 36 Hours (viz) while Third'd the 29th at about 5 in the Morning he Died. About sunset the Officers present, being about 20 in Number, were Assign'd a Comfortable Room in a House Nigh at hand, where I Laid down on a Chaff Bed, but Slept very Little.

Wednesd: the 28th: In the Morning a Cirgeon was sent to Dress the Wounds of the Prisoners, he also gave Capt Jewett some Physick, & Attended on him several Times this Day; But Majr: Brown was the Officer that Principally Attended us here on all Occasions, & Treated us with great Humanity &

Complisance; Genll: Grant also was so good as to make us a
Present of a Side of Mutton, & order'd his Negro to Cook it
for us; This Day there was a Considrable Firing of Small Arms
&c the Perticulars of which, we were not able to learn; Capt
Jewett Decay'd Gradually through the whole Day, but was
not sopos'd Dangerous, while near Night, I sat with him
most of the Night, & slept but very Little; the Capt: had his
senses, while about 2 in the Morning, & was sensible of his
being near his End, often Repeating that it was hard work to
Die, he also Desired me to see him Buried with Deacence as
far as our present Circumstances would Admit, & write the
Circumstances of his Death to his Wife; for 2 or 3 hours before he Died, he was somewhat Delirious, & Talk'd somewhat
Irrational, he was also speechless for some short Time before
he Expired.

Henry Strachey:
Memorandum on Meeting Between
Lord Howe and the American Commissioners

11th. Septr. 1776.

LORD HOWE received the Gentlemen on the Beach — Dr. Franklin introduced Mr. Adams and Mr. Rutledge — Lord Howe very politely expressed the Sense he entertained of the Confidence they had placed in him, by thus putting themselves in his hands —

A general and immaterial Conversation from the Beach to the House — The Hessian Guard saluted, as they passed —

A cold dinner was on the Table — dined — the Hessian Colonel present — Immediately after dinner he retired —

Lord Howe informed them it was long since he had entertained an opinion that the Differences between the two Countries might be accommodated to the Satisfaction of both — that he was known to be a Well Wisher to America — particularly to the Province of Massachusetts Bay, which had endeared itself to him by the very high Honors it had bestowed upon the Memory of his eldest Brother — that his going out as Commissioner from the King had been early mentioned, but that afterwards for some time, he had heard no more of it — That an Idea had then arisen of sending several Commissioners, to which he had objected — that his Wish was to go out singly and with a Civil Commission only, in which case, his Plan was to have gone immediately to Philadelphia, that he had even objected to his Brother's being in the Commission, from the Delicacy of the Situation and his desire to take upon himself all the Reproach that might be the Consequence of it — that it was however thought necessary that the General should be joined in the Commission for reasons which he explained — (having their hands upon the Two Services) — and that he, Lord Howe should also have the naval Command, in which he had acquiesced — that he had hoped to reach America before the Army had moved, and did not doubt but if their Disposition had been the same as expressed in their Petition to the King, he should have been able to have brought about an Accomodation to the Satisfaction of both Countries — that he thought the Petition was a sufficient Basis to confer upon — that it contained Matter, which, with Candour & Discussion might be wrought into a Plan of Permanency — that the Address to the People, which accompanied the Petition to His Majesty, tended to destroy the good Effects that might otherwise have been hoped for from the Petition — that he had however still flattered himself that upon the Grounds of the Petition, he should be able to do some good —

[Mr. Rutledge mentioned (by way of Answer to Lord Howe's Remark upon that point) that their Petition to the King contained all which they thought was proper to be addressed to His Majesty, — that the other Matters which could not come under the head of a Petition and therefore could not with Propriety be inserted, were put into the Address to the People, which was only calculated to shew them the Importance of America to Great Britain — and that the Petition to King was by all of them meant to be respectful]

That they themselves had changed the ground since he left England by their Declaration of Independency, which, if it could not be got over, precluded him from all Treaty, as they must know, and he had explicitly said so in his Letter to Dr. Franklin, that he had not, nor did he expect ever to have, Powers to consider the Colonies in the light of Independent States — that they must also be sensible, that he could not confer with them as a Congress — that he could not acknowledge that Body which was not acknowledged by the King, whose Delegate he was, neither, for the same reason, could he confer with these Gentlemen as a Committee of the Congress — that if they would not lay aside that Distinction, it would be improper for him to proceed — that he thought it an unessential Form, which might for the present lie dormant — that they must give him leave to consider them merely as Gentlemen of great Ability, and Influence in the Country — and that they were now met to converse together upon the Subject of Differences, and to try if any Outline could be drawn to put a stop to the Calamities of War, and to bring forward some Plan that might be satisfactory both to America and to England — He desired them to consider the Delicacy of his Situation — the Reproach he was liable to, if he should be understood by any step of his, to acknowledge, or to treat with, the Congress — that he hoped they would not by any Implication commit him upon that Point — that he was rather going beyond his Powers in the present Meeting —

[Dr. Franklin said You may depend upon our taking care of that, my Lord]

That he thought the Idea of a Congress might easily be thrown out of the Question at present, for that if Matters could be so settled that the King's Government should be reestablished, the Congress would of course cease to exist, and if they meant such Accommodation, they must see how unnecessary & useless it was to stand upon that Form which they knew they were to give up upon the Restoration of legal Government —

[Dr. Franklin said that His Lordship might consider the Gentlemen present in any view he thought proper — that they were also at liberty to consider themselves in their real Character — that there was no necessity on this occasion to distinguish between the Congress and Individuals — and that the Conversation might be held as amongst friends —

The Two other Gentlemen assented, in very few Words, to what the Doctor had said —]

Lord Howe then proceeded — that on his Arrival in this Country he had thought it expedient to issue a Declaration, which they had done him the honor to comment upon — that he had endeavored to couch it in such Terms as would be the least exceptionable — that he had concluded they must have judged he had not expressed in it all he had to say, though enough, he thought, to bring on a Discussion which might lead the way to Accommodation — that their Declaration of Independency had since rendered him the more cautious of opening himself — that it was absolutely impossible for him to treat, or confer, upon that Ground, or to admit the Idea in the smallest degree — that he flattered himself if That were given up, their was still room for him to effect the King's Purposes — that his Majesty's most earnest desire was to make his American Subjects happy, to cause a Reform in whatever affected the Freedom of their Legislation, and to concur with his Parliament in the Redress of any real Grievances — that his Powers were, generally, to restore Peace and grant Pardons, to attend to Complaints &c Representations, and to confer upon Means of establishing a Re Union upon Terms honorable & advantageous to the Colonies as well as to Great Britain — that they knew We expected Aid from America — that the Dispute seemed to be only concerning the Mode of obtaining it —

[Doctor Franklin here said, — *That* we never refused, upon *Requisition.*]

Lord Howe continued — that their Money was the smallest Consideration — that America could produce more solid Advantages to Great Britain — that it was her Commerce, her Strength, her Men, that we chiefly wanted —

[Here Dr. Franklin, said with rather a sneering Laugh, Ay, my Lord, we have a pretty considerable Manufactory of *Men* — alluding as it should seem to their numerous Army.]

Lord Howe continued — it is desirable to put a stop to these ruinous Extremities, as well for the sake of our Country, as yours — when an American falls, England feels it — Is there no way of treading back this Step of Independency, and opening the door to a full discussion?

Lord Howe concluded with saying that having thus opened to them the general Purport of the Commission, and the King's Disposition to a permanent Peace, he must stop to hear what they might chuse to observe.

Dr. Franklin said he supposed His Lordship had seen the Resolution of the Congress which had sent them hither — that the Resolution contained the whole of their Commission — that if this Conversation was productive of no immediate good Effect, it might be of Service at a future time — that America had considered the Prohibitory Act as the Answer to her Petition to the King — Forces had been sent out, and Towns destroyed — that they could not expect Happiness now under the *Domination* of Great Britain — that all former Attachment was *obliterated* — that America could not return again to the Domination of Great Britain, and therefore imagined that Great Britain meant to rest it upon Force — The other Gentlemen will deliver their Sentiments —

Mr. Adams said that he had no objection to Lord Howe's considering him, on the present Occasion, merely as a private Gentleman, or in any Character except that of a British Subject — that the Resolution of the Congress to declare the Independency was not taken up upon their own Authority — that they had been instructed so to do, by *all* the Colonies — and that it was not in their power to treat otherwise than as independent States — he mentioned warmly his own Determination not to depart from the Idea of Independency, and spoke in the common way of the Power of the Crown, which was comprehended in the Ideal Power of Lords & Commons.

Mr. Rutledge began by saying he had been one of the oldest Members of the Congress — that he had been one from the beginning — that he thought it was worth the Consideration of Great Britain whether she would not receive greater Advantages by an Alliance with the Colonies as independent States, than she had ever hitherto done — that she might still enjoy a *great Share* of the Commerce — that she would have their raw Materials for her Manufactures — that they could protect the West India Islands much more effectually and more easily than she can — that they could assist her in the Newfoundland Trade — that he was glad this Conversation had happened, as it would be the occasion of opening to Great Britain the Consideration of the Advantages she might derive from America by an Alliance with her as an independent State, before anything is settled with other foreign Powers — that it was impossible the People should consent to come again under the English Government — he could answer for South Carolina — that Government had been very oppressive — that the Crown Officers had claimed Privilege and confined People upon pretence of a breach of Privilege — that they had at last taken the Government into their own hands — that the People were now settled and happy under that Government and would not (even if they, the Congress could desire it) return to the King's Government —

Lord Howe said, that if such were their Sentiments, he could only lament it was not in his Power to bring about the Accommodation he wished — that he had not Authority, nor did he expect he ever should have, to treat with the Colonies as States independent of the Crown of Great Britain — and that he was sorry the Gentlemen had had the trouble of coming so far, to so little purpose — that if the Colonies would not give up the System of Independency, it was impossible for him to enter into any Negociation —

Dr. Franklin observed that it would take as much time for them to refer to, and get an answer from their Constituents, as it would the Commissioners to get fresh Instructions from home, which he supposed might be done in about 3 Months —

Lord Howe replied it was in vain to think of his receiving Instructions to treat upon that ground —

After a little Pause, Dr. Franklin suddenly said, well my Lord, as America is to expect nothing but upon total unconditional Submission —

[Lord Howe interrupted the Doctor at the Word Submission — said that Great Britain did not require unconditional Submission, that he thought what he had already said to them, proved the contrary, and desired the Gentlemen would not go away with such an Idea —

Memdn — Perhaps Dr. Franklin meant Submission to the Crown, in opposition to their Principle of Independency.]

And Your Lordship has no Proposition to make us, give me leave to ask whether, if *we* should make Propositions to Great Britain (not that I know, or am authorised to say we shall) You would receive and transmit them.

Lord Howe said he did not know that he could avoid receiving any Papers that might be put into his hands — seemed rather doubtful about the Propriety of transmitting home, but did not say that he would decline it —

Ambrose Serle:
Journal, August 22–September 15, 1776

THURSDAY, 22d.

Early this Morning the English Troops, the Highlanders, & Preston's Light Horse, landed on Long Island. The Disembarkation was effected upon the flat Shore, near Gravesend, without the least Resistance; the inhuman Rebels contenting themselves with burning as much of the People's Corn as they could (tho' the great Rains wch fell last night very happily prevented much of their Design), with driving off their Cattle as far as their Time would permit, and doing as much Injury to the Inhabitants, who are generally well disposed, as they possibly could. The Soldiers & Sailors seemed as merry as in a Holiday, and regaled themselves with the fine apples,* which hung every where upon the Trees in great abundance. After the landing was pretty well effected, I went with two or three Gentlemen on Shore to Mr. De Nuys's House, opposite the Narrows, whose Family were rejoiced at the Deliverance from the Tyranny they had so long undergone from the Rebels. It was really diverting to see Sailors & Apples tumbling from the Trees together.

The General pushed on to his Post, and was joined by great Numbers of the People. Every thing, relative to the Disembarkation, was conducted in admirable Order, and succeeded beyond our most sanguine Wishes.

The Island seems extremely fertile, and the Country rather flat. There were some fine Cattle still remaining; and proper Precautions were taken to prevent our People from Plundering.

I was just now told an affecting Instance of the villainous Barbarity of the Rebels, which cannot be recited without Indignation. A little Boy, belonging to one of our officers, playing by himself opposite the Jersey Shore, about 7 or 8 of

---

*These are chiefly what are called Newtown Pippins, and appear to me to be Descendants of our Broad nose Pippins, softened by the Soil.

the cowardly Riflemen came down slily, and discharged their Peices upon him. One of the Shot killed him; upon which they gave three Huzzas & retired. A Turk would detest so dirty an action. This is not War, supposing their Cause good, but Murder; and, upon a defenceless innocent Child, a most cruel, dastardly & infamous Murder. Such Villains would run away from the very appearance of *Men*.

Mrs. De Nuys told me, that her Family had 700 of these People to feed for some time together, before the Arrival of the Troops. If any Complaints were made of their Impositions or Insolence; the Complainants wd. be immediately stygmatized for Tories, & all their Property subjected to Confiscation for "the Good of the Cause."

In a Word, the Disembarkation of about 15,000 Troops, upon a fine Beach, their forming upon the adjacent Plain, a Fleet of above 300 Ships & Vessels with their Sails spread open to dry, the Sun shining clear upon them, the green Hills and Meadows after the Rain, and the calm Surface of the Water upon the contiguous Sea and up the Sound, exhibited one of the finest & most picturesque Scenes that the Imagination can fancy or the Eye behold. Add to all this, the vast Importance of the Business and of the Motions of the Day; and the mind feels itself wonderfully engaged by the Variety & Greatness of the objects; but finds, or shd. find, in the midst of all, that there is no assurance or Dependence in these things, but in Him only, who saveth by many or by few, and who giveth the Victory when, & where, & how, he pleaseth. In this Frame, a man may be disappointed of his present Wish, but not of his Hope or future Expectation. He may err in his Judgement; but he is right in his Heart.

FRIDAY, 23d. AUGUST.

We could see the Rebels this Morning, retiring, carrying off, and burning; the Country seemed covered with Smoke. Some of the Sailors, belonging to the Transports, having got on Shore & plundered; Orders were given by the Admiral that no Boats should go on Shore without particular Directions or without an officer. The General, as well as the Admiral, returned Thanks to particular officers of the Fleet

for their Activity & Assistance yesterday in the Debarkation
of the Troops: And, what may perhaps animate the Seamen
more particularly to distinguish themselves, the Admiral directed that Lists of the Names of such as assisted in the
Debarkation, should be given in to him by their respective
officers.

Last Night a great Fire was seen up the North River; from
what Cause unknown.

We have heard this Evening, that a Detachment of the
Army upon long Island have taken a Redoubt this Morning
from the Rebels, with the Loss of one Hessian killed & two
or three wounded. A Captain of the Engineers received a
slight Wound in the Hand.

About three or four Weeks since, ruminating where this
stupendous Fleet could be stationed during Winter to the
best Advantage for the Service, as well as its own Security,
and knowing long since, that it has been ever deemed impracticable for any Ships to remain in this Harbor or Sound
during Winter, on account of the vast Quantities of Ice
driven up and down by the Tides; a Thought struck me, that
if the Kill van Kull, a Channel of Water between New York
Sound & Rariton Bay, were well secured at each End where
the Width is the least, it would not only be defended from
the Drifts of Ice, but be capacious enough for all the
Shipping, which it might be thought necessary to keep here
during the extreme Severity of the Winter, which is of no
long Continuance. I communicated my Ideas to Mr. Hunter,
the master of the Eagle & a very ingenious Man, and wished
him to turn his Thoughts to the Practicability of the Matter
and to examine the Depth of Water in the Channel, in order
to see how well it would answer in that Respect for any of
the Men of War. Mr. Hunter readily fell in with my Notion,
and, at my Request, examined the Soundings and drew a
Plan of the Channel, together with a Scheme of the best
means for carrying the whole, if necessary, into Execution. I
advised him to present it to Lord H. which he complied
with.

The Rebels made more Conflagrations to-day of the poor
Farmers' Stacks of Corn and other Property. We could see
Columns of Smoke arise to a great Extent.

SATURDAY, 24th. AUGUST.

The passing of the Bill for confining Convicts to hard Labor within the Realm instead of transporting them to America, is a very just and politic Step, which ought to have been taken 50 Years ago. I read the account of it with great Pleasure in the Papers, wch the last Packet brought me. The Emigrations, voluntary & involuntary, from the British Islands, have been really alarming and inconsiderately allowed. The People are the Wealth & Strength of a State; and we have been suffering that Wealth & Strength to pass from us to the Colonies, who are too strong (beyond their original Design) already. In the Years 1771 & 1772 the number of Passengers from the North of Ireland, as it appears by the *Belfast News Letter*, amounted to near 18,000; and it is added, that the greatest Part of these Emigrants paid their Passage, which at £3.10. each, amounted to above £60,000. Most of them were People employed in the Linen manufacture, or Farmers, and of some Property, which they turned into Money and carried with them. By an account, which I have likewise seen, communicated by an Hon. & Right Revd. Bp. in the North of Ireland, above 33,000 Persons have quitted that Country for America from the Year 1770 to the Year 1774: and most of these were (what is termed) *Scots-Irish*, Presbyterians in Religion, disposed absolutely to the present Faction against Government, and many of them now principal agitators in these Confusions.

The Acts likewise, which have permitted Naturalization in the Colonies, when matters are settled, should be entirely abrogated.

A Party of about 15 Highlanders, routed a Lieutenant and about 30 Rebels; the Lieutenant & most of the men were taken Prisoners.

Another Party was attacked by a Body of Hessians & Light Infantry, who killed and wounded about 200 of the Rebels, with the Loss only of 2 or 3 Men.

SUNDAY, 25th. AUGUST.

Early this Morning the main Body of the Hessians passed over in Flat Boats from Staten to Long Island. They left enough behind them for the Defence of the Island. I was very sorry to be informed (I think by Ld. Dunmore) that these

People had committed already several Depredations, and even upon the Friends of Government. If a private Individual may be allowed to wish any thing in public Measures, I should have rejoiced if the Rebellion could have been reduced without Foreign Troops at all; for I fear our Employment of these upon this Service will tend to irritate and inflame the Americans infinitely more than two or three British Armies upon such an Occasion. Some Deference is to be paid to the Goodwill of Mankind; and it cannot be Policy to extort that by the most odious kind of Force, which may be obtained any other way. But, perhaps, there was no Alternative, which alone renders the Measure excusable.

MONDAY, 26th.

Nothing material occurred to-day: Great Preparations only were making, by Sea & Land; and every thing directed to be in readiness for an Attack, which in itself & in its Consequences is of the utmost Importance.

TUESDAY, 27th.

General Howe, having under his Command about 18,000 Men upon Long Island, began to move about 9 o'Clock last Night, in order to come up with the Rebels early in the Morning. He formed his Army into 3 Divisions, about 5,000 under Genl. Grant, which marched nearly along the Coast, 4,000 under Genl. Clinton, which came up in a Column from Jamaica Plain, and the rest under himself from Flat bush, which formed a Circuit & came round upon the Rebels a still farther Way. The Rebels, relying upon their Numbers, which were indeed very great, ventured for the first Time to keep the Field. The Morning was cool clear & pleasant; so that I was able to see almost the whole Process through a Perspective from the Poop of the admiral's Ship. The Detachment under Genl. Grant first fell in with them, near the Water-side, about 6 o'Clock in the Morning; and a smart Canonade continued till after Genl. Clinton's Detachment came over the Tops of the Hills. The Rebels, with Colors flying, formed themselves in a Line upon a very advantageous rising Ground, and by their great Superiority of numbers would have been able to have flanked the Troops under Grant if they had attacked them closely in that Situation. The two

Bodies therefore (as the Rebels did not chuse to quit their Ground & Grant had been ordered to advance no farther) stood looking at each other, almost without a Shot, for about an Hour. At length Genl. Howe with his Forces came round upon them, and, if they had not speedily retired from their Ground, would have closed them within three Fires. In retiring, Genl. Grant pressed upon them, and a sharp though short and shuffling Encounter passed between them. The Rebels abandoned every Spot as fast, I should say faster, than the King's Troops advanced upon them. One of their officers (Ld. Stirling, as I afterwards found) did indeed make an Effort to form a considerable Line of them in a ploughed Field; but they had scarce formed when down came the Troops upon the Ground, and the Poltroons ran in the most broken disgraceful and precipitate manner at the very first Fire. The Soldiers followed them with Spirit, and, as the Ground was pretty clear, cut them down in a terrible manner before any of them could get off from it. After this they made no Attempt to stand, but dispersed themselves as fast as they could. Some ran into the Woods; some posted towards their own Quarters; others, rather more bold though not more brave, fired, as they ran or as they could find Cover, from Walls and Hedges; and many were killed and taken Prisoners. The Number of these is yet unknown. Of our People, we have but 54 killed, and about 140 wounded, but very few dangerously. One of the General's Aid de Camps waited upon the Admiral with this Intelligence, and praised the conduct of all the Troops both British & Hessian in the highest Degree. From what I saw myself, nothing could exceed their Spirit & Intrepidity in attacking the Enemy. In one thing only they failed — they could not run so fast as their Foes, many of whom indeed were ready to run over each other. This 'tis presumed will be their last, as 'tis their first Effort to fight us upon plain Ground, if a woody Country can be called so. Our advanced Guards came close up to their Lines; so that they are now cut off from their Intercourse with the rest of Long Island. The Wretches burnt & destroyed Houses & Barns as they retired, and those especially whose Proprietors they believed were attached to G. Britain. Ignoble Warfare becoming only such ignoble Minds! The Conflagration was very great and in the Dusk of the Evening wore an awful appearance.

The Ships likewise made a Feint of attacking the Town; and many of the principal men of War got under Way and sailed backwards & forwards for great Part of the morning. This diverted some of the Force of the Rebels to another Consideration. Capt. Hammond only in the Roebuck went high enough to exchange a Shot or two with Red Hook, which, it was believed, did no Harm on either Side.

The Ships are stationed ready to sail up to the Town, and are prepared to enter upon Action.

WEDNESDAY, 28th. AUGUST.

By accounts recd. this Morning the Number of the Killed, Wounded & Prisoners of the Rebels is considerable indeed: Exact Returns are not yet made.

In the Afternoon, our People penetrated farther upon the Rebels about Brookland and the Ferry: The Firing was very continual & very hot, and lasted till dark night. We could only see imperfectly at a Distance, and impatiently wait to know the Event.

How melancholy is the Reflection, that the Folly & Wickedness of Man, under the abused Titles of Prudence & Patriotism, shall ruin the finest Countries, and proceed, as far as they may, to desolate the Earth! A little Pains & a little common Honesty might have induced a meeting with the King's Commissioners, and have settled all Differences with Amity & Ease. But — *Quos Deus vult perdere, priùs dementat.*

THURSDAY, 29th. AUGUST.

The Firing yesterday Evening was occasioned by the Rebels attempting to prevent our People from throwing up their Works & making a covered Way to the round Fort. There was more Noise than Damage. We had only two men slightly wounded.

Lord Dunmore came on board & dined this Day. He had much Conversation with me respecting the Rebels, the Country, the mode of carrying on the War, & such like Matters.

Ld. Stirling (so called) & Mr. (called Genl.) Sullivan, late one of the Members of the Congress, were taken among other Prisoners; the whole of which amounted to about 1200.

They were admitted to dine with the Admiral, with whom they both, and particularly Sullivan, had much Conversation. I had also a great deal of Discourse with them both, in which, by the softest Words & manner I could, I labored to convince them of their Error, how the People in America had been duped by artful Insinuations, and what real Desire the Mother-Country had ever had of bringing matters to a pacific Conclusion. They both acknowledged they had either misconceived the affair, or were misinformed, and that they had ever understood that G. Britain had but one simple Idea, on the Subject, which was their absolute Submission. I then opened to them the Intention of the Commission, which was Peace & Settlement, and explained how necessary it was to their own Interest & Welfare to propose and even intreat an accommodation. To this they seemed to agree. Sullivan, with great art but not with art sufficient to impose upon or delude any man acquainted with the Subject, expatiated upon the internal Strength and Resources of America, and of her Capability of maintaining the War for a long Time. To all Discourse of this kind, I countermined with the Power & Opulence of Great Britain, and argued the Incapacity of America from the Necessity of their running into Debt for 10 Years to come, in order to support the War of the present Year, and in order to support it another, they must run at least 15 Years further forward still, with the greater & increasing Improbability or Difficulty of discharging it. After this, I dwelt a good deal upon the insidious Arts wch designing men had employed to inflame the Americans, and upon the great Industry they had used to prevent the Circulation of the Truth. I could not help saying (I told him) that such men, whoever they were, were not only Foes to Great Britain, but to America chiefly, and to all Humanity itself; that a good Cause needed no such bad means to support it; and that a true Cause always coveted, never avoided, the Light, in order that its Truth might appear. Lastly, I regretted, that the Conduct of the matter was lodged in such intemperate Hands, and, that if ever affairs were adjusted, it must be placed with cooler minds & more considerate Heads. My whole Discourse was as soft as possible in its manner, and as strong as I could make it in the matter. They seemed to feel a good Deal, and came down vastly in their Style & Air, which at first was rather lofty & warm. I engaged myself to them in this way, and am persuaded that if those, who meant well among them, were properly discoursed with, and singly, a good Effect might be produced. — But all things are in the Hand of GOD, who (says M. Rollin excellently) "as the sole arbiter of all human Events and Lord of all, determines the Fate of Empires, prescribes the Form of them, regulates their Limits, marks out their Duration, and makes the very Passions and Crimes of Men subservient to the Execution of his gracious & just Designs;" and, "by the secret Springs of his admirable Wisdom, disposes at a Distance, and without man's being sensible of it, the Preparations for the great Work to which all the rest relates, which is the Establishment of his Church, & Salvation of his Elect."

A Captain, two Lieutenants, an Ensign, and 50 Privates of New York Men came over to our Army this Day, and enlisted under its Banners. Those we had before did immense Service in the Battle, both as Scouts & Assistants; and the army was highly obliged to them for their loyal Assiduity & Conduct.

A Party of above 400 Men, whom the Rebels had sent into Long Island to cut the Throats of all the Cattle, were, upon the Information of the Country People, pursued by Sir Wm. Erskine, and wholly cut off or taken Prisoners.

Friday 30th. August.

Sullivan was allowed to go up to the Town this morning under a Flag of Truce, to confer with Washington & to procure himself some Necessaries.

Soon afterwards, we were most agreeably surprized to find, that the Rebels had entirely abandoned Long Island, and left every thing of Bulk and Weight behind them; soon after which our People began to fire from Red Hook upon Nutting Island. This hasty Evacuation surprized us the more, as they had constructed Forts, Redoubts and Intrenchments without End. Not a Foot of Ground was unfortified. If they had been disposed, they might have given us an Immensity of Trouble, have delayed our Operations, & cut off a vast number of our men. Before Night they also abandoned Nutting Island, upon which likewise they had spent a great Deal of Labor. Our

People harassed them in this last Retreat by their great Guns from Brookland Ferry, Red Hook, and other Places. In the Evening some of our People, who were sent up to the Town with a Letter, by a Flag of Truce, directed to Sullivan (who is to set out to-morrow morning for the Congress at Philadelphia), observed a great Firing of Musquetry & much noise in the Town, from which they concluded, as our Troops could not possibly be there, that they were all in Confusion among themselves. The Ships of War had weighed Anchor in the Evening, and sailed up towards the Town, which, together with the rapid Progress of the Troops, 'tis imagined has occasioned a Panic. From these & some other Circumstances, I am inclined to believe we shall obtain a favorable Issue to our Business. The Ships cast anchor off Nutting Island, the Night coming on apace, and the army and other arrangements not being immediately ready for a great Operation.

We lost in the late Engagement 54 Killed, all of them of the Light Infantry, and about 140 Wounded, most of them very slightly. In the number of the Killed were 1 Colonel, 2 Captains and 1 Lieutenant. The Rebels lost upwards of 3400 men, killed, wounded & taken Prisoners. Of these last we have so many, that we are perplexed where to confine them. They lost near 100 officers. Sullivan said to me, in reciting the Conduct of the Battle, "General Howe was too old for us." The Rebels behaved very ill as men; and their officers, to make them fight, were obliged to push them on with their Swords. A hopeful Rabble, & worthy of their Cause! The Hand of GOD seems every way upon them; rent with Distractions, about 3000 sick of a contagious Disorder, distressed in their Circumstances, and all in a Panic, they have little to hope & every thing to fear. Sullivan promised me to mention Mr. Stanhope's Situation, and to do what he could for his Release from Captivity.

SATURDAY, 31st. of AUGUST.

Several of the Transports were ordered up, with Flat-boats, &c. to be near the Men of War, and to be ready, on occasion, to take in Troops. Though we were so near the Town, the Rebels did not fire a Gun upon us from the Fort, which was thought to be rather extraordinary. Several men in Boats, passing over to Nutting Island to take off some Sheep and other Things which they had left behind them, were fired upon by two of the Ships and one of our Batteries on Long Island; but probably without Effect. The Rebels, in return, fired one Gun which remained upon Nutting Island, but very wide of their Mark.

The Orpheus came in to-day from a Cruize.

I have great Doubts, and great Reason to doubt, of the Sincerity of those, who manage the Rebels, with regard to their Desire after Pacification. Nor can I see, upon revolving the Subject continually in my mind, the Possibility of obtaining a permanent Settlement, if any Settlement at all, by mere Treaty. They themselves say, and probably with more Reason than they say many things, that "if G. Britain cannot conquer them, she cannot govern them." In other Words it is saying, that while she maintains the Superiority of her Power, so long only will they obey her. But to let affairs revert again to their old Channel, may indeed skin over the Sore for a Time, but in a very few Years & perhaps at a more critical Season than the present, this Notion of Independence will increase with their Increase, and be strengthened with their Strength; so that our Superiority will become still more problematical. I believe, nobody can abhor Bloodshed more than myself, and no man can be a more hearty Friend to the civil & religious Liberty of Mankind than I am; but, considering G. Britain and America as *one* Empire, it is necessary for the common Welfare that they shd. be governed by the *same* Supreme Power, and that America should even be obliged, if necessary, to submit to it, as much as any other Part of the State; that we may have a Union of Polity among ourselves, and that the young Scion may not draw off the Sap from or exhaust the old Tree. It is the Interest of America itself, that this order should prevail, and that it may be out of the Power of a Set of low, factious Persons to disturb the general Tranquility, whenever it may serve the Purposes of their Interest or Ambition. If an accommodation be made upon any other Ground, I can foresee the Evils that will naturally ensue to my native Country, from the restless Temper of the Americans, from their Rivalry in Trade, and from the Envy they will always bear to the Restraint of our commercial Laws, while they have any Prospect of over-turning them by raising Factions & Tumults either at Home or abroad. At present, I am sure they are too haughty, either to rescind some of their own Resolutions, or to agree to the most essential of the British Claims, both of which must be done, ere it be possible to form the very shadow of an Agreement. But — *in apricum proferet otas.*

SUNDAY, 1st. SEPTEMBER.

The Congress, either stimulated by their Preachers, or "to cajole the godly Party," are very ready in ordering Days of Fasting & Prayer. Religion is an Honor to man, if it be true Religion and truly used. But, employed in the Service of Sedition & Rebellion, and for the Subversion of an Empire, it is turned into an Abuse, the more diabolical as it pretends to be the more sanctimonious. 'Tis frequent Matter of astonishment to me, how men that avow to believe the Bible & to preach the Gospel of Xt, which is only & entirely the Gospel of Peace, can deliberately rush into Tumult, Confusion & Bloodshed, and, under the Pretence of a Sanction from that Gospel, act in all Cases directly opposite to the Letter & Spirit of it. To such Preachers, one might address the Words of the Poet,

> —— O who shall believe,
> But you misuse the Rev'rence of your Place,
> Employ the Countenance & Grace of Heav'n,
> As a false Favorite doth his Prince's Name
> In Deeds dishon'rable? You've raised up,
> Under the counterfeited Zeal of God,
> The Subjects of his Substitute, the King,
> And both against the Peace of Heav'n and Him
> Strove to upswarm them.

I walked this afternoon with Ld. Dunmore, Ld. Drummond, &c. over the Rebel Fortifications at Red Hook, which are truly laborious & exceedingly strong — so strong, that a Handful of determined men might have kept off a very large Army for a long Time. From thence we went to a round Fort, wch the Rebels had constructed with vast Labor at

Brookland. Standing on an Eminence, it commanded all the
Country for a great way round. This, and the Parts adjacent,
is the most beautiful & fertile Spot I have yet seen in America.
It is impossible to express the Devastations, which the
Hessians have made upon the Houses & Country Seats of
some of the Rebels. All their Furniture, Glasses, Windows,
and the very Hangings of the Rooms are demolished or de-
faced. This with the Filth deposited in them, make the
Houses so offensive, that it is a Penance to go into them. Add
to all this, putrid dead Bodies are lying in the Fields about the
Country, as the Army has hardly had Time to bury them.
From Brookland Battery, wch the Rebels have constructed
with a great apparatus, it seems, for the use of His Majesty's
Troops, I had a fine View of the Town facing the East River,
of the Fort, and even of the Distribution of the Rebels. Our
People on this Battery could soon lay the Town in Ruins,
were it any Part of our operations.

   We were informed, by a Gentleman of the Town, a Refugee
here, that the Reason of the precipitate abandonment by the
Rebels of these advantageous Posts was founded in the Sight
of two of our Ships appearing in the Sound near a Place called
Hell-Gate, & in the apprehension of their being entirely surrounded. So hasty was their Flight, that in getting over from
Long Island to the Town, many of them were the means of
drowning each other: Our Army pressed on them in the Rear,
wch quickened their Pace, and rendered their Distress very
extreme. Some of them were half distracted with the Fright.
A little Spirit & Perseverance would soon bring this Country
to Reason or Subjection. And though I am an utter Enemy to
all Tyranny, I am persuaded that absolute Submission would
be eventually the Interest of this People, because it would
take the Power out of improper Hands, and prevent the Land
from becoming an Aceldama, a Field of Blood, perhaps for
ages.

MONDAY, 2d. SEPTEMBER.

The Generals Howe, Clinton, &c. reconnoitring the Shores
about Hell Gate, were fired upon by the Rebels, but (though
only at 4 or 500 Yards Distance) without any Hurt. A great
Part of their Army has left New York, and retired towards

King's bridge, and farther back into the Country. Nothing terrifies these People more than the Apprehension of being surrounded. They will not fight at any Rate, unless they are sure of a Retreat. Their army is the strangest that ever was collected: Old men of 60, Boys of 14, and Blacks of all ages, and ragged for the most part, compose the motley Crew, who are to give the Law to G. Britain and tyrannize over His Majesty's Subjects in America.

Genl. Howe came on board the Eagle this morning. The Loss of the Rebels, by the Destruction or Captivity of those who were scattered in the Woods, now amounts to near 4000 men. To see dead Bodies scattered up and down the Fields, and to view the Distresses of the Inhabitants of the Country, some of whom are perhaps innocent of the Guilt which incurred all this Vengeance, would, I shd think, terrify all the mock-Patriots in the World, from the precipitate Commencement of a civil War. They have also 7000 Men sick in their Army, 4000 of which are in the Environs of New York.

This morning a Party of Hessians took Possession of Governor's Island, which, though the Rebels had fortified it with immense Labor, they abandoned without the least Compulsion.

A Frigate, the Rose, commanded by the brave Capt. Wallace, assisted by Capt. Dickson, received orders to pass up the East River this night, with the Flat-Boats, &c.

Capt. Wallace dined on board the Eagle, and entered fully into the Consequences of the present War with America. I could not but concur in his Opinion, that America has grown rich at the Expence, & not to the Advantage of G. Britain; that the northern Americans in particular are rather Rivals to our Trade than Merchants in it, and that if a considerable Reduction take Place in the Strength & opulence of America, it will render her the longer dependent upon G. Britain. The Americans have quarrelled with the old System, while they grew so rich & powerful under it as to bid us Defiance; for which Reason we may justly quarrel with it too, and insist upon another, which will bring them, & keep them when brought, into a closer Union & Dependence with the Parent State. If, on the contrary, a pacific accommodation ensue upon the former Terms, we may indeed obtain Quiet for the present Generation, but our Posterity will bitterly regret, that for our own Ease we patched up a Building, which in some future (and not very distant) Storm will tumble into Ruins upon them. The Americans unjustly provoked us & began the War; and we ought never to finish it, till we have put out of their Power to involve us in the Expence & Bloodshed of another.

TUESDAY, 3d. SEPTEMBER.

A Mr. Griffiths, with his Son, and another man, all from Connecticut, came on board the Eagle late last Night, by whom we learn both the Poverty and Inveteracy of the People of that Colony in general. Their Stock of Cloathing in particular is almost exhausted; and they must suffer extremely in the ensuing Winter. Having in general taken up Arms, they have neglected the Tillage of their Lands during the last Year, and therefore must either subsist upon their old Stock, or be supplied from other Parts of America.

The Dissenting Preachers of all men are the most extraordinary in their Conduct. They inculcate War, Bloodshed & Massacres, as though all these were the express Injunctions of Jesus Christ; and they call for Destruction upon the loyal Subjects and Army of their rightful Sovereign, like so many Arbiters of the Vengeance of Heaven, or so many Disposers of the divine Decrees. One of these People lately, in a Prayer before his Congregation, desired God to destroy the British Fleet, as he did the Egyptians of old in the Red Sea, and that he would gratify his People, in America, with the Sight of our dead Bodies strewed & stinking upon the Sea-Shore. This is one Sample of the true Oliverian Style & Spirit. Here follows another, equally pious, but rather more ridiculous. Another of these Worthies publicly begged of God to espouse the Cause of America, and to confound its Enemies (meaning the King and the British Subjects) with his Judgements; but, if he did not chuse to take so active a Part, he desired, that *he would, at least, stand neuter.* To this Sort of Instruction the Practice of their People is entirely answerable. If a man refuse to go all Lengths with them, for they will suffer no Man to be moderate, they hunt immediately after his Life. Those, who fall into their Hands are either killed upon the Spot, or dragged to their Copper Mines in Connecticut, where they see no Day-Light, and are allowed no Candle but while they eat their Victuals. In this dismal Gloom, surrounded with Terrors equal to Death itself, many have been kept a great while, and are now confined. In short, the Bitterness of these Tyrants on the one hand, and the Wretchedness of the Country on the other, are inexpressibly great and unparalleled. An Insurrection in Turkey could not be attended with more Barbarity; and I don't recollect any, that has been attended with so much.

A great Firing was heard last night from the Town upon the Rose & the Boats, which were ordered to sail up the East River. One Shot passed through the Rose, and another beat off one of her anchors, without doing any other Damage. The Rebels fired two Pieces of Ordnance upon her to-day from a Battery opposite Bushwyck; and wounded two or three Men. The Boats got safe into Newtown Creek, and, as 'tis supposed, unperceived by the Enemy, through the favorable Darkness of the Night.

The Woods near Brookland are so noisome with the Stench of the dead Bodies of the Rebels, whom the Hessians and the Highlanders followed thither & destroyed, that they are quite inaccessible.

Five men came off last Night in a Boat from New York, who confirm our former Intelligence, that the Rebels are in a State of Animosity, Feud, and Distrust, among themselves.

WEDNESDAY 4th. SEPTEMBER.

Ld. Drummond introduced Mr. Ludlow, one of the Judges of this Colony, to Lord H. this afternoon. He seemed a sensible Man, and gave some good Information, respecting the Stock, &c. upon Long Island, and the Fears & Submissions of its Inhabitants, many of whom are returned to their Possessions intreating Favor and Protection.

THURSDAY, 5th. SEPTEMBER.

Taking a Walk with some others on Long Island, we roamed down to a Battery near Bushwyck Creek, where we had not been five minutes, before the Rebels began firing upon us with their Cannon. One of the Shot whizzed very near my Head, but providentially did no Damage to any body. We soon retired from this hostile Station, and went round by Brookland, and into the Dutch Church there. But very few Houses are upon this Spot; so that the People, who frequent it, must come from very great Distances. Many Descendants of the Dutch yet remain, much unmixed, in New York Colony, and especially upon Long Island. The Dutch were the original Settlers, before its Capture or Cession to K. Charles the 2d.: and the Dutch Language is still very much in Use among them.

In the Evening Capt. Davis, of the Repulse Frigate, took me for an Airing, first upon the Water between Governor's Island & New York City and not far from its Batteries; too near in my own Opinion, though I made no objection, lest it should be imputed to Cowardice, with which, I thank God, I am not much troubled, when called to Duty or not out of it. We afterwards walked to Brookland Battery, where there was a heavy Canonade going on; and the Shot flew very thick over our Heads, and passed through several Houses not far from us. We returned to the Ship by the Way we came, and, through God's Goodness, without Hurt. The Mosquitos were exceedingly troublesome; and, with my Boots on my Legs, Gloves on my Hands, & Handkerchief round my Head, could I scarce defend myself from their most offensive Stinging.

The Lord Hyde Packet sailed down to the Hook to-day, and is intended to depart for England to-morrow, in which Major Cuyler embarks, who is entrusted with the Dispatches for Government.

The Friends of Govt. on Long Island, with Col. Oliver Delancey at their Head, are raising a great Body of militia to co-operate with and serve under the Army. I should hope, that another Campaign, *vigorously* and *rightly* pursued, would go far in the Suppression of this most unnatural & flagitious Rebellion.

FRIDAY, 6th. SEPTEMBER.

Major Holland called upon me this Morning. We had various Discourse upon American affairs, and the Conduct of the War. We perfectly agreed in opinion, that our Hostilities must be pushed warmly & unintermittingly, that the Rebels may have neither Time to recover from their Panic, nor to fortify their Ground; that no Dependence is to be made upon the Generosity of their Tempers, which has never appeared even among each other, but, instead of it, a Spirit of Litigiousness and Acrimony, which divides the nearest Relatives, upon trivial occasions, in the most inveterate Law-Suits & Contentions; and that no Impression is to be made upon them otherwise than by Fear and an apprehension of Superiority. All this is the very Character of the Indians; and is, I really believe, very much effected by the nature of the Climate. They have a Tartness of Temper without Firmness, and an ardent Warmth of Soul, not animated, however, by true Courage. They are too impatient to be brave, and too insidious to be noble, free and generous. What seems to have borne an appearance of that kind, may, I think, be more fairly traced from a Pride & Insolence of Heart, than a Soul of true Sensibility & Kindness.

For the Credit of Religion, I was sorry to hear that a Mr. Wheelock, who has been made useful in enlightening the minds of the Indians with the Principles of the Xtian Religion, should have rendered himself an injurious Instrument, by poisoning the affections of His Majesty's Subjects with Sentiments of Disloyalty & Rebellion. For my own Part, it infinitely exceeds all my Comprehension, how these People, if they are sincere (and I know not how to suppose them otherwise), can reconcile these Practices with the Duties of Xtianity, wch principally consist in Meekness and Charity towards all men, and expressly in Submission to Kings and to civil Magistrates appointed by the Providence of GOD, with positive Orders of Obedience & Honor. I can only apologize for them at the Expence of their understandings, which have been corrupted by the artful & false Insinuations of designing men, who have represented Religion, Law & Liberty in Danger from G. Britain, when they wd. all have remained in Security but for themselves.

As the Rebels have been making several appearances of attacking Staten Island from Amboy & Elizabeth Town, Major Holland was going thither by orders to contrive the best means of securing it by the Help of the Hessians, in number between 2 and 3000, still left upon it.

The Fleet & Army are now exceedingly well supplied with fresh Provisions & Vegetables from Long Island, which is a pleasing Circumstance both for the Health & Spirit of the Troops. The Hessians, in particular, never fared so well before, and seem remarkably happy in their Situation. Add to all this, the Trees are so loaded with apples, that they seem to defy all the Powers of a fair Consumption.

While I detest the artifices and Conduct of the Leaders in this Rebellion, I sincerely pity, and would as far as it is consistent acquit, those, who, out of a sincere Regard to public Freedom, one of the dearest of all temporal Blessings, have abetted their Proceedings. I regret, that Liberty, honest, virtuous and generous Liberty, should be made the Plea & Pretence for so many infamous Disorders. The End is answerable to the means; and these pretended Fautors of Freedom have introduced, as far as they could, a Part of the most detestable Tyranny in the World. What Tacitus feelingly has drawn of the Servitude of the Roman People under the Rule of Tiberius, and his vile administrator Sejanus, may with great Truth be applied to the Americans under the arbitrary Dictates of the Congress, and the dirty Conduct of their Committees. The Country is "seized with anxiety & Dread; and one Relation fears (and is at Enmity with) another, &c. &c." Annal. L. iii.

The Carysfort, Capt. Robert Fanshaw, an old Schoolfellow with me, arrived this Day from Canada, & brought Dispatches from the Commander in Chief to the Admiral & General.

SATURDAY, 7th. SEPTR.

This Morning, the Fowey, Capt. G. Montagu, came into the Harbor from North Carolina.

Great Preparations have been making all this Day; and about 80 Flatbottomed Boats were made ready for a further Debarkation of Troops, and for a further attack upon the Rebels.

A slight alarm happened to-night from the Enemy's Boats approaching too near; they were soon driven back by the Musketry in our Boats. Their Intention was, as we apprehended, to bring down 2 or 3 Fire-ships to set adrift in the Fleet.

SUNDAY, 8th. SEPTR.

Preparations still making for another Attack. A brisk Canonade all the morning upon one of the Rebel Batteries, which was soon silenced.

The General dined on board. He informed us, that the Rose had received many Shot in her Hull & masts, but had not lost one man: Three only of his Crew were slightly wounded.

The Rebels are so nigh, that they have called out several Times, and were heard distinctly by our People. After bestowing a few opprobrious Names, they told our Soldiers; "Ah! we won't run away now." To which our men only replied; "We don't design you shall." — They have drawn up, we hear, their main Force to Kingsbridge, which separates York Island from the Continent by its narrow Channel, either to secure their Retreat, or to make a Stand against our Army in a Fortification wch is represented to be extremely strong.

MONDAY, 9th. SEPTR.

This Morning Sullivan returned upon his Parole, in a Boat bearing a Flag of Truce.

Walked over Governor's or Nutting Island this Afternoon & took a View of the Rebel Fortifications and Intrenchments. These are as extensive as the Island itself, and have been constructed with immense Labor and some Art. There are several Forts, Cannon Proof, with many Platforms & Embrazures, stockaded and intrenched on every side: To the Sound, in particular, they seem impregnable. Next to the Works themselves, nothing astonishes our People more than their sudden Abandonment. Our Engineers have unspiked all their Cannon but two, and fitted & opened Embrazures this afternoon opposite the Fort, which the Rebels perceived, but did not fire upon them, as our Men every Moment expected.

The Season having been rather rainy, the Musketoes are innumerable upon the Shore, least of all on board, and are exceedingly troublesome. The Swarms of them destroy the Pleasure of walking.

Further Preparations making for a formidable Attack; and the several Ships, under Orders to cover the Boats, fitting themselves for the Business. Many Deserters come off constantly, who represent Things in a State of Perturbation with the Rebels.

I could not forbear smiling to-day, when I heard of the wonderful Change of Sentiment, wch has taken place in some eminent Persons, who, before they left England, were remarkable for the Warmth of their Zeal in Favor of the Americans. They reverse, in that respect, the Observation of the Poet; for

> *Et coelum, et animum mutaverunt.*

They thought better, both of the Cause and the People, till they had more thoroughly examined the one, and actually seen the other, upon the Spot. They find the Object to have long been alienation and Independence; and they perceive the Leaders of the Faction to be, for the most part, men of low or of suspicious Characters.

TUESDAY, 10th. SEPTR.

Walked on Shore this morning. The Hessians were marching down towards the North West Point of the Island near Hell-Gate.

The Merlin Sloop, Capt. Burnaby, with 6 or 7 Merchant Vessels, and two Prices, came in this Afternoon from a Cruize.

WEDNESDAY, 11th. SEPTR.

This Morning Lord H. went to

Govr. Wentworth came on board this morning, &, in the course of Conversation, informed me, that Sullivan, exalted as he now is, was once a very low & insignificant Person, that he worked even for himself as a Labourer, that he afterwards served an Attorney as a menial Servant, in whose Kitchin first & afterwards in his office he picked up a Smattering of the Law, and that finally, by Chicane & the worst Sort of legal Conduct, he raised himself to a Degree of Distinction in New Hampshire. — From the View I have had of the man, as well as by his Conversation, there is nothing improbable in all this; but the contrary. Govr. Wentworth also assured me (though I recd. his Intelligence with some Latitude knowing the personal Pique of the Gentleman) that Peter Livius Esq. (lately of New Hampshire, but now Chief Justice at Montreal) was chief Instigator of the present Troubles at New Portsmouth, & that he has almost legal Proof to convict him of it.

A Flag of Truce came from the Town this Afternoon, with Letters, Cloaths, & Money (hard Cash, not *Congress Notes*) for some of the Rebel Prisoners. Among them was a most illiterate Letter from Putnam to a Mr. Chew, in our army.

THURSDAY, 12th. SEPTR.

A severe Canonade was heard on board this Morning, supposed to be Horn's Hook, where our People are dislodging the Rebels, and are already in Possession of two Islands near the Isle of York Shore. We have lost one Sailor, who was killed as he lay sleeping on the Grass by a Cannon Ball. An Engineer lost an Arm; and two or three other slight Accidents occurred.

This Afternoon Capt. Wilkinson in the Pearl, a fine Frigate of 32 Guns, arrived from Quebec. He brought us very agreeable News from Genl. Carleton, viz. That General Burgoyne was almost ready to embark on Lake Champlain, and probably would be embarked by the middle of August, with an Army of about 14,000 Men, of which 10,000 were Regulars and about 1000 Indians; and that, if it were necessary, he could bring with him 15 or 20,000 Canadians. Capt. Wilkinson convoyed several Transports with upwards of 500 Rebel Prisoners on board, with whom we know not what to do. He also informed us, that he spoke with a Ship on the 27th. of July, who had seen the Second Division of the Hessians at Sea, and that they may hourly be expected to arrive.

One daily hears mortifying Accounts of the bitter Tyranny of the Rebels over the loyal Subjects in their Power. Such men are no Enemies to absolute Rule: they only hate it in others, but ardently pursue it for themselves. From the Beginning, as soon as they had the least Authority, they have been uniformly Persecutors, though (strange to tell) they pretended to leave their mother-Country upon the Account of Persecution. A flagrant Instance of this appeared in the infant State of the New England Colonies; for to these I chiefly allude; so early as the Year 1657. The Assembly at Boston made a Law against Quakers, the Substance of wch was; "That whoever brought any Quaker, knowing him to be such, should pay 40 Shillings an Hour for such Concealment; and any Quaker there should forfeit £100. That those who concealed a Quaker, after the first Conviction, if a man, was to lose one Ear, and a second Time the other; a Woman, each Time to be severely whipped, and the third Time, man or woman, to have their Tongues bored through with a red hot Iron: Besides, every Quaker, who should become such in the Colony was subjected to the like Punishments." At length, finding this not enough, they made it Death for a Quaker to appear in the Province; and accordingly hanged some. Yet these, and men like these, are our noisy Advocates for civil & religious Liberty!

FRIDAY, 13th. SEPTEMBER.

We heard a great Firing this Morning upon the Land, and were afterwards told, that it arose from our Troops making good their Landing on the opposite Shore, and the Islands in the East River near Hell Gate.

In the Afternoon, the Phoenix, Capt. Parker, of 44 Guns, the Orpheus of 32 Guns, Capt. Hudson, the Carysfort of 28 Guns, Capt. Fanshaw, and the Roebuck of 44 Guns, Capt. Hammond, sailed up the East River up to Bushwyck Bay. The Fort fired 4 or 5 Guns faintly upon them, as also a Battery upon a red Bank of high Land just above the Town; and were retorted upon very warmly by our Batteries on Governor's Island & Brookland. The Ships passed along under their Topsails, for the most Part; and, in supreme Contempt of the Rebels and their Works, did not fire a Gun. It was a fine Sight, if one could have divested one's Thoughts of the melancholy Reflection, that some Fellow-Creatures Lives were either taking away or in Danger, on account of the Villainy of the Rebel Leaders & Abettors. We could not perceive that the Ships recd. the least Damage; by an account afterwards we found, that the Phoenix had one man killed upon her Forecastle.

Sullivan set out for the Congress on the 31st. of August, and returned on the 9th. of Septr., as I have noted. He says, that when he mentioned to the Congress Ld. Hs. Desire of treating with them, they asked him for his Testimonials, that Ld. H had such a Desire. He confessed, he had no written Proof, but such verbal Assurances, that no Doubt could be had of his Lp's

Sincerity; and he expatiated a great Deal upon the Happiness & Advantage of bringing matters to a pacific & speedy Conclusion, and that there was no such thing as a Design formed against their Liberties, which he could assure them of from his Lp, whose Veracity & Honor not even themselves could question. He was ordered to withdraw for a while; and, upon being called in again, they desired him to recite what he had before said, which he punctually did. They then asked him, if Lord H. meant to treat with them as independent States; to which he replied, It was the farthest from his Lordship's Thoughts. After some Altercation, they resolved to send a Committee of three of the Congress to wait upon Lord H. at Amboy on the 11th. of September. The three, that came, were *Franklin*, *Samuel Adams*, & *Routledge*. From the Complexion of the agents, it was easy to foresee what would be the Event of the Business. They met, they talked, they parted. And now, nothing remains but to fight it out against a Set of the most determined Hypocrites & Demagogues, compiled of the Refuse of the Colonies, that ever were permitted by Providence to be the Scourge of a Country.

The Americans have long since boasted of their ability to bring 80 or 100,000 Men into the Field against His Majesty's Troops. I find it the vainest Boast, that the vainest Thraso ever made. As a Proof, this Year they have been obliged, at four several times, to draw men by Force from Long Island, and by Force have kept them together; that they have never amounted to many more than 20,000, even upon these compulsive Terms; and that when these are dispersed or overthrown, they will find it rather difficult (and particularly after the ensuing Winter) to form any Army at all. And if they could bring 100,000 men into the Field, wch it is impossible for them to bring or to maintain, H. majesty's Troops need be in no great Concern about them.

SATURDAY, 14th. SEPTR.

Late last Night arrived Capt Jordan in the Galatea of 20 Guns from Plymouth, which Place she left on the 10th. of July. He brought us Advices, that the Hessians were only sailing from England, when he left it, and that, being in heavy-sailing Dutch Transports, we cannot expect their Arrival here for a great while to come, and especially if they come into the Course of the equinoctial Winds, by which they may be probably driven to the West India Islands, and not be able therefore to sail hither before the Spring. He also brought an account, that the Sea to the South-East from hence, & about Bermuda, and to the Lat. of 32°., is greatly infested by American Privateers, who have taken several of our West India merchant men, and that the Rebels are fitting out every Vessel that can sail for that Purpose. This Intelligence was very unpleasant altogether. A few such swift-sailing Ships as the Galatea would soon disperse or destroy these Free-booters; and 'tis presumed they will be employed.

From all I see & with whomsoever I converse, I plainly perceive, that nothing will serve with this People but the most determined Conduct. Calmness & Moderation are construed into Embarrassment & Timidity. Without Generosity themselves, they seem to act as if they believed there was no such Principle in the World. What one of their own People [Mr. Cotton Mather, in his Magnalia, L.vii.c.3.] said of Rhode Island, may, in some respects, be applied to most of the New Englanders in particular; "They are a Colluvies of Antinomians, Familists, Anabaptists, Anti-sabbatarians, Arminians, Socinians, Quakers, Ranters, and every thing but Roman Catholics, & true Christians; *bona terra, mala gens.*" To which may be added the Observation of Bp. Berkeley, who lived for a considerable Time upon the Spot, that "as for their morals, he apprehended there was nothing to be found in them, that shd. tempt others to make an Experiment of their Principles, either in Religion or Government."

Five Transports sailed up the East River this Evening to join the Man of War, who went up last Night. Many Shot were exchanged upon the Occasion. I saw a House or Part of a House in the Town tumble down, by a Ball from one of our Ships or Batteries. Three men of War were to have passed up the North River at the same time, but were prevented by an accident.

SUNDAY, 15th. SEPTR.

This Morning about 7 o'Clock, the Renown of 50 Guns, Capt. Banks, the Repulse of 32 Guns, Capt. Davis, & the

Pearl of 32 Guns, Capt. Wilkinson, with the Schooner, Lieut. Brown, sailed up the North River. The Morning was fine, the Tide flowed, and there was a fresh Breeze. The Rebels began their Canonade as furiously as they could, but apparently with very little Effect, as their Guns were but poorly served. The Ships, as these were the grand Batteries of the Enemy, returned a heavy Fire, and struck the Walls of the Batteries and the Sods of Earth, which the Rebels had raised, very frequently. What other Damage our People did them, we as yet know not; but, 'tis observed, that, except for beating down particular Structures, or clearing the Way for other operations, Cannon have but a very small or precarious Effect. The great Business is always accomplished by the minor Implements of War.

About a Quarter before 9, the Ships came to an Anchor in the North River, in view of the Fleet, at about 4 or 5 Miles Distance above it, and beyond the principal Works of the Enemy.

A Transport, during the Affair upon the North River, went up the East River & joined the other Ships, almost without Molestation.

The whole Scene was awful & grand; I might say, beautiful, but for the melancholy Seriousness which must attend every Circumstance, where the Lives of Men, even the basest Malefactors, are at Stake. The Hills, the Woods, the River, the Town, the Ships, and Pillars of Smoke, all heightened by a most clear & delightful morning, furnished the finest Landschape that either art and nature combined could draw, or the Imagination conceive.

After this affair had subsided for a little while, a most tremendous Discharge of Cannon from the Ships began (as was concerted) in the East River, in order to cover the Landing of the Troops upon New York Island. So terrible and so incessant a Roar of Guns few even in the Army & Navy had ever heard before. Above 70 large Pieces of Cannon were in Play, together with Swivels & small arms from the Ships, while the Batteries added to the uproar upon the Land. The Rebels were apparently frightened away by the horrid Din, and deserted the Town & all their Works in the utmost Precipitation. The King's Forces took Possession of the Place, incredible as it may seem, without the Loss of a Man. Nothing could equal the Expressions of Joy, shewn by the Inhabitants, upon the arrival of the King's officers among them. They even carried some of them upon their Shoulders about the Streets, and behaved in all respects, Women as well as Men, like overjoyed Bedlamites. One thing is worth remarking; a Woman pulled down the Rebel Standard upon the Fort, and a Woman hoisted up in its Stead His Majesty's Flag, after trampling the other under Foot with the most contemptuous Indignation. I first espied both Circumstances from the Ship, and could not help paying the first Congratulations to Lord H. upon the Occasion. The Spirit and Activity of the Troops & Seamen were unequalled: Every man pressed to be foremost, consistent with Order, and to court Distinction. The dastardly Behaviour of the Rebels, on the other Hand; sinks below Remark. The Ground, where our People landed, was far from being advantageous; the Tide rapid; the Current unequal; the Shore shallow; and themselves obliged to march up on Ground, where these Poltroons had been at Work to entrench themselves for several months. Providentially, the Wind coming in with a fine Breeze from the S. W. wch it had not done before since we have been here, and wch was the most favorable Circumstance our People could have desired, enabled the Boats to carry over the Forces almost in a Direct Line, and return in like manner for the second Division, notwithstanding the Rapidity of the Current. Thus this Town and its Environs, wch these blustering Gentleman had taken such wonderful Pains to fortify, were given up in two or three Hours without any Defence, or the least appearance of a manly Resistance.

In the Evening the Admiral ordered up the Mercury of 24, and the Fowey of 20 Guns, to lie close to the Town, to prevent the Transport Boats from going on Shore & plundering, wch many of them appeared very ready to do.

Philip Vickers Fithian:
Journal, September 15, 1776

SUN: 15

Our Battalion was ordered to the Alarm Post by half after two; it is said the Enemy are moving downwards nearer New-York — At seven a firing begun below & was most quick & heavy, the Wind brisk at S.W. We soon found that three Ships were proceeding up N. River — We could see the firing from Powles-Hook, & soon they came in plain View, roaring up the River; they came to an Anchor about five Miles below, the Strength of the Flood running & the Wind brisk; so that they have other Intentions than proceeding up the River; it is to hinder us from removing our Stores, out of New-York — And it is now a Certainty that all the Sick, & Stores which are not necessary for present Use, are removing from the City, so that if we are compell'd, we may leave it with as little Loss as possible.

Between eight & nine the Drums beat "to Arms." Our Army seem eager to attack their Enemies, wherfore, when called, they fly to their Guns & Accoutrements.

There is something forceably grand in the Sound of Drums & Fifes, when they are calling such an Army as ours to contend with another of perhaps equal Force! Whenever they come together the Death of many must be the Consequence — And this thought with all its Pomp of serious Grandieur, is ever associated with the Call to Arms when the two Armies lie so near each other, & daily expect an Action! —

The Battalions of our Brigade paraded, & grounded their Arms, when orders came that a strong Guard should be placed over them, & the Men retire into their Tents & sleep, as it is probable they must be up all the coming Night.

All our Cannon that are not immediately wanted in the Forts, are drawn into a Valley out of Sight from the Enemy, should they come up the River.

A little before twelve on the East-River began a Cannonade which soon grew to be the heaviest I ever heard; Cannons on a continual roar! — but we are at five Miles Distance. Soon after an Express came foaming & ordered all the Troops to march downwards as the Enemy has landed — Again the Drums rattle to Arms, to Arms! — We marched down & found the Report true; — But Shame to *Connecticut* Valour; it is said, & I believe is true, that two Brigades of Connecticut Militia fled from one hundred & fifty *Regulars*! — Yes, they fled.

His Excellency: the General was enraged; It is said he was for a short Time exceeding angry.

Our Brigade by Order of Gen: *Mifflin* who was present, halted on the Heights on this Side Harlem, & formed. But the Road was filled with armed Men moving promiscuously as tho' sick towards Kings-Bridge. The Gen: however to oppose them detached off Men & formed a Guard from Harlem-River to North-River, with firm & strict Order to let none pass but Women, & those who were indeed sick — The Guard stood with fixed Bayonets & charged; soon however a vast Body collected, & the Father of Confusion himself could not have stirred a greater Hubbub. Some swore — some begged & pleaded — & some like timorous Children cry'd — But Oaths & Cries could not be heard — The Gen: appointed Officers & gave them a Station, & ordered them to form; or if they refused, he swore he would discharge the Field-Pieces upon them! — But thus they continued thronging till Evening — Our Lads I hope will stand; For the Honour of their State; for the Safety of the Land, & for their own Reputation, I hope they will stand.

Tools were given out & our People went composedly, amidst all the Confusion, to throwing up an Entrenchment.

But New-York we have lost this Day; the Enemy entered about three o Clock; & we have abandoned the Works on this Side; Just Heaven thy Judgments are equal — We are a sinful Nation, O Lord. But is it written in thy Book concerning us that we must always fly before our Enemies? — Must this great, & formerly happy Country, submit at Length to despotic Domination? — Must Oceans of our Blood yet stain our own Land? Must not the widowed Lovers, & the fatherless Orphans for a long Time to come cease to increase! — We pray, good Lord for thy interposing Mercy; O spare us, & spare our Land —

I pray my God I may never see another such a Sabbath — The Cries of Women, the Groans of the Wounded, the Confusion of *All*! Swearing most profanely in every Quarter of the Army.

I met with Mr. Evans towards Evening; poor Boy, he will grow used to retreating.

Gen: Washington came up to the Lines before Night; viewed them, & how they were manned, with much Attention.

Our Battalion were ordered to lie in the Trenches, with their Arms secure — for their Encouragement the Evening is fine, the Wind at N.W. brisk; & coold with a Shower —

After Dark we returned to our Quarter to rest — *Stephen Ranney* was in the Lines opposite to where the Shiping lay & where the Enemy landed — He assures us that the Grape-Shot struck round him thick as tho a Person at the Distance of a few Rods had thrown his hand full of small Stones! But he is yet spared.

Benjamin Trumbull:
Journal, September 15–16, 1776

A Little after Day Light on Sunday Morning Septr, 15 Two Ships of the Line and three Frigates drew up near the Shore within Musket Shot of the Lines and entrenchments and came to Anchor there in a proper Situation to fire most furiously upon our Lines. In this Situation they lay entirely quiet till about 10 o'Clock. During this Time boats were passing from the Island to the Ships and men put on Board, and about 100 Boats full of men came out of New Town Creek and made towards the Shore. When Things were thus prepared, The Ships about 10 o'Clock after Firing a Signal Gun began from the mouths of near an 100 Canon a most furious Canonade on the Lines, which Soon levelled them almost with the Ground in some Places, and buried our men who were in the Lines almost Sand and Sods of Earth and made such a dust and Smoke that there was no possibility of firing on the Enemy to any advantage, and then not without the utmost Hazzard, while the Canon poured in Such a tremendous Fire on the Lines the Ships from their round Tops kept up a Smart Fire with Swivels loaded with Grape Shot which they were able to fire almost into the entrenchments they were so near. The boats all this Time kept out of the reach of the Musquetry and finally turning off to the Left a little north of the Lines in the Smoke of the Ships made good their Landing without receiving any anoyance from our Troops. They soon marched up to the main Road and formed across it and on the hills above our Troops in order to cut off their Retreat. The Continental Troops now Left the Lines & there being no General orders given how to form them that they might Support Each each other in a General Attack, or any Disposition made for it, they attempted an escape round the Enemy in the best manner they could, and generally made their Escape.

Colonels Selden, Hart, and Tompson were taken with Major Porter, and Brigadier Major Wyllys and an 150, or 200 men, were either Killed or taken. Some Canon, Tents, Flower and a great Deal of Baggage fell into the Enemies Hands. This on the whole was an unfortunate Day to the American States. The loss was owing principally to a Want of Wagons & Horses to remove the Guns and Baggage and to the Situation of the Troops Left behind, and the neglect in the officers, in not forming some proper plan of Defence.

The Army was principally called off to the Northward and had been in a State of Retreat from the City for some Days all the Field Pieces had been removed out of the Town and most of the Artilery Companies. And though few Canon had been left in the Forts to keep up the Farce of Defence and Oppo- sition, yet there was not one that could anoy the Shiping or be brought on to the Assistance of the Infantry. They could see nor expect any Assistance from the Troops above as y^y were all retreating. Officers and men had Expected that their Retreat would be cut off unless they could fight their Way through them wc yy thout very dangerous and precarious. In such a Situation it was not reasonable to expect that they would make any vigorous Stand. The men were blamed for retreating and even flying in these Circumstances, but I image the Fault was principally in the General Officers in not dis- posing of things so as to give the men a rational prospect of Defence and a Safe retreat should they engage the Enemy. And it is probable many Lives were saved, and much to the Army prevented in their coming off as yy did tho' it was not honourable. It is admirable that so few men are lost.

Monday Septr 16. A large body of the Enemy advanced to- wards our Lines, Supposed to be three or four Thousand, and a little before Twelve oClock a very Smart and Heavy Fire Commenced between them and our Rangers and riflemen on the Advanced posts. This was sustained by the Rangers Bravely till they were reinforced from the Lines, when the fire grew more sharp and Heavy on both Sides, and continued in the whole for 2 or three Hours, in which Time the Enemy were several Times considerably broken and formed anew, and finally were driven by the Americans about 2 miles, though they were often reinforced. Our men by this Time

were much Fatigued, and had some of them almost Spent
their Ammunition, and the General Thought best to order
them to retreat. But few men were Killed and wounded on
the Side of the Provincials considering the Heat and duration
of the Action. It was Supposed after the Action that not more
than 20, or 25 men were killed and about 50 Wounded, but by
the Returns afterwards, as far as I could learn about   were
killed, and about   wounded.

It appeared by the blood and trails of the Enemy where
they retreated that their Loss was considerable. Our Troops
had the honour of behaving well, and the issue of the Battle
gave Spirit to them.

Frederick MacKenzie:
Diary, September 20–22, 1776

20th Sept — A little after 12 o'Clock last night a most dreadful fire broke out in New York, in three different places in the South, and windward part of the town. The Alarm was soon given, but unfortunately there was a brisk wind at South, which spread the flames with such irresistible rapidity, that notwithstanding every assistance was given which the present circumstances admitted, it was impossible to check its Progress 'till about 11 this day, when by preventing it from crossing the Broad-way at the North part of the town, it was stopped from spreading any further that way, and about 12 it was so far got under that there was no danger of its extending beyond those houses which were then on fire. It broke out first near the Exchange, and burnt all the houses on the West side of Broad Street, almost as far as The City Hall, & from thence all those in Beaver Street, and almost every house on the West side of the town between the Broad way and the North River, as far as The College, amounting in the whole to about 600 houses, besides several Churches, particularly Trinity Church, the principal one in town.

On its first appearance two Regiments of the 5th brigade went into town, and some time after, a great number of Seamen from the Fleet were sent on shore under proper officers by order of Lord Howe, to give assistance. About daybreak the Brigade of Guards came in from Camp, but from the absence of the regular Firemen, the bad state of the Engines, a want of buckets, and a Scarcity of Water, the efforts of the Troops and Seamen, tho' very great, could not prevent the fire from spreading in the manner it did. The first notice I had of it was from the Sentry at Genl Smith's quarters at Mr Elliot's house, who called me up about 10 Clock and said New York was on fire; on going to the window I observed an immense Column of fire & smoke, and went and

Detail of the Guards, New York. 20th Septr 1776

Guards	C	S	S	C	D	P
Main	1	2	3	3	2	50
North ferry	.	1	1	1	1	30
New Barracks	.	1	1	1	1	30
Naval Stores	.	1	1	3	1	36
Prison	.	1	1	1	1	24
Bridewell	.	.	1	1	.	9
Jail	.	.	1	1	.	9
New Hospital	.	.	1	1	.	12
Vauxhall Battery	.	.	1	1	.	12
Church Battery	.	.	1	1	.	12
Harrison's brewery	.	.	.	1	.	6
Fort George	.	.	.	1	.	6
Provision Store	.	.	.	1	.	6
Wood Store	.	.	.	1	.	6
Buncker's hill Redoubt . . .	.	.	.	1	.	3
Major Genl Vaughan	.	.	1	.	.	6
Total	1	6	13	19	6	257

called Genl Smith, who said he would follow me into town as soon as possible. I dressed myself immediately and ran into town, a distance of two miles, but when I got there the fire had got to such ahead there seemed to be no hopes of stopping it, and those who were present did little more than look on and lament the misfortune. As soon as buckets & Water could be got, the Seamen and the troops, assisted by some of the Inhabitants did what they could to arrest its progress, but the fresh wind, and the combustible nature of the materials of which almost all the houses were built, rendered all their efforts vain.

From a variety of circumstances which occurred it is beyond a doubt that the town was designedly set on fire, either by some of those fellows who concealed themselves in it since the 15th Instant, or by some Villains left behind for the purpose. Some of them were caught by the Soldiers in the very act of setting fire to the inside of empty houses at a distance from the fire; many were detected with matches and combustibles under their Clothes, and combustibles were found in several houses. One Villain who abused and cut a woman who was employed in bringing water to the Engines, and who was found cutting the handles of the fire buckets, was hung up by the heels on the spot by the Seamen. One or two others who were found in houses with fire brands in their hands were put to death by the enraged Soldiery and thrown into the flames. There is no doubt however that the flames were communicated to several houses by means of the burning flakes of the Shingles, which being light, were carried by the wind to some distance and falling on the roofs of houses covered with Shingles, (which is most generally the case at New York,) and whose Inhabitants were either absent or inattentive, kindled the fire anew. The Trinity Church, a very handsome, ancient building, was perceived to be on fire long before the fire reached the adjacent houses, and as it stood at some distance from any house, little doubt remained that it was set on fire wilfully.

During the time the Rebels were in possession of the town, many of them were heard to say they would burn it, sooner than it should become a nest for Tories — and several Inhabitants who were most violently attached to the Rebel cause have been heard to declare they would set fire to their own houses sooner than they should be occupied by The King's troops.

No assistance could be sent from the Army 'till after daybreak, as the General was apprehensive the Rebels had some design of attacking the Army.

It is almost impossible to conceive a Scene of more horror and distress than the above. The Sick, The Aged, Women, and Children, half naked were seen going they knew not where, and taking refuge in houses which were at a distance from the fire, but from whence they were in several instances driven a second and even a third time by the devouring element, and at last in a state of despair laying themselves down on the Common. The terror was encreased by the horrid noise of the burning and falling houses, the pulling down of such wooden buildings as served to conduct the fire, (in which the Soldiers & Seamen were particularly active and useful) the rattling of above 100 wagons, sent in from the Army, and which were constantly employed in conveying to the

Common such goods and effects as could be saved;—The confused voices of so many men, the Shrieks and cries of the Women and children, the seeing the fire break out unexpectedly in places at a distance, which manifested a design of totally destroying the City, with numberless other circumstances of private misery and distress, made this one of the most tremendous and affecting Scenes I ever beheld.

The appearance of the Trinity Church, when completely in flames was a very grand sight, for the Spire being entirely framed of wood and covered with Shingles, a lofty Pyramid of fire appeared, and as soon as the Shingles were burnt away the frame appeared with every separate piece of timber burning, until the principal timbers were burnt through, when the whole fell with a great noise.

20th Sept—The 3rd Battalion of Light Infantry, and the 2nd & 6th brigades received orders last night to be in readiness to march this Morning at 6 oClock. They were to have made an attack on Paulus hook this morning, under cover of the fire of three Ships of War, and were to have been commanded by Lord Percy. But the fire last night put a stop to the attempt for the present.

21 Septr—The troops mentioned yesterday as intended for an attack on Paulus hook, were to have marched again this morning at Six, for that purpose, but the wind not permitting the Ships of War to come up to their Stations, the attack was postponed.

22nd Sept—The Army continues in the same position.

400 men began to work this morning at McGowan's house, where we have begun to construct some works for the defence of our right.

The 3rd Battalion of Light Infantry, the 2nd & 6th brigades, and Stirn's brigade of Hessians, marched from Camp at 9 o'Clock this morning to Greenwich, where part of them embarked in the flatboats, in order to cross the River & make an attack on Paulus hook; but the wind being unfavorable for the Men of war to come up to cover the attack, it was thought adviseable to postpone it, especially as it appeared by the Rebels' firing at some ships in the River, that they still had some Cannon there. The troops therefore disembarked and returned to Camp.

As the Rebels saw plainly for some days past that it was intended to attack the post, they struck their Camp there yesterday, and sent off most of their baggage and some of their Cannon. It is therefore probable that if the troops had rowed across the River, they would have retired in time to have secured their retreat across the Neck.

A person named Nathaniel Hales, a Lieutenant in the Rebel Army, and a native of Connecticut, was apprehended as a Spy, last night upon Long Island; and having this day made a full and free confession to the Commander in Chief of his being employed by Mr Washington in that capacity, he was hanged at 11 o'Clock in front of the Park of Artillery. He was about 24 years of age, and had been educated at the College of Newhaven in Connecticut. He behaved with great composure and resolution, saying he thought it the duty of every good Officer, to obey any orders given him by his Commander in Chief; and desired the Spectators to be at all times prepared to meet death in whatever shape it might appear.

CAPTURE OF FORT WASHINGTON:
NEW YORK, NOVEMBER 1776

Robert Auchmuty to the Earl of Huntingdon

1777, Jan. 8. Chittley Court, Pall Mall — The following account lately came to my hands. And as it is more particular than any I have seen, think it may be agreeable to your Lordship.

"Nov. 25, 1776. — Fort Washington is certainly one of the strongest places that can be conceived, as well from its peculiar advantageous situation as from the endless lines, redoubts and other works that surround it, in which the rebels have exerted all their art, and the most surprising labour, to guard every place where they could imagine it possible to approach the fort. In short it was rendered impregnable as far as nature and art could contribute to make it so. The honour of reducing this important place was solicited by General Knephausen, in which he was indulged by General Howe. Everything therefore being prepared, agreeable to the most masterly disposition, the attack was begun at daybreak on Saturday morning the 15th instant. A detachment of Hessians with cannon marched round from General Howe's army by Kingsbridge along the clear road (which you will remember is a kind of causeway) through a hollow way, commanded on both sides by very steep craggy hills on which the rebels had redoubts, which enfiladed the whole length of the valley. The Hessians with great firmness marched through this way until they came to the north end of the steep mountain on Harlem River, on the left side, which they began to climber up, notwithstanding the heavy fire from the rebels on the top of the hills, and after very great difficulties and labours gained the summit; which as soon as the rebels saw they ran away towards the fort with great precipitation. At the same time that this Hessian detachment marched round by Kingsbridge, the 43rd and 71st, two Highland regiments, pushed over Harlem or Kingsbridge River in flat bottomed boats about two miles and a half below Kingsbridge, and directly opposite to the most rugged and steep part of the mountain, where the rebels had

230

raised no works, thinking it utterly impossible for any human being to climb up a rocky precipice nearly perpendicular. There however these brave North Britons landed, and with incredible labour scrambled up by means of small bushes growing out through the cracks of the rocks on the side of the mountain; all the while sustaining a heavy fire from the rebels at the top; which as soon as they had reached, they began a very spirited attack upon the rebels, who were in the bushes on top of the mountains, driving them from behind trees and rocks; and by this means greatly facilitating the operations of the Hessians, who had very hard work, some to scramble over the rocks, and fight all the way, in order to make way for others who was to drag their cannon along a very steep road, commanded on all sides. All these difficulties were at last overcome by firmness, patience, and the most manly perseverance, and they had the pleasure of soon dispersing all the rebels they could find in their route, who ran towards the fort in the utmost panic. These operations you will observe were on the north and east side of the rebels' works. But the success of them would, in all human probability, have been very precarious, had it not been for Lord Percy's attack of the very strong lines on the heights on the Harlem side; in which the chief body of the rebels had planted themselves. For at the same instant that the Hessians and Highlanders began their attack, his Lordship with the brigades under his command attacked the lines with singular bravery, rushing into them with the greatest fury, and driving the rebels from line to line, and from work to work, till he had got them crammed up in the fort, before the Hessians and Highlanders could get to it with their cannon. About one o'clock this was the situation of the wretches, who seeing themselves surrounded on all sides by the troops with fixed bayonets, and the cannon within two hundred paces, sent out a white flag, begging the general would not fire upon them, for that they were consulting about surrendering, which they were not long about. By 4 o'clock they had laid down their arms, delivered themselves up prisoners, and the troops took possession of the fort, with everything in it. What number of them were killed I can't exactly learn, some say 600, others about half that number. But the prisoners amount to upwards

of three thousand men, all of them from Pensylvania, Maryland, and Virginia. When Washington ran away from Kingsbridge they had, it seems, been 5,000 men, all southern
people, which were the best troops in the rebels' army, who
refusing to go into New England had engaged to defend this
strong place to the last extremity. But that some of them had
gone over to Fort Constitution a day or two before, and
taken with them a great deal of provisions, stores and ammunition. The loss of our army on this occasion was really trifling, about seventy killed and a hundred wounded, which
is very surprising. This grand point being gained, by which
York Island and a great part of the province was cleared from
the rebels, General Howe, I think, on the morning of the
20th instant landed 5,000 men under the command of Lord
Cornwallis up the North River on the Jersey shore, a few
miles above the other famous fortification, called Fort Constitution or Fort Lee. His Lordship immediately marched to
attack this place, and got to it by 1 o'clock the same day, but
found it had been evacuated by the rebels so precipitately that
the pots were left absolutely boiling on the fire, and the tables
spread for dinner of some of their officers. In the fort they
found but twelve men, who were all dead drunk. There were
forty or fifty pieces of cannon found loaded, with two large
iron sea mortars and one brass one, with a vast quantity of
ammunition, provision and stores, with all their tents standing. His Lordship finding this pressed forward as quick as
he could toward Hackinsack new bridge. But the people
belonging to the fort had the heels of him. However, on
the road he met with 3 or 4,000 fresh hands coming from
Newark to assist in garrisoning the forts. To these gentry the
troops distributed a couple of rounds, and set them a scampering, leaving behind them several brass field pieces and their
baggage; and as they marched along, found the roads thick
strewed with muskets, knapsacks, etc. But the number of cattle taken in the Hackinsack meadows, which had been driven
from Pensylvania and some parts of the Jerseys for the use of
the grand rebel army, is truly astonishing, and amount to
many thousands. His Lordship's face seems to be set towards
Philadelphia, where he will meet with no kind of opposition.
I hope he will be at Amboy or Brunswick to-morrow or next

day, if it will leave off raining. You see, my dear sir, that I have not been mistaken in my judgment of this people. The southern people will no more fight than the Yankees. The fact is that their army is broken all to pieces, and the spirits of their leaders and their abettors is also broken. However, I think one may venture to pronounce that it is wellnigh over with them. All their strongholds are in the hands of his Majesty's troops. All their cannon and mortars, and the greatest part of their stores, ammunition, etc. are gone. The people in the country almost universally sick of it, in a starving condition, and cannot help themselves. And what is to become of them during the approaching inclement season God only knows."

In addition to which there is another letter from very good authority dated the 4th Dec., in which the writer says, "Tomorrow General Howe sets off to join Lord Cornwallis, who is now at Brunswick." From which I conclude, if the weather will permit, the general intends for Philadelphia.

George Washington to Lund Washington

Falls of Delaware So. Side

Dear Lund,   10th Decr 1776.

Hurried as I am and distressed by a number of perplexing circumstances I will write you a few Lines in acknowledgment of yr Letters of the 20th & 26th Ulto.

I wish to Heaven it was in my power to give you a more favourable Acct of our situation than it is — our numbers, quite inadequate to the task of opposing that part of the Army under the Command of Genl Howe, being reduced by Sickness, Desertion, & Political Deaths (on & before the first Instt, & having no assistance from the Militia) were obliged to retire before the Enemy, who were perfectly well informd of our Situation till we came to this place, where I have no Idea of being able to make a stand, as My numbers, till joind by the Philadelphia Militia did not exceed 3000 Men fit for duty — now we may be about 5000 to oppose Howes whole Army, that part of it excepted which saild under the Comd. of General Clinton. I tremble for Philadelphia, nothing in my opinion but General Lee's speedy arrival, who has been long expected, thô still at a distance (with about 3000 Men) can save it. We have brought over, and destroyed, all the Boats we could lay our hands on, upon the Jersey Shore for many Miles above and below this place; but it is next to impossible to guard a Shore for 60 Miles with less than half the Enemys numbers; when by force, or Stratagem they may suddenly attempt a passage in many different places. at present they are Incamp'd or quarterd along the other shore above & below us (rather this place for we are obliged to keep a face towards them) for fifteen Miles.

If you can get some Holly Trees to plant upon the Circular Banks in the manner, or rather thicker than I did a year or two ago I should be glad of it — or if good & well set Holly can not be had then young & strait bodied Pines will do. If you have a mind to try the Sycamore upon some of the cross

Banks in the Neck, or elsewhere I have no objection to the
experiment; but it runs in my head that I have heard of some
objection to the Sycamore — near to, or upon the Land of
Colo. Warner Lewis in Gloucester, I have seen neglected
hedges of it; but to what cause I know not. perhaps Colo.
Fieldg Lewis (who I think it was told me they did not answer)
can tell. The honey locust must, I should think, be better, if
to be had.

If you can get a good match (and a young horse) for the
Stallion, I should like it very well — but let the match be
good, & the Horse handsome. the hurried situation I am in
at present allows me no time, or indeed any body to spare, to
send the Horses I promis'd — Mrs Washington must therefore make the old greys serve her a little while longer, I think
if there can be any possible shift made, without buying
Linnen for the Negros at the enormous price you speak of, it
ought to be attempted, as the price is too heavy to be borne
with (if it be possible to avoid it) without making the poor
Negros suffer too much — this I would not do to save any expence, as they certainly have a just claim to their Victuals and
cloaths, if they make enough to purchase them.

Decr 17th Ten Miles above the Falls. This Letter was wrote
in order to send you by the last Post, but in the multiplicity
& hurry of my business I forgot that I had wrote it, and
therefore it was not sent.

I have since moved up to this place to be more convenient
to our great and extensive defence of this River. hitherto by
our destruction of the Boats, and vigilance in watching the
Fords of the River above the Falls (which are now rather
high) we have prevented them from crossing; but how long
we shall be able to do it, God only knows, as they are
still hovering about the River, and if every thing else fails
will wait till the first of Jany when their will be no other Men
to oppose them but Militia, none of which but those
from Philadelphia mentiond in the first part of this Letter,
are yet come (tho I am told some are expected from the back
Counties) when I say none but Militia, I am to except the
Virginia Regiments & the shatterd remains of Smallwoods
which by fatiegue, want of Cloaths &ca &ca are reduced to

nothing; Weedons which was the strongest, not having more than between One hundd & thirty & 40 Men fit for duty; the rest being in the Hospitals. The unhappy policy of short Inlistments, and a dependance upon Militia will, I fear, prove the downfall of our cause, tho early pointed out with an almost Prophetick Spirit.

Our Cause has also received a severe blow in the Captivity of General Lee — Unhappy Man! taken by his own Imprudence! going three or four Miles from his own Camp to lodge, & within 20 of the Enemy; notice of which by a rascally Tory being given, a party of light Horse siez'd him in the Morning after travelling all Night & carried him off in high triumph, and with every Mark of Indignity — not even suffering him to get his Hat, or Sartout Coat. the Troops that were under his Command are not yet come up with us, though I think they may be expected to morrow. A large part of the Jerseys have given every proof of disaffection that a people can do, & this part of Pensylvania are equally inemical; in short your immagination can scarce extend to a situation more distressing than mine — Our only dependance now, is upon the Speedy Inlistment of a New Army; if this fails us, I think the game will be pretty well up, as from disaffection, and want of spirit & fortitude, the Inhabitants instead of resistance, are offering Submission, & taking protections from Genl Howe in Jersey.

I send you by Mr Mercer a very pretty Mare, but rather too small (if she had ever been broke to it) for the draft — I also send you a very likely, as well as a very good Horse to match the Bay you have for Mrs Washington; but as he has been badly cut, he is exceeding troublesome, being very vicious; as much so I think after Mares, as any Stallion I ever met with — buy the Horse you spoke of, & if you have any Money to spare, of mine, I should be glad to have it laid out in young Mares for Breeders.

Matters to my view, but this I say in confidence to you, as a friend, wears so unfavourable an aspect (not that I apprehend half so much danger from Howes Army, as from the disaffection of the three States of New York, Jersey & Pensylvania) that I would look forward to unfavorable Events, & prepare Accordingly in such a manner however as to give no alarm or suspicion to any one; as one step towards it, have my Papers in such a Situation as to remove at a short notice in case an Enemy's Fleet should come up the River—When they are removd let them go immediately to my Brothers in Berkeley.

Since writing the above I have determind to send Mrs Washington another Horse for her Chariot, which with the one before mentiond, the one you have, and the one you are to buy, will make a very good set, if you can purchase a good one and likely—the two I send are exceeding good Horses, and Young, the lightest of the two Bays is an exceeding tough, hardy horse as any in the World, but rather lazy—he will do well for the Postilian before.

My best remembrance to all friends with sincere regard I am Yr Affecte friend

P.S. If you could exchange the old Greys for young Mares, it would be a good way of getting quit of them. If I never did, in any of my Letters, desire you to Plant locusts across from the New Garden to the Spinning House as the Wall is to run from the end of the Sunk Wall (& on that side of it next the Quarter) as also as the other Wall from the old Garden gate to the Smoke House or Hen House (and on the lower side of it) I must request it now in this Letter. let them be tall and strait bodyed about Eight or ten feet to the first Limbs— plant them thick enough for the limbs to Interlock when the Trees are grown for Instance 15 or 16 feet a part.

The young Gentlemen who carry my Horses home should be assisted by you in getting to Fredericksburg—may be they would purchase some of yr Greys.

Thomas Paine:
The American Crisis, Number I

December 19, 1776

THESE are the times that try men's souls: The summer soldier and the sunshine patriot will, in this crisis, shrink from the service of his country; but he that stands it NOW, deserves the love and thanks of man and woman. Tyranny, like hell, is not easily conquered; yet we have this consolation with us, that the harder the conflict, the more glorious the triumph. What we obtain too cheap, we esteem too lightly: — 'Tis dearness only that gives every thing its value. Heaven knows how to set a proper price upon its goods; and it would be strange indeed, if so celestial an article as FREEDOM should not be highly rated. Britain, with an army to enforce her tyranny, has declared, that she has a right (*not only to* TAX) but "*to* BIND *us in* ALL CASES WHATSOEVER," and if being *bound in that manner* is not slavery, then is there not such a thing as slavery upon earth. Even the expression is impious, for so unlimited a power can belong only to GOD.

Whether the Independence of the Continent was declared too soon, or delayed too long, I will not now enter into as an argument; my own simple opinion is, that had it been eight months earlier, it would have been much better. We did not make a proper use of last winter, neither could we, while we were in a dependent state. However, the fault, if it were one, was all our own; we have none to blame but ourselves*. But no great deal is lost yet; all that Howe has been doing for this month past is rather a ravage than a conquest, which the spirit of the Jersies a year ago would have quickly repulsed, and which time and a little resolution will soon recover.

---

*"The present winter" (meaning the last) "is worth an age, if rightly employed, but if lost, or neglected, the whole Continent will partake of the evil; and there is no punishment that man does not deserve, be he who, or what, or where he will, that may be the means of sacrificing a season so precious and useful." COMMON SENSE.

I have as little superstition in me as any man living, but my secret opinion has ever been, and still is, that GOD almighty will not give up a people to military destruction, or leave them unsupportedly to perish, who had so earnestly and so repeatedly sought to avoid the calamities of war, by every decent method which wisdom could invent. Neither have I so much of the infidel in me, as to suppose, that HE has relinquished the government of the world, and given us up to the care of devils; and as I do not, I cannot see on what grounds the king of Britain can look up to heaven for help against us: A common murderer, a highwayman, or a housebreaker, has as good a pretence as he.

'Tis surprising to see how rapidly a panic will sometimes run through a country. All nations and ages have been subject to them: Britain has trembled like an ague at the report of a French fleet of flat bottomed boats; and in the fourteenth century the whole English army, after ravaging the kingdom of France, was driven back like men petrified with fear; and this brave exploit was performed by a few broken forces collected and headed by a woman, Joan of Arc. Would, that Heaven might inspire some Jersey maid to spirit up her countrymen, and save her fair fellow-sufferers from ravage and ravishment! Yet panics, in some cases, have their uses; they produce as much good as hurt. Their duration is always short; the mind soon grows thro' them, and acquires a firmer habit than before. But their peculiar advantage is, that they are the touchstones of sincerity and hypocrisy, and bring things and men to light, which might otherwise have lain for ever undiscovered. In fact, they have the same effect on secret traitors, which an imaginary apparition would upon a private murderer. They sift out the hidden thoughts of man, and hold them up in public to the world. Many a disguised Tory has lately shewn his head, that shall penitentially solemnize with curses the day on which Howe arrived upon the Delaware.

As I was with the troops at fort Lee, and marched with them to the edge of Pennsylvania, I am well acquainted with many circumstances, which those, who lived at a distance, know but little or nothing of. Our situation there was exceedingly cramped, the place being on a narrow neck of land between the North river and the Hackensack. Our force was inconsiderable, being not one fourth so great as Howe could bring against us. We had no army at hand to have relieved the garrison, had we shut ourselves up and stood on the defence. Our ammunition, light artillery, and the best part of our stores, had been removed upon the apprehension that Howe would endeavour to penetrate the Jersies, in which case fort Lee could be of no use to us; for it must occur to every thinking man, whether in the army or not, that these kind of field forts are only for temporary purposes, and last in use no longer than the enemy directs his force against the particular object, which such forts are raised to defend. Such was our situation and condition at fort Lee on the morning of the 20th of November, when an officer arrived with information, that the enemy with 200 boats had landed about seven or eight miles above: Major General Green, who commanded the garrison, immediately ordered them under arms, and sent express to his Excellency General Washington at the town of Hackensack, distant by the way of the ferry six miles. Our first object was to secure the bridge over the Hackensack, which laid up the river between the enemy and us, about six miles from us and three from them. General Washington arrived in about three quarters of an hour, and marched at the head of the troops towards the bridge, which place I expected we should have a brush for; however they did not chuse to dispute it with us, and the greatest part of our troops went over the bridge, the rest over the ferry, except some which passed at a mill on a small creek, between the bridge and the ferry, and made their way through some marshy grounds up to the town of Hackensack, and there passed the river. We brought off as much baggage as the waggons could contain, the rest was lost. The simple object was to bring off the garrison, and to march them on till they could be strengthened by the Jersey or Pennsylvania militia, so as to be enabled to make a stand. We staid four days at Newark, collected in our outposts with some of the Jersey militia, and marched out twice to meet the enemy on information of their being advancing, though our numbers were greatly inferiour to theirs. Howe, in my little opinion, committed a great error in generalship, in not throwing a body of forces off from Staaten Island through Amboy, by which means he might have seized all our stores at Brunswick, and intercepted our march into Pennsylvania: But, if we believe the power of hell to be limited, we must likewise believe that their agents are under some providential controul.

I shall not now attempt to give all the particulars of our retreat to the Delaware; suffice it for the present to say, that both officers and men, though greatly harassed and fatigued, frequently without rest, covering, or provision, the inevitable consequences of a long retreat, bore it with a manly and a martial spirit. All their wishes were one, which was, that the country would turn out and help them to drive the enemy back. Voltaire has remarked, that king William never appeared to full advantage but in difficulties and in action; the same remark may be made on General Washington, for the character fits him. There is a natural firmness in some minds which cannot be unlocked by triffles, but which, when unlocked, discovers a cabinet of fortitude; and I reckon it among those kind of public blessings, which we do not immediately see, that GOD hath blest him with uninterrupted health, and given him a mind that can even flourish upon care.

I shall conclude this paper with some miscellaneous remarks on the state of our affairs; and shall begin with asking the following question, Why is it that the enemy hath left the New-England provinces, and made these middle ones the seat of war? The answer is easy: New-England is not infested with Tories, and we are. I have been tender in raising the cry against these men, and used numberless arguments to shew them their danger, but it will not do to sacrifice a world to either their folly or their baseness. The period is now arrived, in which either they or we must change our sentiments, or one or both must fall. And what is a Tory? Good GOD! what is he? I should not be afraid to go with a hundred Whigs against a thousand Tories, were they to attempt to get into arms. Every Tory is a coward, for a servile, slavish, self-interested fear is the foundation of Toryism; and a man under such influence, though he may be cruel, never can be brave.

But before the line of irrecoverable separation be drawn between us, let us reason the matter together: Your conduct is an invitation to the enemy, yet not one in a thousand of you has heart enough to join him. Howe is as much deceived by you as the American cause is injured by you. He expects you will all take up arms, and flock to his standard with muskets on your shoulders. Your opinions are of no use to him, unless you support him personally; for 'tis soldiers, and not Tories, that he wants.

I once felt all that kind of anger, which a man ought to feel, against the mean principles that are held by the Tories: A noted one, who kept a tavern at Amboy, was standing at his door, with as pretty a child in his hand, about eight or nine years old, as most I ever saw, and after speaking his mind as freely as he thought was prudent, finished with this unfatherly expression, *"Well! give me peace in my day."* Not a man lives on the Continent but fully believes that a seperation must some time or other finally take place, and a generous parent would have said, *"If there must be trouble, let it be in my day, that my child may have peace;"* and this single reflection, well applied, is sufficient to awaken every man to duty. Not a place upon earth might be so happy as America. Her situation is remote from all the wrangling world, and she has nothing to do but to trade with them. A man may easily distinguish in himself between temper and principle, and I am as confident, as I am that GOD governs the world, that America will never be happy till she gets clear of foreign dominion. Wars, without ceasing, will break out till that period arrives, and the Continent must in the end be conqueror; for, though the flame of liberty may sometimes cease to shine, the coal never can expire.

America did not, nor does not, want force; but she wanted a proper application of that force. Wisdom is not the purchase of a day, and it is no wonder that we should err at first sitting off. From an excess of tenderness, we were unwilling to raise an army, and trusted our cause to the temporary defence of a well meaning militia. A summer's experience has now taught us better; yet with those troops, while they were collected, we were able to set bounds to the progress of the enemy, and, thank GOD! they are again assembling. I always considered a militia as the best troops in the world for a sudden exertion, but they will not do for a long campaign. Howe, it is probable, will make an attempt on this city; should he fail on this side the Delaware, he is ruined; if he succeeds, our cause is not ruined. He stakes all on his side against a part of ours; admitting he succeeds, the consequence will be, that armies from both ends of the Continent will march to assist their suffering friends in the middle States; for he cannot go every where, it is impossible. I consider Howe as the greatest enemy the Tories have; he is bringing a war into their country, which, had it not been for him and partly for themselves, they had been clear of. Should he now be expelled, I wish, with all the devotion of a Christian, that the names of Whig and Tory may never more be mentioned; but should the Tories give him encouragement to come, or assistance if he come, I as sincerely wish that our next year's arms may expell them from the Continent, and the Congress appropriate their possessions to the relief of those who have suffered in well doing. A single successful battle next year will settle the whole. America could carry on a two years war by the confiscation of the property of disaffected persons, and be made happy by their expulsion. Say not that this is revenge, call it rather the soft resentment of a suffering people, who, having no object in view but the GOOD of ALL, have staked their OWN ALL upon a seemingly doubtful event. Yet it is folly to argue against determined hardness; eloquence may strike the ear, and the language of sorrow draw forth the tear of compassion, but nothing can reach the heart that is steeled with prejudice.

Quitting this class of men, I turn with the warm ardour of a friend to those who have nobly stood, and are yet determined to stand the matter out: I call not upon a few, but upon all; not on THIS State or THAT State, but on EVERY State; up and help us; lay your shoulders to the wheel; better have too much force than too little, when so great an object is at stake. Let it be told to the future world, that in the depth of winter, when nothing but hope and virtue could survive, that the city and the country, alarmed at one common danger, came forth to meet and to repulse it. Say not, that thousands are gone, turn out your tens of thousands; throw not the burthen of the day upon Providence, but *"shew your faith by your works,"* that GOD may bless you. It matters not where you live, or what rank of life you hold, the evil or the blessing will reach you all. The far and the near, the home counties and the back, the rich and the poor, shall suffer or rejoice alike. The heart that feels not now, is dead: The blood of his children shall curse his cowardice, who shrinks back at a time when a little might have saved the whole, and made *them* happy. I love the man that can smile in trouble, that can gather strength from distress, and grow brave by reflection. 'Tis the business of little minds to shrink; but he whose heart is firm, and whose conscience approves his conduct, will pursue his principles unto death. My own line of reasoning is to myself as strait and clear as a ray of light. Not all the treasures of the world, so far as I believe, could have induced me to support an offensive war, for I think it murder; but if a thief break into my house, burn and destroy my property, and kill or threaten to kill me, or those that are in it, and to *"bind me in all cases whatsoever,"* to his absolute will, am I to suffer it? What signifies it to me, whether he who does it, is a king or a common man; my countryman or not my countryman? whether it is done by an individual villain, or an army of them? If we reason to the root of things we shall find no difference; neither can any just cause be assigned why we should punish in the one case, and pardon in the other. Let them call me rebel, and welcome, I feel no concern from it; but I should suffer the misery of devils, were I to make a whore of my soul by swearing allegiance to one, whose character is that of a sottish, stupid, stubborn, worthless, brutish man. I conceive likewise a horrid idea in receiving mercy from a being, who at the last day shall be shrieking to the rocks and mountains to cover him, and fleeing with terror from the orphan, the widow and the slain of America.

There are cases which cannot be overdone by language, and this is one. There are persons too who see not the full extent of the evil that threatens them; they solace themselves with hopes that the enemy, if they succeed, will be merciful. It is the madness of folly to expect mercy from those who have refused to do justice; and even mercy, where conquest is the object, is only a trick of war: The cunning of the fox is as murderous as the violence of the wolfe; and we ought to guard equally against both. Howe's first object is partly by threats and partly by promises, to terrify or seduce the people to deliver up their arms, and receive mercy. The ministry recommended the same plan to Gage, and this is what the Tories

call making their peace; *"a peace which passeth all understanding" indeed!* A peace which would be the immediate forerun-
ner of a worse ruin than any we have yet thought of. Ye men
of Pennsylvania, do reason upon those things! Were the back
counties to give up their arms, they would fall an easy prey to
the Indians, who are all armed: This perhaps is what some
Tories would not be sorry for. Were the home counties to deliver up their arms, they would be exposed to the resentment
of the back counties, who would then have it in their power
to chastise their defection at pleasure. And were any one State
to give up its arms, THAT State must be garrisoned by all
Howe's army of Britons and Hessians to preserve it from the
anger of the rest. Mutual fear is a principal link in the chain
of mutual love, and woe be to that State that breaks the compact. Howe is mercifully inviting you to barbarous destruction, and men must be either rogues or fools that will not see
it. I dwell not upon the vapours of imagination; I bring reason to your ears; and in language, as plain as A, B, C, hold up
truth to your eyes.

I thank GOD that I fear not. I see no real cause for fear. I
know our situation well, and can see the way out of it. While
our army was collected, Howe dared not risk a battle, and it
is no credit to him that he decamped from the White Plains,
and waited a mean opportunity to ravage the defenceless
Jersies; but it is great credit to us, that, with an handful of
men, we sustained an orderly retreat for near an hundred
miles, brought off our ammunition, all our field-pieces, the
greatest part of our stores, and had four rivers to pass. None
can say that our retreat was precipitate, for we were near three
weeks in performing it, that the country might have time to
come in. Twice we marched back to meet the enemy and remained out till dark. The sign of fear was not seen in our
camp, and had not some of the cowardly and disaffected inhabitants spread false alarms thro' the country, the Jersies had
never been ravaged. Once more we are again collected and
collecting; our new army at both ends of the Continent is recruiting fast, and we shall be able to open the next campaign
with sixty thousand men, well armed and cloathed. This is our
situation, and who will may know it. By perseverance and fortitude we have the prospect of a glorious issue; by cowardice

and submission, the sad choice of a variety of evils — a rav-aged country — a depopulated city — habitations without safety, and slavery without hope — our homes turned into barracks and baudy-houses for Hessians, and a future race to provide for whose fathers we shall doubt of. Look on this picture, and weep over it! — and if there yet remains one thoughtless wretch who believes it not, let him suffer it un-lamented.

Thomas Rodney: Diary, December 18–25, 1776

December 18th 1776

To-day we reached the City of Philadelphia and were quartered in the house of Samuel Emllens at the corner of Walnut Street and the Dock. All the company are in good health and spirits but some have blistered feet.

When we arrived at Philadelphia it made a horrid appearance, more than half the houses appeared deserted, and the families that remained were shut up in their houses, and nobody appeared in the streets.

There was no military of any kind in the City, only Gen. Putnam, who was there to give orders to any militia that might come in. I had a sentinel placed at the General's door, and others to guard the City that night, and then went to the Coffee house, but there was no one there.

After sometime I found Bradford and made him bring a bowl of punch and some biscuit, and I sat in a box alone. I asked Bradford what was the reason no one appeared, and he said that they expected the British in every moment and were afraid.

I told them they need not be afraid, I would engage to guard the City that night, but he soon ran out again, seeming afraid to stay, and I sat in a box alone; but afterwhile Capt. Fortner came to peep in, and seeing an officer in the Coffee house, took me to be a British officer, and went round secretly to Bradford, who told him who it was, and then they both came in; I asked them where all the whigs were, and they said there were but few in town, and they expected the British in town every moment and were afraid to be out. I told them again they need not be afraid. They then went out and brought in a good deal of company and we stayed about an hour and then broke up.

December 19th 1776

This morning I waited on Gen. Putnam, who commands here, and received orders to get ready immediately and march to join Gen. Washington.

To-day we began to draw rations and live as soldiers. The remainder of the day was spent in getting ready to march to headquarters. This evening I was notified by general orders, that all the militia must appear at the General's at 9 o'clock to-morrow morning.

This morning I went to see Joshua Fisher's family, who is uncle to my wife but are quakers and very great tories.

They seemed glad to see me, were all extremely cheerful, said that the contest would soon be over now; that the British would be in town in a day or two and invited me to sup at Thomas Fisher's that evening, which I accepted, and accordingly went.

Thomas, Samuel, and Miers Fisher all supped there with me. The entertainment was exceedingly clever, and they were all particularly friendly to me. After supper several kinds of good wine were placed on the table and I drank, what was usual with me, about three glasses of Madeira.

They then began on the times; they informed me, I believe very truly, of the situation of the British and American armies; told me Gen. Lee was certainly taken prisoner; that there was no prospect that America could make any further exertions.

That it was, therefore, in vain for me to attempt anything more; that now was a favorable time to relinquish all further opposition. — That they would engage, that neither myself nor my brother nor any of my friends should be injured, and that I might expect on the contrary any favor I would ask, as they expected the British in town in a few days and would interest themselves in every degree in my favor; and that it was necessary for myself, my family and friends that I should embrace this favorable occasion and much more to the same effect.

I answered them by pointing out those circumstances that were still favorable to America, and concluded by assuring them that I should not change my determination, that I knew my business and should not return until the British were beaten, but they treated this as levity and concluded that I was an obstinate man, and must be left to take my own way. I told them I was perhaps better informed than they were, and should most certainly proceed in my enterprise; and then as it was now pretty late parted from them and went to my quarters.

December 20th 1776

At 9 o'clock this morning we appeared at the General's door but found no other companies paraded. The General was not up, but his aid appeared, and I requested that the general would dismiss us as we were under marching orders, which he immediately did.

A continual snow fell last night and cleared up with rain and sleet and the weather is very cold. To-day in getting ready to march I went through the City and found it almost deserted by the inhabitants, and looking as if it had been plundered, and scarcely a chair can be had at a public house to sit down in; or a meal of vituals to be had, but to our great joy we saw the streets full of militia and hundreds pouring in every hour.

In the evening I sent the company to the mustermaster with the Lieutenant, who not carrying the muster rolls, the drunken Mustermaster cursed them and sent them back, which vexed them very much.

I gave orders that the company should be ready to march next morning by daylight.

December 21st 1776

This morning early the company paraded and I carried them to the mustermaster and had them mustered, and marched immediately. The roads being very deep we only got to the Red Lion on the Bristol road 13 miles from Philadelphia where we stayed all night.

(Sunday) December 22d 1776

About 2 o'clock to-day we reached Bristol, where the Philadelphia volunteers are encamped. I waited on Gen. Cadwalader, who commands here, to show him my orders, but he was engaged, and upon waiting on the Quartermaster found that there were no quarters in Bristol, but Col. Morris the quartermaster immediately sent us out to William Coxe's and Andrew Allens on the banks of the Neshaminy creek where he appointed our quarters, about 2 miles from Bristol. The Lieutenant and half the company were placed at Mr. Coxes and the other half at Mrs. Allens, who prepared a room for me, and requested that I would stay at her house to prevent her being insulted, as her husband and brothers had fled to the enemy, and she therefore had been insulted some days before. But nothing of this sort happened afterwards, as I would scorn to insult a woman or permit it to be done, for the offence of her husband: we turned out to protect and defend the innocent not to insult them. Our cause is a just one and should be maintained with Justice. Both families treat myself and the whole company with the greatest kindness and politeness.

This evening I received an order from Gen. Cadwalader to wait on him immediately.

I waited on him, and he asked me what number of men I had brought, I told him 35. He asked me if that was all. I told him it was, and I thought they were enough, and asked him how many he had there, and how many General Washington had left. He said he had had 1200 but many had gone off one way or another, but he supposed there was still 800 left; that General Washington had about 1500 and there was some more, that had been under Gen. Lee, who was taken prisoner. That his capture had damped the spirit of the army very much, and everything looked very gloomy.

I told him I was sorry for Gen. Lee because I knew him personally and had a regard for him, but I did not view his capture as unfavorable but as an advantage; that too much confidence had been put in General Lee, that this must have greatly embarrassed the commander in chief, as he was afraid to do anything without consulting Gen. Lee, but now he would be at liberty to exert his own talents.

He asked what could be done. I answered, that in an enterprise a small number was best, that 500 men was enough to surprise any of the British Posts on the Delaware, he then said that General Washington intended some enterprise of that sort but was waiting for men to make him strong enough, and that Gen. Reed had gone down to Philadelphia to see what militia had come in, and on his return, if there was any prospect of success something would be done.

I replied that there was no occasion for more men, that there was enough for any enterprise, and the measure ought not to be delayed a moment on that account, for now was a favorable time, and I had not the least doubt of success, but if men were wanting, there would soon be enough, for the roads were full from Virginia and Pittsburgh to Philadelphia.

Upon this, Gen. Cadwalader's countenance began to flame and he asked me if I would stay there. I told him I was ordered to headquarters and wanted to get there to urge expedition. He said the Commander in Chief had directed him to stop all militia there, and if I would stay he would send an express to him. I told him if he would send an express and write what I had said, to the General, and he said I might stay, then I would do so. So Gen. Cadwalader sent an express immediately to the General and I returned to my quarters at Mrs. Allens.

In the night the express returned with orders from General Washington that I might stay at this post and Gen. Cadwalader sent the express out to my quarters and I accordingly appeared at Bristol, where Gen. Cadwalader informed me that he wanted us to join a party of Philadelphia militia that night, to make a tour into the Jersey and harrass the enemy, and asked me if the men were fit to go. I told him that a number of them were, and would willingly go, but as we had marched a hundred and odd miles, some few of them were too much jaded, which I begged he would permit me to leave. However, when he heard they had marched so far he would not permit any of us to go.

The rest of the troops paraded at 2 o'clock that night, but an express from Col. Griffin informing them he was not prepared to join them stopped the expedition.

December 23d 1776

This morning at 9 o'clock I waited on the General and just as I reached there he received a second express from Gen. Washington countermanding our going over the River, and informing him that he had determined on his plan of attacking the British posts on Christmas night, and would not have any of the troops harrassed in the meantime, but that they should be prepared against that time for the enterprise, and he would send his plan in a day or two; this was communicated to me by Gen. Cadwalader and I was rejoiced and assured him we should certainly be successful.

The General pressed me much to be with him, and seemed much animated with my decided sentiments.

December 24th 1776

We continued in our quarters this day and refreshed ourselves a little from the fatigue of a long march.

I waited on the General this morning and he privately communicated to me all the important information, and spoke with the utmost openness, when we were alone, his own sentiments.

He requested me to dine with him, but I could not take the time and he then asked that I would dine with him tomorrow.

December 25th 1776

I waited on the General this morning and was informed by him that he had obtained leave of General Washington to join my company to his Brigade and ordered that the company should be ready to receive marching orders tonight.

Yesterday the Quartermaster General, at Bristol, sent wagons down to Coxes and Allens to take all their grain and forage but I would not permit them to touch it unless they bought it, so they left it and went away.

To-day a Brigade of New England Continental troops were sent down to quarter here, and the Quartermaster came down to turn out both families, but I would not allow them to be disturbed and wrote to Gen. Cadwalader for instructions.

When Gen. Hitchcock, the commander, was informed of the matter, he politely replied he would not attempt to disturb them nor would he put the families to any inconvenience. Mr. Cox, thereupon, offered the field officers one of his rooms and Mrs. Allens house for the rest of his officers, upon my agreeing to move to his house, and Mrs. Allen, in consideration of such civilities, consented to do the same.

About dark I received orders to march immediately to Neshaminy ferry and await orders.

We march off immediately without the knowledge of the families where we were staying and met Col. Matlack at the ferry, he being the advance party of the brigade from Bristol. We soon received orders to march to Dunkers ferry on the Delaware, and after we arrived there the whole brigade came up, and also Col. Hitchcock Brigade of New England Regulars.

Our light Infantry Battalion were embarked in boats to cover the landing of the Brigade.

When we reached the Jersey shore we were obliged to land on the ice, 150 yards from the shore; the River was also very full of floating ice, and the wind was blowing very hard, and the night was very dark and cold, and we had great difficulty in crossing but the night was very favorable to the enterprise. We advanced about two hundred yards from the shore and formed in four columns of double files.

About 600 of the light troops got over, but the boats with the artillery were carried away in the ice and could not be got over.

After waiting about 3 hours we were informed that Gens. Cadwalader and Hitchcock had given up the expedition, and that the troops that were over were ordered back. This greatly irritated the troops that had crossed the River and they proposed making the attack without both the Generals and the artillery but it was urged, that if Gen. Washington should be unsuccessful and we also, the cause would be lost, but if our force remained intact it would still keep up the spirit of America; therefor this course was abandoned.

We had to wait about three hours more to cover the retreat, by which time the wind blew very hard and there was much rain and sleet, and there was so much floating ice in the River that we had the greatest difficulty to get over again, and some of our men did not get over that night. As soon as I reached the Pennsylvania shore I received orders to march to our quarters, where I arrived a little before daylight very wet and cold.

George Washington to John Hancock

Sir   Head Quarters Newtown 27th Decemr 1776.

I have the pleasure of congratulating you upon the Success of an Enterprize, which I had formed against a Detatchment of the Enemy lying in Trenton, and which was executed yesterday Morning.

The Evening of the 25th I ordered the Troops intended for this Service to parade back of McKonkey's Ferry, that they might begin to pass as soon as it grew dark, imagining we should be able to throw them all over, with the necessary Artillery, by 12 OClock, and that we might easily arrive at Trenton by five in the Morning, the distance being about nine Miles. But the quantity of Ice, made that Night, impeded the passage of Boats so much, that it was three OClock before the Artillery could all be got over, and near four, before the Troops took up their line of march.

This made me despair of surprizing the Town, as I well knew we could not reach it before the day was fairly broke, but as I was certain there was no making a Retreat without being discovered, and harassed on repassing the River, I determined to push on at all Events. I formed my Detatchment into two divisions one to march by the lower or River road, the other, by the upper or Pennington Road. As the Divisions had nearly the same distance to march, I ordered each of them, immediately upon forcing the out Guards, to push directly into the Town, that they might charge the Enemy before they had time to form. The upper division arrived at the Enemys advanced post, exactly at eight OClock, and in three Minutes after, I found from the fire on the lower Road that, that Division had also got up. The Out Guards made but small Opposition, tho', for their Numbers, they behaved very well, keeping up a constant retreating fire from behind Houses.

We presently saw their main Body formed, but from their Motions, they seem'd undetermined how to act.

Being hard pressed by our Troops, who had already got possession of part of their Artillery, they attempted to file off by a road on their right leading to Princetown, but perceiving their Intention, I threw a Body of Troops in their Way which immediately checked them. Finding from our disposition, that they were surrounded, and that they must inevitably be cut to pieces if they made any further Resistance, they agreed to lay down their Arms. The Number, that submitted in this manner, was 23 Officers and 886 Men. Colo. Rall the commanding Officer and seven others were found wounded in the Town. I dont exactly know how many they had killed, but I fancy not above twenty or thirty, as they never made any regular Stand. Our Loss is very trifling indeed, only two Officers and one or two privates wounded.

I find, that the Detatchment of the Enemy consisted of the three Hessian Regiments of Lanspatch, Kniphausen and Rohl amounting to about 1500 Men, and a Troop of British Light Horse; but immediately, upon the beginning of the Attack, all those, who were not killed or taken, pushed directly down the Road towards Bordentown. These would likewise have fallen into our hands, could my plan have been compleatly carried into Execution. Genl Ewing was to have crossed before day at Trenton Ferry, and taken possession of the Bridge leading out of Town, but the Quantity of Ice was so great, that tho' he did every thing in his power to effect it, he could not get over. This difficulty also hindered Genl Cadwallader from crossing, with the Pennsylvania Militia, from Bristol, he got part of his Foot over, but finding it impossible to embark his Artillery, he was obliged to desist. I am fully confident, that could the Troops, under Generals Ewing and Cadwallader, have passed the River, I should have been able, with their Assistance, to have driven the Enemy from all their posts below Trenton. But the Numbers I had with me, being inferior to theirs below me, and a strong Battalion of Light Infantry being at Princetown above me, I thought it most prudent to return the same Evening, with the prisoners and the Artillery we had taken. We found no Stores of any Consequence in the Town.

In justice to the Officers and Men, I must add, that their Behaviour upon this Occasion, reflects the highest honor upon them. The difficulty of passing the River in a very severe Night, and their March thro' a violent Storm of Snow and Hail, did not in the least abate their Ardour. But when they came to the Charge, each seemed to vie with the other in pressing forward, and were I to give a preferance to any particular Corps, I should do great injustice to the others.

Colo. Baylor, my first Aid de Camp, will have the honor of delivering this to you, and from him you may be made acquainted with many other particulars; his spirited Behaviour upon every Occasion, requires me to recommend him to your particular Notice. I have the Honor to be with great Respect Sir Your most obt Servt

Inclosed you have a particular List of the Prisoners, Artillery and other Stores.

Thomas Rodney: Diary, January 2–4, 1777

Allentown January 2d 1777

This morning we were called up at 2 o'clock under a pretended alarm that we were to be attacked by the enemy but by daylight we were ordered to march for Trenton, and when we reached Crosswicks found that the brigade had gone. We reached Trenton about 11 o'clock and found all the troops from our different posts in Jersey, collected and collecting there under Gen. Washington himself; and the regular troops were already properly disposed to receive the enemy, whose main body was then within a few miles and determined to dispossess us.

Trenton stands upon the River Delaware, with a creek called the Assanpink passing through the town across which there is a bridge.

The enemy came down on the upper side of this creek, through the town, and a number of our troops were posted with Riflemen and artillery to oppose their approach.

The main body of our army was drawn up on a plain below, or on the lower side of the Assanpink, near the bridge, and the main force of our Artillery was posted on the banks and high ground along the creek in front of them.

Gen. Mercers brigade was posted about 2 miles up the creek, and the troops under Gen. Cadwalader were stationed in a field on the right about a mile from the town, on the main road, to prevent the enemy from flanking. We had five pieces of Artillery with our division and about 20 more in the field, near, and at the town. Our numbers were about five thousand and the enemy's about seven Thousand.

The attack began about 2 o'clock and a heavy fire upon both sides, chiefly from the artillery continued until dark.

At this time the enemy were left in possession of the upper part of the town, but we kept possession of the bridge, altho' the enemy attempted several times to carry it but were repulsed each time with great slaughter.

After sunset this afternoon the enemy came down in a very

heavy column to force the bridge. The fire was very heavy and the Light troops were ordered to fly to the support of that important post, and as we drew near, I stepped out of the front to order my men to close up; at this time Martinas Sipple was about 10 steps behind the man next in front of him; I at once drew my sword and threatened to cut his head off if he did not keep close, he then sprang forward and I returned to the front. The enemy were soon defeated and retired and the American army also retired to the woods, where they encamped and built up fires.

I then had the roll called to see if any of our men were missing and Martinas was not to be found, but Leut. Mark McCall informed me, that immediately on my returning to the head of the column, after making him close up, he fled out of the field.*

We lost but few men; the enemy considerably more. It is thought Gen. Washington did not intend to hold the upper part of the town.

January 3d 1777

At two o'clock this morning the ground having been frozen firm by a keen N. West wind secret orders were issued to each department and the whole army was at once put in motion, but no one knew what the Gen. meant to do. Some thought that we were going to attack the enemy in the rear; some that we were going to Princeton; the latter proved to be right. We went by a bye road on the right hand which made it about 16 miles; During this nocturnal march I, with the Dover Company and the Red Feather Company of Philadelphia Light Infantry led the van of the army and Capt. Henry with the other three companies of Philadelphia light Infantry brought up the rear.

The Van moved on all night in the most cool and determined order but on the march great confusion happened in the rear. There was a cry that they were surrounded by the Hessians and several corps of Militia broke and fled towards Bordentown but the rest of the column remained firm and pursued their march without disorder, but those who were

---

*In justice to Martinas I must add that he afterwards joined the Delaware Regiment under Col. David Hall and became a brave and faithful soldier.

frightened and fled did not recover from their panic until they reached Burlington.

When we had proceeded to within a mile and a half of Princeton and the van had crossed Stony Brook, Gen. Washington ordered our Infantry to file off to one side of the road and halt. Gen. Sullivan was ordered to wheel to the right and flank the town on that side, and two Brigades were ordered to wheel to the Left, to make a circuit and surround the town on that side and as they went to break down the Bridge and post a party at the mill on the main road, to oppose the enemy's main army if they should pursue us from Trenton.

The third Division was composed of Gen. Mercers brigade of Continental troops, about 300 men, and Cadwaladers brigade of Philadelphia militia to which brigade the whole of our light Infantry Regiment was again annexed.

Mercers brigade marched in front and another corp of infantry brought up the rear.

My company flanked the whole brigade on the right in an Indian file so that my men were very much extended and distant from each other; I marched in front and was followed by sargeant McKnatt and next to him was Nehemiah Tilton.

Mercers brigade which was headed by Col. Haslet of Delaware on foot and Gen. Mercer on horseback was to march straight on to Princeton without Turning to the right or left.

It so happened that two Regiments of British troops that were on their march to Trenton to reinforce their army there, received intelligence of the movements of the American army (for the sun rose as we passed over Stony brook) and about a mile from Princeton they turned off from the main road and posted themselves behind a long string of buildings and an orchard, on the straight road to Princeton.

The first two Divisions of our army therefore passed wide to the right and left and leaving them undiscovered went on to Princeton.

Gen. Mercers Brigade owing to some delay in arranging Cadwaladers men had advanced several hundred yards ahead and never discovered the enemy until he was turning the buildings they were posted behind, and then they were not more than fifty yards off.

He immediately formed his men, with great courage, and poured a heavy fire in upon the enemy, but they being greatly superior in number returned the fire and charged bayonets, and their onset was so fierce that Gen. Mercer fell mortally wounded and many of his officers were killed, and the brigade being effectually broken, began a disorderly flight.

Col. Haslet retired some small distance behind the buildings and endeavored to rally them, but receiving a bullet through his head, dropt dead on the spot and the whole brigade fled in confusion. At this instant Gen. Cadwalader's Philadelphia Brigade came up and the enemy checked by their appearance took post behind a fence and a ditch in front of the buildings before mentioned, and so extended themselves that every man could load and fire incessantly; the fence stood on low ground between two hills; on the hill behind the British line they had eight pieces of artillery which played incessantly with round and grape shot on our brigade, and the fire was extremely hot. Yet Gen. Cadwalader led up the head of the column with the greatest bravery to within 50 yards of the enemy, but this was rashly done, for he was obliged to recoil; and leaving one piece of his artillery, he fell back about 40 yards and endeavored to form the brigade, and some companies did form and gave a few vollies but the fire of the enemy was so hot, that, at the sight of the regular troops running to the rear, the militia gave way and the whole brigade broke and most of them retired to a woods about 150 yards in the rear; but two pieces of artillery stood their ground and were served with great skill and bravery.

At this time a field officer was sent to order me to take post on the left of the artillery until the brigade should form again, and, with the Philadelphia Infantry keep up a fire from some stacks and buildings, and to assist the artillery in preventing the enemy from advancing.

We now crossed the enemies fire from right to left and took position behind some stacks just on the left of the artillery; and about 30 of the Philadelphia Infantry were under cover of a house on our left and a little in the rear.

About 15 of my men came to this post, but I could not keep them all there, for the enemies fire was dreadful and three balls, for they were very thick, had grazed me; one passed within my elbow nicking my great coat and carried away the breech of Sargeant McKnatts gun, he being close behind me, another carried away the inside edge of one of my shoesoles, another had niched my hat and indeed they seemed as thick as hail.

From these stacks and buildings we, with the two pieces of artillery kept up a continuous fire on the enemy, and in all probability it was this circumstance that prevented the enemy from advancing, for they could not tell the number we had posted behind these covers and were afraid to attempt passing them; but if they had known how few they were they might easily have advanced while the two brigades were in confusion and routed the whole body for it was a long time before they could be reorganized again, and indeed many, that were panic struck, ran quite off.

Gen. Washington having rallied both Gen. Mercers and Gen. Cadwaladers brigade they moved forward and when they came to where the artillery stood began a very heavy platoon fire on the march. This the enemy bore but a few minutes and then threw down their arms and ran.

We then pushed forward towards the town spreading over the fields and through the woods to enclose the enemy and take prisoners.

The fields were covered with baggage which the Gen. ordered to be taken care of.

Our whole force met at the Court House and took there about 200 prisoners and about 200 others pushed off and were pursued by advance parties who took about 50 more.

In this engagement we lost about 20 killed, the enemy about 100 men killed and lost the field.

This is a very pretty little town on the York road 12 miles from Trenton; the houses are built of brick and are very elegant especially the College which has 52 rooms in it; but the whole town has been ravaged and ruined by the enemy.

As soon as the enemy's main army heard our cannon at Princeton (and not 'til then) they discovered our manœuvre and pushed after us with all speed and we had not been above an hour in possession of the town before the enemy's light horse and advanced parties attacked our party at the bridge but our people by a very heavy fire kept the pass until our whole army left the town.

Just as our army began our march through Princeton with all their prisoners and spoils the van of the British army we had left at Trenton came in sight, and entered the town about an hour after we left it, but made no stay and pushed on towards Brunswick for fear we should get there before him, which was indeed the course our General intended to pursue had he not been detained too long in collecting the Baggage and Artillery which the enemy had left behind him.

Our army marched on to Kingston then wheeled to the left and went down the Millstone, keeping that River on our left; the main body of the British army followed, but kept on through Kingston to Brunswick: but one division or a strong party of horse took the road to the left of the Millstone and arrived on the hill, at the bridge on that road just as the van of the American Army arrived on the opposite side.

I was again commanding the van of our army, and General Washington seeing the enemy, rode forward and ordered me to halt and take down a number of carpenters which he had ordered forward and break up the bridge, which was done and the enemy were obliged to return.

We then marched on to a little village called Stone brook or Summerset Court House about 15 miles from Princeton where we arrived just at dusk. About an hour before we arrived here 150 of the enemy from Princeton and 50 which were stationed in this town went off with 20 wagons laden with Clothing and Linen, and 400 of the Jersey militia who surrounded them were afraid to fire on them and let them go off unmolested and there were no troops in our army fresh enough to pursue them, or the whole might have been taken in a few hours.

Our army was now extremely fatigued not having had any refreshment since yesterday morning, and our baggage had all been sent away the morning of the action at Trenton, yet they are in good health and in high spirits.

January 4th 1777

At daylight this morning our army was put in motion and passed on towards Brunswick and crossed the Raritan over a bridge 6 miles above that Town, but the General found the army was too much fatigued to attempt Brunswick as the enemy's main body were so close after us, he therefore changed his course and went on to a place called Pluckemin situated among the mountains of Jersey about 10 miles from the last place. Here he was obliged to encamp and await the coming up of nearly 1000 men who were not able through fatigue and hunger to keep up with the main body, for they had not had any refreshment for two days past and as all our baggage had been left at Trenton the army in this situation was obliged to encamp on the bleak mountains whose tops were covered with snow, without even blankets to cover them. Most of this army were militia and they bore all this with a spirit becoming Freemen and Americans.

Pluckemin Jan. 4th 1777

To-day we continued here and our troops were pretty well supplied with provisions and in the evening most of those who had laged behind came up. Here Sergeant McKnatt was accidentally shot through the arm by one of our own people, who fired off his musket to light a fire and as there was not one surgeon in the whole army I was forced to dress it myself and the next day got one of the prisoners to do it. The surgeons not being informed of the movement of the army at Trenton did not hear of it until daylight and then were so frightened that they fled towards Philadelphia for their lives.

Nicholas Cresswell:
Journal, January 5–17, 1777

Scotland, Loudoun County, Virginia — Sunday, January 5th, 1777. This happens to be Mr. Neilson's Birthday, as well as mine, We spent it as happily as our situation would admit. We are of the same opinion in political matters, which makes it the more agreeable. *Monday, Jan. 6th, 1777.* News that Washington had taken 760 Hessian prisoners at Trenton in the Jerseys. Hope it is a lie. This afternoon hear he has likewise taken six pieces of Brass Cannon. *Tuesday, Jan. 7th, 1777.* The news is confirmed. The minds of the people are much altered. A few days ago they had given up the cause for lost. Their late successes have turned the scale and now they are all liberty mad again. Their Recruiting parties could not get a man (except he bought him from his master) no longer since than last week, and now the men are coming in by companies. Confound the turncoat scoundrels and the cowardly Hessians together. This has given them new spirits, got them fresh succours and will prolong the War, perhaps for two years. They have recovered their panic and it will not be an easy matter to throw them into that confusion again. Volunteer Companies are collecting in every County on the Continent and in a few months the rascals will be stronger than ever. Even the parsons, some of them, have turned out as Volunteers and Pulpit Drums or Thunder, which you please to call it, summoning all to arms in this cursed babble. D— them all.

Wednesday, January 8th, 1777. This is a most unhappy country. Every necessary of life is at an extravagant price, some of them indeed is not to be had for money. Poor people are almost naked. Congress or Committee of Safety or some of those infernal bodies have issued an Order that every one that is fortunate enough to be possessed of two coats is to give one to their naked soldiers. Grain now begins to bear a good price, owing to such great quantities being distilled and the small proportion that is in the ground. I am persuaded there will be a famine very soon as well as a War. *Saturday, Jan.*

11th, 1777. Very cold weather for three days. Almost stupid for want of employment. *Sunday, Jan. 12th, 1777.* News that the *Slebers* Ships had taken 30,000 suits of clothes, that were intended to clothe Our Army for the Winter. Believe it is a lie. However, it serves the rascals' purpose to entice the people to enlist. *Tuesday, Jan. 14th, 1777.* News, that Washington had entirely routed our Army and the few that had escaped had been obliged to take refuge on board the ships. This must certainly be a lie. *Wednesday, Jan. 15th, 1777.* I am exceedingly kindly treated here, and am very happy in the company of Mr. Neilson, but the thought of receiving such unmerited kindness from an entire stranger, whom in all probability it will never be in my power to repay, makes me uneasy. *Thursday, Jan. 16th, 1777.* Intend to go to Leesburg to-morrow. I am unhappy every where. The late news has increased my anxiety to be at home that I may have an opportunity to be revenged of these miscreants.

Leesburg, Loudoun County, Virginia — Friday, January 17th, 1777. Left Mr. Neilson's. Got to Leesburg to my old lodgings. Dined and spent the evening at Mr. Kirk's, who begs me to make him the model of a machine for driving piles into the River to build wharfs upon. Their late successes have made him believe that they will have a free and open trade to all parts of the World very soon. Such is the instability of human affairs. Six weeks ago this gentleman was lamenting the unhappy situation of the Americans and pitying the wretched condition of their much-beloved General, supposing his want of skill and experience in military matters had brought them all to the brink of destruction. In short, all was gone, all was lost. But now the scale is turned and Washington's name is extolled to the clouds. Alexander, Pompey and Hannibal were but pigmy Generals, in comparison with the magnanimous Washington. Poor General Howe is ridiculed in all companies and all my countrymen abused. I am obliged to hear this daily and dare not speak a word in their favour. It is the Damd Hessians that has caused this, curse the scoundrel that first thought of sending them here.

Jabez Fitch: Narrative

A Narative
of the treatment with which the American Prisoners
were Used who were taken by the British & Hessian
Troops on Long Island York Island &c 1776
With some occasional Observations thereon

Dear Bro:

As one of the most malencholy Ideas attending a State of Confinment in Exile like ours, is that of being seperated from all Connection with those whom the Laws of Nature hath made most Desireable & agreable to us; & for whose Wellfare & happiness we are naturally fill'd with the greatest Anxiety of mind, but yet are Deprived even of the agreable priviledge of Inteligence from them; It may therefore be suppose'd that any one who hath fallen into so unfortunate a Situation, would gladly Embrace an oppertunity of communicating any material Inteligence to a Friend.

Having according to my Usual Custom, kept a Diery during the Course of my Captivity; making a brief memorandum of such Occurrancys as happen'd within my Observation, by the help of which, together with such perticular Circumstances as were yet Retain'd in my Memory &c, I have form'd the following Narative & Observations, with a Design of communicating them to my Friends at home, if Divine Providence should present a favourable Oppertunity for that purpose; The many Disadvantages attending the Circumstance of my writing, may be a sufficient Appoligy for the Vulgar & Irregular manner in which they appear; But as to the certainty of Facts therein contain'd, I have been myself personally knowing to most of them, and such as did not happen within my personal Observation, I have collected from Authors whose truth & Verassity is not in the least to be Doubted.

If this should be so fortunate as to reach you, I hope after reading it, you will communicate it to my Family &c, but Desire that it may not be lost or Destroyed, as it may be Useful to me hereafter in Case I should be so happy as to Survive this Captivity. Wishing all happiness to my Friends in perticular, & my Country in general

I am Dear Sr:

New Lots 2nd: Your Affectionate Bro:
of Aprill 1777.   Jz: Fitch
To Elisha Fitch Esqr:

A Narative &c.

It appears by the various Usage, with which we have been treated during the course of our tedious Imprisonment, that Divine Providence hath not been more perticular, in forming the different Features, & various Statures of Mankind, than it hath been in the formation of the various Dispositions & capacitys of the mind; Nor doth there appear to ocular view, a greater Distinction between the well proportion'd Courtier or Citizen, in a Deacent & Beautifull dress & the most deform'd Hessian Butcher, or Amarican Savage, in their murdering or hunting Uniforms, than an attentive Observer may Discover, betwixt the Person whose mind is annimated with Sentements of Virtue, Humanity and Friendship to Mankind in Genll:, and the Insolent Clown who knows no satisfaction, but in Acts of Cruelty, Slaughter & Rapine. Each of the foregoing Characters, have frequently fell within our observation during the course of our confinement; The former treating us with Politeness humanity & acts of friendship, Endeavouring to minister to our relief, and thereby alleviating (as much as possible) our sufferings; While the latter were ever treating us with the most savage Insolence, Malace & Cruelty, Endeavouring to Augment (as much as possible) & make every part of our sufferings, as great as their narrow Capacitys could Raise them.

It also appears, that many with whom we have been concern'd, who seem'd clothd with the greatest appearance of Gentelism, & dispos'd to shew the greatest Acts of Humanity & Friendship; by a short times Experience, are found to have their Harts & Tongues placed at as great a distance from Each other, as the Citys of London in Europe, & New York in

Amarica; in consequence of which, it hath not been uncommon for us to find, that on the fairest promises of Assistance & Relief, on any perticular Exigence, no more hath been seen or hear'd of the fair Promiser (perhaps) for some Weeks or Months; & then if through accident or necessity, they happen to fall in our way, a very slighty or Evasive appology, is sufficient to Justifie their neglect of poor Prisoners, who are altogather in their Power; they also seem'd to Expect that we gratefully Acknowledge to them, every favour that we Receive, even from the Almighty himself.

It would be Impossible to Reherse the many Instances of Insult, with which we have been treated, especially in the forepart of our Captivity, when those unthinking Mercinarys vainly sopos'd they had little more to do, than Ravage a Rich & plentiful Country, Deserted by its Inhabitants; & also to treat us (who were so unfortunate as to fall into their hands) with as much Insolence as their narrow, th'o savage Capacitys were capable of; Yet it ought to be mention'd, to the Honour of some (both of the Army & Inhabitants) who treated us with humanity, & Endeavoured to protect us from the Insults of others; I myself was so happy, as to fall at first into the hands of a party of this kind when taken prisoner; It was part of the 57th: Regt: who used me with some degree of Civility, alth'o some perticular Offrs: were very liberal of their favourite Term (Rebel) & now & then did not forget to Remind me of a halter &c; they did not Rob or Strip me of any of my Clothing but took only my Arms & Ammunition, & after keeping me in the Field some time, in confinement with several others, under a strong Guard, was sent off to Genll: Grant's Quarters, at Gowaynas.

In this March we pass'd through the Front of several Brigaids of Hessians, who were peraded on several Emminences in order of Battle: they Indeed made a very Warlike appearance, & as no power appear'd at that time to oppose them, their whole Attention seemed to be fixed on us, nor were they by any means sparing of their Insults; But their Offrs: Escpecially, Represented to the life (as far as their Capacitys would Admit) the conduct of Infernal Spirits, under certain Restrictions; Having pass'd through those savage Insults, we at length came onto a hill nigh to the place where we at first

Engaged the Enimy in the Morning; we were here met by a number of Insolent Soldiers, among whom was one Woman who appear'd remarkably Malicious and attempted several times, to throw Stones at us, when one of our Guard Inform'd me that her Husband had been kill'd in this Day's Action; We were then conducted down to a Barn, near the water side, where we were drove into a Yard among a great number of Offrs: & men who had been taken before us; soon after we came here, Capt: Jewett with a number of others, were brought in, & confin'd with us; Capt: Jewett had Recd: two Wounds with a Bayonet after he was taken, & Strip'd of his Arms & part of his Clothes, one in the Brest & the other in the Belly, of which he Languished with great pain untill the thirdsday following when he Died; Sargt: Graves was also Stab'd in the Thigh with a Bayonet, after he was taken with Capt: Jewett, of which wound he recovered, alth'o he afterward perish'd in Prison with many hundred others at N. York.

While we were here confin'd, we were Visited by many Regular Offrs:, by whom we were ask'd many Questions; some of them seem'd Inclin'd to Insult us, alth'o they might think it in a Polite manner; one of whom Asserted to us with great Confidence, that many of our principle Offrs: had a permission from Government, to accept Commissions in the Continental Service &c.

After being some time confin'd in this Yard, Capt: Jewett & some others who were wounded, were ordered to some other place in order to have their Wounds dress'd, & I see no more of them this Night.

When it began to grow dark, the Offrs: who were here confin'd, were ordered to an adjacent House, where we were kept confin'd in a very durty Room the two following Days & Nights; while we were here, we were visited by a number of Regular Offrs:, some of whom treated us with proper Respect, and others with mean & low lived Insolence, Despising & Rideculing the mean appearance of many of us who had been strip'd & abused by the Savages under their comd:, nor did they forget to Remind us of the British Laws against Rebellion, Treason &c, with many of their own learned Comments thereon, which seem'd to give them wonderfull Consolation.

Early next morning, Capt: Jewett came to us in excessive pain with his wounds which had already been Dress'd, but yet notwithstanding the applications of several of the Enimys Cirgions, Especially one Doctr: Horn (a young Scotch Gentn:) who treated him with great Civility & tenderness he Languished while the Thirdsday following (viz) the 29th: of Augt: at about 5 oClock in the Morning, when he Expired, & was Buried in our Orchard nigh to sd: House at about 8 the same morning, with as much Deacence as our present Situation would Admit; I myself was Indulg'd by Genll: Grant at the application of Majr: Brown who Attended us in this place, to Attend the Captain's Funeral; The aforesaid Majr: Brown, treated us with the greatest Civility & Complesance, during our confinment in this place, & Endeavour'd to make our accommodation, as agreable as possable; Genll: Grant also was so good as to send us (with his Compliments) two Quarters of Mutton well Cook'd, & several Loaves of Bread, which were very Acceptable to us, as most of us had eat nothing since the Monday before.

On Thirdsday the 29th some time afternoon, Majr: Brown Inform'd us that we were soon to be sent on Board the Fleet, & that the Passific (a large Transport Ship) was prepared to Receive us; About the same time, a number of Officers & men, belonging to the Navy came on shore in order to conduct us on Board, & at about 4 oClock we were ordered into the Boats, being oblig'd to Wade about two hundred Yards on the Flats before we came to Water sufficient to flote the Boats, it also Rain'd very hard most of the time while we were crossing the Bay for the Passific lay over on the other side, close under Statten Island.

The Offrs: being about 24 or 25 in number, were carried chiefly in one Boat, & the men being between 3 & 4 hundred in several other Boats and had their hands tied behind them.

In this Cituation we were carried by several Ships where there appear'd great numbers of Women on Deck, who were very liberal of their Curses & Execrations; they were also not alittle noisey in their Insults, but Clap'd their hands & Use'd other peculiar gestures in so Extraordinary a manner that they were in some Danger of leaping overboard in this surprising Extacy; But at Length we arriv'd at the Passific, which was a very large Transport Ship; We clim up her side & soon after we came on Board, found that our accomodations were to be but very Coarse, for notwithstanding Majr: Brown had Inform'd us while we were at Gowoynis, that the Offrs: were to have the Liberty of the Cabbin &c yet Mr: Dun (the Master of the Ship) acquainted us that we were all, both Offrs: & men without Distinction to be shut down below Deck; Accordingly at about Sunset we were all drove down the Hatches, with as many vile Curses & Execrations, as that Son of perdition, with his Infernal Understrappers could Express; When we came down into this Dungeon, we found but very Indifferent Quarters, for both the lower Decks were very full of Diert, & the Excessive Rains that had fell of late, had drove in so plentifully as to Quite cover them, so that a great number of men treading the Durt & water togather, soon made the Morter or mud near half over our shoes; Besides all those inconveniances, there was no kind of platform, or places prepared for our Lodging, but what was so Clutter'd with Artillery, Carriages, rough pieces of Timber Riging &c, that there was not a sufficiency of Room for a Man to lay between them, nor was there a sufficiency of Room in the whole assign'd us, for but little more than one half of our number, any how to lay down at one time. To add yet more (if possible) to our Calamity, some time in the Evening a number of the Infernal Savages came down with a Lanthorn, & loaded two small pieces of Cannon with grape shot, which were plac'd Aft of a Bulkhead & pointed thr'o two Ports for that purpose, in such a manner as to Rake the Deck where our people lay; telling us at the same time with many Curses that in Case of any Disturbance or the least noise in the Night, they were to be Imediately fired on the Damn'd Rebbels.

In this unhappy Situation, we pass'd three tedious Nights, nor was the Daytime much more agreable, for alth'o some of us were suffered to come up on Deck part of the Time, yet we were Insulted by those Blackgard Villians, in the most vulgar manner; Nor was our accomodation on acct: of Provision much unsimelar to our other Usage, Espacially in the Necessary Article of Water, of which we were not allow'd any that was fit for a Beast to Drink, alth'o they had plenty of good Water on board, which was Used plentifully by the Seamen &c.

The next morning after we came on Board this Ship, we found there was one Lieut: Dowdswell, with a party of Marines sent on board for our Guard; this Mr. Dowdswell treated us with considrable humanity, & appear'd to be a Gentleman, nor were the Marines in Genll: so Insolent as the Ships Crew.

While I was here confin'd, I requested one Spence (the Mate of the Ship) to do me the favour of laying away a Regimental Coat & Hat (which belong'd to the late Capt: Jewett) in some safe place, on which he had the Impudence to Insult me in the most Rude manner, & Swore by his Maker that no Damn'd Rebbels Clothes should ever be found in his possession; but yet it seems that notwithstanding this firm Resolution, his mind soon Alter'd for although I kept the most critical watch over those Articles, togather with my own watch Coat, which I could not conveniently wear in the Day time, yet among those Artful Thiefs, they were stole from me on Deck, & when search was made for them, I by the generous Assistance of Mr: Dowdswell found them all in the Gun Room, in the Imediate care of this good Mr: Spence who had been so peculiarly cautious in medling with Rebbels' Clothing.

On the 31st: Mr: Loring (the Commasary of Prisoners) came on Board, & took down the names & Rank of the Officers, & names of the men; he treated us with Complasance & gave us Encouragement of further Endulgence; he also Informd us that Col: Clark & many other of our Offrs: were taken & confin'd at Flatbush, & that a Ship would soon be provided for the Reception of all the Offrs: so that they might be by themselves, & not crouded with the Privates without Distinction.

Untill now we had been made to believe that we were to be sent home to Europe in Confinement, & that no Cartell for Exchange of Prisoners, would be Admitted, but we soon found the grose Representations of those Sons of Falsehood, to be so very Extraordinary, that no dependance might be had on any of their Assertions; For we were Informd by them that they had taken three thousand of the Amarican

Prisoners, in the Action of the 27th:, beside great numbers kil'd, which we knew to be a larger number than we had that Day Engagd. They also Inform'd us in a short time after we were taken, that they had either kil'd or taken, almost every Genll: Officer in our Army; And that they had taken New York & Destroy'd great part of the Continantal Army ten times, before they had landed a man on that Island; And that Genll: Burgoine, with a very numerous & powerfull Army, both of English & French, were within a Days March of Genll: Howes Army; That the Indians were ravaging the Fronteer Towns throughout the Country, Sacrifising Men, Women & Children without Distinction; And that the Continantal Congress was broak up with great Confusion, the Members all running off to make their Escape from the British Army; These and many other such false, & Inconsistant Representations, were constantly made to us, nor were those Reports made by the vulgar Soldiers & Sailors only, but frequently Asserted by Offrs: & others who pretended to be Gentn:, with the greatest Confidence.

On Sunday the 1st: of Septr: in the Morning we were Remov'd on board the Ship Lord Rochford, Commanded by one Lambert (an Englishman) This man was Indeed very Sovereign & Tyranacal in most of his conduct, as well as Vulgar & Vile in his Conversation, but yet not so Egregiously Insolent & void of all humanity & Generosity as Mr: Dun, who commanded the Passific, But we soon found our selves more crouded here, than we had been before, this Ship not being more than half so large as the other, on which acct: most of the Offrs: among the Prisoners Lodg'd on the Quarter Deck, & Indeed we thought this priviledge a considrable piece of Indulgence, alth'o some nights we were considrably wet with the Rain &c.

The same day that we were Remov'd on board the Lord Rochford, they hove up & fell down through the Narrows, after which she came too in the Bay, all against Newatrict Meeting house, where she lay while after the Kings Troops took possession of N. York.

Septr: 3rd many of us wrote to our Friends in the Amarican Army, with Expectation of sending our Letters by a Flag of Truce, which we had the promise of being favour'd with; but our Letters (most or all) of them) somehow fail'd reaching our Camp; for though the Offrs: confin'd in other places, afterwards Recd: their Baggage &c in consequence of this Flag yet we who were confin'd on board this Ship, Recd: none of ours; But my own in perticular was unfortunately lost in our Army's Retreat from New York, (as I was afterward Inform'd).

This day our Offrs: who had been confin'd at Flatbush, were brought on board the Snow Mentor, which lay nigh to us, and with which we were all toowell acquainted afterward, for on the 5th: we were Remov'd on board this Snow, which was our Prison for a long time; Our accomodations here were but very Indifferent, alth'o much better than we had had, in Either of the other Ships, for we were now but about Ninety in number, & the Field Offrs: had Liberty of the Cabbin &c, alth'o the other Offrs: had no other place for Lodging, than forward of the Stearage between Decks, & there was but very scant Room for all to lay down at the same time.

This Snow was commanded by one Davis, (a very worthless lowlived fellow,) yet happy for us, his Capacity was not sufficient to do any one much hurt yet we were now and then under an Necessity to holding a severe Wrangle with him on many occasions; We had also a Guard of Marines constantly on board, by whom we were some times highly Insulted.

When we first met on board the Mentor, we spent considrable of our Time in Relating to Each other the perticular Circumstances of our first being Taken, & also the various Treatment, with which we met on that occasion, nor was this a disagreable Entertainment in our Melancholy Situation.

But it seems that most of the Officers & men, who were first confin'd at Flatbush, fell into the hands of the Hessian Troops, & were generally treated in a more Savage manner (if possable) than we who were first confin'd at Gowoynus, & had been most of us taken by the British Troops, & although many had been both Robb'd & Murder'd by them, in a most Scandalous manner, yet it is said that the Hessians generally treated those who fell into their hands, with more Cruelty and Insolence than the Britains; for it seems that the

Hessian Offrs: (though of never so high Rank*) were not in-
active in this Ridiculous practice of striping, Robing,
Insulting & murdering the unfortunate Amaricans who fell
within the limits of their power; The present appearance of
our Offrs: and men, are an Incontestable proof of those
Facts, for many of them yet remain almost Destitute of
Clothes, several having neither Britches Stockings or Shoes;
many of them when first Taken were strip'd Intirely naked alth'o some others present, who had some small degree of humanity in their Composition, were so good as to favour them
with some old durty worn out Garments, Just sufficient to
cover their nakedness, & in this Cituation we were made
Objects of Ridecule for the Diversion of those Foreign
Butchers.

One Sam Talman, (an Indian fellow belonging to the 17th
Regt:) after he was taken & strip'd by the Barbarians, was set
up at a small Distance as a mark for them to shoot at for
Diversion or practice, by which he Recd: two severe wounds,
one in the Neck & the other in the Arm, but alth'o it appear'd that their Skill in the Use of fire Arms was not sufficient to Despatch him in that way, yet it afterward Appear'd
that they were sufficiently Skil'd in the Cruel Art of Starving
with hunger Cold &c, to Destroy him with many hundred
others who perrish'd in N. York.

On the 6th Genll: Woodhull of the Long-Island Malitia,
was sent from the Mentor to the Hospital at Newatrect; he
was an aged Gentleman, & was taken by a party of the
Enemys Light Horse at Jameca, & although he was not taken
in Arms, yet those Bloodthirsty Savages cut & wounded him
in the head, & other parts of the Body, with their Swords in
a most Inhuman manner, of which wounds he Died at the
Hospital; and alth'o the Directors of those Affairs, took but
little care to preserve his Life, yet they were so generous to
his Lady, as to Indulge her with liberty to carry home the
Generals Corpse, and bury it with Deacence.

Soon after this there was a new Disposition made of the

*Corpll: Raymond of the 17th Regt: after being taken & strip'd, was
shamefully Insulted & abused by Genll: Dehighster (in his own Person) who
was so lowlived as to seize Raymond by the Hair of his head, throw him on
the Ground &c.

Prisoners the Europeans being Assign'd a Ship by themselves, most of whom were soon after compel'd to Inlist into the Kings Army; many of the Amaricans were also afterward compel'd by hunger and other cruel Usage from the hands of those Unrelenting Barbarians, to follow the Example of the Europeans, & for want of present sustenance undertake in the Inhuman & Scandalous Employment of Butchering their Countrymen. A memorable Specimen of this was Exhibited not long before they were set on Shore at N. York, when they were kept several Days without any Provision at all, and for the full term of nine Days, not suffered the Priviledge of any fire to Cook what little provision they had.

On the 12th: most of the Officers (who were Prisoners) Recd: a Considrable Quantity of Baggage &c in Consequence of the late Flag which had been sent to N. York at our Request; but I myself, with the other four Offrs: of our Regt:, who had been first sent on board the Passific, did not Receive a single Article, by which we concluded that our Letters had miscarried & of Consequence our Friends had no knowledge whether we had been kil'd or taken in the late Action.

While we lay confin'd at this place we frequently hear'd a heavy fireing of Cannon up toward the City, but more Especially on the 15th: of Septr: when there was a very Extraordinary Canonade, & we were soon after Inform'd that the Kings Troops this day Landed on York Island.

On Saturday the 21st: at about 1 oClock in the morning, we observ'd a very considerable Light to the Northward, which we sopos'd to be the burning of some Buildings, & as it continued while after Daylight, & was then Succeeded by a very great Smoak which lasted most of the Day, we concluded that the fire must be in the City of N. York; This conclusion was soon after confirm'd by many Reports which we hear'd, with the most gross & futile Representation of the Circumstance of this Melancholy Catastrophy, when it was asserted to us with great confidence that the Rebels (as they Insolently cal'd them) had set fire to the City, & that great numbers of them were Detected in the very Act, many of whom were Emediately Hang'd on the spot, & others committed to

Prison in order for Tryal, who would Undoubtedly be put to Death with more formality; These & many other such false & Futile Representations, were made to us on this Occasion; without considering that the Amaricans might have destroyed the Town (if they had been so Inclin'd) without the least hazzard, but a few days sooner, while it was yet in their own Possession; nor was this futile Accusation propagated by the Vulgar & Ignorant only, but Genll: Robertson himself was pleas'd the Intimate something of it, in a Proclamation that he Issued some time after, although he might with Equal Truth & propriety have accused the Amaricans with being the Occasion of the Eclipse of the Sun which happen'd on the 9th: of Jany: following.

While we lay thus confin'd, we were also favour'd with the perusal of Lord & Genll: Howe's famous Proclamation, promiseing to all Amaricans (on certain conditions) the Endulgance of full Power & Previlege of Existance &c; But this Proclamation it seems was for a limmited time, yet his Majestys Commissioners, on the Expiration thereof, were graciously pleas'd to Renew it for the full term of sixty Days longer.

On Sunday the 22nd:, all the Ships which had Prisoners on board, togather with the Experiment & Resolution (Men of War) mov'd up through the Narrows, & came too off between Redhook & Gibbit Island, in the Centre of a great number of Men of War & Friggits, among whom were the Eagle, the Rainbow &c, so that it seems we were now sufficiently guarded against any kind of Casualty, Except Insult, hunger, Sickness or Death.

We were now in plain Sight of the City, & had a perticular prospect of the part where the late Fire had been, although it made but a very Desolate & Melancholy appearance.

On Monday the 23rd: We observ'd the Enemy were very busy in transporting Troops &c over into the Jerseys; the Amaricans having a considrable Camp at that time at Bergen (a small Town up alittle distance from the Water) they had also some small Redouts or Batterys from which we frequently observ'd the firing of Cannon &c but never learnt the consequence; While we lay here we also observ'd the Enemys Destroying the Works which we had Erected at Redhook, they set fire to them about this time, which burnt for several days.

We were also about this time Inform'd that a number of Prisoners, who had been Bro't from Quebec, were soon to be sent out on Exchange; This Inteligence gave us some gleam of hope, that in our turn we should be Endulg'd with the same favour, although we have since found (to our Sorrow) that those affairs have been Conducted with the greatest Partiality.

On tuesday Octr: 1st: all the Ships that had Prisoners on board, with the Resolution (Man of War) mov'd up North River as far as opposite to the Colledge, where they came too, & lay while after the Prisoners were Landed at N. York.

We this Evening Recd: Orders to be in Readiness to Land next morning, (although we were held in suspence while the Monday following) & the next day Capt: Davis Ordered a large Cable coiled away in the place where we had Lodg'd, so that a number of us, had no other Lodging the five following Nights, than on this Cable, which was much more uncomfortable than the Deck itself; The Seamen also about this time began to overhaul the Hold, & hoisted out great numbers of large water Buts, which had lain there many Years, & by striking out the water & Mud, the Decks were kept continually cover'd while we Remain'd on Board; The weather at this time being Chilly & Cold, our circumstances were now rendered much more Disagreable than Usual.

On Fryday the 4th: there was a number of Ships came up to Town, which we sopose had newly arriv'd; many of them had Troops on board, & we observ'd the landing of a number of Light Horse from them; we were also soon after Inform'd that the Kings Army about this time Recd: a considrable Reinforcment; among whom (it was said) was a Regt: of Waldeckers, several of Hanovarians & Brunswickers; we were also Inform'd that Genll: Kniphauson of the Hessians arriv'd about this Time.

On Monday the 7th: at about 4 oClock in the Afternoon, we were Disembark'd & landed at the Ferry stairs, near the Bair Market, where we remain'd on the Wharf wateing for Directions from the Commasary, while near sunset, when Mr. Loring conducted us up to a very large house on the west side of Broad way, & in the corner south of Warren street near Bridewell; where we were assign'd a small yard back of the house, & a Stoop in the Front, for our Walk; we were also Endulg'd with Liberty to pass & Repass to an Adjacent Pump in the Street.

We had sign'd a Parole before we left the Mentor but yet were not Endulg'd with Liberty to walk out, while after the taking of Fort Washington, so that we were confin'd close in this place near six Weeks, & alth'o the Provisions furnish'd us by the Commasary, were insufficient to preserve the Connection between Soul & Body, yet the Charitable People of this City were so good as to afford us very considrable Relief on this acct:; but it was the poor & those in low Circumstances only, who were thoughtfull of our Necessitys, & provisions were now grown scerce & Excessive dear, so that it was Impossable for them to furnish a sufficiency for the whole number of Prisoners, yet their unparrallel'd generosity, was undoubtedly the happy means of preserving many Lives, notwithstanding such great numbers perish'd with Hunger.

When we first came to this house, we found here a number of Amarican Offrs: who had been made Prisoners since we were, among whom were Col: Selden, Col: Hart, Col: Moulton &c; they had been first confin'd for several days in the City Hall, but some time since were Remov'd to this place; Col: Selden had been some time Sick of a Fever; of which he Died the Fryday following, at about 3 oClock in the Afternoon, his Corpse was provided with a Coffin, and Deacently Buried in the New Brick Churchyard the next Day, most of the Offrs: who were Prisoners, were Endulg'd with Liberty to attend his Funeral; In the latter part of his Sickness, he was attended by one Doctr: Thatcher of the British Army, whose humanity & Attention to him, & several other Gentn: who were sick in this place, ought to be remembered with gratitude.

Those Gentn: having been made Prisoners near twenty days later than we were, were able to give us a perticular acct: of their Retreet from Long Island &c, which had been perform'd with much less Loss, than had been Represented to us before; they also Inform'd us of the Death of Majr: Chapman & some others who were kil'd in the Action of the 15th: of

Septr:, when they were made Prisoners in our Army's Retreet from N. York.

When we were first confin'd at this house great numbers of the Inhabitants of the City, were Imprison'd, (chiefly) in consequence of false & Injurious Informations, by their Malicious Neighbours, but time soon Discover'd the Fraud & Malignity, of those Zealous Informers, who were afterward treated with the Neglect & Contempt, that their Conduct had Justly Merreted, & their honest Neighbours were set at Liberty from their unjust Confinment; a Similar Piece of Policy afterward appear'd in the Jerseys, while the Kings Troops made such Rappid progress in that State after the taking of Fort Washington &c, when the pretended friends to British government, in order to Recommend themselves to favour with that party, in the present Contest, Seized on their honest Neighbours, brought numbers of them Prisoners into N. York, pillaged their houses, & Confiscated their Estates; Yet Justice seems soon to persue them in this Zealous Frenzie, when the American Army persuing that of the Europeans, takes possession of the Dwellings of those Malignant Torys, Devoting their Estates to the pious Use of Defending their Country's Just Rights & Libertys; & alth'o many of their Persons were so lucky as to escape the Just Rage of their Injured Countrymen, yet were oblig'd to Sculk away into New York for the protection of the Kings Troops; and are now Reduced from a State of Affluence, to a very scanty subsistance or want of the necessary supports of Life; And are also become Objects of Contempt & Insult, to the British Army, while every honest American views them with the greatest Abhorrance & Detestation.

About the Time we were Landed in N. York, Genll: Howe (having made several unsuccessful Attacks on Fort Washington & the Adjacent Lines of the American Army) Remov'd the main Body of his Troops, up East River, Landing them at or near West Chester, from whence they proceeded to the White Plains &c.

During the aforesd: movements of the Army we hear'd a great Variety of Reports, generally greatly to the disadvantage of the Provinsials; But it seems there was no considerable number of Prisoners bro't into the City, while after the taking of Fort Washington although there were great numbers of wounded (both of Britons & Hessians) who were generally convey'd to the Hospitals in the Night season; Yet notwithstanding all their Endeavours to secreet their bad success, it appear'd by credible Information, that soon after the taking of Fort Washington, their number of wounded in the Hospital here on Long Island, did not amount to less than two thousand; & of consequence we concluded they must needs have had some kil'd, so that the Advantages they had obtain'd, could not be without very considrable Loss.

On Saturd: Novr: 16th: Early in the morning we heard a heavy Canonade up to the Northward, which continued a considerable time; soon after which we were Inform'd again that Fort Washington with a great number of Prisoners was taken by the Kings Troops; But as we had heard the same Report many times before, we at first gave but little Credit to it, yet we soon after found it to be too true, & the Monday following the Prisoners were brought into the City, where they were confin'd in Bridewell & several Churches; some of them were soon after sent on board a Ship for confinement; And on Tuesday the 19th: a number of the Officers were sent to the place of our confinment, among whom were Col: Rawlings Col: Hobby Maj: Williams &c, Rawlings & Williams were wounded; there was also some other wounded Officers bro't here, among whom was one Lieut: Hanson (a young Gentn: from Virginia) who was Shot through the Shoulder with a Musqt: Ball, of which wound he Died the 2nd: of Decr:

By those Gentn: Taken at Fort Washington, we Recd: some late Intelligence from our Army; & among other Important Events, they acquainted us of the Death of Col: Knowlton (a very Usefull Offr:) who was kill'd in an Action on York Island the 16th: of Septr:

During our confinment in this house, we were often Treated with the greatest Insolence by the Kings Troops; & many of the Charitable Inhabitants, who attempted to afford us Assistance, were also Insulted, & frequently deny'd admittance when they came to Visit us; we were also often Insulted in the most lowlived manner, by those who pretended to be friends to Government, and by worthless Refugees of our own Countrymen, who exercis'd their forked tongues, as a continual Scourge for us after we were admitted to Parole.

Novr: 20th most of the Offrs: who were now Prisoners, were Endulg'd with Liberty to walk the Streets &c within the Bounds of the City, from sunrise to sunset; which Endulgence was continued as long as we Remain'd in the City; Nor was this Enlargment at all Disagreable, as we had suffered almost three months in close Imprisonment, great part of which time, we had been in the most disagreable Situation; But yet we frequently met with Insults in the Streets, and when we Visited those friendly People who had used us with humanity, & Visited us in our close Confinment, they were often Insulted on our Acct:

Having obtain'd the aforesd: Endulgence, the first Objects of our Attention, were the poor men who had been unhappily Captivated with us; they had been Landed about the same Time that we were, & confin'd in several Churches & other large Buildings; And alth'o we had often Recd: Inteligence from then, with the most Deplorable Representation of their miserable Situation, yet when we came to Visit them, we found their sufferings vastly superior to what we had been able to Conceive, nor are words sufficient to convey an Adequate Idea of their Unparrallal'd Calamity; Well might the Prophet say, "They that be slain with the Sword are better than they that be slain with hunger for these pine away* &c." Their appearance in genll: Rather Resembled dead Corpses than living men; Indeed great numbers had already arrived at their long home, & the Remainder appear'd far advanc'd on the same Journey; their accomodations were in all Respects, vastly Inferior to what a New England Farmer would have provided for his Cattle, & alth'o the Commasart pretended to furnish them with two thirds of the allowance of the Kings Troops, yet it was often observ'd, that they were cheeted out of one half of that. They were also many times Entirely neglected from Day to Day, & Recd: no provision at all; they were also frequently Impos'd upon in Regard to the Quality, as well as Quantity of their provision, Especially in

*Laments: 4th: 9.

the Necessary article of Bread, of which they often Recd: such Rotten, & mouldy stuff as was Intirely unfit for use.

There was Indeed pretentions of accomodations for the Sick & a large number of the most feeble were Remov'd down to the Quaker Meeting house in Queen Street, where many hundreds of them perish'd, in a much more miserable Situation than the dumb Beasts, while those whose perticular business it was to provide them Relief, paid very little or no attention to their unparallal'd sufferings; This house I understand was under the Superintendance of one Doctr: Debuke, who was an European born, but had dwelt many years in America, & had been (at least), once Convicted of Stealing, in consequence of which (not finding the Country very agreable for his profession) he with many other of like Character had fled here for protection; It was said that this Fellow often made application of his Cane among the Sick, in steed of other medecines.

Nor was there any more Solemnity or Ceremony bestow'd on those miserable Sufferers, after they were dead, than while living, for their Bodys were thrown out on the ground, where they lay almost naked, Expos'd to the Weather (th'o never so Stormy &c) Indeed it was said that some of them were Expos'd to the unnatural Devouring of Swine & other greedy Annimals, in a most Inhuman & Ridiculous manner; however this might be, they were most of them Buried, alth'o it was in a manner very uncommon for the Interment of human Bodys, many of them being thrown into the ground in a heep, almost naked, where they were Slightly cover'd over with Earth.

Although this Beastly treatment of those Senseless Corpses, does not Affect their persons, yet when consider'd in connection with their Usage of the Living, it shews the unnatural, the savage & Inhuman Disposition of the Enemy into whose hands we are fallen; & whose Charecter (notwithstanding all their boasts of Lenity & humanity) will bear a Just comparison to those whose tender mercies are Cruelty.

When we attempted to Visit the Prisoners at the Churches, in their miserable Situation, we were frequently Repuls'd & deny'd Admittance by the Guard, who often treated us with the greatest Insolence, driving us back with their Bayonets,

Swords or Canes; Indeed I have often been in danger of being stabb'd, for attempting to speak with a Prisoner in the Yard.

There was no considrable number of Prisoners sent out while about the 24th: of Decr:, when a large number were Embarkd on board a Ship in order to be sent to New England; what privates of the 17th: Regt: Remain'd living were Included in this number, but about one half of them had already perish'd in Prison; I was also afterward Inform'd, that the Winds proving unfavourable & their accomodations & provision on board the Ship, being very Similar to what they had been provided with before, a large proportion of them yet perrished before they could reach New England; so that it is to be fear'd, but very few of them lived to see their native homes.

Soon after the aforesd: Ship Sail'd for N. England, there was large numbers of Prisoners sent off by Land, both to the Southward & Eastward, so that when the Officers were Remov'd over onto Long Island in the latter part of Jany:, there Remain'd but very few of the privates in the City, Except those who had been Releas'd from their miserable confinment by Death, which number was suppos'd to be about Eighteen hundred.

It may be observ'd that Genll: Robertson (so famous for Politeness & humanity) was commanding Offr: in New York during the aforesd: treatment of the Prisoners.

It was said that Governor Scheene (who had been long confin'd Prisoner in Connecticut) was so humane as to Visit the Prisoners at the Churches, & manifested great dissatisfaction at their Ill usage, & also that several other Gentn: of the British Army had signified the same Disapprobation of their Ill treatment; yet I was never able to learn that the poor Sufferers Recd: any Advantage thereby.

Novr: 25th: Mr: Rapellye, a Rich Tory who had belong'd to Brookline, on Long Island, & had been taken up, on acct: of being Inimical to his Country, & lately confin'd at Norwich in Connecticut, but had obtained liberty to Return to this City on Parole of honour, under pretence of furnishing a number of the Prisoners here, who belong'd to that Neighbourhood, with Necessarys for their Support, I myself being Included in the aforesd: number; This Mr: Rapellye came to our Quarters & treated us with great Complasance making us many fair promises of affording us Assistance & Relief; but as he had but Just arriv'd, he must have a little time to make the necessary preperation for that purpose, & would call on us again very soon.

Soon after this the New England Officers, having Recd: but very little Cash from their friends in the Country, since they had been Captivated, & most of them who had Watches & other valuable Articles which had escaped the pillaging of the Troops, had been obleg'd to dispose of them, to procure the Necessary supports of Life, the poor men confin'd in the Churches &c, being in a perrishing Condition for want of support; The aforesd: Officers therefore Requested liberty for one of their number to go home on Parole, to procure money &c for the whole; & in Consequence of this Request, Majr: Wells was Endulg'd with Liberty to go to Connecticut for that purpose, & the Officers wrote to their friends by him, for such Assistance as they thought would be needfull: but we who had Recd: such fair promises from Mr: Rapellye, wrote to our Friends that we had Dependance on him for Assistance; but I have not yet been able to learn, that this fair promisor hath paid any other attention to his Engagement, than to Renew the Lye as often as any applications hath been made to him by the Offrs:, for Assistance; & although some of our Friends were so good as to send us some Relief by Majr: Wells, notwithstanding our Dependance on Mr: Rapellye, yet we might have all perrish'd, for all any assistance from him; But yet it seems that his Conduct is all of a piece for I understand that he has paid no more Regard to his honour, in Returning to Norwich according to his Parole, than he has to his many promises made to us, for I am Inform'd that he yet Remains in New York or at Brookline.

I am also Inform'd that one Mr: Jones of New York who had likewise been confin'd at Norwich with Mr: Rapellye, & on the same acct:, obtain'd Liberty to Return to New York soon after him; & that on his leaving Norwich, he generously offer'd his Land Lord (Mr: Witter) to afford Assistance to such of the Prisoners as he should Recommend for that purpose, whereupon Mr: Witter Desired him to furnish Lieut: Brewster & another Bror: in Law of his, (who were then Prisoners in New York) with such Assistance as their circumstances should Require, which Mr: Jones Engaged punctually to perform, in Consequence of which Engagement, Mr: Witter neglected to send a sum of money &c, which he had then prepared for that purpose, by Majr: Wells, who was then at home, & soon to set off for New York; But he (Mr: Witter) wrote to Lieut: Brewster by the Major, that he might depend on being supplied by Mr: Jones, according to the aforesd: Engagement; Yet it seems that this good Mr: Jones (like his Bror: Rapellye) when he became Restored to his Butlership Remembered not Joseph; nor did he pay the least Regard to his aforesd: Engagement, for after Lieut: Brewster had several times apply'd for some Assistance, agreable thereto, he was at length Inform'd that Mr: Jones had Remov'd with his Family, to the Eastward part of Long-Island.

The two foregoing Instances are sufficient, to give a Just Idea of the honour and Gratitude of the New York Torys.

Novr: 28th: Col: Allen came to our Quarters he had been Employ'd in the Northern Army, the forepart of the War, & was taken Prisoner in som part of Canada about fourteen Months before; from whence he was Transported to Europe (being kept in Irons) after which he was brought to America while the British Fleet lay down at Sandy hook last Summer, from whence he was sent back to Hallyfax, & now is again bro't back to this place, where he had lately Arriv'd & this Day came on Shore; he gave us a perticular, & very entertaining acct: of many of his Adventures; and hath since been an agreable Companion, to us in our Tribulations.

Decr: 2nd: several Offrs: Recd: Letters from their Friends in the American Army, by some of which, we were Inform'd that some hard money had been prepared to be sent in here for the Use of some of the Prisoners, but that the Commanding Offr: had Refused to suffer it to be brought in; who this over cautious American Genll: was, we were not able to learn with certainty, but whoever he was, we are not greatly Obleg'd to him, for his peculiar Frugality.

the 15th: We were Inform'd that Genll: Lee was taken Prisoner, which Rept: we gave but little credit too for several Days, but finally found it too well Evidenc'd for Disbelief.

On the 16th: Lt: Col: Clark of the 17th: Regt: Died at about one in the Morning; & his Corpse was Deacently Intered the Evening following, in the new Brick Church Yard; A large number of the Officers who were Prisoners, Attended his Funeral; He had been sick of a lingering Disorder most of the Time since we were Landed from on board the Mentor.

the 17th: Doctr: Kyes (a Prisoner from Connecticut) was taken Sick of the Small Pox at our Quarters; he was Remov'd a few days after, to an Hospital prepared for that Purpose, where he Died on Sunday the 29th: as I was afterward Inform'd.

The Smallpox now being considerably spread in the City, several of us who had not had that Infectious Distemper, Remov'd our Quarters to several other places where we thought ourselves less Expos'd to the Infection; & were admited into the Familys of our Charitable Friends, where we were Entertain'd as long as we continued in the City, with the greatest humanity & Tenderness; although many of us were at present able to make them but a very Indifferent Reward for their peculiar generosity.

Soon after this, many of our Offrs: who had not had the Small pox, took the Infection by Inoculation, most of whom had the Desease very favourably.

Decr: 23rd: Majr: Wells Return'd from Connecticut, & bro't considerable Sums of money, & some Clothing for the Use of the Prisoners; We also Recd: (by him) a great number of Letters as well as other agreable Inteligence from our Friends in the Country.

After the taking of Fort Washington, a considerable part of the Kings Army cross'd North River, with an Intention of trying their fortune in the Jerseys; On which the Amaricans Evacuated Fort Lee, & Retreeted before them to the Interior parts of the State; But whether this Retreet was a movement of Necessity, or Policy, we have not (as yet) been able to Learn; although the former hath been assign'd with great Assurance in all publications, as well as common Report here, yet the Consequences of this movement carrying a very considerable appearance of the latter, we yet Remain in Doubt; nor Indeed do we much care what the Cause was, since we have it from good Authority, that the consequences thereof, hath been favourable to the Americans, for notwithstanding all our Sufferings of every kind, & the Tedious delay of our Exchang &c, yet we esteem ourselves Embark'd in the common cause, & Expect to stand or fall with our Country.

About the same time that the aforesd: Division of the Kings Army march'd into the Jerseys, another considerable Division thereof, were Embark'd on Board a Fleet prepared for that purpose; & soon After Sail'd from this Port; The place of their Destination was for some time conceal'd from us, but we afterward were Inform'd, that they took possession of Rhode Island, which the Americans had evacuated; But yet it seems that Genll: Howe found himself under an necessity of Recalling the greater part of this Division of the Army, before the Expiration of the Winter, in order to Reinforce the other Division in the Jerseys.

During the aforesd: movements, the wonted Insolence of the Troops & Torys was by no means atall abated, while they with peculiar satisfaction were continually using the word Rebel with the same degre of pleasure & propriety, that the Roman Clergy &c in Europe had done the word, Heretic, in some of the late Centurys; The newspapers, which seem to be the only Oricle of these people, & from which they collect their Articles of Faith, will give a tolerable Idea of their manner of Address &c; for Indeed there appears to be a very considerable degree of Consistancy, between their Faith & Manners; I shall therefore Insert a short passage from their Prophet Hugh Gaine, which is contained in that part of his Prophesy Dated Decr: 9th: 1776 & is as follows (viz) "It is said by some persons who have lately seen the Rebel Forces that they are the most pitiable collection of Ragged Dispirited Mortals, that ever pretended to the name of an Army, that not three thousand even of these are to be found" &c.

But it is to be observ'd, that notwithstanding this Despicable Representation of the American Army, from such undoubted Authority, yet it was but a few days after, when we were Credibly Inform'd, that a whole Brigaid of Hessians, with a considerable number of British Troops, had been

Intirely cut off at Trentown, most of whom were taken prisoners with a large Quantity of Artilery, Baggage &c, by this
small number of "pitiable Ragged & Dispirited Mortals," &
also that another Game of the same kind had been playd at
Princetown, & some other places in that Neighbourhood, &
that the whole had been Affected without any great
Slaughter; those Reports by various ways & means, soon became so well confirm'd, that we could not doubt the Truth of
them; then was there some little silent Rejoicing, among us
poor Despicable Mortals of the Captivity, scatter'd up &
down in this Seashan.

Soon after this (viz) on the 8th: of Jany: 1777, I accidantally
happen'd in at a house where I had often been treated with
great Civility, & seting with the good Woman of the house,
& some others who were also Disciples (though privately, for
fear &c) when there came in an Elderly Gentn:, whom I soon
discover'd to be a Chaplain in the Kings Army, & it seems by
his discourse, that he had lately Return'd from the Jerseys;
Indeed it was somewhat of an agreable Entertainment to me,
to sit & silently Observe the peculiar Mixture of Fraud,
Falacy, Superstition & Enthusiasm, of this Simple Clergy-
man's Composition, while he with many Artificial Sighs, &
heavy Groans, Related his own personal adventures since he
had left this City; he also gave some Genll: acct: of several late
actions that had happen'd in the State, the truth & Varasity of
which, I no more Doubted, than if I had Read them from the
prophet H. Gaine. He Represented his own Fatigues during
those late movements, to have been so great, that he had
scarcely had oppertunity to undress himself for Sleep the
whole time, alth'o he had been out four or five Weeks; & that
he had not undertaken to preach but once, during the whole
time, & was then fired on by the Rebels before the conclusion
of Service. He also Inform'd us that a small party of Hessians
at Trentown, whose commanding Officer could not be made
to believe that they were in Danger, had suffered themselves
to be Surprised, & that some of them had been taken
Prisoners by the Rebels; & that the 17th: Regt: had been
Attacked at Princetown by a very numerous Army of the
Rebels; But yet notwithstanding the vast superiority of the
latter in numbers, it could not be said that they had obtain'd

a Victory; He then concluded his Narative in a very malencholy Tone, & with a Countenance full of Artificial Sanctity, observing that it was to be fear'd that this Trifling Success of the Rebels, had so Elated them, that it would have a tendency to protract the War; & that he was very apprehensive that his Majestys Commissioners most Gracious Proclamation would be suffered by the Rebels to Run out without their Attention, the Consequences of which would be very, &c, &c, &c.

But I may here Observe, that I was so fortunate as to Obtain Inteligence by this Gentlemans Servt: who had constantly attended him in his late Adventures, & whose appearance in Regard to Simplicity, Indeed much Resembled that of his Master, alth'o he appeard to have ten times as much Integrity; This Servt: gave much the same acct: of the several late actions, that we had already Recd: by various ways; & alth'o his Master had Represented the 17th Regt: to have made such a Myraculous stand before the Americans, yet this servt: Inform'd us that almost the whole Regt: had been Either kil'd or taken.

But since I have began to Introduce those worthy Author's Relation of Facts, I will also proceed to Insert another more lengthy Paragraph, from this Celebrated one among the four hundred & fifty (viz) the Prophet H. Gaine, which runs thus "The Continantal Currancy is so sunk in its Credit, that none of the Farmers will take it in Connecticut; & Necessarys are now only to be Obtaind by the Barter of Commoditys. Salt is not to be had in Connecticut under the Rate of forty Shillings lawfull per Bushel, which however must be paid in Produce. They have every Prospect of a Famine, as their last Crop of Wheat is more entirely blasted than has ever been known in the Memory of Man. In short the whole Course of things has been so much against the Cause, that to use the Impious Expression of one of their Preachers before his Audience, it seems as if God almighty was really turned Tory."

I shall only Observe on the foregoing Paragraph, that although Majr: Wells was in Connecticut at the time of the Date of this prophetic Declaration, & on his way back to New York pass'd through almost the whole State, yet on his Return, he acquainted us with none of the above Facts, but quite the Reverse; and also that we have Repeatedly Recd:

Inteligence from undoubted Authors, from those parts, which perfectly agree with the Majors Representation; so that on the whole we are somewhat apprehensive that the foregoing acct: may possably be subject to Error, notwithstanding the great authority from whence it comes; & that since they "from the prophet even unto the Priest, every one dealeth falsely" perhaps it is a Lye.

But I shall yet proceed, & ensert a 3rd: Paragraph from this Inexhaustable Fund of Intelligence, which is as follows, "The running Disorder, which has lately very much Infested the Rebel Army, we hear has broak out in Rhode Island, & carried off many persons belonging to that Colony, it has one peculiarity like the Sweating Sickness in King Edward the Sixth's time; for as that affected English men alone in all parts of the World, this Disease Attacks only Rebels."

As to the Sweating Sickness above Referr'd to, perhaps very few Armys (if any) that have ever appear'd on Earth since War was first Introduce'd, could be sopos'd to be less Infested with any thing of the kind, than the British Troops with their Auxiliarys now in America: But as to the other (viz) the running Disorder, perhaps this pious Informer had forgot, or never heard of the peculiar Scene which appear'd at Concord in April 1775, & also another more general Attack made by this Disorder, on the main Body of the British Army at Boston in March 1776; This Attack was so very general, that it hath been said by some curious Observers, that there was not a single Offr: or Soldier in that part of the Army that escaped the Disease; Nor does it Indeed appear that the Britans & Hessians have been perfectly free from this Disorder, in the Jerseys the Winter passd, alth'o it might be with gratitude Acknowleged, that the very humane Applications of Genll: Washington, hath preserv'd many of them from that Ridiculous Disease, by an Effectual medicine called by the name of Captivity; This Medicine I know to be somewhat harsh & Severe, having taken an excessive large Portion of it myself; But however hope that they may have a Suitable preparation of it, & that both they & the Americans may Receive benefit thereby.

But I shall further Observe, that there is no one sort of people within the Bounds of my Observation, that have been

so much subject to this running Disorder, as those called
Torys, who have been frequently Observed to "Flee when
none persue," and as there are none who may with so great
propriety be call'd Rebels, as those who are Enimical to their
Country, it is a Question worthy of Observation, whether
these may not be within the meaning of the prophet in the
foregoing Paragraph; & as it is not uncommon to find certain
Ambiguous & figurative Expressions in prophesy, & as I mean
not to be Dogmatical, or over confident in Regard to their
Explanation, I shall not therefore undertake to determine this
Important Question, but would rather refer it to the Vener-
able Priest, whom I have had occasion to mention in some of
the foregoing pages, whose wise & learned Comments on the
Mysterys contain'd in the prophesies of the Prophet Hugh
Gaine, might Doubtless be very Serviceable to the Cause.

Jany: 20th: the Offrs: who were Prisoners on Parole in
N. York, Recd: Orders to Remove over to Kings County on
Long Island; A number of the Northern Offrs: cross'd the
Ferry the same day, & another party the Day following; & on
the 23rd: most of the New England Offrs: cross'd the Ferry,
& were ordered to New Lots in the Town of Flatbush, where
we were Billetted generally by two, or three in a house,
among the Inhabitants. There being yet a large number of
American Offrs:, they were Distributed in the Towns of
Gravesend, Newatrict, Flatlands & Flatbush, & were Indulg'd
with Liberty of the Respective Towns, in which we were
Billetted; But a number of the Officers had not yet Recover'd
of the Smallpox, & some were sick of other Disorders, who
were Endulg'd with Liberty to continue in the City until they
Recover'd, most of whom were afterward sent off to us in the
several Towns aforesd:

This new Disposition, was somewhat Disagreable to many
of us, as we had now contracted considerable Acquaintance in
the City, & were most of us in comfortable Quarters, with
Familys who had treated us with great Civility, & shewn us
many favours. We had also had our Exoectations greatly
raised with hope of a speedy Exchange, which now seem'd to
Vanish, or appear at a greater Distance. There was also various
Conjectures in Regard to the Reasons or Cause of this
Removal, some supposing it to have Originated from the

Malignity of the Torys & Refugees, of whom there was now great plenty in the City, who were continually Discovering their Rage & Disapprobation of every kind of Endulgence allow'd the Prisoners; Others were of opinion that it was only design'd for our greater Enlargment, & that we might be accomodated with more agreable Quarters than we had yet been provided with; Indeed it was said that Genll: Howe had lately Recd: a very Spiritted Letter from Genll: Sullivan of the American Army, shewing the highest Resentment at the Illtreatment of the Prisoners,

But whatever might be the occasion of the aforesd: Disposition, the Consequences thereof prov'd favourable to us for being Billitted among the Inhabitants, as hath already been Observ'd, we generally found ourselves in much more agreable circumstances, than what we had yet been Endulg'd with; The limits of our Confinment being much larger than what we had Enjoy'd in N. York, we were under a greater Advantage for Exercise, and could also Visit Each other at our pleasure, without Interruption or being Expose'd to the Savage Insults, with which we had been so often Treated; For alth'o in this place of our Confinment, we were not Strangers to this kind of Treatment, yet it generally proceeded from worthless Refugees and Vagrants, who are Despise'd even by the Inhabitants & by the British Troops themselves as well as by us; And alth'o the Inhabitants are chiefly Torys, & those who have the highest opinion of British Government and Administration, yet they are of a very Pasific Disposition, & not much Inclin'd either to Fighting, or to Insult those who Dissent from their Opinions in political matters.

Soon after we Remov'd over to Long Island, we hear'd of the Death of Col: Piper (a very worthy Gentn: from Pensylvania) who had been made Prisoner in the Action of the 27th: of Augt:, and had for some time been Sick of a Fever in New York. We also about the same time hear'd of the Death of Capt: Fellows of Tolland in Connecticut who had been made Prisoner in our Armys Retreet from N. York, & under pretence that he had been somehow susspected of having been concerned in the late fire, he was kept close Prisoner in the City Hall untill a few Days before we Remov'd over to this Island; by means of which long and uncomfortable Confinment, he contracted such a complication of Disorders, as to End his Days soon after he came out of Prison.

There has also a number of other Offrs: Died During the course of our confinement, which I have not yet taken notice of in this Narative, most of whom I have not been able to learn the perticular time of their Death; among whom were Capt: Peoples from Pennsylvania; Capt: Booy & Lt: Butler from Maryland; those three Gentn: were wounded in the Action of the 27th: of Augt: & Died on Long Island; Lt: Makepeace of the 17th Regt: was also wounded the same Day of which wound he Died at Flatbush the 6th of Octr:; Lt: Moore of Symsbury in Connecticut Died of Sickness in N. York the 3rd: of Novr:; Lt: Wheatley of Norwich, Lt: Williams of Chatham, Lt: Whiting of Stratford, & Lt: Gaylord of some part of Connecticut all Died in N. York.

John Peebles: Diary, February 13–24, 1777

Thursday 13th Febry. Cloudy weather looks like rain or snow intended to have gone ashore to finish business & buy some things we want but got orders to get under way directly, & a Pilot came aboard to carry us to Amboy, a good many of the officers & men ashore no word of Serjt. Stewart with the cloathing, got under way about noon & went down to Red Hook below Governors island where the Agent & the Rest of the ships came to anchor those we left ashore coming aboard every opportunity, — being hurried away sooner than we expected were not at all provided with any thing to Eat & Drink so sent to Town & got a couple dozen wine & some cold meat whh was all they could get, in the afternoon cold & snowy —

Friday 14th. Febry. Hard frost & a sharp north wind got under way about 10 AM. & stood down thro' the Narrows, then giving the Bank to Starboard a wide birth hawled up to westward & stood up Rariton River or Bay a crooked channel & sometimes in 2 1/2 fathom, passed a man of war ye. Raven & a parcel of victualers lying at Princes Bay; the Mercury got aground there — about 2 P.M. came to anchor about a mile or more from Amboy the Tide turng about 8 most of the ships got under way again & turn'd up nearer to the Town, a Brig with the Horses aground at the point Staten island

Saturday 15th. Febry. hard frost & a cold N.W. wind in the forenoon warp'd up opposite to Amboy but it blew too hard to get near the Town, about 1 P.M. went ashore on Staten island to try to get some fresh stock being quite out, we made a range of 5 or 6 miles into the Country & got nothing but a few eggs & a little butter. din'd at the Sign of the Ship on hung beeff & Eggs & return'd to the ship about 9 oclock at night — The Commanders went ashore to Amboy & return'd in the Eveng. but no word of our landing nor where we are to go. Amboy and Brunswick & the villages between are occupied by our Troops but never move out except

in large Parties, Elizabeth Town Woodbridge &ca are in possession of the Rebels who take every opportunity to harrass
our forraging Parties, but generally come off with the
worst — Genl. Vaughan Commands here at Amboy, Lord
Cornwallis at Brunswick &ca. the Commander in Chief is expected here on Monday or Tuesday —

Sunday 16th. Febry. the Weather more mild got the ship
hauled over to the Amboy side among the rest, — Capt. Skelly
& some of 71st. acquaintances came aboard to see us, two of
their Battns are here the other at Bonamtown with the 33d.
the 42d. at Piscataway. they say everything is very scarce in
the Country here & they live almost entirely on salt provision. — the afternoon turns cloudy, most of the Gentlen.
gone ashore its going to snow, Snow & sleet in the afternoon —

Monday 17th. Febry. Clear weather & gentle frost wind
NW no orders for landing yet. some of our men turning sick
& no doctor to attend them our surgeon having left us at
New York, sent for the Surgn. of the Light Infantry, who
comes & visits them — Most of our Gentlen. gone ashore
Eight of us aboard at dinner & had nothing but a little bit of
salt pork. Reviewed the Mens arms & ammunition, they are
compleated to 60 rounds P man & two spare flints. 4 firelocks
wants some mending   They have it ashore that Washington
is drawing in his out posts & collecting his army in order to
retire across the Delaware.

Tuesday 18th. Febry. a cold sharp Northwind & frost   got
out the new cloathing & put it on the men, just as it is, having no time to get it fitted. it is in general too little for
the men, set the Taylors to work to put on hooks & Eyes &
turn up the corner of the skirt which is all that can be done
at present —

Wednesday 19th. Febry. hard frost & cold NW wind   went
ashore with some of our folks to take a walk & dine at the
Tavern, sent Ms. Gennes to the Hospital, but they would not
admit a sick Woman — They have thrown up 3 or 4 redouts
with 2 pieces of Cannon in each, & have out lying picquets
beyond these. — the British Regts. here (Vizt. the 4th.

Brigade & 71th) are very weak in Numbers having lost a good many by the Enemy in that affair at Princetown and are very sickly, so that the duty of defence comes pretty hard — got but an indifferent dinner at the Tavern, the wine pretty good, club 18/ York — in the Evening according to custom some of the lads met at passdice & lost & win a few hundreds — General Howe arrived with his suite in the afternoon in a sloop from N. York & went to Genl. Vaughans who lodges at the Govrs. House. Mrs. Franklin still at home, her Husband prisoner in Connecticut — Yesterday Colo Mawhood went out with 800 on a foraging party when one Desaquilliers an officer of Ary. having gone before with two light horse men was wounded & taken prisoner,

Thursday 20 Febry. I believe last night was the hardest frost we have had this winter, a sharp NW wind, inclement Wr. for the out lying Picquets & sentries, the Genl. & his suite left this in the morng. for Brunswick Escorted by the Light Infantry & two Battns. the Troops from Bonam Town met them at the crossroads & took the Genl. under their charge, sometime after they parted, Those from Amboy in taking a turn in the Country fell in with some of the Rebels & drove them with a little firing in which we had two or three men wounded. the alarm came into Town on which the 35th. & the Waldeckers turn'd out & march'd a little way but they soon got notice that the affair was all over & they return'd, the whole came in soon after —

Friday 21st. Still hard frost & bitter cold, wind at NW in coming aboard last night from dining with Capt. Skelly I stepp'd into a little skiff that was so crank that with the least motion to one side she heel'd & I tumbled into the water, I scrambled out again & got aboard but it was devilish cold — went ashore & dined with Skelly today again, he & the Laird of McLeod in a mess, two fine young fellows — Capt. Duncan Campbell emigrants return'd from t'other side the Country where he had been with a flag to get his wife & family from Burlington but he was stopped by the way carried into PrinceTown blind folded & ordered to return by Putnam — The Troops from Rhode Island took a walk ashore

Saturday 22d. Febry. the weather a little more moderate
still cold & clear, a proportion of Bedding deliver'd out to the
Troops on board, which looks like remaining there, sent to
New York for our Grenr. Caps & some other articles, Serjt.
Stewart gone for ours

Sunday 23d. Febry a fine clear frosty morng. not so cold
The Troops from Rhode Island went ashore early this morning — vizt 3d. Light Infantry & Grens. & the 3d. Brigade, &
marched into the Country with a few field pieces & a train of
waggons to bring forrage, the whole under the Command of
Colo Mawhood, when we had got a few miles beyond
Woodbridge Colo: Campbell of the 52d. was detatch'd with 4
or 500 men to the left to make a Sweep into the Country, he
got 4 Compys. of Grrs. with him, having ask'd for ours to be
one of them, & I was order'd with 20 men to be the advance
guard. — when we had marched about a mile & a half to the
Westward, I discover'd a body of the Rebels on a hill which I
acquainted Colo: Campbell of, Very well says he I'll manou-
vre them, he accordingly gave orders for the Detatchment to
form & desir'd me to move on the edge of a wood in our
front, as we came forward the Rebels disappeared, & I kept
moving on thinking the whole detachment were coming after,
but it seems they made a turn to the left while I went on in
the tract of the Enemy, & soon after saw a body of them go
into a wood where they halted, I sent a Corpl. to Colo:
Campbell to acquaint him of their situation, but the detatchmt. being a good way off at this time he was long a coming back, — the Rebels seeing my small party drawn up &
nobody near them sent out about 30 or 40 to bring us on to
engage, I went up & met them & receiv'd their fire from
behind a fence. I moved on to a fence in front & order'd my
men to fire, which we continued to do at each other for a few
minutes when they gave way. I believe at seeing the Detatchmt. coming up for I don't think we hit above 3 or 4 of
them. I had two wounded: when the Detatchmt. came near I
mov'd off to the left where a party of them were driving off
some Cattle & sheep & some straglers firing at us, I then
form'd & gave them a plattoon & two or 3 rounds after,
which made them take to their heels. Colo: Campbell sent up

& order'd me to retire back to the detatchmt. which I accordingly did, they having withdrawn towards the left, he form'd his troops again in a field in the rear & to the left withall, & moving on still more to the left we saw another body of the Rebels coming down thro a Swamp & making straight for a wood, Colo: Campbell hurried us on, I suppose to get betwixt the wood & them, but they got into the wood before we could get within shot of them, he then order'd me up to a fence at the edge of the wood with my little party which were reduced now to 14 or 15, we went up to the fence under the beginning of their fire, we posted ourselves there & kept up as much fire as we could two Grenadr. compys 42d. & 28th. came up to our support but began their fire at too great a distance; when they got up to the fence they soon found themselves gall'd by a fire on their right, & those in our front being all posted behind trees almost flank'd the 42d. Compy. in this Situation the men are droping down fast when they (the 2 Compys.) got orders to retire which I hear'd nothing off. I remain'd at my post till I had not one man left near me, except Jno. Carr lying wounded, & fired away all my Cartridges, when seeing the Rascals coming pretty close up I took to my heels & ran back to the Compy. under a heavy fire which thank God I escaped, as I fortunately did all the rest of the day — in this affair we had the worst of it for want of that support we had reason to expect from the rear, where the 52d Regt. were drawn up but did not move on tho' Colo Campbell says he left orders for them so to do, but it seems in the interim Colo: Mawhood had sent orders fro them to retire or move to the right, however they came down at last together with some others & gave a heavy volley into the wood which cleared it of the Rebels, Colo: Mawhoods division were drawn towards this scene of Action but what they had to do in their thether I can't say — the Rebels being now gone off we got the wounded brot. up to the road taken some care of & put into Waggons. The enemy seeing a disposition to march back showed themselves again in our rear which occasion'd a counter march to oppose them, but on our facing them they retired with firing a few shot, we moved on again, the men much fatigued & harrassed a great many of them quite knock'd up; shortly after we got into the main road the Rebels appear'd in our rear & rear flanks & harrass'd the Grenadrs. that form'd the rear guard very much. we were at last obliged to halt & fire some Cannon amongst them which set them a scampering, as we came near Woodbridge we found a large body of them in a wood posted to oppose us in front. upon discovering them we fired a few pieces of Cannon into the wood and then formed a line in front which moved on to the wood & pour'd in their fire, which made them the Rebels quicken their steps to their right, to which they began to move when this front line moved on to charge them. they fired some scattering shots in going off which did little hurt, we then got into the road again & moved on without further molestation & got into to Amboy between 7 & 8 oclock much fatigued —

Monday 24th. Febry. it came on to snow & blow last night, which it continues still to do very hard, the worst day of wr. we have seen this winter — In the affair of yesterday we have lost 69 killed & wounded & 6 missing, our Compy. has 2 Sergts. 1 Corpl. & 20 wounded & 1 killed, 2 Drrs. missing; went ashore in Eveng. & saw the wounded men several of them in a very dangerous way poor fellows, what pity it is to throw away such men as these on such shabby ill managed occasions. Capt. Gr: & I call'd on Colo McDonald to thank him for his civility & attention to the wounded men of our Compy. Colo: Campbell sent for Capt. Graham to speak to him, to talk over the affair of yesterday & to let him know where the fault lay of our not being supported

Abigail Adams to John Adams

Braintree March 8 1777

We have had very severe weather almost ever since you left us. About the middle of Febry. came a snow of a foot and half deep upon a Level which made it fine going for about 10 day's when a snow storm succeeded with a High wind and banks 5 and 6 feet high. I do not remember to have seen the Roads so obstructed since my remembrance; there has been no passing since except for a Horse.

I Have wrote you 3 Letters since your absence but whether you have ever received one of them I know not. The Post office has been in such a Situation that there has been no confiding in it, but I hear Hazard is come to put it upon a better footing.

We know not what is passing with you nor with the Army, any more than if we lived with the Antipodes. I want a Bird of passage. It has given me great pleasure to find by your Letters which I have received that your Spirits are so Good, and that your Health has not sufferd by your tedious journey. Posterity who are to reap the Blessings, will scarcly be able to conceive the Hardships and Sufferings of their Ancestors. — "But tis a day of suffering says the Author of the Crisis, and we ought to expect it. What we contend for is worthy the affliction we may go through. If we get but Bread to eat and any kind of rayment to put on, we ought not only to be contented, but thankfull. What are the inconveniencies of a few Months or years to the Tributary bondage of ages?" These are Sentiments which do Honour to Humane Nature.

We have the Debates of Parliament by which it appears there are Many who apprehend a War inevitable and foresee the precipice upon which they stand. We have a report Here that Letters are come to Congress from administration, and proposals of a treaty, and some other Stories fit to amuse children, but Experienced Birds are not to be caught with chaff. What is said of the english nation by Hume in the Reign of Harry the 8th may very aptly be applied to them now, that they are so thoroughly subdued that like Eastern Slaves they are inclined to admire even those acts of tyranny and violence which are exercised over themselves at their own expence.

Thus far I wrote when I received a Letter dated Febry. 10, favourd by —— but it was a mistake it was not favourd by any body, and not being frank'd cost me a Dollar. The Man who deliverd it to my unkle brought him a Letter at the same time for which he paid the same price. If it had containd half as much as I wanted to know I would not have grumbld, but you do not tell me How you do, nor what accommodations you have, which is of more consequence to me than all the discriptions of cities, states and kingdoms in the world. I wish the Men of War better imployd than in taking flower vessels since it creates a Temporary famine Here, if I would give a Guiney for a pound of flower I dont think I could purchase it. There is such a Cry for Bread in the Town of Boston as I suppose was never before Heard, and the Bakers deal out but a loaf a day to the largest families. There is such a demand for Indian and Rye, that a Scarcity will soon take place in the Country. Tis now next to imposible to purchase a Bushel of Rye. In short since the late act there is very little selling. The meat that is carried to market is miserabley poor, and so little of it that many people say they were as well supplied in the Seige.

I am asshamed of my Country men. The Merchant and farmer are both alike. Some there are who have virtue enough to adhere to it, but more who evade it.

John Burgoyne: Proclamation

By JOHN BURGOYNE, Esq; &c. &c. Lieut. General of his
Majesty's Forces in America, Colonel of the Queen's
Regiment of Light Dragoons, Governor of Fort-William,
in North-Britain, one of the Representatives of the
Commons of Great-Britain in Parliament, and com-
manding an Army and Fleet in an Expedition from
Canada, &c. &c. &c.

THE Forces entrusted to my Command are designed to act
in concert, and upon a common Principle, with the numerous
Armies and Fleets which already display, in every Quarter of
America, the Power, the Justice, and, when properly sought,
the Mercy of the King; the Cause in which the British Arms
are thus exerted, applies to the most affecting Interest of the
human Heart: And the Military Servants of the Crown, at
first called for the sole Purpose of restoring the Rights of the
Constitution, now combine with the Love of their Country,
and Duty to their Sovereign, the other extensive Incitements,
which spring from a due Sense of the general Privileges of
Mankind. To the Eyes and Ears of the temperate Part of the
Public, and to the Breasts of suffering Thousands in the
Provinces, be the melancholy Appeal — Whether the present
unnatural Rebellion, has not been made the Foundation of
the compleatest System of Tyranny that ever GOD, in his
Displeasure, suffered for a Time, to be exercised over a
froward and stubborn Generation: Arbitrary Imprisonments,
Confiscation of Property, Persecution and Torture, unprecedented in the Inquisitions of the Romish Church, are among
the palpable Enormities that verify the Affirmative: These are
inflicted by Assemblies and Committees, who dare to profess
themselves Friends to Liberty, upon the most quiet Subject,
without Distinction of Age or Sex, for the sole Crime, often
from the sole Suspicion, of having adhered in Principle to the
Government under which they were born, and to which, by

every Tie divine and human, they owe Allegiance. To consummate these shocking Proceedings the Profanation of Religion is added to the most profligate Prostitution of common Reason! The Consciences of Men are set at naught, and Multitudes are compelled not only to bear Arms, but also to swear Subjection to an Usurpation they abhor. — Animated by these Considerations, at the Head of Troops in the full Powers of Health, Discipline and Valour, determined to strike where necessary, and anxious to save where possible, I, by these Presents, invite and exhort all Persons, in all Places where the Progress of this Army may point, and by the Blessing of God I will extend it FAR, to maintain such a Conduct as may justify me in protecting their Lands, Habitations, and Families. The Intention of this Address is to hold forth Security, not Depredation, to the Country; to those whose Spirit and Principle may induce them to partake the glorious Task of redeeming their Countrymen from Dungeons, and re-establishing the Blessings of legal Government, I offer Encouragement and Employment, and upon the first Intelligence of their Association, I will find Means to assist their Undertakings. — The domestic, the industrious, the infirm, and even the timid Inhabitants, I am desirous to protect, provided they remain quietly at their Houses; that they do not suffer their Cattle to be removed, or their Corn or Forage to be secreted or destroyed; that they do not break up their Bridges or Roads, or by any other Act, directly or indirectly, endeavour to obstruct the Operation of the King's Troops, or supply or assist those of the Enemy. Every Species of Provision brought to my Camp, will be paid for at an equitable Rate, in solid Coin. — In Consciousness of Christianity, my Royal Master's Clemency, and the Honour of Soldiership, I have dwelt upon this Invitation, and wished for more persuasive Terms to give it Impression; and let not People be led to disregard it by considering the immediate Situation of my Camp. I have but to give Stretch to the Indian Forces under my Direction, and they amount to Thousands, to overtake the hardened Enemies of Great-Britain; I consider them the same wherever they may lurk. —If notwithstanding these Endeavours and sincere Inclination to assist them, the Phrenzy of Hostility should remain, I trust I shall stand ac-

quitted in the Eyes of God and Men, in denouncing and ex-
ecuting the Vengeance of the State against the wilful Outcast.
The Messengers of Justice and of Wrath await them in the
Field, and Devastation, Famine, and every concomitant
Horror that a reluctant but indispensible Prosecution of
Military Duty must occasion, will bar the Way to their
Return.

J. Burgoyne.

Camp at the River Bongrett, June 23d, 1777.
By Order of his Excellency the Lieutenant General,
    Robert Kingston, Sec'ry.

William Digby:
Journal, July 24–October 13, 1777

July 24th. We marched from Skeensborough, and tho but 15 miles to Fort Anne, were two days going it; as the enemy had felled large trees over the river, which there turned so narrow, as not to allow more than one battow abreast, from whence we were obliged to cut a road through the wood, which was attended with great fatigue and labour, for our wagons and artillery. Our heavy cannon went over Lake George, as it was impossible to bring them over the road we made, and were to join us near Fort Edward, in case the Enemy were to stand us at that place, it being a good road for cannon and about 16 miles. — Fort Anne is a place of no great strength, having only a block house, which though strong against small arms is not proof against cannon. We saw many of their dead unburied, since the action of the 8th, which caused a violent stench. One officer of the 9th regiment, Lieut Westrop was then unburied, and from the smell we could only cover him with leaves. At that action, the 9th took their colours, which were intended as a present to their Colonel Lord Ligonier, They were very handsome, a flag of the United States, 13 stripes alternate red and white, with thirteen stars in a blue field representing a new constellation. In the evening, our Indians brought in two scalps, one of them an officer's which they danced about in their usual manner. Indeed, the cruelties committed by them, were too shocking to relate, particularly the melancholy catastrophe of the unfortunate Miss McCrea, which affected the general and the whole army with the sincerest regret and concern for her untimely fate. This young lady was about 18, had a pleasing person, her family were loyal to the King, and she engaged to be married to a provincial officer, in our Army, before the war broke out. Our Indians, (I may well now call them Savages) were detached on scouting parties, both in our front and on our flanks, and came to the house where she resided; but the scene is too tragic for my pen. She fell a sacrifice to the savage passions of these blood thirsty monsters, for the particulars of which, I shall refer the reader to General Burgoyne's letter, dated 3rd September, to General Gates, which he will find on page 316, with his manner of acting on that melancholy occasion. I make no doubt, but the censorious world, who seldom judge but by outward appearances, will be apt to censure Gen Burgoyne for the cruelties committed by his Indians, and imagine he countenanced them in so acting. On the contrary, I am pretty certain it was always against his desire to give any assistance to the savages. The orders from Lord George Germaine to General Carlton, on Lieutenant General Burgoyne's taking the command of the Army were as follows. "As this plan cannot be advantageously executed without the assistance of Canadians and Indians, his majesty strongly recommends it to your care, to furnish him with good and sufficient bodies of these men, and I am happy in knowing that your influence among them is so great, that there can be no room to apprehend you will find it difficult to fulfill his majesty's intentions." General Burgoyne, afterwards says in parliament: "As to the Indian alliance, he had always at best considered it as a necessary evil. He determined to go to the soldiers of the State, not the executioners. He had been obliged to run a race with the congress in securing the alliance of the Indians. They courted and tempted them with presents, as well as the British. He had in more instances than one controled the Indians &c."

28th.   We marched from Fort Anne, but could only proceed about 6 miles, the road being broke up by the enemy and large trees felled across it, taking up a long time to remove them for our 6 pounders, which were the heavyest guns with us. We halted at night on an eminence, and were greatly distressed for water, no river being near, and a report that the enemy had poisoned a spring at a small distance; but it was false, as our surgion tried an experiment on the water and found it good.

29th.   Moved about 6 or 7 miles farther, and had the same trouble of clearing the road, as the day before. We encamped within a mile of Fort Edward, on the banks of the Hudson river. It was a very good post, and we expected it would have been disputed. There, the road from Fort George then in our possession joined us, and being in possession of that post secured our heavy guns &c coming from Fort George. It was supposed we should not go much farther without them. Our tents were pitched in a large field of as fine wheat as I ever saw, which in a few minutes was all trampled down. Such must ever be the wretched situation of a Country, the seat of war. The potatoes were scarce fit to dig up, yet were torn out of the ground without thinking in the least of the owner.

30th.   We moved on farther to a rising ground about a mile south of Fort Edward, and encamped on a beautiful situation from whence you saw the most romantic prospect of the Hudson's river; intersperced with many small islands, and the encampment of the line about 2 miles in our rear. There is a fine plain about the Fort, which appeared doubly pleasing to us, who were so long before buried in woods. On the whole, the country thereabout wore a very different appearance from any we had seen since our leaving Canada, and from that Fort to Albany, about 46 miles, the land improves much, and no doubt in a little time will be thickly settled. The enemy were then encamped about 4 miles from us; but it was not thought they intended to make a stand. At this time a letter appeared addressed to General Burgoyne, I believe found nailed to a tree. There was no name signed, yet it was thought — (how true heaven only knows) — to be wrote by brigadier general Arnold, who opposed our fleet the preceding year on Lake Champlain, and was then second in command under General Gates. He first tells him, not to be too much elated on his rapid progress, as all he had as yet gained was an uncultivated desert, and concludes his letter by desiring him to beware of crossing the Hudson's river, making use of that memorable saying, "Thus far shalt thou go and no farther." We heard by some intelligence from the enemy's camp, that Genls St Clair & Schyler were ordered before a committee of their congress, to account for their reasons of evacuating Ticonderoga. As yet, the fickle Goddess Fortune had smiled upon our arms, and crowned our wishes with every kind of success, which might easyly be seen from the great spirits the Army in general were in; and the most sanguine hopes of conquest, victory &c. &c. were formed of crowning the campaign with, from the general down to the private soldier; but alas! this life is a constant rotation of changes; and the man, who forms the smallest hopes, has generally the greatest chance of happiness. In the evening, our Indians had a skirmish with an advance party of the enemy. It was a heavy fire for about half an hour, when the latter fled with loss. During our stay there, many of the country people came to us for protection. Those are styled by the enemy torys, and greatly persecuted if taken after fighting against them.

August 9th. We moved on to Fort Miller 9 miles nearer Albany, and which the enemy evacuated some days before. What I could see and learn is, that few of the forts situated on the Hudson River in that part, are proof against cannon; they being built during the last war in order to defend stores and amunition from the inroads of the Indians, who frequently came down in large numbers, plundering and scalping our first settlers residing contiguous to that river, and were full sufficient to withstand any attack made with small arms. I then heard the very disagreeable news of our regiment (53d) being ordered back to garrison Ticonderoga and Fort George. I was much concerned at it, as in all probability I should not see them again during the war, which must be attended with many inconveniences; but as it was their tour of duty, there was no putting it over tho ever so disagreeable, which it certainly was to every officer in the regiment. We had many sick at this time of fevers & agues so common to the climate. Cap. Wight, to whose company I belonged, was so ill as not to be able to go on with us, and many other officers were seized with those disorders, as the heats then were very severe and violent, particularly in a camp. All sorts of meat were tainted in a very short time, and the stench very prejudicial, and cleanlyness about our camp was a great consideration towards the health of the army. I there received a letter from an officer of ours, who had been wounded at Hubberton, 7th July, in which he informed me that before they were removed to Ticonderoga, the wolves came down in numbers from the mountains to devour the dead, and even some that were in a kind of manner buried, they tore out of the earth; the great stench thro the country being the cause of their coming down, and was enough to have caused a plague. —

10. An express came thro the woods from Genl Clinton, who was supposed to be coming up the river from New York, but did not hear what it contained. Our heavy guns were then shortly expected from Fort George, as moving them was very tedious; a 24 pounder taking many horses to draw it. We had a carrying place to bring over our battows, which was attended with great fatigue and trouble, and were also obliged to make rafts or scows to convey heavy stores &c down the river Hudson. About this time, Cornet Grant of Genl Burgoyne's regm't of Light Dragoons, the 16th, made an unsuccessful attempt to go express to Gen Clinton, and was obliged to return thro the woods, running many risques of falling into their hands, to the very great dissatisfaction of Gen Burgoyne.

11th. A large detachment of German troops consisting of Gen Reidzels dragoons who came dismounted from Germany, a body of Rangers, Indians & voluntiers, with 4 pieces of cannon, went from our camp on a secret expedition; their route was not publicly known, but supposed for to take a large store of provisions belonging to the enemy at Bennington, and also horses to mount the dragoons. During the night there was a most violent storm of Thunder, Lightening, wind & rain. It succeeded a very hot day, and was so severe that the men could not remain in their tents, as the rain poured quite through them. Ours stood it better; our horses tore down the small sheds formed to keep the heat of the sun from them, being so much frightened. About day break it cleared up, and a great heat followed, which soon dried all our cloths &c.

13th. We moved 3 miles and encamped at a post called Batten Kill, a strong situation bordering on the river Hudson, intended for the army to cross over. Our corps crossed the river with a good deal of trouble, and encamped about 2 miles west of it. The troops crossed in battows, which was very tedious, as we had but few. About a mile below, the horses and baggage forded it with some difficulty, the water being high from a great fall of rain, which came on during the preceding night, in consequence of which, the troops were put into barracs built there for 1000 men by Gen Schyler. His house was a small way in our front, and the best we had as yet seen in that part, and much superior to many gentleman's houses in Canada. It was intended we should move the next day to an eminence a little distance, which was reckoned a good post, and where there was plenty of forage for the army.

16th.   Our orders for marching were countermanded and others given out for us, to move at 3 o'clock next morning. As I was upon no particular duty, I rode back to the line, who, with Gen Burgoyne were at Fort Miller, and in the evening returned to our camp, crossing over our new bridge of boats, which was almost then finished. At night I mounted an advanced picquet, and had orders to return to camp next morning at Revally Beating, day break. Nothing extraordinary passed during the night, every thing quiet about our post, and on going to return in the morning received orders, — the 17th — to remain, as the corps was not to move that day, and to keep a very sharp look out; on which we naturally supposed something extraordinary had happened. Soon after an engineer came out to us with a number of men to throw up a breast work. Still it looked suspicious; but we were soon made acquainted with the melancholy report, that the detachment, which marched from us on the 11th were all cut to pieces by the enemy at Bennington, their force being much superior. Our 4 pieces of cannon were taken, two 6 pounders & two 3 pounders. I fear the officer who commanded, a German, took post in a bad situation, and was surrounded by the enemy after expending all his amunition. Our Albany voluntiers behaved with great bravery; but were not seconded by the Germans and Savages; and it was much regretted British were not sent in their place. The express also informed us that the enemy was greatly elated in consequence of the above, and were upon the move; but where he could not tell. Our situation was not the best, as from the great fall of rain our bridge was near giving way by the flood, which almost totally cut off our communication with Genl Burgoyne and the line. Our post was also far from a good one, being surrounded and commanded by hills around — Gen Frazier not intending to remain there above a night or two. About 4 in the evening our picquet was relieved by Lord Balcarres and the Battallion of light Infantry, who were to lie on their arms there during

the night. Our orders were, to be in readiness to recross the
river next morning at day break, and during the night, to remain accoutred and ready to turn out at a moments warning.
The rain still continued.

18.   Our bridge was carried down by the water, and to
complete all, the ford where our horses crossed over the 15th
was impassable — The river being swelled so much. We had a
few battows and a large scow for our cannon; so began to
cross; but it was a most tedious piece of work, and late at
night before every thing was over — when we lay on our
arms — not as yet being exact as to the motions of the enemy.

19.   We encamped on our former strong post Batten Kill.
On this occasion, the Indians in Congress with Mr Luc at
their head, with an old Frenchman, who had long resided
amongst them, declared their intention of returning to their
respective homes, their interpreter informing the general
(speaking figuratively in the Indian manner) that on their first
joining his army, the sun arose bright, and in its full glory;
that the sky was clear and serene, foreboding conquest and
victory; but that then, that great Luminary was surrounded
and almost obscured from the sight by dark and gloomy
clouds, which threatened by their bursting to involve all nature in a general wreck and confusion. This the general (tho
in his heart he despised them for their fears and might have
sentenced Mr Luc by a general Court Martial to an ignominious death for desertion) yet parted with them seemingly
without showing his dislike, fearing, perhaps, their going over
to the enemy. On which some companies of rangers were ordered to be raised in their place. At this time, many of the inhabitants, who before came into our camp for protection,
calling themselves Torys, went from us over to the enemy,
who we hoped soon to make pay dear for their late success at
Bennington. It is scarce to be conceived the many difficulties
we had to encounter in carrying on a war in such a country,
from the tediousness of removing provisions stores &c, and
the smallness of our numbers were much diminished by sending parties back and forward from fort George to our camp.

22nd.   A few Germans deserted, one of whom was taken
and suffered death. Various were the reports then circulating
thro our camp, not of the most pleasing kind, which might

easily be perceived on the faces of some of our great men, who I believe began to think our affairs had not taken so fortunate a turn as might have been expected; as to my opinion, it was of very little consequence compared to so many abler judges; certain it was, as an Indian express arrived —

28th — to our camp, that Col. St Leger was obliged to retire with his small army to Oswego, in his return towards Canada; but I forgot, I should first have mentioned the nature and cause of his expedition. Lieut Col St Leger, 34th regmt, left Canada about the time we did, with a command of near 700 regulars; viz 100 men from the 8th regmt; 100 from the 34th regmt; Sir John Johnston's regmt of New York, 133; and the Hannau Chasseurs, 342, with a body of Canadians and Indians and some small pieces of Cannon. He was to go by Lake Ontario, and to come down the Mohock river on the Back settlements to take fort Stanwix &c, and to join us at Albany. This was the plan settled by Lord George Germain, as you will see in his letter to Gen Carlton, dated Whitehall March 6th 1777; but why that expedition miscarryed I cannot pretend to say; as the conduct of Col. St Leger by common report, which was all I could depend upon, did him every kind of injustice in the plan concerted by him for carrying his orders into execution. Our accounts also from Genl Howe, or rather our hearing nothing about his proceedings to the Southward, was another cause of disappointment, as it was but natural to suppose, that had he done nothing very great with so large a body of troops under his command — said to be near 40,000 — we could not easyly penetrate into the enemy's country with one eighth of that number; so that upon mature deliberation, and agreeable to the general's express orders, it was determined by him to drop all sorts of communication with Canada — the Army being too small to afford parties at the different posts between us, and Ticonderoga — and by forcing his way by the greatest exertion possible, fight for the wished for junction with the Southern army; and also to remain on our present ground till provisions stores &c were all up previous to so material a movement. In my opinion, this attempt showed a glorious spirit in our General, and worthy alone to be undertaken by British Troops, as the eyes of all Europe, as well as Great

Britain were fixed upon us; tho some disatisfied persons with us did not scruple to give it the appellation of *rashness*, and were of opinion, that we should have remained at Fort Edward entrenched, until we heard Genl Clinton was come up near Albany; and then pushed on to co operate with him. Our great design & wish then was to draw on a general engagement, which we hoped would be decisive, as by their unbounded extent of country they might, by avoiding it, protract the war.

September 2nd.   Went out with a large forraging party, as was the custom every morning, and marched 9 miles towards the enemy before we could procure any; it then turning very scarce from our remaining so long on that post. We halted at an exceeding good house near the road, which was deserted by its master and family on our approach. The furniture was good, and which I might have appropriated to what use I pleased. About 3 o'clock we returned to our camp with some hay, not without some odd thoughts on the fortune of war, which levels all distinctions of property, and which our present situation pictured strongly.

4th.   A drummer, who went from our camp as a flag of truce to Genl Gates, returned, and the following letters which passed from Gen Gates to Genl Burgoyne, with his answers and Gates' account of the Bennington affair to their congress, I shall here insert for the amusement of the reader —

To the honourable, the continental congress.

Your excellencies will perceive by the inclosed letters, that the glorious victory at Bennington has reduced the boasting stile of Gen Burgoyne so much, that he begins in some degree to think and talk like other men.

HEAD QUARTERS OF THE KING'S ARMY
UPON HUDSON RIVER *August 30 1777.*

SIR. — Major Genl Reidzel has requested me to transmit the inclosed to Lieut Coll Baum, whom the fortune of war put into the hands of your troops at Bennington. Having never failed in my attention towards prisoners, I cannot entertain a doubt of your taking this opportunity to show me a return of civility; and that you will permit the baggage and servants of such officers, your prisoners, as desire it, to pass to them unmolested. It is with great concern, I find myself obliged to add to this application a complaint of the bad treatment the provincial soldiers in the king's service received after the affair at Bennington. I have reports upon oath that some were refused quarter after having asked it. I am willing to believe this was against the order and inclination of your officers; but it is my part to require an explanation, and to warn you of the horrors of retaliation, if such a practice is not in the strongest terms discountenanced. Duty and principle, Sir; make me a public enemy to the Americans, who have taken arms, but I seek to be a generous one, nor have I the shadow of resentment against any individual, who does not induce it by acts derogatory to those maxims upon which all men of honor think alike. Persuaded that a Gentleman of the station to which this lettter is addressed will not be comprised in the exception I have made — I am personally, Sir,

Your most humble servant,

JNo BURGOYNE.

HEAD QUARTERS OF THE ARMY OF THE
UNITED STATES *Sep. 2nd.*

SIR. Last night I had the honour of receiving your excellency's letter of the 30th August. I am astonished you should mention inhumanity, or threaten retaliation. Nothing happened in the action of Bennington, but what is common when works are carried by Assault. That the savages of America should in their warfare mangle and scalp the unhappy prisoners, who fall into their hands, is neither new nor extraordinary; but that the famous Lieut General Burgoyne, in whom the fine gentleman is united with the soldier and the scholar, should hire the savages of America to scalp Europeans and the descendants of Europeans; nay more, that he should pay a price for each scalp so barbarously taken, is more than will be believed in England until authenticated facts shall in every gazette convince mankind of the truth of this horrid tale. — Miss McCrea, a young lady lovely to the sight, of virtuous character and amiable disposition, engaged to be married to an officer in your army, was with other women and children taken out of a house near Fort Edward, carried into the woods, and there scalped and mangled in the most shocking manner. Two parents with their six children, were all treated with the same inhumanity while quietly residing in their once happy and peaceful dwelling. The miserable fate of Miss McCrea was partly aggravated by her being dressed to receive her promised husband; but met her murderers employed by you. Upwards of one hundred men, women and children have perished by the hands of these ruffians, to whom it is asserted, you have paid the price of blood. Inclosed are letters from your wounded officers, prisoners in my hands, by whom you will be informed of the generosity of their Conquerers. Such cloathing, necessaries, attendants &c. which your excellency pleases to send to the prisoners shall be carefully delivered. I am, sir, your most

Humble servant
H. GATES.

Sir. I received your letter of the 2d inst, and in consequence of your complying with my proposal, have sent the baggage, servants &c of those officers, who are prisoners in your hands. I have hesitated, sir, upon answering the other paragraphs of your letter. I disdain to justify myself against the rhapsodies of fiction, and calumny, which from the first of this contest, it has been an unvaried American policy to propagate; but which no longer impose upon the world. I am induced to deviate from this rule in the present instance, lest my silence should be construed an acknowledgement of the truth of your allegation, and a pretence be thence taken for exercising future barbarities by the American troops. Upon this motive, and upon this alone, I condescend to inform you, that I would not be conscious of the acts, you presume to impute to me, for the whole continent of America, tho. the wealth of worlds were in its bowels and a paradise on its surface. It has happened, that all my transactions with the Indian nations last year and this, have been open, clearly heard, distinctly understood and accurately minuted by very numerous, and in many parts, very prejudiced audiences. So diametrically opposite to truth is your assertion that I have paid a price for scalps, that one of the first regulations established by me at the great Council in May, and repeated and enforced, and invariably adhered to since, was that the Indians should receive compensation for prisoners, because it would prevent cruelty, and that not only such compensations should be witheld, but a strict account demanded for scalps. These pledges of Conquest — for such you well know they will ever esteem them — were solemnly and peremptorily prohibited to be taken from the wounded and even the dying, and the persons of aged men, women and children, and prisoners were pronounced sacred even, in assaults. — Respecting Miss McCrea; her fall wanted not the tragic display you have laboured to give it, to make it as sincerely abhorred and lamented by me, as it can possibly be by the tenderest of her friends. The fact was no premeditated barbarity, on the contrary, two chiefs who had brought her off for the purpose of security, not of violence to her person, disputed who should be her guard, and in a fit of savage passion in the one from whose hands she was snatched, the unhappy woman became the victim. Upon the first intelligence of the events, I obliged the Indians to deliver the murderer into my hands, and tho to have punished him by our laws and principles of justice would have been perhaps unprecedented, he certainly should have suffered an ignominious death, had I not been convinced, by circumstances and observation beyond the possibility of a doubt, that a pardon under the terms I prescribed and they accepted, would be more efficatious than an execution to prevent similar mischiefs. The above instance excepted, your intelligence respecting cruelties of the Indians is absolutely false. You seem to threaten me with European publications, which affect me as little as any other threats you could make, but in regard to American publications, whether the charge against me, (which I acquit you of believing), was pencilled from a gazette or for a gazette, I desire and demand of you, as a man of honour, that should it appear in print at all, this answer may follow it. I am Sir,

Your humble servant,
JNo. BURGOYNE.

6th. We were pretty credibly informed by accounts which came from the enemy, and were depended upon, that in the action near Bennington, 16th August, we had killed, wounded, prisoners and missing—including wounded in our hospitals, who escaped—near 1000 men. It was then expected we should shortly move, as the magazines of provisions and other stores were mostly up, and our new bridge over the Hudson river was near finished. Our removal from that post was also very necessary, in respect of procuring forage, which began then to turn very scarce; indeed, I wonder we did so well, as it was amazing the great quantity of hay, Indian corn &c we were obliged to provide for so great a number of cattle. Potatoes and all other vegetables were long before consumed, and very few fresh provisions to be got then. A few of our wounded officers and men from the hospitals of Ticonderoga joined the army; also captain Wight and others, who suffered from fever and such disorders, came up. The weather then began to turn cold in the mornings and evenings, which was but badly calculated for the light cloathing of the army, most of our winter apparel being sent from Skeensborough to Ticonderoga in July. Many officers had also sent back their tents and markees, of which I was one, and in their place substituted a soldier's tent, which were then cold at nights though a luxury to what we after experienced

10th. About 11 o'clock, an express arrived with intelligence that the enemy were on the move, and had advanced from their camp at Half Moon to Still water, a few miles nearer us, but they might have saved themselves that trouble, as we should soon have been up with them. He also informed us that in consequence of that unfortunate affair at Bennington, they were joined by some thousands of Militia, who in all probability would have remained neuter had we proved successful. From these accounts we threw up more works to protect our camp till ready to move towards them; after which we should be as liable to an attack in our rear as front, and the waiting to secure every store &c against such an attack, caused our being so long on that post

11th. We received orders to be in readiness to cross the Hudson river at a moment's warning; but all that day was a continued fall of heavy rain, which continued till the 13th, when the morning being very fine, the army passed over the Bridge of boats and encamped on the heights of Saratoga. We encamped in three columns in order of Battle. The duty here turned very severe, such numbers being constantly on either guards or picquets; during that day and the next we had many small alarms, as parties of theirs came very near our camp; but a few companies soon sent them off.

15th.   Moved about 3 miles nearer the enemy, and took post on a strong position late in the evening, and had just time to pitch our camp before dark; about 11 at night we received orders to stand to our arms, and about 12 I returned to my tent and lay down to get a little rest, but was soon alarmed by a great noise of fire, and on running out saw Major Ackland's tent and markee all in a blaze, on which I made the greatest haste possible to their assistance, but before I could arrive, Lady Harriot Ackland, who was asleep in the tent when it took fire, had providentially escaped under the back of it; but the major was much burned in trying to save her. What must a woman of her rank, family and fortune feel in her then disagreeable situation; liable to constant alarms and not knowing the moment of an attack; but from her attachment to the major, her ladyship bore everything, with a degree of steadiness, and resolution, that could alone be expected from an experienced veteran.

16th.   A detachment with about 2000 men with 6 pieces of cannon attended Gen Burgoyne on a reconnoitering party towards the enemy. We remained out till near night, and fired our evening gun at sun set to make them imagine we had taken post so much nearer them; and afterwards returned to our camp with the gun. We heard Gen Gates had been there the preceding day attended by a corps of riflemen. It was then pretty certain and generally believed, and indeed wished for, that we should shortly have a decisive engagement, — I say wished for, as they never would allow us to go into winter quarters, till we had gained some great advantage over them; should that be the case, many of the country people would join us, but not till then — they choosing to be on the strongest side.

17th.   The whole moved about 9 in the morning, and tho we were marching till near night, we came but 3 miles nearer them — we going a great circuit thro thick woods, for such is all that country — in order to keep possession of the heights, we lay on our arms not having light or time to pitch our tents.

18th.   About 11 in the morning, we heard the report of small arms at a small distance. It was a party of the enemy, who surprised some unarmed men foraging not far from our camp. They killed & wounded 13, and then retreated on our sending a party to oppose them; and during that day and night we were very watchful and remained under arms.

19th.   At day break intelligence was received, that Colonel Morgan, with the advance party of the enemy, consisting of a corps of rifle men, were strong about 3 miles from us; their main body amounting to great numbers encamped on a very strong post about half a mile in their rear; and about 9 o'clock we began our march, every man prepared with 60 rounds of cartridge and ready for instant action. We moved in 3 colums, ours to the right on the heights and farthest from the river in thick woods. A little after 12 our advanced pic-quets came up with Colonel Morgan and engaged, but from the great superiority of fire received from him — his numbers being much greater — they were obliged to fall back, every officer being either killed or wounded except one, when the line came up to their support and obliged Morgan in his turn to retreat with loss. About half past one, the fire seemed to slacken a little; but it was only to come on with double force, as between 2 & 3 the action became general on their side. From the situation of the ground, and their being perfectly acquainted with it, the whole of our troops could not be brought to engage together, which was a very material disad-vantage, though everything possible was tried to remedy that inconvenience, but to no effect, such an explosion of fire I never had any idea of before, and the heavy artillery joining in concert like great peals of thunder, assisted by the echoes of the woods, almost deafened us with the noise. To an uncon-cerned spectator, it must have had the most awful and glori-ous appearance, the different Battalions moving to relieve each other, some being pressed and almost broke by their su-perior numbers. This crash of cannon and musketry never ceased till darkness parted us, when they retired to their camp, leaving us masters of the field; but it was a dear bought victory if I can give it that name, as we lost many brave men, The 62nd had scarce 10 men a company left, and other regi-ments suffered much, and no very great advantage, honor excepted, was gained by the day. On its turning dusk we were near firing on a body of our Germans, mistaking their dark clothing for that of the enemy. General Burgoyne was every where and did every thing that could be expected from a brave officer, & Brig gen. Frazier gained great honour by exposing himself to every danger. During the night we remained in our ranks, and tho we heard the groans of our wounded and dying at a small distance, yet could not assist them till morning, not knowing the position of the enemy, and expecting the action would be renewed at day break. Sleep was a stranger to us, but we were all in good spirits and ready to obey with cheerfulness any orders the general might issue before morning dawned.

20th.   At day break we sent out parties to bring in our wounded, and lit fires as we were almost froze with cold, and our wounded who lived till the morning must have severely felt it. We scarce knew how the rest of our army had fared the preceding day, nor had we tasted victuals or even water for some time before; so sent parties for each. At 11 o'clock, some of our advanced sentrys were fired upon by their rifle men, and we thought it the prelude to another action; but they were soon silenced. It was Gen Phillips and Fraziers opinion we should follow the stroke by attacking their camp that morning; and it is believed, as affairs after turned out, it would have been better for the army to have done so; why it was not attended, to I am not a judge; tho I believe Gen Burgoyne had material objections to it, particularly our hospitals being so full and the magazines not properly secured to risque that movement. About 12 the general reconnoitered our post and contracted the extent of ground we then covered to a more secure one nearer the river, which we took up in the evening — our left flank near the Hudson river to guard our battows and stores, and our right extending near two miles to heights west of the river, with strong ravines, both in our front and rear, the former nearly within cannon shot of the enemy. On our taking up this ground, we buried numbers of their dead. Their loss must have been considerable, as the fire was very severe. Contiguous to our ground was a fine field of Indian corn, which greatly served our horses, who had but little care taken of them the last 2 days, and many were

killed the 19th. At night, half stood to their arms, and so relieved each other, in which time of watch we could distinctly
hear them in the wood between us felling trees; from which
we supposed they were fortifying their camp, which by all accounts, and the situation of the country, we had reason to believe was very strong.

21st. Their morning gun, from its report, seemed almost as
near as our own, and soon after we heard them beating their
drums frequently for orders. At 12 we heard them huzzaing in
their camp, after which they fired 13 heavy guns, which we
imagined might be signals for an attack; and which would be
the most fortunate event that we could have wished, our position being so very advantageous. Soon after we found it was
a Feu-de-joy, but for what cause we could not tell, In the
evening, an express was sent thro the woods to Gen Clinton,
informing him that if he could not advance nearer to Albany,
by which movement many troops then opposing us would be
drawn off to stop his progress, we should be obliged to return
to Ticonderoga by 12th October at farthest, as our provisions
would not allow of our remaining there beyond that period.
At 6 in the evening we encamped. It rained very heavy, and
the general often expressed his desire that the men would take
some rest — being greatly harassed after their great fatigue —
to make them the better able to bear what might follow. The
night was constant rain, and we lay accoutred in our tents

22nd. Formed a bridge of boats across the Hudson, on
the left flank of our line. A spy from the enemy was taken
near our camp, and we had reason to suppose there were
many others around. He informed that they had a report
Gen Burgoyne was killed on the 19th, which must have arose
from Capn Green, one of the aid de camps, being wounded
and falling from his horse near the general. About noon
there was a confused report of Gen Clinton's comeing up the
river, and it must be owned Gen Burgoyne was too ready to
believe any report in our favour. Orders were given for our
cannon to fire 8 rounds at mid night from the park of
Artillery. It was done with a view of causing the enemy to
draw in their out posts expecting an attack, at which time 2
officers in disguise were sent express to Gen Clinton with
messages to the same effect as was sent the 21st. The inten-

tion answered, as they stood to their works all that night which was constant rain.

23rd. It was said we were to strengthen our camp and wait some favourable accounts from Gen Clinton, and accordingly began to fell trees for that purpose. I visited our hospitals, which were much crowded, and attended the Auctions of our deceased officers, which for the time caused a few melancholy ideas, though still confirmed me in believing that the oftener death is placed before our eyes the less terrible it appears. All kinds of supplies and stores from Canada were then entirely cut off, as the communication was dropped, and the variety of reports and opinions circulating were curious and entertaining, as I believe our situation was rather uncommon; it was such at least as few of us had before experienced. Some few thought we should be ordered to retreat suddenly under cover of some dark night, but that was not thought probable, as it would be cruel to leave the great numbers of sick and wounded we had in such a situation; we also were certain our general would try another action before a retreat was thought on. Others said we waited either to receive a reinforcement from Ticonderoga or Gen Clinton, which last might have some weight, but as to the former, we knew there were too few troops there to be able to spare us any. Others again thought when the enemy saw us determined to keep our ground and heard of Gen Clinton's movements, they would draw off part of their great force to oppose him; but that was not thought very probable by their receiving so large reinforcements daily to their camp. On the whole, I believe most people's opinions and suppositions were rather founded on what they wished, than on any certain knowledge of what would happen; time only, that great disposer of all human events, could alone unfold to us what was to come. Our few remaining Indians appeared very shy at going out on any scouting parties, indeed, I always took them for a people, whose very horrid figure had a greater effect on their enemy than any courage they possessed, as their cruel turn often assured me they could not be brave, Humanity & pity for the misfortunes of the wretched, being invariably the constant companions of true courage; theirs is savage and will never steadily look on danger. We there got some news papers of the enemy taken from a deserter, in which there was an account of the 19th, by a Mr. Wilkinson, adjutant genl. to their army, very partially given, saying we retreated the 19th from the field of battle, which was absolutely false as we lay that night on the same ground we fought on, as a proof of which, we buried their dead the morning of the 20th — they not venturing near. He concludes with a poor, low expression, saying, "On the 20th the enemy lay very quietly licking their sores."

24th. At day break they fired on our German picquet and killed 3 men, but this alarm gave us no unnecessary trouble, as we were always under arms an hour before day and remained so till it was completely light. During the night it rained heavy, and on the 26th, many bodies not buried deep enough in the ground appeared, (from the great rain), as the soil was a light sand, and caused a most dreadful smell. We still continued making more works. A report was circulated that Ticonderoga was taken, but not believed. I shall here insert Gen Gates' orders to his troops which we received by a deserter —

HEAD QUARTERS OF THE ARMY OF THE
UNITED STATES *September 26. 1777.*

"The public business having so entirely engaged the attention of the General, that he has not been properly at leisure to return his grateful thanks to Gen. Poors & Gen Learned's Brigades, to the regiment of rifle men, to the corps of light infantry and to Col° Marshall's regiment for their valiant behaviour in the action of the 19th inst, which will for ever establish and confirm the reputation of the arms of the United States; notwithstanding the General has been so late in giving this public mark of honour and applause to the brave men, whose valour has so eminently served their country, he assures them the just praise he immediately gave to the Honorable, the Continental Congress, will remain a lasting record of their honour and renown.

"By the account of the enemy; by their embarrassed circumstances; by the desperate situation of their affairs, it is evident they must endeavour by one rash stroke to regain all they have lost, that failing, their utter ruin is inevitable. The

General therefore intreats his valiant army, that they will, by the exactness of their discipline, by their alertness to fly to their arms on all occasions, and particularly by their caution not to be surprised, secure that victory, which Almighty Providence (if they deserve it) will bless their labour with."

27th. We received the unwelcome news that a letter from Gen Clinton to Gen Burgoyne (it was not an answer to his of the 21st) had fallen into the hands of the enemy. On the express being taken he swallowed a small silver bullet in which the letter was, but being suspected, a severe tartar emetic was given him which brought up the ball. We also heard they were in possession of Skeensboro' and had a post both there and at Hubberton. We also received accounts of their making an attack upon Ticonderoga and taking prisoners part of the 53rd regiment; but this was not properly authenticated. In the evening our few remaining Indians left us.

28th. A large detachment was ordered out to forage for the army, which was greatly wanting, as all our grass was ate up and many horses dying for want. We brought in some hay without any skirmish, which we expected going out.

29th. About day break our picquet was fired on from the wood in front, but the damage was trifling. I suppose seldom two armies remained looking at each other so long without coming to action. A man of theirs in a mistake came into our camp in place of his own, and being challenged by our sentry, after recollecting himself, "I believe," says he, "I am wrong and may as well stay where I am." That he might be pretty certain of.

30th. We had reason to imagine they intended to open a battery on our right; they also fired three morning guns in place of two, which caused us to expect a reinforcement, which was soon confirmed by a deserter who came over to us. That evening 20 Indians joined us from Canada; our horses were put on a smaller allowance

October 2nd. Dispatches were received from Brigadier General Powell, who commanded at Ticonderoga with his account of their attempt on that place, and being at length repulsed with loss they retreated over the mountains.

3rd. Dispatches from Ticonderoga were taken by the enemy coming thro the woods directed by an Indian.

4th. Our picquet was fired upon near day break, but as our own posts were strong, and we all slept with our clothes on; it was but little minded. Here the army were put on a short allowance of provisions, which shewed us the general was determined to wait the arrival of general Clinton, (if possible), and to this the troops submitted with the utmost cheerfulness.

5th. A small party of our sailors were taken by the enemy, also about 20 horses, that strayed near their lines. The weather continued fair and dry since 26th September.

6th. I went out on a large forage for the army, and took some hay near their camp. On our return we heard a heavy fire and made all the haste possible with the forage. It was occasioned by some of our ranger's falling in with a party of theirs; our loss was trifling. At night we fired a rocket from one of our cannon at 12 o'clock, the reason I could never hear for doing so. In general it is a signal between two armies at a small distance, but that could not have been our case. During the night there were small alarms and frequent popping shots, fired by sentrys from our different outposts.

7th. Expresses were received from Ticonderoga, but what the purport of them were I could never learn. A detachment of 1500 regular troops with two 12 pounders, two howitzers and six 6 pounders were ordered to move on a secret expedition and to be paraded at 10 o'clock, though I am told, Major Williams (Artillery) objected much to the removal of the heavy guns; saying, once a 12 pounder is removed from the Park of artillery in America (meaning in the woods) it was gone. From some delay, the detachment did not move till near one o'clock, and moved from the right of our camp; soon after which, we gained an eminence within half a mile of their camp, where the troops took post; but they were sufficiently prepared for us, as a deserter from our Artillery went over to them that morning and informed them of our design. This I have since heard, and it has often surprised me how the fellow could be so very exact in his intelligence, as were I taken prisoner, I could not (had I ever so great a desire) have informed them so circumstantially. About 3 o'clock, our heavy guns began to play, but the wood around being thick, and their exact knowledge of our small force, caused them to advance in great numbers, pouring in a superiority of fire from Detachments ordered to hang upon our flanks, which they tried if possible to turn. We could not receive a reinforcement as our works, General Hospital Stores, provisions &c would be left defenceless, on which an order was given for us to retreat, but not before we lost many brave men. Brigadier General Frazier was mortally wounded which helped to turn the fate of the day. When General Burgoyne saw him fall, he seemed then to feel in the highest degree our disagreeable situation. He was the only person we could carry off with us. Our cannon were surrounded and taken — the men and horses being all killed — which gave them additional spirits, and they rushed on with loud shouts, when we drove them back a little way with so great loss to ourselves, that it evidently appeared a retreat was the only thing left for us. They still advanced upon our works under a severe fire of grape shot, which in some measure stopped them, by the great execution we saw made among their columns; during which, another body of the enemy stormed the German lines after meeting with a most shameful resistance, and took possession of all their camp and equipage, baggage &c &c, Colo Bremen fell nobly at the head of the Foreigners, and by his death blotted out part of the stain his countrymen so justly merited from that days behaviour. On our retreating, which was pretty regular, considering how hard we were pressed by the enemy, General Burgoyne appeared greatly agitated as the danger to which the lines were exposed was of the most serious nature at that particular period. I should be sorry from my expression of *agitated*, that the reader should imagine the fears of personal danger was the smallest cause of it. He must be more than man, who could undisturbed look on and preserve his natural calmness, when the fate of so many were at stake, and entirely depended on the orders he was to issue. He said but little, well knowing we could defend the lines or fall in the attempt. Darkness interposed, (I believe fortunately for us) which put an end to the action. General Frazier was yet living, but not the least hopes of him. He that night asked if Genl Burgoynes army were not all cut to pieces, and being informed to the contrary, appeared for a moment pleased, but spoke no more. Captn Wight (53 Grenadiers), my captain, was shot in the bowels early in the action. In him I lost a sincere friend. He lay in that situation between the two fires, and I have been since informed lived till the next day and was brought into their camp. Major Ackland was wounded and taken prisoner with our Quarter master General, and Major Williams of the Artillery. Sir Francis Clerk fell, Aid de camp to the general, with other principal officers. Our Grenadier Company out of 20 men going out, left their Captain and 16 men on the field. Some here did not scruple to say, General Burgoyne's manner of acting verified the rash stroke hinted at by General Gates in his orders of the 26th; (see page 324) but that was a harsh and severe insinuation, as I have since heard his intended design was to take post on a rising ground, on the left of their camp, — the 7th — with the detachment, thinking they would not have acted on the offensive, but stood to their works, and on that night our main body was to move, so as to be prepared to storm their lines by day break of the 8th; and it appears by accounts since, that Gen Gates would have acted on the defensive, only for the advice of Brigadier General Arnold, who assured him from his knowledge of the troops, a vigorous sally would inspire them with more courage than waiting behind their works for our attack, and also their knowledge of the woods would contribute to ensure the plan he proposed. During the night we were employed in moving our cannon Baggage &c nearer to the river. It was done with silence, and fires were kept lighted to cause them not to suspect we had retired from our works where it was impossible for us to remain, as the German lines commanded them, and were then in possession of the enemy, who were bringing up cannon to bear on ours at day break. It may easily be supposed we had no thought for sleep, and some time before day we retreated nearer to the river. Our design of retreating to Ticonderoga then became public.

8th.   Took post in a battery which commanded the country around, and the rest of the army surrounding the battery and under cover of our heavy cannon. About 8 in the morning we perceived the enemy marching from their camp in great numbers, blackening the fields with their dark clothing. From the height of the work and by the help of our glasses, we could distinguish them quite plain. They brought some pieces of cannon and attempted to throw up a work for them, but our guns soon demolished what they had executed. Our design was to amuse them during the day with our cannon, which kept them at a proper distance, and at night to make our retreat, but they soon guessed our intentions, and sent a large body of troops in our rear to push for the possession of the heights of Fort Edward. During the day it was entertaining enough, as I had no idea of artillery being so well served as ours was. Sometimes we could see a 12 pounder take place in the centre of their columns, and shells burst among them, thrown from our howitzers with the greatest judgment. Most of their shot were directed at our bridge of boats, as no doubt they imagined we intended to retreat that way; but their guns were badly served. About 11 o'clock general Frazier died, and desired he might be buried in that battery at evening gun firing. So fell the best officer under Burgoyne, who from his earliest years was bred in camps, and from the many engagements he had been in, attained a degree of coolness and steadiness of mind in the hour of danger, that alone distinguishes the truly brave man. At 12 o clock some of their balls fell very near our hospital tents, pitched in the plain, and from their size, supposed to attract their notice, taking them perhaps for the general's quarters, on which we were obliged to move them out of the range of fire, which was a most shocking scene, — some poor wretches dying in the attempt, being so very severely wounded. At sun set general Frazier was buried according to his desire, and general Burgoyne attended the service, which was performed I think in the most solemn manner I ever before saw; perhaps the scene around, big with the fate of many, caused it to appear more so, with their fireing particularly at our battery, during the time of its continuance. About 11 at night, the army began their retreat, General Reidzel commanding the Van guard, and Major General Phillips the rear, and this retreat, though within musket shot of the enemy and encumbered with all the baggage of the army, was made without loss. Our battallion was left to cover the retreat of the whole, which from numberless impediments did not move until near 4 o'clock in the morning of the 9th, and were then much delayed in breaking up the bridges in our rear. This was the second time of their being

destroyed that season — the first by the enemy to prevent our
pursueing them. What a great alteration in affairs! Our hospitals full of sick and wounded were left behind, with a letter
from general Burgoyne to general Gates, in which he tells him
he makes no doubt of his care to the sick and wounded, conscious of his acting in the same manner himself had the fortune of war placed it in his reach. During our march, it
surprised us their not placing troops on the heights we were
obliged to pass under, as by so doing, we must have suffered
much. We came up with the general and the line about 9 in
the morning at Davagot, seven miles from the enemy. It then
began to rain very hard and continued so all day. We halted
till near 3 in the evening, which surprised many; about which
time, a large body of the enemy were perceived on the other
side the river, and supposed to be on their way to Fort
Edward in order to obstruct our crossing at that place, on
which we were immediately ordered to march after burning
all unnecessary baggage, camp equipage and many wagons
and carts, which much delayed our line of march. Here Lady
Harriot Ackland was prevailed to go to the enemy, or I might
rather say, it was her wish to do so, her husband, the major,
being a prisoner. She was conducted to general Gates by a
chaplain, and received, I am informed, by him with the greatest politeness possible; indeed he must have been a brute to
have acted otherwise. We waded the Fish Kiln near Schylers
house, about 8 o'clock that night, — the enemy having destroyed the Bridge some days before — and took post soon after on the heights of Saratoga, where we remained all night
under constant heavy rain, without fires or any kind of shelter
to guard us from the inclemency of the weather. It was impossible to sleep, even had we an inclination to do so, from
the cold and rain, and our only entertainment was the report
of some popping shots heard now and then from the other
side the great river at our Battows.

    10th.   Preparations were made early in the morning to
push for the heights of Fort Edward, and a detachment of artificers we sent under a strong escort to repair the bridges and
open the road to that place. The 47th regiment, Captain
Frazier's marksmen and MacKay's provincials were ordered
for that service; but about 11 o clock, intelligence was received

that the enemy were surrounding us, on which it was resolved to maintain our post, and expresses were sent to recall the 47th regiment &c. We burned Schyler's house to prevent a lodgement being formed behind it, and almost all our remaining baggage, rather than it should fall into their hands. Here again the discontented part of the army were of opinion that our retreat was not conducted so well as it might have been, and that in place of burning our bridge of boats over the Hudson, which we left on fire on our retreating the night of the 8th, from whence it was evident to the enemy which side of the river we intended to keep on, and would oblige us to ford the Hudson opposite to where they had a force; consequently would be attended with a disadvantage. We should have crossed our bridge on the night of the 8th to gain the Fort Edward side of the river, and would have nothing to delay our march — we moving so many hours before they were apprized of our motions. They also declared our halting so long at Davagot, the 9th within 7 miles of the enemy, was the cause of our being surrounded, as even then we had time to have pushed on, and the day being so constant rain was in our favour, as had we attempted to ford the river at Saratoga, the small arms of the enemy, as well as ours must have been so wet, that but few would go off, and they knew our superiority at the bayonet. They also said that even the 10th by spiking our cannon and destroying all our baggage &c a paltry consideration in comparison, in our circumstances — we might have made our retreat good to Fort George, saving the troops and Musquetry: but even then it was not certain that vessels were prepared to convey us over the lake; in which case it would have been a worse post than Saratoga for the army. These were the opinions of unsatisfied and discontented men, who never approved of anything that turned out contrary to their expectations. Had Burgoyne been fortunate, they would not have dared to declare them; as he was unsuccessful, they set him down guilty. However, all thoughts of a retreat were then given over, and a determination made to fall nobly together, rather than disgrace the name of British troops; on which we immediately changed our ground a little, and under the protection of that night, began to entrench ourselves, all hands being ordered to work. We were called together and desired to tell our men that their own safety, as well as ours, depended on their making a vigorous defence; but that I was sure was an unnecessary caution,—well knowing they would never forfeit the title of Soldiers. As for the Germans, we had but a poor opinion of their spirit since the night of the 7th. Certain our situation was not the most pleasing; but we were to make the best of it, and I had long before accustomed and familiarized my mind to bear with patience any change that might happen. The men worked without ceasing during the night, and without the least complaining of fatigue, our cannon were drawn up to the embrasures and pointed ready to receive them at day break.

11th.   Their cannon and ours began to play on each other. They took many of our Battows on the river, as our cannon could not protect them. We were obliged to bring our oxen and horses into our lines, where they had the wretched prospect of living but a few days, as our grass was all gone, and nothing after but the leaves of the trees for them; still they continued fireing into us from Batteries they had erected during the night, and placed their riflemen in the tops of trees; but still did not venture to storm our works. At night we strengthened our works and threw up more.

12th.   Our cattle began to die fast and the stench was very prejudicial in so small a space. A cannon shot was near taking the general, as it lodged quite close to him in a large oak tree. We now began to perceive their design by keeping at such a distance, which was to starve us out. I believe the generals greatest wish, as indeed it ought to be, was for them to attack us, but they acted with much greater prudence, well knowing what a great slaughter we must have made among them: they also knew exactly the state of our provisions, which was sufficient for but 4 or 5 days more, and that upon short allowance. In the evening, many of our Canadian drivers of wagons, carts and other like services, found means to escape from us. At night, I ventured to take a little sleep which had long been a stranger to me, and tho but a short time could be spared between our watches, yet I found myself much refreshed. We were all in pretty good health, though lying in wet trenches newly dug must be very prejudicial to the constitution, and tho it might not affect it for the time, yet rheumatism afterwards would be the certain consequence.

13th.   Their cannon racked our post very much; the bulk of their army was hourly reinforced by militia flocking in to them from all parts, and their situation, which nearly surrounded us, was from the nature of the ground unattackable in all parts; and since the 7th the men lay constantly upon their arms, — Harassed and fatigued beyond measure, from their great want of rest. All night we threw up Traverse to our works, as our lines were enfiladed or flanked by their cannon.

John André:
Journal, August 31–October 4, 1777

31st   Lieutenant-Colonel Bird with 150 men, marched at 4 o'clock this morning to the surprise of a party of Militia said to be at Ellis's Tavern; he was thence to proceed to Middleneck, between the forks of Bohemia River, to drive in cattle. There were no Militia at Ellis's Tavern nor was any one to be seen on the road, but a few affrighted people who probably had not had time to make their escape, and three or four people on horseback, who retired before us and stopped at every rising ground to see if the Troops continued advancing; some had arms, but they did not appear accoutred as Light Dragoons. The Detachment proceeded to Middleneck, crossing two mill-dams, the one upon a branch of Bohemia Creek the other on a rivulet running into the branch. At each of the passes Colonel Bird left a party, and posted a strong detachment between them on the road leading to Warwick. Colonel Bird marched with the remainder to the lower part of the Neck (George's Wharf) from whence a good quantity of cattle was taken. From the want of expertness in the drivers, only 350 sheep, fifty-five horned cattle and about twenty-four horses or mules were brought in. Several people assisted in bringing in their cattle and of their own accord drove it to Camp next day. Some Hessians belonging to a baggage guard demolished a whole flock of sheep which the owners were voluntarily driving to us. Colonel Bird's Detachments returned to Camp at 4 o'clock in the afternoon.

The remainder of General Knyphausen's Command crossed the ferry this morning and encamped with the 3rd Brigade.

Sept. 1st   Great complaints were made of the plunder committed by the Troops — chiefly by the Hessians.

2d   The Corps under General Knyphausen marched to Carson's Tavern, five miles from Cecil Church. Detachments of 100 men each marched to the right and left of the Column, at about half a mile distance to collect cattle. The piquets formed the advanced Guard. A few Rebel Light Dragoons were seen on the road, and two or three Militiamen in arms picked up. At a mill near Carson's, sixty barrels of flour were taken. The inhabitants were in general fled and a great deal of cattle driven off.

3d   General Knyphausen marched to Aikens's Tavern a village four miles from Carson's. The main body of the Army under Sir William Howe had just passed this place and marched towards Iron Hill when General Knyphausen came up. By this time a considerable drove of cattle had been collected and was a very seasonable supply to the other Column, which had none. The whole however, had a very narrow escape, having gone near half a mile on a road leading to the Enemy's posts.

The van of Sir William Howe's Column, consisting, of Chasseurs and Light Infantry, fell in with a body of about 500 Rebels posted a little beyond Aiken's on the road to Iron Hill. They disposed of themselves amongst some trees by the roadside, and gave a heavy fire as our Troops advanced, but upon being pressed ran away and were pursued above two miles. At first retreating they fired from any advantageous spot they passed, but their flight afterwards became so precipitate that great numbers threw down their arms and blankets. Amongst their dead were two or three Officers. A wounded man who was left on the field was found to be quite drunk. It seems the whole had received an extraordinary quantity of strong liquor, and that the detachment was composed of Volunteers and looked upon as a Corps from which great exertions were to be expected. They were commanded by a General Maxwell. The attempts made by our Troops to get round them were defeated by their being unable to pass a swamp. Of the Chasseurs and Light Infantry, the only Troops engaged, three or four were killed and twelve or fourteen wounded.

4th   A grand Guard of Cavalry mounted.

5th   Some men of Ferguson's Corps fired by mistake on a patrole of Light Dragoons and wounded a man and a horse.

6th   A Corps left at the head of Elk under Major-General Grant, joined the main body of the Army with a train of provisions for several days. They were encamped, 1st Brigade in front of the 4th Brigade, and 2d Brigade rear the 40th Regiment. That day the camp equipages, excepting the bell tents, was sent on board the transports at the head of Elk, and from henceforward all communication with the shipping ceased. A Regulation was made by General Grey for the method of hutting for the 3d Brigade.

The general reports concerning Washington's Arms were that they were posted between Brandywine & Christien Creeks; that he had a body of men at Christien Bridge up to which gondolas came, and that Wilmington, which he had in his rear, was fortified and covered by gallies in either Creek

7th　Several deserters came in. They said that Washington had advanced towards Newport, and all insisted that their General was in the intention to stand an action. They rendered this intelligence more to be relied on by quoting part of his Order. The Light Dragoons who deserted from the Rebels sold their horses by auction at a very advanced price.

8th　The Army marched in three Divisions and by the left at daybreak, passing Newark and White Clay Creek they came in a march of about ten miles to the New Garden Road, where they were encamped.

9th　The Army received Orders to be in readiness to march at 1 o'clock in the afternoon in two Columns. The Troops, however, did not move till sunset. The 3d and 4th Brigades were at first in the right-hand Column, but the road being found very bad, were ordered, together with a Brigade of Artillery and the baggage of that Column, to turn back and take the road General Knyphausen had marched. This movement was attended with a great deal of trouble and protracted the march of the Brigade in the rear till near 3 o'clock the next day. It was fortunate we had not an enterprizing well-informed Enemy near us. The line of baggage was produced, by the badness of the road and insufficiency of the horses, to a very great length, and the 4th Brigade, which was in front of it, had by quickening their pace to reach General Knyphausen, gained so much upon the carriages that there was a space of two or three miles between them. It was with some difficulty at a crossroad that it was ascertained which way the front of the Column had passed. General Howe's Column had reached Kennet's Square early in the morning and the whole was encamped there (10 miles).

10th & 11th   The Army marched in two Columns under Lord Cornwallis and General Knyphausen. (Sir William Howe was with the former) and proceeded to the forks of Brandywine, crossed the ford there and by a circuit of about fifteen miles came upon the Enemy's right flank, near Birmingham Meeting House. The latter took the straight road to Chad's Ford, opposite to which the Rebel Army lay.

The design, it seemed was that General Knyphausen, taking Post at Chad's Ford, should begin early to cannonade the Enemy on the opposite side, thereby to take up his attention and make him presume an attack was then intended with the whole Army, whilst the other Column should be performing the *détour*. Lord Cornwallis's wing being engaged was to be the signal for the Troops under General Knyphausen to cross the ford when they were to push their advantage. The event fell little short of the project. General Knyphausen posted himself early in the day on the heights opposite the Rebel Army. This was distributed on all the most advantageous eminences overlooking the ford which lay beneath. On one of these hills they had thrown up a small breastwork with two Guns, one a 12-pounder, and beneath this, flanking the ford and road, another battery of three guns and a howitzer. Felled trees obstructed the passage at other fords near this place. It was not without some opposition that General Knyphausen took up his ground, and whilst he was there a body of 2000 men crossed the river and came upon his right. They were driven back by one or two Regiments.

On the left, Sir William Howe drawing near Birmingham found the Rebels posted on the heights to oppose him. Washington had drawn part of his Army here about two hours before, on receiving the first intimation of General Howe's approach. At about 4 o'clock the attack began near the Meeting House. The Guards were formed upon the right, the British Grenadiers in the Centre, and the Light Infantry and Chasseurs on the left. The Hessian Grenadiers supported

the Guards and British Grenadiers, and the 4th Brigade supported the Light Infantry and the left of the Grenadiers. The
3d Brigade under General Grey was the Reserve. The Guards
met with very little resistance and penetrated to the very
height overlooking the 4-gun battery of the Rebels at Chad's
Ford, just as General Knyphausen had crossed. The Hessian
Grenadiers were to their left and not so far advanced. The
British Grenadiers divided after passing Birmingham Meeting
House, the 1st Battalion inclining to the right and the 2d
pushing about a mile beyond the village of Dilworth. The
Light Infantry and Chasseurs inclined to the left, and by this
means left an interval which was filled up by part of the 4th
Brigade. The Light Infantry met with the chief resistance at a
hill on which the Rebels had four pieces of cannon. At the
end of the day the 2d Battalion Grenadiers received a very
heavy fire; the 64th Regiment, which was near them was engaged at the same time. The Rebels were driven back by the
superior fire of the Troops, but these were too much exhausted to be able to charge or pursue. The Reserve moved
centrically in the rear of the whole and inclined successively to
the parts most engaged.

General Knyphausen, as was preconcerted, passed the ford
upon hearing the other Column engaged, and the Troops
under him pushed the Enemy with Equal Success. Night and
the fatigue the Soldiers had undergone prevented any pursuit. It is remarkable that after reconnoitering after the action, the right of General's Howe's Camp was found close on
General Knyphausen's left, and nearly in a line, and in forming the General Camp next day, scarce any alteration was
made.

We took this day eleven pieces of ordnance, five French
brass guns, three Hessian and three American, viz: a brass 6-
pounder, a howitzer an iron gun of a particular construction.
The ammunition waggons, horses, &c. were likewise taken.

12th   Parties were sent from the different Regiments to
find their wounded in the woods and bury their dead. The
village of Dilworth was fixed upon for the Hospital. General
Grant with the 1st and 2d Brigades and Rangers marched to
Concord (two miles).

13th   Lord Cornwallis with the Light Infantry and Grenadiers marched to Concord and proceeded from thence with General Grant towards Chester. The 15th and 64th Regiments took post at Concord. The 17th Regiment took possession of Wilmington.

14th   The wounded were conveyed to Wilmington, which place was fixed upon for the General Hospital. A great many deserters came in the 12th and 13th. The Rebel Army was said to be at Derby.

15th   Surgeons came from the Rebel Army to attend their wounded. They went with their patients to the Turk's Head (5 miles). Two men, one of the Light Infantry and one of the Grenadiers, were executed at Lord Cornwallis's Camp for plunder.

16th   The Army marched from Brandywine to Goshen. The greatest part of the day it rained excessively hard. The 3rd. Brigade, Battalion of Donop, and Rangers, covered the baggage, which from the badness of the road could not all get up that evening. Some shots were fired on the Column at the Turk's Head five miles from Brandywine, where a soldier of the 33rd Regiment was killed and another wounded; an Officer was likewise slightly wounded.

There was a good deal of firing heard in the direction of Lord Cornwallis's Corps, which was now near the White Horse on the Lancaster Road. The Rebels were said to be within a mile or two of the White Horse. We found that at the time the firing was heard several of the Militia made their appearance and were driven off by the advanced Corps. A few of them were taken prisoners, amongst which were two Officers, and fifteen or twenty killed.

17th   A Colonel and a Major of the Rebels were taken this morning in a house, by a single Light Dragoon.

The Troops received Orders to be ready to march on the shortest notice. At 3 o'clock the Orders were given for marching, but part of the Artillery having taken a wrong road and the night promising rain, the march was deferred till 3 o'clock the next morning. The 1st 3rd Brigades only marched this evening. They joined Lord Cornwallis near the White Horse on the Lancaster Road.

18th   The Army marched to White Horse, and after a short halt proceeded to Trudusfrin on the road to Swedes' Ford on the Schuylkill. On this march we passed over the ground thru' which the Rebels had gone very recently. It should seem that after the affair of Brandywine they had marched to Chester, Derby, Philadelphia and Germantown; that they had re-crossed the Schuylkill at Swedes' Ford, had come to White Horse and from thence had suddenly turned to the right to gain the Schuylkill again near the Yellow Spring, where they crossed it a third time.

19th   The main Army of the Rebels was said to be at Coventry on the Reading Road. A Brigade under a General Wayne was said to be very near us, for the purpose of attacking our Rear on the next march. An order was given for marching the next morning, but was afterward countermanded. Three Companies of Light Infantry, who the preceding day had taken possession of 4000 barrels of flour at Valley Forge, were this day reinforced by the Grenadiers, 1st Battalion Light Infantry, and the Guards. A report prevailed in Camp that Sir William Erskine was taken. It was without any foundation; he returned to Camp from reconnoitering, and brought in 150 horses. Deserters from the Rebels came in daily. Three Artillery men who were straggling this morning fell into the Enemy's hands. In the Store at Valley Forge were taken, besides the 4000 barrels of flour, a great quantity of camp-kettles, axes, horseshoes, nails &c.

20th   Intelligence having been received of the situation of General Wayne and his design of attacking our Rear, a plan was concerted for surprising him, and the execution entrusted to Major General Grey. The troops for this service were the 40th and 55th Regiments, under Colonel Musgrave, and the 2d Battalion Light Infantry, the 42d and 44th Regiments under General Grey. General Grey's Detachment marched at 10 o'clock at night, that under Colonel Musgrave at 11. No soldier of either was suffered to load; those who could not draw their pieces took out the flints. We knew nearly the spot where the Rebel Corps lay, but nothing of the disposition of their Camp. It was represented to the men that firing discovered us to the Enemy, hid them from us, killed our friends and produced a confusion favorable to the escape of the Rebels and perhaps productive of disgrace to ourselves. On the other hand, by not firing we knew the foe to be wherever fire appeared and a charge ensured his destruction; that amongst the Enemy those in the rear would direct their fire against whoever fired in front, and they would destroy each other. General Grey's Detachment marched by the road leading to White Horse, and took every inhabitant with them as they passed along. About three miles from Camp they turned to the left and proceeded to the Admiral Warren, where, having forced intelligence from a Blacksmith, they came in upon the out sentries, piquet and Camp of the Rebels. The sentries fired and ran off to the number of four at different intervals. The piquet was surprised and most of them killed in endeavoring to retreat. On approaching the right of the Camp we perceived the line of fires, and the Light Infantry being ordered to form to the front, rushed along the line putting to the bayonet all they came up with, and, overtaking the main herd of the fugitives, stabbed great numbers and pressed on their rear till it was thought prudent to order them to desist. Near 200 must have been killed, and a great number wounded. Seventy-one Prisoners were brought off; forty of them badly wounded were left at different houses on the road. A Major, a Captain, and two Lieutenants were amongst the prisoners. We lost Captain Wolfe killed and one or two private men; four or five were wounded, one an Officer, Lieut. Hunter of the 52d Light Company

It was about 1 o'clock in the morning when the attack was made, and the Rebels were then assembling to move towards us, with the Design of attacking our baggage.

Colonel Musgrave marched a different way and took post on the Philadelphia Road at the Paoli. It was thought he would have first fallen in with their outposts. By our attacking them on the flank next to Colonel Musgrave's Post, they retired the opposite way and his Detachment saw nothing of them.

A second Brigade had joined Major Wayne the evening before, and 1500 Militia under Smallwood lay at the White Horse. We took eight waggons and teams with flour, biscuit and baggage; their guns we could not overtake. The Detachment returned to Camp by daybreak by the Paoli and the road Colonel Musgrave had marched.

Wayne's Corps consisted of

1st Battalion Pens'a — Chambers		
2d Battalion Pensa' — late DeHaas	Hartley	
7th Battalion Pens'a — Grier		
10th Battalion Pens'a — Hubley		
Hartley's Rovers		Wayne
4th Battalion Pens'a — Butler		
5th Battalion Pens'a — Johnson	Humpton	
8th Battalion Pens'a — Broadhead		
11th Battalion Pens'a — Humpton		

21st The Army marched from Trudusfrin to Valley Forge and was posted in an extent of three miles from Fatland Ford to some distance beyond Moore Hall. Large bodies of the Enemy were seen on the opposite shore; they frequently fired on our Sentries.

22d There was reason to believe the Enemy had quitted the opposite side of the river. In the evening the Guards passed the river at Fatland Ford and the Hessian Chasseurs and some Grenadiers passed at some distance above Moore Hall. Some Light Dragoons crossed at dusk at Long Ford. The guns of the Hessians and those of the 3rd Brigade fired a few shot across the river opposite their Encampments to deceive the Enemy with respect to the ford at which it was intended the Army should pass. The Hessians and Light Dragoons returned at night. At the rising of the moon the Troops were in readiness to march and at . . . o'clock began crossing at Fatland Ford.

23d At . . . o'clock the Troops, artillery and baggage had all passed and were drawn up on the opposite shore. As soon as the men had dried themselves, the whole marched and proceeded to Norrington where the Army was encamped, with their right on the Reading Road, and their left to the Schuylkill. A Battalion of Light Infantry was posted at Swedes' Ford. Three hundred Militia who were stationed there quitted it as the Army drew near. They left five iron 12-pounders on travelling carriages, some ammunition, stores, and a pair of Colours were found in the neighborhood. Washington was said to be at the 32-mile Stone from Philadelphia on the Reading Road.

24th The Army remained at Norrington. A few persons

came in from Philadelphia. Several deserters came in from Washington's Army.

25th   The Army marched in two Columns to German Town, and encamped on the heights near that place. On the march some Militia were seen in front of the right-hand Column.

A good many people came in from Philadelphia; most of them represented that place as in the greatest confusion and expressed fears of its being burnt.

A few Rebel Dragoons with a Captain were taken by a party of Burgoyne's. A Commodore fell into our hands the same day. Some waggons and a considerable magazine of hay were taken possession of within two miles of Philadelphia, and four iron 12-pounders on field carriages were found in the woods near German Town. Major Washington was said to be at Pottsgrove. It rained very hard at night.

26th   This morning the British and Hessian Grenadiers marched at 8 o'clock towards Philadelphia and took possession of the town. The Rebels had withdrawn part of their shipping to Burlington, and rested in hopes of opposing ours with armed vessels, gondolas &c., which lay near a fort on Mud Island, seven miles below Philadelphia.

27th   The *Delaware*, Rebel frigate, attempted to pass the town in her way to Burlington, or was approaching to fire upon the town, but ran ashore and struck to the Grenadiers, who brought down their field guns and two 12-pounders to bear upon her. Howitzers were likewise brought against her. A schooner which was coming up at the same time also struck, but as we were not able to take possession of her, she got off in the night. Another frigate, seeing the fate of the *Delaware*, would not venture near enough to receive much damage, but returned to her station near Mud Island. There has been since great reason to believe their intention was to set fire to the town. Alexander, the Captain of the *Delaware*, was put in jail.

The Militia, of which there were skulking parties about the right of our Encampment, wounded three or four men and two Officers of Wemys's Corps. Washington was supposed to be beyond Perkiomy Creek.

28th   Sir William Howe visited Philadelphia. A Lieutenant

and fifty Seamen came from Wilmington to man the *Delaware* Frigate.

29th   A soldier of Wemys's Corps was executed for desertion.

30th   General Grey visited Philadelphia. Major Galloway (a man of considerable property in this province) valued the number of inhabitants who have quitted Philadelphia, at one-sixth; some respectable Quakers said one-third.

Some operations were making at this time near the mouth of Schuylkill towards opening the communication with the ships. Lieutenant-Colonel Stirling marched from German Town with the 10th and 42d Regiments, in order to take possession of some Rebel works at Billingsport below Mud Island, on the Jersey shore of Delaware.

30th   Deserters continued coming in; they related that on the 28th Major Washington fired a *feu de joie* and administered rum to his Army, on account of a victory gained over General Burgoyne.

Oct 1st   Other Deserters came in; they said the reverse of former accounts, and insisted that Burgoyne had had great success.

2d   Lieutenant Colonel Stirling took possession of Billingsport; about 300 Militia who were in it having evacuated the work and spiked the cannon.

3rd   Our communication with the ships was only by land.

4th   Some intimations had been received the 3rd of the designs of the Rebels to attack us, which were very little credited. In the morning of the 4th a Rebel flanker was taken prisoner by a sentry from a Light Infantry piquet. The patroles of the 1st Light Infantry fell in with a party of the Rebels, some men of which they took prisoners; they learnt from them that Washington's whole Army had marched the preceeding evening from the 19th mile-stone; that he was within a very small distance and was to begin his attack immediately. Whilst this intelligence was circulating, their first onset began upon the 2d Light Infantry and the 40th Regiment. These not only maintained themselves a great while, but drove the Rebels off repeatedly, till, from their unsupported position, fresh bodies of men appeared and pressed on both their flanks and rear. The Light Infantry then fell back and the 40th Regiment, under Lieutenant-Colonel Musgrave, threw themselves into a house from the avenues to which they had driven the Rebels. They here for upwards of an hour resisted the efforts of the Enemy, who in vain brought several pieces of cannon upon them and attempted to storm the house, until released by the 44th Regiment. The 1st Light Infantry, who were on the right of the line, were attacked soon after, and the 4th Regiment, which was on their left and had moved forward from their Encampment, was engaged at the same time. In this quarter the Rebels did not gain ground upon the Troops. The line now began to move in support of the advanced Corps, the Guards, 28th and 27th Regiments were drawn towards the right of the 4th Regiment and 1st Light Infantry. The 37th and 15th Regiments were moved from the 4th and 3rd Brigade across German Town to the left of the 5th and 55th, which had marched forward inclining somewhat to the right, and by that means were formed to the left of the 4th Regiment and 1st Light Infantry, the Corps attacked. Thus the 1st and 2d Brigades, consisting of only the 4th, 49th, 5th, and 55th, and the 1st Light Infantry, supported on the right by the Guards* 28th and 27th Regiments, and on the left by the 37th and 15th, formed the right wing and fell under the command of Major-General Grant, and as far as from the irregularity of an action they could be considered as forming a line, their front was North-east and towards Abingdon. The 37th, 5th, and 15th were the only Regiments engaged, and on this side the Enemy was repulsed and pursued a considerable distance. General Grant, finding it not possible to come up with them, left Abingdon to his right and marched his Column to White-marsh Church, where he joined Lord Cornwallis's rear.

On the left and on the West side of German Town the 4th and 3rd Brigades and Hessians moved forward from their Encampment in a direction parallel with the Village. This as far as near the market-place, was occupied by the Rebels, who had pressed on upon the retreat of the 2d Light Infantry, leaving the 40th Regiment besieged in their rear. The 4th

*These Regiments having been detached from their Brigades, as likewise the 40th, 10th and 42d, are not considered when the Brigades are mentioned. The 23d Regiment was also detached.

Brigade received Orders by inclining to their right to enter German Town and drive the Enemy from it. From some misunderstanding, or from receiving some fire, they did not immediately go into the village, but halted on the skirts of it, and kept up a very heavy fire against a distant Column they had some intimation of in front. The 17th and 44th Regiments were therefore ordered to wheel to the right and drive out the Rebels. This was executed, the 44th crossing the village and moving up the skirts on the opposite side, and the 17th moving up the street. General Grey headed the 44th Regiment. Lord Cornwallis came up as the Rebels had retired, and took the command of the left wing, with which he pursued as far as Whitemarsh Church, leaving a Corps at Chestnut Hill. At Chestnut Hill the 2d Battalion Grenadiers, who had marched from Philadelphia, joined Lord Cornwallis. The 2d Light Infantry, having received the submissions of about 150 men, who found themselves cut off by the 44th crossing German Town above them, marched forward at some distance on the right of the 44th, and fell in with the left Column near Whitemarsh Church. The Grenadiers were pushed across Wisahicon Creek, but received orders to retire again and bring up the rear of the Column, which was marched back to German Town and encamped on the same ground it had left. The Rebels were each equipped with a piece of white paper in his hat, which made us imagine they meant a surprise by night. Their disposition for the attack is not easily traced; it seems to have been too complicated; nor do their Troops appear to have been sufficiently animated for the execution of it in every part, altho' the power of strong liquor had been employed. Several, not only of their Soldiers but Officers, were intoxicated when they fell into our hands. Besides the attacks above mentioned a Column showed themselves to the Jägers, and another came within sight of the Guards, but did not wait to be engaged. We supposed the Rebels to have lost between 200 and 300 killed, with the proportion of wounded. On our side about 300 were killed or wounded. Amongst the killed were Brigadier General Agnew and Lieutenant-Colonel Bird of the 15th Regiment. We took 380 prisoners, whereof fifty were Officers. It has been said since that the 2d Light Infantry and 40th Regiment had been left unsupported through some mistake, for that the 55th and 5th Regiments had been ordered to move towards them and again unfortunately countermanded and drawn off to the right.

John Glover to
Jonathan Glover and Azor Orne

CAMP 3 M. above STILLWATER,
Sept. 21st, 1777.

DEAR SIRS:

I have just time to inform you that the 18th inst. we marched out with 3000 men to attack the enemy, who were encamped on the Heights about 2 miles from us; found it not practicable as they had taken an advantageous post; however we drew up in line, in full view of them, with a design to draw them out & there tarried till dark without doing any thing further. The next day (the 19th) sent out large scouting parties, some of which fell in with those of the enemy. A brisk firing came on; this happened about 1 o'clock. We re-enforced till we had about 3000 engaged. The enemy re-enforced till they brought their whole force into action, consisting of 7000, Gen. Burgoyne at their head, who was wounded through his shoulder.

The battle was very hot till 1/2 past 2 o'cl'k; ceased about half an hour, then renewed the attack. Both armies seemed determined to conquer or die. One continual blaze, without any intermission till dark, when by consent of both parties it ceased. During which time we several times drove them, took the ground, passing over great numbers of their dead and wounded. Took one field piece, but the woods and bush was so thick, & being close pushed by another party of the enemy coming up, was obliged to give up our prize. The enemy in their turn sometimes drove us. They were bold, intrepid and fought like heroes, and I do assure you Sirs, our men were equally bold and courageous & fought like men, fighting for their all. We have taken about 70 prisoners, among which are two officers.

By three deserters this moment come in, we are informed the enemy suffered much, having two Regt's almost cut off &

that their killed wounded and missing were 700, among which were a great proportion of officers.

We have 202 wounded, 101 killed and missing, among whom is Lt. Cols. Cobwin and Adams & Lt. Thomas, Capt. Allen & Ensign Foster killed, Capt. Bell mortally wounded. A considerable number more were killed, whose names I have not been able to get. *   *   *

We are in a very confused situation, which you must reasonably conceive.

I am Sirs
yr most obed. servt.

N. B. Sent a copy of the above to Gen. Heath, and another to Col. Johonnot.

——

CAMP 3 miles above STILLWATER,
29th Sept. 1777.

DEAR SIRS:

Since my last letter to you we have had two flags of truce from the enemy, by which we have received an account of their killed and wounded in the battle of the 19th, 746, among which is a great proportion of officers. But the truth has not come out yet, as I'm fully persuaded, & it's the opinion of all the Gen. Officers, that they must have suffered a great many more.

We had 20 taken prisoners, of which seven were wounded. Gen. Burgoyne sent a return of their names by the flag, with a very polite letter to Gen. Gates, who returned as polite a one, with a list of 70 prisoners, 30 odd of which were wounded. These I think will ballance the 20.

We had 81 officers and men killed dead on the spot and 202 wounded, many of which are since dead, in the whole 303 — a very inconsiderable number, when we consider how hot the battle was & how long it continued, being 6 hours without any intermission, saving about half an hour between 2 and 3 o'clock.

The enemy have remained very quiet ever since at about one mile distance, not attempting to advance one step. We are continually harrassing them by driving their pickets, bringing off their horses &c.

We have taken 30 prisoners since the battle, and as many more deserted.

Our men are in fine spirits, are very bold and daring, a proof of which I will give you in an instance two nights past.

I ordered 100 men from my Brigade to take off a picket of about 60 of the enemy, who were posted about half a mile from me, at the same time ordered a covering party of 200 to support them. This being the first enterprise of this kind, & as it was proposed by me, I was very anxious for its success. I therefore went myself. The night being very foggy and dark, could not find the enemy till after day. When I made the proper disposition for the attack, they went on like so many tigers, bidding defiance to musket balls and bayonets. Drove the enemy, killed 3, and wounded a great number more, took one prisoner, 8 Packs, 8 Blankets, 2 guns, 1 sword, and many other articles of Plunder without any loss on our side.

Matters can't remain long as they now are. Burgoyne has only 20 days provision. He must give us battle in a day or two, or else retire back.

The latter I think he'll endeavor to do; in either case I think, with the blessing of Heaven he must be ruined.

We are now between 10 & 11000, strong, healthy and in fine fighting cue, I am fully satisfied they will fight hard, when called to action. God grant that every man may do his duty, and be crowned with success, which will put an end to our trouble in this quarter; at least this campaign, and I am inclined to think forever. My compliments to your good ladies, families and all friends, and believe me to be respectfully,

> yr friend & most obedt. servt.,

N. B. This moment 4 Hessian deserters came in who say that 1/2 the company agreed to come off with them, & that we may expect a great many more very soon.

John Adams to Abigail Adams

York Town Pennsylvania,
Septr. 30. 1777 Tuesday

My best Friend

It is now a long Time, since I had an Opportunity of writing to you, and I fear you have suffered unnecessary Anxiety on my Account. — In the Morning of the 19th. Inst., the Congress were allarmed, in their Beds, by a Letter from Mr. Hamilton one of General Washingtons Family, that the Enemy were in Possession of the Ford over the Schuylkill, and the Boats, so that they had it in their Power to be in Philadelphia, before Morning. The Papers of Congress, belonging to the Secretary's Office, the War Office, the Treasury Office, &c. were before sent to Bristol. The President, and all the other Gentlemen were gone that Road, so I followed, with my Friend Mr. Merchant of Rhode Island, to Trenton in the Jersies. We stayed at Trenton, until the 21. when We set off, to Easton upon the Forks of Delaware. From Easton We went to Bethlehem, from thence to Reading, from thence to Lancaster, and from thence to this Town, which is about a dozen Miles over the Susquehannah River. — Here Congress is to sit.

In order to convey the Papers, with safety, which are of more Importance than all the Members, We were induced to take this Circuit, which is near 180 Miles, whereas this Town by the directest Road is not more than 88 Miles from Philadelphia. This Tour has given me an Opportunity of seeing many Parts of this Country, which I never saw before.

This Morning Major Throop arrived here with a large Packett from General Gates, containing very agreable Intelligence, which I need not repeat, as you have much earlier Intelligence from that Part than We have.

I wish Affairs here wore as pleasing an Aspect. — But alass they do not.

I shall avoid every Thing like History, and make no Reflections.

However, General Washington is in a Condition tolerably respectable, and the Militia are now turning out, from Virginia, Maryland and Pensilvania, in small Numbers. All the Apology that can be made, for this Part of the World is that Mr. Howes march from Elke to Philadelphia, was thro the very Regions of Passive obedience. The whole Country thro which he passed, is inhabited by Quakers. There is not such another Body of Quakers in all America, perhaps not in all the World.

I am still of Opinion that Philadelphia will be no Loss to Us.

I am very comfortably situated, here, in the House of General Roberdeau, whose Hospitality has taken in Mr. S A, Mr. G and me. My Health is as good as common, and I assure you my Spirits not the worse for the Loss of Philadelphia.

Biddle in the Continental Frigate at S. Carolina has made a noble Cruise and taken four very valuable W.I. Prizes.

Continue to write me by the Post, and I shall pay my Debts.

Samuel Shaw to Francis Shaw

Artillery Park, Skippack, about twenty-four miles
west from Philadelphia, September 30th, 1777.
DEAR SIR,

When I wrote to you last, our affairs wore rather a clouded
aspect; our misfortune at Brandywine occasioned some small
depression of spirits in our army, which we hoped a successful
turn would carry off. But, though this desirable event has not
yet happened, the temporary gloom seems to be entirely dispelled, and our camp is as cheerful as ever. Since that time, we
have had (I don't know that I ought to call it the misfortune)
the mortification of seeing the enemy possess themselves of
Philadelphia. From the account sent our good friends in
Boston, they must naturally have been led to expect the news
of another battle before that of the loss of the city; and I believe the General intended fully they should have had one
more scrabble for it. In this, however, he was disappointed.
We recrossed the Schuylkill the 14th instant, in hopes to gain
some advantage by it; the next day but one after that the enemy advanced, and our army was formed in order of battle;
but, rain coming on very fast, the General filed off, choosing
to avoid an action in which the discipline of the enemy in the
use of their bayonets (the only weapon that could then be of
any service, and which we were by no means generally supplied with) would give them too great a superiority. The hot-
headed politicians will no doubt censure this part of his
conduct, while the more judicious will approve it, as not only
expedient, but, in such a case, highly commendable. It was,
without doubt, chagrining to a person of his fine feelings to
retreat before an enemy not more in number than himself;
yet, with a true greatness of spirit, he sacrificed them to the
good of his country. We marched all night through as heavy
a rain as ever fell, which damaged the greater part of the ammunition then with us. It was shortly after judged necessary
to return on the other side of the river, that we might the

better be able to counteract the enemy, and prevent them from crossing. This was effected in good order, and a party, under General Wayne, was left to harass their rear, should they attempt to ford. It is not my province to judge of the conduct of this party; I shall only relate facts. It was surprised by the enemy about one o'clock in the morning of the 22d instant, who rushed upon them with fixed bayonets and cutlasses, drove them off the ground, killed fifty-six on the spot, and wounded and took a proportionable number.

In the above surprise, my friend Randall, after getting one of his pieces away, was taken while he was anxiously exerting himself for the security of that, and another, which, under cover of the night, was also got off. On finding himself in their hands, he endeavoured to escape, but the enemy prevented it by knocking him down and stabbing him in eight places. His wounds not admitting of his being carried with them, they left him at a house near the scene of action, and took his parole to return when called for, unless exchanged. It is no less true than remarkable, that a continued series of ill-luck has constantly attended poor Randall; who, no sooner than he finds himself at liberty to oppose the enemies of humanity and justice, has, by some perverse trick of Fortune, been thrown into their hands, and bound, by the strongest tie that can affect a man of honor, not to act against them. His good conduct on all, and the most trying, occasions, joined with my long acquaintance and friendship, interests me exceedingly in his behalf, and makes me anxious for his exchange, — both as it will be very grateful to him, and, I really think, beneficial to his country.

To return. Had there been no other object but that of preventing Mr. Howe from fording the river, Philadelphia might at this time, perhaps, have remained ours. But, instead of crossing, as we expected, he moved by his left up the river, which made it necessary we should do the same with our right, in order to cover our magazines, then at Reading, it being by no means improbable he would attempt destroying them. Of this manœuvre, though under such circumstances very essential on our part, he took advantage; for, by a forced march, he returned in the night of the 22d instant, and crossed his whole army before morning. This being effected, and we left eight miles in his rear, his proceeding to the city could be attended with little or no hazard, unless we chose to attack him at a manifest disadvantage. This was by no means advisable, and Philadelphia, of course, fell into his hands. Here, again, some blustering hero, in fighting his battles over a glass of madeira, may take upon him to arraign the conduct of our general, and stigmatize the army as cowards. Leaving such to enjoy their own sagacity, it must appear obvious to men of sense and reflection, duly impressed with the importance of the great contest in which we are engaged, that a general action ought, on no pretence, to be risked under disadvantageous circumstances; nor should the safety of a single city be brought in competition with the welfare of posterity. Giving these considerations due weight, the absurdity of risking too much is evident; for, should we miscarry, posterity would execrate, and the world call us fools.

* * *

Such being the situation of affairs, the inquiry naturally arises, What is to be done? are the enemy peaceably to remain in Philadelphia? I hope not. We have received reinforcements of regular troops (exclusive of between three and four thousand militia) more than will make up for our loss at Brandywine, and a desire of obtaining satisfaction pervades the whole army. Our lads are unwilling to relinquish their prospects of yet having the city for winter-quarters, and the good news from the northward adds fuel to the flame. A spirit of emulation gains ground daily, and the general wish is for a fair opportunity to signalize themselves. Under the influence of such a temper, I am persuaded our troops, when again called to action, will acquit themselves well. The time, I think, cannot be far distant. There remains much to be done on our part, and it would be infamous in Mr. Howe to content himself as yet with what he has done.

On a comparison of circumstances in this and our army at the northward, it pretty plainly appears that the campaign, take it together, has not been too favorable to the enemy. Fortune seems to have relented; and, at a time when Mr. Burgoyne, puffed up by his too easy acquisition of Ticonderoga, was threatening us with 'devastation, famine, and every concomitant horror which a reluctant, but indispensable, prosecution of military duty must occasion,' checked him in his mad career, and gave a new face to our affairs in that quarter. This, while it is considered as a just punishment to the arrogant, may teach us that ——

————

October 3d, sunset.

I received your letter, and have only time to say, God bless my dear parents. I shall write you again.

————

October 13th.

It is with much satisfaction I embrace this opportunity of finishing my long and almost tedious letter. When I began the foregoing, I knew of no conveyance; and, being interrupted while writing, let it lie till the 3d instant, when Captain Randall told me he should set off the next morning for Boston. Time was precious, the army just beginning to march, and not a moment to spare, which obliged me to conclude in the abrupt manner I did. He has called to see me on his way home (having been detained by his wounds), which has afforded me opportunity of giving you a short sketch of our late affair with Mr. Howe.

Our whole army, exclusive of the necessary guards left for the security of the camp, began its march, in four columns, on the evening of the 3d instant, about six o'clock, by different roads, some of them being distant sixteen and eighteen miles, and the nearest to the enemy fourteen. Their pickets were attacked about daylight the next morning, and, after being reinforced by the light infantry of the whole line, were driven back, reinforcement and all, upon their main body. The attack of the pickets gave the alarm, and the resistance they made afforded the main body time to form, and recover a little from their surprise, which could not have been greater had they seen an army drop from the clouds to oppose them. Our lads, encouraged by so prosperous a beginning, pushed on with the utmost resolution, and broke the reinforcement coming to the relief of the pickets and light infantry. This was the critical moment; had things gone on in the same train five minutes longer, we, perhaps, at this time should have been in quiet possession of Philadelphia. But it was otherwise; unfortunately, at that most important juncture, an exceeding thick fog arose, which, joined to the smoke, made it impossible to discern objects at the distance of thirty yards, and, the firing continuing on all quarters, it was impossible, in such circumstances, to distinguish, while on the right, whether the firing heard was from our left and centre, or from the enemy. This was a very disagreeable situation for new troops, and, the ammunition being chiefly spent, our general ordered a retreat, which was performed in good order, bringing off the artillery, wagons, and wounded.

Besides the above, I know of no other reasons which can be assigned for our leaving the ground, unless we conclude that it was not the will of Heaven we should succeed, and by *one* bold push purchase the inestimable blessing of Freedom. This, and this only, seems to be a consolation for the loss of victory, even after it was in our grasp, and is at the same time so comfortable a persuasion that I shall always cherish it. "The ways of Heaven are dark and intricate," and, though we cannot fathom the designs of infinite wisdom, it becomes us, notwithstanding, to acquiesce in its dispensations. For my own part, I am so fully convinced of the justice of the cause in which we are contending, and that Providence, in its own good time, will succeed and bless it, that, were I to see twelve of the United States overrun by our cruel invaders, I should still believe the thirteenth would not only save itself, but also work the deliverance of the others. This, however, is not the case. From the bravery, and, I may add, the discipline, of our troops, much may be expected. In the late engagement they did their duty, maintaining the action upwards of two hours and a half, teaching themselves and the world this useful truth, founded on experience, that *British troops* are proof against neither a surprise nor a vigorous attack. Our loss I believe to be much less than at Brandywine. The enemy's, by accounts from the city and by deserters, has been great; some say twelve hundred, some sixteen hundred, others, two thousand or more, killed and wounded. General Agnew was killed on the spot, as also was Colonel Bird, of the fifteenth regiment; General Grant was wounded. On our part, General Nash, mortally wounded, is since dead, with some other brave officers. General Sullivan's division behaved gallantly; he lost two aid-de-camps, dead of their wounds. We had three officers of artillery wounded, viz. Captain Frothingham, Captain-Lieutenant Hewman, and Lieutenant Parsons, who are all likely to do well. A proportion of privates were killed and wounded.

Our army is now encamped in a good part of the country, about twenty-six miles from Philadelphia, is in good spirits, and expects soon to have the other watch.

Though 't is something late in the day, I must, however, congratulate you on the success of our arms at the northward, — particulars of which you, without doubt, have heard. This by way of balance, as I have to sympathize with you on the loss of our forts on the North River, an event which might have been attended with fatal consequences, had it happened early in the year. The drawing of troops for reinforcing this army so weakened our posts in that quarter, that it was a great temptation to the enemy to risk a little. However, I hope they will yet be disappointed in their main object, which is conjectured to be the relieving Burgoyne, as it is not improbable there may be soon a very good account of him; if not, the hazard the enemy would run by leaving General Putnam in their rear must make them extremely cautious how they venture to his assistance.

———

15th, 8 o'clock, morning.

An important piece of intelligence arrived last night in camp. Burgoyne has received another check. Great part of his camp, nine pieces of brass cannon, and upwards of five hundred prisoners, have fallen into our hands. This, without doubt, will induce Clinton to return again to New York, as it is too late for him to relieve Burgoyne, who, to all human appearance, must be ruined. This news increases the ardor our troops have to engage the enemy, which we seem to be under a double obligation to do, — first for our country, and next for our own honor, which seems very nearly concerned; as great things are justly expected from us in this quarter, from the main American army.

Robert Morton:
Diary, September 16–December 14, 1777

Philada., September 16th, 1777. — This afternoon about 4 o'clock, I, in company with my agreeable Friend Dr. Hutchinson, set off on a journey to Reading, on business relating to the Friends now confined there on their way to Winchester in Virginia. We rode about 4 Hours in an excessive hard rain, when we arrived at Thomson's Tavern, about 20 miles from Philada., where upon Enquiry we found nothing to our Satisfaction, the house being filled with militia. From thence we went to Mrs. Toy's, in the upper Reading Road, who, apologizing for her not being able to accommodate us, directed us to an old Dutchman's, about 1/4 of a mile from her house. Upon asking him for lodgings he at first hesitated, thinking we were military officers, but upon scrutinizing us he found we made a different appearance, and introduced us with many apologies for the meanness of his house, the badness of his beds, and other excuses of the same nature. We thanked him for his kindness, and kindly accepted of his mean tho' grateful Fare. In the morning we crossed Skippack though very rapid, and proceeded on to Perkioming, where we found it dangerous to pass owing to the rapidity of the stream and the inconvenience attending the swimming of our horses. We enquired the distance of the head of the creek, and found it was about 20 miles, and in our way had to cross many small creeks which were impassable at that time without great danger. Upon mature deliberation we thought it most advisable to proceed to Pawling's Ferry upon Schuylkill, which having raised above 8 feet perpendicularly, and great number of trees and other rubbish coming down so fast, the Boatman would not go over. Every safe means of proceeding on our journey being now out of our power, and sensible that our consequence at Reading would be inadequate to the risque we run, both of ourselves and our horses, we determined to proceed home, where we arrived about 6 o'clock Wed. Ev'g after an agreeable journey and no other misfortune than a fall from my horse, which hurt my left arm, which I hope shall soon be recovered of. 17th and 18th included in the above.

Sept. 19th. — This morning, about 1 o'clock, an Express arrived to Congress, giving an acco. of the British Army having got to the Swedes Ford on the other side of the Schuylkill, which so much alarmed the Gent'n of the Congress, the military officers and other Friends to the general cause of American Freedom and Independence, that they decamped with the utmost precipitation, and in the greatest confusion, insomuch that one of the Delegates, by name Fulsom, was obliged in a very *Fulsom* manner to ride off without a saddle. Thus we have seen the men from whom we have received, and from whom we still expected protection, leave us to fall into the hands of (by their accounts) a barbarous, cruel, and unrelenting enemy.

This afternoon we rec'd a letter from my Father, I. P., informing us that Alex. Nesbit, who was one of the Guards, had arrived at Reading with advices from the Executive Council of this State, from which they were apprehensive we were to be deprived of a hearing, and sent off to Winchester immediately.

O Philada. my native City, thou that hast heretofore been so remarkable for the preservation of thy Rights, now sufferest those who were the Guardians, Protectors, and Defenders of thy Youth, and who contributed their share in raising thee to thy present state of Grandeur and magnificence with a rapidity not to be paralleled in the World, to be dragged by a licentious mob from their near and dear connections, and by the hand of lawless power, banished from their country unheard, perhaps never more to return, for the sole suspicion of being enemies to that cause in which thou art now engaged; hadst thou given them even the form of a trial, then thou wouldst have been less blameable, but thou hast denied them that in a manner more tyrannical and cruel than the Inquisition of Spain. Alas, the day must come when the Avenger's hand shall make thee suffer for thy guilt, and thy Rulers shall deplore they Fate.

Sept. 20th. — Went with Charles Logan to his Plantation,

and returned about 5 o'clock; my mother rec'd a letter from my Father, giving a particular Acco. of his Journey to Reading, and the Treatment they rec'd there, being all confined in one house, but kindly treated by their Friends, who are residents there from this City, and as much hated and despised by the deluded multitude.

Sept. 21st. — Nothing remarkable this day.

Sept. 22nd. — This morning I saw Benj. Bryan, who has just returned from Thos. McKean, Esq's, Chief Justice of this State, by whom I understand that the Executive Council have deprived the Justices of executing part of their Offices, by virtue of an Act of Gen'l Assembly passed last week, to suspend the Granting of Writs of Habeas Corpus, to persons who are taken up on suspicion of being inimical to the United States. He made many professions of his disapprobation of the unprecedented measure, and would willingly, were it in his power, grant them a hearing, but as the Council had prevented him, he would receive no payment for the granting the writs. An instance worthy of imitation. This morning they went about to the inhabitants seeking for Blankets, Cloathes, &c. From some they rec'd a little, but not generally so. They got one from us. My mother rec'd a letter from my father, I. P., dated 20th inst., giving an acco. of the Prisoners moving from Reading on their way to the place of Banishment. The two armies having moved up Schuylkill yesterday, it is thought the British have crossed the river, a heavy cannonade being heard this evening it is supposed near to Potts Grove.

Sept. 23rd. — Employed this day in making hay. In the evening the inhabitants were exceedingly alarmed by an apprehension of the City being set on fire. The British troops being within 11 miles of the City, caused the disturbance, and gave rise to those womanish fears which seize upon weak minds at those occasions — Set up till 1 o'clock, not to please myself, but other people.

Sept. 24th. — This day 4 Row Gallies were set up at 4 cross streets with 2 field pieces at Market Street Wharf to annoy the enemy on their march thro this City, but they not coming according to expectation, they fell down with the tide about 12 o'clock. N. B. Yesterday, in the evening a number of horses were taken out of the City to prevent them from falling into the hands of the enemy.

Sept. 25th. — This morning the news arrived of the British army being about 5 miles from the City. In the evening they sent a letter to T. Willing desiring him to inform the inhabitants to remain quietly and peaceably in their own dwellings and they should not be molested in their persons or property. Set up till 1 o'clock patrolling the streets for fear of fire. 2 men were taken up who acknowledged their intentions of doing it.

Sept. 26th. — About 11 o'clock A.M. Lord Cornwallis with his division of the British and Auxiliary Troops amount'g to about 3000, marched into this city, accompanied by Enoch Story, Jos. Galloway, Andw. Allen, William Allen and others, inhabitants of this city, to the great relief of the inhabitants who have too long suffered the yoke of arbitrary Power; and who testified their approbation of the arrival of the troops by the loudest acclamations of joy. Went with Chas. Logan to Head Quarters to see his Excell'y Gen. Sir Wm. Howe, but he being gone out, we had some conversation with the officers, who appeared well disposed towards the peaceable inhabitants, but most bitter against, and determined to pursue to the last extremity the army of the U.S. The British army in this city are quartered at the Bettering House, State House and other Places, and already begin to show the great destruction of the Fences and other things, the dreadful consequences of an army however friendly. The army have fortified below the town to prevent the armed vessels in our River coming to this city — likewise have erected a Battery at the Point. This day has put a period to the existance of Continental money in this city. "Esto Perpetua."

Sept. 27th. — About 9 o'clock this morning 1 Ship of 34 guns, 1 of 18, 4 Row gallies and a schooner came opposite to the Batteries erected in this city, who fired upon them when at a proper distance. The engagement continued for an hour when the Frigate got aground and struck to the British troops. The other ship immediately made sail and got off with the 4 gallies, the schooner coming down was fired at several times, when a shot struck her foremast and carried it away, which bro't her to and run her aground, when all the men on board escaped. This execution was done by 4 pieces of

Artillery. This afternoon about 3 o'clock an engagement happened near my Uncle's plantation, between 100 C. Troops and 30 British, the Con. troops gave way, their loss unknown. 3 officers and 1 private wounded, and 1 private killed on the side of the British, whom I see —

Sept. 28th. — About 10 o'clock this morning some of the Light Dragoons stationed near Plantation broke open the house, 2 desks, 1 Book Case and 1 closet besides several drawers and other things, and ransacked them all. I apply'd to their officer, who informed me that if the men were found out they should be severely punished.

I have been informed that a soldier this day rec'd 400 lashes for some crime, which I do not know.

Sept. 29th. — Went with Dr. Hutchinson to Israel Pemberton's Plantation where we found a destruction similar to that at our Plantation, 3 closets being broke open, 6 doz. wine taken, some silver spoons, the Bedcloaths taken off 4 Beds, 1 rip'd open, the Tick being taken off, and other Destruction about the Plantation. The officers were so obliging as to plant a centry there without application. Upon our return home we pass'd thro' part of the camp and saw a man hanging.

Sept. 30th. — This morning my mother and I went to Col. Harcourt, Com. of the Light Dragoons, near our plantation, to make intercession for the men who are apprehended for breaking and ransacking our plantation and house. The Col. upon my application, behaved very unlike a Gent'n by asking me "what I wanted" in an ungenteel manner, and told me he could not attend to what I had to say, and said that the trial was coming on and I must attend to prosecute them. I informed him there was a lady who would be glad to speak with him. He then came to my mother and behaved in a very polite genteel manner, and assured her that he could not admit her application as the orders of the General must be obeyed, and that the soldiers were not suffered to commit such depredations upon the King's subjects with impunity. Some of the British troops came to my mother's pasture on 6th and 1st days last and took away 2 loads of hay without giving a Rec't or offering Paym't.

We had a verbal acco't this morning of the Prisoners being seen on 4th day last at Carlisle on their way to Banishment.

It is reported that the Con. Troops have erected several batteries on the other side of the River to annoy and distress their enemy. One at White Hill, one at Trenton, and one nearer to the city.

Oct. 1st. — The man who was found guilty of robbing our Plantation rec'd punishment this day, which was —— lashes. The man found coming out of Mary Pemberton's plantation House is sentenced to be executed. M. P. has petitioned the Gen'l for a mitigation of the punishment. The British are erecting batteries from Delaware to Schuylkill on the north side of the city. Great numbers of officers and men belonging to the Row Gallies have deserted their posts at this time of approaching danger; and, among the rest, to his eternal disgrace and immediate death, if taken by the Con's, is Dr. Dun, Jr., who, I am told, served as Surgeon Gen'l to the Fortifications upon the River.

Oct. 2nd. — The Quarter M. Gen'l of the Light Horse took 1 load of hay from our Pasture, which he promises to give a Rec't for the 2 loads taken before by order of the Quarter Master, 2d Batt. Grenadiers, he has given me a Rec't for 100 lbs. which 2 loads Jacob declares was near 1000 lbs. 'Tis said Lord Howe with the Fleet arrived in the River last week.

Oct. 3rd. — 10 of the Row Gallies men have deserted and come up this morning, who gave an acco of the Forts at Billingsport and Red Bank being taken and a universal disaffection among the men. Enoch Story is appointed to administer the oath of allegiance to those who come in and put themselves under his Majesty's protection. A foraging party went out last week towds Darby and brought in a great number of cattle to the great distress of the inhabitants. A paper is handing about to be signed by the inhabitants agreeing to take the old lawful money, which I signed. The following report is this day prevalent concerning the defeat of Gen'l Gates near Albany — Gen'l Washington on last 1st day ordered a feu-de-joie to be fired in his camp by way of rejoicing for a victory obtained by Gen'l Gates over Burgoyne on the 18th Ulto. A letter is come to town, the postscript of which being wrote in Irish, gives an acco. of a Battle being fought on the 18th of Sept. in which Gen'l Gates was successful, that Gen'l Burgoyne returned on the 19th to bury his dead, which brot.

on a general engagement in which Burgoyne was successful, and that he was advancing towards Albany. A man is arrived in town who left Albany since the 19th, and says that there was no acco. of Burgoyne advancing when he left it. An intercepted letter of Dr. Potts is arrived in Town which says that he was going to Albany to establish a Hospital for the sick and wounded. From which Accot. if true, we may infer that there has been an engagement, but which party is successful is dubious.

Oct. 4th. — This morning early the picquet of the British near Germantown was surprised by the Americans, which brought on a very severe engagement in which the British lost 500 men killed and wounded and the Americans about 400 prison'rs, their killed and wounded is uncertain. I went this morning to the plantation, from thence to the middle ferry, where I saw a number of the citizens with about 30 of the Light Dragoons on Foot watching the motions of the enemy on the other side. I waited there about an hour during which time there were several shots from both sides without much execution, when 3 columns of the Americans with 2 field pieces appeared in sight marching tow'ds the River. The Dragoons were order'd under arms and an express sent off for a reinforcement immediately, after which the Americans fired a field piece attended with a volley of small arms. I thought it most advisable to leave the Ground, and rode off as fast possible. The Americans afterwards came down to the River side with 2 Field Pieces, which they fired with some small arms and run and left them; soon after they returned and brought them back without any considerable loss, 1 man being wounded on their side and none on the other. The British in the engagement of this morn'g lost a Gen'l Agnew, Col. Bird, and 1 Lieut. Col. besides an amazing number wounded; the loss of the Americans is undetermined, as they carryed off as many of their killed and wounded as they could. It is reported that Gen'l Wayne is among the slain.

Oct. 5th. — This morning I went to Germantown to see the destruction, and collect if possible a true acco. of the Action. From the acco's of the Officers and Sold'rs it appears that the Americans surprised the picquet guard of the English, which consisted of the 2d Batt. Grenadiers, some Infantry, and the

40th Regt., altogether about 500. The English sustained the fire of the Americans for near an hour (their numbers unknown), when they were obliged to retreat, the ammunition of the Grenadiers and infantry being expended. The 40th Regt. retreated to Chew's House, being about 120 men, and supported the fire of the Americans on all sides. The Americans came on with an unusual firmness, came up to the Doors of the House, which were so strongly barricaded they could not enter. One of the Americans went up to a window on the N. side of the house to set fire to it, and just as he was putting the Torch to the window he rec'd a Bayonet thro. his mouth, which put an end to his existence. The Americans finding the fire very severe retreated from the house. A small party of the Americans which had gone in near the middle of Germantown and had sustained the fire in the street for some time, perceived the British coming up in such numbers that they retreated. Gen'l Grey with 5000 men pursued them to the Swedes Ford, his men being much fatigued and very hungry, and the Americans running so fast, that he gave over the chase and returned to his old encampment. The greatest slaughter of the Americans was at and near to Chew's Place. Most of the killed and wounded that lay there were taken off before I got there, but 3 lay in the field at that time opposite to Chew's Place. The Americans were down as far as Mrs. Mackenet's Tavern. Several of their balls reached near to Head Qur's, from all which Accos. I apprehend with what I have heard that the loss of the Americans is the most considerable. After I had seen the situation of Chew's House, which was exceedingly damaged by the Balls on the outside, I went to Head Qur's, where I saw Major Balfour, one of Gen'l Howe's Aid de camps, who is very much enraged with the people around Germantown for not giving them intelligence of the advancing of Washington's Army, and that he should not be surprised if Gen'l Howe was to order the country for 12 miles round Germantown to be destroyed, as the People would not run any risque to give them intelligence when they were fighting to preserve the liberties and properties of the peaceable inhabitants. On our setting off we see His Excellency the Gen'l att'd by Lord Cornwallis and Lord Chewton, the Gen'l not answ'g my expectations.

Oct. 6th. — A heavy firing this morning down by Billings-port; I went to see the wounded soldiers now in this City, some at the Seceeder meeting house, some at the Presbyterian meeting house in Pine Street, some at the Play House, and some, and those the most, at the Penns'a Hospital, where I see an Englishman's leg and an American's arm cut off. The American troops are mostly at 2 new houses in Fourth Street near to the Presbyterian meeting house, amt'g to about 30 and not so much attended to as might be. The British have about 300 wounded in this city. A heavy firing all this evening, supposed to be at the Forts down the river. An acco. come of the fleets being in the River.

Oct. 7th. — A certainty of the Fleets being below, 14 men have deserted from the Row Gallies, who give an acco. of their disabling a British Brig last ev'g, and that the men be-longing to the American Fleet would desert were it in their power. News arrived this morning of 3000 men being arrived at New York, and 5000 at Quebec. No further intelligence of Burgoyne's movements. No certain acco. of the Chevaux de Frise being as yet raised. The wounded Americans in this city are removed to the State House.

Oct. 8th. — Admiral Howe is arrived at Chester. David Sproat is come to town, who reports that there is a letter in the fleet from Gen. Clinton to Gen. Howe, giving an acco. of Gen. Burgoyne defeating Gen. Gates, and that he is now on his march to Albany. I went to see Doc. Foulke amputate an American soldier's leg, which he completed in 20 minutes, while the physician at the military hospital was 40 ms. per-forming an operation of the same nature. A report that some of the Chevaux de Frise are raised.

Oct. 9th. — A heavy cannonade last night and this morning. The British are about to open Batteries to bombard the Fort at Mud Island. Cap. Ewald call'd this morning with a letter from my uncle, N. L., dated New Jersey, Dec. 12th, 1776, at which time many in Jersey were apprehensive that the British would take possession of this city as soon as the river was fas-tened by the ice, but Gen'l Washington's taking the Hessians at Trenton turned the scale against them, disconcerted their measures, and prevented their coming that winter. At the time of his coming into the house I was not within, but being sent for, and presenting myself to him, he handed me ye letter, and behaved in other respects much like a gentleman. After a long conversation and he offering to go, I invited him to dine with us, but he politely excused himself and promised to wait upon us when he again comes to the City, being stationed at the Widow Lewis' Plantation.

Oct. 10th. — Nothing remarkable this day.

Oct. 11th. — A heavy cannonade this morning. A report that the battery erected by the British on Province Island was taken. Went with a number of Gent'n to Hollander Creek's mouth, where we had a sight of the American Fleet and 5 of the British lying a little way below the Chevaux de Frise. From all appearances the British Fort was not taken, as from the Acco's of numbers who were present at the time of the American Boats landing at the Fort (the acco's of their numbers are various and contradictory) and the boats returning without their men and the Gondolas 2 hours afterwards firing upon the Fort, it is reasonable to conclude that the Report is groundless and that the Fort is not taken.

Oct. 12th. — About 1 o'clock this morning, the inhabitants were alarmed by the cry of fire, which happened at a stable above the Barracks, supposed to have been occasioned by a number of Hessians lodging in the Stable, but was happily extinguished notwithstanding the inactivity of the inhabitants, and a 3 story adjoining house which caught 3 Times, in less than 2 hours. Went this afternoon to the middle Ferry at Schuylkill, where I see a man from Chester who said that last night about 300 militia came into that town and took off the Sheriff of Sussex, whom Governor McKinley some time since advertised with a reward of 300 Dol's. Several Acco's at this ferry of the Americans approaching this City, particularly one who said that they were within 7 miles and that his Brother was taken off.

Oct 13th. — This morning about 1 o'clock there was the most severe cannonade that has yet been heard, near Province Island, supposed to be from the British ship, upon the American ships and battery. I went down there this morning and perceive the British ships to have altered their stations and come up higher, the American fleet nearly in the same place they were some time since. This ev'g I see a man from

Chester County who says that Gen'l Potter with 1600 militia is now in Newton Township about 16 miles from this City.

Oct. 14th. — This ev'g my mother rec'd a letter from my Father, J. P. dated 1 and 6 inst. by which we find that the prisoners had arrived at Winchester, that the people were very much enraged at them and declared that they should not stay there long; that they had petitioned Gov. Henry of Vir. and the Congress for a Releasement from their confinement and their return to their families. The British are erect'g a strong Battery upon Province Island, and they suppose will be completed and opened this morning.

Oct. 15th. — A heavy firing this morning near to Province Island. The American Fort is abandoned by a number of their men who have carried a great deal of their Stores, Baggage, &c. to Redbank and the American Fleet is moved further up the River. The Americans came down to the middle Ferry upon Schuylkill and cut the rope about 4 o'clock this morning, which caused some platoon firing between them and the Light Dragoons.

Oct. 16th. — Some bombs were this day thrown at the American Fort, and it is reported set fire to their Barracks. The Americans are fortifying at Red Bank. The British at Wilmington have marched to take their Fort. Provisions are very scarce. Good beef sells for 2/6 Mutton 2/6 Veal 2/ Butter 7/6. A prospect of starvation.

This day the English Battery burnt some of the Barracks belonging to the American Fort.

Oct. 17th. — No remarkable occurrence this day.

Oct. 18th. — Went to the mouth of Hollanders Creek this morning, where I had a view of the American and 4 of the British Fleets. The upper and lower British Batteries fired several times at the Mud Island Fort, but I believe without execution. The American Fort returned the fire. The lower English Battery fired 3 Bombs. The American Fleet lay nearly under Red Bank to be out of the way of the bombs. The American Flag was this day hoisted at Red Bank. The British troops that left Wilmington and were supposed to have gone to take Red Bank y's ev'g came up as far as Geo. Gray's Ferry and bro. a number of their sick and wounded into Town. A smart platoon firing this ev'g above Germantown.

Oct. 19th. — A firing this morning at the fort. Went this afternoon to the Plantation. When I had got as far as I. Pemberton's Place, I see about 100 Hessians com'g down the road on a foraging, or rather plundering, party. As soon as they came to the corner of the road, their com. gave them permission to take all the cabbage and Potatoes they could find. Being afraid y't they would take our cabbage, I applied for a guard to the House and Garden, which was immediately granted, and by that means prevented our cabbage from being plundered. After they had taken all Jno. King's Cabbage and Potatoes they marched off. Bro't our cabbage home. It was surprising to see with what rapidity they run to, and with what voraciousness they seized upon Jno. King's Cabbage and Potatoes, who remained a silent spectator to their infamous depredations.

Oct. 20th. — Went to the plantation to see about the potatoes, &c., and when I got to the corner of ye road I see another party of Hessians com'g down with Horses, Carts, bags, &c., to carry off Hay, potatoes, &c. The com'r rode up to Jno. King's House, and I followed him. He said he was come by orders of the General to take the Hay and Potatoes. I told him who it belonged to, but to no purpose. By this time a guard which Col. Harcourt had sent came up and declared they should not take it. From thence they went to J. Bringhurst's Place where they took all the Hay and most of ye Potatoes which belonged to the Tenant, to the great distress of the family. I went a little further and see a number of Hessians crossing over the bridge of boats lately made for that purpose, with Bennett of W—n, a prisoner. 14 of the Eng. flat bottomed boats came by the Che-de-Frise this morning, which occasioned some firing. I went this afternoon to see the British encampment, which extends in nearly a line from Delaware to Schuylkill. The reason of their leaving Germantown was because their lines were too extensive for the number of ye men. The troops appeared in good spirits, good health and heartily desirous for the fleets getting up that they might pursue General Washington. The most heavy firing at the fort y't we have had yet: On 1st day, the 19th, Gen'l Howe came to his quarters at Jno. Cadwalader's house in consequence of the Army contracting their lines. The B. Camp is below Kensington. We see a number of the Con. troops about 1/2 mile from the British Piquet, having exchanged several shots.

Oct. 21st. — This morning about 2500 Hessians, under the Command of Count Donop, crossed the River in order to attack Red Bank, and marched from Cooper's Ferry tow'ds Haddonfield. No firing this day at the fort.

Oct. 22nd. — Went to the Plantation this morning and found that the British had taken 1 load of hay without paying or giving a Rec't. A number of the British have crossed the lower ferry in expectation of an attack with the Continental Troops, and keeping a communication open with Chester. The British have taken 2 more loads of hay upon the same conditions as the first. Last 7th day I rec'd a Rec't for the load of hay taken for the Light Horse, which I omitted mentioning at that time. The Hessians having taken all the Stores belonging to the A. Army at Haddonfield, proceeded on tow'ds Red Bank.

Oct. 23rd. — 5th day of the week. An acco. is just arrived of Count Donop having attacked the fort at Red Bank, and his being repulsed 3 times with the loss of about 300 killed and wounded; and the great Count, who petitioned for the command in order to signalize himself and his famous Hessians, rec'd a fatal blow of which he shortly died. The wounded are brot. to town, and a number of Grenadiers and infantry gone over to make another effort. From this instance we see the important effects of despising the American army, and of Red Bank not being possessed by the British at the time they took Billingsport. This morning 20 of the British ships moved nearer to the fort in order to do more execution than they have yet been able to do. After the British batteries, erected on Province Island, and the British ships had been firing near 6 hours at the Mud Island Fort, the Augusta, a new 64 Gun Ship, by some means or other, caught fire and burnt near 3 hours and then blew up; and the Zebra, a 16 gun sloop, likewise caught fire, and about 3 o'clock in the afternoon likewise blew up, to the great amazement of the inhabitants and the disappointment of the soldiery, who having a number of troops embarked to storm the fort, and which in all probability would have surrended in 1/2 an hour and the beseiged fallen victims to their vengeance. The Hessians this morning broke open the Plantation house, but did no considerable damages. The British that crossed Schuylkill yesterday, have returned and broke up the bridge at Gray's ferry, where they are erect'g a Facine Battery to defend the pass instead of carry'g it to the upper ferry, where its proximity to ye camp would render it more conveniently protected and where, from the situation of the ground, it would be impossible to demolish it from the opposite side.

Oct. 24th. — No firing this morning. The Hessians and British Soldiers have taken above 50 Bus. of our Potatoes, notwithstanding the gracious proclamation of his Excell'y to protect the peaceable inhabitants in a quiet possession of their property. The ravages and wanton destruction of the soldiery will, I think, soon become irksome to the inhabitants, as many who depended upon their vegetables, &c. for the maintenance of their families, are now entirely and effectually ruined by the soldiers being permitted, under the command of their officers, to ravage and destroy their property. I presume the fatal effects of such conduct will shortly be very apparent by the discontent of the inhabitants, who are now almost satiated with British clemency, and numbers of whom, I believe, will shortly put themselves out of the British protection; I mean not to dictate to men of whose superior abilities I have a just appreciation, but had the necessities of the army justified the measures, and they had paid a sufficient price for what they had taken, then they would have the good wishes of the people, and perhaps all the assistance they could afford; but contrary conduct has produced contrary effects, and if they pursue their present system, their success will be precarious and uncertain. It is reported that Count Donop, after he had taken a view of the American Fort, found it impossible to take it without great loss; but as his orders were peremptory, he must take it or nobly fall in the attack. He del'd his watch and purse to Lord Bute's natural son, and then bro. on the attack; being soon after wounded, he fainted and he died.

Oct. 25th. — Great part of this day employed at Plantation taking down the fences to prevent the soldiery taking them. A report is this day prevalent, that Gen'l Burgoyne with 4000 men, surrendered prisoners of War on the 15th inst.

Oct. 26th. — This day employed at Plantation taking down the fences. About 3 o'clock P.M., a small party of the Americans, chiefly militia, attacked a sentry of the British upon the Hill opposite Ogden's house at the middle ferry, which bro. on a smart firing between them and the British Picket. It continued about 15 min., when a Regiment marched over the Bridge to reinforce them. Upon their appearance, the Americans marched off, and the firing ceased.

Oct. 27th. — Nothing remarkable this day.

Oct. 28th. — Remarkably rainy weather, and nothing very material except that the English had burnt the Town of Esopus in New York Province.

Oct. 29th. — A firing at the fort about 1 o'clock.

Oct. 30th and 31st, and Nov. 1st. — These three days employed at the plantation taking up the posts and rails. A report in town that Esopus, in the Province of New York, was burnt, and that a number of the inhabitants had fired upon the British troops from out of the windows, for which reason the town was set on fire, and guards placed at all the avenues to prevent the inhabitants from making their escape, which, if true, is an instance not to be paralleled in the annals of any nation who have so long boasted of their civilization, and yet proffer no milder conditions than servitude or death. The Americans have advanced to the borders of Schuylkill on acco. of the British at the destruction of their bridge being obliged to retreat to this side, which has occasioned a smart firing from each side. Having mentioned all that is necessary of my particular affairs, I shall now take a review of the conduct of the great, and candidly deliver my sentiments concerning their measures, and my opinion of their success provided they pursue them. Previous to their taking this city, their Gen'l published a proclamation warranting security and protection to those who should quietly remain in their dwellings, and thereby give a convincing proof of their attachment to his Majesty's government. Relying on the General's candor and generosity, they embraced the benefit of his proclamation, and remained quietly in their dwellings, expecting him to afford them that protection which the subjects of the British Empire are of right entitled to, but alas! melancholy experience has convinced them of the contrary, and the

ruin of numbers has stamped it with infallible certainty. After
they had, without much opposition, taken possession of the
City, they sent a number of troops and took possession of
Billingsport, and at the same time might have possessed Red
Bank with a very inconsiderable loss had not their confidence
dictated to the contrary. The City being well fortified, they
erected batteries on the Province Island, to silence the Mud
Island Fort, they fired to no purpose till the 23 ult., when 3
ships and the batteries engaged the Fort. After a few hours firing, the Augusta, 64 gun ship, and a small sloop blew up. The
same morning ye Count Donop, with a body of Hessians, attacked the Fort at Red Bank and was repulsed, with a great
number killed and wounded, himself mortally, and now
among the slain. Here we have an additional instance of the
experience of their confidence. As the last resource they are
building 2 Floating Batteries, to make another attempt, and if
that should fail, the consequences will be dreadful. But as by
their expectations heightened by their confidence they will
make great efforts, it is highly probable they will take the fort
and their shipping come to the city. The Fort or bomb-
battery was, by the last rain, so overflowed that the men were
up to their middles in water. A certain acco. arrived by one of
Gen'l Burgoyne's captains sent for the purpose, that on the
16th ult., the army consisting of 3500 men, 13,000 stand of
arms, 40 pieces brass cannon, and marched out with the honors of war and surrendered themselves prisoners.

Nov. 2nd. — This afternoon I took a walk to see the camp,
and went by the way of Schuylkill where we see some of the
Americans on the other side. The soldiers appeared clean and
neat.

Nov. 3rd. — No occurrence remarkable this day, a firing in
the eve'g. We rec'd a letter from Winchester giving an acco.
of the Friends, that they had a large room to dine in, that
they were all very healthy, and that they had rec'd no answer
to their address to Gov. Henry, and their remonstrance to
Congress.

Nov. 4th. — An acco. of Burgoyne's surrender given out to
day in General orders. The terms of capitulation are, "That
the army should march out of their entrenchments and pile
up their arms on the Bank of the Hudson River, that the men

should march to, and encamp as nearly as convenient to the Town of Boston, there to remain at the expense of Congress till transports should be sent to carry them to G. B.," agreed to on the 16th Oct. 1777. Burgoyne's army ammo. to 1900 British, 1600 Germans, Gates' Army to 16,000 men Con. and Militia. For the Particulars see Humphrey's paper, Nov. 5th.

Nov. 5th. — Nothing remarkable this day. Have heard that one of the floating batteries was launched yesterday. They report that the Fort is to be attacked the beginning of next week.

Nov. 6th. — No remarkable occurrence. Men employed at Plantation cutting our wood.

Nov. 7th. — Nothing remarkable this day.

Nov. 8th. — A report prevails that the British have, by orders evacuated Rhode Island. I went this morning to see the floating batteries upon the banks of Schuylkill, one of which had been launched the day before and was found very leaky and insufficient for that purpose. They are now repairing her, expecting to be ready to make the attack in a few days. A proclamation is at last published to prevent the soldiers plundering the inhabitants, and persons appointed to patrole.

Nov. 9th. — No remarkable occurrence. *10th.* Monday Morning, a smart firing this morning at the Fort.

Nov. 11th. — Went to the mouth of Schuylkill and see the firing between the Mud Island Fort and the British Batteries upon Province Island. This ev'g 2 Brigs and 2 Sloops came from the fleet with provisions for the Army and went up Schuylkill.

Nov. 12th, Fourth day. — This day a severe firing by which the American Barracks was several times set on fire, but soon extinguished. I went this ev'g down to Province Island where I see the 2 Brigs, one called the Lord Howe and the other the Betsy, and the 2 sloops. One of the floating batteries has got to the mouth of Schuylkill and the other at Everley's, preparing with all possible dispatch and we may soon expect a general attack to be made upon the Fort.

Nov. 13th. — A firing this day on the Fort. *14th.* Ditto.

Nov. 15th, 7th day of the week. — This morning about 11 o'clock the Vigilant and 6 more ships of war came up and attacked the fort together with the 6 gun, 2 do:, and other batteries on Province Island. The Vigilant took her station between the Province and Mud Islands and the other 6 ships just above the Hog Island. The firing continued till 6 o'clock P.M., and then ceased, being returned but seldom by the American Fort. The damage which the Fort sustained by an almost incessant fire for 7 hours, which burnt the Barracks, knocked down the Block Houses, dismounted the cannon and otherwise rendered the Fort untenable, obliged the besieged to evacuate and retire to Red Bank. The damage sustained by the British Ships and Batteries is unknown, but the Vigilant was huld several times by the Gondolas. Thus by American perseverence and the Fort's situation a British Army of 12,000 men and a fleet of 300 sail had been detained in their operations near 7 weeks by a power far inferior to theirs and which has always appeared contemptible in the eyes of men who have uniformly despised the Americans as a cowardly insignificant set of People. We rec'd a letter from my father by way of Wilmington giving an acco. of their being enlarged and permitted to ride 6 miles from their Dwellings. The British Troops entered the Mud Island fort this morning the 16th inst., and by the appearance of the Fort apprehended the Americans must have lost great numbers killed and wounded. They found a flock of sheep and some oxen in the Fort, besides 18 pieces of Cannon.

Nov. 18th. — This ev'g Lord Cornwallis with 2500 men marched over the Bridge at the middle ferry, with intentions as is supposed to attack the Fort at Red Bank. The next morning on their march tow'ds Darby they surprised the American Piquet, who retreated to the House called the Blue Bell and fired from the windows and killed 2 Grenadiers, some of the Grenadiers rushed into the House, bayoneted five, and the others would have shared the same fate had not the officers interfered.

Nov. 19th. — This ev'g a Body of Hessians marched over Schuylkill.

Nov. 20th. — A report this day that the Americans last night set fire to the 2 floating batteries. A fireship, gondola, Armed ship or Floating battery, unknown which belonging to the Americans, was this afternoon seen on fire between the city and Gloucester point. The cause of her being fired is unknown, she burnt for several hours and extinguished without doing further damage. We, this morning, rec'd a letter from my Father dated at Winchester the 12th inst., informing us that they had rec'd no intelligence from hence these 6 weeks, expressing an earnest solicitude for our welfare in this time of general calamity and distress; but they had rec'd an answer from Gov. Henry to their remonstrance by which they apprehended they are not to be sent further, but we imagine they have rec'd an answer by no means conducive to their releasem't. They had seen a Baltimore paper doubtless filled with gross misrepresentations and falsehoods respecting our situation, which, added to their not hearing from us for such a length of time, must have occasioned alarming apprehensions concerning us. That on the 24 ulto. the roaring of cannon had been heard within 100 miles of the city; that he had wrote 15 letters since their arrival at Winchester, 5 only of which we have received. A firing heard this evening supposed to be at Red Bank.

Nov. 21st. — This morning about 4 o'clock the inhabitants were alarmed by a very severe firing, which proved to be from the Delaware Frigate at the Gondolas as they passed the town on the other side of the river. I walked down to the wharf and see all the American Navy on fire coming up with the flood tide, and burning with the greatest fury. Some of them drifted within 2 miles of the town and were carried back by the ebb tide. They burnt nearly 5 hours; 4 of them blew up. This manœuvre is supposed to have been occasioned by the British having taken Red Bank. The Gondolas passed by in the fog. Lord Corwallis being joined in the Jerseys by 4000 men from the fleet, it is said is to proceed to Burlington, to cross the Delaware and come in the rear of Washington's Army.

Nov. 22d. — Seventh day of the week. This morning about 10 o'clock the British set fire to Fair Hill mansion House, Jon'a Mifflin's and many others amo'tg to 11 besides out houses, Barns, &c. The reason they assign for this destruction of their friends' property is on acco. of the Americans firing from these houses and harassing their Picquets. The generality of mankind being governed by their interests, it is reasonable to conclude that men whose property is thus wantonly destroyed under a pretence of depriving their enemy of a means of annoying y'm on their march, will soon be converted and become their professed enemies. But what is most astonishing is their burning the furniture in some of those houses that belonged to friends of government, when it was in their power to burn them at their leisure. Here is an instance that Gen'l Washington's Army cannot be accused of. There is not one instance to be produced where they have wantonly destroyed and burned their friends' property. But at the last action at Germantown with the same propriety as the British, could have destroyed B. Chew's house, and then would have injured a man who is banished in consequence of his kingly attachment. On the other side they have destroyed most of the houses along the lines, except Wm. Henry's, which remains entire and untouched, while J. Fox's, Dr. Moore's, and several others are hastening to ruin, so that if they want to make any distinction, it is in favor of their open, professed and determined enemies. I went to the top of c. steeple and had a prospect of the fires. A passage being made through the chevaux de frize, several sloops came up to the city this evening. Price of provisions in market on the day of the fleet's coming to the city, Beef w—, Pork —, Veal —, Butter —.

Nov. 23d. — Several reports concerning Lord Cornwallis' expedition, but not to be depended upon. The kitchen at Evergreen burnt by the carelessness of some Hessian soldiers that were in it. The numbers of people who have by permission of Washington been going to Pennapack for these some weeks past for flour at 40 sh. per cwt., c. m., are now stopped by his order.

Nov. 24th. — Twenty or thirty sail of vessels came up this morning from the fleet that the city now begins to receive. People in expectation that Germantown will be shortly burnt.

Nov. 25th. — The fleet daily arriving in great numbers. Burnt about one-half of a house near Gloucester belonging to one Hogg, a person that is reported to be an American Patriot. Lord Cornwallis, with the detachm't under his command, arrived in town this ev'g and brought over 400 head of cattle from the Jerseys.

Nov. 26th. — This morning I had an opportunity of seeing 63 sail of vessels coming to the city between this and the

Point. Lord Howe arrived in town this morning. It is supposed that none of the larger vessels will come up to the city. From all appearances I am of opinion that the Army will not follow Gen'l Washington this winter. A report that additional number of soldiers are to be quartered on the inhabitants this winter. Rob't Ritchie of this city, merch't, is apprehended and secured on suspicion of giving intelligence to Gen'l Washington's Army.

Nov. 27th, 28th, 29th, 30th. — These 4 days the fleet coming up in great numbers. Some part of the army have marched over Schuylkill, and reports are prevalent that the main part of the army will soon move off. The Americans are moving off their heavy cannon. Gen'l Washington, it is said, is going to Virginia in a few weeks, and the command to devolve upon Gen'l Gates. Great exertions are making, both by the men and women of this city, to support the credit of the paper money legally issued. The women are determined to purchase no goods with hard money. Some of those who agreed to receive paper money have refused it for their goods, and among the rest some of our Society.

Dec. 1st, 2nd, 3rd. — Numbers of the Fleet daily arriving. None of the large ships have yet come up. A contest has subsisted in this City since the arrival of the fleet, concerning the legal Paper Currency. The English merchants that came in the fleet will not dispose of their goods without hard money, alleging that no bills are to be bought, no produce to be obtained, and no method can be adopted by which they can send remittances. Numbers of the most respectable inhabitants are using all their influence to support it, and numbers of others who have no regard for the public good, are giving out the hard money for what they want for immediate use, thus purchasing momentary gratifications at the expense of the Public, for if the circulation of this money should be stopt, many who have no legal money but paper, and have no means of obtaining gold and silver, will be reduced to beggary and want, and those who are so lost to every sense of honor, to the happiness of their fellow citizens, and eventually their own good, as to give out their hard money, either for the goods of those who are newcomers, or in the public market where it is now exacted for provisions, will, by their evil example, oblige those who possess hard money, to advance it and ruin the credit of the other money for the present. The consequence of which must be that we shall be shortly drained of our hard cash, the other money rendered useless, no trade by which we can get a fresh supply, our ruin must therefore be certain and inevitable. This depreciation of the Paper Currency will not only extend its baneful influence over this City, but over all the continent, as the friends of government and others have been collecting this legal tender for several mo's past, expecting that in those places in the possession of the British Army it will be of equal value with gold and silver. But from the enemies of the British constitution among ourselves, who give out their hard money for goods, from the almost universal preference of private interest to the public good, and from a deficiency of public virtue, it is highly probable the paper money will fall, and those newcomers having extracted all our hard money, will leave us in a situation not long to survive our Ruin. Reports prevail, I suppose with some foundation, that the British Army are to march tomorrow. By the packet which sailed the first of this month for England, I wrote a letter to Dr. Fothergill in answer to one he wrote my father, also to Jno. and R. Barclay, acknowld'g the rec't of theirs of ye 1st Jany. last. Welsh, the Deputy Barrack Master, seized upon the house at Chestnut Street, late T. W.'s, for the 64th Regt. to put their baggage in it. I applied to Mr. Robinson the Barrack Master, and he ordered the house to be immediately del'd up.

Dec. 4th. — 5th day of the week. This evening about 8 o'clock, the British Army under the com'd of his Ex'y Sir Wm. Howe, marched out of the entrenchments and advanced towards Germantown, leaving a few regiments to keep possession of the City. Their advanced party arrived at Chestnut Hill about daylight, the rear of the army about leaving Germantown. On their march they took an American picket and a Brig. Gen'l Erwin of the P. Militia. A report that they had an engagement on Chestnut Hill. The Continentals at Frankford, not hearing of the British advancing till 12 o'clock, moved off to Germantown, when they took Christ'r Sower, Jun., who went with a division of the Army to that place.

6th. — Several of the inhabitants went out to day and brought in provision.   *7th.* — No certain acco. of the situation of the armies.

Dec. 5th. — No reports to be depended upon concerning the armies.

Dec. 6th. — Nothing material.

Dec. 7th. — Gen'l Erwin came in with a few Continental troops as prisoners yesterday morning. A heavy firing this day.

Dec. 8th. — Several reports about the armies, but this ev'g, to the great astonishment of the citizens, the army returned. The causes assigned for their speedy return are various and contradictory, but ye true reason appears to be this, that the army having marched up to Washington's lines near to White Marsh, and finding him strongly posted, thought it most prudent to decline making the attack. The Hessians on their march committed great outrages on the inhabitants, particularly at John Shoemaker's, whom they very much abused. Bro't off about 700 head of cattle, set fire to the house on Germantown Road, called the Rising Sun, and committed many other depredations, as if the sole purpose of the expedition was to destroy and to spread desolation and ruin, to dispose the inhabitants to rebellion by despoiling their property, and to give their enemies fresh cause to alarm the apprehensions of the people by these too true melancholy facts. John Brown of this city, is now confined in Lancaster gaol for carrying a verbal message to Rob't Morris from Thos. Willing, the purport of which was, that if the Congress would rescind independence, they should be put into their situation in 1763. This is said to have come from Gen'l Howe to T. W. R. Morris communicated it to Congress; they demanded the name of the person who bro. the message, ordered him, thro. the council of safety, to be imprisoned for his attempting to lull them into security by these fallacious proposals. Flour excessively scarce at 23/9 pr Quarter of cwt, Beef 3/9, Mutton 2/3, Veal 3, Pork 2/3. The poor are very much necessitated, are turned out of the Bettering house, put into Fourth Street meeting house, the Lodge, and the Carpenters' Hall. No prospect of the paper money being established. Joseph Galloway, Esq., is appointed Superintendent General with three other citizens as magistrates, to regulate the police of the City. Jos. Parker is dead at Lancaster. A report that the

British Army is to go to Wilmington in a few days. Several boats have come up with provisions, one to day with ab't 200 Hogs, some sheep, fowls, &c., from Dover.

Dec. 9th, 10th. — This Evg., Lord Cornwallis, with a division of the Enemy, marched over Schuylkill.

Dec. 11th. — This morning, Gen'l Washington left his strongholds, which he demolished, and marched over Schuylkill to watch Cornwallis' movements. A firing this morning on the Lancaster Road.

Dec. 12th — Provisions scarce, people daily going out for it. Hard to pass the paper money.

Dec. 13th. — Nothing material.

Dec. 14th. — This Evg., Dr. D. Smith returned from Winchester, to the great amazement of his friends and fellow-citizens, having been confined better than 3 mos. He says that the Lieutenant of the County told them they were at liberty to go where they pleased. He, with the knowledge of his fellow-prisoners, left them on 2nd day last. This extraordinary and unexpected affair may occasion the remainder being more closely confined, or else have a discharge with a permission to return home. It appears that no orders have been given concerning them, since the election of our new council, by the Assembly. The British Army, on their last excursion to Abington and Chester County, plundered a number of the inhabitants of everything they had upon their farms, and abused many old, inoffensive men. Some of them have applied for redress, but have not obtained it. Dr. Hutchinson entered into the Am. Army, as a surgeon, with 22/6 Con. money per diem. Paper money entirely dropt, and not passable.

Sarah Wister:
Journal, October 19–December 12, 1777

Oct the 19th 1777 seconday, now for new and uncommon scenes. as I was laying in bed. and ruminating on past and present events, and thinking how happy I shou'd be if I cou'd see you. Liddy come running into the room. and sai'd there was the greatest drumming fifing and rattling of Waggons that ever she had heard, what to make of this we were at a loss. we dress'd and downstairs in a hurry, our wonder ceas'd the britsh had left Germantown and our Army were marching to take possession. it was the general opinion they wou'd evacuate the capitol, sister Betsy myself and GE. went about a half mile from home. where we cou'd see the army pass, thee will stare at my going, but no impropriety in my *opine*, or I wou'd not have gone. we made no great stay but return'd with excellent appetites for our breakfast. several officers call'd to get some refreshment, but none of consequence till the afternoon cousin Prissa and myself were sitting at thee door I in a green skirt dark short gown, &c. two genteel men of the military order rode up to the door. your servant ladies, &c ask'd if they cou'd have quarters for Genl Smallwood. aunt Foulke thought she cou'd accomodate them as well as most of her nieghbours said they cou'd, one of the officers dismounted and wrote Smallwoods quarters over the door which secur'd us from straggling soldiers, after this he mounted his steed and rode away. when we were alone our dress and lips were put in order for conquest and the hopes of adventures gave brightness to each before passive countenance thee must be told of a Dr Gould who by accident had made an acquaintance with my father a sensible conversible man. a carolinian and had come to bid us adieu on his going to that State daddy had prevail'd upon him to stay a day or two with us, in the evening his Gen'ralship come with six attendants, which compos'd his family, a large gaurd of soldiers,

a number of horses and baggage Waggons. the yard and
house was in confusion, and glitterd with military equip-
ments. Gould was intimate with Smallwood and had gone
into Jesse's to see him while he was there, there was great
running up and down stairs, so I had an opportunity of seing
and being seen. the former the most agreable to be sure. one
person in particular attracted my notice. he appear'd cross and
reserv'd, but thee shall see how agreably disappointed I was.
Dr Gould usherd the gentlemen in to our parlour and intro-
duc'd them. Genl Smallwood Capt Furnival Major Stodard
Mr Prig Capt Finley and Mr Clagan. Col Wood and Col Line
these last two did not come with the Genl they are virginians
and both indispos'd, the Genl and suite are Marylanders be
assur'd I did not stay long with so many men but secur'd a
good retreat heart safe so far. some sup'd with us. others at
Jesse's they retir'd about ten in good order. how new is our
situation, I feel in good spirits tho surrounded by an Army
the house full of officers, yard alive with soldiers. very peacable sort of men tho', they eat like other folks, talk like them,
and behave themselves with elegance, so I will not be afraid
of them. that I wont. adieu I am going to my chamber to
dream I suppose of bayonets and swords, sashes, guns, and
epaulets.

3 day morn. Oct, 20th. I dare say thee is impatient to know
my sentiments of the officers, so while somnus embraces them
and the house is still, take there characters according to thier
rank the General is tall portly wel made a truly martial air the
behaviour and manner of a gentleman, a good understanding
& great humanity of disposition constitute the character of
Smallwood Col Wood. from what we hear of him and what
we see, is one of the most amiable of men tall and genteel an
agreable countenance and deportment. these following lines
will more fully characterize him

> How skill'd he is in each obliging art
> The mildest manners with the bravest heart

The cause he is fighting for alone tears him from the society
of an amiable wife and engaging daughter. with tears in his
eyes he often mentions the sweets of domestic life. Col Line
is not married so lett me not be too warm in his praise least

you suspect he is monstrous tall, & brown but has a certain somthing in his face and conversation very agreable he entertains the highest notions of honour. is sensible and humane and a brave officer he is only seven and twenty years old. but by a long indisposition and constant fatigue looks vastly older and almost worn to a skeleton, but very lively and talkative. Capt Furnival I need not say more of him than that he has excepting one or two the handsomest face I ever seen, a very fine person fine light hair and a great deal of it adds to the beauty of his face. Well here comes the glory the major so bashful so famous &c. he shou'd come befor the captain but never mind. I at first thought the major cross and proud but I was mistaken. he is about nineteen, nephew to the Genl and acts as Major of brigade to him, he cannot be extolld for the graces of person but for those of the mind he may justly be celebrated, he is large in his person manly and an engaging countenance and address. Finley is wretched ugly, but he went away last night so shall not particularize him. nothing of any moment to day. no acquaintance with the officers Col Wood and Line and Gould din'd with us I was dress'd in my chintz and lookd smarter than night before

fourth day Oct 21st. I just now met the major, very reservd nothing but Good morning or your servant madam. but Furnival is most agreable he chats every opportunity but luckily has a wife, I have heard strange things of the Major. worth a fortune of thirty thousand pounds independant of anybody the major more over is vastly bashful. so much so he can hardly look at the ladies, (excuse me good sir I really thought you were not clever if tis bashfulness only we will drive that away)

fifthday sixthday and seventhday pass'd the Genl still here the major still bashful.

firstday evening prepare to here amazing things the Genl was invited to dine, was engag'd, but Col Wood Line — Majr Stodard and Dr Edwards din'd with us. in the afternoon and Stodard addressing himself to mamma pray ma'am do you know Miss Nancy Bond, I told him of the amiable girl's death. This major had been at Philada College. in the evening I was diverting Johny at the table when he drew his chair to the table and began to play with the child, I ask'd him if he knew. N. Bond no ma'am but I have seen her very often one word brought on another and we chatted the greatest part of the evening he said he knew me directly as he seen me. told me exactly where we liv'd, it rains now so adieu,

secondday 26th oct. a very rainy morning so like to prove the officers in the house all day. secondday afternoon the General and officers drank tea with us. and stay'd part of the evening after supper I went into aunts where sat the Genl Col Line and Major Stodard. so lidy and me seated ourselves at the table in order to read a verse book, the Maj was holding a candle for the Genl who was reading a newspaper. he look'd at us turn'd away his eyes. look'd again, put the candle stick down, up he jump'd out of the door he went. well said I to Lydy he will join us when he comes in. presently he return'd and seated himself on the table. pray ladies is there any songs in that book yes many, cant you favr me with a sight of it, no major tis a borrow'd book. Miss Sally cant you sing, no, thee may be sure I told the truth there. Liddy saucy girl told him I cou'd he beg'd and I deny'd. for my voice is not much better than the voice of a raven. we talk'd and laugh'd for an hour he is very clever amiable and polite. he has the softest voice never pronounces the R at all. I must tell thee to day arriv'd Col Guest and Major Letherberry the former a smart widower the latter a lawyer a sensible young fellow and will never swing for want of tongue, Dr Diggs come secondday a mighty disagreable man. we were oblig'd to ask him to tea, he must needs prop himself between the major and me, for which I did not thank him, after I had drank tea I jump'd from the table and seated myself at the fire the M. —— follow'd my example, drew his chair close to mine and entertain'd me very agreably. Oh Debby I have a thousand things to tell thee. I shall give thee so droll an account of my adventures that thee will smile, no occasion of that sally methinks I hear thee say. for thee tells me every triffle, but child thee is mistaken for I have not told thee half the civil things that are said of us *sweet* creatures at General Smallwoods quarters, I think I might have sent the gentlemen to thier Chambers. I made my adieus and home I went.

third day morn a polite good morning from the M. —— very sociable than ever. no wonder, a stoic cou'd not resist such affable damsels as we are, thirdday eve. Octr 27, we had again the pleasure of th' Genl, and suit at afternoon tea, he (the Genl I mean) is most agreable so lively so free and chats so gaily that I have quite an esteem for him, I must steel my heart. Capt Furnival is gone to Baltimore the residence of his belove'd wife, the Major and I had a little chat to ourselves this eve, no harm. I assure thee he and I are friends, this eve, came, a parson belonging to the Army he is, how shall I describe him, near seven foot high thin and meagre not a single personal charm very few mental ones. he fell violently in love with liddy at first sight, the first discover'd conquest that has been made since the arrival of the Genl, come shall we chat about Col Guest he's very pretty a charming person. his eyes are exceptionable very stern and he so rolls them about that mine allways fall under them, he bears the character of a brave officer, another admirer of Liddys and she is of him when will sallys admirers. appear ah that indeed, why Sally has not charms sufficient to peirce the heart of a Soldier, but still I won't dispair who knows what mischief I yet may do. Well Debby heres Dr Edwards come again, now we shall not want clack for he has a perpetual motion in his head and if he was not so clever as he is, we shou'd get tired,

fourth day oct. 28th, nothing material engag'd us to day.

fifthday Oct 29th, I walk'd into aunts this evening I met the Major, well thee will think I am writing his history but not, so, pleas'd with the encounter, Liddy Betsy, Stodard and myself seated by the fire and chatted away an hour in lively agreable conversation, I cannot pretend to write all he said, but he shone in every subject that was talkd of.

sixthday eve. Oct 30th, nothing of consequence.

seventhday Oct 31st a most charming day. I walk'd to the door. reciev'd the salutation of the morn, from Stodard and other officers, as often as I go to the door so often have I seen the major we chat passingly as a fine day Miss Sally. Yes very fine Major. seventhday night another very charming conversation with the young Marylander, he seems possest of very amiable manners, sensible and agreable — he has by his unexceptionable deportment engag'd my esteem

firstday morn, Lidy Betsy and a TL. prisoner of this State

went to the Mill, we made very free with some continental flour. we were pow'derd mighty white to be sure home we came. Col Wood was standing at a window with a young officer, he gave him a push forward as much as to say observe what fine girls we have here for all I do not mention Wood as often as he deserves it is not that we are not sociable we are very much so and he is often at our house dines or drinks tea with us every day, Liddy and I had kind of an adventure with him this morn. we were in his chamber chatting about our little affairs, and no idea of being interrupted we were standing up each an arm on a chest of drawers the door bang'd open. — Col Wood. was in the room. we started, the colour flew into our faces. and crimson'd us over the tears flew into my eyes. it was very silly but his coming was so abrupt he was between us and the door Ladies do not be scar'd I only want somthing from my portmantue I beg you not to be disturb'd, we ran by him like two partridges into mammas room threw ourselves in to chairs and reproach'd each other for being so foolish as to blush and look so silly I was very much vex'd at myself. so was Liddy the Col laugh'd at us and it blew over. the army had orders to march to day the regulars accordingly did Genl Smallwood had the command of Militia at that time and they being in the rear were not to leave their encampment till secondday. observe how Militaryish I talk no wonder. when I am surrounded by people of that order. the Genl. Colonels. Wood Line Guest Crawford. Majors Stoddard and Letherberry din'd with us to day. after dinner Liddy Betsy and thy smart journaliser put on thier bonnets, determin'd to take a walk we left the house I naturally look'd back when behold the two Majors seem'd debating whether to follow us or not. Liddy said we shall have their attendance but I did not think so they opend the gate and came fast after us, they overtook us about ten pole from home and beg'd leave to attend us no fear of a refusal. they enquird where we were going to nieghbour Roberts's. we will introduce you to his daughters you us to Genl Stevens the affair was concluded and we shortened the way with lively conversation our intentions of going to Roberts was frustrated as the rain that had fall'n lately had rais'd Wisahicken too high to attempt crossing it on foot. we alterd the plan of our ramble. left the road and walk'd near two miles thro' the woods. M. Letherberry observing my locket repeated with the energy of a comedian

On her white neck a sparkling cross she wore
That jews might kiss or infidels adore

I reply'd my trinket bore no resemblance to a cross. tis somthing better, ma'am, tis nonsense to pretend to recount all that was said my memory is not so obliging, but it is sufficient that nothing happend during our little excursion, but what was very agreable and intirely consistent with the strictest rules of politeness & decorum. I was vex'd a little at tearing my muslin petticoat I had on my white whim, quite as nice as a first day in town. we return'd home safe. Smallwood. Wood and Stodard drank tea with us. and spent the greatest part of the evening. I declare this genl is very entertaining so good naturd so good humour'd, yet so sensible I wonder he is not married are there no ladies form'd to his taste. some people my dear think that theres no difference between good nature and good humour. but according to my opinion they differ widely good nature consists in a naturally amiable and even disposition free from all peevishness and fretting, it is accompany'd by a natural gracefulness a manner of doing and saying everything agreably, in short it steals the senses and captivates the heart. good humour. consists in being pleas'd and who wou'd thank a person for being chearful if they had nothing to make them other ways, good humour is a very agreable companion for an afternoon but give me good nature for life. adieu tonight

secondday morn November 1st, today the Militia marches and the Genl and officers leave us high ho. I am very sorry for when you have been with agreable people tis impossible not to feel regret when they bid you adieu perhaps for ever. when they leve us we shall be immur'd in solitude the Major looks dull secondday noon about two o clock the Gen and Major come to bid us adieu, with daddy and mammy they shook hands very friendly to us they bow'd politely our hearts were full I thought major was affected good by miss Sally spoken very low. he walk'd hastily and mounted his horse. they promis'd to visit us soon. we stood at the door to take a last look all of us very sober the major turn'd his horses head and rode back dismounted I have forgot my pistols pass'd us and run up stairs he came swiftly back as if wishing through inclination to stay by duty compell'd to go. he remounted his horse farewell ladies till I see you again canter'd away. we look'd at him till the turn in the road hid him from our sight, amiable major clever fellow good young man was echo'd from one to the other I wonder whether we shall ever see him again he has our wish for his safety. Well heres uncle Miles heartily glad of that am I his family are well and at reading. secondday even Jesse who went with the Genl return'd I had by him a letter from my dear Polly Fishbourn she is at George Emlens, head quarters is at their house, we had compliments from the Genl and Major they are very well dispos'd of at Evan Merediths six miles from here. I wrote to Polly by uncle Miles who waited upon Genl Washington next morn.

3rd day morn Novem,b 2d. it seems strange not to see our house as it us'd to be we are very still no rattling of Waggons glittering of musquets the beating of the distant drum is all we hear. Cols Wood Line Guest and M. Letherberry are still here the two last leave to day. Wood and Line will soon bid us adieu amiable Wood he is esteem'd by all that know him every body has a good word for him.

here I skip a week or two nothing of consequence occurring, Wood & Line are gone some time since arriv'd two officers Lieutenant Lee and Warring Virginians I had only the salutations of the morn from them Lee is not remarkable one way or the other Warring an insignificant piece enough. Lee sings prettyly and talks a great deal how good turkey hash and fry'd homany is (a pretty discourse to entertain the ladies) extolls Virginia and execrates Maryland which by the by I provok'd them too for tho' I admir'd both Virga. and Maryd, I laugh'd at the former and prais'd the latter ridiculed there manner of speaking, I took great delight in tiezing them I believe I did it some times ill natur'dly, but I dont care. they were not I am certain almost first rate gentlemen (how different from our other officers) but they are gone to Virginia where they may sing dance and eat turkey hash and fry'd homny all day long if they chuse. nothing scarcely lowers a man in my opinion more than talking of eating what they love and what they hate Lee and Warring were proficients in this science, eneough of them.

Decem. 5th sixthday oh gracious Debby I am all alive with fear. the English have come out to attack (as we imagine) our army. they are on Chestnut hill our army three mile this side, what will become of us. only six mile distant, we are in hourly expectation of an engagment. I fear we shall be in the midst of it heaven defend us from so dreadful a sight. the battle of Germantown and the horrors of that day are recent in my mind. it will be sufficiently dreadful if we are only in hearing of the firing to think how many of our fellow creatures are plung'd into the boundless ocean of eternity few of them prepar'd to meet thier fate but they are summon'd befor an all merciful judge from whom they have a great deal to hope.

seventhday december 6th. no firing this morn. I hope for one more quiet day. seventhday noon 4 o' clock I was much alarm'd just now. setting in the parlour indulging melancholy reflections when somebody burst open the door, sally here's major Stodard I jump'd, our conjectures were various concerning his coming, the poor fellow from great fatigue and want of rest together with being expos'd to the night air. had caught cold which brought on a fever. he cou'd scarcely walk and I went into aunts to see him. I was surpriz'd, instead of the lively alert blooming Stodard who was on his feet the instant we enter'd, he look'd pale thin and dejected too weak to rise a bow. and how are you miss sally. how does thee do Major I seated myself near him inquir'd the couse of his indisposition, ask'd for the genl. receiv'd his compliments not willing to fatigue him with too much chat I told him adieu to night aunt hannah Foulke senr adminester'd something, Jesse assisted him to his chamber he had not lain down five minutes before he was fast asleep. adieu I hope we shall enjoy a good nights rest.

firstday morn decemr. 7th. I trip'd into aunts there sat the major rather more like himself. how natural it was to see him good morning miss sally, good morrow major how does thee do to day? Major. I feel quite recover'd Sally Well I fancy this indisposition has sav'd thy head this time. Major, no ma'am for if I hear a firing I shall soon be with them. that was heroic. about eleven I dress'd myself silk and Cotton gown. it is made

without an apron I feel quite awkardish, and prefer the girlish
dress. firstday afternoon a Mr Seaton and Stodard drank tea
with us. he and me had a little private chat after tea, in the
eve, Seaton, went into aunts mamma went to see Prissa who
is poorly. papa withdrew to talk to some strangers, Liddy just
then came in so we engag'd in an agreable conversation I
beg'd him to come and give us a circumstancial account of the
battle if there shou'd be one. I certainly will ma'am if I am
favour'd with life, Liddy unluckyly took it into her head to
blunder out somthing about a person being in the kitchen,
who had come from the army. Stodard ever anxious to hear
jump'd up goodnight to you Ladies was the word and he disappear'd but not for ever. Liddy thee hussy what busyness had
thee to mention a word of the army. thee see's it sent him off.
thy evil genius prevaild and we all feel the effects of it. Lord
bless me said Lidy I had not a thought of his going or for ten
thousand worlds I wou'd not spoke. but we cannot recall the
past. well we laugh'd and chatted at a noisy rate till a summons for Liddy, parted us. I sat negligently on my chair
thought brought on thought and I got so low spirited that I
cou'd hardly speak the dread of an engagement our dreadful
situation (if a battle shou'd ensue) we shou'd be in join'd to
my anxiety for P. Fishbourn and family who wou'd be in the
midst of the scene, was the occasion and yet I did not feel half
so frightened as I expected to be, tis amazing how we get rec-
oncild to such things six months ago. the bare idea of being
within ten aye twenty miles of a battle wou'd almost distracted
me and now tho' two such large armys are within six miles of
us. we can be cheerful and converse calmly of it, it verifies the
old proverb that "Use is second nature" I forgot one little
piece of intelligence in which the girls say I discover'd a particular partiality for our Marylander but disclaim anything of
the kind these saucy creatures are for ever finding out wonders
and for metamorphosing mole hills in to mountains.

> Friendship I offer pure and free
> And who with such a freind as ME
> Cou'd ask or wish for more.

if they charg'd thee with vanity sally it wou'd not be very unjust, Debby Norris, be quiet no reflections or I have done,

but the piece of intelligence sally. is just coming Debby. in the afternoon we distinctly heard platoon firing every body was at the door. I in the horrors. the Armies were as we judgd engag'd, very composdly. says the Major to our servant will you be kind eneough to saddle my horse. I shall go. accordingly the horse was taken from the hospitable quiet barn to plunge into the thickest ranks of war. cruel change. Seaton insisted to the Major that the armies were still nothing but skirmishing with the flanking parties do not go we happen'd (us girls I mean) to be standing in the kitchen the Maj. passing thro' in a hurry and I forsooth discover'd a strong partiality by saying oh major thee is not going. he turn'd round yes I am Miss Sally. bow'd and went into the road. we all pitied him the firing rather decreas'd and after perswasions inumerable from my father and Seaton. and the firing over he reluctantly agreed to stay ill as he was he wou'd have gone it shew'd his bravery. of which we all believe him possess'd of a large share.

secondday Decemr 8th. rejoice with us my dear the British have returnd to the city charming news this. may we ever be thankful to the Almighty disposer of events for his care and protection of us while surrounded with dangers

Major went to the army nothing for him to do so return'd 3d or 4th day I forget which he was very ill kept his chamber most of the day in the even' I seen him he has a violent sore mouth I pity him mightyly but pity is a poor remedy.

fifthday Decemr 11th. our Army mov'd as we thought to go into winter quarters, but we hear there is a party of the enemy gone over Schuyllkill so our army went to look at them I observ'd to Stodard so you are going to leave us to the English yes hahaha leave you for the E. he has a certain indifference about him somtimes that to strangers is not very pleasing, he somtimes is silent for minutes one of these silent fits was interrupted the other day by his clasping his hands and exclaiming aloud oh My God I wish this war was at an end. noon the M. gone to Camp. I dont think we shall see him again. well strange creature that I am here have I been going on without giving the an account of two officers one who will be a principal character thier names are Capt Lipscomb and a Mr Tilly the former a tall genteel man very delicate from an indisposition and has a softness in his Countenance, that is very pleasing and has the finest head of hair I ever saw. tis light shining auburn; the fashion of his hair was this negligently ty'd, and waving down his back, well may it be said

Loose flow'd the soft redundance of his hair.

He has not hitherto shewn himself a ladies man tho' he is perfectly polite now let me attempt to characterize Tilly, he seems a wild noisy mortal, tho' I am not much acquainted with him he appears bashful when with girls, we disipated the Majors bashfulness. but I doubt we have not so good a subject, now he is above the common size rather genteel an extreme pretty ruddy face, hair brown and a sufficiency of it, a very great laughter, and talks so excessively fast that he often begins sentences without finishing the last which confuses him very much and then he blushes and laughs and in short he keeps me in perpetual good humour but the creature has not address'd one civil thing to me since he came. but I have not done with his accomplishments yet for he is a musician that is he plays on the German flute and has it here. fifthday night the family retir'd take the adventures of the afternoon as they occurd, Seaton and Capt Lipscomb drank tea with us. while we sat at tea, the parlour door was open'd in came Tilly, his appearance was elegant he had been riding the evening had given the most beautiful glow to his cheeks and blow'd his hair carelessly round his face oh my heart thought I be secure. the caution was needless I found it without a wish to stray, when the tea equipage was remov'd the conversation turnd on politicks a subject I avoid. I gave Betsy a hint I rose she followd and we went to seek Lydy, we chatted a few minutes at thee door. the moon shone with uncommon Splendour our spirits were high, I propos'd a walk. the girls agreed, when we reach'd the Poplar tree, we stop'd: our ears were assail'd by a number of voices, a party of Lighthorse said one the English perhaps lets run home. no no said I be heroines, at last two or three men on horseback came in sight, we walk'd on, the well known voice of the Major saluted our hearing with how do you Ladies, we turn'd ourselves about with one accord, he not relishing the idea of sleeping on the banks of the Schuylkill had return'd to the Mill we chatted along the road till we reach'd our hospitable mansion,

Stodard dismounted and went into Jese's parlour. I sat there
a half hour. he is very amiable Seaton Lipscomb Tilly and my
father hearing of his return and impatient of the news came in
at one door while I made my exit at the other I am vex'd at
Tilly who has his flute and does nothing but play the fool he
begins a tune, plays a note or so then stops, well after awhile
he begins again, stops again, will that do Seaton hah hah hah.
he has given us but two regular tunes since he arriv'd, I am
passionatly fond of music how boyish he behaves.

Sixthday Decemr. 12th, 1777 I run into aunts this morn to
chat with the girls, Major Stodard join'd us in a few minutes,
I verily believe the man is fond of the ladies, and what to me
is astonishing he has not discover'd the smallest degree of
pride. whether he is artful eneough to conceal it under the
veil of humility or whether he has none is a question, but I
am inclin'd to think it the latter. I really am of opinion that
there is few of the young fellows of the modern age exempt
from vanity, more especially those who are bless'd with exterior graces. If they have a fine pair of eyes they are ever rolling
them about a fine set of teeth, mind they are great laughers,
a genteel person, for ever changing thier attitudes to shew
them to advantage, oh vanity! vanity! how boundless is thy
sway! but to resume this interview with Major Stodard, we
were very lively and sprightly, I was darning an apron upon
which he was pleas'd to compliment me. well miss Sally what
wou'd you do if the British were to come here do exclaim'd I
be frighten'd just to death, he laugh'd and said he wou'd escape thier rage by getting behind the representation of a
British Grandadier which you have upstairs, of all things I
shou'd like to frighten Tilly with it pray ladies lets fix it in his
chamber tonight, if thee will take all the blame we will assist
thee that I will he reply'd, and this was the plan we had
brought some weeks ago a B. Grandadier from Uncle Miles's
on purpose to divert us. it is remarkably well executed six foot
high and makes a martial appearance. this we agreed to stand
at the door that opens into the road, (the house has four
rooms on a floor with a wide entry running through) with another figure that would add to the deciet one of our servants
was to stand behind them. others were to serve as occasion
offer'd, after an half hours converse in which we rais'd our

expectiations to the highest pitch we parted, if our scheme answers I shall communicate in the eve till then adieu tis dining hour. sixthday night never did I more sincerely wish to possess a descriptive genius than I do now. all that I can write will fall infinitely short of the truly diverting scene that I have been witness too to night, but as I mean to attempt an acount I had as well shorten the preface and begin the story. in the beginning of the even I went to Liddy and beg'd her to secure the swords and pistols which were in thier parlour. the Marylander hearing our voices join'd us. I told him of my proposal whether he thought it a good one or not I cant say but he approv'd of it, and Liddy went in and brought her apron full of swords & pistols. when this was done Stodard join'd the officers we girls went and stood at the first landing of the stairs. the Gentlemen were very merry and chatting on public affairs when Seatons Negro (observe that Seaton being indispos'd was appriz'd of the scheme) open'd the door candle in his hand and said theres somebody at the door that wishes to see you who all of us? said Tilly yes sir answer'd the boy, they rose (the Major as he afterwards said almost dying with laughing) and walk'd into the entry Tilly first in full expectation of news the first object that struck his view was a British soldier in a moment his ears were saluted with "is there any Rebel officers here" in a thundering voice, not waiting for a second word he darted like lightening out at the front door, through the yard bolted o'er the fence swamps fences thorn hedges and plough'd fields no way impeded his retreat, he was soon out of hearing the woods echo'd with which way did he go stop him surround the house, the amiable Lipscomb had his hand on the latch of the door. intending to attempt his escape, Stodard considering his indisposition acquainted him with the deciet, we females ran down stairs to join the general laugh. I walk'd into Jesses parlour there sat poor Stodard (whose sore lips must have reciev'd no advantage from this) almost convuls'd with laughing rolling in an arm chair he said nothing I believe he cou'd not have spoke. Major Stodard said I go call Tilly back he will lose himself indeed he will, every word interrupt with a ha ha, at last he rose and went to the door and what a loud voice could avail in bringing him back he try'd, figure to thyself this

Tilly of a snowy even: no hat shoes down at heel, hair unty'd flying across meadows creeks and mudholes flying from what — why a bit of painted wood. but he was ignorant of what it was the idea of being made a prisoner wholly engross'd his mind and his last resource was to run after a while we being in rather more composure, and our bursts of laughter less frequent yet by no means subsided, in full assembly of girls and officers Tilly enter'd the greatest part of my risibility turn'd into pity, inexpressible confusion had taken intire possession of his countenance, his fine hair hanging dishevell'd down his shoulders. all splash'd with mud yet his fright confusion and race had not divested him of his beauty, he smil'd as he trip'd up the steps, but twas vexation plac'd it on his features joy at that moment was banish'd from his heart. he briskly walk'd five or six steps, then stopt and took a general survey of us all. Where have you been Mr Tilly? ask'd one officer (we girls were silent) I really imagind said Stodard that you were gone for your pistols I follow'd you to prevent danger an excessive laugh at each question, which it was impossible to restrain pray where were your pistols Tilly. he broke his silence by the following expression You may all go to the D——l I never heard him utter an indecent expression before at last his good nature gain'd a compleat acendance over his anger and he join'd heartily in the laugh I will do him the justice to say that he bore it charmingly no cowardly threats, no vengeance denouncd Stodard cought hold of his coat come look at what you ran from and drag'd him to the door. he gave it a look said it was very natural and by the singularity of his expressions gave fresh couse for diversion, we all retir'd to our different parlours for to rest our faces if I may say so well certainly these military folks will laugh all night, such screaming I never did hear adieu to night,

George Washington: General Orders

Head Quarters, at the Gulph, December 17, 1777.
Parole Warwick.   Countersigns Woodbridge, Winchester.
The Commander in Chief with the highest satisfaction expresses his thanks to the officers and soldiers for the fortitude and patience with which they have sustained the fatigues of the Campaign. Altho' in some instances we unfortunately failed, yet upon the whole Heaven hath smiled on our Arms and crowned them with signal success; and we may upon the best grounds conclude, that by a spirited continuance of the measures necessary for our defence we shall finally obtain the end of our Warfare, Independence, Liberty and Peace. These are blessings worth contending for at every hazard. But we hazard nothing. The power of America alone, duly exerted, would have nothing to dread from the force of Britain. Yet we stand not wholly upon our ground. France yields us every aid we ask, and there are reasons to believe the period is not very distant, when she will take a more active part, by declaring war against the British Crown. Every motive therefore, irresistably urges us, nay commands us, to a firm and manly perseverance in our opposition to our cruel oppressors, to slight difficulties, endure hardships, and contemn every danger. The General ardently wishes it were now in his power, to conduct the troops into the best winter quarters. But where are these to be found? Should we retire to the interior parts of the State, we should find them crowded with virtuous citizens, who, sacrificing their all, have left Philadelphia, and fled thither for protection. To their distresses humanity forbids us to add. This is not all, we should leave a vast extent of fertile country to be despoiled and ravaged by the enemy, from which they would draw vast supplies, and where many of our firm friends would be exposed to all the miseries of the most insulting and wanton depredation. A train of evils might be enumerated, but these will suffice. These considerations make it indispensibly necessary for the army to take such a position,

as will enable it most effectually to prevent distress and to give the most extensive security; and in that position we must make ourselves the best shelter in our power. With activity and diligence Huts may be erected that will be warm and dry. In these the troops will be compact, more secure against surprises than if in a divided state and at hand to protect the country. These cogent reasons have determined the General to take post in the neighbourhood of this camp; and influenced by them, he persuades himself, that the officers and soldiers, with one heart, and one mind, will resolve to surmount every difficulty, with a fortitude and patience, becoming their profession, and the sacred cause in which they are engaged. He himself will share in the hardship, and partake of every inconvenience.

To morrow being the day set apart by the Honorable Congress for public Thanksgiving and Praise; and duty calling us devoutely to express our grateful acknowledgements to God for the manifold blessings he has granted us. The General directs that the army remain in it's present quarters, and that the Chaplains perform divine service with their several Corps and brigades. And earnestly exhorts, all officers and soldiers, whose absence is not indispensibly necessary, to attend with reverence the solemnities of the day.

Albigence Waldo:
Diary, December 11–29, 1777

December 11.—At four o'clock the Whole Army were Order'd to March to Swedes Ford on the River Schuylkill, about 9 miles N. W. of Chestnut Hill, and 6 from White Marsh our present Encampment. At sun an hour high the whole were mov'd from the Lines and on their march with baggage. This Night encamped in a Semi circle nigh the Ford. The enemy had march'd up the West side of Schuylkill—Potter's Brigade of Pennsylvania Militia were already there, & had several skirmishes with them with some loss on his side and considerable on the Enemies. An English Serj. deserted to us this Day, and inform'd that Webb's Regt kill'd many of their men on 7th, that he himself took Webb's Serj. Major who was a former Deserter from them, and was to be hanged this day.

I am prodigious Sick & cannot get any thing comfortable—what in the name of Providence am I to do with a fit of Sickness in this place where nothing appears pleasing to the Sicken'd Eye & nausiating Stomach. But I doubt not Providence will find out a way for my relief. But I cannot eat Beef if I starve, for my stomach positively refuses to entertain such Company, and how can I help that?

December 12.—A Bridge of Waggons made across the Schuylkill last Night consisting of 36 waggons, with a bridge of Rails between each. Some skirmishing over the River. Militia and dragoons brought into Camp several Prisoners. Sun Set—We were order'd to march over the River—It snows—I'm Sick—eat nothing—No Whiskey—No Forage—Lord—Lord—Lord. The Army were 'till Sun Rise crossing the River—some at the Waggon Bridge & some at the Raft Bridge below. Cold & uncomfortable.

December 13.—The Army march'd three miles from the West side of the River and encamp'd near a place call'd the

Gulph and not an improper name neither, for this Gulph seems well adapted by its situation to keep us from the pleasures & enjoyments of this World, or being conversant with any body in it. It is an excellent place to raise the Ideas of a Philosopher beyond the glutted thoughts and Reflexions of an Epicurian. His Reflexions will be as different from the Common Reflexions of Mankind as if he were unconnected with the world, and only conversant with immaterial beings. It cannot be that our Superiors are about to hold consultations with Spirits infinitely beneath their Order, by bringing us into these utmost regions of the Terraqueous Sphere. No, it is, upon consideration for many good purposes since we are to Winter here — 1st There is plenty of Wood & Water. 2dly There are but few families for the soldiery to Steal from — tho' far be it from a Soldier to Steal. 4ly There are warm sides of Hills to erect huts on. 5ly They will be heavenly Minded like Jonah when in the Belly of a Great Fish. 6ly They will not become home Sick as is sometimes the Case when Men live in the Open World — since the reflections which will naturally arise from their present habitation, will lead them to the more noble thoughts of employing their leisure hours in filling their knapsacks with such materials as may be necessary on the Journey to another Home.

December 14. — Prisoners & Deserters are continually coming in. The Army which has been surprisingly healthy hitherto, now begins to grow sickly from the continued fatigues they have suffered this Campaign. Yet they still show a spirit of Alacrity & Contentment not to be expected from so young Troops. I am Sick — discontented — and out of humour. Poor food — hard lodging — Cold Weather — fatigue — Nasty Cloaths — nasty Cookery — Vomit half my time — smoak'd out of my senses — the Devil's in't — I can't Endure it — Why are we sent here to starve and Freeze — What sweet Felicities have I left at home; A charming Wife — pretty Children — Good Beds — good food — good Cookery — all agreeable — all harmonious. Here all Confusion — smoke & Cold — hunger & filthyness — A pox on my bad luck. There comes a bowl of beef soup — full of burnt leaves and dirt, sickish enough to make a Hector spue — away with it Boys — I'll live like the Chameleon upon Air. Poh! Poh! crys Patience within

me — you talk like a fool. Your being sick Covers your mind
with a Melanchollic Gloom, which makes every thing about
you appear gloomy. See the poor Soldier, when in health —
with what cheerfulness he meets his foes and encounters every
hardship — if barefoot, he labours thro' the Mud & Cold
with a Song in his mouth extolling War & Washington — if
his food be bad, he eats it notwithstanding with seeming content — blesses God for a good Stomach and Whistles it into
digestion. But harkee Patience, a moment — There comes a
Soldier, his bare feet are seen thro' his worn out Shoes, his
legs nearly naked from the tatter'd remains of an only pair of
stockings, his Breeches not sufficient to cover his nakedness,
his Shirt hanging in Strings, his hair dishevell'd, his face meagre; his whole appearance pictures a person forsaken & discouraged. He comes, and crys with an air of wretchedness &
despair, I am Sick, my feet lame, my legs are sore, my body
cover'd with this tormenting Itch — my Cloaths are worn
out, my Constitution is broken, my former Activity is exhausted by fatigue, hunger & Cold, I fail fast I shall soon be
no more! and all the reward I shall get will be — "Poor Will
is dead." People who live at home in Luxury and Ease,
quietly possessing their habitations, Enjoying their Wives &
families in peace, have but a very faint Idea of the unpleasing
sensations, and continual Anxiety the Man endures who is in
a Camp, and is the husband and parent of an agreeable family. These same People are willing we should suffer every
thing for their Benefit & advantage, and yet are the first to
Condemn us for not doing more!!

   December 15. — Quiet. Eat Pessimmens, found myself better
for their Lenient Opperation. Went to a house, poor & small,
but good food within — eat too much from being so long
Abstemious, thro' want of palatables. Mankind are never truly
thankfull for the Benefits of life, until they have experienc'd
the want of them. The Man who has seen misery knows best
how to enjoy good. He who is always at ease & has enough
of the Blessings of common life is an Impotent Judge of the
feelings of the unfortunate. . . .

   December 16. — Cold Rainy Day, Baggage ordered over the
Gulph of our Division, which were to march at Ten, but the
baggage was order'd back and for the first time since we have

been here the Tents were pitch'd, to keep the men more comfortable. Good morning Brother Soldier (says one to another) how are you? All wet I thank'e, hope you are so (says the other). The Enemy have been at Chestnut Hill Opposite to us near our last encampment the other side Schuylkill, made some Ravages, kill'd two of our Horsemen, taken some prisoners. We have done the like by them. . . .

December 18. — Universal Thanksgiving — a Roasted pig at Night. God be thanked for my health which I have pretty well recovered. How much better should I feel, were I assured my family were in health. But the same good Being who graciously preserves me, is able to preserve them & bring me to the ardently wish'd for enjoyment of them again.

Rank & Precedence make a good deal of disturbance & confusion in the American Army. The Army are poorly supplied with Provision, occasioned it is said by the Neglect of the Commissary of Purchases. Much talk among Officers about discharges. Money has become of too little consequence. The Congress have not made their Commissions valuable Enough. Heaven avert the bad consequences of these things!!

*　　　*　　　*　　　*　　　*　　　*

up the Bristol Road & so got out unnoticed. He inform'd that Cornwallis was embark'd for England, and that some High-landers had gone to N. York for Winter Quarters.

There is nothing to hinder Parties of the like kind above mention'd, continually coming out between Delaware and Schuylkill, and plundering and destroying the Inhabitants.

Our brethren who are unfortunately Prisoners in Philadelphia meet with the most savage and inhumane treatments that Barbarians are Capable of inflicting. Our Enemies do not knock them in the head or burn them with torches to death, or flee them alive, or gradually dismember them till they die, which is customary among Savages & Barbarians. No, they are worse by far. They suffer them to starve, to linger out their lives in extreem hunger. One of these poor unhappy men, drove to the last extreem by the rage of hunger, eat his own fingers up to the first joint from the hand, before he died. Others eat the Clay, the Lime, the Stones of the Prison Walls. Several who died in the Yard had pieces of Bark, Wood,

Clay & Stones in their mouths, which the ravings of hunger
had caused them to take in for food in the last Agonies of
Life! "These are thy *mercies*, O Britain!"

December 21. — Preparations made for hutts. Provisions
Scarce. Mr. Ellis went homeward — sent a Letter to my Wife.
Heartily wish myself at home, my Skin & eyes are almost
spoil'd with continual smoke. A general cry thro' the Camp
this Evening among the Soldiers, "No Meat! No Meat!" —
the Distant vales Echo'd back the mellancholly sound — "No
Meat! No Meat!" Immitating the noise of Crows & Owls,
also, made a part of the confused Musick.

What have you for your Dinners Boys? "Nothing but Fire
Cake & Water, Sir." At night, "Gentlemen the Supper is
ready." What is your Supper Lads? "Fire Cake & Water, Sir."
Very poor beef has been drawn in our Camp the greater part
of this season. A Butcher bringing a Quarter of this kind of
Beef into Camp one day who had white Buttons on the knees
of his breeches, a Soldier cries out — "There, there Tom is
some more of your fat Beef, by my soul I can see the
Butcher's breeches buttons through it."

December 22. — Lay excessive Cold & uncomfortable last
Night — my eyes are started out from their Orbits like a
Rabbit's eyes, occasion'd by a great Cold & Smoke.

What have you got for Breakfast, Lads? "Fire Cake &
Water, Sir." The Lord send that our Commissary of Purchases
may live on Fire Cake & Water, 'till their glutted Gutts are
turned to Pasteboard.

Our Division are under Marching Orders this morning. I
am ashamed to say it, but I am tempted to steal Fowls if I
could find them, or even a whole Hog, for I feel as if I could
eat one. But the Impoverish'd Country about us, affords but
little matter to employ a Thief, or keep a Clever Fellow in
good humour. But why do I talk of hunger & hard usage,
when so many in the World have not even fire Cake & Water
to eat.

The human mind is always poreing upon the gloomy side
of Fortune, and while it inhabits this lump of Clay, will always
be in an uneasy and fluctuating State, produced by a thousand
Incidents in common Life, which are deemed misfortunes,
while the mind is taken off from the nobler pursuit of matters

in Futurity. The sufferings of the Body naturally gain the Attention of the Mind, and this Attention is more or less strong, in greater or lesser souls, altho' I believe that Ambition & a high Opinion of Fame, makes many People endure hardships and pains with that fortitude we after times Observe them to do. On the other hand, a despicable opinion of the enjoyments of this Life, by a continued series of Misfortunes, and a long acquaintance with Grief, induces others to bear afflictions with becoming serenity and Calmness.

It is not in the power of Philosophy however, to convince a man he may be happy and Contented if he will, with a *Hungry Belly.* Give me Food, Cloaths, Wife & Children, kind Heaven! and I'll be as contented as my Nature will permit me to be.

This Evening a Party with two field pieces were order'd out. At 12 of the Clock at Night, Providence sent us a little Mutton, with which we immediately had some Broth made, & a fine Stomach for same. Ye who Eat Pumkin Pie and Roast Turkies, and yet Curse fortune for using you ill, Curse her no more, least she reduce your Allowance of her favours to a bit of Fire Cake, & a draught of Cold Water, & in Cold Weather too.

December 23. — The Party that went out last evening not Return'd to Day. This evening an excellent Player on the Violin in that soft kind of Musick, which is so finely adapted to stirr up the tender Passions, while he was playing in the next Tent to mine, these kind of soft Airs it immediately called up in remembrance all the endearing expressions, the Tender Sentiments, the sympathetic friendship that has given so much satisfaction and sensible pleasure to me from the first time I gained the heart & affections of the tenderest of the Fair. A thousand agreeable little incidents which have Occurr'd since our happy connection, and which would have pass'd totally unnoticed by such who are strangers to the soft & sincere passion of Love, were now recall'd to my mind, and filled me with these tender emotions, and Agreeable Reflections, which cannot be described, and which in spite of my Philosophy forced out the sympathetic tear. I wish'd to have the Musick Cease, and yet dreaded its ceasing, least I should loose sight of these dear Ideas, which gave me pain and pleasure at the same instant. Ah Heaven why is it that our harder fate so often deprives us of the enjoyment of what we most wish to enjoy this side of thy brighter realms. There is something in this strong passion of Love far more agreeable than what we can derive from any of the other Passions and which Duller Souls & Cheerless minds are insensible of, & laugh at — let such fools laugh at me.

December 24. — Party of the 22d not returned. Hutts go on Slowly — Cold & Smoke make us fret. But mankind are always fretting, even if they have more than their proportion of the Blessings of Life. We are never Easy, allways repining at the Providence of an Allwise & Benevolent Being, Blaming Our Country or faulting our Friends. But I don't know of any thing that vexes a man's Soul more than hot smoke continually blowing into his Eyes, & when he attempts to avoid it, is met by a cold and piercing Wind.

December 25, Christmas. — We are still in Tents — when we ought to be in huts — the poor Sick, suffer much in Tents this cold Weather. But we now treat them differently from what they used to be at home, under the inspection of Old Women and Doct. Bolus Linctus. We give them Mutton & Grogg and a Capital Medicine once in a While, to start the Disease from its foundation at once. We avoid Piddling Pills, Powders, Bolus's Linctus's Cordials and all such insignificant matters whose powers are Only render'd important by causing the Patient to vomit up his money instead of his disease. But very few of the sick Men Die.

December 26. — Party of the 22d not Return'd. The Enemy have been some Days the west Schuylkill from Opposite the City to Derby. Their intentions not yet known. The City is at present pretty Clear of them. Why don't his Excellency rush in & retake the City, in which he will doubtless find much Plunder? Because he knows better than to leave his Post and be catch'd like a d——d fool cooped up in the City. He has always acted wisely hitherto. His conduct when closely scrutinised is uncensurable. Were his Inferior Generals as skillfull as himself, we should have the grandest Choir of Officers ever God made. Many Country Gentlemen in the interior parts of the States who get wrong information of the Affairs & state of our Camp, are very much Surprized at Gl Washington's delay to drive off the Enemy, being falsely inform'd that his Army consists of double the Number of the Enemy's — such wrong information serves not to keep up the spirit of the People, as they must be by and by undeceiv'd to their no small disappointment; — it brings blame on his Excellency, who is deserving of the greatest encomiums; it brings disgrace on the Continental Troops, who have never evidenced the least backwardness in doing their duty, but on the contrary, have cheerfully endur'd a long and very fatigueing Campaign. 'Tis true they have fought but little this Campaign; which is not owing to any Unwillingness in Officers or Soldiers, but for want of convenient Opportunities, which have not offer'd themselves this Season; tho' this may be contradicted by many; but Impartial Truth in future History will clear up these points, and reflect lasting honour on the Wisdom & prudence of Genl Washington. The greatest Number of Continental Troops that have been with his Excelly this Campaign, never consisted of more than Eleven thousand; and the greatest Number of Militia in the field at Once were not more than 2000. Yet these accounts are exaggerated to 50 or 60,000. Howe, by the best, and most authentic Accounts has never had less than 10,000. If then, Genl Washington, by Opposing little more than an equal Number of young Troops, to Old Veterans has kept his Ground in general, Cooped them up in the City, prevented their making any considerable inroads upon him, Killed and wounded a very considerable number of them in different Skirmishes, and made many proselytes to the Shrine of Liberty by these little successes, and by the prudence, calmness, sedateness & wisdom with which he facilitates all his Opperations. This being the case, and his not having wantonly thrown away the lives of his Soldiers, but reserved them for another Campaign (if another should Open in the Spring) which is of the utmost consequence This then cannot be called an Inglorious Campaign. If he had risk'd a General Battle, and should have proved unsuccessfull, what in the name of Heaven would have been our case this Day. Troops are raised with great difficulty in the Southern States, many Regiments from these States do not consist of one hundred men. What then was the grand Southern Army before the N. England Troops joined them and if this Army is Cut off where should we get another as good. General Washington has doubtless considered these matters & his conduct this Campaign has certainly demonstrated his prudence & Wisdom.

This Evening, cross'd the Schuylkill with Dr Coln — eat plenty of Pessimmens which is the most lenient, Sub Acid & Subastringent fruit, I believe that grows.

December 27. — My horse shod. A Snow. Lodg'd at a Welchman's this Night, return'd to Camp in the morning of 28th. Snow'd last Night.

December 28. — Yesterday upwards of fifty Officers in Genl Greene's Division resigned their Commissions — Six or Seven of our Regiment are doing the like to-day. All this is occasion'd by Officers Families being so much neglected at home on account of Provisions. Their Wages will not by considerable, purchase a few trifling Comfortables here in Camp, & maintain their families at home, while such extravagant prices are demanded for the common necessaries of Life — What then have they to purchase Cloaths and other necessaries with? It is a Melancholly reflection that what is of the most universal importance, is most universally neglected — I mean keeping up the Credit of Money.

The present Circumstances of the Soldier is better by far than the Officers — for the family of the Soldier is provided for at the public expence if the Articles they want are above the common price — but the Officer's family, are obliged not only to beg in the most humble manner for the necessaries of Life, — but also to pay for them afterwards at the most exorbitant rates — and even in this manner, many of them who depend entirely on their Money, cannot procure half the material comforts that are wanted in a family — this produces continual letters of complaint from home. When the Officer has been fatiguing thro' wet & cold and returns to his tent where he finds a letter directed to him from his Wife, fill'd with the most heart aching tender Complaints, a Woman is capable of writing — Acquainting him with the incredible difficulty with which she procures a little Bread for herself & Children — and finally concluding with expressions bordering on dispair, of procuring a sufficiency of food to keep soul & Body together through the Winter — that her money is of

very little consequence to her — that she begs of him to consider that Charity begins at home — and not suffer his family
to perish with want, in the midst of plenty. When such,
I say — is the tidings they constantly hear from their families — What man is there — who has the least regard for his
family — whose soul would not shrink within him? Who
would not be disheartened from persevering in the best of
Causes — the Cause of his Country, — when such discourage-
ments as these ly in his way, which his Country might remedy
if they would?

December 28. — Building our Hutts.

December 29. — Continued the Work. Snow'd all day pretty
briskly. — The party of the 22d return'd — lost 18 men, who
were taken prisoners by being decoyed by the Enemies Light
Horse who brought up the Rear, as they Repass'd the Schuylkill to the City. Our party took 13 or 14 of their Horsemen. The Enemy came out to plunder — & have strip'd
the Town of Derby of even all its Household furniture. Our
party were several times mixed with the Enemy's horse — not
knowing them from our Connecticut Light Horse — their
Cloaks being alike.

So much talk about discharges among the Officers — & so
many are discharged — his Excellency lately expressed his fears
of being left Alone with the Soldiers only. Strange that our
Country will not exert themselves for his support, and save so
good — so great a Man from entertaining the least anxious
doubt of their Virtue and perseverance in supporting a Cause
of such unparallel'd importance!!

All Hell couldn't prevail against us, If Heaven continues no
more than its former blessings — and if we keep up the Credit
of our Money which has now become of the last consequence. If its Credit sinks but a few degrees more, we shall
then repent when 'tis too late — & cry out for help when no
one will appear to deliver. We who are in Camp, and depend
on our Money entirely to procure the comforts of life — feel
the Importance of this matter — He who is hording it up in
his Chest, thinks little more of it than how he shall procure
more.

John Laurens to Henry Laurens

Headquarters, Valley Forge,
January 14, 1778

I barely hinted to you my dearest Father my desire to augment the Continental Forces from an untried Source — I wish I had any foundation to ask for an extraordinary addition to those favors which I have already received from you I would sollicit you to cede me a number of your able bodied men Slaves, instead of leaving me a fortune — I would bring about a twofold good, first I would advance those who are unjustly deprived of the Rights of Mankind to a State which would be a proper Gradation between abject Slavery and perfect Liberty — and besides I would reinforce the Defenders of Liberty with a number of gallant Soldiers — Men who have the habit of Subordination almost indelibly impress'd on them, would have one very essential qualification of Soldiers — I am persuaded that if I could obtain authority for the purpose I would have a Corps of such men trained, uniformly clad, equip'd and ready in every respect to act at the opening of the next Campaign — The Ridicule that may be thrown on the Colour I despise, because I am sure of rendering essential Service to my Country — I am tired of the Languor with which so sacred a War as this, is carried on — my circumstances prevent me from writing so long a Letter as I expected and wish'd to have done on a subject which I have much at heart — I entreat you to give a favorable Answer to

Your most affectionate

———

Headquarters, Valley Forge.
February 2, 1778

My dear Father.

The more I reflect upon the difficulties and delays which are likely to attend the completing our Continental Regiments — the more anxiously is my mind bent upon the Scheme which I lately communicated to you — the obstacles to the execution of it had presented themselves to me, but by no means appeared insurmountable — I was aware of having that monster popular Prejudice open-mouthed against me — of undertaking to transform beings almost irrational into well disciplined Soldiers — of being obliged to combat the arguments and perhaps the intrigues of interested persons — but zeal for the public Service and an ardent desire to assert the rights of humanity determined me to engage in this arduous business, with the sanction of your Consent — my own perseverance aided by the Countenance of a few virtuous men will I hope enable me to accomplish it —

You seem to think my dear Father, that men reconciled by long habit to the miseries of their Condition, would prefer their ignominious bonds to the untasted Sweets of Liberty, especially when offer'd upon the terms which I propose — I confess indeed that the minds of this unhappy species must be debased by a Servitude from which they can hope for no Relief but Death — and that every motive to action but Fear, must be nearly extinguished in them — but do you think they are so perfectly moulded to their State as to be insensible that a better exists — will the galling comparison between themselves and their masters leave them unenlighten'd in this respect — can their Self-Love be so totally annihilated as not frequently to induce ardent wishes for a change —

You will accuse me perhaps my dearest friend of consulting my own feelings too much — but I am tempted to believe that this trampled people have so much human left in them, as to be capable of aspiring to the rights of men by noble exertions, if some friend to mankind would point the Road, and give them a prospect of Success — If I am mistaken in this, I would avail myself even of their weakness, and conquering one fear by another, produce equal good to the Public — You will ask in this view how do you consult the benefit of the Slaves — I answer that like other men, they are the Creatures of habit, their Cowardly Ideas will be gradually effaced, and they will be modified anew — their being rescued from a State of perpetual humiliation — and being advanced as it were in the Scale of being will compensate the dangers incident to their new State — the hope that will spring in each mans mind respecting his own escape — will prevent his being miserable — those who fall in battle will not lose much — those who survive will obtain their Reward —

Habits of Subordination — Patience under fatigues, Sufferings and Privations of every kind — are soldierly qualifications which these men possess in an eminent degree.

Upon the whole my dearest friend and father, I hope that my plan for serving my Country and the oppressed Negro-race will not appear to you the Chimara of a young mind deceived by a false appearance of moral beauty — but a laudable sacrifice of private Interest to Justice and the Public good —

You say that my own resources would be small, on account of the proportion of women and children — I do not know whether I am right for I speak from impulse and have not reasoned upon the matter — I say Altho my plan is at once to give freedom to the Negroes and gain Soldiers to the States; — in case of concurrence I shd: sacrifice the former interest, and therefore wd. change the Women and Children for able bodied men — the more of these I could obtain the better but 40 might be a good foundation to begin upon —

It is a pity that some such plan as I propose could not be more extensively executed by public Authority — a well chosen body of 5000 black men properly officer'd to act as light Troops in addition to our present establishment, might give us decisive Success in the next Campaign —

I have long deplored the wretched State of these men and considered in their history, the bloody wars excited in Africa to furnish America with Slaves — the Groans of despairing multitudes toiling for the Luxuries of Merciless Tyrants — I have had the pleasure of conversing with you sometimes upon the means of restoring them to their rights — When can it be better done, than when their enfranchisement may be made conducive to the Public Good, and be so modified as not to overpower their weak minds —

You ask what is the General's opinion upon this subject — he is convinced that the numerous tribes of blacks in the Southern parts of the Continent offer a resource to us that should not be neglected — with respect to my particular Plan, he only objects to it with the arguments of Pity, for a man who would be less rich than he might be —

I am obliged my dearest Friend and Father to take my leave for the present, you will excuse whatever exceptionable may have escaped in the course of my Letter — and accept the assurances of filial Love and Respect of

Your

John Laurens to Henry Laurens

Valley Forge, May 7, 1778

My dear Father.

I have to ask pardon for omitting in my last to thank you for the striped dimity which you were so kind as to send me — it did not occur to me 'till it was too late to recall the messenger, and my uneasiness was the greater as I had been frequently a delinquent in this way —

Yesterday we celebrated the new alliance with as much splendor as the short notice would allow — divine service preceded the rejoicing — after a proper pause, the several brigades marched by their right to their posts in order of battle — and the line was formed with admirable rapidity and precision — three Salutes of Artillery, thirteen each, and three general discharges of a running fire by the musketry, were given in honor of the King of France; — the friendly European powers — and the United American States — loud huzzas

the order with which the whole was conducted — the beautiful effect of the running fire which was executed to perfection — the martial appearance of the Troops — gave sensible pleasure to every one present — the whole was managed by signal, and the plan as formed by Baron de Steuben succeeded in every particular, which is in a great measure to be attributed to his unwearied attention and to the visible progress which the troops have already made under his discipline —

a cold collation was given afterwards at which all the officers of the Army & some Ladies of the neighborhood were present — Triumph beamed in every countenance — the greatness of mind and policy of Louis XVI were extol'd — and his long life tosted with as much sincerity as that of the British King used to be in former times — The General received such proofs of the love and attachment of his officers as must have given him the most exquisite feelings —

But amid all this inundation of Joy, there is a conduct observed towards him by certain great men which as it is humiliating must abate his happiness — I write with all the freedom of a person addressing himself to his dearest friend, and with all the unconstraint of a person delivering an unconsequential private opinion — I think then the Commander in chief of this Army is not sufficiently informed of all that is known by Congress of European Affairs — is it not a galling circumstance for him to collect the most important intelligence piece-meal and as they choose to give it, from Gentlemen who come from York — apart the chagrin which he must necessarily feel at such an appearance of Slight — it should be considered that in order to settle his plan of operations for the ensuing campaign, he should take into view the present state of European Affairs — and Congress should not leave him in the dark — if ever there was a man in the world whose moderation and Patriotism fitted him for the command of a Republican Army he is — and he merits an unrestrained confidence —

You will receive Copies of Letters from and to the General respecting Monsieur de la neuville — if I recollect right that Gentleman aims at the rank of Brigadier — this I can venture to assure you the General does not think either politic or proper to be granted to him — I took the liberty of mentioning this, that the Generals Letter which is couched in polite terms might not induce an opinion of his approving the demands of Mr de la neuville — the General thinks him a man of merit and liberal sentiments — but that he looks too high —

I take the liberty which is allowed when the restraint of officiality is laid to say many things which cannot with propriety be said in public Letters — and am with as much respect for you in your public capacity as love and friendship in our private relation

your

Ambrose Serle: Journal, March 9–June 19, 1778

MONDAY, 9th.

This Evening, Mr. Jos. Wanton had a long Conversation with me upon public Affairs; upon my "Address to the Colonies" (written in June 1776, but not published), which he solicited me to print; upon another Address from the Town to Lord H. at his Departure, wch I took the Liberty to say was unnecessary and not to be desired; upon corresponding with me in future; and (hinc illae lachrymae) upon the Subject of his own Losses & Expectations wch I told him must necessarily be postponed & submitted, not to the admiral, but elsewhere. I entered pretty fully into the Propriety & Expediency of supporting Govt. wch as much tended in effect to the Interest & Happiness of the Colonies, as of the Parent-State; and that a moderate Tax upon any People, both by keeping them constantly employed, by rendering them therefore more attached to those who procure them Employment, and by inducing a more vigorous Spirit of Industry, really profited a Country at large, tended to make them quiet & happy, and effected that Subordination & Distinction of Ranks in Society, wch is so much wanted here.

He gave me an Account of the Number of Inhabitants in this Colony, according to Census, made in the Years 1730 and 1774. The last was done, in order to answer certain Queries proposed by Lord Dartmouth, when Secry of State, which, as the Troubles were then breaking out, were never sent him from this Colony.

In the Town of *Newport* alone,

anno—1730 . . . . 3843 Inhabitants.
anno—1774 . . . . 9290, or 1596 Families.

In the Colony of *Rh. Island*.

anno—1730 17,935
anno—1774 59,500

Nothing can more plainly prove the Force of political Institutions upon the Conduct of a People, than the manners and Temper of the Inhabitants of this Island, wch was governed perhaps in the most truly democratic mode of any in the World. They are vulgar in their Behaviour, yet affect what they think Politeness, which is a sort of Rudeness that suits so ill with it, that they are never more irksome than when they offer to be civil. Generosity of Spirit is certainly not among their Virtues: They don't seem to feel an exalted Sentiment, nor are they troubled with refined Sensibilities. Their Religion is altogether problematical. They have almost every Sect of it here: Nor do they seem to think, that Unity & Concord are essential Branches of it. In short, they do not appear to merit much Confidence in any Shape. Smuggling, Trade, Republicanism, Dissensions, and Luxury, have spoiled their manners, & rendered them disagreeable Companions for the most part, as well as bad Subjects. As human Nature is the same every where, I can only impute all this to the Errors of their Government, which operates as strongly upon a People, as Education upon Individuals.

SUNDAY, 15th. MARCH.
Came on board the Eagle. A Rebel Colonel (Johannet), who came down in a Flag of Truce, dined with the Admiral. A mean-looking Fellow, but apparently not destitute of abilities, or rather of that low Cunning, which is the Characteristic of the New England People. He was very careful to use the Term *State* for the old Word *Colony*, and sate with his Uniform (Blue & Buff) in all the native Confidence of his Countrymen. A Commissary came with him from Genl. Burgoyne.

MONDAY, 16th.
Recd. a Lr from Revd. Mr. Inglis of N. York, by the Sphynx, wch arrived last night. Remained all this Week on board, expecting to sail: The Diamond arrived on Friday from the Delaware, and the Isis from N. York, the last of which brought an Account of the arrival of the Janry. Packet at N. York, on Saturday the 14th. inst, and of our Letters being forwarded thence by the Daphne, upon a Supposition that we had sailed to Philadelphia. Vague accounts were brought of various Commotions at Home & Changes here.

MONDAY, 23d.

About 12 o'Clock this Day, we sailed from Rh. Island with a fair Wind. About 3 we were abreast of Block Island, on the Western Side, about 4 or 5 miles distant. The Face of this Island, wch is about 10 miles long, and 5 or 6 broad, appears perfectly bare of Trees & even Shrubs, though there are about 70 Families scattered over it, most of whom are poor, & live partly by Fishing, and partly by raising Provisions for Newport & Rh. Island, of wch it is a Dependency. The Soil seems poor & sandy, & rises into easy Hills. On the East & West Sides it has two Bays, which are sometimes used as Roads in tempestuous Weather, though the Shelter is but indifferent. It is erroneously laid down in most of the Charts. It bears S of Point Judith; but it is often marked at S.S.E. about 7 Leagues.

On Tuesday, when we approached within a few Leagues of Sandy Hook, a strong Gale of Wind at E. accompanied with a Fog, obliged us to stand out to Sea, & drave us off the mouth of the Delaware. By the Sunday morning following, the 29th. instant, we were again in Sight of the Hook, but a violent Gale from the East compelled us to stand off again. With Difficulty & Hazard we worked off from the Jersey Shore, very near us to the Leeward, by the Use of our main Sail, wch in about two Hours' Time, by the Increase of the Storm, was rent from Top to Bottom, though quite new. Happily we had then made a considerable offing, or the Consequences might have been fatal to us all. The Storm raged all the Day & succeeding Night, increasing (as it seemed) every Hour; and the Sea rose to a most awful Degree. About 11 at Night, when all was dark & dismal, the Sea broke upon our Quarter, carried away part of the Gallery, and filled the Ward-Room with Water. The Tables, Chairs, Trunks, Boxes, Books, Cloaths, &c. driving in the Torrent from Side to Side, made a most tremendous & melancholy Scene. The Ship, not having been caulked for a long Time, was so leaky & took in so much Water every where, that it gave us all very alarming Apprehensions. I lay in my Bed, resigned to GOD'S Will, without much Anxiety, either for Life or Death. I considered, that He knew what was best, & could do nothing but what was right. My chief Concern was for my dear Family &

Friends.* — Towards morning, the Wind subsided; but the Swell was tremendous, & continued several Days. We were now to the Southward of Chesapeak Bay, driven between 2 & 300 miles from our Port, to which we were almost all the Week working up again. On Saturday *April* 4th. we appeared off the Hook again, & fired a Gun for a Pilot, who came off in the afternoon; but the Wind turning contrary we were obliged to anchor out of the Hook, where we lay till Monday in the afternoon (April 6th.) when we weighed and got safely in. — We found afterwards, that this Storm had done immense Damage at N. York & along the Coast.

TUESDAY, APRIL 7th.

Two or three small armed Vessels, with Troops on board, arrived last night from Egg Harbor, where they had destroyed some Salt Works, erected by the Rebels, and other Stores, to the Value of near £30,000, without the least Inconvenience. Enterprizes on the Coast, by small Detachments, would annoy the Rebels exceedingly, and with great Facility on our Part. — This morning I sailed up to Town in a Schooner, and was gladly recd. by my good Friend Mr. White, Govr. Tryon, & others. The next Day I employed in removing Papers from Ld. H's House, from whence he is removing all his Effects, and in visiting Acquaintances. I had a long Conference with Genl. Tryon, who seems resolved upon sailing for England, through Disgust at being slighted here. I deplored the evident Want of Harmony & Confidence in some principal Commanders. Govr. T. had sent me a Letter stating some Particulars, imagining I shd. not come up to N. York. All men seem persuaded, that a Revolution will happen shortly in the chief Command, and that a different mode of carrying on the War will be in consequence adopted. I dined with Commodore Hotham. In the Evening, I was visited by Govr. T. Mr Ch. Justice Smyth, Mr. Foxcroft, &c. with great Expressions of Civility. A Licenser of the Press I found established at N. York at 20s. per Day — a useless office & an addl. Expence!

*Mr. Addison's excellent Ode in *Spect.* No. 489. is very applicable to my Situation on this Day.

Thursday, April 9th.

Took Leave of my N. York Friends, and sailed to the Hook in Commodore Hotham's Tender. I got on board the Eagle before Sunset. In the Evening, some Vessels arrived from Rh. Island in five Days, which brought an Account of the Destruction of the Rebel Frigate Columbus of 32 Guns, in attempting to get out from Providence. The Sphynx, Capt. Graham, drave her on Shore, & burnt her.

Monday, 13th.

This afternoon, the Andromeda, Capt. Bryne, arrived at Sandy Hook in 7 Weeks from Portsmouth, and brought Expresses to the admiral & General, the Substance of wch were, a Declaration of the Parliament relative to the Exercise of the Right of Taxation in America, and a Bill for empowering H.M. to send out Commrs with full Powers to treat with the Rebels, to suspend certain Acts of Parliament, to cause a Cessation of Hostilities *by Land*, to grant Pardons, and to make & unmake Governors. Lord & General H. are nominated among the Commrs. Intelligence was also brought, but not confirmed, that the French Court has signed a Treaty with the Rebel agents, & that in consequence a Declaration of War was looked upon as inevitable. This News afforded me much Uneasiness for the Honor and Interest of my King & Country. Lord H. was pleased to desire me to revolve in my Mind, whether I would chuse to serve under the new Commission, informing me at the same time of his own Intentions in that particular; but added, that his Determinations need not influence me, who had the Interests of a Family to pursue, and my Fortune yet to make. I readily answered, with Thanks for his Lordship's condescending attentions to me & Care for my Welfare, That as I came out with him, with him I should wish to return, and that, exclusive of all Delicacy wch I might feel upon his Account, I should not desire to stay on my own, as I did not conceive it possible for me to gain either Credit or Advantage by yielding my poor Abilities to the measure upon the Carpet. He smiled, and seemed to approve of my Resolution, which indeed appeared very acceptable to Him.

TUESDAY, 14th. APRIL.

As these Bills of Parliament were inclosed in a Letter from the Secry of State, signifying His Majesty's Commands, that they should be published as much as possible in the Colonies, I was employed this morning in transcribing them for Sir Henry Clinton, that they may be printed immediately at New York. I had some further Conversation with Lord H. this Morning on the Subject of them, and upon the utter Improbability of their having any good Effect. To add to our Vexation, Intelligence came in, that the Congress, fearful of the Consequences of the War, to the Support of wch they feel their Resources unequal, are retiring, with all their Effects, to the Back Country over the mountains about Fort Pitt. Thus, when our Point was almost gained, we are throwing all down again by Concessions, founded on Timidity & that, if accepted of, in their unlimited Ground, will eventually weaken & supplant, if not ruin, the Nation. All our Friends here will be disheartened; and matter of Triumph or Good can happen to none, but their Persecutors & our Foes. And after all, this Cement (should one be formed) will prove like that in Nebuchadnezzar's Image; for Republican Presbyterianism can never heartily coalesce with Monarchy & Episcopacy. — Wrote to the Superintendant at N. York, relative to a Complaint made by a Mr. S. Martin of Whitehaven, respecting the Expertation of Prize Tobacco, and upon the Expertation of some Goods brought in by some Refugees from No. Carolina.

By a Vessel, wch arrived this afternoon from the W. Indies, we learnt, that the Rebel Frigate, the Randolph, wch sailed with 4 more armed Vessels from Charles Town in order to plunder Tobago, fell in at night with the Yarmouth of 64 Guns, which she took for a small Frigate, and threatened to sink her if she did not immediately surrender to the Congress, to wch the Yarmouth made no Reply but from her Guns. The Randolph and the others fired most furiously upon her, but upon the Yarmouth's opening her lower Deck Tier, the Randolph was sunk at the first Broadside, & in sinking blew up. Another was believed to share the same Fate, as at Daylight only three of the five could be seen. Four Days afterwards in cruizing about, the Yarmouth fell in with a Part of the Randolph's Wreck, with four men, each of a different Nation, upon it, whom she took up almost starved, and found that these were all that escaped of 305 which was the Randolph's Crew, under one Biddle a notorious Rebel. Another of the Rebel Frigates (the Alfred) has been taken & carried into Barbadoes by the Ariadne & Ceres, who also chased the Raleigh, in company of the Alfred, which escaped. Many of their Privateers also have been taken about the W. India Islands. The Seaforth chased a piratical Vessel under the Guns of a French Fort at Martinique, which fired upon her. The Fire was returned, several of their Guns dismounted, & the Vessel was cut out of the Harbor.

We learnt, that the Febry Packet arrived at the Delaware last Wednesday.

FRIDAY 17th.

About noon we sailed from Sandy Hook, and the next Day in the Evening, after a fair & pleasant Passage, anchored off the Cape Henlopen. On Sunday 19th. about 4 in the morning we weighed & sailed up Delaware Bay till about 1 o'Clock, when the Wind coming ahead we were obliged to come to an Anchor in the Passage among the Shoals, near the Shears. We met the Greyhound going out for New York in order to convey Sir H. Clinton to Philadelphia to relieve Sr. Wm. Howe, who is resolved upon setting out for England as soon as possible. On Monday 20th. we lay at Anchor all Day, the Wind being contrary.

TUESDAY, 21st. APRIL.

The Wind coming fair this afternoon, we set sail & reached Bombay Hook, where we anchored.

WEDNESDAY, 22d.

Sailed early this morning, & reached off Newcastle by Noon, where we anchored, because the Tide was too much fallen for the Eagle to pass over Wilmington Bar.

Received from the Pearl Frigate my Letters from England by the January & Febry Packets, with Abundance of political Communication.

Towards Evening, at Flood, we weighed & made Sail up to Marcus Hook, where we anchored for the Night.

THURSDAY, 23d.

Sailed this morning up to Billingsport, where the Eagle moored. The Admiral went up immediately after to Philadelphia.

FRIDAY, 24th.

Walked on Shore at Billingsport, where about 200 Provincials have refortified the Post, though very frequently disturbed by the Rebels. In an Excursion, yesterday, they had one man killed & two or three wounded.

SATURDAY, 25th.

Sailed this morning, in the Eagle's Pinnace, to Philadelphia. Dined with Ld. & Gl. H. at Head Quarters. Spent the Evening with my sensible Friend Mr. Galloway, with whom I had much Conversation on the present State of Affairs. He deplored the Languor of our Proceedings, & insisted on the Possibility of crushing Washington's Force, if not the Rebellion, by one or two spirited Exertions: That some Thousands, in that case, of the Countrymen wd defend this Province by their own Force, if entrusted with Arms, being stripped of them by the Rebels; and that he, and others through him, had offered upon those Conditions to raise very large Quotas of men, who would not be any Expence to Govt. We then discoursed upon the Resources of this Country, which are now really exhausted, the whole present Debt, involved in the Paper Currency, being greater than the whole present Worth of all the Property, real & personal, in the Country, being but little less than 40 millions Sterling. And as to men, allowing the number of Inhabitants at the Beginning of the Rebellion to have been what the Rebels estimated — 3 millions White & Black; by the best Calculation, the number of fighting men of both kinds could not amount at first to more than about 220,000. Of these (and these mostly, if not entirely, Whites) not less than 50,000 have perished by the End of the Year 1777, upon a nigh Computation, by Sickness & the Sword, the People here not having the requisite *Stamina* to endure the Rigors of Campaigns. The Camp Diseases, being contagious, have carried off great numbers of other People, who had no medicines to assist them; the little to be procured being all taken up for the Use of the Rebel-Army. Since the Beginning of this Year, they have lost by Desertion, Disease & the Sword, near 4000 men, who can be accounted for by us, besides those, who are gone off unknown. There then remain not many more than 150,000; and one third of these at least may be estimated *Blacks*. We have then 100,000. Of these we must make a Division into Friends, Enemies, and moderate or Neuters, and of the last it is presumed, as in all other Cases of the kind, there are most; possibly, one half of the whole. But, saying, one third, and allowing that we have 20,000 Friends scattered over this Continent (though it may be credited we have many more), it then proves very clearly, *why* Mr. Washington's Army is at so low an Ebb, and *why* such Extremities are used to compel men to join it. It also proves, that the present British Force, duly exerted, has but little to fear; and that this unnatural Outrage, deprived of foreign Assistance & destitute of internal Succours, could not possibly last long, and of course that Peace might soon be restored to this distracted Land. We then talked over our favorite System of Polity, wch tended to make the People free & united, and we observed & wished, that out of all these Ruins, such a Structure might be raised, as might not only be beautiful, but compact all the Parts together with such Strength & Order, as to render it illustrious, permanent & complete. — But this Desideratum the prevailing Folly & Madness will too probably prevent!

SUNDAY, 26th. APRIL.
Attended divine Service at X church, & afterwards dined with Capt. Hammond.

MONDAY, 27th.
Dined at Mr. Galloway's, after an Airing in his Carriage along the Banks of the Schuylkill, wch are very pleasant. In the Evening, we recd. an Account, that the Congress have absolutely refused to treat with *any* Commrs, that may be sent out from England, but upon the Ground of Independency. It was only what I expected, & therefore afforded me no Surprize. Those wicked men must lose all their Consequence

upon a Reconciliation, if not the very means of Subsistence. — The Paper was immediately forwarded to Ld. H. though late, and by him sent after the Packet, which was overtaken at Bombay Hook. — The Army & People of the Town seemed glad of this Resolution.

TUESDAY, 28th.

Visited the College, and was shewn Rittenhouse's Orrery by the famous Dr. Smith, Montgomery's Panegyrist. This College was built for a Place of Worship by Mr. Whitefield in the year 1740, but, upon the Failure of his People, purchased & applied to the present Use. It is a heavy, ill-constructed Pile, with little Convenience & no Ornament. Walked over the Town, & viewed the public Buildings, which, excepting two or three, are all for the Purposes of Religion: of these there are many, and some of them large & not inelegant. The whole Town affords a Curiosity, when it is considered, that, not a Century since, the Site of it and all the adjacent Country was one continued Wood, the Resort of Savages & the Habitation of wild Beasts. It stands upon a fertile Plain, which is covered with Villas, Fields & Gardens. It exhibits very strikingly, what Encouragement has been given to this Country, & what Neglect has been bestowed upon our own. If the Subjects we have lost by migrating hither, had been kept at Home, either employed in our Manufactures or the Cultivation of our own Wastes in the three Kingdoms; they would have afforded so much more real Riches & Strength to the State, wd. have contributed to the public Burdens, and not have drained us of millions in foreign Wars. This may be said for the wild, visionary, destructive Spirit of Colonization, wch, like a Scion, encouraged at the Root, first impairs & at last destroys the Substance & Strength of the original Tree!

For several Days, I amused myself in walking about the Country, within the Lines, once over the Schuylkill, & once over to the Jersies; which near Philadelphia are exceedingly pleasant, & particularly upon the Banks of the Delaware.

THURSDAY, 7th. MAY.

Sir Henry Clinton arrived in the Greyhound from N. York, by which I recd. Lrs from Govr. Tryon, &c. containing their opinions of present affairs.

FRIDAY, 8th. MAY.

Early this Morning, we recd. Advices by the Porcupine
Frigate, Capt. Finch, that France had been base enough to
conclude a Treaty of Commerce with our profligate & abandoned Rebels about the Middle of March, & that in consequence a War with that Power, & therefore with Spain, was
inevitable. May the GOD of Hosts be with us, and He, who
governs Battles, our Refuge! Surely, the righteous One, will
not prosper the Iniquity of our Enemies, nor suffer a Cause,
founded in Falshood, Baseness, & Rebellion, to succeed. *The
Judge of the whole Earth will do Right.*

Dined at Ld. H's with Sr. H. Clinton.

MONDAY, 11th.

Wrote for the Packet, wch is to sail in a Day or two. This
Evening Mr. Strachey called upon me, & told me, that it was
fixed, that he shd. go Home with Sr. Wm. Howe in the
Andromeda, and after Variety of Discourse relative to our &
the new Commission, in which he expressed some Disgust at
his not being nominated one of the Commrs rather than
Secry, wch his Friends at Home had refused for him, he
talked of what I intended or wished to do on the Occasion.
Perceiving that he was sounding me, I answered frankly, that
I wished to get Home as much as He could, & even by
the same Conveyance, if there was Room. We changed the
Conversation to other matters, & parted.

TUESDAY, 12th. MAY.

Lord H. after Breakfast called me aside, and gave me a long
& full account of the Disgust wch Govt. had conceived from
his Brother's Conduct, and of his own Intentions to resign his
Command, tho' the Admty had expressed strong Wishes for
his continuing in a Service, where he had been so eminently
& undeniably useful. He then told me, that as the Commission, we came out with, was now at an End, our Attendance in this Country was no longer necessary, & therefore
that Mr. Strachey wd. embark with the General, and that I
might sail in the next Ship of War for England, wch wd. be
the Porcupine, & wch probably might carry the news of the
Event of an Expedition upon the Rebels, now in meditation.

I thanked his Ldp for his Favor, & told him that my Wishes of remaining here terminated with his, & must be guided by them, &c. &c.

Afterwards saw Mr. Galloway, & had long Conversation with him on my Departure, his own Situation, & the Posture of affairs. Many kind Expressions of Friendship & good Correspondence passed between us, relative to our Separation. I believe, his Esteem for me is perfectly cordial, & sincere, as mine is for him.

Men's Spirits are differently agitated on the News & the Bills; but those of our Friends rather desponding & low. — Some seem dissatisfied with the Caprices (as they term them) of the new General.

The Soil of this Province, so far as I have had an opportunity of observing, confirms the Accounts I had received of its being better than of any other in America. There is a very striking Difference, in this respect, on each Side of the Delaware. In Pensylvania, the Land has a strong mixture of Loam, which has a Substratum of Clay: In Jersey, The Soil is a light Sand, like that of most of the Colonies. A Gardener here told me, that Cabbages, Colliflowers, & many other of useful Plants, degenerated here; and that the Soil required constantly fresh Recruits from Europe. The Laurestinus, Rosemary, & several other Shrubs, which endure the Winter very well in England, must be preserved in a Green-house here during that Season; while, on the contrary, several Plants, which require more Heat than we have in England to bring them to maturity, succeed very well in this Country, and even as far Northwards as New Hampshire. So great are the Extremities of the two Seasons!

THURSDAY, 14th.

Had some Conversation with Mr. Andw Allen. His most material Remark was, that from the Persuasion, that five Sixths of the Province were against the Rebels, our Army had only to drive off Washington & to put arms into the Hands of the well-affected, and the Chain of Rebellion would be broken; especially if we restored the Province to the King's Peace, suffered the Assembly to act, & to accept of those Terms, & propose those Contributions, which had been offered: That this wd affect all the Southern Colonies; & that then the Northern Colonies could not long stand out.

Recd. Information by Mr. Chads, one of the agents of Transports, that certain Persons in the Commissary General's Department, having first given Receipts to several Farmers about this Town for Quantities of Hay taken to H.M. Use, when the Receipts were brought for Payment, offered *blank* Receipts for their Signature; some of which were signed by the Farmers, but others among them, and in particular some Quakers, abhorring the Iniquity or disliking the Impropriety of the matter, refused, tho' threatened with the Loss of their Property, & have not been paid to this Day. Mr. Stuyvesant of N. York informed me, last year, that he was compelled to do the like, & that it had been done by many Farmers in Long Island. — *O tempora! O mores!**

MONDAY, 18th.

This afternoon was exhibited a strange kind of Entertainment, wch the Projectors styled a Meschianza or Medley, consisting of Tilts & Tournaments, in Honor of the General upon his Departure. It cost a great Sum of money. Our Enemies will dwell upon the Folly & Extravagance of it with Pleasure. Every man of Sense, among ourselves, tho' not unwilling to pay a due Respect, was ashamed of this mode of doing it.

WEDNESDAY, 20th. MAY.

Early this morning, a Detachment of 4000 Men marched out to attack the Marquis de la Fayette, who with about the same number of Rebels had ventured over the Schuylkill to a Spot within about 12 miles of Philadelphia; but, through some mistake on our Side or Information given the Rebels, they ran off & forded the River before our People could come up with them. The commanding officer exceedingly blamed by the army.

Had a long Conversation with my Friend Mr. G. respecting affairs, on wch we were rather sad. He mentioned, that all the

---

*This extraordinary matter Mr. Galloway has likewise assured me of from several, indeed many, incontestible Proofs, particularly from a Mr. Turner, one of the Proprietary's late Council & a very considerable Person in the Province, who, with sevl. others, have not been paid their Dues, merely because they wd. not sign these blank Receipts.

important Intelligence wch he had procured thro' the Winter for the Genl. had not cost Govt. £500; whereas Skinner (according to Col. Innis) had disbursed £12000 upon that account in the Jersies during the former year. — The Plan of seizing Livingston & his Council — the Congress, &c. &c. &c.

THURSDAY, 21st.

Very uneasy this morning on the Information by Mr. G. of a Conversation, wch passed between Genl. H. and one of the first Magistrates (Schumacher) in this City, who waited to take Leave of him. Upon representing the Uneasiness wch prevailed among the loyal Subjects on Account of the Rebels, the Genl. advised him "to make his Peace with the States, who, he supposed, would not treat them harshly; for that it was probable, on Account of the French War, the Troops would be withdrawn." This was soon circulated about the Town, & filled all our Friends with melancholy on the Apprehension of being speedily deserted, now a Rope was (as it were) about their necks, & all their Property subject to Confiscation. — The Information chilled me with Horror, and with some Indignation when I reflected upon the miserable Circumstances of the Rebels, &c.

FRIDAY, 22d.

A Confirmation of the sad Intelligence of yesterday was communicated to Mr. Galloway by Sr. Wm. Erskine from Sr. Wm. Howe & Sr. H. Clinton. It filled my poor Friend, as might be expected with Horror & melancholy on the View of his deplorable Situation; exposed to the Rage of his bitter Enemies, deprived of a Fortune of about £70,000, and now left to wander like Cain upon the Earth without Home, & without Property. Many others are involved in the like dismal Case for the same Reason — attachment to their King & Country, & opposition to a Set of daring Rebels, who might soon be crushed by spirited Exertions. — I now look upon the Contest as at an End. No man can be expected to declare for us, when he cannot be assured of a Fortnight's Protection. Every man, on the contrary, whatever might have been his primary Inclinations, will find it his Interest to oppose & drive us out of the Country. — I endeavored to console, as well as to advise my Friend. I felt for him & with him. Nothing remains for him but to attempt Reconciliation with (what I may *now* venture to call) *the United States of America*; which probably may not succeed, as they have attainted him in Body & Goods by an Act of the Legislature of Pennsylvania. — O Thou righteous GOD, where will all this Villainy end!

Mr G. summoned the magistrates of the Town, & imparted the sad news, wch filled many an honest & loyal Heart with Grief & Despair.

SATURDAY, 23d.

Had a long Conversation this morning with Ld. H. upon this measure of leaving the Town, & particularly upon the Subject of my poor Friend Mr. Galloway. I told him, that the Congress, if they knew their Business, had only one measure more to take, which is, to publish a Genl. Amnesty, and they drive us from this Continent forever. He assented, & expressed great Emotions of Sorrow upon the Event, & all the Readiness to assist Mr. G. in his Power. — I had afterwards some Conversation with Mr. G. to whom I recommended from Lord H. to propose the making his Peace with the present Powers, who, probably from his Weight & Influence, would be glad to accept him, as well because of the gaining his Countenance & That of his Friends & settling their administration quietly, as of avoiding the making any desperate Enemies; That this Negotiation must be set on Foot immediately, as the Friends of Govt. must prepare for Embarkation, in Case of a Refusal; That the only way seemed to be, to profess candidly to the Congress, that it was true, He & they had adhered to the old Constitution while they thought it possible to live under its Protection; but that, being deserted, they would as faithfully adhere to the present Establishment; That a Treaty of this kind, if effected, would be far better than throwing himself upon the Favor of our Govt. wch seemed sufficiently perplexed upon that Score already; & That, for the worst Event, the Admiral would set apart a Transport for him & his. It was a mournful Business; and nothing but misery & Sorrow are to be seen in the Town.

SUNDAY, 24th. MAY.

This Day the Genl. Sr. Wm. Howe departed from Philadelphia, & the Command devolved upon Sr. H. Clinton, who presently afterwards sent a message by Col. Innes to my Friend Mr. G. expressing his Desire to see him. This was what I expected, & mentioned before to him, as a necessary object upon his assuming the Command. So many Reasons & Circumstances occur against the abandonment of the Town, that, notwithstanding appearances, some of the most sensible cannot credit it. Their fortifying the principal Redoubt, Bomb Proof, is certainly very remarkable. I sat down in the Evening, & suggested in writing 13 (as I think) cogent Reasons, for Mr. G. to use with Sr. Henry, against the Abandonment of this central Province, wch appeared so convincing to us, that we recd. a Gleam of Hope that this terrible measure may be averted.

MONDAY, 25th.

My Friend Mr. G. had two long Conferences with Sr. H. Clinton, in wch he imparted every Intelligence of this Country in his Power, & much to his Satisfaction. From the Tenor of these Conferences our minds seemed more satisfied than before, that no imprudent Steps wd. be taken. All the Communications, formerly made, were not left with the present General; so that he must find his own Way. The poor Inhabitants still distressed, & preparing for Flight. — Dined at Mr. Galloway's, and afterwards had a pleasant Ride upon the Banks of the Schuylkill.

TUESDAY, 26th.

Sr. Wm. Erskine called upon Mr. G. & Mr. G. afterwards upon Sr. H. Clinton. The Result was, that it appears, that the K. under his Sign Man. has ordered the abandonment of Philad. & the march of the Army Northwards, to co-operate with Sir Guy Carleton. — This damped our Spirits. — Many People come in, who assert that nine tenths of the People are weary of the Rebellion and the tyrannical oppression of their new Governors, and wd. take up arms in our Behalf, if they had them; That the Indians & others are driving all before them in the Back-Country; That Washington has sent off his heavy Baggage from his present Camp, from wch he is ready to run, his People being almost ever under arms; That he has sent to the Jersies, apprehending we mean to pass through them, to raise the militia to annoy us; That the Rebels are in

high Spirits upon the Occasion, & mean to throw in a Body
of the militia, as soon as we have left the Town. &c. Had
much Discourse with Mr. G. upon all these & other matters,
and particularly upon the Settlement of a Correspondence between us. We talked over the Idea, suggested to him by some
Friends, of presenting a meml. of Consideration to Admn. to
be backed by Sr. W. H. wch we thought it best for the present to delay for sevl. Reasons.

The Town in great Distress was occupied in preparing for
our Departure.

THURSDAY, 28th.

Lord H. returned this Day to Town, in order to view the
Embarkation, with whom I dined. Recd. a Letter by the Eagle
Packet from my dear Wife, who is full of Solicitude &
Expectation for my Return. In the Evening fell into Company
with Sr. Wm. Erskine, who seems much dejected on the present Posture of affairs, & presses the General to make an Alert
upon Washington at any & at every Risque, that the Country,
wch is fully disposed, may protect itself. He thinks with Mr.
Galloway, though he does not speak like him, and is sure,
that, if his Ideas were followed, the Rebellion wd. soon be at
an End: But that if we depart hence, without doing something, it will end in our Confusion. He says, that Desertion
begins to prevail among the Soldiers, which is only what was
expected.

Wrote Lrs to Washington & Laurens (Presidt. of Congress)
inclosing Acts of Parliamt. for empowering Commrs to treat,
abrogating all Acts of Taxation, & the Act for altering the
Govt. of Mass. Bay, wch, 'tis most likely, will be treated with
the Contempt given to former Overtures of Reconciliation.

SUNDAY, 31st.

This morning the D. of Cumberland Packet arrived, &
brought Advices to the 4th. of April from England. A general
War appeared inevitable in Europe; and no more Forces are to
be sent out to America, but Part of them to be withdrawn. —
This News perplexed the Friends of Govt. here, & induced
them to think seriously of a negotiation with the present
Powers. My Friend Mr. G. much distressed upon the Subject.
I hinted to him, that probably by making his Peace now, he

might have it in his Power, with other Friends, when the madness of the Times was abated, to be a mediator between the two Countries, whose Interests being really one, and bring about a happy Union of Constitution & Polity. At present he could only be to them a ruined Enemy, & to us an inefficient Friend. — He seemed to form his Resolution accordingly.

MONDAY, 1st. JUNE.

Two Regiments, with Waggons, Horses & Baggage, passed over to Jersey from the City. The Distress of the Inhabitants in general inexpressibly great, as before, on the nearer Prospect of our Departure. They wish for that Act of Oblivion & Amnesty, wch the Congress (if they are wise) will pass; and then there is an End of British Power in this Country, but what can be obtained by mere Force of Arms, without a Friend to assist or guide us.

Genl. Grey, Sr. Wm. Erskine, Col. Patterson, &c. dined with us. Col. Patterson, in Discourse after Dinner, mentioned his Commission to negotiate an Exchange of Prisoners with Washington, and expressed some Delicacy to be used in the mode of adjusting a matter, wch Commrs, appointed on both Sides, had failed in the Execution of before. Genl. Grey answered, that too much Refinement & altercation with such men as Washington & his People had been used already, or affairs had never been in their present Situation; That there was but one mode of settling any thing effectually with them, and that this was by the Sword; That with respect to the Cartel, Washington might be told, & told truly, that if he wd. not exchange Man for Man, as well as officer for officer, it wd. be absolutely necessary for us to put our Prisoners into the Holds of the Vessels, for Want of Room & Tonnage, and the Consequences of their Sickness or Death must then be imputed to him; and That this Necessity being known, the Clamor of the Prisoners' Friends wd. be so importunate, that Washn. might probably be obliged to exchange them; whereas, were we to set them free without this adjustment, these very Fellows wd. have arms immediately put into their Hands to annoy us. — Sr. W. E. observed, that the Time of Lenity was now over, and we had already suffered sufficiently

by it; That the Rebels were never in so low a State, with respect to Strength & Resources, as at present (in wch G. Grey
concurred); That this Abandonment of the Town, so void of
all Honor, Spirit & Policy, made him miserable in himself &
ashamed of the name of a Briton; That he never was accused
of Rashness, but wd. answer with his Life, either to crush the
Rebels, if they stayed in their Works, in 48 Hours, or disperse
& drive them entirely out of this Province over the Susquehannah in 10 Days; That then he cd. & wd. raise the
Country 9 or 10 to 1 against the Rebels, & put it out of their
Power to recover themselves in this Province again, by breaking this great & central Link of the Chain; That the Rebels
were nothing compared with our Army in any respect; and
that, humanly speaking, we might even now (as we could
have done long since) "put our Foot upon them" & soon settle the Controversy. All this the two Generals spoke with
much Warmth, and strong Resentment of the Disgrace, wch
was arising to their Country & to the British Arms. The rest
of us were silent, but, I believe, greatly pleased.

The Rebel Frigate, the Providence, lately slipt past our
Ships at Rh. Island & got clear off; so that they have now
three out, & only three to send out, that we know off—the
Raleigh, the Warren & Providence.

TUESDAY, 2d. JUNE.

By a Conversation with Mr. Andw. Allen this morning, I was
informed, that the present assembly of this Province consists
of the lowest of the People; that these were chosen only by 153
Electors, whereas there are more than 30,000 in the Province;
that the Representatives for Philadelphia County, the richest
& most populous of all, were appointed by 17 Electors, & that
this whole Business was done at a low Tavern; that Genl.
Wayne (of the Rebels) and many others of the first officers are
exceedingly exasperated against them for the Violence of their
Acts & Proceedings as well as for the meanness of their
Persons, and has declared, that they shd not long proceed in
this way, but that He & his Corps wd. turn them out or "cut
the Throats of the Rascals, he did not care wch;" and that the
Leaders of the Army were promoting an Act of General
Amnesty & Oblivion. On the other hand, that many principal

People, who, being deprived of Arms both for themselves & Connections, intended to step forward upon the British Army routing or dispersing the Rebels, wch they thought wd. have been done, as it might have been with Ease, long ago, to the amount of nine Tenths of the Inhabitants of the whole Province, have sent into their Friends in Town to know what they were to expect, and upon being told, that we are evacuating the Country here, have been obliged to take the Oaths of Allegiance to the States on the 1st. of June; so that in future these People who wd. have fought for us and covered the Province are now at best neutrals, & can yield us no assistance in future, if we shd. want them.

Wednesday, 3d. June.

A vague Report came into Town by People out of the Lines, that the Rebels have recd. an Account from France, by the way of Boston, that England & France are reconciled, & that Canada is to be ceded to the French. News, perhaps too good to be true!

Fell in company with Mr. Israel Pemberton, the first man among the Quakers here, with whom I had a long Conversation upon the affairs & Politics of this Country. He was one of the twenty lately imprisoned by the Rebels. He professed, that he ever held, that the British Parlt. had no constitutional Right to tax America, but that he was equally averse to the violent Proceedings of the People here and particularly to the atrocious Act of Independency. In my answer to much matter of this kind, I reasoned with him, That every Part of any State or Empire ought in Justice & Policy to contribute its Share to the public Strength & Protection, or some wd. be unduly oppressed, and consequently the whole be weakened & exposed. This he allowed. I then urged, that if the *mode* only of levying this Contribution was a Grievance, some other Arrangement might have been suggested, by which the End cd. have been answered, and all Parties satisfied; That G. Britain having proposed one mean for this Purpose wch was disliked, it was incumbent on the Colonists, if they sincerely wished for Peace, to have proposed another; and that this was expected from the first Congress till their adoption of the *Suffolk* Resolves; after wch, it was perceived, that as they began in

Faction & Intemperance, they would end in Rebellion & Independency. My Quaker neither wanted Art or Words, but endeavored, with Dexterity enough, to turn off the Edge of my Arguments by some other matter, when they seemed to be cutting too close; but I chose to prevent him. — It was an agreeable amicable Conference, in wch we mutually expressed our Wishes for Accommodation & a speedy Termination to the Horrors of War. He mentioned that Gates, Washington, & some other principal officers of the Rebel-army freely gave out their Desire for a Treaty, when he passed through their Camp on his Return home: But the Congress cannot part with their Power & sink into former Obscurity.

Many Ships, &c. fell down the River, on wch I took a pleasant Airing in a Whale-Boat before Dinner.

THURSDAY, 4th.

The King's Birth-day. The Guns fired as usual, but there was not that Demonstration of Hilarity upon the Occasion, wch Respect to His Majesty wd. have induced, but for our melancholy Removal.

Recd. Lrs from my Friends Govr. Tryon & Mr. White at N. York, dated 24 & 25 May, by which I find that the Friends of Govt. there are involved in the common Gloom.

An evident Delay is made in the Embarkation; People hope, for some good Reason: One supposes, from a Wish for further news from England; Another, for a sudden Expedition agst the Rebels.

Sr. Js. Wallace in the Experiment has taken a Rebel Frigate, the Portsmouth, of 22 Guns, lately from that Port.

FRIDAY, 5th.

Mr. Loring, Commissary of Prisoners, shewed me a List of Rebels taken between the Landing upon Long Island and the End of Decr. 1777, of wch the Total was near 6000*; above 2000 of them have been released (1800 & upwards of those taken at Fort Washington) upon their Parole, and the Rebels refuse to return us a man in their Room — such is their Insult towards us! We deserve it all by our own stupid Conduct towards them. Any other Power upon Earth wd. have acted dif-

*NB. Those, taken at Sea, are not included.

ferently & crushed the Rebellion in its Egg. — Loring went out yesterday to negotiate the Exchange of some particular Prisoners. He rode over the Schuylkill 16 miles before he met with any Post of the Rebels. At length he & his Party were stopped by a Col. Morgan, who recd. their Lrs & forwarded them to Washington. Upon this Lee & one Hamilton, one of Wn's. Aid de Camps, came down, & behaved very well; though they all seemed very dull, & wished very much for Peace. Morgan went so far as to say, that 99 in a 100, were of the same Sentiment & wd. be glad to give up Independency upon the Terms offered by the acts, and that none (as he expressed it) but a few low dirty Rascals who had got into the Lead of affairs were for it. They were afraid however it was too late now, though they were extremely distressed & perplexed upon the Subject. Lee called one of our Company aside for a minute, & told him, that he was very unhappy in and very averse to the present Course of affairs, & that he might assure Ld. Howe, that he had acted entirely as he had promised him, & wished for nothing so much as to promote every Idea of Peace. — Morgan & the rest of the Rebel-officers said, that Grant deserved to be hanged for his Conduct in the attempt upon Fayette's Corps, who were actually surrounded or cut off in their Retreat by our Troops, when he suffered them to escape, that they the Rebels gave them all up (3000 of them) for lost, & that not one of them cd. have got away, if there had been but ordinary management; an Event wch wd. have entirely ruined them, as they were the best of their army. — I can only say — Alas! & perhaps nothing more will be said to any body. Follies & Blunders without End!

Recd. a Lr. from Mr. Chew at N. York, giving an account of the Rebel Vessels in Connecticut, where they are busy in fitting whatever they can for the Sea.

Washington is said to be moving. Sr. Guy Carleton (by Information sent me by my Friend Govr. Tryon) has taken Ticonderoga & Mount Independence, and killed & taken 600 of the Rebels. This, afterwards, proved to be, like many others at this time, a false Report.

News came up this Evening, that Ld. Carlisle, Mr. Eden & Govr. Johnstone, the new Commrs arrived this morning off Bombay Hook. They sailed on the 21st. of April. This

Intelligence revived the Hopes of my Friend Galloway, to
whom I immediately communicated it.

SATURDAY, 6th. JUNE.

The Commrs came up this Evening, as also did Lord Cornwallis, &c. Major Drummond arrived, & brought me news
from my Family. The Spirits of the Town seem revived upon
the Occasion; People conceiving a Hope, that they shall not
now be abandoned. Variety of Accounts of affairs at Home,
the War with France, the Raising the militia, &c.

My agent, in his Letter, gave me Pain by informing me,
that as "no new Secretaries go out with the Commrs, he concluded I shd. be detained in America." I mentioned it to Ld.
H. and my Desire of returning Home, to wch he answered, it
wd. depend perhaps on my own Choice. I begged to rely
upon him for any Facility I might want for that purpose.

SUNDAY, 7th.

The Commrs were saluted this morning by the Artillery. They
had a long Conference with Ld. H. and afterwards dined with
us. I had some Conversation with them, particularly Govr.
Johnstone, upon public affairs, upon the Debt & Resources
of the Colonies, & such like Subjects. — My Friend Galloway
had afterwards a Conversation with this last Gentleman in the
Evening, and expressed no great admiration of his political
Ideas; one of wch was rather extraordinary, That the Assemblies of these Colonies shd. meet as formerly, to each of wch
two Representatives shd. be sent over from G. Britain, and
from each assembly one should be admitted into the
Parliament; that Taxation shd. be entirely given up, but that
the Parliament shd. have Authority to bind in all other Cases;
and that this wd. lay the Foundation of (what he called) a
"Foederal Union." Mr. G. represented, in its true light, the
absurdity & Impracticability of such a Scheme, and told him
that no foederal Union cd. subsist but between Independent
States, and that to propose it wd. be a virtual acknowledgemt.
of American Independency.

MONDAY, 8th.

Wrote a Letter for Ld. H. to the new Commrs, communicating his Intention to decline from serving in the new Com-

mission, & also to the Secry of State for the same Purpose, in which he told him that as He was "become unworthy of that Place in H.M. Confidence, by wch he had before the Honor to be distinguished, & had been recently encouraged to hope he might still retain (alluding to a Lr. from Ld. N. signifying that he was to be *first* Commr, which was not attended to), he shd. avail himself of the Permission to return to England, wch his impaired State of Health had obliged him to solicit, "but that he shd. not fail of continuing equally assiduous, in the meantime, to promote the great Purpose of H.M. Commission, to the utmost of his Power."

A newspaper of Jersey was put into my Hands, containing a most diabolical Message of the Rebel Governor Livingston to his Assembly for the Extirpation of all H.M. liege Subjects in that Province. I never read a more virulent or indecent Performance.

The Commrs intend to dispatch Mr. Ferguson, one of their Secretaries, with a Notice of their arrival to the Congress to-morrow. *Parturiit mons, nascitur mus.*

TUESDAY, 9th. JUNE.

At a meeting, which Loring our Commissary held with Boudinot the Rebel Commissary, it was this Day agreed, that we shd. receive in Exchange above 2200 of our men, wch were due to us upon the Cartel Account from the Rebels; but none of them belonging to the Convention, made with Genl. Burgoyne.

Laurens, President of the Congress, returned An answer to-day, dated at York Town on the 6th. instant, to Ld. Howe's Lr of the 27th. ult. inclosing to the Congress the Acts of Parliament, in wch he says, "Yr Lp may be assured, that when the King of G.B. shall be *seriously* disposed to put an End to the unprovoked & cruel War, waged against these United States, Congress will readily attend to such Terms of Peace as may consist with the Honor of Independent Nations, the Interest of their Constituents, and the sacred Regard they mean to pay to Treaties." — Small Hopes from this of these rebellious Tyrants being likely to treat with Commrs! The moment an Agreement is made, the Demagogues must sink into their former Obscurity.

THURSDAY, 11th.

Some strange Propositions were handed about this morning, as the fundamental Terms of the Treaty; one of wch gave up that Palladium of our Commerce the Navigation Act, and almost all the rest were absurd or contradictory. They were said to originate from Govr. Johnstone.

SUNDAY, 14th.

Several Ships & Frames upon the Stocks were burnt, to prevent their being employed against us by the Rebels.

The Commrs & Mrs. Eden dined with us, & two of their Secretaries, Dr. Fergusson & Mr. Lewis. — I was told by Mr. Galloway, that J——e brought over Washington's Picture in the Lid of a Snuff-Box, wch he presented to *somebody** out of the Lines; that in Conversation with him, he was very inquisitive about the Value of Lands & landed Security in this Country, & expressed his Intention of selling what he has in England & sitting down here. Mr. G. was much surprized at this Discourse, and assured me that it is the manner of his Conversation about the Town, which has given great offence to the King's loyal Subjects, who speak of him with great Reproaches. I shall not easily forget the Dispatches brought over to Thos. Willing, long concerned in the Rebellion. A man of this kind is not likely to be solicitous for the Interest & Honor of my dear Country.

Went to the Quaker's Meeting in the Evening. Several of their Friends & one of their Preachers, a serious good man, called upon me afterwards. We had a long Conversation together, wch turned upon that Unity of Spirit wch the Grace of GOD induces among all his People, whatever be their Denominations, and that the nearer we are in Truth to Him, the nearer likewise we shall be in Love towards each other. We parted with great Demonstration of Regard, probably never to see each other upon Earth again. Anthony Benezet brought them to me: The Preacher's name was Emlin.

*A Mrs. Ferguson, a Woman noted for her Virulence in the Cause of Rebellion.

MONDAY, 15th.

Took leave of my Friends at Philadelphia. The Embarkation of the Troops to Jersey proceeded, as before.

TUESDAY, 16th.

Departed this Morning from Philadelphia in an armed Sloop, in order to join the Eagle at Newcastle; but the Wind being contrary could reach no lower down than Marcus Hook, where we came to Anchor, under the Porcupine's Guns, for the Night, it not being safe to proceed.

WEDNESDAY, 17th.

Early this Morning sailed from Marcus Hook, & arrived at the Eagle about Noon. The Day most excessively hot.

THURSDAY, 18th. JUNE.

After a Gust of Wind, attended with Thunder & Lightning, usual in this Country, the morning was pleasant & cool. The Wind likewise changed to the Northwards, wch favored the Descent of the Vessels, which have been going down for several Days.

About 8 o'Clock this morning, the last Detachment of the Troops, consisting of about 5000 men, closed the Evacuation of Philadelphia & the Embarkation to the Jersies from Gloucester Point, about 2 miles below the Town, which was effected without the least molestation from the Rebels. The Precaution was taken to destroy the Bridge wch led over the marshes to Gloucester Point. The Bridge over Schuylkill, formed of cut masts, was destroyed a few Days before; and another Bridge, for the same Place, constructed formerly by the Rebels, was burnt at Mud Island. In coming down, the Vigilant ran ashore upon the Spit opposite Mud Island, wch occasioned some Delay; though it was a happy Circumstance for a Detachment of about 180 men, whose Retreat was cut off from Billingsport by a Party of 500 Rebels, & who were taken off by the Flat-Boats, however injurious the Delay was to the Sinking of the Vessels, filled with Stones, to obstruct the two narrow Channels, which Business was not so well effected by the strong Flux of the Tide.

FRIDAY, 19th.

This morning all the men of War, Ships, &c. came down. The
Eagle unmoored & came down to the Pea-Patch below
Newcastle; but the Wind falling scanty, she was obliged to anchor. It grieved me much to see so many doleful Faces passing by me, flying from their Homes, and not knowing where
next to lay their Heads.

Ld. H. mentioned very kindly my Departure in the Porcupine for England; and I immediately prepared for the Voyage.
We had a long Conversation upon his Situation & my own.
He told me, among many other matters, that, excepting from
Lord D. he had received neither Confidence nor Civility from
any member of a——n; & that he shd. take an opportunity
to thank his Ldp for it. He particularly instanced the mortifi-
cations he had recd. from the two Principals, with whom he
officially corresponded; that his Brother had recd. many
more, & that the most honbl. & just thing they could do for
Sr. W. H. would be to bring him to a Tryal, wch His Lp
seemed by the Tenor of his Discourse rather to expect. As to
me, he liberally told me, that I might say what I pleased respecting what I had seen & heard; to which I answered, I shd.
very reluctantly meddle with Opinions, & shd. confine myself
as much as possible to Facts, wch came under every man's
Observation upon the Spot. I hinted to him, that notwithstanding the present aukward appearance of things, it might
be found expedient for the public Service to place him at the
Head of the naval Department, for wch, without Flattery,
perhaps no man was so well qualified as himself. To this he
answered, that he believed he shd retire & meddle no more
with public affairs, by wch People often get immense Trouble
& Hazard with little Thanks: That indeed, if he had succeeded in the Object of his Peace-Commission, the public
Voice might have called him to that Station, as an honorable
Reward, wch now, at the probable Beginning of a War, was a
Post of too much Labor & Care, for him in his present State
of Health, to execute or desire. He said, it wd. also have been
highly advantgeous to myself and other Parties concerned, if
we had met with the desired Success by negotiation; but that,
matters standing as they are, he was sorry to think I must
be obliged to recommend myself by my applications in my

former Station. I immediately replied, that I ought not to re-
pine at falling where no man rose; and that I had a mind prepared for the most untoward Circumstances of human Life,
contented to take my Lot & bear my Part in the genl. misfortune. After other Conversation of similar Import, I withdrew.

In the Evening, I wrote a parting Letter to my Friend Mr.
Galloway, lest, through sudden Departure, I should not have
an opportunity of seeing him.

The Continental Congress: Response to British Peace Proposals

In CONGRESS.
June 13, 1778.

AN express arrived with a letter of the 11th, from General Washington, which was read, and a packet in which it was inclosed, together with other papers, a letter signed 'Carlisle, William Eden, G. Johnstone,' dated 'Philadelphia, June 9, 1778,' and directed 'to his excellency, Henry Laurens, the president, and other members of the congress;' which letter was read to the words, 'insidious interposition of a power, which has from the first settlement of these colonies been actuated with enmity to us both; and notwithstanding the pretended date or form of the French offers,' inclusive; whereupon the reading was interrupted, and a motion was made not to proceed farther, because of the offensive language against his most christian majesty. Debates arising thereon,

Ordered, that the consideration of the motion be postponed, and congress adjourned till ten o'clock on Monday June 16.

Congress resumed the consideration of the motion respecting the letter from the commissioners of the king of Great Britain, which being postponed,

A motion was made, 'That the letter from the commissioners of the king of Great Britain lie on the table.' Passed in the negative.

On the motion—Resolved, 'That the letter and the papers accompanying it be read.' Whereupon a letter of the 9th, and one dated June, 1778, both signed, 'Carlisle, William Eden, G. Johnstone,' and a paper indorsed, 'Copy of the commission for restoring peace, &c. to the Earl of Carlisle, Lord Viscount Howe, Sir William Howe, or in his absence Sir Henry Clinton, William Eden, and George Johnstone,' were read, and also three acts of the British parliament, one intitled, 'An act for repealing an act passed in the 14th year of his present Majesty's reign, intitled, an act for the better regulating the government of the province of Massachusett's-bay, in New-England,' the other two the same as the bills already published. The letters are as follow:

To his excellency Henry Laurens, the President, and other
    Members of Congress.

    Gentlemen, With an earnest desire to stop the further effusion of blood and the calamities of war, we communicate to you, with the least possible delay after our arrival in this city, a copy of the commission with which his Majesty is pleased to honour us, as also the acts of parliament on which it is founded; and at the same time that we assure you of our most earnest desire to re-establish, on the basis of equal freedom and mutual safety, the tranquillity of this once happy empire, you will observe, that we are vested with powers equal to the purpose, and such as are even unprecedented in the annals of our history.

    In the present state of our affairs, though fraught with subjects of mutual regret, all parties may draw some degree of consolation, and even an auspicious hope from the recollection that cordial reconciliation and affection have, in our own and other empires, succeeded to the contentions and temporary divisions not less violent than those we now experience.

    We wish not to recall subjects which are now no longer in controversy, and will reserve to a proper time of discussion both the hopes of mutual benefit, and the consideration of evils that may naturally contribute to determine your resolutions as well as our own on this important occasion.

    The acts of parliament which we transmit to you, having passed with singular unanimity, will sufficiently evince the disposition of Great Britain, and shew that the terms of agreement, in contemplation with his majesty and with his parliament, are such as come up to every wish that North America, either in the hour of temperate deliberation, or of the utmost apprehension of danger to liberty, has expressed.

    More effectually to demonstrate our good intentions, we think proper to declare, even in this our first communication, that we are disposed to concur in every satisfactory and just arrangement towards the following among other purposes:

'To consent to a cessation of hostilities, both by sea and land. To restore free intercourse, to revive mutual affection, and restore the common benefits of naturalisation through the several parts of this empire. To extend every freedom to trade that our respective interests can require. To agree that no military force shall be kept up in the different states of North America, without the consent of the general congress, or particular assemblies. To concur in measures calculated to discharge the debts of America, and raise the value and credit of the paper circulation.

'To perpetuate our union, by a reciprocal deputation of an agent or agents from the different states, who shall have the privilege of a seat and voice in the parliament of Great Britain; or, if sent from Britain, to have in that case a seat and voice in the assemblies of the different states to which they may be deputed respectively, in order to attend to the several interests of those by whom they are deputed.

'In short, to establish the power of the respective legislatures in each particular state, to settle its revenue, its civil and military establishment, and to exercise a perfect freedom of legislation and internal government, so that the British states throughout North America, acting with us in peace and war, under our common sovereign, may have the irrevocable enjoyment of every privilege that is short of a total separation of interest, or consistent with that union of force, on which the safety of our common religion and liberty depends.

'In our anxiety for preserving those sacred and essential interests, we cannot help taking notice of the insidious interposition of a power, which has from the first settlement of these colonies been actuated with enmity to us both. And notwithstanding the pretended date, or present form, of the French offers to America, yet it is notorious, that these were made in consequence of the plans of accommodation previously concerted in Great Britain, and with a view to prevent our reconciliation, and to prolong this destructive war.

'But we trust that the inhabitants of North-America, connected with us by the nearest ties of consanguinity, speaking the same language, interested in the preservation of similar institutions, remembering the former happy intercourse of good offices, and forgetting recent animosities, will shrink from the thought of becoming an accession of force to our late mutual enemy, and will prefer a firm, free, and perpetual coalition with the parent state to an insincere and unnatural foreign alliance.

'This dispatch will be delivered to you by Dr. Ferguson, the secretary to his majesty's commission; and, for further explanation and discussion of every subject of difference, we desire to meet with you either collectively or by deputation, at New-York, Philadelphia, York-Town, or such other place as you may propose. We think it right, however, to apprize you, that his majesty's instructions, as well as our own desire, to remove from the immediate seat of war, in the active operations of which we cannot take any part, may induce us speedily to remove to New-York; but the commander in chief of his majesty's land-forces, who is joined with us in this commission, will, if it should become eligible, either concur with us in a suspension of hostilities, or will furnish all necessary passports and safe conduct, to facilitate our meeting, and we shall of course expect the same of you.

'If after the time that may be necessary to consider of this communication, and transmit your answer, the horrors and devastations of war should continue, we call God and the world to witness, that the evils which must follow are not to be imputed to Great Britain; and we cannot without the most real sorrow anticipate the prospect of calamities which we feel the most ardent desire to prevent. We are, with perfect respect, Gentlemen, your most obedient and most humble servants,

Carlisle, W. Eden, G. Johnstone.

To his Excellency Henry Laurens, President, and other
　　Members of Congress.

Gentlemen, The dispatch inclosed with this, was carried this morning to the nearest post of General Washington's army by Dr. Ferguson, Secretary to his Majesty's commission for restoring peace, &c. but he, not finding a passport, has returned to this place. In order to avoid every unnecessary delay, we now again send it by the ordinary conveyance of your military posts; as soon as the passport arrives, Dr. Ferguson shall wait upon you according to our first arrangement. We are, with perfect respect, gentlemen, your most obedient and most humble servants,

Carlisle, W. Eden, G. Johnstone.

Ordered, that they be referred to a committee of five.

Eodem Die, P. M. The committee to whom were referred the letters and papers from the Earl of Carlisle, &c. Commissioners from the King of Great Britain, reported the draft of a letter, which was read.

Resolved, that the consideration thereof be postponed till to-morrow.

June 17th, 1778. Congress resumed the consideration of the draft of the letter, in answer to the letter and papers received from the Earl of Carlisle, &c. Commissioners from the King of Great Britain, which was unanimously agreed to, and is as follows:

To their Excellencies the Right Hon. the Earl of Carlisle,
  William Eden, and George Johnstone, Esqrs. Commissioners from his Britannic Majesty, Philadelphia.

I have received the letter from your Excellencies of the 9th instant, with the inclosures, and laid them before Congress. Nothing but an earnest desire to spare the farther effusion of human blood could have induced them to read a paper, containing expressions so disrespectful to his Most Christian Majesty, the good and great ally of these states, or to consider propositions so derogatory to the honour of an independent nation.

'The acts of the British parliament, the commission from your Sovereign, and your letter, suppose the people of these states to be subjects of the crown of Great Britain, and are founded on an idea of dependence, which is utterly inadmissible.

'I am further directed to inform your Excellencies, that Congress are inclined to peace, notwithstanding the unjust claims from which this war originated, and the savage manner in which it hath been conducted; they will therefore be contented to enter upon a consideration of a treaty of peace and commerce, not inconsistent with treaties already subsisting, when the King of Great Britain shall demonstrate a sincere disposition for that purpose. The only solid proof of this disposition will be an explicit acknowledgement of the independence of these states, or the withdrawing his fleets and armies. I have the honour to be, your Excellencies most obedient and humble servant,

HENRY LAURENS, President.

York-Town, July 17, 1778.

Resolved unanimously, that Congress approve the conduct of General Washington, in refusing a passport to Dr. Ferguson. Published by order of Congress.

CHARLES THOMSON, Sec.

Henry Laurens to Horatio Gates

York, June 17, 1778

Dear Sir—

I troubled you with a few private Lines on the 13th by Crugier.

Congress have not determined their answer to the British Commissioners Address, although I foresee it will be a very short one—when that is finished the whole will probably be published, in the mean time I consider Sir your situation & distance from the Center of intelligence & conclude that the following brief account of the Address will not be unacceptable.

There is rather a repletion in the direction of the Paper leaving no room for cavil on that score.

The Commissioners after the necessary preface observe— "That in the present state of our affairs tho' fraught with subjects of mutual regret all parties may derive some consolation & even auspicious hope from recollecting that cordial reconciliation & affection have in our own & other Empires succeeded to contention & temporary division not less violent than those we now experience.

they wish not to recall subjects now no longer in controversy, observe that the Acts of Parliament which they transmit & refer to, passed with singular Unanimity.

they are willing to consent to a cessation of hostilities by Sea & Land.

to extend every freedom of Trade that our respective Interests can require. (who is to adjust this point) to agree that no Military forces shall be kept up in the States without our Consent.

to concur in measures calculated to discharge the debts of America & to raise the Credit & Value of the Paper circulation. to perpetuate our Union by a reciprocal Deputation in Parliament & in the several General Assemblies.

In short to establish the Power of the Respective Legislatures in each particular <u>State</u>, to settle its revenues its Civil &

Military establishment & exercise a perfect freedom of Legislation & internal Government so that the British <u>States</u>
throughout North America acting with us in Peace & War
under one common Sovereign may have the irrevocable enjoyment of every privilege that is short of a total seperation of
Interests or consistent with that Union of force on which the
safety of our common Religion & Liberty depends — "

The French Court are illiberally charged with insidious
practices — this gives much offence —

If all the fine things now offered had been tendered some
time ago, admitting their solidity, there can be no doubt but
that the People of America would joyfully have embraced the
proposition — but now what answer can be given but that
which was returned to the foolish Virgins — "the Door is
shut" more especially when we reflect that there is no solidity — because all is to be transmitted to Parliament for Ratification "And until such Ratification no such regulation
matter or thing shall have any other force or effect or be carried further into Execution than is hereafter mentioned"
here's a Boy's Card House tumbled down by a Breath —

"If," say Lord Carlisle, Willm. Eden & Gēo Johnstone
Esquires, "after the time that may be necessary to consider
this communication & transmit your answer the horrors &
devastations of War should continue We call God & the
World to Witness that the Evils which must follow are not to
be imputed to Great Britain" — to whom are the past to be
imputed? but are they not now in the very moment of pretended attempts to establish Peace burning ravaging &
murdering?

they seem to mistake our understanding as once they did
our Resolution —

Colonel Malcom waits I must stop short & assure you I am
with great Esteem Dear Sir Your obliged & hum̄ servt

John André: Journal, June 16–July 5, 1778

1778

June   In consequence of the determination taken to evacuate Philadelphia, the 5th Brigade (26th, 63d, 7th) 46th and 55th Regiments, Simco's and Stirn's Brigade, were passed over the Delaware at Cooper's Ferry and the waggons with provision and stores for the march packed there under their cover.

17th   The Army received Orders to parade at 6 in the afternoon at their Brigade parades; from these they were marched to the works, behind which they lay on their arms.

18th   Before daybreak, General Grant with the 1st and 2d Brigade and the Hessian Grenadiers marched in different columns to Glocester Point, where he crossed the Delaware in flat boats.

At sunrise the 3rd and 4th Brigades and the Guards were put in motion and came to Glocester Point, where they also crossed. The Grenadiers and Light Infantry passed last. The *Vigilant* was stationed a little above the point, and her guns could graze the neck of land thro' which the Troops passed, so as to render the embarkation very secure. No shot was fired, nor did an Enemy appear until the whole were on the opposite shore. The 46th and 55th marched the same morning from Cooper's Ferry to Glocester Point, where they joined their respective Brigades.

As soon as the Troops were passed, General Knyphausen, with the Hessian Grenadiers and the 1st and 2d Brigades, marched to Haddonfield. Lord Cornwallis with the Light Infantry, British Grenadiers, Guards and 3d and 4th Brigade followed soon after and halted for the night within two miles of Haddonfield.

19th   General Leslie with the Corps from Cooper's Ferry brought up the waggons of the Army to Haddonfield, where they were left, the General proceeding with his Corps to Foster Town. Lord Cornwallis's Column moved before day break and, passing Haddonfield soon after General Leslie, came to Evesham. The Grenadiers on coming to their ground found a Captain of Militia expiring; he had been shot by the Queen's Rangers.

20th The Troops at Evesham were under arms at 4 o'clock in the morning, and at 5 marched, proceeding through Foster Town to Mount Holly, a little way beyond Foster Town.

General Leslie's Corps joined the rear of the Column. The Rebels, supposed about 900 in number, under General Maxwell, had quitted Mount Holly the morning before. General Knyphausen having in the evening of the 19th moved the train across a deep ravine a mile and a half on his road from Haddonfield, marched early the 20th to Moorestown, and on the 21st came to Mount Holly and encamped with the remainder of the Army now assembled in one body. Colonel Allen's Corps was posted at a pass in the rear on Rancocas Creek.

22d The Army was under arms at 4 o'clock in the morning, and marched soon after through Slab Town to the *Black Horse*. General Leslie with the 5th Brigade took an intermediate road between that of the Column and Burlington, where it was supposed there might be some Rebel Troops; by that means flanking the baggage. The 5th Brigade afterwards fell into the Black Horse Road and brought up the rear. We learnt at the *Black Horse* that Maxwell, with a large body of men, had quitted that place at 2 in the morning. Several papers were found warning us to beware of being *Burgoyned*. A deserter was executed on the march.

23d The Army marched in two Columns, the 5th Brigade under General Leslie forming the advance of that on the left. Lord Cornwallis, who commanded that Column, proceeded to the *Rising Sun*, 4½ miles and turning to the right marched to Crosswicks, 3½ miles. Near the *Rising Sun* the Rebels had destroyed a bridge, which it took some time to repair. At Crosswicks a piquet of the Enemy fired at the head of the Column, and retired to join a body on the other side of the Creek (Crosswicks Creek) the bridge over which they hastily destroyed. The Queen's Rangers followed them very soon. but they retreated with great speed after firing a few shot across the rivulet. A Captain of Simco's was dangerously

wounded. One or two of the Enemy were found killed by
grape shot from a 3-pounder brought on a height in front of
Crosswicks whilst the bridge was repairing. The 16th Dragoons, supported by a Battalion of Grenadiers and Light
Infantry, were pushed in pursuit two miles on the Allentown
Road, as far as another creek where the Enemy were at work
destroying the Bridge. Simco's Corps pursued at the same
time some distance on the Allentown Road.

General Leslie with the 5th Brigade masked the Bordentown Road when the Column turned off at the *Rising Sun*.
He afterward proceeded to Bordentown, where he lay on his
arms all night. The Rebels cannonaded his Corps from a
wood on the opposite side of a creek which enters the
Delaware there, but without effect. A Jäger was wounded by
a musket shot.

General Knyphausen hutted about two miles on the right
of Crosswicks.

24th   General Leslie joined Lord Cornwallis at 6 in the
morning, and the Division marched immediately after and
came to Allentown, four miles. A good deal of attention was
paid to enforcing the Orders respecting plunder, and also the
Battalion horses and followers of the Army not mixing in the
line of march.

25th   The Troops received Orders to be under arms at 4
o'clock, and marched by the left as soon as the baggage had
got into the front. This reversion of the order of march took
up some time, and it was late before the rear was in motion.
The Queen's Rangers during this time masked the Prov-
incetown Road, and the Chasseurs, who had been posted
on the West side of Doctor's Creek, were withdrawn to the
same side with the Army. A body of the Enemy soon showed
themselves, and passing thro' the village advanced a little towards the Jägers, but were dispersed again by a shot or two
from their 3-pounders. It was said Morgan's Corps of Rifle
men were close at hand. The ground of the Encampment on
which the rear was detained was very open, and some Cavalry
was kept ambuscaded a little time, in hopes of cutting off
some of the most adventurous in pressing on the Column.
They were withdrawn again without having had an opportunity of trying their success. As the Rear quitted the ground a

few of the Rebels possessed themselves of the house which had been Lord Cornwallis's Quarters, but were very speedily dislodged by a gun of the Light Infantry.

The Division halted at Upper Freehold (the *Rising Sun*).

26th   Lord Cornwallis's Division marched in the same order as the preceeding day, at 5 o'clock. There was a little firing as the rear was put in motion. The Division halted within two miles of Freehold or Monmouth Court House. The roads the Army had marched thro' were in general very sandy, and the land, except in the neighborhood of Allentown, deemed poor. The weather, which after the first two or three days' march, which were rainy, was very sultry, and as we approached Freehold water was very scarce. The Rebels had added to this by stopping up the wells. From several concurring testimonies there was little doubt of Washington having crossed the Delaware and gained Princetown or Cranberry. It was asserted he had passed at Coryel's Ferry on the 21st three days after our crossing at Glocester point.

Since Black Horse Camp, General Knyphausen's Division, consisting of the 1st and 2d Brigades, British 17th Dragoons and Brigade of Stirn, marched in a Column on our right thro' Recceles Town and Embles town. That Column had with them the provision train, pontoons and part of Artillery. On the 25th General Knyphausen fell into the Monmouth Road about five miles beyond the *Rising Sun*, and the next day took a Camp at Freehold connected with the other Division.

27th   The Army halted at Freehold.

28th   General Knyphausen marched from Freehold at 4. The baggage joined and followed his Division. Simco's Corps and the 5th Brigade took post on the Cranberry Road. At 5 o'clock Lord Cornwallis moved. Parties of Horse and Foot appeared on the heights to the left of the Cranberry Road, and Colonel Simco with two or three Companies was sent along the skirt of the wood, to endeavour to get around them. He fell in with a very superior body of Militia, whom he charged with his mounted Company, killing or wounding several of them. Himself and three or four of his own were wounded, but all brought off.

As the rear of Lord Cornwallis's Division moved off the ground on which General Knyphausen had been encamped, the Enemy began to shew themselves. At first only a few of their Light Horse appeared; a Corps soon came out of the wood to the left, but a few cannon-shot made them retire again, and their Light Horse only continued to follow. Some of these having ventured so far as to afford a chance of intercepting them, two or three Troops of the 16th Dragoons charged into the fields after them, but found a large body of Infantry ambuscaded, who gave them a heavy fire and obliged them to retreat. Immediately after this a Column appeared to out left and Rear, marching very rapidly and in good order. The 1st Light Infantry were fronted about to the advancing Enemy, the Guards, Hessian and British Grenadiers were halted and faced to the left, and Orders being sent to the 3d, 4th and 5th Brigades to return and be ready to support, the whole began moving back. The Rebel Corps as soon retreated, nor was a shot scarcely fired until we had recrossed the Cranberry Road. The Troops found themselves now arranged with the Light Infantry on the right, the Guards in the centre and the Grenadiers to the left. The Hessian Grenadiers were in the rear of the Light Infantry, and the 3rd and 4th Brigade supported the Grenadiers and Guards. The Guards first fell into action by receiving a very heavy fire from a wood on their right. They soon dislodged the Enemy from it, and drove them as far as they had strength to pursue. The Enemy had yet cannon and Troops on an advantageous height in front, from which it was necessary to force them. The Grenadiers were therefore led on, and the Rebels were driven back across a deep morass, upon their main Army. This was not effected without loss, but more from heat and fatigue under which many died, than from the Enemy's shot. To this height our cannon, consisting of twelve 6-pounders, two medium 12-pounders, and two howitzers, were brought and opposed to that of the Enemy, whose whole force occupied the opposite hills. Whilst the Guards and Grenadiers were engaged the Light Infantry, pressing forward on the right upon the Cranberry Road, had headed the Swamp which divided the two Armies, and gained an eminence very near the Enemy's left flank, but without meeting any opposition. The 3d Brigade, upon the attack of the Guards, moved into the woods on their right and penetrated across the morass to the hill, where the Light Infantry took post a few minutes after. The Hessian Grenadiers and 4th Brigade remained as a second line, and the 5th Brigade kept in the rear as a reserve. In this situation the cannonade took place which lasted until the evening, when the Troops were withdrawn to a new position half a mile to the rear, where they lay on their arms in a convenient arrangement for proceeding on their march, and better covered from some guns the Enemy had brought round at a considerable distance on our left, and fired with a great elevation. A body of the Rebels attempted to possess themselves of the hill from which the Grenadiers were retiring; but were immediately attacked and put to flight with some loss. Another Corps was as unsuccessful in endeavoring to annoy the Light Infantry as they recrossed the swamp; after this they did not venture to advance. The wounded were brought into the village of Freehold, and those whose cases would admit of it, brought away when the Division marched.

At twelve o'clock the Division marched from Freehold, and in the morning joined Major General Grant and General Knyphausen within five miles of Middletown.

29th   General Knyphausen marched to Middletown.

30th   Lieutenant General Lord Cornwallis marched at 3 in the morning and joined the other Division at Middletown. The 1st, 2d, 5th and Stirn's Brigade were sent forward to occupy the heights of Neversink, and the baggage received Orders to follow. At 10 in the evening the remainder of the Troops marched to the heights.

31st   The Troops were arranged on the heights and the embarkation of baggage, stores, &c, began. During the succeeding days the embarkation was carried on.

A bridge of boats was thrown across the gap in the Isthmus, which till lately had connected Sandy Hook with the main, and the Troops were marched into the Hook and embarked on board transports.

The 3d, 4th and 5th Brigades were landed on Long Island; the 1st and 2d on Staten Island and the Guards, Hessians and Cavalry on York Island.

Thus was completed a March of many miles thro' the Enemy's country, in defiance of every obstacle they threatened or attempted to throw in our way; nor was it only by repelling and pursuing them at Freehold that a superiority both of skill and powers was shewn; but throughout the whole march they were perplexed in their conjectures by the secrecy observed respecting our route and by false movements made to deceive them; neither could their Militia or Light Troops with their boasted knowledge of the country and dexterity in hovering round us, find an opportunity to give the least annoyance to a Column of eight or ten miles in length.

James McHenry:
Journal, June 18–July 23, 1778

Valley Forge —18 June

Early this morning by intelligence from McLane, Sir Henry Clinton and the British army evacuated Philadelphia and took post on the Jersey side.

Everything being arranged for our march — a division under General Lee proceeded towards the Delaware in the evening.

19th. The whole army in motion. — March to Norringtown Township. Encamp on Stony run. Head Quarters at a Doctor Shannons.

A good farm house — good cheer — and a pretty situation.

A letter from Genl. Dickinson to his Excellency — The enemy, the General writes, at Eyres Town, three miles below Montholly. — The militia collecting to give them opposition. Some little skirmishing — The enemy repairing a bridge which our people had broke down.

20th. March at 4 o'clock in the morning. — Hault at Mordecai Moors, about 7 miles from Shannons, and 22 miles from Philadelphia. — A beautiful country & Every where the marks of industrious & happy inhabitants.

In going to Moors, we cross the Skippach and North Wales road. —

The army encamps for the night 8 miles from Moors and 25 from Philadelphia.

Head Quarters at a Jonathan Fells.

A rainy evening. Let me see, what company have we got within doors. — A pretty, full-faced, youthful, playfull lass. — The family quakers, meek and unsuspicious. — Hamilton, thou shalt not tread on this ground — I mark it for my own. Enter not this circle.

— The pretty girl gives me some excellent milk, and sits and chats with me till bedtime. — She was too innocent a subject for gallantry, so I kissed her hand — telling her that we should be all gone before she got up — but not to forget that one man is often more dangerous to a woman than a whole army.

In the morning, as we were about to move, we were stopped by a deputation from the Seneca, Tuscorora, and Oneida Indians, who requested an audience of the Genl.

Their speaker informed the General that the Indians which he represents are now at war with the Americans, but that this circumstance did not prevent him from trusting himself with his enemy when in search of the warrior Astiarix, whom he understood was a prisoner with the Americans. As he came upon a peaceful errand, he had relied upon protection, and he had got it. As he came to seek his friend and a warrior, he was sure that the great American warrior would not withhold his friend whom he sought. They were both great warriors and must know each other and must both be inspired by the same generous sentiments. I ask nothing, but Astiarix, and I do not ask him but upon such conditions as you may impose. We are willing to deliver up one of your chiefs in his stead, or to ransom him with our property. You can ask no more. But if this will not do, and you should have doomed Astiarix to die, I am sure he will not forget the nation to which he belongs, nor his great deeds in battle. You may torment him — but he will always be Astiarix and his nation will never forget his ashes, nor forgive the hand which scatters them to the winds.

His Excellency replied to this bold and animated speech through the interpreter — that *he* did not know anything of the warrior, Astiarix — that perhaps he might be in Virginia — that if a prisoner, his life was safe: — that he was sorry to be at war with the Senecas, Tuscororas & Oneidas, and that he wished to bury the hatchet, &c. &c. — He then desired the Indians to observe the army (which was drawn up and ready to march) — suggesting that if peace could not be made upon reasonable terms with the Indians, he must send these men, pointing to the troops, to make it. — The Indians then took leave, and the army took up its line of march.

10 o'clock.

Additional waggons ordered for the tents which were weat and heavier in consequence.

A rapid morning's march. The heat excessive. — Some of the soldiers die suddenly. Reach Coryels ferry. Encamp on the Pennsylvania side.

The General crosses — with the spare baggage and artillery.

Headquarters at one Holcombs in the Jersey. Here are some charming girls — But one of the drums of the guard more a favorite than Hamilton.

Division of Lee and Wayne 4 miles in advance of Coryels.

General Arnold advises that the Enemy's advanced guard commanded by Gen. Leslie consists of 2,000 — main body 5,000 — rear guard 2,000 — under Knyphausen. Their shipping below Rudy Island.

22d. Gen. Dickinson writes that the enemy advance — That he is at the draw bridge 4 miles below Trenton, and preparing for a vigorous defense of that post. — The enemy's superiority in horse making it impossible for our handful of cavalry to stand their ground.

Genl. du Portail, Engineer, ordered forward to reconnoitre a position near Princetown.

Sourland hills and Rocky hill reported by the Engineer. The nearest part of the former chain of hills 5 miles distant from Princetown — running in the direction of North by East. Rocky hill has the advantage in point of water. — The roads of retreat from Sourland must be opened towards Aimwel road — the country rocky and difficult.

The army cross Coryels. General Lee reconnoiters a position about 6 miles from the ferry.

23d. The army takes the road from the Stone Schoolhouse to Rocky hill. Hault near Sourland hights — Hopewell. 4 miles from Princetown.

Rocky hill reconnoitered. A good position relative to Kingston in case that should be the enemy's route. The Millstone river unfordable — steep craggy ground under the right flank. — The order of march — 3 o'clock. 600 men detached under Col. Morgan to hang on the enemy in conjunction with the militia.

24. In consequence of intelligence from Gen. Dickinson we remain on the ground we took yesterday — The day spent in digesting intelligence and in decyphering the enemy's intentions.

1400 picked men ordered to march towards the enemy under Brigadier General Scott.

General Arnold orders Jackson's detachment to cross the Delaware.

Gen. Cadwallader endeavors to induce the Philadelphia Volunteers to march with him to the enemy's rear.

The seventh day since the evacuation of Philadelphia and the enemy tent near Allen's Town. This gives rise to a conjecture that their slow movement is not the consequence of obstructions — broken bridges &c., but that it proceeds from a desire to give us battle. I don't think so.

Gen. Dickinson writes that the enemy failed in an attempt to rebuild a bridge 4 miles from Trenton, owing to the fire of his militia.

— A Council of war. — The majority against putting the enemy in a situation which might bring on a general engagement. — The General however determines to attack.

25th. March to Rocky hill. Cross the Millstone by a bridge, and hault at Kingston.

Breakfast at Mrs. Berians — good tea and agreeable conversation.

A dinner in the woods. — The General receives advice that the English right column marched from Imleys Town by the road to Monmouth court house.

The Marquiss de la Fayette is detached to support Scott, with 2000 men — with orders to take command of the whole detached troops.

The young Frenchman in raptures with his command and burning to distinguish himself moves towards the enemy who are in motion.

It is night before the main body of our army marches, and then only to Laurens's, 4 miles from Kingston.

26. March to Cranberry, and hault 7 miles from Laurence's farm. — A heavy rain.

The armies at no great distance from each other. Our troops anxious to engage. — The enemy encamped at Monmouth court house in two lines, and in a strong position.

27. March early in the morning 6 miles on the road to English Town. — The enemy still on the ground at Monmouth.

The Marquiss files off by the left of English Town to put us in a situation to co-operate.

Major Gen. Lee thinks himself overlooked as being an old officer, in the commands being given to the Marquiss. To prevent disunion, Lee is detached with 2 brigades to join the Marquiss, and as senior officer to the command.

His detachment consists of 5,000 men, four-fifts of whom were picked for this service.

Morgan hovering on the enemy's right flank, and the militia under Gen. Dickinson on their left.

Their right stretched about one mile and a half beyond Monmouth court house — in the parting of the roads leading to Shrewsberry and Middletown — and their left along the road from Allen Town to Monmouth about 3 miles on this side the court house. Their right flank skirted by a small wood — their left by a thick forest & morass running towards their rear. And their front covered by a wood and for a considerable extent to the left with a morass.

Tonight Gen. Lee receives orders to attack as soon as they begin their march.

28th.   The Baron Steuben and Col. Laurens reconnoitre, find the encampment up, and their rear formed at the court house. They appear ready to march. Gen. Lee informed of this by Col. Laurens.

Gen. Lee moves his men to the attack — but is repulsed and retreats.

Detail of the Engagement.

The enemy advanced two regiments by files into the woods near the court house — These being reported to Genl. Lee as heavy columns he immediately ordered a hault and Varnum's Brigade to repass a bridge which they had just crossed. The enemy were now more closely reconnoitred and Gen. Lee ordered the troops to advance. But our advance troops had got into disorder — were much exhausted by marching and countermarching and the moment lost for attacking the enemy. They had now formed their order of battle and came on briskly to the charge with the cavalry in front.

Our few horse were charged by their whole cavalry and were obliged to give way till supported by the infantry.

Livingston & Col. Steuart were ordered to turn their left—when the enemy charged their front—These regiments were then ordered to fall back and form in the village. From thence they retired to Rus house and the rest of the detachment through the woods.

Genl. Lee again ordered a retreat leaving a fine defile unguarded.

In this juncture Genl. Washington met the detachment having received no notice of the order for retreat. He was much surprised, chagrinned and disappointed—and instantly preceiving there was no time to be lost—for the enemy were in full view and full march to improve the advantage they had gained over Lee's detachment—he directed some of the disordered troops to form, till the main body could take a position of support.

The moment was critical and the safety of the whole army depended upon a firm opposition.

Col. Steuart & Col. Ramseys troops were nearest the General—He encouraged the men—he took the officers by the hand—he told them how much depended on a moments resistance, and he said he was satisfied every thing would be attempted. Col. Ramsey and Col. Steuart gave him assurances of their utmost exertions, and in that instant the whole was involved in the smoke of battle.

As these two regiments were to sustain the assault of the whole British line, it is not to be supposed they could make a long opposition.—They were obliged to give way and retreated into the woods—but not before they had given our main body time to form and take an advantagious ground.

Two Regiments of Varnums Brigade, under Lt. Col. Olney received the next shock of the enemy who keep advancing. The British cavalry dashed upon them with great impetuosity, but could not stand a cool and well directed fire from our troops. This opposition did Olney great honor.

We had now everything disposed for a general action—Our center was covered by a morass—the left commanded an extent of open ground on the flank which made it difficult for the enemy to turn in rear—& the right was covered by a ravine and close wood.

Lord Stirling commanded our left wing and Genl. Greene the right.

Olney was at length obliged to give way — but he did it with great dignity — Livingston who acted on his right was very powerful in his fire and did much execution.

Lord Stirling planted a battery of cannon on the right of his wing, and made a detachment of Infantry under Col. Scilly and Col. Barker of the 1st Virginia Regt. which penetrated the woods and fell vigorously on the enemy's right flank. — This obliged the enemy to give way.

After this small repulse they appeared in motion towards our left.

Gen. Wayne kept them at bay in front, having occupied a barn and orchard, which he defended with bravery. At this instant, when they pressed upon Wayne and on all sides, Gen. Green took possession of a piece of ground on their left with a brigade under the immediate command of Gen. Woodford

It was now the fate of our army was to be decided — the firing was supported with equal vigor — and neither party seemed inclined to give way — all was dubious — when Gen. Greene opened a battery of cannon which enfiladed the enemy — , This and Gen. Wayne's fire at length forced them to retire with considerable loss — and gave us the ground upon which they had fought, and all their wounded and killed.

Night set in and we . . .

Gen. Washington meets the retreating troops — they are rallied — and the day is disputed in a variety of places — with great gallantry and spirit. We gain the field of battle — and at evening the two front lines of the two armies within musket shot of each other rest upon their arms.

Failing in an attempt to turn the enemy's flank — we composed ourselves to sleep behind the line of battle under a large tree.

29. Bury the dead. Col. Burmer on our side — a Capt. of the Artillery &c. — and Col. Moncton on the part of the enemy with the honors of war — and about 245, of the enemy's privates.

The enemy gain the hights of Middletown and we return to Englishtown.

Capt. Plunket makes a Capn. Kennedy, formerly a Dr. in Baltimore a prisoner & brings him to Head Quarters. — obtains permission for Kennedy to go in on parole — Kennedy having done some favors for Plunket when a prisoner.

The soil near English Town sandy — and water very scarce.

Gen. Lee ordered under an arrest for retreating — misbehaviour &c.

30th.   The army marches to Spottswood. Pass through Brunswick — and make Head Quarters at Ross Hall. The mistress of the house a pretty widdow.

A fine prospect comprehending Brunswick from Ross Hall. This place still exhibits marks of war, and the remains of some elegant houses in ruins along the banks of the Raritan.

We rest ourselves on this ground till the 5th. The 4 being the anniversary of Independence it is celebrated with a feu de joye. The fire from the two lines of the army with the intermingled discharge of cannon animating and brilliant.

In our route to Paramus where a part of the army had encamped in order to rest and refresh we had an opportunity of seeing the falls of Pasaic.

We crossed an old bridge very much out of repair on the Pasaic river, and in about half a mile, reached the falls. The river is about 40 yards broad — The cleft of the falls is from 4 to 12 feet broad.

The rock into which the water tumbles is of considerable extent, and covered in general with herbage — some trees, and shrubbery. But besides the great chasm into which it precipitates — there are several large fissures in the rock, whose singularity combine with the falls to render the whole an interesting spectacle. One sees A smooth and gentle sheet of water hurrying down into the great aperture or cleft, while, at the same time several lesser portions seem to steal from different parts of the ledge, all rudely encountering each other in a descent of near seventy feet, till reaching the bottom they dash together with all the indignation of combatants. — One end of the cleft being closed the water rushes out from the other with great rapidity, and is received into a large bason, where it loses all its rage and assumes the polish of a miror.

The conflict and dashing of the water against the sides of the rock in its fall, produces a fine spray, that issuing from the cleft appears at a distance like a thin body of smoke, while viewed in the sunshine from the edge of the chasm it exhibits a beautiful rainbow.

When the water leaves the bason it spreads itself into a pretty broad channel and continues its course uninterrupted to New Ark Bay.

A little above the falls the water glides over some rocks raised across the channel in a pretty trembling manner, as if to suggest to the spectators the shock which it is about to en- counter. —

One cannot help observing that the apertures or dismem- berments in the rock, of which there are several, all run in the same direction. You may descend into some of them by means of earth and stones till you get to a great depth. On each side you are defended by a perpendicular and smooth wall of stone, overgrown with moss. There one enjoys a de- lightful coolness which no sun can render disagreeable. Over head you see vines and the branches of trees which of them- selves would form a perfect shade.

I wished for more time to examine the various beauties of a place well formed for love — for lettered ease — and con- templation. I wished to investigate the cause which seemed to have changed the course of a river — and made such dismem- berments in an immense rock. Was it as old as creation — The effect of the deluge, or the production of a volcano or earth- quake? — But a soldier has other objects to fill up the measure of his idle hours — more amusing but rarely so commendable.

Adieu, gentle Pasaic, less noisy and boisterous than famed Niagara — less stupendous also — though, perhaps not less curious or interesting — till days of returning leisure security come round (if such I am ever to enjoy), when I promise — to make thee a second visit. — But I was interrupted by a call from the General, and I may never see thee more, Charming Pasaic, — Adieu!

I found the General & suite seated under a large spreading oak — within view of the spray diversified by a beautiful rain- bow.

A fine cool spring bubled out most charmingly from the bottom of the oak. The travelling canteens were immediately emptied, and a sudden repast spread before us consisting of cold ham—tongue—and excellent biscuit. With the assistance of a little spirit we composed some grog—over which we chatted away a very cheerful hour, and then took leave of the friendly oak—its refreshing spring—and the meek falls of Pasaic.

From this romantic spot we passed through a fertile country to Paramus. We stopped at a Mrs. Watkins's, whose house was marked for headquarters.—But the General receiving a note of invitation from a Mrs. Provost to make her Hermitage, as it was called, the seat of his stay while the army remained at Paramus, we only dined with Mrs. Watkins and her two handsome daughters.

At our new quarters we found some fair refugees from New York on a visit to the lady of the Hermitage. Here we talked and walked and laughed—and frolicked—and gallanted away four days and four nights, and would have gallanted—and frolicked and laughed—and walked and talked, I believe, for ever, had not the General given orders for our departure.

It was about 6 o'clock the next morning when we bad adieu to the Hermitage, coasting it through narrow and stony roads, to a place called *Haverstraw* in the State of New York.

July

15. Our quarters was engaged at the house of a Col. Hays, formerly a Mr. Smith's. The house stands about one mile from the North River on an eminence commanding the view of a large extent of water—a considerable part of Chester County and some of the hights of Duchess.

After dinner I took a ride to a pond or lake about half a mile from the North river on the top of a large mountain. To get to it you must ride round the base of a high chain of rocks which border on the North river. We were obliged to ascend slowly and after about three miles riding came to a fine level and cultivated country. On this ground which is greatly elevated above the water of the North river—we discovered the lake. It is large and abounds in some excellent fish;—there are several farm houses along its banks which add considerably to the beauty of the scene. . . .

21st. The army remained on the same ground.

22d. Wednesday. Varnum & Glovers Brigades march for ——

23. Jacksons detachment, consisting of part of three regiments, march for Gen. —— The whole under the Marquiss la fayette amounting to near 2,000 men.

John Laurens to Henry Laurens

Englishtown, N.J., June 30, 1778

My dear Father

I was exceedingly chagrined that public business prevented my writing to you from the Field of battle, when the General sent his dispatches to Congress — the delay however will be attended with this advantage that I shall be better able to give you an account of the enemys loss — tho I must even now content myself with a very succinct relation of this affair — the situation of the two Armies on Sunday was as follows — Genl Washington with the main body of our army was at 4 miles distance from Englishtown — Genl Lee with a chosen advanced Corps was at that Town — the Enemy were retreating down the Road which leads to Middle Town, their flying Army composed, (as it was said,) of 2 batallions of british grenadiers — 1 Hessian Grendrs — 1 batalion of light infantry — 1 Regiment of Guards — 2 brigades of foot — 1 Regt. of Dragoons — and a number of mounted and dismounted Jagers — the Enemy's Rear was preparing to leave Monmouth Village, which is at 6 miles from this place — when our advanced Corps was marching towards them — the Militia of the Country, kept up a random returning fire with the Hessian Jagers, no mischief was done on either side — I was with a small party of horse reconnoitring the enemy in an open space before Monmouth when I perceived two parties of the enemy advancing by files in the woods on our right and left, with a View as I imagined of enveloping our small party, or preparing the way for a skirmish of their horse — I immediately wrote an account of what I had seen to the General — and expressed my anxiety on account of the languid appearance of the continental troops under Geñ Lee — some person in the mean time reported to Genl Lee that the Enemy were advancing upon us in two Columns — and I was informed that he had in consequence ordered Varnums brigade which was in front to repass a bridge which it had passed — I went

myself & assured him of the real state of the case—his reply
to me was, that his accounts had been so contradictory, that
he was utterly at a loss what part to take—I repeated my account to him in positive distinct terms and returned to make
farther discoveries—I found that the two parties had been
withdrawn from the woods and that the enemy were preparing to leave Monmouth—I wrote a second time to Genl
Washington—Genl Lee at length gave orders to advance—
the Enemy were forming themselves on the Middletown
Road, with their light infantry in front, and Cavalry on the
left flank—while a scattering distant fire was commenced between our flanking parties and theirs—I was impatient, and
uneasy at seeing that no disposition was made, and endeavored to find out Genl Lee to inform him of what was doing,
and know what was his disposition—he told me that he was
going to order some troops to march below the Enemy and
cut off their retreat—two Pieces of Artillery were posted on
our right without a single foot soldier to support them—our
men were formed piecemeal in front of the Enemy—and
there appeared to be no general plan or disposition—calculated on that of the Enemy, the nature of the ground, or any
of the other principles which generally govern in these
cases—the Enemy began a cannonade from two parts of their
line—their whole body of horse made a furious charge upon
a small party of our Cavalry and dissipated them, and drove
them till the appearance of our infantry and a judicious discharge or two of Artillery made them retire precipitately—
three Regiments of ours that had advanced in a plain open
country towards the enemys left flank, were ordered by Gen
Lee to retire and occupy the village of Monmouth they were
no sooner formed there, than they were ordered to quit that
post and gain the woods—one order succeeded another, with
a rapidity and indecision calculated to ruin us—the enemy
had changed their front and were advancing in full march toward us—our men were fatigued, with the excessive heat—
the artillery horses were not in condition to make a brisk
retreat—a new position was ordered—but not generally
communicated—for part of the Troops were forming on
the right of the ground, while others were marching away,
and all the Artillery driving off—the enemy after a short halt

resumed their pursuit—no Cannon was left to check their progress—a Regiment was ordered to form behind a fence and as speedily commanded to retire—all this disgraceful retreating—passed without the firing of a Musket—over ground which might have been disputed Inch by Inch—we passed a defile—and arrived at an eminence beyond which was defended on one hand by an impracticable fen—on the other by thick woods where our men must have fought to advantage—here fortunately for the honor of the Army, and the welfare of America—Genl. Washington met the troops retreating—in disorder, and without any plan to make an opposition—he ordered some pieces of Artillery to be brought up to defend the pass—and some troops to form and protect the pieces—the Artillery was too distant to be brought up readily so that there was but little opposition given here—a few shot though and a little skirmishing in the wood checked the Enemys career—The Genl expressed his astonishment at this unaccountable Retreat, Mr Lee indecently replied that the attack was contrary to his advice and opinion in council— we were obliged to retire to a position which though hastily reconnoitred, proved an excellent one—two Regiments were formed behind a fence in front of the position—the enemys horse advanced in full charge with admirable bravery—to the distance of forty paces—when a general discharge from these two Regiments—did great execution among them, and made them fly with the greatest precipitation—the Grenadiers succeeded to the attack—in this spot the action was hottest, and there was considerable Slaughter of British Grenadiers—The General ordered Woodfords brigade with some Artillery to take possession of an eminence on the enemys left and cannonade from thence—this produced an excellent effect—the enemy were prevented from advancing on us—and confined themselves to cannonade with a shew of turning our left flank—our artillery answered theirs—with the greatest vigour—the general seeing that our left flank was secure—as the ground was open and commanded by it—so that the enemy could not attempt to turn us without exposing their own flank to a heavy fire from our artillery, and causing to pass in review before us, the force employed for turning us—in the mean time Genl Lee continued retreating—Baron Steuben was order'd to form the broken troops in the rear—The Cannonade was incessant, and the General ordered parties to advance from time to time, and engage the British Grenadiers—and Guards—the horse shewed themselves no more—the Grenadiers shewed their backs and retreated every where with precipitation—they returned however again to the charge and were again repulsed—they finally retreated and got over the strong pass where as I mentioned before Genl Washington first rallied the troops—we advanced in force and continued Masters of the ground—the Standards of Liberty were planted in Triumph on the field of battle—we remained looking at each other with the defile between us till dark—& they stole off in silence at midnight—

We have buried of the enemys slain 233, principally Grenadiers—forty odd of their wounded whom they left at Monmouth fell into our hands—several officers are our prisoners—among their killed are Col. Moncton of the Grenadiers, brother to Genl. Moncton, a Captain of the guards and several Captains of Grenadiers—we have taken but a very inconsiderable number of prisoners for want of a good body of horse—deserters are coming in as usual—Our officers and men behaved with that bravery which becomes freemen and have convinced the world that they can beat british Grenadiers—to name any in particular wd be a kind of injustice to the rest—there are some however who came more immediately under my view, whom I will mention that you may know them—B. Genl Wayne—Col. Barber, Col. Stewart, Col Livingston—Col Oswald of the Artillery—Capt. Doughty—deserve well of their country and distinguished themselves nobly—

the enemy buried many of their dead that are not accounted for above—and carried off a great number of wounded—

I have written diffusely and yet I have not told you all—Genl. Lee I think must be tried for misconduct—however as this is a matter not generally known, tho' it seems almost universally wished for—I would beg you my dear father to say nothing of it—

You will oblige me much by excusing me to Mr Drayton for not writing to him—I congratulate you my dear Father upon this seasonable victory and am ever your most dutiful and affectionate

———

Brunswick, N.J., July 2, 1778

My dear father.

I had the pleasure of writing to you the day before yesterday from English Town — but through some mistake my letter was not delivered to the express — altho it was written in a hurry, I recollect no circumstance in it relative to our late engagement which farther inquiry and consideration do not confirm — from a second view of the ground, as well as the accounts I have since had of the enemys strength and designs, it is evident to me that Mr Clintons whole flying army would have fallen into our hands, but for a defect of abilities or good will in the Commanding Officer of our advanced Corps —

his precipitate retreat spread a baneful influence every where — the most sanguine hope scarcely extended farther when the Commander in chief rallied his troops, then to an orderly retreat but by his intrepidity and presence of mind a firm line of Troops was formed on a good position, from whence he cannonaded with advantage, and detached light parties in front who drove the enemy from the field. Genl. Clinton and Lord Cornwallis were both present at the action —

The reason for not pursuing them farther with the main body of our army was that people well acquainted with the Country, said that the strength of the ground would render it impracticable for us to injure them essentially and that the sandy parched soil together with the heat of the sun, would probably occasion us considerable loss — from the specimen of yesterdays march we have reason to think it fortunate that we took the part we have done — the heat of the weather, thirsty soil, and heavy sand, reduced us to the necessity of bringing on many of our weaker men in waggons —

we are now arrived in a delightful country where we shall halt and refresh ourselves — bathing in the Rariton, and the good living of the Country will speedily reestablish us — I wish my dear Father that you could ride along the banks of this delightful Rivers — your zeal for the public Service will

not at this time permit it — but the inward satisfaction which
you must feel from a patriotic discharge of your duty, is infinitely superior to the delights of retirement and ease — I admire your constant virtue and will imitate your example —

Your most affectionate

Col. Morgan writes this day that the rear of the enemy is a
mile below Middletown, that he has had a skirmish with several of their light parties which has cost them some lives — he
had only one man wounded — Desertions continue and I
suppose will be very considerable at the moment of embarkation —

I have seen the General much embarrassed this day, on the
subject of those who distinguished themselves in the battle of
Monmouth — to name a few and be silent with regard to
many of equal merit wd be an injustice to the latter — to pass
the whole over unnoticed wd be an unpardonable slight — in-
discriminate praise of the whole wd be an unfair distribution
of rewards — and yet when men generally conducted themselves so well as our officers did — this method is Allowable,
and is eligible because least liable to give offence — The Merit
of restoring the day is due to the General, and his conduct
was such throughout the affair as has greatly increased my
Love & esteem for him — my three brother aids gained themselves great applause by their activity and bravery — even the
three Secretaries acted as military men on this occasion, and
proved themselves as worthy to wield the sword as the pen —

Genl Steuben his Aids and your son narrowly escaped being surrounded by the british horse early on the morning of
the action — we reconnoitred them rather too nearly, and Ld
Cornwallis sent the Dragoons of his guard to make us prisoners — Genl. Clinton saw the barons stop and the whole pursuit was directed at him — but we all escaped — the dragoons
fearing an ambuscade of Infantry.

We have buried Col. Moncton with the honors of War —

J. Hector St. John Crèvecoeur:
Narrative of the Wyoming Massacre

Soon after my return from this last excursion began the great contest between the mother-country and this. It spread among the lower class like an epidemic of the mind, which reached far and near, as you well know. It soon swallowed up every inferior contest; silenced every other dispute; and presented the people of Susquehanna with the pleasing hopes of their own never being decided by Great Britain. These solitary farmers, like all the rest of the inhabitants of this country, rapidly launched forth into all the intricate mazes of this grand quarrel, as their inclinations, prepossessions, and prejudices led them. It was a fatal era, which has since disseminated among them the most horrid poison; which has torn them with intestine divisions; and has brought on that languor, that internal weakness, that suspension of industry, and the total destruction of their noble beginning.

Many, however, there were who still wished for peace; who still respected the name of Englishman; and cherished the idea of ancient connection. These were principally settled in the upper towns; the inhabitants of the lower ones were strongly prepossessed with the modern opinions. These latter ill brooked that anyone who had come to settle under their patronage should prove their antagonists, and, knowing themselves to be the strongest party, were guilty of many persecutions, — a horrid policy. Every order was destroyed; the new harmony and good understanding which began to prevail among them were destroyed. Some of the inhabitants of the upper towns fell victims to this new zeal; gaols were erected on these peaceful shores where many sticklers for the old government were confined. But I am not going to lead you through the disgusting details of these scenes with which your papers have been filled, for it would be but a repetition of what has been done from one end of the continent to the other. This new ebullition of the mind was everywhere like one and the same cause; and therefore everywhere produced the same effects.

Many of those who found themselves stripped of their property took refuge among the Indians. Where else could they go? Many others, tired of that perpetual tumult in which the whole settlement was involved, voluntarily took the same course; and I am told that great numbers from the extended frontiers of the middle provinces have taken the same steps, — some reduced to despair, some fearing the incursions with which they were threatened. What a strange idea this joining with the savages seems to convey to the imagination; this uniting with a people which Nature has distinguished by so many national marks! Yet this is what the Europeans have often done through choice and inclination, whereas we never hear of any Indians becoming civilized Europeans. This uncommon emigration, however, has thrown among them a greater number of whites than ever has been known before. This will ere long give rise to a new set of people, but will not produce a new species, — so strong is the power of Indian education. Thus war, tyranny, religion mix nations with nations; dispeople one part of the earth to cause a new one to be inhabited.

It will be worthy of observation to see whether those who are now with the Indians will ever return and submit themselves to the yoke of European society; or whether they will carefully cherish their knowledge and industry and gather themselves on some fertile spot in the interior parts of the continent; or whether that easy, desultory life so peculiar to the Indians will attract their attention and destroy their ancient inclinations. I rather think that the latter will preponderate, for you cannot possibly conceive the singular charm, the indescribable propensity which Europeans are apt to conceive and imbibe in a very short time for this vagrant life; a life which we civilized people are apt to represent to ourselves as the most ignoble, the most irksome of any. Upon a nearer inspection 'tis far from being so disgusting. Innumerable instances might be produced of the effect which it has had not only on poor illiterate people, but on soldiers and other persons bred to the luxuries and ease of a European life.

Remember the strong instance of the people taken at Oswego during the last war, who, though permitted to return home, chose to remain and become Indians. The daughters of these frontier people will necessarily marry with the young men of the nation in which they have taken refuge; they have now no other choice. At a certain age Nature points out the necessity of union; she cares very little about the colour. By the same reason and in consequence of the same cause the young Europeans will unite themselves to the squaws. 'Tis very probable, therefore, that fishing, hunting, and a little planting will become their principal occupations. The children that will spring from these new alliances will thoroughly imbibe the manners of the village, and perhaps speak no other language. You know what the power of education is: the Janissaries, though born of Frank parents, were by its impulse rendered the most enthusiastic enemies of the Christian name.

Some time after the departure of these people a few Indians came down under the sanction of a flag to demand their effects, representing that they had been so much disturbed in their huntings that they were not able to maintain so many of them; that, had they their cows and horses, they would give them land enough to raise their own bread. But instead of complying with this just request, in the hour of the utmost infatuation they seized these ambassadors, whipped them, and sent them away. Ignorant, as we suppose them to be, yet this treatment inflamed them to most bitter revenge, and awakened those unguided passions which are so dreadful among this haughty people. Notwithstanding this high insult, the nation sent a second and more numerous embassy than the first. Colonel Dyer, a member of Congress for the province of Connecticut, expostulated with them by letter, and pointed out the injustice and impolicy of their proceedings, but in vain. Though they should have been astonished at a step so new and extraordinary as this second embassy, yet they attempted to seize them. Two only were apprehended and confined; the rest made their escape.

A short time before this the Congress had ordered a body of four hundred men to be raised, in order to cover more effectually the frontiers of this long-extended settlement. The people readily enlisted, and this regiment was soon com-

pleted. But what was their surprise and alarm when it was ordered to join General Washington's headquarters! They then,
but too late, began to emerge from that state of blindness in
which they seemed to have been plunged. They began to fear
lest their ill-judged conduct should bring down at last the
vengeance of a much larger body of assailants than they could
well repel. The absence of this regiment, composed of the
flower of their youth, not only left them very much exposed
but even seemed to invite the enemy. As they had foreseen it,
it hastened the long-premeditated storm which had been
gathering. The Europeans who had taken refuge among the
natives united with them in the same scheme which had been
anteriorly proposed, and set on foot by the commandant of
Niagara; they were, therefore, joined by several English officers and soldiers. The whole body of these assailants seemed
animated with the most vindictive passions, a sacrifice to
which many innocent families as well as guilty ones were
doomed to fall. As no bard has as yet appeared to sing in
plaintive strains: "Mourn, Susquehanna! mourn thy hapless
sons, thy defenceless farmers slaughtered on thy shores!" shall
I be excused in following my feelings and in finishing the
short account of their final catastrophe as my untutored but
honest impulse directs?

> Oh Man! thou hast made the happy earth thy hell,
> Filled it with cursing cries and deep exclaims;
> If thou delight to view thy heinous deeds,
> Behold this pattern of thy butcheries.

The assailants formed a body of about eight hundred men
who received their arms from Niagara; the whites under the
conduct of Colonel Butler, the Indians under that of Brant.
After a fatiguing march, they all met at some of the upper
towns of the Susquehanna, and while they were refreshing
themselves and providing canoes and every other necessary
implement, parties were sent out in different parts of the
country. Some penetrated to the west branch and did infinite
mischief; it was easy to surprise defenceless, isolated families
who fell an easy prey to their enemies. Others approached the
New England settlements, where the ravages they committed
were not less dreadful. Many families were locked up in their

houses and consumed with all their furniture. Dreadful scenes were transacted which I know not how to retrace. This was, however, but the prelude of the grand drama. A few weeks afterwards, the whole settlement was alarmed with the news of the main body coming down the river. Many immediately embarked and retired into the more interior parts of Pennsylvania; the rest immediately retired with their wives and children into the stockade they had erected there some time before.

Meanwhile the enemy landed at Lackawanna or Kingston, the very place where the stockade was erected. Orders were immediately issued by their commanders for the rest of the militia to resort to them. Some of the most contiguous readily obeyed; distance prevented others. Colonel Butler, seeing they had abandoned their dwellings, proposed to them to surrender and quit the country in a limited time. It was refused by the New England people, who resolved to march out and meet them in the open fields. Their number consisted of five hundred and eighty-two. They found the enemy advantageously situated, but much weaker in numbers, as they thought, than had been reported. This encouraged them; they boldly advanced; and the Indians as sagaciously retreated. Thus they were led on to the fatal spot where all at once they found themselves surrounded. Here some of the New England leaders abandoned them to their evil destiny. Surprised as they were at this bad omen, they still kept their ground and vigorously defended themselves until the Indians, sure of their prey, worked up by the appearance of success to that degree of frenzy which they call courage, dropped their guns and rushed on them with the tomahawk and the spear. The cruel treatment they expected to receive from the wrathful Indians and offended countrymen animated them for a while. They received this first onset with the most undaunted courage, but, the enemy falling upon them with a redoubled fury and on all sides, they broke and immediately looked for safety in flight.

Part of them plunged themselves into the river with the hopes of reaching across, and on this element a new scene was exhibited not less terrible than that which had preceded it. The enemy, flushed with the intoxication of success and victory, pursued them with the most astonishing celerity, and, being naked, had very great advantage over a people encumbered with clothes. This, united with their superiority in the art of swimming, enabled them to overtake most of these unfortunate fugitives, who perished in the river pierced with the lances of the Indians. Thirty-three were so happy as to reach the opposite shores, and for a long time afterwards the carcasses of their companions, become offensive, floated and infested the banks of the Susquehanna as low as Shamokin. The other party, who had taken their flight towards their forts, were all either taken or killed. It is said that those who were then made prisoners were tied to small trees and burnt the evening of the same day.

The body of the aged people, the women and children who were enclosed in the stockade, distinctly could hear and see this dreadful onset, the last scene of which had been transacted close to the very gates. What a situation these unfortunate people were in! Each wife, each father, each mother could easily distinguish each husband and son as they fell. But in so great, so universal a calamity, when each expected to meet the same fate, perhaps they did not feel so keenly for the deplorable end of their friends and relations. Of what powerful materials must the human heart be composed, which could hold together at so awful a crisis! This bloody scene was no sooner over than a new one arose of a very similar nature. They had scarcely finished scalping the numerous victims which lay on the ground when these fierce conquerors demanded the immediate entrance to the fort. It was submissively granted. Above a hundred of them, decorated with all the dreadful ornaments of plumes and colour of war, with fierce and animated eyes, presented themselves and rushed with impetuosity into the middle of the area, armed with tomahawks made of brass with an edge of steel. Tears relieved some; involuntary cries disburdened the oppression of others; a general shriek among the women was immediately heard all around.

What a spectacle this would have exhibited to the eyes of humanity: hundreds of women and children, now widows and orphans, in the most humble attitude, with pale, dejected countenances, sitting on the few bundles they had brought with them; keeping their little unconscious children as close to them as possible; hiding by a mechanical instinct the babies of their breasts; numbers of aged fathers oppressed with the unutterable sorrow; all pale, all trembling, and sinking under the deepest consternation were looking towards the door — that door through which so many of their friends had just passed, alas! never more to return. Everyone at this awful moment measured his future punishment by the degree of revenge which he supposed to animate the breast of his enemy. The self-accusing consciences of some painted to them each approaching minute as replete with the most terrible fate. Many there were who, recollecting how in the hour of oppression they had insulted their countrymen and the natives, bitterly wept with remorse; others were animated with the fiercest rage. What a scene an eminent painter might have copied from that striking exhibition, if it had been a place where a painter could have calmly sat with the palette in his hands! How easily he might have gathered the strongest expressions of sorrow, consternation, despondency, and despair, by taking from each countenance some strong feature of affright, of terror, and dismay, as it appeared delineated on each face. In how many different modes these passions must have painted themselves according as each individual's temper, ardent or phlegmatic habit, hurried or retarded the circulation of the blood, lengthened or contracted the muscles of his physiognomy.

But now a scene of unexpected humanity ensues, which I hasten to describe, because it must be pleasing to peruse and must greatly astonish you, acquainted as you are with the motives of revenge which filled the breasts of these people, as well as with their modes of carrying on war. The preceding part of this narration seems necessarily leading to the horrors of the utmost retaliation. Happily these fierce people, satisfied with the death of those who had opposed them in arms, treated the defenceless ones, the women and children, with a degree of humanity almost hitherto unparalleled.

In the meanwhile the loud and repeated war-shouts began to be re-echoed from all parts; the flames of conflagrated houses and barns soon announced to the other little towns the certainty of their country's defeat; these were the first marks of the enemies' triumph. A general devastation ensued, but not such as we read of in the Old Testament where we find men, women, children, and cattle equally devoted to the same blind rage. All the stock, horses, sheep, etc., that could be gathered in the space of a week, were driven to the Indian towns by a party which was detached on purpose. The other little stockades, hearing of the surrender of their capital, opened their gates and submitted to the conquerors. They were all immediately ordered to paint their faces with red, this being the symbol established then, which was to preserve peace and tranquillity while the two parties were mingled together.

Thus perished in one fatal day most of the buildings, improvements, mills, bridges, etc., which had been erected there with so much cost and industry. Thus were dissolved the foundations of a settlement begun at such a distance from the metropolis, disputed by a potent province; the beginning of which had been stained with blood shed in their primitive altercations. Thus the ill-judged policy of these ignorant people and the general calamities of the times overtook them and extirpated them even out of that wilderness which they had come twelve years before to possess and embellish. Thus the grand contest entered into by these colonies with the mother-country has spread everywhere, even from the sea-shores to the last cottages of the frontiers. This most diffusive calamity, on this fatal spot in particular, has despoiled of their goods, chattels, and lands, upwards of forty-five hundred souls, among whom not a third part was ever guilty of any national crime. Yet they suffered every extent of punishment as if they had participated in the political iniquity which was attributed to the leaders of this unfortunate settlement. This is always the greatest misfortune attending war. What had poor industrious women done? What crime had their numerous and innocent children committed?

> Where are heaven's holiness and mercy fled?
> Laughs heaven at once at virtue and at Man?
> If not, why that discouraged, this destroyed?

Many accused the King with having offered a reward for the scalps of poor inoffensive farmers. Many were seized with violent fevers, attended with the most frantic rage, and died like maniacs; others sat in gloomy silence and ended their unhappy days seemingly in a state of insensibility; various were the ultimate ends of some of these people.

Towards the evening of the second day a few Indians found some spirituous liquor in the fort. The inhabitants, dreading the consequence of inebriation, repaired to Brant who removed every appearance of danger. After this everyone was permitted to go and look for the mangled carcass of his relation and to cover it with earth. I can easily imagine or conceive the feelings of a soldier burying the bodies of his companions, but neither my imagination nor my heart permit me to think of the peculiar anguish and keen feelings which must have seized that of a father, that of a mother avidly seeking among the crowd of slain for the disfigured corpse of a beloved son, the throbbing anguish of a wife — I cannot proceed.

Yet was it not astonishing to see these fierce conquerors, besmeared with the blood of these farmers, loaded with their scalps hardly cold, still swelled with the indignation, pride, and cruelty, with which victory always inspires them, abstain from the least insult and permit some rays of humanity to enlighten so dreadful, so dreary a day?

The complete destruction of these extended settlements was now the next achievement which remained to be done, in order to finish their rude triumph, but it could not be the work of a few days. Houses, barns, mills, grain, everything combustible to conflagrate; cattle, horses, and stock of every kind to gather; this work demanded a considerable time. The collective industry of twelve years could not well be supposed, in so great an extent, to require in its destruction less than twelve days. During that interval both parties were mixed together, and neither blows nor insults tarnished the duration of this period; a perfect suspension of animosities took place. The scattered inhabitants, who came to take the benefit of the Painter proclamation, all equally shared in the protection it imparted. Some of the Indians looked for those families which were known to have abhorred the preceding tyranny. They found the fathers and mothers, but the young men were killed; they bestowed on them many favours. The horrors of war were suspended to give these unhappy people full leisure to retire.

Some embarked in boats, and, leaving all they had behind them, went down the river towards Northumberland, Paxtung, Sunbury, etc., to seek shelter among the inhabitants of Pennsylvania; others, and by far the greatest number, were obliged to venture once more on foot through the great wilderness which separated them from the inhabited part of the province of New York. They received the most positive assurances that they would meet with no further injuries, provided they kept themselves painted in this long traject. This was the very forest they had traversed with so much difficulty a few years before, but how different their circumstances! 'Tis true they were then poor, but they were rich in hopes; they were elated with the near approach of prosperity and ease. Now that all-cheering, that animating sentiment was gone. They had nothing to carry with them but the dreadful recollection of having lost their all, their friends, and their helpmates. These protecting hands were cold, were motionless, which had so long toiled to earn them bread and procure them comfort. No more will they either hold the plough or handle the axe for their wives and children, who, destitute and forlorn, must fly, they hardly know where, to live on the charity of friends. Thus on every side could you see aged parents, wives, and a multitude of unhappy victims of the times, preparing themselves as well as they could to begin this long journey, almost unprovided with any kind of provisions.

While the faithful hand is retracing these mournful events in all the various shades of their progressive increase, the humane heart cannot help shedding tears of the most philanthropic compassion over the burning ruins, the scattered parts of a society once so flourishing, now half-extinct, now scattered, now afflicted by the most pungent sorrow with which the hand of heaven could chastise them.

For a considerable time the roads through the settled country were full of these unhappy fugitives, each company slowly returning towards those counties from which they had formerly emigrated. Some others, still more unfortunate than others, were wholly left alone with their children, obliged to carry through that long and fatiguing march the infants of their breasts, now no longer replenished as before with an exuberant milk. Some of them were reduced to the cruel necessity of loading the ablest of them with the little food they were permitted to carry. Many of these young victims were seen bare-headed, bare-footed, shedding tears at every step, oppressed with fatigues too great for their tender age to bear; afflicted with every species of misery, with hunger, with bleeding feet, every now and then surrounding their mother as exhausted as themselves. "Mammy, where are we going? Where is father? Why don't we go home?" "Poor innocents, don't you know that the King's Indians have killed him and have burnt our house and all we had? Your uncle Simon will perhaps give us some bread."

Hundreds were seen in this deplorable condition, yet thinking themselves happy that they had safely passed through the great wilderness, the dangers of which had so much increased the misfortunes of their situation. Here you might see a poor starved horse as weak and emaciated as themselves, given them perhaps by the enemy as a last boon. The poor beast was loaded with a scanty feather-bed serving as a saddle which was fastened on him with withes and bark. On it sat a wretched mother with a child at her breast, another on her lap, and two more placed behind her, all broiling in the sun; accompanied in this pilgrimage of tribulation by the rest of the family creeping slowly along; leading at a great distance behind a heifer once wild and frolicsome but now tamed by want and hunger; a cow, perhaps, with hollow flanks and projecting ribs closed the train; these were the scanty remains of greater opulence. Such was the mournful procession, which for a number of weeks announced to the country, through which they passed, the sad disaster which had befallen them. The generous farmers sent their wagons to collect as many as they could find, and convey them to the neighbouring county, where the same kindness was repeated. Such was their situation, while the carcasses of their friends were left behind to feed the wolves of that wilderness on which they had so long toiled, and which they had come to improve.

Peter Oliver: from "The Origin & Progress of the American Rebellion"

Much hath been said, & many Exclamations thrown out, even in Parliament, by some popular Orators in the Opposition, against employing the Indians, to whom they gave the Appellation of, *Savages*. Savage is a convertible Term. It properly designated a Person who acts contrary to the Principles of Humanity: An Englishman who hath been educated in Rules of civil Society, may, by a certain Tenor of Conduct, contract a Savageness of Manners which may exceed any Action which an Indian hath been guilty of; as you may, by & by, see, if you please, in the Appendix. Every Nation hath something Peculiar in its Mode of War. An Indian prefers the Mode of fighting behind a Tree, or of skulking in Bushes. He prefers the Hatchet, the scalping Knife & the Tomahawk, to the Bayonet, the Sword & the Cutlass. His Weapons give, at least, as sudden, if not a less painfull Death, than the Englishman's Weapons. It is true, he doth not discover what is called english Courage, of standing undaunted in open Field to be shot at; he rather chuses to be safe in his own Person, whilst he destroys the Person of his Enemy; but this is all, the Custom of Particular Nations. If you incline to put him to Death in a painfull Manner, he will convince You, that he can undergo the most excruciating Torture, without a Groan. This perhaps would be called, by a civilized European, a *Savage Temper*. The Definition of Courage is arbitrary. As to taking the Scalp off a dead Man, it will not give any great Pain; & this is the Trophy of their Victory, which they return Home with as their Voucher; & as to any Damage it may do to a dead Person, it is of no more Consequence than taking off the Shirt of his Garment.

This Scalping Business hath been encouraged, in the Colonies, for more than a Century past. Præmiums have been given, frequently, by the *Massachusetts* Assemblies, for the

Scalps of Indians, even when they boasted loudest of their Sanctity; & I have seen a Vessell enter the Harbor of *Boston*, with a long String of hairy Indian Scalps strung to the rigging, & waving in the wind; but I never heared of an Englishmans scalping an Englishman, untill the Battle of *Lexington* told the savage Tale. And in the last Century, a War was waged with the Indian King *Philip*, who would have been equal to *Julius Cæsar* had their Education been equal. A certain Warrior had acquired a great & a just Fame in his Victories over the French & the Indians, & had hunted King *Philip* down at last; but his Enmity subsisted, after he had killed him; for he most shamefully cut off his Hand, to preserve it as a Trophy; & not contented with so mean a Revenge, he condescended, in a spitefull Manner to chop his backside with a Hatchet; insulting the dead, whilst in the Operation, with ignominious Language. This seemed to be done with the Air of savage Cowardice; as it doth not look fair to attack a Man behind; unless an Attack upon a dead Body will exculpate a Man from Cowardice. Whether King *Philip*, or the Province who employed this Warrior, found any Fault with this mean & base Transaction, the History is silent.

But let Opposition roar, as loud as they please, against the employing Indians in the present Contest with Rebellion; they cannot but remember, that Gen. *Amherst* employed them, under the Sanction of their late Patron, against the French of *Canada*; & surely, there cannot be a worse & baser Enemy than a Rebel, to whom the English Law has assigned the most ignominious Punishment. Besides, those very Men, whom the Opposition have encouraged in this Revolt, appointed a Committee to meet the *Iroquois*, or *Five Nations*, at *Albany*, in Order to engage them against their old Ally, *Great Britain*. Each Party met; &, agreeable to the ancient Custom of such Treaties, the Indians had the usual Frolick of the roasted Ox. The Parties then met upon their Business. The Commissioners proposed to the Indians, that they should join them against their Mother Country; but no Bribe was offered. The Indians were silent; the Convention was adjourned. The Blankets and other Presents were prepared against the next Meeting, to the Value of above £2000 Sterlg. The next Meeting came, according to appointment. The presents were made, & when the Indians had full possession of them, they made this Reply, vizt. "This is a Quarrell between Father & Children; we shall not meddle with it." Thus were these notable Commissioners outwitted in Indian Cunning. But they profited of their Disappointment, for the *Saratoga* Convention will be a standing Witness of the Infidelity of an american rebel Treaty.

Another Example was set, for the Use of the scalping Knife, by these very Men; who never complained of the Use of it untill they were disappointed in their Aims to bring it into Fashion. There was a Tribe of Indians who lived about 150 Miles from *Boston*, at a Place called *Stockbridge*, who were incorporated with the English Settlers. These Indians were brought down into the Rebel Incampments near *Boston*. They would approach nigh to the british Lines, & there flourish their scalping Knives, & yell, by Way of Insult. But these new Allies did not continue, for any Length of Time, among them; they were too fond of Liquor; they grew troublesome to them; there was no Bush fighting to employ them in; & they were dismissed. Hence forward, let Patriotick Oratory & american Complaints, about the scalping Knife & Indian Savages, be controled by everlasting Silence.

George Washington to Henry Laurens

Fredericksburgh, November 14, 1778.
Dear Sir: This will be accompanied by an official letter on the subject of the proposed expedition against Canada. You will perceive I have only considered it in a military light; indeed I was not authorised to consider it in any other; and I am not without apprehensions, that I may be thought, in what I have done, to have exceeded the limits intended by Congress. But my solicitude for the public welfare which I think deeply interested in this affair, will I hope justify me in the eyes of all those who view things through that just medium.

I do not know, Sir, what may be your sentiments in the present case; but whatever they are I am sure I can confide in your honor and friendship, and shall not hesitate to unbosom myself to you on a point of the most delicate and important Nature.

The question of the Canadian expedition in the form it now stands appears to me one of the most interesting that has hitherto agitated our National deliberations. I have one objection to it, untouched in my public letter, which is in my estimation, insurmountable, and alarms all my feelings for the true and permanent interests of my country. This is the introduction of a large body of French troops into Canada, and putting them in possession of the capital of that Province, attached to them by all the ties of blood, habits, manners, religion and former connexion of government. I fear this would be too great a temptation, to be resisted by any power actuated by the common maxims of national policy. Let us realize for a moment the striking advantages France would derive from the possession of Canada; the acquisition of an extensive territory abounding in supplies for the use of her Islands; the opening a vast source of the most beneficial commerce with the Indian nations, which she might then monopolize; the having ports of her own on this continent independent on the precarious good will of an ally; the engrossing the whole trade of New found land whenever she pleased, the finest nursery of seamen in the world; the security afforded to her Islands; and finally, the facility of awing and controuling these states, the natural and most formidable rival of every maritime power in Europe. Canada would be a solid acquisition to France on all these accounts and because of the numerous inhabitants, subjects to her by inclination, who would aid in preserving it under her power against the attempt of every other.

France acknowledged for some time past the most powerful monarchy in Europe by land, able now to dispute the empire of the sea with Great Britain, and if joined with Spain, I may say certainly superior, possessed of New Orleans, on our Right, Canada on our left and seconded by the numerous tribes of Indians on our Rear from one extremity to the other, a people, so generally friendly to her and whom she knows so well how to conciliate; would, it is much to be apprehended have it in her power to give law to these states.

Let us suppose, that when the five thousand french troops (and under the idea of that number twice as many might be introduced,) were entered the city of Quebec; they should declare an intention to hold Canada, as a pledge and surety for the debts due to France from the United States, or, under other specious pretences hold the place till they can find a bone for contention, and in the meanwhile should excite the Canadians to engage in supporting their pretences and claims; what should we be able to say with only four or five thousand men to carry on the dispute? It may be supposed that France would not choose to renounce our friendship by a step of this kind as the consequence would probably be a reunion with England on some terms or other; and the loss of what she had acquired, in so violent and unjustifiable a manner, with all the advantages of an Alliance with us. This in my opinion is too slender a security against the measure to be relied on. The truth of the position will intirely depend on naval events. If France and Spain should unite and obtain a decided superiority by Sea, a reunion with England would avail very little and might be set at defiance. France, with a numerous army at command might throw in what number of land forces she thought proper to support her pretensions; and England without men, without money, and inferior on her favourite element could give no effectual aid to oppose them. Resentment, reproaches, and submission seem to be all that would be left us. Men are very apt to run into extremes; hatred to England may carry some into an excess of Confidence in France; especially when motives of gratitude are thrown into the scale. Men of this description would be unwilling to suppose France capable of acting so ungenerous a part. I am heartily disposed to entertain the most favourable sentiments of our new ally and to cherish them in others to a reasonable degree; but it is a maxim founded on the universal experience of mankind, that no nation is to be trusted farther than it is bound by its interest; and no prudent statesman or politician will venture to depart from it. In our circumstances we ought to be particularly cautious; for we have not yet attained sufficient vigor and maturity to recover from the shock of any false step into which we may unwarily fall.

If France should even engage in the scheme, in the first instance with the purest intentions, there is the greatest danger that, in the progress of the business, invited to it by circumstances and, perhaps, urged on by the solicitations and wishes of the Canadians, she would alter her views.

As the Marquis clothed his proposition when he spoke of it to me, it would seem to originate wholly with himself; but it is far from impossible that it had its birth in the Cabinet of France and was put into this artful dress, to give it the readier currency. I fancy that I read in the countenances of some people on this occasion, more than the disinterested zeal of allies. I hope I am mistaken and that my fears of mischief make me refine too much, and awaken jealousies that have no sufficient foundation.

But upon the whole, Sir, to wave every other consideration; I do not like to add to the number of our national obligations. I would wish as much as possible to avoid giving a foreign power new claims of merit for services performed, to the United States, and would ask no assistance that is not indispensible. I am, etc.

George Washington to Benjamin Harrison

Head Qrs., Middle Brook, December 18, 1778.
My dear Sir: You will be so obliging as to present the inclosed
to the House when oppertunity, and a suitable occasion offers. I feel very sensibly the late honorable testimony of their
remembrance; to stand well in the good opinion of my
Countrymen constitutes my chiefest happiness; and will be
my best support under the perplexities and difficulties of my
present Station.

The mention of my lands in the back Country was more
owing to accident than design; the Virga. Officers having sol-
licited leave for Colo. Wood to attend the Assembly of that
commonwealth with some representation of theirs respecting
their claims, or wishes, brought my own matters (of a similar
nature) to view; but I am too little acquainted with the minu-
tiæ of them to ground an application on or give any trouble
to the Assembly concerning them. Under the proclamation of
1763, I am entitled to 5000 Acres of Land in my own right;
and by purchase from Captn. Roots, Posey, and some other
Officers, I obtained rights to several thousands more, a small
part of wch. I patented during the Admn. of Lord Dunmore;
another part was (I believe) Surveyed, whilst the major part
remains in locations; but where (without having recourse to
my Memms.) and under what circumstances, I know not at
this time any more than you do, nor do I wish to give trouble abt. them.

I can assign but two causes for the enemys continuance
among us, and these balance so equally in my Mind, that I
scarce know which of the two preponderates. The one is, that
they are waiting the ultimate determination of Parliament; the
other, that of our distresses; by which I know the Commissioners went home not a little buoyed up; and sorry I am to
add, not without cause. What may be the effect of such large
and frequent emissions, of the dissentions, Parties, extravagance, and a general lax of public virtue Heaven alone can
tell! I am affraid even to think of It; but it appears as clear to

me as ever the Sun did in its meredian brightness, that America never stood in more eminent need of the wise, patriotic, and Spirited exertions of her Sons than at this period and if it is not a sufficient cause for genl. lamentation, my misconception of the matter impresses it too strongly upon me, that the States seperately are too much engaged in their local concerns, and have too many of their ablest men withdrawn from the general Council for the good of the common weal; in a word, I think our political system may, be compared to the mechanism of a Clock; and that our conduct should derive a lesson from it for it answers no good purpose to keep the smaller Wheels in order if the greater one which is the support and prime mover of the whole is neglected. How far the latter is the case does not become me to pronounce but as there can be no harm in a pious wish for the good of ones Country I shall offer it as mine that each State wd. not only choose, but absolutely compel their ablest Men to attend Congress; that they would instruct them to go into a thorough investigation of the causes that have produced so many disagreeable effects in the Army and Country; in a word that public abuses should be corrected, and an entire reformation worked; without these it does not, in my judgment, require the spirit of divination to foretell the consequences of the present Administration, nor to how little purpose the States, individually, are framing constitutions, providing laws, and filling Offices with the abilities of their ablest Men. These, if the great whole is mismanaged must sink in the general wreck and will carry with it the remorse of thinking that we are lost by our own folly and negligence, or the desire perhaps of living in ease and tranquility during the expected accomplishment of so great a revolution in the effecting of which the greatest abilities and the honestest Men our (i.e. the American) world affords ought to be employed. It is much to be feared my dear Sir that the States in their seperate capacities have very inadequate ideas of the present danger. Removed (some of them) far distant from the scene of action and seeing, and hearing such publications only as flatter their wishes they conceive that the contest is at an end, and that to regulate the government and police of their own State is all that remains to be done; but it is devoutly to be wished that a sad reverse of this may not fall upon them like a thunder clap that is little expected. I do not mean to designate particular States. I wish to cast no reflections upon any one. The Public believes (and if they do believe it, the fact might almost as well be so) that the States at this time are badly represented, and that the great, and important concerns of the nation are horribly conducted, for want either of abilities or application in the Members, or through discord and party views of some individuals; that they should be so, is to be lamented more at this time, than formerly, as we are far advanced in the dispute and in the opinn. of many drawg. to a happy period; have the eyes of Europe upon us, and I am perswaded many political Spies to watch, discover our situation, and give information of our weaknesses and wants.

The story you have related of a proposal to redeem the paper money at its present depreciated value has also come to my ears, but I cannot vouch for the authenticity of it. I am very happy to hear that the Assembly of Virginia have put the completion of their Regiment upon a footing so apparently certain, but as one great defect of your past Laws for this purpose, has lain in the mode of getting the Men to the Army, I shall hope that effectual measures are pointed out in the present, to remedy the evil and bring forward all that shall be raised. The Embargo upon Provisions is a most salutary measure as I am affraid a sufficiency of flour will not easily be obtained even with money of higher estimation than ours. adieu my dear Sir.

P.S. Phila. 30th. This Letter was to have gone by Post from Middle brook but missed that conveyance, since which I have come to this place at the request of Congress whence I shall soon return.

I have seen nothing since I came here (on the 22d. Instt.) to change my opinion of Men or Measrs. but abundant reason to be convinced, that our Affairs are in a more distressed, ruinous, and deplorable condition than they have been in Since the commencement of the War. By a faithful labourer then in the cause. By a Man who is daily injuring his private Estate without even the smallest earthly advantage not common to all in case of a favourable Issue to the dispute. By one who wishes the prosperity of America most devoutly and sees or thinks he sees it, on the brink of ruin, you are beseeched most earnestly my dear Colo. Harrison, to exert yourself in endeavouring to rescue your Country, by, (let me add) sending your ablest and best Men to Congress; these characters must not slumber, nor sleep at home, in such times of pressing danger; they must not content themselves in the enjoyment of places of honor or profit in their own Country, while the common interests of America are mouldering and sinking into irretrievable (if a remedy is not soon applied) ruin, in which theirs also must ultimately be involved. If I was to be called upon to draw A picture of the times, and of Men; from what I have seen, heard, and in part know I should in one word say that idleness, dissipation and extravagance seem to have laid fast hold of most of them. That Speculation, peculation, and an insatiable thirst for riches seems to have got the better of every other consideration and almost of every order of Men. That party disputes and personal quarrels are the great business of the day whilst the momentous concerns of an empire, a great and accumulated debt; ruined finances, depreciated money, and want of credit (which in their consequences is the want of every thing) are but secondary considerations and postponed from day to day, from week to week as if our affairs wore the most promising aspect; after drawing this picture, which from my Soul I believe to be a true one I need not repeat to you that I am alarmed and wish to see my Countrymen roused. I have no resentments, nor do I mean to point at any particular characters; this I can declare upon my honor for I have every attention paid me by Congress than I can possibly expect and have reason to think that I stand well in their estimation but in the present situation of things I cannot help asking: Where is Mason, Wythe, Jefferson, Nicholas, Pendleton, Nelson, and another I could name; and why, if you are sufficiently impressed with your danger, do you not (as New Yk. has done in the case of Mr. Jay) send an extra Member or two for at least a certain limited time till the great business of the Nation is put upon a more respectable and happy establishmt. Your Money is now sinking 5 pr. Ct. a day in this City; and I shall not be surprized if in the course of a few months a total stop is put to the currency of it. And yet an assembly, a concert, a Dinner, or

Supper (that will cost three or four hundred pounds) will not only take Men of from acting in but even from thinking of this business while a great part of the Officers of your Army from absolute necessity are quitting the Service and the more virtuous few rather than do this are sinking by sure degrees into beggery and want. I again repeat to you that this is not an exaggerated acct.; that it is an alarming one I do not deny, and confess to you that I feel more real distress on acct. of the prest. appearances of things than I have done at any one time since the commencement of the dispute; but it is time to bid you once more adieu. Providence has heretofore taken us up when all other means and hope seemed to be departing from us, in this I will confide. Yr. &ca.

Stephen De Lancey to
Cornelia Barclay De Lancey

SAVANNAH JANY 14TH 1779

Long have I wish'd my dearest Cornelia for the Departure of a Vessel from this Place that I might communicate to you the glad Tidings of my Health and Safety but much more for the Arrival of one from N York that I might hear from you. How anxious every Hour passes that cannot indulge us with the Knowledge of the Situation of those we love, I flatter myself you have experienced. Tho' my dearest wife I wish you all the Happiness that you deserve or any Being is capable of experiencing, yet I cannot help owning (from the Frailty of Human Nature) that I should not be pleased at the Idea of your enjoying perfect Satisfaction in my Absence. Your Affection is the great Object of my Heart and while I possess that it will always furnish those Sentiments which will render my Presence necessary to you. Never since I was yours have I met with so great a Trial of Philosophy. What pleasure the external Objects here might afford me were you present with me, I will not pretend to say, but a mere military Life is for me a very dull Scene. I may say with a favorite Author of Yours, the inimitable Thompson,

> "All my Labour is to kill the Time,
> "And Labour dire it is, & weary woe

Our Passage was long and Tempestuous, seldom fair for twenty four Hours together and the slow Mode of sailing necessary to keep a fleet from separation rendered it very disagreably tedious. (I was agreably disapointed in not being in the least Sea Sick). After we had been at Sea more than a Month we arrived at the Light House at the Entrance of the River Savannah, from whence we proceeded to a Place near the Town in flat Boats and landed on a Causeway in a Rice Plantation which was form'd out of a Swamp on the Banks of

the River. This narrow Passage led up to a House situated on
an Eminence very steep. Had the Rebels been there in Force
with Cannon, it would in my opinion have been impracticable to have made good the Landing. In Consequence of the
very strong Ground, we should have been obliged to ascend
in Opposition to the Rebels and by the narrow Passage thro'
the Swamp in approaching the Eminence. But from great
want of Generalship they had but thirty men at this strong
Post. We had a Captain and three Men of the Light Infantry
of the 71st Regt killed at this Place when the Rebels immediately retreated. The main Body of our Army then advanced
towards the Town, on this Side of which the Rebels appear'd
with a good Front, and we expected they would have behaved
better than usual but were deceived. By a quick and well conducted March of the Light Infantry of the 71st and the New
Corps, under the Command of Sir James Beard, round a
Swamp, the Rebels were so intimidated that they fled with
the utmost Consternation, leaving us in quick Possession of
the Town. Forty Officers and upwards of Five hundred Men
were killed or taken in a Space of Time almost incredible.
We took Possession of the Town with the trifling Loss I first
mention'd.

The Town of Savannah is situated on the Banks of the
River of that Name on a Sand Bank of which your Shoes are
full in crossing a Street. The Inhabitants have been extremely
wealthy, as appears from the great Profusion of Elegant
Furniture we found in the Town and the great Quantity of
Cattle, Hogs, Poultry etc. with which their Plantations are
stock'd. Almost all the People had deserted their Habitations
but are daily coming in and receiving Protections for their
Persons and Property. The Government here established is to
the greatest Degree lenient, so that I conclude it is imagined
they will be sooth'd into a Change of Sentiments and receive
Money and Property as Greater Goods than Rebellion and
Poverty. Our Troops are extended in different Ports upwards
of thirty Miles from the Town along the River. My quarters
are Eight Miles from the Town—a very bad House but
Plenty of Provisions. Colonel Brewerton is from the Regiment with a separate Command. At present not any Rebels
are in arms in this Province. They have collected a small Force

in South Carolina I suppose to prevent a Passage over the River. A Movement will soon take Place when we shall be sent, in Consequence of our Weakness to do Garrison Duty in the Town. General Provost with all the Troops from St. Augustine is but twelve Miles from this Place and expected before Night. Colonel Innes is Commandant of the Town here, for which Station he appears well adapted and gives universal Satisfaction. His Behavior is easy and affable and he dispatches Business in a very expeditious Manner. Captain Moore is Barrack Master, very usefull and also well adapted to it. I can at present communicate nothing of what is intended in the Military Line but by every Opportunity I shall inform you of all things within my Knowledge. I am now sitting with the Windows open without any Fire, although the Inhabitants have complain'd of the Severity of the Weather and I suppose you are ordering more Wood to the Fire.

The People here are sallow and in general disgusting. Pale faces and large swolen Bellies proceeding from the Fever and Ague seem to be the Characteristics of the Georgia Ladies and their Speech is so Negroish that I cannot help imagining that some of them cannot boast of a Number of Ancestors thoroughly White. This is not the Case with all; I am told they have fine Women tho I have seen very few. The Negro's and Negro Women are inhumanly treated, are two-thirds naked, and are very disgusting to the Eye and another Sense, Tho I begin to be more habituated to the Sight, yet I cannot be to the great Cruelty made Use of to the poor ignorant Wretches. Indeed the Title of the Overseer is a sufficient Explanation of the Whole. He is stiled a Negro Driver. These circumstances of Cruelty to these People render the Persons who exercise it disagreable, nay odious to me. When a Set of People can sit down enjoying all the Luxuries of Life without feeling the least Sensation or Compunction for the Sufferings of those poor Wretches whose Lives are render'd Miserable and Constitutions destroyed for those Purposes, I must conclude them Obdurate, Selfish, and Unfeeling to the greatest Degree imaginable. At what an Expence of Life and Happiness do we eat Rice and Sugar! One thing more I must add, that their Diet is almost entirely on Rice and sweet Potatoes as they are allowed Meat but once a Year.

I am ever wishing, my dearest wife, to be able to send to you for your Use some of the Good things that we have in the greatest Profusion here and which I am much afraid you will want. Indeed it gives me great Pain to think that you want anything which I enjoy, for tho I am a great advocate for the Principle of Selfishness as the prime Motive to Action in every Body, yet I can so far wrest the argument as to wish you to enjoy every thing to satisfy my feelings. By the next opportunity I shall transmit a Bill for Money, as my Expences here are very limited, and happy I shall be to be able to furnish you with any thing for your Ease and Happiness which the Narrowness of my Circumstances has too frequently prevented.

Present my Compliments to your Mother and my best Love to Nancy and Tom. Inform him that I depend on him to oversee everything for you, tho' I know his Love for you and Friendship for me will dictate the Utmost Assiduity for us; desire him to present my Love to Susan and tell her to prepare to romp with me when I come back. Remember me to Heathcote Johnston and all friends. If Jacob behaves well, tell him I mention'd him.

God grant you my ever dear Wife uninterrupted Health and may you and my family be his peculiar Care and if it should be his Will to take any of our Children to himself may you be endued with Resolution to bear it as on you all my Happiness depends. I mean to write to Mrs. Cruger; if I do not, tell her nothing but something unavoidable could have prevented what my great Attachment and her Goodness would always dictate.

> I am My most dear Wife
> Yours

George Rogers Clark:
Narrative of the March to Vincennes

EVERYTHING being now ready, on the 5th of February, after receiving a lecture and absolution from the priest, etc., we crossed the Kaskaskia river with one hundred and seventy men; marched about three miles and encamped, where we lay until the 8th (refer to Major Bowman's journal for the particulars of this march), and set out, the weather wet, but, fortunately, not cold for the season, and a great part of the plains under water several inches deep. It was difficult and very fatiguing marching. My object now was to keep the men in spirits. I suffered them to shoot game on all occasions, and feast on it like Indian war-dancers — each company, by turns, inviting the others to their feasts — which was the case every night, as the company that was to give the feast was always supplied with horses to lay up a sufficient store of wild meat in the course of the day, myself and principal officers putting on the woodsmen, shouting now and then, and running as much through the mud and water as any of them. Thus, insensibly, without a murmur, were those men led on to the banks of the Little Wabash, which we reached on the 13th, through incredible difficulties, far surpassing anything that any of us had ever experienced. Frequently the diversions of the night wore off the thoughts of the preceding day. This place is called the two Little Wabashes. They are three miles apart, and from the heights of the one to that of the other, on the opposite shore, is five miles — the whole under water, generally about three feet deep, never under two, and frequently four.

We formed a camp on a height which we found on the bank of the river, and suffered our troops to amuse themselves. I viewed this sheet of water for some time with distrust, but, accusing myself of doubting, I immediately set to work, without holding any consultation about it, or suffering anybody else to do so in my presence, ordered a pirogue to be built immediately and acted as though crossing the water would be only a piece of diversion. As but few could work at the pirogue at a time, pains were taken to find diversion for the rest to keep them in high spirits, but the men were well prepared for this attempt, as they had frequently waded further in water, but, perhaps, seldom above half-leg deep. My anxiety to cross this place continually increased, as I saw that it would at once fling us into a situation of a forlorn hope, as all ideas of retreat would, in some measure, be done away with; that if the men began, after this was accomplished, to think seriously of what they had really suffered, that they prefer risking any seeming difficulty that might probably turn out favorable, than to attempt to retreat, when they would be certain of experiencing what they had already felt, and if the weather should but freeze, altogether impracticable, except the ice would bear them.

In the evening of the 14th, our vessel was finished, manned and sent to explore the drowned lands on the opposite side of the Little Wabash with private instructions what report to make, and, if possible, to find some spot of dry land. They found about half an acre and marked the trees from thence back to the camp, and made a very favorable report.

Fortunately the 15th happened to be a warm, moist day for the season. The channel of the river where we lay was about thirty yards wide. A scaffold was built on the opposite shore which was about three feet under water, and our baggage ferried across and put on it; our horses swam across and received their loads at the scaffold, by which time the troops were also brought across, and we began our march through the water. Our vessel was loaded with those who were sickly, and we moved on cheerfully, every moment expecting to see dry land, which was not discovered until we came to the little dry spot mentioned. This being a smaller branch than the other, the troops immediately crossed and marched on in the water, as usual, to gain and take possession of the nighest height they could discover. Our horses and baggage crossed as they had done at the former river, and proceeded on, following the marked trail of the troops. As tracks could not be seen in the water, the trees were marked.

By evening we found ourselves encamped on a pretty height in high spirits, each party laughing at the other in consequence of something that had happened in the course of this ferrying business, as they called it. A little antic drummer afforded them great diversion by floating on his drum, etc. All this was greatly encouraging, and they really began to think themselves superior to other men, and that neither the rivers nor the seasons could stop their progress. Their whole conversation now was concerning what they would do when they got about the enemy. They now began to view the main Wabash as a creek, and made no doubt but such men as they were could find a way across it. They wound themselves up to such a pitch that they soon took St. Vincent, divided the spoil, and before bedtime were far advanced on their route to Detroit.

All this was no doubt pleasing to those of us who had more serious thoughts. We were now, as it were, in the enemy's country — no possibility of a retreat if the enemy should discover and overpower us, except by the means of our galley, if we should fall in with her.

We were now convinced that the whole of the low country on the Wabash was drowned, and that the enemy could easily get to us, if they discovered us and wished to risk an action; if they did not, we made no doubt of crossing the river by some means or other. Supposing Captain Rogers had not got to his station, agreeable to his appointment, that we would, if possible, steal some vessels from houses opposite the town, etc. We flattered ourselves that all would be well, and marched on in high spirits.

On the 17th, dispatched Mr. Kennedy and three men off to cross the river Embarrass (this river is six miles from St. Vincennes), and, if possible, to get some vessels in the vicinity of the town, but principally if he could get some intelligence. He proceeded on, and getting to the river found that the country between that and the Wabash overflowed. We marched down below the mouth of the Embarrass, attempting, in vain, to get to the banks of the Wabash. Late in the night, finding a dog shot, we encamped, and were aroused, for the first time, by the morning gun from the garrison. We continued our march, and about two o'clock, 18th, gained the banks of the Wabash, three leagues below the town, where we encamped; dispatched four men across the river on a raft to find land, if possible, march to the town, if possible, and get some canoes. Captain W. McCarty with a few men set out privately the next day in a little canoe he had made, for the same purpose. Both parties returned without success. The first could not get to land, and the captain was driven back by the appearance of a camp. The canoe was immediately dispatched down the river to meet the galley, with orders to proceed day and night; but, determined to have every string to my bow I possibly could, I ordered canoes to be built in a private place, not yet out of hopes of our boat arriving — if she did, those canoes would augment our fleet; if she did not before they were ready they would answer our purpose without her.

Many of our volunteers began, for the first time, to despair. Some talked of returning, but my situation now was such that I was past all uneasiness. I laughed at them, without persuading or ordering them to desist from any such attempt, but told them that I should be glad they would go out and kill some deer. They went, confused with such conduct. My own troops I knew had no idea of abandoning an enterprise from the want of provisions, while there was plenty of good horses in their possession; and I knew that, without any violence, the volunteers could be detained for a few days, in the course of which time our fate would be known. I conducted myself in such a manner that caused the whole to believe that I had no doubt of success, which kept their spirits up.

This last day's march (February 21st) through the water was far superior to anything the Frenchmen had an idea of. They were backward in speaking, said that the nearest land to us was a small league called the sugar camp, on the bank of the river. A canoe was sent off and returned without finding that we could pass. I went in her myself and sounded the water; found it deep as to my neck.

I returned with a design to have the men transported on board the canoes to the sugar camp, which I knew would spend the whole day and ensuing night, as the vessels would pass but slowly through the bushes. The loss of so much time to men half starved was a matter of consequence. I would have given now a great deal for a day's provision or for one of our horses. I returned but slowly to the troops, giving myself time to think. On our arrival all ran to hear what was the report. Every eye was fixed on me. I unfortunately spoke in a serious manner to one of the officers. The whole were alarmed without knowing what I said. They ran from one to another, bewailing their situation. I viewed their confusion for about one minute, whispered to those near me to do as I did, immediately put some water in my hand, poured on powder, blackened my face, gave the warwhoop and marched into the water, without saying a word. The party gazed and fell in, one after another, without saying a word, like a flock of sheep. I ordered those near me to begin a favorite song of theirs. It soon passed through the line and the whole went on cheerfully.

I now intended to have them transported across the deepest part of the water, but when about waist deep one of the men informed me that he thought he felt a path — a path is very easily discovered under water by the feet. We examined and found it so, and concluded that it kept on the highest ground, which it did, and, by taking pains to follow it, we got to the sugar camp without the least difficulty (and what gave the alarm at the former proved fortunate), where there was about half an acre of dry ground, at least not under water, where we took up our lodging.

The Frenchmen we had taken on the river appeared to be uneasy at our situation. They begged that they might be permitted to go in the two canoes to town in the night. They said that they would bring from their own houses provisions without a possibility of any person knowing it; that some of our men should go with them, as a surety of their good conduct; that it was impossible that we could march from the place until the water fell; that would not be for a few days, for the plain, for upward of three miles, was covered two feet deep.

Some of the selected believed that it might be done. I would not suffer it. I never could well account for this piece of obstinacy and give satisfactory reasons to myself or anybody else why I denied a proposition apparently so easy to execute and of so much advantage, but something seemed to tell me that it should not be done, and it was not.

The most of the weather that we had on this march was moist and warm for the season. This was the coldest night we had. The ice, in the morning, was from one-half to three-quarters of an inch thick near the shores and in still waters. The morning was the finest we had on our march. A little after sunrise I lectured the whole. What I said to them I forget, but it may be easily imagined by a person who could possess my affections for them at that time. I concluded by informing them that surmounting the plain, that was then in full view, and reaching the opposite woods, would put an end to their fatigue; that in a few hours they would have a sight of their long wished for object, and immediately stepped into the water without waiting for any reply. A huzza took place. We generally marched through the water in a line; it was much easiest. Before a third entered, I halted, and, further to prove the men, having some suspicion of three or four, I hallooed to Major Bowman, ordering him to fall in the rear with twenty-five men and put to death any man who refused to march, as we wished to have no such person among us. The whole gave a cry of approbation that it was right, and on we went. This was the most trying of all the difficulties we had experienced. I generally kept fifteen or twenty of the strongest men next myself, and judging from my own feelings what must be that of others. Getting about the middle of the plain, the water about knee deep, I found myself sensibly failing, and as there were here no trees nor bushes for the men to support themselves by, I doubted that many of the most weak would be drowned. I ordered the canoes to make the land, discharge their loading, and play backward and forward, with all diligence, and pick up the men, and to encourage the party; sent some of the strongest men forward with orders when they got to a certain distance to pass the word back that the water was getting shallow, and when getting near the woods to cry out "land." This stratagem had its desired effect. The men, encouraged by it, exerted themselves almost beyond their abilities — the weak holding by the stronger, and frequently one with two others' help, and this was of infinite advantage to the weak. The water never got shallower, but continued deepening — even when getting to the woods, where the men expected land. The water was up to my shoulders, but gaining the woods was of great consequence. All the low men, and the weakly, hung to the trees and floated on the old logs until they were taken off by the canoes. The strong and tall got ashore and built fires. Many would reach the shore, and fall with their bodies half in the water, not being able to support themselves without it.

This was a delightful, dry spot of ground, of about ten acres. We soon found that the fires answered no purpose, but that two strong men taking a weaker one by the arms was the only way to recover him, and, being a delightful day, it soon did. But fortunately, as if designed by Providence, a canoe of Indian squaws and children was coming up to town, and took through part of this plain as a nigh way. It was discovered by our canoes as they were out after the men. They gave chase and took the Indian canoe, on board of which was near half a quarter of a buffalo, some corn, tallow, kettles, etc. This was a grand prize and was invaluable. Broth was immediately made and served out to the most weakly with great care; most of the whole got a little, but a great many gave their part to the weakly, jocosely saying something cheering to their comrades. This little refreshment and fine weather, by the afternoon, gave new life to the whole.

Crossing a narrow, deep lake in the canoes and marching some distance, we came to a copse of timber called the Warrior's Island. We were now in full view of the fort and town, not a shrub between us, at about two miles' distance. Every man now feasted his eyes and forgot that he had suffered anything, saying that all that had passed was owing to good policy and nothing but what a man could bear, and that a soldier had no right to think, etc., passing from one extreme to another, which is common in such cases. It was now we had to display our abilities. The plain between us and the town was not a perfect level. The sunken grounds were covered with water full of ducks. We observed several men out on horseback, shooting of them, within a half mile of us, and sent out as many of our active young Frenchmen to decoy and take one of these men prisoner in such a manner as not to alarm the others, which they did. The information we got from this person was similar to that which we got from those we took on the river, except that of the British having that evening completed the wall of the fort, etc., and that there were a good many Indians in town.

Our situation was now truly critical — no possibility of retreating in case of defeat — and in full view of a town that had, at this time, upward of six hundred men in it, troops, inhabitants and Indians. The crew of the galley, though not fifty men, would have been now a reinforcement of immense magnitude to our little army (if I may so call it), but we would not think of them. We were now in the situation that I had labored to get ourselves in. The idea of being made prisoner was foreign to almost every man, as they expected nothing but torture from the savages if they fell into their hands. Our fate was now to be determined, probably in a few hours. We knew that nothing but the most daring conduct would insure success. I knew that a number of the inhabitants wished us well; that many were lukewarm to the interest of either; and I also learned that the grand chief, the Tobacco's Son, had, but a few days before, openly declared, in council with the British, that he was a brother and friend to the big knives. These were favorable circumstances, and as there was but little probability of our remaining until dark undiscovered, as great numbers of fowlers go out in the day, and that we now see and hear them through the plains around us, I determined to begin the career immediately, and wrote the following placard to the inhabitants and sent it off by the prisoner just taken, who was not permitted to see our numbers:

To the Inhabitants of Post Vincennes:

GENTLEMEN — Being now within two miles of your village with my army, determined to take your fort this night, and not being willing to surprise you, I take this method to request such of you as are true citizens and willing to enjoy the liberty I bring you, to remain still in your houses; and that those, if any there be, that are friends to the king of England, will instantly repair to the fort and join his troops and fight like men. And if any such as do not go to the fort should hereafter be discovered that did not repair to the garrison, they may depend on severe punishment. On the contrary, those who are true friends to liberty may expect to be well treated as such, and I once more request that they may keep out of the streets, for every person found under arms, on my arrival, will be treated as an enemy.

(Signed)   G. R. CLARK.

I had various ideas on the supposed results of this letter. I knew that it could do us no damage, but that it would cause the lukewarm to be decided, encourage our friends and astonish our enemies; that they would, of course, suppose our information good, and our forces so numerous that we were sure of success — and this was only a piece of parade; that the army was from Kentucky and not from the Illinois, as it would be thought quite impossible to march from thence, and that my name was only made use of. This they firmly believed until the next morning, when I was shown to them by a person in the fort who knew me well — or that we were a flying party that only made use of this stratagem to give ourselves a chance to retreat. This latter idea I knew would soon be done away with. Several gentlemen sent their compliments to their friends, under borrowed names, well known at St. Vincent, and the persons supposed to be at Kentucky. The soldiers all had instructions that their common conversation, when speaking of our numbers, should be such that a stranger overhearing must suppose that there were near one thousand of us.

We anxiously viewed this messenger until he entered the town, and in a few minutes could discover by our glasses some stir in every street that we could penetrate into, and great numbers running or riding out into the commons, we supposed to view us, which was the case. But what surprised us was, that nothing had yet happened that had the appearance of the garrison being alarmed — no drum nor gun.

We began to suppose that the information we got from our prisoners was false, and that the enemy already knew of us and were prepared. Every man had been impatient — the moment had now arrived. A little before sunset we moved and displayed ourselves in full view of the town, crowds gazing at us. We were flinging ourselves into certain destruction — or success; there was no midway thought of. We had but little to say to our men, except in calculating an idea of the necessity of obedience, etc. We knew they did not want encouraging, and that anything might be attempted with them that was possible for such a number — perfectly cool, under proper subordination, pleased with the prospect before them, and much attached to their officers. They all declared that they were convinced that an implicit obedience to orders was the only thing that would ensure success, and hoped that no mercy would be shown the person who should violate them, but should be immediately put to death. Such language as this from soldiers to persons in our station must have been exceedingly agreeable. We moved on slowly in full view of the town; but, as it was a point of some consequence to us to make ourselves appear as formidable as possible, we, in leaving the covert that we were in, marched and countermarched in such a manner that we appeared numerous.

In raising volunteers in the Illinois, every person who set about the business had a set of colors given him, which they brought with them to the amount of ten or twelve pairs. These were displayed to the best advantage; and as the low plain we marched through was not a perfect level, but had frequent raisings in it seven or eight feet higher than the common level, which was covered with water, and as these raisings generally ran in an oblique direction to the town, we took the advantage of one of them, marching through the water under it, which completely prevented our men being numbered. But our colors showed considerably above the heights, as they were fixed on long poles procured for the purpose, and at a distance made no despicable appearance; and as our young Frenchmen had, while we lay on the Warrior's Island, decoyed and taken several fowlers, with their horses, officers were mounted on these horses and rode about, more completely to deceive the enemy. In this manner we moved, and directed our march in such a manner as to suffer it to be dark before we had advanced more than half way to the town. We then suddenly altered our direction, and crossed ponds where they could not have suspected us, and about eight o'clock gained the heights back of the town. As there was yet no hostile appearance, we were impatient to have the cause unriddled.

Lieutenant Bailey was ordered, with fourteen men, to march and fire on the fort. The main body moved in a different direction and took possession of the strongest part of the town. The firing now commenced on the fort, but they did not believe it was an enemy until one of their men was shot down through a port as he was lighting his match, as drunken Indians frequently saluted the fort after night. The drums now sounded and the business fairly commenced on both sides. Reinforcements were sent to the attack of the garrison, while other arrangements were making in town, etc.

We now found that the garrison had known nothing of us; that, having finished the fort that evening, they had amused themselves at different games, and had retired just before my letter arrived, as it was near roll-call. The placard being made public, many of the inhabitants were afraid to show themselves out of the houses for fear of giving offense, and not one dare give information.

Our friends flew to the commons and other convenient places to view the pleasing sight, which was observed from the garrison and the reason asked, but a satisfactory excuse was given; and, as a part of the town lay between our line of march and the garrison, we could not be seen by the sentinels on the walls. Captain W. Shannon and another being some time before taken prisoner by one of their raiding parties and that evening brought in, the party had discovered at the sugar camp some signs of us.

They supposed it to be a party of observation that intended to land on the height some distance below the town. Captain Lamothe was sent to intercept them. It was at him the people said they were looking when they were asked the reason of their unusual stir. Several suspected persons had been taken to the garrison. Among them was Mr. Moses Henry. Mrs. Henry went, under the pretense of carrying him provisions, and whispered him the news and what she had seen. Mr. Henry conveyed it to the rest of his fellow-prisoners, which gave them much pleasure, particularly Captain Helm, who amused himself very much during the siege, and, I believe, did much damage.

Ammunition was scarce with us, as the most of our stores had been put on board of the galley. Though her crew was but few, such a reinforcement to us at this period would have been invaluable in many instances. But, fortunately, at the time of its being reported that the whole of the goods in the town were to be taken for the king's use, for which the owners were to receive bills, Colonel Legras, Major Bosseron and others had buried the greatest part of their powder and ball. This was immediately produced, and we found ourselves well supplied by those gentlemen.

The Tobacco's Son being in town with a number of warriors, immediately mustered them, and let us know that he wished to join us, saying that by the morning he would have a hundred men. He received for answer that we thanked him for his friendly disposition, and, as we were sufficiently strong ourselves, we wished him to desist and that we would counsel on the subject in the morning; and, as we knew that there were a number of Indians in and near the town who were our enemies, some confusion might happen if our men should mix in the dark, but hoped that we might be favored with his counsel and company during the night, which was agreeable to him.

The garrison was now completely surrounded, and the firing continued without intermission, except about fifteen minutes a little before day until about nine o'clock the following morning. It was kept up by the whole of the troops — joined by a few of the young men of the town, who got permission — except fifty men kept as a reserve in case of casualty happening, which was many and diverting in the course of the night. I had made myself fully acquainted with the situation of the fort, town, and the parts relative to each. The gardens of St. Vincent were very near, and about two-thirds around it; the fencing of good pickets, well set, and about six feet high where those were watching. Breast-works were soon made by tearing down old houses, gardens, etc., so that those within had very little advantage to those without the fort, and not knowing the number of the enemy, thought themselves in a worse situation than they really were.

The cannons of the garrison were on the upper floors of strong block-houses, at each angle of the fort, eleven feet above the surface, and the ports so badly cut that many of our troops lay under the fire of them within twenty or thirty yards of the walls. They did no damage, except to the buildings of the town, some of which they much shattered, and their musketry, in the dark, employed against woodsmen covered by houses, palings, ditches, the banks of the river, etc., was but of little avail and did no damage to us, except wounding a man or two, and as we could not afford to lose men, great care was taken to preserve them sufficiently covered and to keep up a hot fire in order to intimidate the enemy as well as to destroy them. The embrasures of their cannons were frequently shut, for our riflemen, finding the true direction of them, would pour in such volleys when they were open that the men could not stand to the guns — seven or eight of them in a short time got cut down. Our troops would frequently abuse the enemy in order to aggravate them to open their ports and fire their cannons, that they might have the pleasure of cutting them down with their rifles, fifty of which, perhaps, would be leveled the moment the port flew open, and I believe that if they had stood at their artillery the greater part of them would have been destroyed in the course of the night, as the most of our men lay within thirty yards of the wall, and in a few hours were covered equally to those within the walls and much more experienced in that mode of fighting. The flash of our guns detected them, perhaps, the instant the man moved his body. The moment there was the least appearance at one of their loop-holes, there would probably be a dozen guns fired at it.

Sometimes an irregular fire, as hot as possible, was kept up from different directions for a few minutes, and then only a continual scattering fire at the ports as usual, and a great noise and laughter immediately commenced in different parts of the town by the reserved parties, as if they had only fired on the fort a few minutes for amusement, and as if those continually firing at the fort were only regularly relieved. Conduct similar to this kept the garrison eternally alarmed. They did not know what moment they might be stormed or [   ], as they could plainly discover that we had flung up some entrenchments across the streets, and appeared to be frequently very busy under the bank of the river, which was within thirty feet of the walls.

The situation of the magazine we knew well. Captain Bowman began some works in order to blow it up in case our artillery should arrive, but as we knew that we were daily liable to be overpowered by the numerous bands of Indians on the river, in case they had again joined the enemy (the certainty of which we were unacquainted with), we resolved to lose no time but to get the fort in our possession as soon as possible. If our vessel did not arrive before the ensuing night, we resolved to undermine the fort, and fixed on the spot and plan of executing this work, which we intended to commence the next day.

The Indians of different tribes that were inimical had left the town and neighborhood. Captain Lamothe continued to hover about it, in order, if possible, to make his way good into the fort. Parties attempted in vain to surprise him. A few of his party were taken, one of which was Maisonville, a famous Indian partisan. Two lads, who captured him, tied him to a post in the street, and fought from behind him as a breastwork — supposing that the enemy would not fire at them for fear of killing him, as he would alarm them by his voice. The lads were ordered, by an officer who discovered them at their amusement, to untie their prisoner and take him off to the guard, which they did, but were so inhuman as to take part of his scalp on the way. There happened to him no other damage. As almost the whole of the persons who were most active in the department of Detroit were either in the fort or with Captain Lamothe, I got extremely uneasy for fear that he would not fall into our power, knowing that he would go off if he could not get into the fort in the course of the night.

Finding that, without some unforeseen accident, the fort must inevitably be ours, and that a reinforcement of twenty men, although considerable to them, would not be of great moment to us in the present situation of affairs, and knowing that we had weakened them by killing or wounding many of their gunners, after some deliberation we concluded to risk the reinforcement in preference of his going again among the Indians. The garrison had at least a month's provisions, and if they could hold out, in the course of that time he might do us much damage. A little before day the troops were withdrawn from their positions about the fort, except a few parties of observation, and the firing totally ceased. Orders were given, in case of Lamotte's approach, not to alarm or fire on him without a certainty of killing or taking the whole. In less than a quarter of an hour he passed within ten feet of an officer and a party who lay concealed. Ladders were flung over to them, and as they mounted them our party shouted. Many of them fell from the top of the walls — some within and others back; but as they were not fired on they all got over, much to the joy of their friends, which was easily discovered by us; but, on considering the matter, they must have been convinced that it was a scheme of ours to let them in, and that we were so strong as to care but little about them or the manner of their getting into the garrison, our troops hallooing and diverting themselves at them while mounting, without firing at them, and being frequently told by our most blackguard soldiers of the scheme, and reason for suffering them to get into the fort — which on reflection they must have believed — but we knew that their knowledge of it could now do us no damage, but rather intimidate them. However, the garrison appeared much elated at the recovery of a valuable officer and party.

The firing immediately commenced on both sides with double vigor, and I believe that more noise could not have been made by the same number of men — their shouts could not be heard for the firearms; but a continual blaze was kept around the garrison, without much being done, until about daylight, when our troops were drawn off to posts prepared for them, from about sixty to a hundred yards from the garrison. A loophole then could scarcely be darkened but a rifleball would pass through it. To have stood to their cannon would have destroyed their men without a probability of doing much service. Our situation was nearly similar. It would have been imprudent in either party to have wasted their men, without some decisive stroke required it.

Thus the attack continued until about nine o'clock on the morning of the 24th. Learning that the two prisoners they had brought in the day before had a considerable number of letters with them, I supposed it an express that we expected about this time, which I knew to be of the greatest moment to us, as we had not received one since our arrival in the country; and, not being fully acquainted with the character of our enemy, we were doubtful that those papers might be destroyed, to prevent which I sent a flag, with a letter, demanding the garrison and desiring Governor Hamilton not to destroy them, with some threats of what I would do in case that he did if the garrison should fall into my hands. His answer was that they were not disposed to be awed into anything unbecoming British subjects.

The firing then commenced warmly for a considerable time, and we were obliged to be careful in preventing our men from exposing themselves too much, as they were now much animated, having been refreshed during the flag. They frequently mentioned their wishes to storm the place and put an end to the business at once. This would at this time have been a piece of rashness. Our troops got warm.

The firing was heavy, through every crack that could be discovered in any part of the fort, with cross shot. Several of the garrison got wounded, and no possibility of standing near the embrasures. Towards the evening a flag appeared, with the following proposition:

Governor Hamilton proposes to Colonel Clark a truce for three days, during which time he proposes there shall be no defensive work carried on in the garrison, on condition that Colonel Clark shall observe, on his part, a like cessation of any offensive work. That is, he wishes to confer with Colonel Clark as soon as can be, and promises, that, whatever may pass between these two and another person, mutually agreed upon to be present, shall remain secret till matters be finished, as he wishes that, whatever the result of their conference, it may be to the honor and credit of each party. If Colonel Clark makes a difficulty of coming into the fort, Lieutenant-Governor Hamilton will speak to him by the gate.

(Signed)   HENRY HAMILTON.
24th February, 1779.

I was greatly at a loss to conceive what reason Governor Hamilton could have for wishing a truce of three days on such terms as he proposed. Numbers said it was a scheme to get me into their possession. I had a different opinion and no idea of his possessing such sentiments, as an act of that kind would infallibly ruin him, but was convinced that he had some prospect of success, or otherways, of extricating himself.

Although we had the greatest reason to expect a reinforcement in less than three days that would at once put an end to the siege, I yet did not think it prudent to agree to the proposals, and sent the following answer:

Colonel Clark's compliments to Governor Hamilton, and begs leave to inform him that he will not agree to any other terms than that of Mr. Hamilton surrendering himself and garrison prisoners at discretion. If Mr. Hamilton is desirous of a conference with Colonel Clark, he will meet him at the church, with Captain Helm, 24th February, 1779.

G. R. CLARK.

We met at the church, about eighty yards from the fort—Lieutenant-Governor Hamilton, Major Hay, superintendent of Indian affairs; Captain Helm, their prisoner; Major Bowman and myself. The conference began. Governor Hamilton produced articles of capitulation, signed, that contained various articles, one of which was that the garrison should be surrendered on their being permitted to go to Pensacola on parole. After deliberating on every article, I rejected the whole. He then wished that I would make some proposition. I told him that I had no other to make than what I had already made—that of his surrendering as prisoners at discretion. I said that his troops had behaved with spirit, that they could not suppose they would be worse treated in consequence of it, with their viewing us as savages; that if he chose to comply with the demand, though hard, perhaps the sooner the better; that it was in vain to make any proposition to me; that he, by this time, must be sensible that the garrison would fall; that both of us must [   ] that all blood spilled for the future by the garrison as murder; that my troops were already impatient, and called aloud for permission to tear down and storm the fort; if such a step was taken, many, of course, would be cut down, and the result of an enraged body of woodsmen breaking in must be obvious to him —it would be out of the power of an American officer to save a single man.

Various altercations took place for a considerable time. Captain Helm attempted to moderate our fixed determination. I told him he was a British prisoner, and it was doubtful whether or not he could, with propriety, speak on the subject. Governor Hamilton then said that Captain Helm was from that moment liberated, and might use his pleasure. I informed the captain that I would not receive him on such terms; that he must return to the garrison and await his fate. I then told Governor Hamilton that hostilities should not commence until fifteen minutes after the drums gave the alarm. We took our leave and parted but a few steps when the governor stopped, and, politely, asked me if I would be so kind as to give him my reasons for refusing the garrison on any other terms than those I had offered. I told him I had no objections in giving him my real reasons, which were simply these: That I knew the greater part of the principal Indian partisans of Detroit were with him; that I wanted an excuse to put them to death, or otherwise treat them, as I thought proper; that the cries of the widows and the fatherless on the frontiers, which they had occasioned, now required their blood from my hands, and that I did not choose to be so timorous as to disobey the absolute commands of their authority, which I looked upon to be next to divine; that I would rather lose fifty men than not to empower myself to execute this piece of business with propriety; that if he chose to risk the massacre of his garrison for their sakes, it was at his own pleasure, and that I might, perhaps, take it into my head to send for some of those widows to see it executed.

Major Hay paying great attention, I had observed a kind of distrust in his countenance, which, in a great measure, influenced my conversation during this time. On my concluding, "Pray, sir," said he, "who is that you call Indian partisans?" "Sir," I replied, "I take Major Hay to be one of the principals." I never saw a man in the moment of execution so struck as he appeared to be — pale and trembling, scarcely able to stand. Governor Hamilton blushed, and, I observed, was much affected at his behavior in our presence! Major Bowman's countenance sufficiently explained his disdain for the one, and his sorrow for the other. I viewed the whole with such sentiments as I supposed natural to some men in such cases. Some moments elapsed without a word passing, as we could now form such disposition with our troops as render the fort almost useless. To deface that then could be no danger of course; supposed it prudent to let the British troops remain in the fort until the following morning. We should not have had such suspicions as to make so much precaution, but I must confess that we could not help doubting the honor of men who could condescend to encourage the barbarity of the Indians, although almost every man had conceived a favorable opinion of Governor Hamilton. I believe what effected myself made some impression on the whole, and I was happy to find that he never deviated, while he staid with us, from that dignity of conduct that became an officer in his situation. The morning of the 25th approaching, arrangements were made for receiving the garrison (which consisted of seventy-nine men), and about ten o'clock it was delivered in form, and everything was immediately arranged to the best advantage on either side. From that moment my resolutions changed respecting Governor Hamilton's situation. I told him that we would return to our respective posts; that I would reconsider the matter, and that I would let him know the result. If we thought of making any further proposals than that of his surrendering at discretion, he should know it by the flag — if not, to be on his guard at a certain beat of the drum. No offensive measures should be taken in the meantime. Agreed to, and we parted.

What had passed being made known to our officers, it was agreed that we should moderate our resolutions. The following articles were sent to the garrison and an answer immediately returned:

In the course of the afternoon of the 24th the following articles (Major Bowman's MS. journal) were signed and the garrison capitulated:

1. Lieutenant-Governor Hamilton engages to deliver up to Colonel Clark Fort Sackville, as it is at present, with all the stores, etc.

2. The garrison are to deliver themselves as prisoners of war and march out, with their arms and accoutrements, etc.

3. The garrison to be delivered up at ten o'clock tomorrow.

4. Three days' time to be allowed the garrison to settle their accounts with the inhabitants and traders of this place.

5.   The officers of the garrison to be allowed their necessary baggage, etc.

Signed at Post St. Vincent, 24th February, 1779.

Agreed, for the following reasons: The remoteness from succor, the state and quantity of provisions, etc.; unanimity of officers and men in its expediency, the honorable terms allowed, and, lastly, the confidence in a generous enemy.

(Signed)   HENRY HAMILTON,
          Lieutenant-Governor and Superintendent.

The business being now nearly at an end, troops were posted in several strong houses around the garrison and patroled during the night to prevent any deception that might be attempted. The remainder, off duty, lay on their arms, and, for the first time for many days past, got some rest.

During the last conference a party of about twenty warriors who had been sent to the falls for scalps and prisoners, were discovered on their return, as they entered the plains near the town, and, there being no firing at this time, they had no suspicion of an enemy. Captain John Williams was ordered to meet and salute them. He went on, meeting them. The Indians supposed it a party of their friends coming to welcome them, gave the scalp and war-whoop and came on with all the parade of successful warriors. Williams did the same, approaching each nearer. The Indians fired a volley in the air; the captain did so, approaching within a few steps of each other; the chief stopped, as being suspicious; Captain Williams immediately seized him. The rest of the Indians saw the mistake and ran. Fifteen of them were killed and made prisoners. Two partisans and two prisoners were released and the Indians tomahawked by the soldiers and flung into the river.

We after this learned that but one of this party ever returned who got off, so that seventeen must have been destroyed. It was known by us that mostly the whole of them were badly wounded, but, as we yet had an enemy to contend with of more importance than they were, there was no time for pursuit, and spent but a few moments in executing the business before Captain Williams drew off his party and returned. Of course, the Indians who did not immediately fall, or were taken, got off.

One reason why we wished not to receive the garrison until the following morning was its being late in the evening before the capitulation was signed, and the number of prisoners that we should have, when compared to our own small force, we doubted the want of daylight to arrange matters to advantage, and we knew we could now prevent any misfortune happening.

On viewing the inside of the fort and stores, I was at first astonished at its being given up in the manner it was, but weighing every circumstance I found that it was prudent, and a lucky circumstance, and probably saved the lives of many men on both sides. As the night passed we intended to attempt undermining it, and I found it would have required diligence to have prevented our success. If we had failed in this, on further examination I found that our information was so good that in all probability the first hot shot, after the arrival of our artillery, would have blown up the magazine, and would at once have put an end to the business, as its situation and the quantity of powder in it was such that it must have nearly destroyed a great part of the garrison. We yet found ourselves uneasy. The number of prisoners we had taken, added to those of the garrison, was so considerable when compared to our own numbers, that we were at a loss how to dispose of them so as not to interfere with our future operations.

Alexander Hamilton to John Jay

Dear Sir,

Col Laurens, who will have the honor of delivering you this letter, is on his way to South Carolina, on a project, which I think, in the present situation of affairs there, is a very good one and deserves every kind of support and encouragement. This is to raise two three or four batalions of negroes; with the assistance of the government of that state, by contributions from the owners in proportion to the number they possess. If you should think proper to enter upon the subject with him, he will give you a detail of his plan. He wishes to have it recommended by Congress to the state; and, as an inducement, that they would engage to take those batalions into Continental pay.

It appears to me, that an expedient of this kind, in the present state of Southern affairs, is the most rational, that can be adopted, and promises very important advantages. Indeed, I hardly see how a sufficient force can be collected in that quarter without it; and the enemy's operations there are growing infinitely serious and formidable. I have not the least doubt, that the negroes will make very excellent soldiers, with proper management; and I will venture to pronounce, that they cannot be put in better hands than those of Mr. Laurens. He has all the zeal, intelligence, enterprise, and every other qualification requisite to succeed in such an undertaking. It is a maxim with some great military judges, that with sensible officers soldiers can hardly be too stupid; and on this principle it is thought that the Russians would make the best troops in the world, if they were under other officers than their own. The King of Prussia is among the number who maintain this doctrine and has a very emphatical saying on the occasion, which I do not exactly recollect. I mention this, because I frequently hear it objected to the scheme of embodying negroes that they are too stupid to make soldiers. This is so far from appearing to me a valid objection that I think their want of cultivation (for their natural faculties are probably as good as ours) joined to that habit of subordination which they acquire from a life of servitude, will make them sooner became soldiers than our White inhabitants. Let officers be men of sense and sentiment, and the nearer the soldiers approach to machines perhaps the better.

I foresee that this project will have to combat much opposition from prejudice and self-interest. The contempt we have been taught to entertain for the blacks, makes us fancy many things that are founded neither in reason nor experience; and an unwillingness to part with property of so valuable a kind will furnish a thousand arguments to show the impracticability or pernicious tendency of a scheme which requires such a sacrifice. But it should be considered, that if we do not make use of them in this way, the enemy probably will; and that the best way to counteract the temptations they will hold out will be to offer them ourselves. An essential part of the plan is to give them their freedom with their muskets. This will secure their fidelity, animate their courage, and I believe will have a good influence upon those who remain, by opening a door to their emancipation. This circumstance, I confess, has no small weight in inducing me to wish the success of the project; for the dictates of humanity and true policy equally interest me in favour of this unfortunate class of men.

When I am on the subject of Southern affairs, you will excuse the liberty I take, in saying, that I do not think measures sufficiently vigorous are persuing for our defence in that quarter. Except the few regular troops of South Carolina, we seem to be relying wholly on the militia of that and the two neighbouring states. These will soon grow impatient of service and leave our affairs in a very miserable situation. No considerable force can be uniformly kept up by militia — to say nothing of many obvious and well known inconveniences, that attend this kind of troops. I would beg leave to suggest, Sir, that no time ought to be lost in making a draft of militia to serve a twelve month from the States of North and South Carolina and Virginia. But South Carolina being very weak in her population of whites may be excused from the draft on condition of furnishing the black batalions. The two others may furnish about 3,500 men and be exempted on that account from sending any succours to this army. The states to the Northward of Virginia will be fully able to give competent supplies to the army here; and it will require all the force and exertions of the three states I have mentioned to withstand the storm which has arisen and is increasing in the South.

The troops drafted must be thrown into batalions and officered in the best manner we can. The supernumerary officers may be made use of as far as they will go.

If arms are wanted for these troops and no better way of supplying them is to be found, we should endeavour to levy a contribution of arms upon the militia at large. Extraordinary exigencies demand extraordinary means. I fear this Southern business will become a very *grave* one.

With the truest respect & esteem I am Sir Your most Obed servant

Want of time to copy it, will apologise for sending this letter in its present state.

Head Quarters   March 14th. 79

George Washington to Henry Laurens

Middle brook, March 20, 1779.

Dear Sir: I have to thank you, and I do it very sincerely, for your obliging favors of the 2d. and 16th Inst.; and for their several inclosures, containing articles of intelligence. I congratulate you most cordially on Campbells precipitate retreat from Fort Augusta. What was this owing to? it seems to have been a surprize even upon Williamson. but I rejoice much more on acct. of his disappointed application to the Creek Indians; this I think, is to be considered as a very important event, and may it not be the conjectural cause of his (Campbells) hasty return; this latter circumstance cannot but be a fresh proof to the disaffected (in that Country) that they are leaning upon a broken reed; severe examples should, in my judgment, be made of those who were forgiven former offences and again in Arms against us.

The policy of our arming Slaves is, in my opinion, a moot point, unless the enemy set the example; for should we begin to form Battalions of them, I have not the smallest doubt (if the War is to be prosecuted) of their following us in it, and justifying the measure upon our own ground; the upshot then must be, who can arm fastest, and where are our Arms? besides, I am not clear that a discrimination will not render Slavery more irksome to those who remain in it; most of the good and evil things of this life are judged of by comparison; and I fear a comparison in this case will be productive of much discontent in those who are held in servitude; but as this is a subject that has never employed much of my thoughts, these are no more than the first crude Ideas that have struck me upon the occasion.

I had not the smallest intimation of Monsr. Gerards passing through Jersey till I was favoured with your Letter, and am now ignorant of the cause, otherwise than by conjecture. The inclosed I return, as Mr. Laurens left this some days ago for Philadelphia, on his way to the Southward.

Mrs. Washington joins me in respectful compliments to you, and with every sentiment of regard and attachment. I am etc.

Samuel Shaw to Francis and Sarah Shaw

June 28, 1779

I wish, seriously, that the ensuing campaign may terminate
the war. The people of America seem to have lost sight entirely of the noble principle which animated them at the commencement of it. That patriotic ardor which then inspired
each breast,—that glorious, I had almost said godlike, enthusiasm,—has given place to avarice, and every rascally practice which tends to the gratification of that sordid and most
disgraceful passion. I don't know as it would be too bold an
assertion to say, that its depreciation is equal to that of the
currency,—*thirty for one.* You may perhaps charitably think
that I strain the matter, but I do not. I speak *feelingly.* By the
arts of monopolizers and extortioners, and the little, the very
little, attention by authority to counteract them, our currency
is reduced to a mere name. Pernicious soever as this is to the
community at large, its baneful effect is more immediately experienced by the *poor* soldier. I am myself an instance of it.
For my services I receive a nominal sum,—dollars at *eight*
shillings, in a country where they pass at the utmost for
fourpence only. If it did not look too much like self-applause,
I might say that I engaged in the cause of my country from
the purest motives. However, be this as it may, my continuance in it has brought me to poverty and rags; and, had I fortune of my own, I should glory in persevering, though it
should occasion a sacrifice of the last penny. But, when I consider my situation,—my pay inadequate to my support,
though within the line of the strictest economy,—no private
purse of my own,—and reflect that the best of parents, who,
I am persuaded, have the tenderest affection for their son,
and wish to support him in character, have not the means of
doing it, and may, perhaps, be pressed themselves,—when
these considerations occur to my mind, as they frequently do,
they make me serious; more so than my natural disposition

would lead me to be. The loss of my horse, by any accident whatever (unless he was actually killed in battle, and then I should be entitled only to about one third of his value), would plunge me in inextricable misfortune; two years' pay and subsistence would not replace him. Yet, the nature of my office renders it indispensable that I should keep a horse. These are some of the emoluments annexed to a military station. I hardly thought there were so many before I began the detail; but I find several more might be added, though I think I have mentioned full enough.

Believe me, my dear and honored parents, that I have not enumerated these matters with a view to render you uneasy. Nothing would give me more pain, should they have that effect; but I think communicating one's difficulties always lessens, and, of course, makes them more tolerable; and I fancy it has already had some influence on me. I feel much easier than when I began to write, and more reconciled to my lot. It is true I shall see many persons grown rich at the end of the war, who at the commencement of it had no more than myself; but I shall not envy them. I must, notwithstanding, repeat my wish that this campaign may put an end to the war, for I much doubt the virtue of the people at large for carrying it on another year. Had the same spirit which glowed in the breast of every true American at the beginning of the controversy been properly cherished, the country, long ere now, had been in full enjoyment of the object of our warfare, — 'peace, liberty, and safety.' But, as matters are at present circumstanced, it is to be feared these blessings are yet at a distance. Much remains to be done for the attainment of them. The recommendations of Congress, in their late address to the inhabitants of the States, should be in good earnest attended to. We are not to stand still and wait for salvation, but we must exert ourselves, — be industrious in the use and application of those means with which Heaven has furnished us, and then we may reasonably hope for success.

"A Whig": To the Public

Pennsylvania Packet, August 5, 1779

AMONG the many errors America has been guilty of during her contest with Great-Britain, few have been greater, or attended with more fatal consequences to these States than her lenity to the Tories. At first it might have been right, or perhaps political; but is it not surprising that, after repeated proofs of the evils resulting therefrom, it should still be continued? We are all crying out against the depreciation of our money, and entering into measures to restore it to it's original value, while the Tories, who are one principal cause of the depreciation, are taken no notice of, but suffered to live quietly among us. I can no longer be silent on this subject, and see the independence of my country, after standing every shock from without, endangered by internal enemies. Rouse, America! your danger is great — great from a quarter where you least expect it. The Tories — the Tories will yet be the ruin of you. 'Tis high time they were separated from among you. They are now busily engaged in undermining your liberties. They have a thousand ways of doing it, and they make use of them all. Who were the occasion of this war? the Tories. Who persuaded the tyrant of Britain to prosecute it in a manner before unknown to civilized nations and shocking even to barbarians? the Tories. Who prevailed on the savages of the wilderness to join the standard of the enemy? the Tories. Who have assisted the Indians in taking the scalp from the aged matron, the blooming fair one, the helpless infant, and the dying hero? the Tories. Who advised, and who assisted in burning your towns, ravaging your country, and violating the chastity of your women? the Tories. Who are the occasion that thousands of you now mourn the loss of your dearest connections? the Tories. Who have always counteracted the endeavours of Congress to secure the liberty of this country? the Tories. Who refused their money when as good as specie, though stamped with the image of *his most sacred Majesty*? the Tories. Who continue to refuse it? the Tories. Who do all in their power to depreciate it? the Tories. Who propagate lies among us to discourage the Whigs? the Tories. Who corrupt the minds of the good people of these States by every species of insidious counsel? the Tories. Who hold a traiterous correspondence with the enemy? the Tories. Who daily send them intelligence? the Tories. Who take the oaths of allegiance to the States one day, and break them the next? the Tories. Who prevent your battalions from being filled? the Tories. Who dissuade men from entering the army? the Tories. Who persuade those who have enlisted to desert? the Tories. Who harbour those who do desert? the Tories. In short, who wish to see us conquered, to see us slaves, to see us hewers of wood and drawers of water? the Tories And is it possible, my countrymen, that you should suffer men, who have been guilty of all these and a thousand other calamities which this country has experienced, to live among you! To live among you did I say? Nay, do they not mix in your Assemblies? Do they not insult you with their impudence? Do they not hold traiterous Assemblies of their own? Do they not walk the streets at noon-day, and taste the air of Liberty? In short do they not enjoy every privilege of the brave soldier who has spilt his blood, or the honest patriot who has sacraficed his all in your righteous cause? Yes, — to your eternal shame be it spoken they do. Those very men, who wish to entail slavery on your country, are caressed and harboured among you. — Posterity will not believe it; if they do, they will curse the memory of their fore-fathers for their shameful lenity. Do you ever expect any grateful return for your humanity, if it deserves that name? Believe me, not a spark of that or any other virtue is to be found in a Tory's breast. For what principle can that wretch have who would sell his soul to subject his country to the will of the greatest tyrant the world at present produces? 'Tis time, my countrymen, to rid ourselves of these bosom-vipers. An immediate separation is necessary. I dread to think of the evils every moment is big with, while a single Tory remains among us. May we not soon expect to hear of plots, assassinations, and every other species of wickedness their malice and rancour can suggest? For what can restrain those who have already imbrued their hands in their country's blood? Did not that villain Matthews, when permitted to live among us at New-York, plot the assassination of General Washington? He did; he was detected, and had he received his deserts, he would now have been in gibbets, instead of torturing our unfortunate friends, prisoners in New-York, with every species of barbarity. Can you hear this, and still harbour a Tory within these walls? For my own part, whenever I meet one in the street, or at the Coffee-house, my blood boils within me. Their guilt is equalled only by their impudence. They strut, and seem to bid defiance to every one. In every place, and in every company they spread their damnable doctrines and then laugh at the pusillanimity of those who let them go unpunished. I flatter myself, however, with the hopes of soon seeing a period to their reign, and a total end to their existence in America. Awake, Americans, to a sense of your danger. No time is to be lost — Instantly banish every Tory from among you. Let these walls, let America be sacred alone to freemen. Drive far from you every baneful wretch who wishes to see you fettered with the chains of tyranny. Send them where they may enjoy their beloved slavery in perfection. Send them to the island of Britain, there let them drink the cup of slavery and eat the bread of bitterness all the days of their existence — There let them drag out a painful life, despised and accursed by those very men whose cause they have had the wickedness to espouse — Never let them return to this happy land — Never let them taste the sweets of that independence which they strove to prevent — Banishment, perpetual banishment, should be their lot. But, say some, we allow the Tories are as bad and indeed much worse than you have represented them; but how can we banish them? They have taken the oaths and are under the protection of the laws. Some of these miscreants, 'tis true, have put on a sham repentance, and have dared to call the Almighty to witness to their perjuries — Perjuries I call them, for have we not seen hundreds of them taking the oaths of allegiance one day and breaking them the next, or the first safe opportunity? Nay, do they not tell you to your faces, that no faith is to be kept with Rebels, with which name they have still the effrontery to insult you? Are men who act on principles like these to be trusted? Do you think them less able, or less willing to assist the enemy than heretofore? No, my friends, on the least turn of fortune against us, those men whom you now trust so near you, would convince you your confidence and lenity had been misplaced — They would soon forget the oaths with which they now amuse you — They would hail the enemy to your capital — They would welcome him to your habitations — They would point out those among you who had been active in your country's cause, and if unfortunately any were obliged to stay, and submit to the mercy of the enemy, a prison, or a dungeon and irons would be their portion. Then, tho' too late, you would repent your shameful lenity and your reliance on their oaths. But, say others, who are worked on more by their fears than their reason, if we send them to the enemy, they will encrease their strength, and be embodied against us. Fear not this, my countrymen; they may eat the bread and spend the money of their idol King, but will never be of any material injury to you in the field. They will never be formidable as soldiers. Their wicked principles make cowards of them all. They never were — they never will be, of service to the enemy in battle. They never could be brought to storm the works, or stand the fire of Americans in the open field. Their cowardice, I repeat it, will secure you from any danger you may apprehend from their embodying against you; but nothing can prevent the thousand mischiefs they can do while among you. Think of these things betimes, my countrymen, before it be too late, and you and your posterity forever have reason to repent your lenity to the Tories.

A WHIG.

Philadelphia, July 30, 1779.

William Barton:
Journal, August 27–September 14, 1779

Friday, 27th. At half past eight began marching, and proceeded two miles in the order of the day before. Halted in consequence of their being a defile, which our artillery, horses, &c., could not pass until repaired, from 11 o'clock A. M. till 4 in the afternoon. We passed the defile, and after marching quarter of a mile our Regiment was ordered back to assist the horses in passing, till 11 o'clock P. M. the whole having got up, though not without considerable destruction of the bags with flour and other stores. Then proceeded about three miles, and halted with the army, about one o'clock in the morning, about three miles from Shamong, on an old Indian settlement near some large fields of corn, said to be planted at the expense of the King of Britain, and many smaller ones said to belong to the Indians: with beans, squashes, potatoes, &c., on which our soldiers feasted sumptuously, it being a good substitute for bread which was a scarce article with us. Distance about six miles. Course of march this day, N. NW. The country as level as any I have marched through, except the defile; chiefly woods, but indifferent.

28th, Saturday. Continued marching until 3 P. M.: some ammunition wagons being broke and left behind for the purpose of gathering the corn and destroying what we did not make use of. Proceeded one mile and forded the Cahuga creek at crotch deep—very rapid. Marched half a mile farther and re-crossed the creek again, where it was something deeper than at the other place, and extremely rapid, so as to carry down some of our men, and many of our pack horses, with the loss of three of the latter drowned, and a very considerable loss of flour, baggage, &c. At sunset arrived at Shamong; at nine our baggage came up. Here we encamped for the night; distance three miles. On the march between the places of fording, some Indians were seen and fired on by our flanks, when they ran off. This day the army was allowed no flour on account of the great quantity of corn, beans, &c. Course northwest.

Sunday 29th.   Proceeded very slowly two miles, occasioned by the roughness of the way, which we had to clear for the artillery, baggage, &c., to pass. Here we halted for one hour and a half, until the artillery, &c., should raise a difficult height, at which time an advanced party of our riflemen discovered the enemy throwing up some works on the other side of a morass, and a difficult place through which we had to pass. It appears this was intended for an ambuscade, it being on a small height, where some logs, etc. were laid up, covered with green bushes, which extended half a mile. On the right was a small town which they had destroyed themselves, making use of the timber, etc. in the above works. Moved one mile and a quarter, after all was in readiness, and within a quarter of the works, when some small parties of riflemen were sent to divert them by firing at long shot on their works. After the ground was well reconnoitered, the artillery was advanced on their left. At the same time Gen'l Poor with his brigade was endeavoring to gain their rear around their left; Gen'l Hand's brigade was following in rear of Poor. Our brigade was kept as a reserve, as was also Gen. Clinton's, until their rear should be gained; but they having a party posted on a very considerable height, over which our right flanks had to pass, we were discovered by them. Previous to this, some shells and round shot were thrown among them in their works, which caused them to give several yells, and doubtless intimidated them much. But at this discovery they gave a most hideous yell and quit their works, endeavoring to prevent Gen'l Poor's ascending the height, by a loose scattering fire; but our troops pressing forward with much vigor, made them give way, leaving their dead behind, (amounting to eleven or twelve) which were scalped immediately. We likewise took one white man, who appeared to be dead, and was stripped, when an officer came up and examined him, said he was not wounded, gave him a stroke and bade him get up; he immediately rose up and implored mercy, and was kept a prisoner some time. In the evening a negro was taken. Their number wounded not known. Two or three of ours killed, and thirty-four or five wounded. Among the latter was Major Titcomb, Capt. Cloise, and Lt. Allis. At half after three the firing ceased, and the army proceeded one mile and a half to a considerable town pleasantly situated under the mountains on the side of the creek, consisting of about twenty huts. The number of the enemy uncertain, but from the best intelligence from the prisoners, the whites were about two hundred, the Indians five. They were commanded by Butler and Brant, who had been waiting some days our approach. It appears their expectations were great, from their numbers, situation, etc. The prisoners likewise inform us they had been kept on an allowance of seven ears of corn per day each, although there is a very great abundance of corn, beans, potatoes, squashes, etc., for several miles on the creek, upon which our whole army has subsisted for days. We had nevertheless to destroy some hundred bushels. Here was found a deal of plunder of theirs, such as blankets, brass kettles, etc.

*   *   *

Monday, 30th.   At the request of Maj. Piatt, sent out a small party to look for some of the dead Indians—returned without finding them. Toward morning they found them and skinned two of them from their hips down, for boot legs; one pair for the Major the other for myself. On the other side this mountain was a town said to be of the best buildings we had passed. It was destroyed by Gen. Poor the evening of the engagement.

Tuesday, 31st.   Proceeded about six miles and halted for one hour, destroying a small town of huts on a branch of Kihuga Creek, which we forded. On our way thither burnt two houses, the best buildings I have seen since I left Wyoming. Here we left the Kihuga, and proceeded four miles through a level piece of pine land, thinly timbered, with many cranberry ponds, and large flats grown up with grass of considerable heighth. Encamped on one of these at sunset.

Wednesday, September 1st.   At eight in the morning continued our march through a level pine lane, as the afternoon before, for two or three miles, when we began to ascend a mountain, on which we marched, ascending and descending several different times; then came into a very thick swamp, chiefly white and spruce pines. After marching one mile in the swamp, was under the necessity of halting for one hour, until a road was cleared for the artillery to pass; then proceeded after halting, through difficulties of the way, for five miles, in which time we forded a creek, that ran through the swamp, fifteen different times. About sunset came to a clear flat, uncultivated, rich, and well timbered. Near dark again entered a swamp; very difficult and bad marching, our pack and other horses still increasing the mud so as to make it impassable, through darkness, etc. Some, however, attempting it, were mired down with flour and baggage, where many lay all night; in this manner the road was strewed for about 4 miles. Had the savages availed themselves of this opportunity, it must have proved very fatal to us, for they might with ease have destroyed a great part of our provisions, with a party very inconsiderable. Thus continued our march until 12 o'clock at night, when we arrived at French Catherine, an Indian town, deserted by them a few hours before our troops came in; march as disagreeable as I have experienced; sometimes up to our knees in mud and mire, and so dark as not to be able to keep the path by any other means than being close to our front man. When we arrived, our situation still disagreeable, not having our baggage or any covering, and in expectation of being attacked every moment until morning, — men exceedingly fatigued, having marched fourteen miles with fifteen days' flour on their backs, exclusive of their other pack.

Thursday, 2nd. About sunrise a squaw was discovered, to appearance upwards of one hundred years of age, who lay in the woods. She had been left by the Indians the day before, and was so decrepid as not to be able to walk. She was, after examination, by order of the General, put on horse-back, and told to follow her companions, with a letter, but could not ride. She informed us that they had only gone a little way into the woods, and as they expected us not to tarry any time here, might return again: in consequence of which I was ordered out with a party of two hundred to search the woods adjacent, at 11 o'clock, A. M., as the army was to lay here this day for the refreshment of troops and collecting the horses and baggage. After marching three miles and a half, came to a large flat, near the Senakee lake; proceeded as far as we could for the mire, then turned about, knowing we were in the wrong path, and sent out a couple of Indians for the purpose of finding the path, which they did, and returned. We then marched through a swamp for one and a half miles, and halted one hour; when detached Capt. Boman, with fifty men, to the lake, when we again marched and ascended a mountain, where we had a view of the lake, and then took a circuit march over mountains, etc. Returned to camp, after marching ten or eleven miles without making any discovery, more than where they had driven off a number of horses and cattle, several of which were taken this day.

Catharine is the most important Senakee town we have met with since entering their nation. It derived its name from *French Catharine*, who in her infancy was taken from Canada by the savages, and became accustomed to their manners, marrying an Indian chief, who was said to be half French himself, from which marriage she claimed this part of the country. Here she raised a great number of horses for sale — its situation a rich flat on the side of a creek. The corn and beans raised here afforded us one day's subsistence. The great quantity of corn, &c., which is raised here more than usual, was occasioned by the British giving a premium to encourage them in raising it, so as to enable them to come down on our frontiers.

This squaw likewise said they had a long debate whether they should stay and deliver themselves up to our army or not, but at length it was determined not, the warriors saying they would scalp them if they did. Here was made up a small hut for the old squaw on the side of the creek, having destroyed all the huts belonging to the place at our departure, leaving her a plenty to subsist on. She appeared very thankful when she found we did not kill or misuse her.

Friday, 3rd. Marched at half past eight, A. M.; for two miles something mountainous; then through a very large, level tract of land bordering on the Senakee lake; its timber walnut, ash, hichory and oak, by far the largest tract of good land in one body I have yet seen. About five P. M. arrived at encamping ground, which was in the woods. A short time after our halt some men discovered a corn-field; went to it, and found the Indians had just then quit it, leaving corn roasting at the fires, which occasioned there being a scout sent out, who discovered some of them by a fire near a small town, but the enemy making the discovery previous to this, retreated to the town as was supposed, and the scout returned. This evening, orders were given for to march at half past five in the morning, without the usual signals. Distance 12 miles, N. NW. course.

Saturday, 4th.   In the morning it rained, by which means we did not march until half after ten, when we proceeded to Apple town, which was on fire at our arrival. Passed it two or three hundred yards and halted on a mountain near a corn-field, which was soon stripped of its beans, &c. Here we had a prospect of the lake for upwards of twenty miles in length and about three in breadth, the most beautiful I have ever seen. In a short time proceeded until sunset through a good rich land, much the same as the day before, having only two difficult defiles. Distance about 12 miles; course north.

Sunday, 5th.   Proceeded marching through land much the same as the day before, passing two or three defiles, and arrived at an old settled place called Kendae, at 3 P. M. It appeared to be the oldest town we have yet passed, here being a considerable orchard; trees very old, as are the building, very pleasantly situated about quarter of a mile from the lake, on a high piece of ground; some of the best buildings, in number about thirty, with several small fields of corn, which were very insufficient for all our troops, having drawn but half allowance since we left Shamong. A much larger quantity is said to be on the other side of the lake, but we having no boats or any convenience, it being about five miles across, could not get any of that. There was taken a white man, who had by them been made prisoner at Wyoming, in 1777. He informed us the enemy had left this two days before our arrival. He likewise said they had a reinforcement at this place of two or three hundred, who were very anxious to fight us; the others said they had fought enough, and did not choose to do any more. In the evening the whole army discharged their firelocks by order.

Monday, 6th.   I was sent out with a detachment under

Maj. Hollinshead, for the purpose of collecting horses, cattle, &c., many of them having strayed the night before, on account of which the army was detained until 2 P. M., when we proceeded three miles, land continuing rich and fertile as before; encamped in the woods near the lake. Here a great plenty of pea vines, which our horses and cattle feed on. This day have intelligence that the garrison at Powles Hook was surprised and taken.

Tuesday, 7th.   Proceeded about eight miles, halting near the outlet of the lake for one hour and a half, then crossed it near middle deep. The lake is said to be forty miles in length and from two to five in breadth, very beautiful, without a single island in it, its course N.W. and S.E. After crossing as before, proceeded one mile and halted one hour; having a long defile to pass, was expecting an attack. From thence proceeded two miles through a very thick wood, and came on the back of a town a little after sundown, called Cunnesedago, still expecting they would defend their town, it being the capital of their nation, but they were all fled. The town consists of fifty or upwards very good huts, regular and compact, much more than any we have seen before. Here was found a white male child about three years of age, supposed to have been taken from our frontiers. It can speak Indian very well, and understand English, but not talk it. Victuals being given, it appeared to have been nearly starved, and would doubtless have injured itself had it not been restrained. An officer of ours has taken it with the intention to bring it up. This lake runs into lake Kihuga, and from thence into St. Lawrence river.

Wednesday, 8th.   Continued for the purpose of gathering corn, beans, &c.

Thursday, 9th.   Proceeded one mile through a very thick swamp, when we came to some up-land, which appeared to have been cleared, and was grown up with Indian grass and some ash bushes, over which we travelled for two or three miles, when we again entered a swamp, which we travelled through for five miles and halted on a piece of high ground for the night. This morning a detachment was sent down to Tioga consisting of fifty men, who were to escort all the sick, invalids, &c. and likewise all the horses that were not able to carry packs. Thirty odd were nevertheless left at this place, that could not be got farther.

Friday, 10th. Came to a lake called by some Genessee, which is from one to three miles in width, and about ten in length, and very shallow. Proceeded and crossed the outlet at half leg deep, and twenty yards across. It lies nearly north and south. After crossing had a long defile to pass and came to a considerable town of about twenty huts, which were all on fire when we came in sight; marched one mile past the town and encamped for the night, near some corn-fields, at 4 P. M. Distance of this day's march about ten miles. Course West.

Saturday, 11th. Passed many defiles, the ground being rougher than any we have yet passed since we left Catharine, and the up-land more indifferent. Arrived at four o'clock at Onyauyah, where was a large quantity of corn. In sight of this town is a lake lying to the south; here we encamped. Marched fourteen miles this day, course nearly west. Here was left a small garrison, with most of our baggage, horses, &c.

Sunday, 12th. Came to a small lake from a quarter to half a mile wide and three in length, distance about five miles. Crossed the outlet at knee deep, (fifteen yards across) went five and a half miles farther and encamped for the night on a high ground newly cleared.

Monday, 13th. At half past 4, morning, proceeded one mile and a half; came to a considerable town, Canesaah, consisting of from sixteen to twenty huts and halted for the troops to get some refreshment and to build a bridge cross a creek; meantime a party of twenty-six men, commanded by Lt. Boyd, was sent out to a town about six miles for discovery, at which place he arrived without molestation. Here an Indian was killed and scalped by his party. He then despatched two men to inform us what had happened; after they had gone two miles they saw five Indians. They immediately run back and told the Lieutenant what they had seen, who marched on to the place with all speed, when he discovered some few of them who retreated; he pursued and killed one of them. The men then went to scalp him, which caused some dispute who should have it; at the same instant the enemy rose up from their ambuscade, when the action commenced, but they being much superior in numbers, caused him and one or two others to surrender, though not until the rest were all killed and got off. About the same time, Capt. Lodge, surveyor of the road, with a small party was discovered about one mile beyond, where the party was building a bridge. They were fired on by the Indians and one of his men wounded. The rest ran off and were pursued so closely that one of them drew out his tomahawk and was close on the heels of one of our men, when a sentinel from the party at the bridge fired at the Indian, which caused them all to run off. Major Poor immediately pushed on, hearing the firing, and found the knapsacks, &c. of the Indians, who had all run off on his approach. At two o'clock, the bridge being completed, we marched on to a town, Casawavalatetah, where we arrived about dark, in expectation of an attack, and encamped. Land continuing very fertile; at both of these places was a large quantity of corn, at the former we did not destroy all.

Tuesday, 14th.   Early in the morning was ordered to destroy the corn, which we did by throwing the ears into the creek which runs close to the town, and is a branch of the Canisee river, which empties into the lake Ontario about fourteen miles hence. At two P. M. marched and crossed the creek, and forded the main branch of Canisee and proceeded four miles down to the Chenisee castle, where we arrived about four P. M. At this place was Lieut. Boyd and one soldier found, with their heads cut off. The Lieutenant's head lay near his body; the scalp was entirely cut off; his body appeared to have been whipped and pierced in many different places. The other's head was not found. A great part of his body was skinned, leaving his ribs bare.

John Paul Jones to Benjamin Franklin

On board the Ship of War
Serapis at Anchor without the Texel
Octr. 3d. 1779.

Honoured and dear Sir

When I had the honour of writing to you on the 11th. August Previous to my departure from the Road of Groa I had before me the most flattering prospect of rendering essential service to the common Cause of France & America. I had a full confidence in the Voluntary inclination & ability of every Captain under my Command to assist and support me in my duty with Cheerful Unremitting Emulation — and I was persuaded that every one of them would persue Glory in preference to Interest. Whether I was or was not deceived will best appear by a simple relation of circumstances. — The little Squadron under my command consisting of the Bon home Richard of 40 Guns the Alliance of 36 Guns the Pallas of 32 Guns the Serf of 18 Guns & the Vengeance of 12 Guns Join'd by two Privateers the Monsieur & the Grandvelle Sailed from the Isle of Groa at Day Break on the 14th. of August the same day we spoke with a large Convoy bound from the Southward to Brest on the 18th. we took a large Ship belonging to Holland laden chiefly with Brandy and Wine that had been destined from Barcelona for Dunkirk and taken eight days before by an English Privateer — The Captain of the Privateer Monsieur took out of this Prize such Articles as he pleased in the Night and the next day being astern of the Squadron & to windward he actually wrote Orders in his proper Name and sent away the Prize under one of his own Officers — This however I superceeded by sending her for L'Orient under my Orders in the character of Commander in Chief — The evening of the Day following the Monsieur Seperated from the Squadron — On the 20th. we saw and Chased a large Ship but could not come up with her She being to Windward — On the 21st we saw and Chased another Ship that was also to

Windward and thereby Eluded our pursuit the Same afternoon we took a Brigantine Called the May Flower laden with
Butter & Salt Provision bound from Limerick in Ireland for
London; this Vessel I Immediately expedited for L'Orient.
On the 23 we saw Cape Clear and the S. West Part of Ireland
that Afternoon it being Calm I sent some Armed Boats to
take a Brigantine that appeared in the N.W. Quarter — soon
after in the evening it became necessary to have a Boat a
Head of the Ship to Tow as the Helm could not prevent her
from laying across the Tide of Flood which would have driven
us into a deep and dangerous Bay Situated between the Rocks
on the south called the Skillicks and on the North called the
Blaskets — The Ships Boats being absent I sent my own Barge
a head to tow the Ship — The Boats took the Brigantine She
being called the Fortune and Bound with a Cargo of Oil
Blubber & Staves from Newfoundland for Bristol — This
Vessel I Ordered to proceed immediately for Nants or St.
Malo. — Soon after Sunset the Villains who Towed the Ship
cut the tow Rope and Decamped with my Barge. — Sundry
Shot were fir'd to bring them too without effect — In the
mean time the master of the Bon homme Richard without
Orders Manned one of the Ships Boats & with 4 Soldiers pursued the Barge in Order to stop the deserters — The Evening
was then Clear & Serene — but the Zeal of that Officer Mr.
Cutting Lunt induc'd him to pursue too far, and a Fog which
came on soon afterwards Prevented the Boat from Rejoyning
the Ship altho I caused Signal Guns to be frequently fired —
the Fog & Calm continued the next day till towards the
Evening — In the Afternoon Captain Landais came on board
the Bonhomme Richard and behaved towards me with great
disrespect Affirming in the most indelicate language and manner that I had lost my Boats and People thro' imprudence in
sending Boats to take a Prize — He persisted in his reproaches
tho' he was assured by Messieurs De Wybert & Chamillard
that the Barge was actually Towing the Ship at the time of the
Elopement and had not been sent in pursuit of the Prize —
He was affronted because I would not the Day before Suffer
him to Chase without my Orders and to approach the dangerous Shore I have already mentioned, where he was an entire Stranger and where there was not a Sufficient wind to

govern a Ship—He told me that he was the only American in
the Squadron and was determined to follow his own Opinion
in Chasing when and where he thought proper and in every
other matter that concerned the Service—and that if I continued in that Situation three days longer the Squadron
would be Taken &c, By the advice of Captain Cottineau and
with the free consent and Approbation of M. De Verage I
sent the Serf in to Reconnoitre the Coast and endeavour to
take up the Boats and People the next day while the
Squadron stood off and on in the S.W. Quarter in the best
Possible Situation to intercept the Enemies Merchant Ships
whether outward or Homeward Bound.—The Cerf had on
board a Pilot well acquainted with the Coast and was Ordered
to Join me again before Night,—I approached the Shore in
the Afternoon but the Serf did not appear—This induced me
to stand off again in the Night in order to return and be re-
joyned by the Serf the Next Day—but to my great concern
and disappointment tho' I ranged the Coast along and
hoisted our private Signal neither the Boats nor the Serf
Joined me—The evening of that day the 26th. brought with
it Stormy Weather with an appearance of a Severe Gale from
the South West Yet I must declare I did not follow my own
Judgment but was led by the assertion which had fallen from
Captain Landais when I in the evening made a Signal for to
steer to the Northward and leave that Station, which I wished
to have Occupied at least a Week longer—The Gale increased
in the Night with the thick Weather—To prevent seperation
I carried a Toplight and fired a Gun every Quarter of an hour, I
carried also a Very moderate Sail and the Course had been
clearly Pointed out by a Signal before Night. Yet with all this
precaution I found myself accompanied only by the Brigantine Vengeance in the Morning—the Grand Velle having
remained astern with a Prize as I have since understood the
Tiller of the Pallas broke after MidNight in which disenabled
her from keeping up—but no apology has yet been made in
behalf of the Alliance.—On the 31st we saw the Flannin
Islands Situated near the Lewises on the N.W. Coast of
Scotland and the next morning off Cape Wrath we gave
Chase to a Ship to Windward at the same time two Ships appearing in the N.W. Quarter which proved to be the Alliance

and a Prize Ship which She had taken bound as I Understood from Liverpool for Jamaica.—The Ship which I chased brought too at Noon—She proved to be the Union Letter of Mark bound from London for Quebec with a Cargo of Naval Stores on Account of Government, Adapted for the Service of the British Armed Vessels on the Lakes. The Public dispatches were lost as the Alliance very imprudently hoisted American Colours tho' English Colours were then Flying on board the Bon homme Richard.—Captain Landais sent a small Boat to ask whither I would Man the Ship or he should—as in the latter Case he would suffer no Boat nor Person from the Bon homme Richard to go near the Prize.—Ridiculous as this appeared to me I yielded to it for the sake of Peace and received the Prisoners on board the Bon homme Richard while the Prize was manned from the Alliance.—In the Afternoon another Sail appeared and I immediately made the Signal for the Alliance to Chase—but instead of Obeying He wore and laid the Ships Head the other way; The next morning I made a Signal to speak with the Alliance to which no attention was shewn—I then made Sail with the Ships in Company for the second Rendezvous which was not far distant and where I fully expected to be Join'd by the Pallas and the Serf—The 2d. of Sepr. we saw a Sail at Day break and gave Chase—That Ship proved to be the Pallas and had met with no Success while seperated from the Bon homme Richard—On the 3d. the Vengeance brought too a small Irish Brigantine bound homewards from Norway.

The same evening I sent the Vengeance in the N.E. Quarter to bring up the two Prize Ships that appeared to me to bee too near the Islands of Schetland—while with the Alliance & Pallas I endeavoured to Weather Fair Isle and to get into my second Rendezvous where I directed the Vengeance to Join me with the three Prizes. The Next Morning having weathered Fair Isle and not seeing the Vengeance nor the Prizes—I spoke the Alliance and ordered her to Steer to the Northward and bring them up to the Rendezvous. On the morning the 5th the Alliance appeared again and had brought too 2 very Small Coasting Sloops in Ballast but without having Attended properly to My Orders of Yesterday.— The Vengeance Joined me soon after And informed me that in consequence of Captain Landais Orders to the Commanders of the two Prize Ships they had refused to follow him to the Rendezvous. I am to this moment Ignorant what Orders these Men received from Capt. Landais — nor Know I by Virture of what Authority he ventured to give his Orders to Prizes in my Presence and without either my Knowledge or Approbation. Captain Ricot further informed me that he had Burnt the Prize Brigantine because that Vessel Proved leaky and I was sorry to understand afterwards that the Vessel was Irish Property the Cargo was the Property of the Subjects of Norway —

In the evening I sent for all the Captains to come on board the Bon homme Richard to consult on future Plans of Opperation. Captains Cottineau & Ricot Obeyed me, but Captain Landais Obstinately refused and after sending me Various uncivil Messages wrote me a very extraordinary letter in Answer to a written Order which I had sent him on finding that he had trifled with my Verbal Orders —

The next day a Pilot Boat came on board from Shetland by which Means I received such advices as induced me to change a Plan which I otherwise meant to have Pursued, And as the Serf did not appear at my second Rendezvous I determined to steer towards the 3d. in hopes of meeting her there — In the Afternoon a Gale of Wind came on which continued four Days without intermission. In the 2d. Night of that Gale the Alliance with her 2 little Prizes Again seperated from the Bon homme Richard —

I had now with me only the Pallas and Vengeance Yet I did not abandon the hopes of performing some Essential service — The Winds continued contrary so that we did not see the Land 'till the Evening of the 13th when the Hills of Chevot in the S.E. of Scotland appeared — The Next day We Chased Sundry Vessels and took a Ship & a Brigantine both from the Firth of Edinborough laden with Coal Knowing that there lay at Anchor in leith Roads an Armed Ship of 20 Guns with two or three fine Cutters — I formed an Expedition against Leith which I purposed to lay under a large Contribution or otherwise to reduce it to Ashes — Had I been alone the Wind being favourable I would have proceeded directly up the Firth and must have Succeeded as they lay there in a State of

perfect indolence and security which would have Prov'd their
Ruin. Unfortunately for me the Pallas and Vengeance were
both at a considerable Distance in the Offing they having
Chased to the Southward — This Obliged me to Steer out of
the Firth again to meet them — The Captains of the Pallas
and Vengeance being come on board the Bon homme
Richard I communicated to them my Project — to which
many difficulties and Objections were made by them — at last
however they appeared to think better of the design after I
had assured them that I hoped to raise a Contribution of
200,000 Pounds Sterling on Leith, and that there was no
Battery of Cannon there to oppose our landing. — So much
time however was unavoidably spent in Pointed Remarks and
Sage Deliberation that Night that the Wind became contrary
in the Morning — We continued Working to windward up the
Firth without being able to reach the Road of Leith till on
the Morning of the 17th. when being almost within Cannon
Shot of the Town having every thing in readiness for a Descent;
a very severe Gale of Wind came on and being directly contrary
Obliged us to bear away after having in Vain endeavoured for
some time to withstand Its Violence the Gale was so severe
that one of the Prizes that had been taken the 14th. sunk to
the Bottom the Crew being with difficulty saved — As the
alarm had by this time reached Leith by means of a Cutter
that had watched our motions that Morning, — & as the
Wind continued contrary (tho' more moderate in the evening)
I thought it impossible to pursue the Enterprize with a good
prospect of success especially as Edinborough where there is
always a Number of Troops is only a Mile distant from Leith;
therefore I gave up the Project — on the 19th. having taken a
Sloop and a Brigantine in Ballast with a Sloop laden with
Building Timber — I Proposed another Project to Mr.
Cottineau which would have been highly Honorable tho' not
Profitable many difficulties were made and our Situation was
represented as being the most Perulous the Enemy he said
would send against us a superiour Force and that if I
Obstinately continued on the Coast of England two days
longer we should all be Taken.

The Vengeance having Chased Along Shore to the Southward Capt. Cottineau said he would follow her with the

Prizes as I was unable to make much Sail having that day been Obliged to strike the Main Topmast to repair its damages and as I afterwards Understood he told M. De Chamillard that unless I Joined them the next Day both the Pallas & the Vengeance would leave that Coast.—I had thoughts of attempting the Enterprize alone after the Pallas had made Sail to Join the Vengeance—I am persuaded even now that I should have succeeded And to the honour of my Young Officers I found them as ardently disposed to the Business as I could desire. Nothing prevented me from pursuing my design but the reproach that would have been cast upon my Character as a Man of prudence had the Enterprize miscarried—It would have been said was he not forewarned by Captain Cottineau & Others—

I made Sail along Shore to the Southward and next Morning took a Coasting Sloop in Ballast which with another that I had taken the Night before I Ordered to be sunk.—In the Evening I again met with the Pallas and the Vengeance off Whitby—Captain Cottineau told me he had sunk the Brigantine and ransomed the Sloop Laden with Building Timber that had been Taken the Day before—I had told Captain Cottineau the day before that I had no Authority to Ransom Prizes—On the 21st. We saw and Chased Two Sail off Flambrough Head—The Pallas Chased in the N. E Quarter while the Bon home Richard followed by the Vengeance Chased in the S.W.—The one I Chased a Brigantine Collier in Ballast belonging to Scarborough was soon Taken and sunk immediately Afterwards—As a Fleet then appeared to the Southward this was so late in the Day that I could not come up with the Fleet before night at length however I got so near one of them as to force her to run ashore between Flamborough Head and the Spurn—soon after I Took another a Brigantine from Holland belonging to Sunderland and at Day light the Next Morning seeing a Fleet Steering towards me from the Spurn I immagined them to be a Convoy bound from London for Leith which had been for some time expected—one of them had a Pendant Hoisted and appeared to be a Ship of Force—They had not however Courage to come on but kept back all except the one which seemed to be Armed and that one

Also kept to Windward very near the Land and on the Edge of Dangerous Shoals where I could not with safety Approach — This induced me to make a Signal for a Pilot and soon afterwards two Pilot Boats came off — They informed me that the Ship that wore a Pendant was an Armed Merchantman And that a Kings Frigate lay there in sight at Anchor within the Humber waiting to take under Convoy a number of Merchant Ships bound to the Northward. The Pilots imagined the Bon homme Richard to be an English Ship of War and consequently communicated to me the Private Signal which they had been required to make — I endeavoured by this means to decoy the Ships out of the Port, but the wind then changing and with the Tide becoming Unfavourable for them; the deception had not the desired Effect; and they wisely put back. — The entrance of the Humber is exceedingly difficult and Dangerous — And as the Pallas was not in sight I thought it imprudent to remain off the Entrance — therefore Steered out again to Join the Pallas off Flamborough Head. In the Night We saw and Chased two Ships untill 3 OClock in the Morning When being at a very small distance from them I made the Private Signal of Reconnoisance which I had given to each Captain before I Sailed from Groa — One half of the Answer only was returned — In this Position both sides lay too till day light When the Ships proved to be the Alliance & the Pallas — On the Morning of that day the 23d. the Brig from Holland not being in sight We Chased a Brigantine that appeared Laying too to Windward — About Noon We saw and Chased a large Ship that appeared coming round Flamborough head from the Northward and at the same time I Manned and Armed one of the Pilots Boats to send in Pursuit of the Brigantine which now appeared to be the Vessel that I had forced ashore — Soon after this a Fleet of 41 Sail appeared off Flamborough Head bearing NNE. This induced me to Abandon the Single Ship which had then Anchored in Burlington Bay; I also called back the Pilot Boat and hoisted a Signal for a general Chase.

When the Fleet discovered us bearing down all the Merchant Ships Crowded Sail towards the Shore. The Two Ships of War that Protected the Fleet at the same time Steered from the Land and made the disposition for Battle — In approaching the Enemy I crowded every Possible Sail and made the Signal for the line of Battle to which the Alliance shewed no Attention. Earnest as I was for the Action I could not reach the Commodores Ship untill Seven in the Evening being then within Pistol Shot when He hailed the Bon homme Richard. We answered him by Firing a Whole Broadside — The Battle being thus begun was continued with Unremitting Fury — Every method was Practiced on both sides to gain an Advantage and Rake each other — And I must confess that the Enemies Ship being much more Manageable than the Bon homme Richard gained thereby several times an advantagious Situation in spite of my best endeavours to prevent it — As I had to deal with an Enemy of greatly Superiour Force I was under the necessity of closing with him to Prevent the Advantage Which he had over me in Point of Manoeuvre — It was my intention to lay the Bon homme Richard athwart the Enemies Bow but as that Opperation required great dexterity in the Management of both Sails and Helm And some of our Braces being Shot away it did not exactly succeed to my wish.

The Enemies Bowsprit however came over the Bon homme Richards Poop by — the Mizen Mast and I made both Ships fast together in that Situation which by the Action the Wind on the Enemies Sails forced her Stern close to the Bon homme Richards Bow so that the Ships lay square alongside of each Other the Yards being all entangled and the Cannon of each Ship touching the Opponents Side when this Position took Place it was Eight OClock Previous to which the Bonhomme Richard had received sundry Eighteen Pound Shot below the Water and leaked very much.

My Battery of 12 Pounders on which I had Placed my Chief dependance being Commanded by Lieut. Dale and Col. Wybert and Manned Principally with American Seamen & French Volunteers; was entirely Silenced and Abandoned — as to the Six old 18 Pounders that formed the Battery of the lower Gun Deck they did no service whatever except firing Eight Shot in all — Two out of them Burst at the first Fire and Killed almost all the Men who were stationed to Manage them.

Before this time too Col. Chamillard who Commanded a
Party of 20 Soldiers on the Poop had Abandoned that Station
after having lost some of his Men.

I had now only two Pieces of Cannon (9 Pounders) on the
Quarter Deck that were not Silenced and not one of the heav-
ier Cannon was fired during the remainder of the Action —
The Purser Mr. Mease who Commanded the Guns on the
Quarter Deck being dangerously Wounded in the head I was
Obliged to fill his Place & with great difficulty Rallied a few
Men and shifted to get over one of the lee Quarter Deck
Guns so that We afterwards played three Pieces of Nine
pounders upon the Enemy The Tops alone seconded the Fire
of this little Battery and held out Bravely during the Whole
Action especially the Main Top where Lieutenant Stack
Commanded. I directed the Fire of one of the three Cannon
against the Main Mast with double Headed Shot while the
other two were Exceedingly well served with Grape &
Canister Shot to Silence the Enemies Musquetry and Clear
her Decks which was at last effected the Enemy were as I have
since Understood on the Instant of Calling out for Quar-
ters — When the Cowardice or Treachery of three of my
Under Officers induced them to call to the Enemy — The
English Commodore Asked me if I Demanded Quarters And
I having Answered him in the most determined Negative
They renewed the Battle with redoubled Fury — They were
unable to stand the Deck but the Fire of their Cannon especially the lower Battery which was entirely form'd of 18
Pounders was incessant. — Both Ships were set on Fire in
Various Places And the scene was dreadful beyond the reach
of Language — To account for the Timidity of my Three under Officers, I mean the Gunner the Carpenter and the
Master at Arms — I must observe that the two First were
slightly Wounded And as the Ship had received Various Shot
under Water And one of the Pumps being shot away
the Carpenter expressed his Fears that she would Sink and the
other two concluded that she was Sinking which Occasioned
the Gunner to run aft on the Poop without my Knowledge to
strike the Colours — Fortunately for me a Cannon ball had
done that before by carrying away the Ensign Staff — He was
therefore reduced to the Necessity of sinking, as he Supposed,

or of Calling for Quarters and he prefered the Latter—All this time the Bon homme Richard had sustained the Action alone And the Enemy tho' much Superior in Force would have been very glad to have got Clear as Appears by their own Acknowledgments and by their having let go an Anchor the Instant that I laid them on Board by which means they would have escaped had I not made them well fast to the Bonhomme Richard; at last, at half past Nine O'Clock the Alliance appeared & I now thought the Battle at an End but to my Utter Astonishment he discharged a Broadside full into the Stern of the Bon homme Richard—We Called to him for Gods sake to forbear Firing into the Bon homme Richard—Yet he passed along the Off Side of the Ship and Continued Firing—There was no Possibility of his Mistaking the Enemy's Ship for the Bon homme Richard there being the most essential difference in their appearance & construction—besides it was then full Moon light, And the Sides of the Bon homme Richard were all Black while the Side of the Prize were Yellow—Yet for the greater security I shewed the Signal of our Reconnoissance by putting out Three Lanthorns, One at the head Another at the Stern and the third in the Middle in a Horrizontal line—Every Tongue cried that He was Firing into the wrong Ship but nothing availed. He passed round firing into the Bon homme Richard's Head, Stern, & Broadside and by one of his Vollies Killed Agreeable to Report several of my best Men and Mortally Wounded an Officer on the Fore Castle only. My Situation was really deplorable the Bon homme Richard received Various Shots under Water from the Alliance the leak gained on the Pumps and the Fire increased Much on board both Ships—Some Officers Persuaded me to Strike of whose Courage and good sense I entertain an High Opinion.—My Treacherous Master at Arms let loose all my Prisoners without my Knowledge and my Prospect became Gloomy Indeed—I would not however give up the Point—The Enemy's Main Mast began to shake, Their Firing decreased Fast Our's rather increased And the British Colours were Struck at half an hour Past Ten O'Clock—This Prize proved to be the British Ship of War the Serapis a New Ship of 44 Guns built on their most approved Construction with two Compleat Batteries one of them of 18 Pounders and Commanded by the Brave Commodore Richard Pearson. — I had yet two Enemies to encounter with far more formidable than the Britons I mean fire and Water. The Serapis was attacked only by the first but the Bon homme Richard was Assailed by both — There was five Feet of Water in the Hold and tho' it was Moderate from the Explosition of so Much Gun Powder Yet three Pumps that remained could with difficulty only Keep the Water from gaining — The Fire broke out in Various Parts of the Ship in spite of all the Water that could be thrown in to quench it and at length broke out as low as the Powder Magazine and within a few Inches of the Powder — In that Dilema I took out the Powder upon Deck ready to be thrown overboard at the last extremity and it was Ten O'Clock the next Day the 24th before the Fire was entirely Extinguished. With respect to the Situation of the Bonhomme Richard The Rudder was cut almost entirely off; the Stern Frame & Transoms Were almost entirely Cut away And the Timbers by the lower Deck especially from the Main Mast towards the Stern being greatly decayed with Age were Mangled beyond my Power of description and A Person must have been an Eye Witness to form a Just Idea of the tremendous Scenes of Carnage Wreck and Ruin which every where appeared — Humanity cannot but recoil from the Prospect of such finished Horror and lament that War should be capable of producing Such fatal Consequences.

After the Carpenters as well as Captain Cottineau and other Men of sense had well examined & Surveyed the Ship which was not Finished before five in Evening I found every Person to be convinced that it was Impossible to Keep the Bon homme Richard Afloat So as to reach a Port if the Wind should increase it being then only a very Moderate Breeze — I had but little time to remove My Wounded which now became Unavoidable and which was effected in the Course of the Night and Next Morning — I was determined to Keep the Bon homme Richard Afloat and if possible to bring her into Port For that purpose the first Lieutenant of the Pallas continued on board with a Party of Men to Attend the Pumps with Boats in waiting ready to take them on board in Case the Water Should gain on them too Fast; The Wind Augmented in the Night and the next Day on the 25th. So that it was impossible to prevent the Good Old Ship from Sinking — They did not abandon her 'till after Nine OClock — The Water was then up to the lower Deck and a little after Ten I saw with inexpressible Grief the last Glimpse of the Bonhomme Richard — No lives were lost with the Ship — but it was impossible to save the Stores of any Sort Whatever — I lost even the best Part of my Cloaths Books and Papers and several of my Officers lost all their Cloaths and Effects.

Having thus endeavoured to give a Clear and Simple relation of the Circumstances and events that have attended the little Armament Under my Command I shall freely submit My Conduct therein to the Cencure of my Superiours and the impartial Public — I beg leave however to Observe that the Force that was put under my Command Was far from being well Composed And as the great Majority of the Actors in it have appeared bent on the pursuit of Interest only; I am exceedingly Sorry that they and I have at all been concerned.

I am in the Highest degree sensible of the Singular Attentions which I have experienced from the Court of France; which I shall remember with Perfect Gratitude Untill the end of my Life — And will always endeavour to Merit while I can consistent with my Honor continue in the Public Service. — I must speak plainly; as I have always been honored with the full confidence of Congress, And as I had also Flattered myself with enjoying in some Measure the Confidence of the Court of France; I could not but be Astonished at the Conduct of M. De Chaumont When in the Moment of my departure from Groa he produced a Paper (a Concordat) for me to Sign in common with Officers Whom I had Commissioned but a few days before. — Had that Paper or even a less dishonourable one been proposed to me at the begining I would have rejected it with Just Contempt, and the Word "Deplacement" Among Others should have been Unnecessary — I cannot however even now suppose that he was Authorized by the Court to make such a bargin with me — Nor can I suppose that the Minister of the Marine Meant that M. De Chaumont should consider me merely as a Colleague with the Commanders of the other Ships And communicated to them not only all he Knew but all he thought respecting our desination and opperations — M. De Chaumont has made me Various Reproaches on account of the Expence of the Bon homme Richard wherewith I cannot think I have been Justly chargeable — M. De Chamillard can attest that the Bon homme Richard was at last far from being well fitted or Armed for War — If any Person or Persons who have been charged with the Expence of that Armament have Acted Wrong the fault must not be laid to my Charge.

I had not the Authority to Superintend that Armament and the Persons who had authority were so far from giving me what I thought necessary that M. De Chaumont even refused among other things to allow me Irons to secure Prisoners of War.

In short while my Life remains If I have any Capacity to render good & Acceptible Services to the Common Cause no Man will step forth with greater Cheerfulness and Alacrity than myself — But I am not made to be dishonoured nor can I accept of the half Confidence of any Man living; of Course I cannot consistent with my Honour and a Prospect of success Undertake Future Expeditions Unless when the Object and distination is communicated to me alone and to no other Person in the Marine line. — In cases where Troops are Embarked a like confidence is due alone to their Commander in Chief — On no other condition will I even under take the Chief Command of a Private Expedition and where I do not command in Chief I have no desire to be in the Secret.

Captain Cottineau Engaged the Countess of Scarborough and took her after an Hours Action While the Bon homme Richard engaged the Serapis — The Countess of Scarborough is an Armed Ship of 20 Six Pounders and was Commanded by a King's Officer —

In the Action the Countess of Scarborough and the Serapis were at a considerable distance asunder and the Alliance as I am Informed Fired into the Pallas & Killed some Men. If it should be asked why the Convoy was Suffered to escape I must answer that I was myself in no Condition to pursue; And that none of the rest shewed any inclination not even M. Ricot who had held off at a distance to Windward during the whole Action; and withheld by Force the Pilot Boat with my Lieutenant and Fifteen Men. — The Alliance too was in a

State to pursue the Fleet not having had a Single Man Wounded or a Single Shot fired at her from the Serapis and only three that did Execution from the Countess of Scarborough at such a distance that One Stuck in the Side and the other two Just touched and then dropped into the Water — The Alliance Killed one Man Only on board the Serapis — As Captain Cottineau charged himself with Manning and Securing the Prisoners of the Countess of Scarborough — I think the Escape of the Baltic Fleet cannot so well be charged to his account.

I should have mentioned that the Main Mast and Mizen Top Mast of the Serapis fell Over Board soon after the Captain had come onboard the Bonhomme Richard.

Uppon the whole the Captain of the Alliance has behaved so very ill in every respect that I must Complain loudly of his Conduct — He pretends that he is authorized to act independent of my Command — I have been taught the contrary; but supposing it to be so his Conduct has been base and unpardonable. M. De Chamillard will explain the Particulars. — Either Captain Landais or myself is highly Criminal and one or the other must be Punished.

I forbear to take any steps with him Untill I have the advice and Approbation of your Excellency. I have been advised by all the Officers of the Squadron to put Landais under Arest but as I have postponed it so long I will bear with him a little longer Untill the return of my Express.

We this Day Anchored here having since the Action been tossed to and fro by contrary Winds — I wished to have gained the Road of Dunkirk on account of our Prisoners but was over Ruled by the Majority of my Colleagues.

I shall hasten up to Amsterdam and there If I meet with no Orders for my Goverment I will take the Advice of the French Ambassador. It is my present intention to have the Countess of Scarborough ready to Transport the Prisoners from hence to Dunkirk Unless it should be found more Expedient to deliver them to the English Ambassador taking his Obligation to send to Dunkirk &c. Immediately an equal Number of Americans. I am under Strong apprehensions that our Object here will fail and that thro' the Imprudence of M. De Chaumont Who has communicated every thing he Knew or thought on the Matter to Persons who cannot help talking of it at a full Table — This is the way he Keeps State secrets. Tho' he never mentioned the Affair to me. I am ever with the Highest Sentiments of grateful Esteem and Respect. Honoured and dear Sir Your very Obliged Friend & very Humble Servant

William Moultrie:
Journal, April 2–May 12, 1780

Sunday, 2d.

Last night the enemy broke ground, and this morning, appeared two redoubts; one nearly opposite the nine gun battery, on the right of the horn-work; and the other, a little to the left of the same, at about twelve hundred yards distance from our lines.

Monday, 3d.

The enemy employed in completing their two redoubts, and erecting one on our left, at an equal distance from the rest.

Tuesday, 4th.

Several deserters within these three or four days, who say the enemy on Thursday last had upwards of twenty men killed and wounded; among the latter, a lieutenant colonel of the 60th regiment; Lord St. Clair badly; and that they are bringing their cannon on the neck: since the appearance of the enemy's works, they have been cannonaded: two ten inch and one seven inch mortars were removed from the Bay, and employed in retarding them. The enemy all this day employed in finishing their redoubts, and throwing up a line of communication.

Wednesday, 5th.

Last night the enemy continued their approaches to Hamstead-hill, on which they erected a battery for twelve cannon; and a mortar battery a little in the rear. The cannon and mortars employed as usual, in annoying their works: the battery from Wappoo, and the gallies, have thrown several shot into town; by which, one of the inhabitants in King-street, was killed.

Thursday, 6th.

The enemy approached from their centre redoubt and erected a five gun battery on the angle, between batteries No. 11 and 12. The Virginians,* under Brigadier General

*About seven-hundred.

Woodford, got in by the way of Addison's-ferry; and some North-Carolina militia under Colonel Harrington.

Friday, 7th.

This afternoon twelve sail of the enemy's vessels, passed Fort Moultrie, under a very heavy fire; one of them, supposed to be a store ship . . . having met with some accident, ran aground in the cove, where she was blown up by her own people: the remainder were ten square rigged vessels; viz. one fifty and two forty-four gun ships; four frigates; two ships, supposed to be store ships; a schooner and sloop anchored under Fort Johnson.

Saturday, 8th.

The enemy employed in finishing their batteries on the right.

Sunday, 9th.

The enemy last night continued their approaches from their redoubt on the left, and threw up a battery for ten cannon, against the angle of our advanced redoubt, and the redan No. 7. Some shot were thrown at the shipping, by our batteries in town, but without effect.

Monday, 10th.

Sir Henry Clinton, and Admiral Arbuthnot summoned the town.

SUMMONS TO MAJ. GEN. LINCOLN.

'April 10th, 1780.

'Sir Henry Clinton, K. B. general and commander in chief of his majesty's forces, laying on the Atlantic, from Nova-Scotia, &c. &c. &c. and Vice-Admiral Arbuthnot, commander in chief of his majesty's ships in North-America, &c. &c. &c. regretting the effusion of blood, and consonant to humanity towards the town and garrison of Charlestown, of the havock and desolation with which they are threatened from the formidable force surrounding them by land and sea. An alternative is offered at this hour to the inhabitants, of saving their lives and property contained in the town, or of abiding by the fatal consequences of a cannonade and storm.

'Should the place in a fallacious security, or its commander in a wanton indifference to the fate of its inhabitants, delay the surrender, or should public stores or shipping be destroyed, the resentment of an exasperated soldiery may intervene; but the same mild and compassionate offer can never be renewed. The respective commanders, who hereby summons the town, do not apprehend so rash a part, as further resistance will be taken, but rather that the gates will be opened, and themselves received with a degree of confidence which will forebode further reconciliation.

'HENRY CLINTON.
'M. ARBUTHNOT.'

FROM GEN. LINCOLN.
'Head-Quarters, Charlestown,
'April 10th, 1780.

'Gentlemen,

'I have received your summons of this date; sixty days have passed since it has been known that your intentions against this town were hostile; in which, time has been offered to abandon it; but duty and inclination point to the propriety of supporting it to the last extremity.

'I have the honor to be,
'Your Excellency's humble servant.
'B. LINCOLN.'

Tuesday and Wednesday, 11th and 12th.

The enemy busied in completing their works and mounting their cannon.

Thursday, 13th.

Between 9 and 10 o'clock this morning, the enemy opened their cannon and mortar batteries. The cannonade and bombardment continued, with short intermissions, until midnight: the gallies and battery at Wappoo also fired. An embrazure at redan No. 7 destroyed; a sergeant and private of the North-Carolina brigade killed; a twenty-six pounder destroyed, and one eighteen pounder dismounted, in the flanking battery, on the right: some women and children killed in town. The enemy's cannon were chiefly twenty-four pounders; and their mortars from five and an half, to ten inches: they threw several carcasses from eight and ten inch mortars, by which two houses were burnt.

Friday, 14th.

The enemy began an approach on the right, and kept up a
fire of small arms. Cannonade and bombard continued. One
sergeant of the North-Carolinians killed by a cannon ball: one
of the militia artillery killed, and one wounded: two matrosses
of the South-Carolina artillery killed.

Saturday, 15th.

The enemy continued approaching on the right: the mortars ordered to the right, and commence a firing immediately,
to annoy them. A continual fire of small arms, cannon, and
mortars. A battery of two guns, opened by the enemy at
Stiles' place, on James-Island. Major Grimball's corps of militia, relieved from the advance redoubt, by a detachment of
continental artillery, commanded by Major Mitchell.

Sunday, 16th.

It is said the enemy attempted to land at Hobcaw-neck
with two gun boats, but were prevented by Col. Malmadie.
Two 18 pounders, a quantity of provisions, and other valuable
articles got out of the wreck of the vessel near Fort Moultrie.

Monday, 17th.

A man, inhabitant of the town, killed by a cannon ball, and
a woman wounded; both from Wappoo battery.

Tuesday, 18th.

The enemy continued a warm firing from their cannon,
mortars, and small arms. Mr. Neyle, aid-de-camp to Gen.
Moultrie, killed by a cannon ball. We advanced a breast-work
to the left of the square redoubt, for riflemen, to annoy
the enemy on their approach. Five men killed by small arms;
and three wounded by a shell: a sentinel at the abbattis had
his arm shot off by one of our own cannon: a twelve
pounder* bursted in the horn-work, by which two men
were much hurt. The enemy ceased throwing large shells. We
hear that our cavalry under General Huger, have been de-

---

*This was one of the guns belonging to the Acteon frigate, that got on
shore while engaged with Fort Moultrie, in 1776, and was burnt. It is remarkable that eight or ten of those guns which we weighed, and mounted on
our lines, were every one of them bursted, after two or three rounds: which
makes me suppose that their being heated by the fire of the ship, and suddenly plunging into the water while red-hot, destroyed their metallic parts,
and left only the dross behind.

feated*; and that we lost between 20 or 30 killed and wounded, among the former was Major Vernier of Paulaski's legion. General Scott with the light-infantry crossed Cooper-river, into town: about 40 Virginians got in last night. The enemy continued their approaches to the right, within 250 yards of the front of the square redoubt: they threw during the night a great number of shells from sixteen royals and Cohorns, chiefly in the North-Carolina camp: one man killed, and two wounded.

Wednesday, 19th.

The enemy began an approach from the left battery, towards our advanced redoubt; and moved some mortars into the former: they also advanced on Hobcaw-neck, and exchanged a few shot with our advance party. Two or three persons killed in town.

Thursday, 20th.

The approaches continued on the left; their mortars removed from their left battery, into their approaches; an eighteen pounder dismounted at Captain Bottard's battery on the right; four of their gallies after dark, moved from Wappoo-creek to the shipping at Fort Johnson, under a very heavy fire from our batteries. The enemy retreated from Hobcaw across Wappataw-bridge, which it is said they have burnt. Two magazines in the batteries commanded by Capt. Sisk, blew up by shells, but no persons hurt.

Friday, 21st.

A flag sent to Sir Henry Clinton.

'Charlestown, April 21st, 1780.

'Sir.

'I am willing to enter into the consideration of terms of capitulation, if such can be obtained as are honorable to the army, and safe for the inhabitants. I have to propose a cessation of hostilities for six hours, for the purpose of digesting such articles.

'I have the honor to be,
'Your Excellency's, &c.
'B. LINCOLN.

'His Ex. SIR HENRY CLINTON.'

---

*This was a shameful surprise, at Monk's-corner, in the open day.

FROM SIR HENRY CLINTON.
Camp before Charlestown, April 21st, 1780.
'Sir,
'Admiral Arbuthnot, who commands the fleet, should have
been addressed jointly with me on this occasion. As I wish to
communicate with him, and as I give my consent to a cessation of hostilities for six hours, I desire an aid-de-camp* may
pass to the ships, with a letter, and my request, that the battery on James'-Island may desist firing.

'I have the honor to be, &c.

'H. CLINTON.'

'Maj. Gen. LINCOLN.'

ARTICLES OF CAPITULATION PROPOSED
BY MAJOR GENERAL LINCOLN.

'Charlestown, April 21st, 1780.

ARTICLE 1.   That all acts of hostilities and works shall cease
between the naval and land forces of Great-Britain and
America, in this state, until the articles of capitulation shall be
agreed on, signed, or collectively rejected.

ART. 2.   That the town, forts and fortifications belonging
to them, shall be surrendered to the commander in chief of
the British forces, such as they now stand.

ART. 3.   That the several troops garrisoning this town and
forts, including the French and American sailors, the French
invalids, the North-Carolina and South-Carolina militia, and
such of the Charlestown militia as may choose to leave this
place, shall have thirty-six hours to withdraw to Lamprier's,
after the capitulation be accepted and signed on both sides;
and that those troops shall retire with the usual honors of
war, and carry off at that time their arms, field-artillery, ammunition and baggage, and such of their stores as they may
be able to transport.

ART. 4.   That after the expiration of the thirty-six hours
mentioned in the preceding article, the British troops before

---

*The aid was permitted to pass to the ships, from Gibbs', round Ashley-
river, to the vessels near Fort Johnson.

the town shall take possession of it, and those now at Wappataw shall proceed to Fort Moultrie.

ART 5.   That the American army thus collected at Lamprier's, shall have ten days, from the expiration of the thirty-six hours before mentioned, to march wherever General Lincoln may think proper, to the eastward of Cooper's-river, without any movement being made by the British troops, or part of them, out of the town or Fort Moultrie.

ART. 6.   That the sick and wounded of the American and French hospitals, with their medicines, stores, the surgeons and director-general, shall remain in the town, and be supplied with the necessaries requisite, until provisions shall be made for their removal, which will be as speedily as possible.

ART. 7.   That no soldier shall be encouraged to desert, or permitted to inlist on either side.

ART. 8.   That the French consul, his house, papers and other moveable property, shall be protected and remain untouched.

ART. 9.   The continental ships of war, Providence, Boston, and Renger, now in this harbor, with the French ship of war, the Adventure, shall have liberty to proceed to sea, with the necessary stores on board, and go unmolested, the three former to Philadelphia and the latter to Cape Francois, with the French invalids mentioned in article three.

ART. 10.   That the citizens shall be protected in their persons and property.

ART. 11.   That twelve months be allowed to those who do not choose to live under the British government, to dispose of their effects, real and personal, in the state, without any molestation whatever, and remove such parts thereof, as they choose, with themselves and families; and during that time, they, or any of them, may have in their option to reside occasionally in town or country.

ART. 12.   That the same protection to their persons and property, and the same time for the removal of their effects be given to the subjects of France and Spain, residing amongst us, as are required for the citizens residing amongst us in the preceding article.

'B. LINCOLN.'

Sir Henry Clinton and Vice-Admiral Arbuthnot
to Major General Lincoln.

'Camp before Charlestown, April 21st, 1780.

'Sir,   8 o'clock at night.

'We have in answer to your third article (for we cannot proceed further) to refer you to our former offer, as terms, which, although you cannot claim, yet we consent to grant. These however, must be accepted immediately, and responsible hostages, of the rank of field-officers, must be sent us as securities, that the custom of war in these cases must be strictly adhered to, that no person of the garrison or inhabitant be permitted to go out, nothing be removed or destroyed, and no ships or vessels pass from the town. All dependant posts are to be included in the surrender, and the hostages to be as answerable for these as the town. Your answer is expected at ten o'clock, at which hour, hostilities will commence again, unless our offers are closed with.

'H. Clinton.

'M. Arbuthnot.'

'Maj. Gen. Lincoln.'

On the summons of Sir Henry Clinton, and Admiral Arbuthnot, General Lincoln called a council of war, of field-officers, on the propriety of evacuating the town. They were of opinion 'that it was unadviseable, because of the opposition made to it by the civil authority and the inhabitants, and because, even if they could succeed in defeating a large body of the enemy posted in their way, they had not a sufficiency of boats to cross the Santee before they might be overtaken by the whole British army.' The council therefore recommended a capitulation.

Saturday, 22d.

Approaches continued on our left in front of the advance redoubt. The enemy kept up a heavy cannonade. Three men wounded.

Sunday, 23d.

Approaches continued on our right and left; those on the right within twenty yards of the wet ditch. About eight at night two deserters from the enemy; they report them to have received a considerable reinforcement* from New-York, and that they detached to day, ten companies of light-infantry to get footing at Haddrell's-point, they say the enemy have lost a number of men by our shells.

Monday, 24th.

A party composed of three hundred men, Virginians and South-Carolinians, under the command of Lieutenant Colonel Henderson, made a sortie upon the enemy's approaches, opposite the advance redoubts at day light, they were completely surprised, and lost about fifteen or twenty men killed with the bayonet, besides twelve persons brought off, seven of whom were wounded. Captain Moultrie killed and two men wounded on our side. The enemy attempted to support their guards from the trenches; but on receiving rounds of grape, made them retreat. The prisoners report their party to have been commanded by Major Hall of the 71st regiment, but no officers were to be found. Colonel Parker killed about eight o'clock, looking over the parapet; two privates killed and seven wounded. The greatest part of the 1st South-Carolina regiment came into garrison this morning, with Colonel C. Pinckney from Fort Moultrie.

Tuesday, 25th.

Between twelve and one this morning, a heavy fire of cannon and musketry, commenced from our advanced redoubt, and the right of the lines occasioned as it was said, by the enemy's advancing in column. It is certain they gave several huzzas, but whether they were out of their trenches, it is not clear; they kept up a very heavy and incessant fire with musketry, for thirty minutes. The enemy threw several light balls into town. Two o'clock P. M. Lord Cornwallis at Mount-Pleasant.

Wednesday, 26th.

The Lord George Germaine, and a sloop, joined the enemy's fleet. The enemy were very quiet all day, and last night; we suppose they are bringing cannon into their third parallel: they are strengthening their approaches: Lord Cornwallis took possession of Mount-Pleasant yesterday.

*Lord Cornwallis with 2500 men.

Brigadier General Du Portail* arrived from Philadelphia. The garrison ordered to be served with the usual quantity of provision; a plentiful supply having been received. One killed; Captain Goodwin of the third South-Carolina battalion, and one private wounded.

On General Du Portail delaring that the works were not tenable, a council was again called upon for an evacuation, and to withdraw privately with the continental troops: when the citizens were informed upon what the council were deliberating, some of them came into council, and expressed themselves very warmly, and declared to General Lincoln, that if he attempted to withdraw the troops, and leave the citizens; that they would cut up his boats, and open the gates to the enemy: this put a stop to all thoughts of an evacuation of the troops, and nothing was left for us, but to make the best terms we could.

Thursday, 27th.

About 1 o'clock in the afternoon, four of the enemy's gallies, an armed sloop, and a frigate, moved down the river, and anchored opposite the mouth of Hog's-Island creek. Five militia men, late of James'-Island, deserted last night from South-bay in a boat. Our post at Lamprier's-ferry, retreated across the river, in the night, to Charlestown, after spiking up four eighteen pounders, they were obliged to leave. One private killed, and five wounded.

Friday, 28th.

Colonel Charles Pinckney is requested to assist General Moultrie in directing and disposing the artillery of the different batteries and works in and about town. Two deserters from the enemy at Hobcaw, brought over by our troops that retreated last night. Some supernumerary officers quitted the garrison. The enemy busy in throwing up their third parallel, within a few yards of the canal. Our fatigue employed in inclosing the horn-work: two privates killed; Lieutenant Campaign of the North-Carolinians, and two privates wounded.

*As soon as General Du Portail came into garrison, and looked at the enemy, and at our works, he declared they were not tenable; and that the British might have taken the town, ten days ago: he wished to leave the garrison immediately, but General Lincoln would not allow him, because it would dispirit the troops.

Saturday, 29th.

We are throwing up a redoubt on the right of the horn-work. The enemy's batteries remarkably silent; they seem to intend erecting two batteries in their third parallel; one at the gate opposite the horn-work, and the other in front of Col. Parker's regiment. A heavy bombardment by the enemy during the night: a deserter from them; who says that they are preparing a bridge to throw over the canal. Captain Templeton of the fourth Georgia battalion, wounded by a shell, of which he died.

Sunday, 30th.

The deserter yesterday further tells us that the huzzas which occasioned the firing last Tuesday morning, were from the enemy's working parties, who thought we were sallying: their engineer, he says, had ordered them, in that event, to give three huzzas, and fall back upon the covering party's, who not having been apprised of it, received them as an enemy; in consequence of which, a considerable number of them were killed and wounded: he affirms the account of the enemy's receiving a reinforcement from New-York, and says their detachment on Hobcaw, amounts to upwards of 2,000; that they look for their shipping up every night; and are preparing a large number of fascines to fill up the canal. Lieutenant Hall of the North-Carolinians wounded; his leg broke by a grape-shot, from our own batteries. Lieutenant Philips of the Virginians wounded in his thigh by a shell.

Monday, May 1st.

Our fatigue employed in erecting another redoubt on the left of the horn-work, and completing the new works. The enemy appear to be about another battery in their third parallel, opposite No. 12, on our right. The garrison congratulated in the general orders of yesterday, on the certainty of large reinforcements being at hand. Five men deserted from the galley last night, Captain Montford of the North-Carolinians wounded, and Mr. Lord,* a volunteer in the con-

*Mr. Lord and Mr. Basquin, two volunteers, were sleeping upon a matrass together, when Mr. Lord was killed by a shell falling upon him, and Mr. Basquin at the same time, had the hair of his head burnt, and did not wake till he was called upon. The fatigue in that advance redoubt, was so great, for

tinental artillery, killed yesterday by a shell, in the advanced redoubt. A smart bombardment during the day.

Tuesday, 2d.

Last night the enemy were making a ditch on the right, to drain our canal. A number of men killed and wounded within these last three or four days; their number not ascertained. A nine pounder bursted at battery No. 12, and a quantity of fixed ammunition blown up by accident at batteries No. 10 and 12. The enemy throw shells at us charged with rice and sugar.*

Wednesday, 3d.

Our fatigue employed in fixing picquets, &c.

Thursday, 4th.

Our rations of meat reduced to six ounces, coffee and sugar allowed to the soldiers. The fire from the enemy's cannon still slack, but they do not spare their shells.

Friday, 5th.

Captain William Mitchell of the continental artillery, badly wounded by a shell.

----

want of sleep, that many faces were so swelled they could scarcely see out of their eyes. I was obliged to relieve Major Mitchell the commanding officer: they were constantly upon the look out for the shells that were continually falling among them, it was by far, the most dangerous post on the lines. On my visit to this battery, not having been there for a day or two, I took the usual way of going in, which was a bridge that crossed our ditch, quite exposed to the enemy, in the mean time, they had advanced their works within seventy or eighty yards of the bridge, which I did not know of; as soon as I had stepped upon the bridge, an uncommon number of bullets whistled about me, on looking to my right, I could just see the heads of about twelve or fifteen men firing upon me, from behind a breastwork, I moved on and got in; when Major Mitchell saw me, he asked me which way I came in, I told him over the bridge, he was astonished, and said, "sir it is a thousand to one that you were not killed," and told me, "that we had a covered way to go out and in," which he conducted me through on my return. I stayed in this battery about a quarter of an hour, to give the necessary orders, in which time we were constantly skipping about to get out of the way of the shells thrown from their howitzers, they were not more than one hundred yards from our works, and throwing their shells in bushels on our front and left flanks.

*They were misinformed if they supposed us in want of those articles.

Saturday, 6th.

From all appearance, Fort Moultrie* is in the hands of the enemy; a British flag was seen flying on the flag-staff.

Sunday, 7th.

The above confirmed. Our principal magazine† near being destroyed, by a thirteen inch shell bursting within ten yards of it.

Monday, 8th.

A second summons from Sir Henry Clinton informing us of the fall of Fort Moultrie, and that the remains of our cavalry were cut to pieces the day before yesterday. The embrazures of the enemies batteries in the third parallel‡ opened last night. Our meat quite out, rice sugar and coffee served out.

———

About eleven o'clock, A. M. on the twelfth of May, we marched out between 1500 and 1600 continental troops, (leaving five or six hundred sick and wounded in the hospitals) without the horn-work, on the left, and piled our arms; the officers marched the men back to the barracks, where a British guard was placed over them; the British then asked where our second division was? they were told these were all the continentals we had, except the sick and wounded; they were astonished, and said we had made a gallant defence. Captain Rochfort had marched in with a detachment of the artillery to receive the returns of our artillery stores: while we

*Fort Moultrie was given up without firing a gun.

†The old magazine behind St. Philip's Church: in consequence of that shell falling so near, I had the powder (10,000 pounds) removed to the north east corner, under the exchange, and had the doors and windows bricked up. Notwithstanding the British had possession of Charlestown so long, they never discovered the powder, although their provost was the next apartment to it, and after the evacuation, when we came into town, we found the powder as we left it.

‡When the enemy's third parallel was completed, we had sand-bags placed upon the top of our lines, for the riflemen to fire through. The sand-bags were about two feet long and one foot thick, we laid down first two of them, three or four inches one from the other, and a third laid upon the top of the two, which made a small loop hole for the riflemen to fire through, the British immediately followed our example: many men were killed and wounded through these holes.

were in the horn-work together in conversation, he said 'sir
you have made a gallant defence, but you had a great many
rascals among you,' (and mentioned names) 'who came out
every night and gave us information of what was passing in
your garrison.' The militia marched out the same day and delivered up their arms at the same place; the continental officers went into town to their quarters, where they remained a
few days to collect their baggage, and signed their paroles,
then were sent over to Haddrell's point. The militia remained
in Charlestown. The next day the militia were ordered to parade near Lynch's pasture,* and to bring all their arms with
them, guns, swords, pistols, &c. and those that did not
strictly comply, were threatened with having the grenadiers
turned in among them; this threat brought out the aged, the
timid, the disaffected, and the infirm, many of them who had
never appeared during the whole siege, which swelled the
number of militia prisoners to, at least, three times the number of men we ever had upon duty: I saw the column march
out, and was surprised to see it so large; but many of them we
had excused, from age and infirmities; however, they would
do to enrol on a conqueror's list. When the British received
their arms, they put them in waggons, and carried them to a
store-house, where we had deposited our fixed ammunition
(about 4,000 pounds) and although they were informed by
some of our officers that the arms were loaded, and several of
them went off before the explosion took place, yet in taking
them out of the waggons they threw them so carelessly into
the store, that some at last set fire to the powder, which blew
up the whole guard of fifty men, and many others that were
standing by; their carcasses, legs, and arms were seen in the
air, and scattered over several parts of the town. One man was
dashed with violence against the steeple of the new independant church, which was at a great distance from the explosion, and left the marks of his body there for several days. The
houses in the town received a great shock, and the window
sashes rattled as if they would tumble out of the frames.

Most of our militia were still together; after delivering up
their arms, they went in a body to assist in extinguishing the

*Where the spring pump now stands.

fire, that had communicated itself to the neighboring houses; and while they were working they were under the dreadful apprehensions lest the magazine should take fire, as the work-house and others that were next to it were in a blaze; at last some timid person called out, that 'the magazine was on fire,' this gave the alarm; every one took fright, both British and Americans, and instantly broke off from work, and run away as fast as possible through the streets, throwing down, and tumbling over each other, and others coming, after tumbling over them, in endeavoring to get as far from the expected explosion, as possible: I have heard some of them say, that although they were so confoundedly frightened at the time, they could not keep from laughing, to see the confusion and tumbling over each other: the alarm was soon brought into the town; I was then in a house, joining St. Michael's church, with some company; I advised the going out of the house, and walking to South-bay, because I was apprehensive, from the great shock which was felt in the houses, from the explosion of 4,000 pounds of powder, that, should the magazine blow up, which had 10,000 pounds of powder in it, many of the houses in town would be thrown down: on my way thither, I met a British officer, who asked me how much powder was in the magazine; I told him 10,000 pounds: 'Sir,' said he, 'if it takes fire, it will blow your town to hell!' I replied, 'I expected it would give a hell of a blast!' The British were very much alarmed at the explosion; all the troops were turned out under arms, and formed: they could not tell what was the matter: some of the British and Hessian officers supposed it was designed by us: I was abused, and taken up by a Hessian officer (whose guard was at Broughton's-battery) he was very angry, and said to me, 'you, General Moultrie, you rebel's have done this on purpose, as they did at New-York;' and ordered his guard to take me a prisoner, into a house near, and placed a sentry at the door, where a number of us were confined; but I soon got a note over a back way, to General Leslie, acquainting him of my situation, upon which he immediately sent one of his aids to me, with an apology, that my confinement was contrary to orders, and ordered the sentry from the door: after a little time, the alarm subsided; they went back, and stopped the progress of the fire: and if they had considered for a moment, they would have found that it was almost impossible for the magazine to take fire from the adjacent houses, because it was inclosed with a high brick wall; and the magazine itself was built of brick, and bomb proof.

The Sentiments of a Lady in New-Jersey

New-Jersey Gazette, July 12, 1780

THE war carried on by the British nation against my native country cannot fail to excite in the humane and virtuous mind sentiments very unfavourable to the authors and instruments of such a variety of complicated evils and misfortunes as we have suffered in the course of it.

The contest, begun on their part without principle, has been prosecuted without humanity. Devoid of those sentiments and that conduct which do so much honour to the civilized nations of Europe even in time of war; they have thrown off all restraint, and fully displayed in their military operations in this part of the world the true characteristicks of their country—a fierce and barbarous spirit, resisting, contrary to the common rule, the ordinary effects which refinement of manners and a high degree of polish usually have on the minds of men in softening them to humanity, constitutes their real character.

Was I unconnected with America by ties of friendship or blood, was I not attached by that love of one's country which is inherent in some degree in every breast, and partakes of the nature of that instinctive affection which we bear to our parents and kindred; was I situated in a distant part of the world, unagitated by the incidents of the day, which are the more interesting the nigher we are to the scene of war, the bare recital of their unjust claims, their cruelties and their crimes would fill my soul with horror, and I should regard them not only as unprovoked aggressors, but as enemies by principle and example to mankind in general.

But as if it were not enough unjustly to spill the blood of our countrymen, to lay waste the fields, to destroy our dwellings and even the houses consecrated and set apart for the worship of the Supreme Being, they have desolated the aged and unprotected, and even waged war against our sex. Who that has heard of the burning of Charlestown in

New-England,—of the wanton destruction of Norfolk and Falmouth,—of their wasting the fine improvements in the environs of Philadelphia,—of the tragical death of Miss M'Crea, torn from her house, murdered and scalped by a band of savages hired and set on by British emissaries,—of the melancholy fate of Mrs. Caldwell, put to death in her own house in the late incursion of the enemy,—and the general havock which at this moment marks their footsteps in their route through a part of this state—but would wish to avert from themselves, their kindred, their property, and their country in general, so heavy misfortunes.

These are truths sufficiently affecting to touch with pity and compassion even hearts hard as marble, and cannot fail to make a deep and lasting impression in the minds of all.

These feelings and these sentiments have been particularly manifested by the Ladies of Philadelphia in their liberal contributions of money towards rendering the situation of the soldiery of the continental army more convenient and comfortable. It is to this class of men we more immediately owe our defence and protection; they have born the weight of the war, and met danger in every quarter; and what is higher praise, they have with Roman courage and perseverance suffered the extremes of heat and cold, the attacks of hunger, and the pain of long and fatiguing marches through parts before unexplored by armies, and which had scarcely ever before born the print of human feet.

It was enough for these brave men to reflect they were engaged in the best and most glorious of all causes, that of defending the rights and liberties of their country, to induce them to behave with so much resolution and fortitude. Their many sufferings so chearfully undergone, highly merit our gratitude and sincere thanks, and claim all the assistance we can afford their distresses. If we have it not in our power to do from the double motive of religion and a love of liberty, what some Ladies of the highest rank in the Court of France every day perform from motives of religion only in the hospitals of the sick and diseased, let us animate one another to contribute from our purses in proportion to our circumstances towards the support and comfort of the brave men who are fighting and suffering for us in the field. We ought to do this if we desire to keep the enemy from our borders, if we wish that there may not be occasion to call forth our husbands, our children, and our dearest friends, to risque their lives again in our defence. I can truly say that I have experienced the most heart-rending anxieties when my relations and friends have been called upon as free citizens to march against the enemy; and the pangs I have suffered on such occasions have made it easy for me to give credit to the account we have in the history of ancient Rome of the two matrons who died for joy, one at the gate of the city, the other at her own house, at the sight of their sons who returned in safety after the battle at the Lake of Thrasymene:—When I say this, I mean only to express the feelings of a woman, my sentiments being ever in favour of that spirit which my countrymen have so often manifested when their services have been required.

Otho Holland Williams:
Narrative of the Battle of Camden

ON the 15th of August, 1780, General Gates issued the following: —

After General Orders — "The sick, the extra artillery stores, the heavy baggage, and such quarter-master's stores, as are not immediately wanted, to march this evening, under a guard, to Waxaws.

"To this order the general requests the brigadier generals, to see that those under their command, pay the most exact and scrupulous obedience.

"Lieutenant Colonel Edmonds, with the remaining guns of the park, will take post and march with the Virginia brigade, under General Stevens; he will direct, as any deficiency happens in the artillery affixed to the other brigades, to supply it immediately; his military staff, and a proportion of his officers, with forty of his men, are to attend him and await his orders.

"The troops will be ready to march precisely at ten o'clock, in the following order, viz: —

"Colonel Armand's advance; cavalry, commanded by Colonel Armand; Colonel Porterfield's light infantry upon the right flank of Colonel Armand, in indian file, two hundred yards from the road; Major Armstrong's light infantry in the same order as Colonel Porterfield's, upon the left flank of the legion.

"Advance guard of foot, composed of the advance pickets, first brigade of Maryland, second brigade of Maryland, division of North Carolina, Virginia division; rear guard, volunteer cavalry, upon the flank of the baggage, equally divided.

"In this order, the troops will proceed on their march this night.

"In case of an attack by the enemy's cavalry in front, the light infantry upon each flank will instantly move up and give, and continue, the most galling fire upon the enemy's horse. This will enable Colonel Armand, not only to support the shock of the enemy's charge, but finally to rout them; the colonel will therefore consider the order to stand the attack of the enemy's cavalry, be their numbers what they may, as positive.

"General Stevens will immediately order one captain, two lieutenants, one ensign, three sergeants, one drum, and sixty rank and file to join Colonel Porterfield's infantry; these are to be taken from the most experienced woodsmen, and men every way the fittest for the service.

"General Caswell will likewise complete Major Armstrong's light infantry to their original number. These must be immediately marched to the advanced posts of the army.

"The troops will observe the profoundest silence upon the march; and any soldier who offers to fire without the command of his officer, must be instantly put to death.

"When the ground will admit of it, and the near approach of the enemy renders it necessary, the army will (when ordered) march in columns.

"The artillery at the head of their respective brigades, and the baggage in the rear.

"The guard of the heavy baggage will be composed of the remaining officers and soldiers of the artillery, one captain, two subalterns, four sergeants, one drum, and sixty rank and file; and no person whatever is to presume to send any other soldier upon that service.

"All bat men, waiters, &c. who are soldiers taken from the line, are forthwith to join their regiments, and act with their masters while they are upon duty.

"The tents of the whole army are to be struck at tattoo."

After writing this order, the general communicated it to the deputy adjutant general, showing him, at the same time, a rough estimate of the forces under his command, making them upwards of seven thousand. That this calculation was exaggerated, the deputy adjutant general could not but suspect, from his own observation. He, therefore, availed himself of the general's orders, to call all the general officers in the army, to a council, to be held in Rugley's Barn — to call also upon the commanding officers of corps for *a field return*; in making which, they were to be as exact as possible; and, as he was not required to attend the council, he busied himself in collecting these returns and forming an abstract for the general's better information. This abstract was presented to the general just as the council broke up, and immediately upon his coming out of the door. He cast his eyes upon the numbers of rank and file *present fit for duty,* which was exactly *three thousand and fifty-two.* He said there were no less than *thirteen* general officers in council; and intimated something about the disproportion between the numbers of officers and privates. It was replied, "Sir, the number of the latter are certainly much below the estimate formed this morning; but," said the general, "these are enough for our purpose." What that was, was not communicated to the deputy adjutant general. The general only added — "there was no dissenting voice in the council where the orders have just been read" — and then gave them to be published to the army.

Although there had been no dissenting voice in the council, the orders were no sooner promulgated, than they became the subject of animadversion. Even those who had been dumb in council, said that there had been no consultation — that the orders were read to them, and all opinion seemed suppressed by the very positive and decisive terms in which they were expressed. Others could not imagine how it could be conceived, that an army, consisting of more than two-thirds militia, and which had never been once exercised in arms together, could form columns, and perform other manœuvres in the night, and in the face of an enemy. But, of all the officers, Colonel Armand took the greatest exception. He seemed to think the *positive* orders respecting himself, implied a doubt of his courage — declared that cavalry had never before been put in the front of a line of battle in the dark — and that the disposition, as it respected his corps, proceeded from resentment in the general, on account of a previous altercation between them about horses, which the general had ordered to be taken from the officers of the army, to expedite the movement of the artillery through the wilderness. A great deal was said upon the occasion; but, the time was short, and the officers and soldiers, generally, not knowing, or believing any more than the general, that any considerable body of the enemy were to be met with out of Camden, acquiesced with their usual cheerfulness, and were ready to march at the hour appointed.

As there were no spirits yet arrived in camp; and as, until lately, it was unusual for troops to make a forced march, or prepare to meet an enemy without some extraordinary allowance, it was unluckily conceived that molasses, would, for once, be an acceptable substitute; accordingly the hospital stores were broached, and one gill of molasses per man, and a full ration of corn meal and meat, were issued to the army previous to their march, which commenced, according to orders, at about ten o'clock at night of the 15th. But I must arrest the progress of the narrative to apologize for introducing a remark, seemingly so trivial. Nothing ought to be considered as trivial, in an army, which in any degree affects the health, or spirits of the troops; upon which often, more than upon numbers, the fate of battles depends. The troops of General Gates' army, had frequently felt the bad consequences of eating bad provision; but, at this time, a hasty meal of quick baked bread and fresh beef, with a desert of molasses, mixed with mush, or dumplings, operated so cathartically, as to disorder very many of the men, who were breaking the ranks all night, and were certainly much debilitated before the action commenced in the morning.

It has been observed, that the direct march of the American army towards Camden, and the prospect of considerable re-enforcements of militia, had induced the commanding officer, Lord Rawdon, to collect there, all the forces under his directions. And it is certain, that the seeming confidence of the American general, had inspired him with apprehensions for his principal post. Lord Cornwallis, at Charlestown, was constantly advised of the posture of affairs in the interior of the country; and, confident that Lord Rawdon could not long resist the forces that might, and probably would, be opposed to him, in a very short time resolved to march himself, with a considerable re-enforcement, to Camden. He arrived there on the 14th, and had the discernment, at once, to perceive that delay would render that situation dangerous, even to his whole force; the disaffection from his late assumed, arbitrary, and vindictive power, having become general through all the country above General Gates' line of march, as well as to the eastward of Santee, and to the westward of Wateree Rivers. He, therefore, took the resolution of attacking the new constituted American army in their open irregular encampment at Clermont. Both armies, ignorant of each other's intentions, moved about the same hour of the same night, and approaching each other, met about half way between their respective encampments, at midnight.

The first revelation of this new and unexpected scene, was occasioned by a smart, mutual salutation of small arms between the advanced guards. Some of the cavalry of Armand's legion were wounded, retreated, and threw the whole corps into disorder; which, recoiling suddenly on the front of the column of infantry, disordered the first Maryland brigade, and occasioned a general consternation through the whole line of the army. The light infantry under Porterfield, however, executed their orders gallantly; and the enemy, no less astonished than ourselves, seemed to acquiesce in a sudden suspension of hostilities. Some prisoners were taken on both sides; from one of these, the deputy adjutant general of the American army, extorted information respecting the situation and numbers of the enemy. He informed, that Lord Cornwallis commanded in person about three thousand regular British troops, which were, in line of march, about five or six hundred yards in front. Order was soon restored in the corps of infantry in the American army, and the officers were employed in forming a front line of battle, when the deputy adjutant general communicated to General Gates the information which he had from the prisoner. The general's astonishment could not be concealed. He ordered the deputy adjutant general to call another council of war. All the general officers immediately assembled in the rear of the line; the unwelcome news was communicated to them. General Gates said, "Gentlemen, what is best to be done?" All were mute for a few moments — when the gallant Stevens exclaimed, "Gentlemen, is it not too late *now* to do any thing but fight?" No other advice was offered, and the general desired the gentlemen would repair to their respective commands.

The Baron De Kalb's opinion may be inferred from the following fact: When the deputy adjutant general went to call him to council, he first told him what had been discovered. "Well," said the baron, "and has the general given you orders to retreat the army?" The baron, however, did not oppose the suggestion of General Stevens; and every measure that ensued, was preparatory for action.

Lieutenant Colonel Porterfield, in whose bravery and judicious conduct great dependance was placed, received, in the first rencontre, a mortal wound, (as it long afterwards proved,) and was obliged to retire. His infantry bravely kept the ground in front; and the American army were formed in the following order: The Maryland division, including the Delawares, on the right — the North Carolina militia in the center — and the Virginia militia on the left. It happened, that each flank was covered by a marsh, so near as to admit the removing of the first Maryland brigade to form a second line, about two hundred yards in the rear of the first. The artillery was removed from the center of the brigades, and placed in the center of the front line; and the North Carolina militia (light infantry) under Major Armstrong, which had retreated at the first rencontre, was ordered to cover a small interval between the left wing and the swampy grounds on that quarter.

Frequent skirmishes happened during the night, between the advanced parties — which served to discover the relative situations of the two armies — and as a prelude to what was to take place in the morning.

At dawn of day (on the morning of the 16th of August) the enemy appeared in front, advancing in column. Captain Singleton, who commanded some pieces of artillery, observed to Colonel Williams, that he plainly perceived the ground of the British uniform at about two hundred yards in front. The deputy adjutant general immediately ordered Captain Singleton to open his battery; and then rode to the general, who was in the rear of the second line, and informed him of the cause of the firing which he heard. He also observed to the general, that the enemy seemed to be displaying their column by the right; the nature of the ground favored this conjecture, for yet nothing was clear.

The general seemed disposed to wait events — he gave no orders. The deputy adjutant general observed, that if the enemy, in the act of displaying, were briskly attacked by General

Stevens' brigade, which was already in line of battle, the effect might be fortunate, and first impressions were important. "Sir," said the general, "that's right — let it be done." This was the last order that the deputy adjutant general received. He hastened to General Stevens, who instantly advanced with his brigade, apparently in fine spirits. The right wing of the enemy was soon discovered *in line* — it was too late to attack them displaying; nevertheless, the business of the day could no longer be deferred. The deputy adjutant general requested General Stevens to let him have forty or fifty privates, volunteers, who would run forward of the brigade, and commence the attack. They were led forward, within forty or fifty yards of the enemy, and ordered to take trees, and keep up as brisk a fire as possible. The desired effect of this expedient, to extort the enemy's fire at some distance, in order to the rendering it less terrible to the militia, was not gained. General Stevens, observing the enemy to rush on, put his men in mind of their bayonets; but, the impetuosity with which they advanced, *firing* and *huzzaing*, threw the whole body of the militia into such a panic, that they generally threw down their *loaded* arms and fled, in the utmost consternation. The unworthy example of the Virginians was almost instantly followed by the North Carolinians; only a small part of the brigade, commanded by Brigadier General Gregory, made a short pause. A part of Dixon's regiment, of that brigade, next in the line to the second Maryland brigade, fired two or three rounds of cartridge. But, a great majority of the militia, (at least two-thirds of the army) fled without firing a shot. The writer avers it of his own knowledge, having seen and observed every part of the army, from left to right, during the action. He who has never seen the effect of a panic upon a multitude, can have but an imperfect idea of such a thing. The best disciplined troops have been enervated, and made cowards by it. Armies have been routed by it, even where no enemy appeared to furnish an excuse. Like electricity, it operates instantaneously — like sympathy, it is irresistible where it touches. But, in the present instance, its action was not universal. The regular troops, who had the keen edge of sensibility rubbed off by strict discipline and hard service, saw the confusion with but little emotion. They engaged seriously in the affair; and, notwithstanding some irregularity, which was created by the militia breaking, pell mell, through the second line, order was restored there—time enough to give the enemy a severe check, which abated the fury of their assault, and obliged them to assume a more deliberate manner of acting. The second Maryland brigade, including the battalion of Delawares, on the right, were engaged with the enemy's left, which they opposed with very great firmness. They even advanced upon them, and had taken a number of prisoners, when their companions of the first brigade (which formed the second line) being greatly outflanked, and charged by superior numbers, were obliged to give ground. At this critical moment, the regimental officers of the latter brigade, reluctant to leave the field without orders, inquired for their commanding officer, (Brigadier General Smallwood) who, however, was not to be found; notwithstanding, Colonel Gunby, Major Anderson, and a number of other brave officers, assisted by the deputy adjutant general, and Major Jones, one of Smallwood's aids, rallied the brigade, and renewed the contest. Again they were obliged to give way— and were again rallied—the second brigade were still warmly engaged—the distance between the two brigades did not exceed two hundred yards—their opposite flanks being nearly upon a line perpendicular to their front. At this eventful juncture, the deputy adjutant general, anxious that the communication between them should be preserved, and wishing that, in the almost certain event of a retreat, some order might be sustained by them, hastened from the first to the second brigade, which he found precisely in the same circumstances. He called upon his own regiment, (the 6th Maryland) not to fly, and was answered by the Lieutenant Colonel, *Ford*, who said—"They have done all that can be expected of them— we are outnumbered and outflanked—see the enemy charge with bayonets." The enemy having collected their corps, and directing their whole force against these two devoted brigades, a tremendous fire of musketry was, for some time, kept up on both sides, with equal perseverance and obstinacy, until Lord Cornwallis, perceiving there was no cavalry opposed to him, pushed forward his dragoons—and his infantry charging, at the same moment, with fixed bayonets, put an end to the contest. His victory was complete. All the artillery, and a very great number of prisoners, fell into his hands — many fine fellows lay on the field — and the rout of the remainder was entire — not even a company retired in any order — every one escaped as he could. If, in this affair, the militia fled too soon, the regulars may be thought almost as blamable for remaining too long on the field; especially, after all hope of victory must have been despaired of. Let the commandants of the brigades answer for themselves. Allow the same privilege to the officers of the corps, comprising those brigades, and they will say, that they never received orders to retreat, nor any order from any *general* officer, from the commencement of the action, until it became desperate. The brave Major General, the Baron De Kalb, fought on foot, with the second brigade, and fell, mortally wounded, into the hands of the enemy, who stripped him even of his shirt; a fate which probably was avoided by other generals, only by an opportune retreat.

The torrent of unarmed militia, bore away with it, Generals Gates, Caswell, and a number of others, who *soon* saw that all was lost. General Gates, at first, conceived a hope that he might rally, at Clermont, a sufficient number to cover the retreat of the regulars; but, the farther they fled the more they were dispersed; and the generals soon found themselves abandoned by all but their aids. Lieutenant Colonel Senf, who had been on the expedition with Colonel Sumpter, returned, and overtaking General Gates, informed him of their complete success — that the enemy's redoubt, on Wateree, opposite to Camden, was first reduced, and the convoy of stores, &c. from Charleston, was decoyed, and became prize to the American party, almost without resistance. That upwards of one hundred prisoners, and forty loaded waggons, were in the hands of the party, who had sustained very little loss; but the general could avail himself nothing of this trifling advantage. The detachment under Sumpter was on the opposite side of the Wateree, marching off, as speedily as might be, to secure their booty — for the course of the firing in the morning, indicated unfavorable news from the army.

The militia, the general saw, were in air; and the regulars, he feared, were no more. The dreadful thunder of artillery and musketry had ceased, and none of his friends appeared. There was no existing corps with which the victorious detachment might unite; and the Americans had no post in the rear. He, therefore, sent orders to Sumpter to retire in the best manner he could; and proceeded himself with General Caswell towards Charlotte, an open village on a plain, about sixty miles from the fatal scene of action. The Virginians, who knew nothing of the country they were in, involuntarily reversed the route they came, and fled, most of them, to Hillsborough. General Stevens pursued them, and halted there as many as were not sufficiently refreshed before his arrival, to pursue their way home. Their terms of service, however, being very short, and no prospect presenting itself to afford another proof of their courage, General Stevens soon afterwards discharged them.

The North Carolina militia fled different ways, as their hopes led, or their fears drove them. Most of them preferring the shortest way home, scattered through the wilderness which lies between Wateree and Pee Dee Rivers, and thence towards Roanoke. Whatever these might have suffered from the disaffected, they probably were not worse off than those who retired the way they came; wherein, they met many of their insidious friends, armed, and advancing to join the American army; but, learning its fate from the refugees, they acted decidedly in concert with the victors; and, captivating some, plundering others, and maltreating all the fugitives they met, returned, exultingly, home. They even added taunts to their perfidy; one of a party, who robbed Brigadier General Butler of his sword, consoled him by saying, "you'll have no further use for it."

The regular troops, it has been observed, were the last to quit the field. Every corps was broken and dispersed; even the boggs and brush, which in some measure served to screen them from their furious pursuers, separated them from one another. Major Anderson was the only officer who fortunately rallied, as he retreated, a few men of different companies; and whose prudence and firmness afforded protection to those who joined his party on the rout.

Colonel Gunby, Lieutenant Colonel Howard, Captain Kirkwood, and Captain Dobson, with a few other officers, and fifty or sixty men, formed a junction on the rout, and proceeded together.

The general order for moving off the heavy baggage, &c. to Waxaws, was not put in execution, as directed to be done, on the preceding evening. The whole of it, consequently, fell into the hands of the enemy; as well as all that which followed the army except the waggons of the General's Gates and De Kalb; which, being furnished with the stoutest horses, fortunately escaped, under the protection of a small quarter guard. Other waggons also had got out of danger from the enemy; but the cries of the women and the wounded in the rear, and the consternation of the flying troops, so alarmed some of the waggoners, that they cut out their teams, and taking each a horse, left the rest for the next that should come. Others were obliged to give up their horses to assist in carrying off the wounded; and the whole road, for many miles, was strewed with signals of distress, confusion and dismay. What added, not a little to this calamitous scene, was the conduct of Armand's legion. They were principally foreigners, and some of them, probably, not unaccustomed to such scenes. Whether it was owing to the disgust of the colonel, at general orders, or the cowardice of his men, is not with the writer to determine; but, certain it is, the legion did not take any part in the action of the 16th; they retired early, and in disorder, and were seen plundering the baggage of the army on their retreat. One of them cut Captain Lemar, of the Maryland infantry, over the hand, for attempting to reclaim his own portmanteau, which the fellow was taking out of the waggon. Captain Lemar was unarmed, having broke his sword in action, and was obliged to submit, both to the loss and to the insult. The tent covers were thrown off the waggons, generally, and the baggage exposed, so that one might take what suited him to carry off. General Caswell's mess waggon afforded the best refreshment; very unexpectedly to the writer, he there found a pipe of good Madeira, broached, and surrounded by a number of soldiers, whose appearance led him to inquire what engaged their attention. He acknowledges, that in this instance, he shared in the booty, and took a draught of wine, which was the only refreshment he had received that day.

But the catastrophe being over, before we pursue a detail of all its distressing consequences, it may be excusable to consider, whether the measures which led to the necessity of fighting a general battle were justifiable: and whether such an event might not have been avoided, at almost any time before the two armies were actually opposed?

If General Gates *intended* to risk a general action, conscious of all circumstances, he certainly made that risk under every possible disadvantage; and a contemplation of those circumstances, would seem to justify Colonel Armand's assertion, made in the afternoon of the day in which the battle was fought — "I will not, said he, say that we have been betrayed; but if it had been the purpose of the general to sacrifice his army, what could he have done more effectually to have answered that purpose?"

Royal Gazette:
"Strayed . . . a whole Army"

September 16, 1780

*The following is said to be a copy of an Advertise-
ment stuck up at the public places in Philadelphia
on the late arrival there of General HORATIO
GATES.*

Millions! — Millions! — Millions!
REWARD,

Strayed, deserted, or stolen, from the Subscriber, on the
16th of August last, near Camden, in the State of South
Carolina, a whole ARMY, consisting of Horse, Foot, and
Dragoons, to the amount of near TEN THOUSAND, (as
has been said) with all their baggage, artillery, waggons,
and camp equipage. The Subscriber has very strong suspicion, from information received from his Aid de Camp, that
a certain CHARLES, Earl CORNWALLIS, was principally
concerned in carrying off the said ARMY with their baggage, &c. Any person or persons civil or military, who will
give information, either to the Subscriber, or to Charles
Thompson, Esq; Secretary to the Continental Congress,
where the said ARMY is, so that they may be recovered and
rallied again, shall be entitled to demand from the Treasurer
of the United States the sum of THREE MILLIONS of
PAPER DOLLARS as soon as they can be spared from the
Public Funds, and ANOTHER MILLION, for apprehending the Person principally concerned in taking the said
ARMY off. — Proper passes will be granted by the President
of the Congress to such persons as incline to go in search
of the said ARMY, — And as a further encouragement, no
deduction will be made from the above reward on account
of any of the Militia, (who composed part of the said
ARMY) not being to be found or heard of, as no depen-

dence can be placed on their services, and nothing but the most speedy flight can ever save their Commander, HORA-TIO GATES, M. G. *And late Commander in Chief of the Southern Army.*

Philadelphia, August 30, 1780

Benedict Arnold:
To the Inhabitants of America

I SHOULD forfeit even in my own Opinion, the place I have so long held in yours, if I could be indifferent to your Approbation, and silent on the Motives which have induced me to join the King's Arms.

A very few words, however, shall suffice upon a Subject so personal, for to the thousands who suffer under the tyranny of the Usurpers in the revolted Provinces, as well as to the great multitude who have long wished for its Subversion, this instance of my Conduct can want no Vindication, as to that class of Men who are Criminally protracting the War from Sinister Views, at the expense of the Public Interest, I prefer their Enmity to their applause. I am only, therefore, Concerned in this address to explain myself to such of my Countrymen as want Abilities or Opportunities to detect the Artifices by which they are duped.

Having fought by your side when the love of our Country animated our Arms, I shall expect from your Justice and Candor, what your deceivers, with more Art and less honesty, will find it inconsistent with their own Views to admit.

When I quitted Domestick happiness for the Perils of the Field, I conceived the rights of my Country in Danger, and that Duty and Honor called me to her Defence — a Redress of Grievances was my only Object and aim; however, I acquiesced in a step which I thought precipitate the Declaration of Independence; to Justify the measure many plausible reasons were urged, which could no longer exist, when Great Britain with the open arms of a Parent offered to embrace us as Children, and grant the wished for redress.

And now that her worst Enemies are in her own bosom, I should change my Principles, If I conspired with their Designs. Yourselves being Judges, was the war the less Just, because Fellow Subjects were considered as our Foes? You have felt the torture in which we raised our arms against a

Brother—God Incline the Guilty protractors of these unnatural Dissentions, to resign their Ambition, and Cease from their Delusions, in Compassion to kindred blood.

I anticipate your question: was not the War a defensive one until the French Joined in the Combination? I answer, that I thought so. You will add, was it not afterwards necessary till the Separation of the British Empire was compleat? By no means; in Contending for the Welfare of my Country, I am free to declare my Opinion, that this End attained, all strife should have ceased.

I lamented therefore the Impolicy, tyranny, and Injustice, which with a Sovereign Contempt of the People of America, studiously neglected to take their Collective Sentiments of the British proposals of Peace, and to negotiate under a suspension of Arms, for an adjustment of differences, as a dangerous Sacrifice of the great Interest of this Country to the Partial Views of a Proud, Antient, and Crafty Foe. I had my suspicions of some imperfections in Our Councils, on Proposals prior to the Parliamentary Commission of 1778; but having then less to do in the Cabinet than the Field (I will not pronounce peremptorily as some may, and perhaps Justly, that Congress have veiled them from the Publick Eye), I continued to be guided in the negligent Confidence of a soldier. But the whole world saw, and all America confessed, the Overtures of the Second Commission exceeded our wishes and expectations. If there was any Suspicion of the National liberality, it arose from its excess.

Do any believe we were at that time really entangled by an Alliance with France? Unfortunate deception! and thus they have been duped by a virtuous Credulity, in the incautious moments of intemperate passion, to give up their fidelity to serve a Nation counting both the will and the power to protect us, and aiming at the Destruction both of the Mother Country and the Provinces. In the Plainess of Common Sense, for I pretend to no Casuistry, did the pretended Treaty with the Court of Versailles amount to more than an Overture to America? Certainly not, because no Authority had been given by the People to conclude it, nor to this very hour have they authorized its ratification—the Articles of Confederation remain still unsigned.

In the firm persuasion, therefore, that the private Judgment of any Individual Citizen of this Country is as free from all Conventional Restraints since, as before the Insidious offers of France, I preferred those from Great Britain, thinking it infinitely wiser and safer to cast my Confidence upon her Justice and Generosity, than to trust a Monarchy too feeble to establish your Independency, so Perilous to her distant Dominions, the Enemy of the Protestant Faith, and fraudulently avowing an affection for the liberties of mankind, while she holds her Native Sons in Vassalage and Chains.

I affect no disguise, and therefore Frankly declare that in these Principles, I had determined to retain my arms and Command for an opportunity to surrender them to Great Britain, and in concerting the Measures for a purpose, in my Opinion, as grateful as it would have been beneficial to my Country; I was only solicitous to accomplish an event of decisive Importance, and to prevent, as much as possible in the Execution of it, the Effusion of blood.

With the highest satisfaction I bear testimony to my old Fellow Soldiers and Citizens, that I find solid Ground to rely upon the Clemency of our Sovereign, and abundant Conviction that it is the generous Intention of Great Britain, not only to have the Rights and privileges of the Colonies unimpaired, together with their perpetual exemption from taxation, but to superadd such further benefits as may consist with the Common prosperity of the Empire. In short, I fought for much less than the Parent Country is as willing to grant to her Colonies, as they can be to receive or enjoy.

Some may think I continued in the struggle of those unhappy days too long, and others that I quitted it too soon. To the first I reply, that I did not see with their Eyes, nor perhaps had so favorable a situation to look from, and that to one Common Master I am willing to stand or fall. In behalf of the Candid among the latter, some of whom I believe serve blindly but honestly in the Ranks I have left, I pray God to give them all the lights requisite to their Own Safety before it is too late; and with respect to that kind of Censurers whose Enmity to me Originates in their hatred to the Principles, by which I am now led to devote my life to the Reunion of the British Empire, as the best and only means to dry up the streams of misery that have deluged this country, they may be assured that, Conscious of the Rectitude of my Intentions, I shall treat their Malice and Calumnies with Contempt and neglect.

NEW YORK, Oct. 7th, 1780.

Benedict Arnold to Lord Germain

NEW YORK 7th OCTOBER 1780.

My Lord,

Conscious of the rectitude of my Intentions (whatever Constructions may have been put on my Conduct,) and convinced of the benevolence and goodness of your Lordship, I am emboldened to request Your Interest and Intercession, that I may be restored to the favor of my most gracious Sovereign; In the fullest Confidence of his Clemency, I most cheerfully cast myself at his Feet, imploring his Royal Grace and Protection.

I have that Confidence in the Goodness of Sir Henry Clinton, That His Majesty will not remain long, uninformed that some considerable time has elapsed, since I resolved to devote my Life and Fortune to his Majesty's Service, and that I was intent to have Demonstrated my Zeal by an Act, which had it succeeded as intended, must have immediately terminated the unnatural Convulsions that have so long distracted the Empire.

Your Lordship will perceive by the enclosed address to the Public, by what principles I have been and am now actuated, to which I shall at present only add my most sacred Assurance that no endeavors of mine shall be wanting to confirm the Profession I make of an unalterable Attachment to the Person, Family and Interests of my Sovereign, and the Glory of his Reign. I enclose another Paper with some imperfect Notes, but will do myself the honor by the next Conveyance to transmit Your Lordship a more full and perfect State of Matters than in my present Confusion and Circumstances I am able to do.

I shall endeavour to merit your Lordships Patronage by my Zeal and Assiduity in His Majesty's Service.

I have the honor to be with the greatest Respect My Lord Your Lordships Most Obedient and most humble servant

The Present State of the American Rebel Army, Navy,
and Finances, with some Remarks.

The present operating Force under the
  immediate Command of general Washington
  as stated by himself to a Council of general
  Officers the 6th. ulto. amounts to . . . . 10,400 men
One Battalion of Continl. troops at
  Rhode Island   500
Two State Regiments of Continl. Militia at
  North Castle   500
                                                            11,400

About one half of these Troops are Militia, whose time of
service expires on the first day of January next, which will reduce the Army engaged for the war to less than Six
Thousand men, exclusive of the Troops in the Southern
Department under General Gates, who may amount to eight
hundred or a thousand regular troops, besides Militia; about
350 Light Horse are included in the above Calculation. All
these troops are illy clad, badly fed, and worse paid having in
general two or three years pay due to them. Many of the best
officers of the Army have resigned, and others are daily following their Example, through Disgust, necessity, and a
Conviction that the Provinces will not be able to Establish
there Independence.

    There has long subsisted a Jealousy between Congress and
the Army. The former have been Jealous of the Power of the
latter, and the latter have thought themselves neglected, and
ill treated by the former, who have excluded the Army from
every Appointment of honor, or profit in the Civil Line. The
Common Soldiers are exceedingly disgusted with the Service,
and every effort to recruit the Army (except by Temporary
Draughts of Militia) has hitherto proved ineffectual. Congress
and General Washington last Spring made the most pressing
Demands on the Colonies to furnish a Body of Troops to
complete the Army to 35,000 men, every Argument was
urged to enforce the Demand, among others that it would
enable General Washington (in conjunction with the French
Troops) to oblige Sir Henry Clinton to evacuate New York —
and thereby put a Period to the War: The Colonies promised

to Comply with the Requisition, every effort was used, but without Success. The Body of the People heartily tired of the war refused to Inlist Voluntarily, and not more than one-third of the men ordered to be Draughted, appeared in the Field. The Distress and Discontents of the People are daily increasing, and the difficulty of Recruiting the Army another year will undoubtedly be greater than ever.

The Navy is reduced to three Frigates, and a few small vessels, who are generally in Port, for want of hands to man them.

The Treasury is entirely empty and the finances are at the lowest Ebb. The Public Debt inclusive of Paper emitted by Congress, and the Colonies, Loan Office Certificates, and Arrears due to the Army, Commissaries and Quarter Masters amounts to upwards of Four hundred Million of Paper Dollars. Congress have lost all Confidence and Credit with the People, who have been too often deceived and duped by them to pay any regard to their promises in future, the different Provinces have very little more Credit with the People than Congress. Their late Emissions of Paper for the payment of which they have given every possible Security, can hardly be said to have any Currency, and is Depreciating Rapidly.

As the result of their Distresses the Eyes of the People are in general opened, they Feel their Error and look back with Remorse to their once happy Condition, and most ardently wish for a reconciliation on Terms safe and honorable to both countries. Many would Return to it with implicit Confidence. Some doubt the Sufficiency of the Powers of the present Commissioners to Offer or Accept Terms for an Established accommodation. It would serve very good uses if the commissioners have Authority for it, to Signify, that the Colonies upon returning to their obedience, shall be restored to their obedience, shall be restored to their Antient Condition with Respect to their Charter, Rights, and Privileges, Civil and Religious, free from British Taxation, and to Invite to Negociation for General Regulations. It will increase the number of Advocates for the reunion.

But the best step is to Vest Commissioners with Decisive Powers on such Settlement as Great Britain may be willing to Establish. There will always be Jealousies seen while a Power is Reserved to Great Britain to approve or disapprove, what Her Commissioners have done. With power in a Sett of Commissioners to bind the Nation as firmly as she would bind herself, by Future Acts of Parliament, I am of opinion that a Pacification would immediately take place.

But should the Artful and Designing who have assumed the Reins of government, continue to have sufficient Influence to mislead the Minds of the People, and continue the Opposition to Government, I am Clearly of Opinion that, an addition of Ten thousand Troops to the American army (including those who may be on their way to America) will be a sufficient Force under the Direction of an Officer of the Experience and abilities of Sir Henry Clinton to put a period to the Contest in the Course of the next Campaign.

I have forgot to mention that the want of Provision in the Army is not owing to the Scarcity of Provision in the country, But to the weakness of the Usurpation in every Colony, without Money or Credit Supplies must be Collected by Force and Terror, wherever the Army are they take without opposition. But this force acts against Itself by Creating internal Enemies, and by making Friends to Great Britain. It is One of the Principal Saps hourly undermining the Strength of the Rebellion.

N. B. In the foregoing Estimate the French Troops at Rhode Island who amount to about 5000 Effectives are not Included.

Alexander Hamilton to John Laurens

c. October 11, 1780

SINCE my return from Hartford, my Dear Laurens, my mind
has been too little at ease to permit me to write to you
sooner. It has been wholly occupied by the affecting and
tragic consequences of Arnold's treason. My feelings were
never put to so severe a trial. You will no doubt have heard
the principal facts before this reaches you; but there are particulars, to which my situation gave me access, that cannot
have come to your knowledge from public report, which I am
persuaded you will find interesting.

From several circumstances, the project seems to have originated with Arnold himself and to have been long premeditated. The first overture is traced back to some time in June
last. It was conveyed in a letter to Col. Robinson; the substance of which was, that the ingratitude he had experienced
from his country, concurring, with other causes, had intirely
changed his principles, that he now only sought to restore
himself to the favour of his king, by some signal proof of his
repentance, and would be happy to open a correspondence
with Sir Henry Clinton for that purpose. About this period he
made a journey to Connecticut, on his return from which to
Philadelphia, he solicited the command of West Point; alleging that the effects of his wound had disqualified him for the
active duties of the field. The sacrifice of this important post
was the atonement he intended to make. General Washington
hesitated the less to gratify an officer who had rendered such
eminent services, as he was convinced the post might be safely
trusted to one, who had given so many distinguished speci-
mens of his bravery. In the beginning of August, he joined
the army, and renewed his application. The enemy, at this
juncture, had embarked the greatest part of their force on an
expedition to Rhode Island; and our army was in motion to
compel them to relinquish the enterprise or to attack New

York in its weakened state. The General offered Arnold the left wing of the army; which he declined on the pretext already mentioned, but not without visible embarrassment. He certainly might have executed the duties of such a temporary command, and it was expected from his enterprising temper, that he would gladly have embraced so splendid an opportunity. But he did not choose to be diverted a moment from his favourite object, probably from an apprehension, that some different disposition might have taken place, which would have excluded him. The extreme solicitude he discovered to get possession of the post, would have led to a suspicion of the treachery, had it been possible from his past conduct to have supposed him capable of it.

The correspondence thus begun was carried on between Arnold and Major André Adjutant General to the British army, in behalf of Sir Henry Clinton, under feigned signatures and in a mercantile disguise. In an intercepted letter of Arnold which lately fell into our hands he proposes an interview, "to settle the risks and profits of the copartnership"; and in the same stile of metaphor, intimates an expected augmentation of the garrison, and speaks of it as the means of extending their traffic. It appears by another letter that André was to have met him on the lines, under the sanction of a flag in the character of Mr. John Anderson. But some cause, or other, not known, prevented this interview.

The 20th. of last month Robinson and André went up the River in the Vulture Sloop of War. Robinson sent a flag to Arnold with two letters; one to General Putnam inclosed in another to himself; proposing an interview with Putnam, or in his absence, with Arnold, to adjust some private concerns. The one to General Putnam was evidently meant as a cover to the other, in case by accident, the letters should have fallen under the inspection of a third person.

General Washington crossed the river, in his way to Hartford, the day these dispatches arrived. Arnold conceiving he must have heard of the flag, thought it necessary for the sake of appearances, to submit the letters to him and ask his opinion of the propriety of complying with the request. The General with his usual caution, though without the least surmise of the design, dissuaded him from it, and advised him to reply to Robinson, that whatever related to his private affairs, must be of a civil nature, and could only properly be addressed to the civil authority. This reference fortunately deranged the plan and was the first link in the chain of events that led to the detection. The interview could no longer take place, in the form of a flag, but was obliged to be managed in a secret manner.

Arnold employed one Smith to go on Board the Vulture the night of the 22d to bring André on shore with a pass for Mr. John Anderson. André came ashore accordingly, and was conducted within a picket of ours to the house of Smith, where Arnold and he remained together in close conference all that night and the day following. At day light in the morning, the commanding officer at Kings ferry, without the privity of Arnold moved a couple of pieces of cannon to a point opposite to where the vulture lay and obliged her to take a more remote station. This event, or some lurking distrust, made the boatmen refuse to convey the two passengers back, and disconcerted Arnold so much, that by one of those strokes of infatuation, which often confound the schemes of men conscious of guilt, he insisted on André's exchanging his uniform for a disguise, and returning in a mode different from that in which he came. André who had been undesignedly brought within our posts in the first instance remonstrated warmly against this new and dangerous expedient. But Arnold persisting in declaring it impossible for him to return as he came, he at length reluctantly yielded to his direction. Smith furnished the disguise, and in the evening passed Kings ferry with him and proceeded to Crompond where they stopped the remainder of the night (at the instance of a militia officer) to avoid being suspected by him. The next morning they resumed their journey Smith accompanying André a little beyond Pine's bridge, where he left him. He had reached Tarry town, when he was taken up by three militia men, who rushed out of the woods and seized his horse.

At this critical moment his presence of mind forsook him. Instead of producing his pass which would have extricated him from our parties and could have done him no harm with his own, he asked the militia men, if they were of the *upper* or *lower* party, distinctive appellations known among the enemy's refugee corps. The Militia men replied they were of the lower party; upon which he told them he was a British officer and pressed them not to detain him, as he was upon urgent business. This confession removed all doubt; and it was in vain he afterwards produced his pass. He was instantly forced off to a place of greater security; where after a careful search there were founded concealed in the feet of his stockings several papers of importance delivered to him by Arnold; among these were a plan of the fortifications of West Point, a memorial from the Engineer on the attack and defence of the place, returns of the garrison, cannon and stores, copy of the minutes of a council of war held by General Washington a few Weeks before. The prisoner at first was inadvertently ordered to Arnold; but on recollection, while still on the way, he was countermanded, and sent to old Salem. The papers were inclosed in a letter to General Washington, which having taken a route different from the one he returned by, made a circuit, that afforded leisure for another letter, through an ill-judged delicacy written to Arnold with information of Anderson's capture, to get to him an hour before General Washington's arrival at his quarters, time enough to elude the fate that awaited him. He went down the river in his barge to the vulture, with such precipitate confusion, that he did not take with him a single paper useful to the enemy. On the first notice of the affair he was persued, but much too late to be overtaken.

Arnold a moment before his setting out, went into Mrs. Arnold's apartment and informed her that some transactions had just come to light which must for ever banish him from his country. She fell into a swoon, at this declaration; and he left her in it to consult his own safety, 'till the servants alarmed by her cries came to her relief. She remained frantic all day, accusing every one who approached her with an intention to murder her child (an infant in her arms) and exhibiting every other mark of the most genuine and agonising distress. Exhausted by the fatigue and tumult of her spirits, her phrenzy subsided towards evening and she sunk into all the sadness of affliction. It was impossible not to have been touched with her situation; every thing affected in female tears, or in the misfortunes of beauty, every thing pathetic in the wounded tenderness of a wife, or in the apprehensive fondness of a mother, and, 'till I have reason to change the opinion, I will add, every thing amiable in suffering innocence conspired to make her an object of sympathy to all who were present. She experienced the most delicate attentions and every friendly office 'till her departure for Philadelphia.

There was some color for imagining it was a part of the plan to betray the General into the hands of the enemy. Arnold was very anxious to ascertain from him the precise day of his return and the enemy's movements seem to have corresponded to this point. But if it was really the case, it was very injudicious. The success must have depended on surprise, and as the officers at the advanced posts were not in the secret, their measures might have given the alarm, and General Washington taking the command of the post might have rendered the whole scheme abortive. Arnold it is true had so dispersed the garrison as to have made a defence difficult, but not impracticable; and the acquisition of West Point was of such magnitude to the enemy, that it would have been unwise to connect it with any other object however great which might make the obtaining it precarious.

André was without loss of time conducted to the Head Quarters of the army, where he was immediately brought before a board of General Officers, to prevent all possibility of misrepresentation or cavil on the part of the enemy. The Board reported, that he ought to be considered as a spy and according to the laws and usages of nations to suffer death; which was executed two days after.

Never perhaps did any man suffer death with more justice, or deserve it less. The first step he took after his capture was to write a letter to General Washington conceived in terms of dignity without insolence and apology without meanness. The scope of it was to vindicate himself from the imputation of having assumed a mean character for treacherous or interested purposes; asserting that he had been involuntarily an impostor, that contrary to his intentions, which was to meet a person for intelligence on neutral ground, he had been betrayed within our posts and forced into the vile condition of an enemy in disguise, soliciting only that to whatever rigor policy might devote him a decency of treatment might be observed, due to a person who though unfortunate had been guilty of nothing dishonorable. His request was granted in its full extent, for in the whole progress of the affair, he was treated with the most scrupulous delicacy. When brought before the Board of Officers, he met with every mark of indulgence and was required to answer no interrogatory, which could even embarrass his feelings. On his part, while he carefully concealed everything that might involve others, he frankly confessed all the facts relating to himself; and upon his confession without the trouble of examining a witness, the Board made their report. The members of it were not more impressed with the candor and firmness mixed with a becoming sensibility, which he displayed than he was penetrated with their liberality and politeness. He acknowledged the generosity of the behaviour towards him, in every respect, but particularly in this, in the strongest terms of manly gratitude. In a conversation with a Gentleman who visited him after his trial, he said he flattered himself he had never been illiberal; but if there were any remains of prejudice, in his mind, his present experience must obliterate them.

In one of the visits I made to him (and I saw him several times during his confinement) he begged me to be the bearer of a request to the General for permission, to send an open letter to Sir Henry Clinton. "I foresee my fate (said he) and though I pretend not to play the hero, or to be indifferent about life; yet I am reconciled to whatever may happen, conscious that misfortune, not guilt, has brought it upon me. There is only one thing that disturbs my tranquillity — Sir Henry Clinton has been too good to me; he has been lavish of his kindness. I am bound to him by too many obligations and love him too well to bear the thought, that he should reproach himself, or that others should reproach him, on the supposition of my having conceived myself obliged by his instructions to run the risk I did. I would not for the world leave a sting in his mind, that should embitter his future days." He could scarce finish the sentence, bursting into tears, in spite of his efforts to suppress them; and with difficulty collected himself enough afterwards to add, "I wish to be permitted to assure him, I did not act under this impression, but submitted to a necessity imposed upon me as contrary to my own inclination as to his orders." His request was readily complied with, and he wrote the letter annexed, and with which I dare say, you will be as much pleased as I am both for the diction and sentiment.

There was something singularly interesting in the character and fortunes of André. To an excellent understanding well improved by education and travel, he united a peculiar elegance of mind and manners, and the advantage of a pleasing person. 'Tis said he possessed a pretty taste for the fine arts, and had himself attained some proficiency in poetry, music and painting. His knowlege appeared without ostentation, and embellished by a diffidence, that rarely accompanies so many talents and accomplishments, which left you to suppose more than appeared. His sentiments were elevated and inspired esteem, they had a softness that conciliated affection. His elocution was handsome; his address easy, polite and insinuating. By his merit he had acquired the unlimited confidence of his general and was making a rapid progress in military rank and reputation. But in the height of his career, flushed with new hope from the execution of a project the most beneficial to his party, that could be devised, he was at once precipitated from the summit of prosperity and saw all the expectations of his ambition blasted and himself ruined.

The character I have given of him is drawn partly from what I saw of him myself and partly from information. I am aware that a man of real merit is never seen in so favourable a light, as through the medium of adversity. The clouds that surround him are shades that set off his good qualities. Misfortune cuts down the little vanities, that in prosperous times served as so many spots in his virtues; and gives a tone of humility that makes his worth more amiable. His spectators who enjoy a happier lot are less prone to detract from it, through envy, and are more disposed by compassion to give him the credit he deserves and perhaps even to magnify it.

I speak not of André's conduct in this affair as a Philosophe, but as a man of the world. The authorised maxims and practices of war are the satire of human nature. They countenance almost every species of seduction as well as violence; and the General that can make most traitors in the army of his adversary is frequently most applauded. On this scale we acquit André, while we could not but condemn him, if we were to examine his conduct by the sober rules of philosophy and moral rectitude. It is however a blemish in his fame, that he once intended to prostitute a flag; about this a man of nice honor ought to have had a scruple, but the temptation was great; let his misfortunes cast a veil over his error.

When his sentence was announced to him, he remarked, that since it was his lot to die there was still a choice in the mode which would make a material difference to his feelings, and he would be happy, if possible, to be indulged with a professional death. He made a second application by letter in concise, but persuasive terms. It was thought this indulgence being incompatible with the customs of war could not be granted and it was therefore determined in both cases to evade an answer to spare him the sensations, which a certain knowlege of the intended mode would inflict.

In going to the place of execution, he bowed familiarly as he went along to all those with whom he had been acquainted in his confinement. A smile of complacency expressed the serene fortitude of his mind. Arrived at the fatal spot, he asked with some emotion, *must* I then die in this manner? He was told it had been unavoidable. "I am reconciled to my fate (said he) but not to the mode." Soon however recollecting himself, he added, "it will be but a momentary pang," and springing upon the cart performed the last offices to himself with a composure that excited the admiration and melted the hearts of the beholders. Upon being told the final moment was at hand, and asked if he had any thing to say, he answered: "nothing, but to request you will witness to the world, that I die like a brave man." Among the extra ordinary circumstances that attended him, in the midst of his enemies, he died universally esteemed and universally regretted.

Several letters from Sir Henry Clinton and others were received in the course of the affair, feebly attempting to prove, that André came out under the protection of a flag, with a passport from a general officer in actual service, and consequently could not be justly detained. Clinton sent a deputation composed of Lt General Robinson, Mr. Elliot and Mr. William Smith to represent as he said the true state of Major

André's case. General Greene met Robinson & had a conversation with him, in which he reiterated the pretence of a flag, urged André's release as a personal favour to Sir Henry Clinton, and offered any friend of ours in their power in exchange. Nothing could have been more frivolous than the plea which was used. The fact was that besides the time, manner, object of the interview, change of dress, and other circumstances, there was not a single formality customary with flaggs and the passport was not to Major André, but to Mr. Anderson. But had there been, on the contrary, all the formalities, it would be an abuse of language to say, that the sanction of a flag for corrupting an officer to betray his trust ought to be respected. So unjustifiable a purpose would not only destroy its validity but make it an aggravation.

André himself has answered the argument by ridiculing and exploding the idea in his examination before the board of officers. It was a weakness to urge it.

There was in truth no way of saving him. Arnold or he must have been the victim; the former was out of our power.

It was by some suspected, Arnold had taken his measures in such a manner, that if the interview had been discovered in the act it might have been in his power to sacrifice André to his own security. This surmise of double treachery made them imagine Clinton might be induced to give up Arnold for André, and a Gentleman took occasion to suggest this expedient to the latter, as a thing that might be proposed by him. He declined it. The moment he had been capable of so much frailty, I should have ceased to esteem him.

The infamy of Arnold's conduct previous to his desertion is only equalled by his baseness since. Besides the folly of writing to Sir Henry Clinton; assuring him that André had acted under a passport from him and according to his directions, while commanding officer at a post, and that therefore he did not doubt he would be immediately sent in; he had the effrontery to write to General Washington, in the same spirit, with the addition of a menace of retaliation, if the sentence should be carried into execution. He has since acted the farce of sending in his resignation. This man is in every sense despicable. Added to the scene of knavery and prostitution during his command in Philadelphia, which the late seizure of his papers has unfolded; the history of his command at West Point is a history of little, as well as great, villainies. He practiced every dirty art of peculation; and even stooped to connections with the suttlers of the garrison to defraud the public.

To his conduct, that of the captors of André forms a striking contrast. He tempted them with the offer of his watch, his horse and any sum of money they should name. They rejected his offers with indignation; and the gold, that could seduce a man high in the esteem and confidence of his country, who had the remembrance of past exploits; the motives of present reputation and future glory to cloak his integrity, had no charm for three simple peasants, leaning only on their virtue and an honest sense of their duty. While Arnold is handed down with execration to future times, posterity will repeat with reverence the names of Van Wert, Paulding and Williams!

I congratulate you my friend on our happy escape from the mischiefs with which this treason was big. It is a new comment on the value of an honest man; and if it were possible, would endear you to me more than ever.

Adieu

Robert Campbell:
Narrative of the Battle of King's Mountain

IN the fall of the year 1780, when the American cause wore a very gloomy aspect in the Southern States, Cols. Arthur and William Campbell, hearing of the advance of Colonel Ferguson along the mountains in the State of North Carolina, and that the Whigs were retreating before him, unable to make any effectual resistance, formed a plan to intercept him, and communicated it to the commanding officers of Sullivan and Washington Counties, in the State of North Carolina. They readily agreed to co-operate in any expedition against Col. Ferguson. Col. Arthur Campbell immediately ordered the militia of Washington Co., Virginia, amounting to near four hundred, to make ready to march under command of Col. Wm. Campbell, who was known to be an enterprising and active officer. Cols. Shelby and Sevier raised a party of three hundred, joined him on his march, and moved with forced marches toward Col. Ferguson. At the same time Cols. Williams, Cleveland, Lacey, and Brandon, of the States of North and South Carolina, each conducted a small party toward the same point, amounting to near three hundred. Col. Ferguson had notice of their approach by a deserter that left the army on the Yellow Mountain, and immediately commenced his march for Charlotte, dispatching at the same time different messengers to Lord Cornwallis with information of his danger. These messengers being intercepted on their way, no movement was made to favor his retreat.

These several corps of American volunteers, amounting to near one thousand men, met at Gilbert Town, and the officers unanimously chose Colonel Campbell to the command. About seven hundred choice riflemen mounted their horses for the purpose of following the retreating army. The balance being chiefly footmen, were left to follow on and come up as soon as they could. The pursuit was too rapid to render an escape practicable. Ferguson, finding that he must inevitably be over-taken, chose his ground, and waited for the attack on King's Mountain. On the 7th of October, in the afternoon, after a forced march of forty-five miles on that day and the night before, the volunteers came up with him. The forenoon of the day was wet, but they were fortunate enough to come on him undiscovered, and took his pickets, they not having it in their power to give an alarm. They were soon formed in such order as to attack the enemy on all sides. The Washington and Sullivan regiments were formed in the front and on the right flank; the North and South Carolina troops, under Cols. Williams, Sevier, Cleveland, Lacey, and Brandon, on the left. The two armies being in full view, the center of the one nearly opposite the center of the other — the British main guard posted nearly half way down the mountain — the commanding officer gave the word of command to raise the Indian war-whoop and charge. In a moment, King's Mountain resounded with their shouts, and on the first fire the guard retreated, leaving some of their men to crimson the earth. The British beat to arms, and immediately formed on the top of the mountain, behind a chain of rocks that appeared impregnable, and had their wagons drawn up on their flank across the end of the mountain, by which they made a strong breast-work.

Thus concealed, the American army advanced to the charge. In ten or fifteen minutes the wings came round, and the action became general. The enemy annoyed our troops very much from their advantageous position. Col. Shelby, being previously ordered to reconnoitre their position, observing their situation, and what a destructive fire was kept up from behind those rocks, ordered Robert Campbell, one of the officers of the Virginia Line, to move to the right with a small company to endeavor to dislodge them, and lead them on nearly to the ground to which he had ordered them, under fire of the enemy's lines and within forty steps of the same; but discovering that our men were repulsed on the other side of the mountain, he gave orders to advance, and post themselves opposite to the rocks, and near to the enemy, and then returned to assist in bringing up the men in order, who had been charged with the bayonet. These orders were punctually obeyed, and they kept up such a galling fire as to compel Ferguson to order a company of regulars to face them, with a view to cover his men that were posted behind the rocks. At this time, a considerable fire was drawn to this side of the mountain by the repulse of those on the other, and the Loyalists not being permitted to leave their posts. This scene was not of long duration, for it was the brave Virginia volunteers, and those under Col. Shelby, on their attempting rapidly to ascend the mountain, that were charged with the bayonet. They obstinately stood until some of them were thrust through the body, and having nothing but their rifles by which to defend themselves, they were forced to retreat. They were soon rallied by their gallant commanders, Campbell, Shelby and other brave officers, and by a constant and well-directed fire of their rifles, drove them back in their turn, strewing the face of the mountain with their assailants, and kept advancing until they drove them from some of their posts.

Ferguson being heavily pressed on all sides, ordered Capt. DePeyster to reinforce some of the extreme posts with a full company of British regulars. He marched, but to his astonishment when he arrived at the place of destination, he had almost no men, being exposed in that short distance to the constant fire of their rifles. He then ordered his cavalry to mount, but to no purpose. As quick as they were mounted, they were taken down by some bold marksmen. Being driven to desperation by such a scene of misfortune, Col. Ferguson endeavored to make his escape, and, with two Colonels of the Loyalists, mounted his horse, and charged on that part of the line which was defended by the party who had been ordered round the mountain by Col. Shelby, it appearing too weak to resist them. But as soon as he got to the line he fell, and the other two officers, attempting to retreat, soon shared the same fate. It was about this time that Col. Campbell advanced in front of his men, and climbed over a steep rock close by the enemy's lines, to get a view of their situation, and saw they were retreating from behind the rocks that were near to him. As soon as Capt. DePeyster observed that Col. Ferguson was killed, he raised a flag and called for quarters. It was soon taken out of his hand by one of the officers on horseback, and raised so high that it could be seen by our line, and the firing immediately ceased. The Loyalists, at the time of their surrender, were driven into a crowd, and being closely surrounded, they could not have made any further resistance.

In this sharp action, one hundred and fifty of Col. Ferguson's party were killed, and something over that number were wounded. Eight hundred and ten, of whom one hundred were British regulars, surrendered themselves prisoners, and one thousand five hundred stand of arms were taken. The loss of the American army on this occasion amounted to thirty killed, and something over fifty wounded, among whom were a number of brave officers. Col. Williams, who has been so much lamented, was shot through the body, near the close of the action, in making an attempt to charge upon Ferguson. He lived long enough to hear of the surrender of the British army. He then said, "I die contented, since we have gained the victory," and expired.

The third night after the action, the officers of the Carolinas complained to Col. Campbell, that there were among the prisoners a number who had, previous to the action on King's Mountain, committed cool and deliberate murder, and other enormities alike atrocious, and requested him to order a court-martial to examine into the matter. They stated that if they should escape, they were exasperated, and they feared they would commit other enormities worse than they had formerly done. Col. Campbell complied, and ordered a court-martial immediately to sit, composed of the Field Officers and Captains, who were ordered to inquire into the complaints which had been made. The court was conducted orderly, and witnesses were called and examined in each case. The consequence was that there were thirty-two condemned. Out of these, nine who were thought the most dangerous, and who had committed the most atrocious crimes, were executed. The others were pardoned by the commanding officer. One of the crimes proven against a Captain that was executed was, that he had called at the house of a Whig, and inquired if he was at home, and being informed by his son, a small boy, that he was not, he immediately drew out his pistol and shot him. The officers on the occasion acted from an honorable motive to do the greatest good in their power for the public service, and to check those enormities so frequently committed in the States of North and South Carolina at that time, their distress being almost unequaled in the annals of the American Revolution.

George Washington:
Circular to the State Governments

Head Quarters, near Passaic Falls, October 18, 1780.
Sir: In obedience to the orders of Congress, I have the honor to transmit you the present state of the troops of your line, by which you will perceive how few Men you will have left after the 1st of Jany. next. When I inform you also that the Regiments of the other Lines will be in general as much reduced as yours, you will be able to judge how exceedingly weak the Army will be at that period, and how essential it is the states should make the most vigorous exertions to replace the discharged Men as early as possible.

Congress are now preparing a plan for a new establishment of their Army which when finished they will transmit to the several States with requisitions for their respective quotas. I have no doubt it will be a primary object with them to have the Levies for the War, and this appears to me a point so interesting to our Independence that I cannot forbear entering into the motives which ought to determine the States without hesitation or alternative to take their measures decisively for that object.

I am religiously persuaded that the duration of the War and the greatest part of the misfortunes and perplexities we have hitherto experienced, are chiefly to be attributed to the System of temporary enlistments. Had we in the commencement raised an Army for the War, such as was within the reach of the Abilities of these States to raise and maintain we should not have suffered those military Checks which have so frequently shaken our cause, nor should we have incurred such enormous expenditures as have destroyed our paper Currency and with it all public credit. A moderate compact force on a permanent establishment capable of acquiring the discipline essential to military operations would have been able to make head against the enemy without comparison better than the throngs of Militia which at certain periods have been, not in the field, but in their way to and from the Field; for from that want of perseverance which characterises all Militia, and of that coercion which cannot be exercised upon them, it has always been found impracticable to detain the greatest part of them in service even for the term, for which they have been called out, and this has been commonly so short, that we have had a great proportion of the time two sets of Men to feed and pay, one coming to the Army and the other going from it. From this circumstance and from the extraordinary waste and consumption of provisions, stores, Camp equipage, Arms, Cloaths and every other Article incident to irregular troops, it is easy to conceive what an immense increase of public expence has been produced from the source of which I am speaking. I might add the diminution of our Agriculture by calling off at critical Seasons the labourers employed in it, as has happened in instances without number.

In the enumeration of Articles wasted, I mention Cloathes. It may be objected that the terms of engagements of the Levies do not include this, but if we want service from the Men particularly in the cold Season we are obliged to supply them notwithstanding, and they leave us before the Cloaths are half worn out.

But there are evils still more striking that have befallen us. The intervals between the dismission of one Army and the collection of another have more than once threatened us with ruin, which humanly speaking nothing but the supineness or folly of the enemy could have saved us from. How did our cause totter at the close of 76, when with a little more than two thousand Men we were driven before the enemy thro' Jersey and obliged to take post on the other side of the Delaware to make a shew of covering Philadelphia while in reallity nothing was more easy to them with a little enterprise, and industry than to make their passage good to that City and dissipate the remaining force which still kept alive our expiring opposition! What hindered them from dispersing our little Army and giving a fatal Blow to our affairs during all the subsequent winter, instead of remaining in a state of torpid inactivity and permitting us to hover about their Quarters when we had scarcely troops sufficient to mount the ordinary Guard? After having lost two Battles and Philadelphia in the following Campaign for want of those numbers and that degree of discipline which we might have acquired by a permanent force in the first instance, in what a cruel and perilous situation did we again find ourselves in the Winter of 77 at Valley Forge, within a days march of the enemy, with a little more than a third of their strength, unable to defend our position, or retreat from it, for want of the means of transportation? What but the fluctuation of our Army enabled the enemy to detach so boldly to the southward in 78 and 79 to take possession of the two States Georgia and South Carolina, while we were obliged here to be idle Spectators of their weakness; set at defiance by a Garrison of six thousand regular troops, accessible every where by a Bridge which nature had formed, but of which we were unable to take advantage from still greater weakness, apprehensive even for our own safety? How did the same Garrison insult the main Army of these States the ensuing Spring and threaten the destruction of all our Baggage and Stores, saved by a good countenance more than by an ability to defend them? And what will be our situation this winter, our Army by the 1st. of January diminished to a little more than a sufficient Garrison for West point, the enemy at liberty to range the Country wherever they please, and, leaving a handful of Men at N York, to undertake Expeditions for the reduction of other States, which for want of adequate means of defense will it is much to be dreaded add to the number of their conquests and to the examples of our want of energy and wisdom?

The loss of Canada to the Union and the fate of the brave Montgomery compelled to a rash attempt by the immediate prospect of being left without Troops might be enumerated in the catalogue of evils that have sprang from this fruitful source. We not only incur these dangers and suffer these losses for want of a constant force equal to our exigencies, but while we labor under this impediment it is impossible there can be any order or œconomy or system in our finances. If we meet with any severe blow the great exertions which the moment requires to stop the progress of the misfortune oblige us to depart from general principles to run into any expence or to adopt any expedient however injurious on a larger scale to procure the force and means which the present emergency demands. Every thing is thrown into confusion and the measures taken to remedy immediate evils perpetuate others. The same is the case if particular conjunctions invite us to offensive operations; we find ourselves unprepared without troops, without Magazines, and with little time to provide them. We are obliged to force our resources by the most burthensome methods to answer the end, and after all it is but half answered: the design is announced by the occasional effort, and the enemy have it in their power to counteract and elude the blow. The prices of every thing, Men provisions &ca. are raised to a height to which the Revenues of no Government, much less ours, would suffice. It is impossible the people can endure the excessive burthen of bounties for annual drafts and substitutes increasing at every new experiment: whatever it might cost them once for all to procure Men for the War would be a cheap bargain.

I am convinced our System of temporary inlistments has prolonged the War and encouraged the enemy to persevere. Baffled while we had an Army in the field, they have been constantly looking forward to the period of its reduction, as the period to our opposition, and the season of their successes. They have flattered themselves with more than the event has justified; for they believed when one Army expired, we should not be able to raise another: undeceived however in this expectation by experience, they still remained convinced, and to me evidently on good grounds, that we must ultimately sink under a system which increases our expense beyond calculation, enfeebles all our measures, affords the most inviting opportunities to the enemy, and wearies and disgusts the people. This has doubtless had great influence in preventing their coming to terms and will continue to operate in the same way, The debates on the ministerial side have frequently manifested the operation of this motive, and it must in the nature of things have had great weight.

The interpositions of Neutral powers may lead to a negotiation this winter: Nothing will tend so much to make the Court of London reasonable as the prospect of a permanent Army in this Country, and a spirit of exertion to support it.

Tis time we should get rid of an error which the experience of all mankind has exploded, and which our own experience has dearly taught us to reject; the carrying on a War with Militia, or, (which is nearly the same thing) temporary levies against a regular, permanent and disciplined force. The Idea is chimerical, and that we have so long persisted in it is a reflection on the judgment of a Nation so enlightened as we are, as well as a strong proof of the empire of prejudice over reason. If we continue in the infatuation, we shall deserve to lose the object we are contending for.

America has been almost amused out of her liberties. We have frequently heard the behavior of the Militia extolled upon one and another occasion by Men who judge only from the surface, by Men who had particular views in misrepresenting, by visionary Men whose credulity easily swallowed every vague story in support of a favorite Hypothesis. I solemnly declare I never was witness to a single instance that can countenance an opinion of Militia or raw troops being fit for the real business of fighting. I have found them useful as light parties to skirmish the Woods, but incapable of making or sustaining a serious attack. This firmness is only acquired by habit of discipline and service. I mean not to detract from the merit of the Militia; their zeal and spirit upon a variety of occasions have intitled them to the highest applause; but it is of the greatest importance we should learn to estimate them rightly. We may expect everything from ours that Militia is capable of, but we must not expect from any, service for which Regulars alone are fit. The late Battle of Campden is a melancholy comment upon this doctrine. The Militia fled at the first fire, and left the Continental troops surrounded on every side and overpowered by numbers to combat for safety instead of Victory. The enemy themselves have witnessed to their Valor.

An ill effect of short enlistments which I have not yet taken notice of, is that the constant fluctuation of their Men is one of the sources of disgust to the Officers. Just when by great trouble fatigue and vexation (with which the training of Recruits is attended) they have brought their Men to some kind of order, they have the mortification to see them go home, and to know that the drudgery is to recommence the next Campaign, In Regiments so constituted, an Officer has neither satisfaction nor credit in his command

Every motive which can arise from a consideration of our circumstances, either in a domestic or foreign point of view calls upon us to abandon temporary expedients and substitute something durable, systematic and substantial. This applies as well to our civil administration as to our military establishment. It is as necessary to give Congress, the common Head, sufficient powers to direct the common Forces as it is to raise an Army for the War; but I should go out of my province to expatiate on Civil Affairs. I cannot forbear adding a few more remarks.

Our finances are in an alarming state of derangement. Public credit is almost arrived at its last Stage. The People begin to be dissatisfied with the feeble mode of conducting the War, and with the ineffectual burthens imposed upon them, which tho' light in comparison to what other nations feel are from their novelty heavy to them. They lose their confidence in Government apace. The Army is not only dwindling into nothing, but the discontents of the Officers as well as the Men have matured to a degree that threatens but too general a renunciation of the service, at the end of the Campaign. Since January last we have had registered at Head Quarters more than one hundred and sixty resignations, besides a number of others that were never regularly reported. I speak of the Army in this Quarter. We have frequently in the course of the Campaign experienced an extremity of want. Our Officers are in general indecently defective in Cloathing. Our Men are almost naked, totally unprepared for the inclemency of the approaching season. We have no magazines for the Winter; the mode of procuring our supplies is precarious, and all the reports of the Officers employed in collecting them are gloomy.

These circumstances conspire to show the necessity of immediately adopting a plan that will give more energy to Government, more vigor and more satisfaction to the Army. Without it we have every thing to fear. I am persuaded of the sufficiency of our resources if properly directed.

Should the requisitions of Congress by any accident not arrive before the Legislature is about to rise, I beg to recommend that a plan be devised, which is likely to be effectual, for raising the Men that will be required for the War, leaving it to the Executive to apply it to the Quota which Congress will fix, I flatter myself however the requisition will arrive in time.

The present Crisis of our Affairs appears to me so serious as to call upon me as a good Citizen to offer my sentiments freely for the safety of the Republic. I hope the motive will excuse the liberty I have taken. I have the honor etc.

TO BE ADDED TO THE LETTER OF DELAWARE

P.S. The foregoing is circular to the several states. Having received no return of your regiment since the affair of Campden, I have it not in my power to transmit any. I can only observe that my accounts make it probable it is greatly reduced. There are in Lee's corps Thirty eight men belonging to your state. I beg leave to suggest that the readiest way to obtain a perfect Return will be by application of your Excellency to the commanding Officer with the Regt.

P.S. to the State of Maryland.

The foregoing is Circular to the several States. I have it not in my power to transmit a very accurate return of the Troops of your State, but I send the best I have received since the late affair at Campden; in which however the remains of the Delaware Regiment are included without being distinguished. I beg leave to suggest that the readiest way to obtain a more perfect one, will be by application from your Excellency to Major General Smallwood.

P.S. to the States of Virginia and North Carolina.

The foregoing is circular to the several states. The circumstances of your line put it out of my power to transmit a return.

P.S. To Pensylvania.

The foregoing is circular to the several states. The observation I make in the first paragraph respecting the comparative strength of the troops would mislead, if applied to your line; for you have a much larger proportion of troops for the war than most of the other states. The Men belonging to Pensylvania in Hazen's regiment is not included in the return I send you, because I believe it will be the intention of Congress to keep this regiment up upon a distinct establishment.

Anthony Allaire:
Diary, October 7–November 25, 1780

Saturday, 7th. About two o'clock in the afternoon twenty-five hundred Rebels, under the command of Brig.-Gen. Williams, and ten Colonels, attacked us. Maj. Ferguson had eight hundred men. The action continued an hour and five minutes; but their numbers enabled them to surround us. The North Carolina regiment seeing this, and numbers being out of ammunition, gave way, which naturally threw the rest of the militia into confusion. Our poor little detachment, which consisted of only seventy men when we marched to the field of action, were all killed and wounded but twenty; and those brave fellows were soon crowded as close as possible by the militia. Capt. DePeyster, on whom the command devolved, saw it impossible to form six men together; thought it necessary to surrender to save the lives of the brave men who were left. We lost in this action, Maj. Ferguson, of the Seventy-first regiment, a man much attached to his King and country, well informed in the art of war; he was brave and humane, and an agreeable companion; in short, he was universally esteemed in the army, and I have every reason to regret his unhappy fate. We had eighteen men killed on the spot; Capt. Ryerson and thirty-two privates wounded of Maj. Ferguson's detachment; Lieut. McGinnis, of Allen's regiment of Skinner's Brigade, killed. Taken prisoners, Two Captains, four Lieutenants, three Ensigns, and one Surgeon, and fifty-four sergeants rank and file, including the mounted men under the command of Lieut. Taylor. Of the militia, one hundred were killed, including officers; wounded, ninety; taken prisoners, about six hundred. Our baggage all taken, of course. Rebels lost Brig.-Gen. Williams, one hundred and thirty-five, including officers, killed; wounded, equal to ours.

Sunday, 8th. They thought it necessary to move us sixteen miles, to one Waldron's plantation, where they halted.

Monday, 9th. Moved two miles and a half to Bullock creek; forded it, and halted on the banks.

Tuesday, 10th. Moved twenty miles and halted in the woods.

Wednesday, 11th. Moved at eight o'clock in the morning; marched twelve miles to Col. Walker's, and halted.

Thursday, 12th. Those villains divided our baggage, although they had promised on their word we should have it all.

Friday, 13th. Moved six miles to Bickerstaff's plantation. In the evening their liberality extended so far as to send five old shirts to nine of us, as a change of linen — other things in like proportion.

Saturday, 14th. Twelve field officers were chosen to try the militia prisoners — particularly those who had the most influence in the country. They condemned thirty — in the evening they began to execute Lieut.-Col. Mills, Capt. Wilson, Capt. Chitwood, and six others, who unfortunately fell a sacrifice to their infamous mock jury. Mills, Wilson, and Chitwood died like Romans — the others were reprieved.

Sunday, 15th. Moved at five o'clock in the morning. Marched all day through the rain — a very disagreeable road. We got to Catawba, and forded it at Island Ford, about ten o'clock at night. Our march was thirty-two miles. All the men were worn out with fatigue and fasting — the prisoners having no bread or meat for two days before. We officers were allowed to go to Col. McDowell's, where we lodged comfortably. About one hundred prisoners made their escape on this march.

Monday, 16th. Moved at two o'clock in the afternoon. Marched five miles; forded the north branch of Catawba and John's river; halted at a Tory plantation.

Tuesday, 17th. Moved at eight o'clock in the morning. Marched fifteen miles; halted at Capt. Hatt's plantation. Three prisoners attempted to make their escape this night; two succeeded — the other was shot through the body.

Wednesday, 18th. About five o'clock in the morning the Rebels executed the man who unfortunately got wounded in attempting to make his escape. We moved at eight o'clock in the morning, and marched eighteen miles to Moravian creek, and halted.

Thursday, 19th. Moved at eight o'clock in the morning; forded Moravian creek, passed by Wilkes Court House, and marched sixteen miles to one Hagwoods' plantation, and halted.

Friday, 20th. Moved at eleven o'clock in the morning; marched six miles to Mr. Sale's plantation, and halted.

Saturday, 21st. Several Tory women brought us butter, milk, honey, and many other necessaries of life. Moved at ten o'clock in the morning, and marched fourteen miles to Mr. Headpeth's plantation, a great Tory, who is at present with Lord Cornwallis. We lodged at Mr. Edward Clinton's, who is likewise with Lord Cornwallis.

Sunday, 22d. Moved at ten o'clock in the morning. Obtained liberty to go forward with Col. Shelby to Salem, a town inhabited by Moravians. Rode ten miles, and forded Yadkin river at Shallow Ford. Proceeded on fourteen miles farther to Salem. Went to meeting in the evening; highly entertained with the decency of those people, and with their music. Salem contains about twenty houses, and a place of worship. The people of this town are all mechanics; those of the other two Moravian settlements are all farmers, and all stanch friends to Government.

Monday, 23d. Lay at Salem in the evening. Two Continental officers slept at the tavern, on their way to join their army, One Mr. Simons, a Lieutenant of Col. Washington's dragoons, was exceeding polite, pitied our misfortune in falling into the hands of their militia.

Tuesday, 24th. Moved at ten o'clock in the morning; marched six miles to the old town called Bethabara. Here we joined the camp again. This town is about as large as the other; but not so regularly laid out. The inhabitants very kind to all the prisoners. This night Dr. Johnson and I were disturbed by a Capt. Campbell, who came into our room, and ordered us up in a most peremptory manner. He wanted our bed. I was obliged to go to Col. Campbell, and wake him to get the ruffian turned out of the room; otherwise he would have murdered us, having his sword drawn, and strutting about with it in a truly cowardly manner.

Wednesday, 25th. The men of our detachment, on Capt. DePeyster passing his word for their good behavior, were permitted to go into houses in the town without a guard.

Thursday, 26th, to Saturday, 28th. Nothing extra.

Sunday, 29th. Col. Cleveland waited on Capt. DePeyster and the rest of the officers, and asked us if we, with our men, would come and hear a sermon at ten o'clock. He marched the militia prisoners from their encampment to the town, and halted them; and sent an officer to our quarters to acquaint us they were waiting for us. We then ordered our men to fall in; marched to the front of the prisoners; the whole then proceeded on to a height about half a mile from the town. Here we heard a Presbyterian sermon, truly adapted to their principles and the times; or, rather, stuffed as full of Republicanism as their camp is of horse thieves.

Monday, 30th. A number of the inhabitants assembled at Bethabara to see a poor Tory prisoner executed for a crime of the following nature, viz: A Rebel soldier was passing the guard where the prisoners were confined, and like a brute addressed himself to those poor unhappy people in this style: "Ah, d—n you, you'll all be hanged." This man, with the spirit of a British subject, answered, "Never mind that, it will be your turn next." But Col. Cleveland's goodness extended so far as to reprieve him.

Tuesday, 30th. Rode to Salem in company with Capt. DePeyster, Dr. Johnson and Mr. Supple. This night very cold; froze ice a quarter of an inch thick—the first this fall.

Wednesday, November 1st. My friend, Dr. Johnson, insulted and beaten by Col. Cleveland for attempting to dress a man whom they had cut on the march. Col. Armstrong relieved Cleveland in the afternoon, and took the command.

Thursday, 2d. Took a walk with Capt. DePeyster, Dr. Johnson and Mr. Taylor to Bathania, three miles from Bethabara. This town contains about thirty houses; it is regularly laid out.

Friday, 3d. Heard by a countryman, who was moving his family over the mountains to Nolachucky, that General Leslie had landed at James river, in Virginia.

Saturday, 4th. Dined at a country house.

Sunday, 5th. Set off from Bethabara in company with Lieut. Taylor, Lieut. Stevenson, and William Gist, a militia-man, about six o'clock in the evening. We marched fifteen miles to Yadkin river; forded it, found it very disagreeable. We continued on twenty miles farther to Mr. Miller's plantation, an exceeding good subject. Here we arrived just at daybreak the next morning.

Monday, 6th. Took up our ground in the bushes, about half a mile from the house. At ten o'clock, we sent Mr. Gist to the house for some victuals. He found Mr. Miller at home, who very readily gave us all the assistance that lay in his power. About two o'clock, he brought us some victuals, which we were very happy to see, being very hungry after our fatiguing march the night before. In conversation, which very naturally run upon the safest way, guides, etc., Mr. Miller told us he knew a militia Capt. Turner, and one or two more subjects, then lying in the bushes, who would be very happy to join Lord Cornwallis; and they were also excellent guides. On this we consulted, and thought it prudent to stay all night. Mr. Miller then fetched us a blanket, and immediately set out to find those people.

Tuesday, 7th. Mr. Miller returned informing us that one of those men would be with us at six o'clock in the evening. We waited till seven, but the man not coming, we thought it prudent to go without him. We set out about half after seven; marched six miles to one Carpenter's. When we arrived there, Mr. Carpenter advised us to remain there the remainder of the night, and he would go to Mr. Miller, and send him again for the men. We then consulted, and thought it best to stay a day or two — then to proceed on, without a guide.

Wednesday, 8th. Lay very snug in the bushes. About four o'clock in the afternoon, Mr. Carpenter returned and told us Mr. Miller was gone in search of a guide, and was to return with an answer as soon as possible. Suffered exceedingly with the cold this day.

Thursday, 9th. Heard of the Rebels following us, but they getting false intelligence, returned again, which was much in our favor. In the course of the day, we thought it would be prudent to get the best directions we could, and proceed on, without a guide, rather than remain too long in one place, lest some of those people might be treacherous. We got direction from Mr. Carpenter for sixty miles, and at six o'clock in the evening, set out; marched thirty miles, and halted in the woods at daybreak.

Friday, 10th. Suffered very much with the cold. At six o'clock in the evening set out again. This night saw the moon in an eclipse, and heard several wolves bark. Passed a Rebel party consisting of twelve or fourteen, who lay about twenty yards from the road by a fire; but very fortunately for us, they were all asleep. We marched thirty miles and arrived at Colbert Blair's, just at daybreak.

Saturday, 11th. It began to rain just after we got to Mr. Blair's. Lucky we were indeed. This good man secreted us in his fodder-house, and gave us the best his house afforded.

Sunday, 12th. Remained at Mr. Blair's; a rainy, disagreeable day.

Monday, 13th. Set out from this good man's fodder-house. He conducted us about three miles to a Mr. F. Rider's, who guided us seven miles farther, over the Brushy Mountains, to Catawba river. Mr. John Murray, who lived on the bank of the river, put us over in a canoe, and conducted us three miles to Mr. Ballou's. This old man was about sixty years of age; but his love for his King and his subjects induced him to get up, although very late at night, and guided us seven miles to a Mr. Hilterbrine's. On the way the old man informed us he had two sons who lay out in the woods, who were anxious to go to our army, and were also good guides. He also told us of one Williams, that was a good guide, and who would be glad to go with us. We told the old man we should be very happy to have them, as the road began to grow more dangerous, and we quite unacquainted with the way. This poor old man expressed a great deal of anxiety for our safety, and at last told us he would go the next day and endeavor to find them, and send them to us. We arrived at Hilterbrine's about six o'clock in the morning of the 14th. He received us with great caution, lest we should be treacherous; but when he found we were British officers he was very kind.

Wednesday, 15th. Just as we were drinking a dish of coffee, on a rock, after dusk, those three young men came to us on horseback, which made us very happy. We set out immediately, and marched twenty miles over the Brushy Mountains, where there was nothing but Indian paths. Crossed several small rivers. We arrived at one Sheppard's plantation, just at daybreak of the 16th. This poor family were so completely stripped of everything they had, by the Rebels, that they could give us nothing but a hoe cake, and some dried beef, which was but a very indifferent repast for hungry stomachs. At six o'clock in the evening set out; marched sixteen miles to Camp's Ford of Second Broad river; forded it, and continued on three and a half miles farther to Island Ford of Main Broad river; forded it, and marched one mile to Capt. Townsend's plantation. This man received three balls in the action on King's Mountain, and was at home on parole. He was very happy to see us, and gave us the best his house afforded.

Friday, 17th. Set out at six o'clock in the evening; marched twelve miles to a Mr. Morris'. Here we were told that a party of Rebels were directly in our front; that we had better remain there that night, in which time we could send Mr. Williams, who was with us, and well acquainted with that neighborhood, to get a militia Capt. Robins, who lay out in the woods, and was going to our army in a day or two. This man was so good a guide that it induced us to stay.

Saturday, 18th. Lay in the woods; fared pretty well.

Sunday, 19th. Mr. Williams returned, but without effecting what he went after. We had a council of safety; found it necessary to proceed on. We got Mr. Murray to guide us to the main road that leads to the Iron Works, which is twelve miles distant. We set out about three o'clock in the afternoon; took by-paths, and got in the main road just at dusk. We crossed Pacolet river, Lawson's Fork, and Tyger river; passed a Rebel guard; marched thirty-seven miles, and arrived at James Duncan's plantation, half an hour before daybreak of the 20th. About ten o'clock Mrs. Duncan rode out to see if she could get any intelligence of our army, and of the Rebel army, that we might shun the latter. Mrs. Duncan returned in less than an hour, with the disagreeable news that the Rebel army was marching within two miles of us, and were going to encamp at Blackstock's, about four miles from us. This news truly discouraged me. About five o'clock in the evening Mr. Duncan came to us with agreeable news — that Col. Tarleton was in pursuit of the Rebels. At six o'clock a Mr. Jackson came to us, and informed us he had seen Col. Tarleton; he had also heard he had had an action with Sumter, who commanded the Rebels, but did not know the particulars. He advised us to go to his house and stay all night, as we would be perfectly safe there, and the next morning go to Mr. Smith's, where we could hear the particulars of the action, as there were some of the Legion wounded there. We agreed to what the man said; staid all night at his house, where we were treated very kindly.

Tuesday, 21st.   Mr. Duncan conducted us to Mr. Smith's, where we found six of the Legion wounded.

Wednesday, 22d.   Set out from Archey Smith's on horseback, which the subjects in that neighborhood supplied us with. They brought us on thirteen miles to one Adair's. Here we dismounted, and those good people returned. We continued thirteen miles to Williams' Fort, which was commanded by Col. Kirkland, who received us very kindly.

Thursday, 23d.   Set out from Col. Kirkland's, who was kind enough to lend us horses as far as Saluda. Left the horses here; crossed in a scow; walked a mile to Col. Mayson's; dined; got horses and rode to Ninety Six. Arrived at Capt. John Barbarie's quarters, about eight o'clock in the evening.

Friday, 24th.   Remained at Ninety Six; nothing extra.

Saturday, 25th.   Set out for Charleston, Where I arrived the 29th of November; nothing worth notice on the journey.

Eno Reeves:
Letterbook Extracts, January 2–17, 1781

Yesterday being the last time we (the officers of the regiment), expected to be together, as the arrangement was to take place this day, we had an elegant Regimental Dinner and entertainment, at which all the Field and other officers were present, with a few from the German Regiment, who had arrived with the men of their regiment that belong to the Penna. Line. We spent the day very pleasantly and the evening 'till about ten o'clock as cheerfully as we could wish, when we were disturbed by the huzzas of the soldiers upon the Right Division, answered by those on the Left. I went on the Parade and found numbers in small groups whispering and busily running up and down the Line. In a short time a gun was fired upon the Right and answered by one on the right of the Second Brigade, and a skyrocket thrown from the center of the first, which was accompanied by a general huzza throughout the Line, and the soldiers running out with their arms, accoutrements and knapsacks. I immediately found it was a mutiny, and that the guns and skyrocket were the signals. The officers in general exerted themselves to keep the men quiet, and keep them from turning out. We each applied himself to his own company, endeavored to keep them in their huts and lay by their arms, which they would do while we were present, but the moment we left one hut to go to another, they would be out again. Their excuse was they thought it was an alarm and the enemy coming on.

Next they began to move in crowds to the Parade, going up to the Right, which was the place appointed for their rendezvous. Lieut. White of our regiment in endeavoring to stop one of these crowds, was shot through the thigh, and Capt. Samuel Tolbert in opposing another party was shot through the body, of which he is very ill. They continued huzzaing and fireing in riotous manner, so that it soon became dangerous for an officer to oppose them by force. We then left them to go their own way.

Hearing a confused noise to the Right, between the line of Huts and Mrs. Wicks, curiosity led me that way, and it being dark in the orchard I mixed among the crowd and found they had broken open the magazine and were preparing to take off the cannon.

January 2 1781.

———

Mount Kemble.

In taking possession of the cannon they forced the sentinel from his post, and placed one of their own men. One of the mutineers coming officiously up to force him away (thinking him to be one of our sentinels) received a ball through the head and died instantly.

A dispute arose among the mutineers about firing the alarms with the cannon, and continued for a considerable time — one party aledging that it would arouse the timid soldiery, the other objected because it would alarm the inhabitants. For a while I expected the dispute would be decided by the bayonet, but the gunner in the meantime slip'd up to the piece and put a match to it, which ended the affair. Every discharge of the cannon was accompanied by a confused huzza and a general discharge of musketry.

About this time Gen. Wayne and several field officers (mounted) arrived. Gen. Wayne and Col. Richard Butler spoke to them for a considerable time, but it had no effect — their answer was, they had been wronged and were determined to see themselves righted. He replied that he would right them as far as in his power. They rejoined, it was out of his power, their business was not with the officers, but with Congress and the Governor and Council of the State; 'twas they had wronged and they must right. With that, several platoons fired over the General's head. The General called out, "if you mean to kill me, shoot me at once, here's my breast," opening his coat. They replied that it was not their intention to hurt or disturb an officer of the Line, (two or three individuals excepted); that they had nothing against their officers, and they would oppose any person that would attempt anything of the kind.

A part of the Fourth Regiment was paraded and led on by Capt. Campbell, to recapture the cannon; they were ordered to charge and rush on — they charged but would not advance, then dispersed and left the officer alone. Soon after a soldier from the mob made a charge upon Lieut. Col. William Butler, who was obliged to retreat between the huts to save his life. He went around one hut and the soldier around another to head him, met Capt. Bettin who was coming down the alley, who seeing a man coming towards him on a charge, charged his Espontoon to oppose him, when the fellow fired his piece and shot the Captain through the body and he died two hours later.

January 2 1781.

————

Mount Kemble.

About twelve o'clock they sent parties to relieve or seize the old Camp guard, and posted sentinels all round the camp. At one o'clock they moved off towards the left of the Line with the cannon and when they reached the centre they fired a shot. As they came down the line, they turned the soldiers out of every hut, and those who would not go with them were obliged to hide 'till they were gone. They continued huzzaing and a disorderly firing 'till they went off, about two o'clock, with drums and fifes playing, under command of the sergeants, in regular platoons, with a front and rear guard.

Gen. Wayne met them as they were marching off and endeavored to persuade them back, but to no purpose; he then inquired which way they were going, and they replied either to Trenton or Philadelphia. He begged them not to attempt to go to the enemy. They declared it was not their intention, and that they would hang any man who would attempt it, and for that, if the enemy should come out in consequence of this revolt, they would turn back and fight them. "If that is your sentiments," said the General, "I'll not leave you, and if you wont allow me to march in your front, I'll follow in your rear."

This day Col. Stewart and Richard Butler joined Gen.

Wayne in hopes they could turn them when they grew cooler, being much agitated with liquor, when they went off, it being New Years day they had drawn half a pint per man. The men have continued going off in small parties all day. About one o'clock one hundred head of cattle came in from the Eastward, which they drove off to their main body, which lay in a wood near Vealtown, leaving a few behind for the use of the officers.

When we came to draw provisions and State stores this day, we found that near half of the men of our regiment had remained.

The men went off very civily last night to what might have been expected from such a mob. They did not attempt to plunder our officers' huts or insult them in the least, except those who were obstinate in opposing them. They did not attempt to take with them any part of the State stores, which appears to me a little extraordinary, for men when they get but little want more.

The militia are called out, they are to assemble at Chatham, in order to oppose the enemy if they come out, or the mutineers if they attempt going to them.

January 2, 1781.

———

Dr Liddel's, Mendem.

On the afternoon of the 2d inst. I procured wagons and moved all the officers' baggage out of camp to Mr. Daniel Drake's on the S—— Road, in Mendem, about three miles from the huts, to which place most of the officers and their boys returned.

The revolted party marched from Vealtown to Middlebrook, and the 3rd went on to Princetown. In the evening an Express arrived from Gen. Wayne, ordering all officers of the Division (a quartermaster and subaltern from each regiment excepted), to press horses and make all possible speed to Pennington. (Ensign Brooke was left behind and I as Quartermaster, of course.) The greater part of the Officers left the night of the 3rd, and the others followed on the fourth. Since this affair Mrs. Wicks and Dr. Liddel's very agreeable families have been kept in continual alarm.

On the 5 inst. as I was obliged to be in camp once every day, I concluded it would be best to move in and stay there, and in consequence of that resolution moved my baggage, and when it had come as far as Dr Liddel's he very kindly offered me the use of his house and to live with his family. I accepted the generous offer with pleasure. Drank tea and spent the afternoon with the agreeable young ladies.

About ten o'clock I walked in to camp to see if all was quiet, and when I came on the parade, I found a number of men assembled, and when I reached our regiment, a signal gun was fired on the right of the Division, and in a short time a large party collected and endeavored to take off the two remaining pieces of artillery. Not finding it convenient they went off about twelve o'clock and left them with us. This party in going off behaved with less noise and more impertinence than the first. They fired on two or three officers as they were going out of camp. About one o'clock I returned from camp to the Doctor's, where I found the family up, with the addition of Mrs. Wicks and her agreeable daughter, almost frightened out of their lives, as some of the mutineers made their appearance around their house and insisted on their showing them where to find horses.

Everything is still again today and the young ladies not much the worse for their fright.

January 6, 1781.

———

Dr Liddel's, Mendem.

We are informed that the mutineers lay at Princetown and intend to await the arrival of some persons from Congress and the Governor of the State. One Sergeant Williams commands the Line, a sergeant is appointed to the command of each regiment, and the first sergeants of each company still keep the command, except in some few instances where they have misbehaved and in consequence turned out. They have likewise a Board of Sergeants, consisting of twelve, a president and secretary, by whom all business is transacted, orders issued, provision returns, &c. They have kept the men in such order on the march and in Princetown as reflects on them the highest honor. But the stragglers who went off in small parties have committed great depredations on the road.

The militia of this and neighboring counties are called out and ordered to rendezvous at Chatham, as well to defend the lines from any attempt of the enemy to penetrate the country at this time as to hinder any of the mutineers from taking that route, should they attempt it. We have certain intelligence that the enemy have reinforced Staten Island with a large body of men to be ready for any movement that may offer. I have spent my time very agreeably in this very pleasant family in the constant company of the ever amiable and very agreeable Miss Betsy Liddel, and very often with the additional happiness of Miss Wicks' company, and sometimes with Col. Spencer's lovely family, which has caused long and perhaps tedious evenings to pass away unnoticed. Capt. William Gray being here at this time, when the ladies did not interfere, with the Doctor and myself would ply the apple-toddy and amuse ourselves with nuts. Thus I have striven to beguile care, for you must know this revolt has given me many uneasy hours.

Yesterday Major Fishbourn went on express from headquarters with dispatches for Gen. Wayne. His Excellency has been expected down from New Windsor, but it was thought most expedient for him to remain.

January 14, 1781.

———

Dr. Liddel's, Mendem.

Last evening Capt. Stake and Steele arrived from Pennington, (where the officers of the Line are quartered), with the following intelligence. The Governor of Pennsylvania, with a Committee composed of a member of Congress, one of the Council, one of the Assembly and a citizen, to settle or treat with our mutineers. Previous to their arrival, three spies who had come from Gen. Clinton (British) were arrested by the revolters, and after being drum'd along the Line were delivered to Gen. Wayne to be tried. They brought a letter from Gen. Clinton to this effect — That if the revolted party would come to Amboy, he was waiting with a great force on Staten Island to receive them; that he would grant them all they could expect from this revolt, that is their arrearages of pay and clothing, make up their depreciation in hard money, with the addition of several guineas to each man. To their immortal honor, they rejected it, and delivered up the messengers as spies, who were tried the evening of the same day and hung the next morning about eight o'clock, and I am informed are to be left hanging till they fall from the gallows.

You know a great number of the men enlisted *for three years or during the war*, which has for a long time given cause of uneasiness in the minds of the soldiers. They claim their discharge at the expiration of three years, while the State claims their services for the war. However, that matter is now given up and proposals made to the non-commissioned officers and soldiers of the Penna. Line to the following purport: That every non commissioned officer and soldier whose enlistment specifies *three years or during the war*, shall be discharged, and that the gratuity of one hundred dollars given by Congress is not looked upon as a bounty. That those enlisted for the war were to remain in service, but that the Governor would endeavor to have something done for them in consideration of the smallness of their bounty, and that they should be indulged with a furlough for a short time. That auditors shall be appointed to settle their accounts of depreciation and certificates given for them as soon as possible. That where the enlistment cannot be produced the soldier's oath shall be taken, with regard to the terms of his enlistment and he discharged thereon accordingly. And if a soldier can prove that he was forced to enlist or any undue advantage taken of him, he shall be discharged. That every one on producing his discharge or furlough to the Clothiers and Commissioners at Trentown, shall receive one shirt, one pair of overalls and a pair of shoes. This was agreed to by the mutineers, and they are to march tomorrow to Trentown, and the Committee to begin their business at once. The paymasters are sent for, who are to bring all enlistments and other regimental papers.

Col. Humpton has arrived at Trentown and has sent up for his baggage — for the purpose of sending which, I have this day been to Squire Dailey's who has promised to send me a wagon tomorrow.

January 14, 1781.

———

Dr. Liddel's, Mendem.

On the 15th inst. Lieut. Col. William Butler received orders from Gen. Wayne to repair to Pennington with all the officers' baggage and the remaining men of the Line. Of the latter, there were not many, as they have been joining the rest in small parties ever since the revolt.

Squire Dailey disappointed me in a wagon, and I wrote to Squire Stiles for one for the Colonel's baggage.

On the morning of 16th breakfasted at Col. Spencer's and got an order on Squire Stiles for three wagons, but on my arrival at his house found a prior order of the Deputy Q. M. from Morristown had deprived me of what he could furnish. I then proceeded to Squire Dailey's at Chatham, who promised me three, which he was to send the following morning. You must know that the mutineers stole my horse and I now have a borrowed one.

I stopped at Lieut. Col. Hay's quarters and was agreeably surprised to find him there as he had arrived in the course of the day from Pennington. The Committee have begun to settle with the men and proceed rapidly.

The 17th I procured a wagon for the Colonel's baggage and gave orders for its setting off the next morning. I awaited the arrival of the teams from Chatham with great impatience, but to my great mortification found myself again disappointed. The teams for twelve miles round this place have been so harrassed since our arrival in quarters, with assisting in drawing the timber for building, drawing forage, provisions and timber for the redoubts, with what the mutineers impressed and what we have employed to move our stores, that a person might almost as well attempt to make a wagon and horses as to procure them otherwise.

January 17, 1781.

Oliver De Lancey: Journal, January 3–21, 1781

On the third of January in the morning received intelligence by an Emissary that the Pensylvanians had Mutinyed in their Camp in Morristown that the alarm Guns had been fired and Beacons lighted. He was immediately dispatched to a Correspondent in New Jersey.

Orders were sent to the British Grenadiers, British Light Infantry, Forty second, Thirty seventh Regiments, Hessian Grenadiers and Hessian Yagers to hold themselves in readiness to march at a moments notice.

On Thursday the fourth of January received the following Intelligence from a Correspondent dated the third of January The Pensylvania Troops Commanded by General Wayne Mutinyed on Monday last, there was an universal complaint in the Camp that they had received no Pay, Cloathing, and a Scanty allowance of Provision, that a great number of these Troops were detained longer than they enlisted for, their terms being expired above ten Months, these complaints led them to mutiny to a Man, about 1500 seized on the Military Magazines, provision and Artillery which consisted of four Field pieces, and in a body marched from their Huts the same day to Vealtown, distant about seven Miles General Wayne followed, but they will not listen to any proposals and persist in going to Congress for redress, or to disband. yesterday they Marched to Middlebrook and this Morning towards Princeton — Two Companys of Riflemen detached from the Pensylvanians and posted at Bottle hill Marched off this Morning to join them — Their officers following them.

The Messenger sent out as above returned with the following Intelligence

The Pensylvania line have been for some time much dissatisfied, on Monday last they turned out in number about 1200 declaring they would serve no longer unless their grievances were redressed, as they had not received either Pay, Cloathing, or Provisions a Riot had ensued in which an Officer was killed and four wounded The Insurgents had five or six wounded. They collected the Artillery Stores, Waggons, Provisions &c &c Marched out of Camp & passed by Wayne's Quarters who sent out a Message to them requesting them to desist or the consequences would prove fatal, they refused & proceeded on their March 'till evening when they took Post on an advantageous piece of ground and Elected Officers from among themselves, appointing a Sergeant Major who was a British Deserter to Command them with the Rank of Major General — On Tuesday they marched to Middlebrook and yesterday to Brunswick where they now are.

On Tuesday morning a Message was sent them by the Officers from Camp, desiring to know their intentions, they refused to receive this Message — A Flag of Truce was sent to the same effect — some said they had served their three years against their inclinations and would continue no longer on any account, others said they would not return unless their grievances were redressed — The Rebels have removed all their Boats to the other side of the Delawar least the Rioters should cross the River — On their first rising the Artillery refused to join, but, being threatened with the Bayonet they consented — Two Companys of Riflemen posted at Bottle hill near Chatham had marched to join them. the Militia not daring to oppose them.

On Thursday Evening three Copys of the following proposals were sent off to the Revolters, one by the Raritan River the others by Newark and Elizabethtown.

It being reported at New York that the Pensylvania Troops and others having been defrauded of their Pay, Cloathing and Provisions are assembled to redress their grievances, and also that notwithstanding the terms of their inlistments are expired they have been forcibly detained in the service where they have suffered every kind of misery and oppression,

They are now offered to be taken under the protection of the British Government, to have their Rights restored free pardon for all former offences, and that Pay due them from the Congress faithfully paid to them, without any expectation of Military service (except it may be voluntary) upon laying down their Arms and returning to their allegiance.

For which purpose if they will send Commissioners to

Amboy they will there be met by People empowered to treat with them & Faith pledged for their security

It is recommended to them for their own safety to move behind South River and whenever they request it a Body of British Troops shall protect them.

It is needless to point out the inability as well as want of inclination in the Congress to relieve them, or to tell them the severitys that will be used towards them by the Rebel leaders should they think of returning to their former Servitude

It will be proved to the Commissioners they may chuse to send that the Authority from whence this comes is sufficient to insure the performance of the above proposals.

> To the person appointed by the Pensylvania Troops
> to lead them in their present struggle for their
> Libertys and Rights.

As soon as the above was dispatched, Orders were immediately sent to the two Battallions of Light Infantry, the British Grenadiers, three Battallions Hessian Grenadiers and the Yagers to march immediately to Denyses Ferry, whence they crossed the 5th to Staten Island and Cantoned on the Road to Richmond except the Yagers who lay on the road to Deckers ferry.

On the 5th I sent out three copies of the proposals and a Verbal Message to the same import to the Pennsylvanians.

A number of men were sent out towards West point the Clove and Morristown to watch the movements that way

On the 6th received a letter acknowledging the receipt of the proposals sent by Newark, informing me they were forwarded by a faithful friend to Princeton where the Pensylvania Troops had halted, that the Rebel Militia were all ordered out and the Jersey Brigade had moved from Pompton to Morristown that General Washington was on his way from West point to see General Wayne.

On the 7th received Information from General Skinner that the Pensylvanians continued their March towards Brunswick and that Wayne was detained a Prisoner among them.

That Col. Dayton with the Jersey Brigade was at Morristown but, hearing the Riflemen and some Light horse had joined the Insurgents he halted fearing a defection among his own Troops and that he heard a man sent with proposals was seen safe within a Mile of the Revolters on Friday Evening.

Information by New York that they were at Rocky hill near Princetown.

On the 8th a man came over by the Blazing Star who said part of them were gone to Trenton.

On the 9th there being an appearance of bad weather the Hessian Grenadiers went back to Long Island.

About twelve o'Clock this day Received a letter from the Jerseys of which the following is an Extract dated Monday Night

The Person I sent to Princetown is just returned which place he left this morning, your address he delivered Saturday evening, the same night two persons arrived with like addresses they were both detained.

The Pensylvania Troops are still at Princetown their number 1700, they keep up order in the Town, no Officer is permitted to come into them but by a Flag of Truce — General Wayne and Governor Reed of Pensylvania had an interview Yesterday and made some proposals, but, they were rejected by the Troops, they require their Pay due in hard money and a discharge

Your offers are now known throughout the Army and will have great influence over the Majority of them, the most sensible people and Officers here think they will yet join you as interest and Policy ought to lead them to it — I am fully satisfied the Congress can not nor will not give them redress, in this case they will come over to you.

The Commander in Chief received Information also this day much to the same purpose as the above letter, dated the 8th at 10 o'clock in the morning.

Received intelligence by New York that came from Morristown and also from Major General Phillips, all which agree that the Revolters are at Princetown, still insisting on the compliance of the Congress to their Demands.

This day I sent out some people from the Refugee Post at Bergen Point and one from the Armed Vessel.

On the 10th the Reports the same, no person came in that could be confided in.

On the 11th Received intelligence by a man who had passed

by the Pensylvanians, that they were at Princetown, still persisting in their demands. the man sent out the 9th returned
this day, reports the situation of the Pensylvanians the same,
says the Guards of Militia along the Coast are so numerous as
to prevent any persons geting in.

On the 12th a party went into the Country, the officer who
Commanded was informed by a friend that a person who had
come from Princetown in the morning, said every thing remained in the same situation we had before heard, they still
refuse all the offers that have been made them; the Party was
fired upon in three or four places

The man sent out was met by a person who informed him
the Rebel Colonel Barber came to Elizabeth Town Yesterday
and reported that eight hundred of the Revolters had absolutely refused to come to any terms; That on Thursday
morning they were supplied with three Waggon loads of
Arms and Ammunition that the whole body were to march
for Trenton and are supposed to be there now — The Militia
had received Orders to follow them — That last night and the
night before the Officers of the Jersey Brigade were under the
necessity of watching their Camp to prevent their people joining the Pensylvanians.

This night received the following intelligence from a
Gentleman who came in and can be depended on. On the 9th
some of the Pensylvanians who had differed in opinion from
the Revolters, told him they were now going to join them
having changed their intention. — That a Sergeant Major of
the 4th Battallion Commanded them, they had not the least
apprehension of the Jersey Troops as they were of the same
sentiments with themselves. — Their demands were for their
arrears of Pay and Cloathing, and those that had inlisted for
three Years insisted on having their discharges, that the depreciation should be made good to them, and should they be
reconciled the Officers they have now appointed from among
themselves are to be continued being determined not to serve
under their late Officers. — They have also stipulated a pardon particularly for all the principle Revolters. One of them a
Deserter from the 7th Regiment said if Congress did not redress their Complaints they knew what course to take — The
Militia of the Jerseys say they are only doing themselves

Justice. General Wayne is kept among them as an hostage. Numbers declare they will not serve Congress at any rate. They have taken two Men one with proposals, the other served as a Guide. They call themselves 2500 but, he thinks from the best accounts they do not exceed 2000 all the Boats are carried to the West Side of the Delawar and kept Guarded. The Militia are ordered out A friend in the Country told him that the reports of their going to Trenton was not true. That two Companys of Riflemen had joined them with one Field piece. some of the insurgents were accidentally killed when they fired upon their Officers, who in general denounce Vengeance against them and declare they will not serve unless an exemplary Punishment is inflicted, it seems the general opinion, that the Jersey Brigade are of the same Sentiments.

On the 13th a man came in from Newark who says they are still at Princetown. The people sent out to them are not yet returned.

On Monday the 15th received the following Intelligence

William Boyce left Philadelphia on Wednesday last, crossed the Delawar on Thursday at Trenton where the Pensylvanians are. he spoke to their out Posts their numbers are said to be from 1500 to 2000 — They demand their back Pay, Cloathing, and the discharges of those whose time of enlistment had expired

There was a Committee of Congress at Barclay's Tavern on the West side of the Delawar in order to adjust matters some were for forcing them, others for submitting to all their Demands — on the West side of the River he was told they were not to be paid for ten days: on the East side they told him it was to be done that day, and they were to have their discharges it however was not decided. They had delivered over two Prisoners taken amongst them with proposals, to the Committee of Congress.

General Wayne is among them as a Prisoner Governor Reed was permitted to have an hours Conversation with him and then sent back to the Committee of Congress. They are Commanded by one Williams, who was a Sergeant Major — They left Princetown on Wednesday last, he met small parties of Soldiers all along the road that seemed to have come from other parts of the Army, some with and some without

Arms. — At Philadelphia the People seemed much alarmed as it was reported they had no money and were disappointed in the Cloathing expected for the Army as Paul Jones who was to convoy it put back to *L'Orient* his Ships being dismasted and in distress. He did not hear that General Washington was at Philadelphia, on the contrary about two miles on the other side Brunswick, he met two Men going with an Express from him to General Wayne, and a Gentleman who was with him and had spoke to the Men sayd Mr. Washington's presence was necessary with his Army as they apprehended a Revolt would take place there.

The Opinion of the people in general is that the Troops are only doing themselves justice — They have killed a Captn Talbot, Tatton and another whose name he does not know There was a report at first of their intention to come over to us but from their moving to Trenton he does not think it likely At Elizabeth Town he heard the two Men taken up were hanged on friday There is a report that five hundred of the Militia are at and about that place.

General Skinner informs me that the Jersey Troops were in the same State as to their Demands, but, have been quieted by a promise of being satisfied in ten days, six of which are elapsed.

Mr. H. informed me that Col. Dayton spread a Report that the Pensylvanians were satisfied, upon which his own people immediately made the same demands, and he was obliged to contradict his own report to quiet them.

On the 15th received a letter from a correspondent saying that the Pensylvanians had not paid that attention to the offers made them by us, which he thought Policy and Interest would have led them to, that he did not imagine Congress would grant them relief, but, force them to submission — That General Washington was not gone to Congress, as he had mentioned in his last letter.

A Man came in who sayd they had left Princetown, but his Intelligence is not to be relied on, he having received it from a Sergeant, who had deserted them and was going home.

The Pensylvanians moving so far from us, and in no instance shewing a disposition to accept of the offers made them. The Commander in Chief returned to Town

No account coming in that could be depended on and no appearance of the Pensylvanians intending any thing in our favour the Troops were ordered to Long Island the 19th.

The same day I was informed from South Amboy, that the Men taken up were people I had sent out, & from the description, I know one of them — They were hanged on friday opposite Trenton where the Pensylvanians still remained not having determined any thing. The 20th received accounts of their being at Trenton, that they were discharging some of them, they having settled with a Committee of Congress

Same Day the account of their being still at Trenton confirmed. The Committee of Congress consists of Genl. Sullivan, Mr. Mathews, Mr. Witherspoon and Mr. Atley. they sit at T. Barclay's Tavern on the Pensylvania side.

Same day a Man I sent out the 7th with a Copy of the proposals got to Princetown on Wednesday where he met a Man, he suspected to be on a similar errand; after some conversation, they found out that their business was the same, they went on together to Trenton to which place the Pensylvanians had Marched. Finding that two Men had been taken up they dropped their Papers, which were carried to Mr. Reed and General Wayne who offered one hundred Guineas reward for the apprehending whoever brought them. One of them being known by a Colonel Hayes and he having intimated to him some suspicions of his designs, they crossed the Delaware and went into Pensylvania where they saw the execution of the two men, whom he describes exactly.

They are commanded by a Sergeant Williams who is a Pensylvanian and had some little property, he was taken Prisoner in the Year 1776 at Princetown and enlisted in one of our Provincial Regiments, raised at that time from which he deserted

There was a Committee of a Sergeant of each Regt. to meet the Committee of Congress, the proposals herewith inclos'd were made to them at Princetown the 7th of January & the answer signed by the Secretary of the Committee of Sergeants was given the 8th and their determination respecting the two prisoners January the 10th at Trenton.

This person adds that they do not intend going home untill every Man is discharged and tho' they lay down their

Arms as they are settled with yet they do not permit them to be taken away but keep a Centry of their own over them

The Pensylvanian Officers are very much dissatisfied, as the Soldiers are allowed to Swear to any thing and their words Credited before any vouched account, which they choose to say they were obliged to sign

He confirms the account of their having on the first of January killed a Captain and wounded another, with a Lieutenant and Ensign, one Soldier was also killed.

They have four pieces of Cannon, they left one spiked at Morristown, he expects the other Man in, who was with him, every moment.

21st. This day a Captain of the 3d Jersey Regiment, who I had corresponded with came over to us he confirms the information of yesterday.

He says they will not stir till they are paid and ask hard Money.

The man who was expected, returned this day his accounts are the same.

He says they have shown no intention of coming to us, but on the contrary declared that should the British interfere, they would take up arms to oppose them as readily as ever.

From all accounts the Country is much alarmed the Militia on the Roads made the Communication more difficult, than at any other time, they having also destroy'd all the Boats Cannoes &c.

George Washington to Philip Schuyler

New Windsor, January 10, 1781.
Dear Sir: Your favor of the 5th. I have had the pleasure to receive. The event, which I have long dreaded would be the consequence of keeping the Army without pay, Cloathing, and (frequently without) Provision, has at length come to pass. On the Night of the first instant a general Mutiny of the Non Comd. and privates of the Pensyla. line (near Morristown) took place; in attempting to suppress which, some Officers lost their lives, and others got wounded, to little effect. The Mutineers Marched off in compact and regular order by Platoons, after possessing themselves of the Artillery and stripping the Magazine of its Stores; declaring it to be their intention to go to Congress, and demand a redress of their Grievances.

Genl. Wayne who Comd., and the Colonels R. Butlar and Stewart, after finding all authority and influence at an end, determined to keep with them and try lenitives; which, by what I can learn, they have practiced to as little effect as either of the other two. The line have halted at Princeton, discovering no inclination to go further; which has a bad aspect, as it is (to them) a favourable intermediate point between Congress and the enemy, and in that view very fit for their purpose of negotiation.

Some powerful considerations, not proper to be communicated in a letter (liable to miscarriage) and the advice of the General Officers at this Post against the measure, strengthened by Governor Clinton's opinion, restrained my setting out for the revolted Troops upon the first notice I had of them. In five minutes I shall step into the Boat for West point, where I have appointed the commanding Officers of Corps to meet me, and think it very probable I shall proceed thence to Morristown, &ca.

Mrs. Washington thanks Mrs. Schuyler, as I do both of you, for your kind and friendly invitation to Albany; the distresses of the Army are too great and complicated, for me to think of private gratifications. Our best wishes attend you, and all around your fireside, and I am etc.

PS. I have this instant receiv'd authentic informn. that the Mutineers have delivered up one of Sir Henry Clintons Emissary's (with his guide) charged with written propositions very favourable to the revolted Troops, tho witht. any intn. I am perswd. of fulfilling them. This is an unequivocal proof of their having no intention to go to the Enemy. A Comee. of Congress are with them.

Nathanael Greene to Alexander Hamilton

Camp on Pedee River
January 10th 1781

My dear Colonel

General de Portail being on his way to the Northward gives me an opportunity to write you; which I should have done before, had not my letters to his Excellency contained as full information of the state of things, as I was able to give from the little time I had been in the department.

When I was appointed to this command I expected to meet with many new and singular difficulties; but they infinitely exceed what I apprehended. This is really carrying on a war in an enemy's Country: for you cannot establish the most inconsiderable Magazine or convey the smallest quantity of Stores from one post to another, without being obligd to detach guards for their security. The division among the people is much greater than I imagined, and the Whigs and Tories persecute each other, with little less than savage fury. There is nothing but murders and devastations in every quarter.

The loss of our Army at Charlestown, and the defeat of General Gates, has been the cause of keeping such shoals of Militia on foot, and their service has been accompanied with such destruction and loss, as has almost laid waste the whole Country. Nothing has been more destructive to the true interest of this Country, than the mode adopted for its defence. Two misfortunes happening one after the other may have rendered it unavoidable the last season; but should it be continued, the Inhabitants are inevitably ruined, and the resources of the Country rendered incapable of affording support to an Army competent to its defence. Government here is infinitely more popular than to the Northward; and there is no such thing as National character or National Sentiment. The Inhabitants are from all quarters of the globe; and as various in their opinions, projects and schemes, as their manners and habits are from their early education. Those in office from a

vanity to be thought powerful join in the measure of imposing upon the public respecting the strength and resources of
these Southern States; and while Congress and the Minister
of France are kept under this fatal delusion I fear little support
will be given to this department. The Inhabitants are numerous but they would be rather formidable abroad than at
home. They are scatterd over such a vast extent of Country
that it is difficult to collect and still more difficult to subsist
them. There is a great spirit of enterprize among the back
people; and those that come out as Volunteers are not a little
formidable to the enemy. There are also some particular
Corps under Sumpter, Marion and Clarke that are bold and
daring; the rest of the Militia are better calculated to destroy
provisions than oppose the Enimy.

At Philadelphia and all my journey through the Country, I
endeavord to impress upon those in power the necessity of
sending cloathing and supplies of every kind immediately to
this Army. But poverty was urged as a plea or bar to every application. They all promised fair; but I fear will do but little:
ability is wanting with some and inclination with others.
Public credit is so totally lost, that private people will not give
their aid, though they see themselves involved in one common ruin. It is my opinion that General Washingtons influence will do more than all the Assemblies upon the
Continent. I always thought him exceeding popular; but in
many places he is little less than ador'd; and universally admir'd. His influence in this Country might possibly effect
somthing great. However I found myself exceedingly well receivd; but more from being the friend of the Generals than
from my own merit.

This Country wants for its defence a small but well appointed Army: organized so as to move with great celerity. It
should consist of about 5000 Infantry and from eight hundred to a thousand horse. The Enimy cannot maintain a large
force in this quarter, neither can we. The resources of the
Country are too small to subsist a large body of troops at any
one point; and to draw supplies from a distance through such
long tracks of barren land, will be next to impossible, unless
the business can be aided by a water transportation; and in
either case, it will be accompanied with an amazing expence.

Could we get a superiority of horse we could soon render it difficult for Lord Cornwallis to hold his position so far in the Country: nor should I be under any apprehension with a much inferior force to his, of taking post near him, if I had but such a body of horse. But the enimy's horse is so much superior to ours, that we cannot move a detachment towards them without hazarding its ruin.

When I came to the Army I found it in a most wretched condition. The Officers had lost all confidence in the General, and the troops all their dicipline. The troops had not only lost their dicipline; but they were so addicted to plundering that they were a terror to the Country. The General and I met at least upon very civil terms; and he expressed the greatest happiness at my being appointed to succeed him. General Smallwood and he were not upon good terms; the former suspected the latter of having an intention to supplant him; but many think without reason. Others again are of opinion his suspicions were well founded; and that Smallwood was not a little mortified at my being appointed to this department; and got outragious when he heard Baron Stuben was coming also. How the matter was I know not; certain it is he is gone home having refus'd to act under Baron Stuben and declares he will not serve at all unless Congress will give him a commission dated at least two years before his appointment. This I think can never happen notwithstanding his private merit and the claim of the State.

The battle of Camden here is represented widely different from what it is to the Northward. Col Williams thinks that none of the General Officers were entitled to any extraordinary merit. The action was short and succeeded by a flight wherein every body took care of themselves as well Officers and soldiers. Not an officer except Major Anderson and one or two Captains that brought off the field of battle a single soldier. The Col also says that General Gates would have shared little more disgrace than is the common lot of the unfortunate notwithstanding he was early off, if he had only halted at the Waxhaws or Charlotte: the first about sixty, and the last about eighty miles, from the field of battle. What little incidents either give or destroy reputation. How many long hours a man may labour with an honest zeal in his

Countrys service and be disgracd for the most triffling error either in conduct or opinion. Hume very justly observes no man will have reputation unless he is useful to society, be his merit or abilities what they may. Therefore it is necessary for a man to be fortunate as well as wise and just. The greater part of the loss of the Maryland line in the action of Cambden happened after they began to retreat: indeed this was the case with all the troops. What gave Smallwood such great reputation was his halt at Salsbury which was nothing but accident. You know there is great parties prevailing in the Maryland Line and perhaps his merit is not a little diminished on that account. I think him a brave and good officer; but too slow to effect any thing great in a department like this, where embarassments are without number, and where nothing can be effected without the greatest promtitude and decision.

This army is in such a wretched condition that I hardly know what to do with it. The Officers have got such a habit of neglegence, and the soldiers so loose and disorderly that it is next to impossible to give it a military complexion. Without clothing I am sure I shall never do it. I call no councils of war; and I communicate my intentions to very few. The Army was posted at Charlotte when I came up with it; and in a Council it had been determined to winter there; but the difficulty of procuring subsistence and other reasons inducd me not only to take a new position, but to make an entire new disposition. All this I effected by a single order having first made the necessary enquiry respecting the new positions by sending a man to examin the grounds and other requisites. If I cannot inspire the Army with confidence and respect by an independant conduct I foresee it will be impossible to instill dicipline and order among the troops.

General Lesly has arrivd and joined Lord Cornwallis whose force now is more than three times larger than ours. And we are subsisting ourselves by our own industry; and I am not without hopes of forming somthing like a Magazine. I am labouring also to get cloathing from every quarter. Baron Stuben is in Virginia; and is indefatigable in equiping and forwarding the Troops from that State. I left General Gist in Maryland for the same purpose; but I have got nothing from there yet; nor do I expect much for Months to come. The

North Carolina State have such a high opinion of the Militia that I dont expect they will ever attempt to raise a single Continental soldier; notwithstanding the most sensible among them will acknowledge the folly of employing Militia.

But I must have tird your patience and therefore will make a full stop concerning matters in this department and enquire how you go on to the Northward. Have you got married: If you have, please to present my best compliments to Mrs Hambleton. If not, to Miss Schuyler; and to the Genl and family in either case. I beg my compliments to General Washingtons family, to General Knox and his family and all other of my acquaintances.

I shall be exceedingly oblige to you if you will communicate to me with great freedom every thing worthy of note that is said or respects this department. Yours Aff

Nathanael Greene to Catherine Greene

Camp on the Pedee January 12th 1781
General de Portail being released from captivity and on his
way to the Northward affords me an opportunity of writing
you (which I have done by every conveyance since I came to
this Country.) Could I have only a single line in return, to let
me know you are well, it would afford me infinite pleasure.
Nothing can exceed my anxiety to know your situation, not
having heard the least syllable from you since I left
Philadelphia.

I have my health exceeding good, being never more hearty
in my life; and could I be useful here, and know that you was
well, I should not be unhappy.

You can have no idea of the distress and misery that prevails
in this quarter. Hundreds of families that formerly livd in
great opulence are now reducd to beggary and want. A
Gentleman from Georgia was this morning with me, to get
assistance to move his wife and family out of the Enemies way.
They have been separated for upwards of eight months, during all which time the wife never heard from her husband, nor
the husband from his wife. Her distress was so great that she
has been obligd to sell all her plate, table linnen and even
wearing apparel, to maintain her poor little children. In this
situation she was tantalised by the Tories, and insulted by the
british. Human misery has become a subject for sport and
ridicule. With us the difference between Whig and Tory is little more than a division of sentiment; but here they persecute
each other with little less than savage fury. When I compare
your situation with those miserable people in this quarter, disagreeable as it may be from our long and distant separation, I
cannot help feeling thankful that your cup has not a mixture
of bitterness like theirs.

A Captain who is now with me and who has just got his
family from near the Lines of the Enemy had his Sister mur-
derd a few days since, and seven of her children wounded, the

oldest not twelve years of age. The sufferings and distress of the Inhabitants beggars all description, and requires the liveliest imagination to conceive the cruelties and devastations which prevail. I will not pain your humanity by a further relation of the distresses which rage in this quarter; nor would I have mentioned them at all, but to convince you that you are not the most unhappy of all creation. God grant us a speedy and happy meeting, by giving to the Country peace, liberty and safety.

In your last letter, you wrote me that you had eight new Shirts and Stocks, and several pair of Stockings; which you intended to have brought to camp with you. As my stock is small, and the difficulty great in getting any here, I wish you to send me all you have. Please to send them in two equal divisions to the care of Mr Pettit in Philadelphia, but dont send them, unless it is by persons who will undertake to have them safely deliverd. Mr Pettit will take care to have them forwarded to me. I am in want of nothing of the clothing kind but shirts, stocks and stockings, these articles I am in want of and shall be more so before those you send can reach me; which cannot be less than three months. Pray be particular in giving an account of the Children; mention who are at home, and who at nursing, and the healths of all. These little anecdotes are pleasing and afford the most agreeable family feelings. I wish to know where you reside, whether at Greenwich, Coventry or at the farm in Westerly. Where is brother Bill Littlefield, and how does he spend his time? I had a letter from him some time since respecting the family interest to the Eastward; which I am not certain that I ever gave an answer to; but you will please to tell him I think he should go down to *Wells* (first getting a power of attorney from his father); and make enquiry respecting the situation of the lands and the sentiments and intention of the settlers, after which it will be best to consult with some good able Lawyer or Lawyers, and then take his measures.

Give my kind love to all friends and believe me to be affectionately yours

Thomas Jefferson: Narrative of Arnold's Raid

RICHMOND, January 13.

A narrative of the late incursion made by the enemy to this place.

ON the 31st of December, a letter from a private Gentleman to General Nelson reached this place, notifying that in the morning of the preceding day, twenty seven sail of vessels had entered the Capes, and from the tenor of the letter, there was reason to expect within a few hours farther intelligence whether they were friends or foes, their force, and other circumstances. General Nelson went immediately into the lower country, with powers to call on the militia in that quarter, or to act otherwise as exigencies should require. The call of the militia from the middle and upper counties was not made till intelligence could be received that the fleet was certainly hostile. No farther intelligence came till the second instant, when the former was confirmed; it was ascertained that they were enemies, and had advanced up James river to Warrasqueak bay. All arrangements were immediately taken for calling in a sufficient body of militia for opposition. In the night of the third, advice was received that they were at anchor opposite James-town, Williamsburg was then supposed to be their object; the wind however, which had hitherto been unfavourable, shifted fair, and the tide being also in their favour, they ascended the river to Kennon's that evening, and with the next tide came up to Westover, having on their way taken possession of the battery at Hoods, by which two or three of their vessels had received some damage, but which was of necessity abandoned by the small garrison of fifty men placed there on the enemy's landing to invest the works. Intelligence of the enemy's having quitted the station at James-town, from which it was supposed they meant to land at Williamsburg, and that they had got in the evening to Kennon's, reached this place at five o'clock in the morning of the fourth, this was the first indication of their meaning to penetrate towards Richmond or Petersburg. As the orders for drawing the militia hither had been given but two days, no opposition was in readiness. Every effort was therefore necessary to withdraw the arms and other military stores, records, &c. from this place: Every effort was accordingly exerted to convey them to the foundery and labaratory, till about sunset of that day, when intelligence was received that the enemy had landed at Westover: From this it appeared that Richmond, and not Petersburg, was their object; it became necessary to remove every thing which remained here, across the river, as well as what had been carried to the foundery and labaratory; which operation was continued till the enemy approached very near. They marched from Westover at 2 o'clock in the afternoon of the 4th, and entered Richmond at one o'clock in the afternoon of the 5th. A regiment of infantry and about fifty horse continued on without halting to the foundery, they burnt that, the boring mill, the magazine, and two other houses, and proceeded to Westham, but nothing being in their power there, they retired to Richmond. The next morning they burnt some buildings of publick and some of private property, with what stores remained in them; destroyed a great quantity of private stores and about 12 o'clock retired towards Westover, where they encamped within the neck the next day. The loss sustained is not yet accurately known. At this place about 300 muskets, some soldiers clothing to a small amount, sulphur, some quarter masters stores, of which 120 sides of leather was the principal article, part of the artificers tools, and 3 waggons; besides which five brass 4 pounders, which had been sunk in the river, were discovered to them, raised and carried off. At the foundery about 5 tons of powder was thrown into the canal, of which there will be a considerable saving by remanufactoring it. Part of the papers belonging to the Auditors office, and the books and papers of the Council office, which were ordered to Westham, but in the confusion carried by mistake to the foundery, were also destroyed. The roof of the foundery was burnt, but the stacks of chimnies and furnaces not at all injured. Within less than 48 hours from the time of their landing and 19 from our knowing their destination they had penetrated 33 miles, done the whole injury, and retired. Our militia, dispersed over a large tract of country can be called in but slowly. On the day the enemy marched to this place, two hundred only were embodied, they were of this town and neighbourhood and were too few to do any thing effectual. The enemy's forces are commanded by the parricide Arnold.

BATTLE OF COWPENS:
SOUTH CAROLINA, JANUARY 1781

Daniel Morgan to Nathanael Greene

Camp near Cain Creek
Dear Sir   Jany 19h 1781.

The Troops I had the Honor to command have been so fortunate as to obtain a compleat Victory over a Detachment from the British Army commanded by Lt Colonel Tarlton. The Action happened on the 17th Instant about Sunrise at the Cowpens. It perhaps would be well to remark, for the Honour of the American Arms, that Altho the Progress of this Corps was marked with Burnings and Devastations & altho' they have waged the most cruel Warfare, not a man was killed, wounded or even insulted after he surrendered. Had not Britons during this Contest received so many Lessons of Humanity, I should flatter myself that this might teach them a little, but I fear they are incorrigible.

To give you a just Idea of our Operations it will be necessary to inform you, that on the 14h Instant having received certain Intelligence that Lord Cornwallis and Lt Colonel Tarlton were both in Motion, and that their movements clearly indicated their Intentions of dislodging me, I abandoned my Encampment at Grindales Ford on Pacolet, and on the 16h in the Evening took Possession of a Post, about seven miles from the Cherokee Ford on Broad River. My original Position subjected me at once to the Operations of both Cornwallis and Tarlton, and in Case of a Defeat, my Retreat might easily have been cut off. My Situation at the Cowpens enabled me to improve any Advantages I might gain, and to provide better for my own Security, should I be unfortunate. These Reasons induced me to take this Post at the Risque of its wearing the face of a Retreat.

I received regular Intelligence of the Enemy's Movements from the Time they were first in Motion. On the Evening of the 16h Ins they took Possession of the Ground I had removed from in the Morning, distant from the Scene of Action about 12 miles. An Hour before Day light one of my Scouts returned and informed me that Lt Colonel Tarlton had advanced within five miles of our Camp. On this Information I hastened to form as good a Disposition as Circumstances would admit, and from the alacrity of the Troops we were soon prepared to receive them. The Light Infantry commanded by Lt Colonel Howard and the Virginia Militia, under the command of Majr Triplette were formed on a rising Ground, and extended a Line in Front. The 3rd Regiment of Dragoons under Lt Colonel Washington, were so posted at such a Distance in their Rear as not to be subjected to the Line of Fire directed at them, and to be so near as to be able to charge the Enemy, should they be broke. The Volunteers of North Carolina, South Carolina & Georgia under the Command of the brave and valuable Colonel Pickens, were situated to guard the Flanks. Majr McDowell, of the N C Volunteers, was posted on the right Flank in Front of the Line 150 yards & Major Cunningham with the Georgia Volunteers on the left at the same distance in Front. Colonels Brandon & Thomas of the S Carolinians were posted on the right of Major McDowell and Colonels Hays and McCall of the same Corps, on the left of Major Cunningham. Capts Tate & Buchannan with the Augusta Riflemen to support the right of the Line.

The Enemy drew up in single Line of Battle 400 yds in Front of our advanced Corps. The first Battalion of the 71st Regt was opposed to our Right; the 7th Regt to our Left. The Infantry of the Legion to our Center. The Light Companies on their Flanks. In Front moved two Peices of Artillery. Lt Colonel Tarlton with his Cavalry was posted in the Rear of his Line. The Disposition of Battle being thus formed, small Parties of Riflemen were detached to skirmish with the Enemy, upon which their whole Line moved on with the greatest Impetuosity shouting as they advanced. McDowell & Cunningham gave them a heavy & galling Fire & retreated to the Regiments intended for their Support. The whole of Colonel Picken's Command then kept up a Fire by Regiments retreating agreable to their Orders. When the Enemy advanced to our Line, they received a well-directed and incessant Fire, but their Numbers being superiour to ours, they gained our Flanks, which obliged us to change our Position.

We retired in good Order about 50 Paces, formed, advanced on the Enemy & gave them a fortunate Volley which threw them into Disorder. Lt Colonel Howard observing this gave orders for the Line to charge Bayonets, which was done with such Address that they fled with the utmost Precipitation, leaving the Field Pieces in our Possession. We pushed our Advantage so effectually, that they never had an Opportunity of rallying, had their Intentions been ever so good.

Lt Colonel Washington having been informed that Tarlton was Cutting down our Riflemen on the left Flank pushed froward & charged them with such Firmness that instead of attempting to recover the Fate of the Day, which one would have expected from an officer of his Splendid Character, broke and fled.

The Enemy's whole Force were now bent solely in providing for their Safety in Flight. The List of their killed, wounded and Prisoners, will inform you with what Effect. Tarlton, with the small Remains of his Cavalry & a few scattering Infantry he had mounted on his Waggon Horses made their Escape. He was Persued 24 miles, but owing to our having taken a wrong Trail at first, we never could overtake him.

As I was obliged to move off of the Field of Action in the mg to secure the Prisoners, I cannot be so accurate as to the killed & wounded of the Enemy as I could wish. From the Reports of an officer I sent to view the Ground, there was 100 non Commissioned officers & Privates & ten commissioned Officers killed and two hundred R and F wounded. We have in our Possession 502 non C. O. & P. Prisoners independent of the wounded, & the Militia are taking up straglers continually. 29 C Officers have fell into our Hands. Their Rank &c &c you will see by an enclosed List. The Officers I have paroled. The Privates I am now conveying by the shortest Rout to Salisburrey. Two Standards, two Field Pieces, 35 Waggons, a travelling Forge, & all their Music are ours. Their Baggage, which was immense, they have in great measure destroyed. Our Loss is inconsiderable, which the enclosed Returns will evince. I have not been able to ascertain Colonel Pickens Loss but know it to be very small.

From our Force being composed of such a Variety of Corps, a wrong Judgment may be formed of our Numbers.

We fought only 800 men, two thirds of which were Militia. The British with their Baggage Guard, were not less than 1150, & these Veteran Troops. Their own Officers confess, that they fought 1037. Such was the Inferiority of our Numbers that our Success must be attributed to the Justice of our Cause & the Bravery of our Troops. My Wishes would induce me to mention the Name of every private Centinel in the Corps I have the honor to Command. In Justice to their Bravery & good Conduct, I have taken the Liberty to enclose you a List of their officers from a Conviction that you will be pleased to introduce such Characters to the World.

Major Giles my Aid & Capt Brookes my Brigade Majr, deserve & have my thanks for their Assistance & Behaviour on this Occasion.

The Baron Glaibeeck who accompanies Major Giles with these Dispatches served with me in the Action as a Volunteer and behaved in such a manner as merits your Attention. I am Dr Sir Yr Ob Servt

George Washington to Robert Howe

West Point, January 22, 1781.

Sir: You are to take the command of the detachment, which has been ordered to march from this post against the mutineers of the Jersey line. You will rendezvous the whole of your command at Ringwood or Pompton as you find best from circumstances. The object of your detachment is to compel the mutineers to unconditional submission, and I am to desire you will grant no terms while they are with arms in their hands in a state of resistance. The manner of executing this I leave to your discretion according to circumstances. If you succeed in compelling the revolted troops to a surrender you will instantly execute a few of the most active and most incendiary leaders.

You will endeavour to collect such of the Jersey troops to your standard as have not followed the pernicious example of their associates, and you will also try to avail yourself of the services of the Militia, representing to them how dangerous to civil liberty the precedent is of armed soldiers dictating terms to their country.

You will open a correspondence with Colonels Dayton and Shreve of the Jersey line and Col Freelinghuosen of the Militia or any others.

Royal Gazette:
"Our Last Will and Testament"

January 31, 1781

IN the NAME of DEVIL AMEN. WE the Congress of America in
Congress assembled, being weak in body, low in credit, and
poor in estate, but rich, high, and strong, in expectation; that
by our hellish faithful behaviour on earth, we shall be advanced to the highest esteem and favour of Satan in his kingdom, do, make, publish and declare, this our Last Will and
Testament, in manner following, that is to say, First and principally we do (as by the strongest tie of duty bound) consign,
our and each of our souls, purely vicious as they are, together
with all, each, and every, the faculty and faculties inseparably
adherent thereto, or to each of them, unto the most highly-
damned Serpent, his Sovereign Majesty of *HELL*, he having
by many titles a just claim thereto. — And it is our Will, that
our Executor hereinafter named, do, as soon as conveniently
may be after our decease, or even before it, cause our names
to be registered among the grand infernal Records of Hell.
And, as touching our worldly wealth, which we have by so
many noble *Frauds*, *Robberies* and *Murders*, amassed together
and concealed, we give, devise, and bequeath, the same unto
and between our two most dearly beloved and most vilely
great and good Allies, the French King and King of Spain, to
hold the same so long as they shall continue to act with the
same uniform conduct, and promote the interest of their
brother Sovereign, to whose kingdom we are hastening in a
swift course of rapidity. — But in default of such conduct in
them or either of them as aforesaid, then we give, devise, and
bequeath, all and whatsoever is before specified in the last be-
fore-mentioned bequest, or the share of such defaulter, to and
among, all, any, or either of the Potentates of Europe, who
shall by his, her, their, any or either of their zeal, (manifested
by real service to our most noble benefactor LUCIFER)

whether under the mask of armed Neutrality, open and avowedly, or otherwise howsoever, cherish, succour, help and comfort all those Americans who shall be inspired with the most noble sentiments of Rebellion, against that great enemy to our Constitution of Hell, GEORGE the THIRD of BRITAIN, whose subjects in the most strange infatuation, look up to *love* and *honour* their KING. In him there is also the most surprising infatuation, that he governs them by their own laws, and wastes all his time to promote their happiness; nor does his infatuation cease here, he loves his Queen and family; and moreover, he is so *righteously* wicked that he loves and fears his GOD. — Now we should make another bequest, that is, of the Land and Soil of North America. — By our Will, by our free Will, it should go to and be divided between our said two great and good Allies; but doubts arising in our *purely vicious* breasts concerning the operation of such bequest, we laid our case respecting the same before the Devil in Council, who just now returned it with his opinion thereunder wrote, in the words following: — *"No part of the Land and Soil of North-America, can be conveyed by your Will: — it is as much out of the power of all Hell to prevent North-America being subject to Britain, as it will be in the power of the King of Spain to hold South America, for that Britain will most assuredly extend her Dominion over the whole."* Now we do nominate and appoint our most infernally noble and dearly beloved *DEVIL*, GUARDIAN to our dear and only *Daughter* MISS *AMERICA REBELLION*, trusting to him the sole care, maintenance, and education of that most *dutiful beautiful* Child. — And we do also nominate and appoint him *sole Executor* of this our Will, made and executed in his presence this Eighteenth day of January, and in the Fifth Year of our *Independency.*

> SIGNED, SEALED, PUBLISHED, DECLARED,
> and DELIVERED by Order of CONGRESS
> *(just now expiring)*,
> CHARLES THOMPSON,
> SECRETARY, (L. S.)

In the evening of the 18th instant, and in the evening of the lustre of their wretchedness, departed this life, to the great grief of all wicked men, their most exalted Excellencies the Congress of America; and about midnight their remains were deposited in a vault prepared for them in the most comfortably-warm regions of infernal misery. By their death, that sweet Babe of Grace, Miss America Rebellion, who from her birth (till the death of her parents) had been nursed and brought up with all the tenderness that such delicate charms, such bewitching beauty, and such perfect deformity could require, is now left a poor helpless Orphan, destitute of friends, and in want of the necessaries of life; nor has the poor soul a rag to cover her —— nakedness.

Nathanael Greene to George Washington

Camp Guilford Court House

Sir   Feb: 9th 1781.

Since I wrote your Excellency by Major Giles, Lord Cornwallis has been constantly in pursuit of the Light Infantry and the prisoners, and is now between the Shallow Ford upon the Yadkin and Salem, one of the Moravian towns; and still pushing into the country with great rapidity.

The moment I was informed of the movements of Lord Cornwallis I put the army in motion on Pedee and left it under the command of Brigr Genl Huger and set out to join the Light Infantry in order to collect the Militia and embarrass the enemy 'till we could effect a junction of our forces.

General Morgan after the defeat of Tarlton had very judiciously made forced marches up into the Country and happily crossed the Catawba the evening before a great rain, which prevented the enemy from following him for several days, during which time the prisoners were got over the Yadkin and on their march for Dan River, which I hope they have passed and are in Virga.

On my arrival at the Lt. Infantry Camp I found them at Sherards Ford on the Catawba. The enemy were a little lower down the river at McCowan's Ford, and the river still so high that they could not cross. We made the best disposition we could to stop them when the river should fall. But the fords were so numerous, and our force so small that we could not effect it. Genl Davidson who had great influence among the Mecklenberg & Roan Militia had made use of all the arguments in his power to get the Militia into the field, but without effect. They had been so much in service and their families so distressed that they were loth to leave home even on the most pressing occasion.

The enemy crossed at McCowen's Ford where Genl Davidson was posted with the greatest part of the Militia who fell by the first discharge. The enemy made good their landing, and the Militia retreated. A place of rendezvous was appointed for the Militia to collect at, who were posted at the different fords up and down the river above 30 miles. Part of them halted at Mrs Tarrences about seven miles short of the place of rendezvous, and were over taken by Tarlton & dispersed. I waited that night at the place appointed for the Militia to collect at, untill morning, but not a man appeared. The light Infantry continued their march to Salisbury and crossed the Yadkin. But before we got over all the baggage and stores the enemy were at our heels. A pretty smart skirmish happened between a party of our riflemen and the advance of the enemy near the ford. We had secured all the boats, and the river was so high that the enemy could not follow us.

Heavy rains, deep creeks, bad roads, poor horses and broken harness as well as delays for want of provisions prevented our forming a junction as early as I expected, and fearing that the river might fall so as to be fordable, I ordered the army to file off to this place where part of them arrived last evening, the rest I hope will be in this night.

The enemy finding they could not cross the Trading Ford, marched up to the Shallow Ford where they passed the night before last, and are within 25 or thirty miles of this place.

As soon as I arrived at the Lt Infantry camp I wrote letters to all the Militia Officers over the mountains and in the upper Country to embody their men and join the Army as early as possible. But very few have joined us, and those principally without arms or amunition. We have no provisions but what we recieve from our daily collections. Under these circumstances I called a council who unanimously advised to avoid an action and to retire beyond the Roanoke immediately. A copy of the proceedings I have the honor to enclose.

I had previously ordered all the stores and heavy baggage to be removed to Prince Edward Court House; and informed Govr Nash of our situation. I have formed a light army composed of the cavalry of the 1 & 3d Regts and the Legion amounting to 240, a detachment of 280 Infantry under Lt Col. Howard, the Infantry of Lt Col Lee's Legion and 60 Virga Rifle Men making in their whole 700 Men which will be ordered with the Militia to harrass the enemy in their advance, check their progress and if possible give us an opportunity to retire without a general action.

The force under Lord Cornwallis consists of between 2500 and 3000 troops including near 300 Dragoons and their mounted Infantry. They have destroyed their waggons, and are compleatly equiped as Light Infantry.

I have the honor to enclose a copy of a letter from Lt Col. Lee, extracts of two letters from Genl Marion and a copy of a letter from a well informed Gentleman respecting the operations at Wilmington.

General Morgan is so unwell that he has left the Army. The enemy since the action of the 17th Ulto have pursued him upwards of 200 Miles. He was obliged to leave the wounded, the arms, waggons and carriages of the artillery taken in the action, but I hope they have not fallen into the hands of the enemy.

I have ordered Genl Marion to cross the Santee River and Genl Sumter to collect the Militia in the upper part of S. Carolina. Genl Pickens has orders to take command of the men in arms in the rear of the enemy.

I have wrote Mr Henery the late Govr of Virginia to collect, if possible, fourteen or 1500 Volunteers to aid us, should the enemy attempt to pursue us beyond the Dan River.

I had the satisfaction to receive your Excellencys dispatches of the 27th of Decr, 2d and 9th Inst. a few days since. I have the honor to be With sentiments of the highest esteem and respect Your Excellency's Most Obedient Humble Servant.

Nathanael Greene to Joseph Reed

Camp near the Iron Works

Dear Sir   March 18th 1781

I have been too much engaged since the enemy crossed the Catabaw to keep up my correspondence regularly with you.

I have had the pleasure to receive several letters from you but no opportunity to answer them. To the best of my remembrance the last time I wrote you was at the Pedee just after Tarltons defeat wherein I informed you that notwithstanding that success we had little to hope and much to fear. The operations since has verified my apprehensions. North Carolinia has been as nearly reducd as ever a State was in the universe and escape. Our force was so small and Lord Cornwallises movments were so rapid that we get no reinforcments of Militia and therefore were obligd to retire out of the State. Upon which the spirits of the people sunk and almost all classes of the Inhabitants gave themselves up for lost. They would not believe themselves in danger until they found ruin at their doors. The foolish prejudice of the formidableness of the Militia being a sufficient barrier against any attempts of the enemy, prevented the Legislator from making any exertions equal to their critical and dangerous situation. Experience has convinced them of their false security. It is astonishing to me how these people could place such a confidence in a Militia scattered over the face of the whole Earth and generally destitute of every thing necessary to their own defences. The Militia in the back Country are formidable, the others are not, and all are very ungovernable and difficult to keep together. As they have generally come out 20,000 might be in motion and not 500 in the field.

After crossing the Dan, and collecting a few Virginia Militia, finding the Enemy had erected their Standard at Hillsborough, and the people began to flock to it from all quarters, either for protections or to engage in their service, I determined to recross at all hazards; and it was very fortunate that I did otherwise Lord Cornwallis would have got several thousand recruits. Seven companies were enlisted in one day. Our situation was desperate at the time we recrossed the Dan, our numbers were much inferior to the enemy, and we were without ammunition provisions or Stores of any kind, the whole having retird over the Stanton River. However, I thought it was best to put on a good face and make the most of appearances. Lt Col Lees falling in with the Tories upon the Haw almost put a total stop to their recruiting service. Our numbers were doubtless greatly magnified and pushing on boldly towards Hillsborough led Lord Cornwallis into a belief that I meant to attack him whereever I could find him. The case was widely different: It was certain I could not fight him in a general action without almost certain ruin. To skirmish with him was my only chance. Those happened dayly, and the enemy sufferd considerably. But our Militia coming out principally upon the footing of Volunteers, they file off dayly after every skirmish, and went home to tell the news. In this situation with an inferior force, I kept constantly in the neighbourhood of Lord Cornwallis, until the 6th when he made a rapid push at our Light Infantry, commanded by Col Williams, who very judiciously avoided the blow. This Manoeuver of the enemy obligd me to change my position. Indeed I rarely ever lay more than two days in a place. The Country being much of a wilderness obligd the enemy to guard carefully against a surprize, and rendered it difficult to surprise us. We had few Waggons with us, no baggage, and only Tents enough to secure our Arms in case of a washing rain.

Here has been the field for the exercise of Genius, and an opportunity to practice all the great and little arts of war. Fortunately we have blunderd through without meeting with any capitol Misfortune. On the 11th of this month I formed a junction at the High Rock Ford with a considerable body of Virginia and North Carolinia Militia, and with a Virginia Regiment of 18 Months Men. Our force being now much more considerable than it had been, and upon a more permanent footing, I took the determination of giving the enemy battle without loss of time and made the necessary dispositions accordingly. The battle was fought at or near Guilford

Courthouse, the very place from whence we began our retreat after the light Infantry joined the Army from the Pedee. The battle was long, obstinate, and bloody. We were obligd to give up the ground, and lost our Artillery. But the enemy have been so soundly beaten, that they dare not move towards us since the action; notwithstanding we lay within ten Miles of them for two days. Except the ground and the Artillery they have gained no advantage, on the contrary they are little short of being ruined. The enemies loss in killed and wounded cannot be less than between 6 & 700. Perhaps more. Victory was long doubtful; and had the North Carlonia Militia done their duty it was certain. They had the most advantageous position I ever saw, and left it without making scarcely the shadow of opposition. Their General and field Officers exerted themselves but the Men would not stand. Many threw away their Arms and fled with the utmost precipitation; even before a gun was fird at them. The Virginia Militia behavd nobly and annoyed the enemy greatly. The horse at different times in the course of the day performed wonders. Indeed the horse is our great safe guard, and without them the Militia could not keep the field in this Country. Col Williams who acts as Adjutant General was very active and to this Officer I am greatly indebted for his assistance. Burnet is one of first Young Men I ever saw and will make one of the greatest Military charactors. I am happy in the confidence of this Army and tho unfortunate I lose none of their esteem. Never did an Army labour under so many disadvantages as They; but the fortitude and patience of the Officers and Soldiery rises superior to all difficulties. We have little to eat, less to drink, and lodge in the woods in the midst of smoke. Indeed our fatigue is excessive. I was so much overcome night before last that I fainted.

Our Army is in good spirits; but the Militia are leaving us in great numbers, to return home to kiss their wives and sweet hearts.

I have never felt an easy moment since the enemy crossed the Catabaw until since the defeat of the 15th; but now I am perfectly easy, being perswaded it is out of the enemies power to do us any great injury. Indeed I think they will retire as soon as they can get off their wounded.

My love to your family and all friends.

You will please to accept this short account until I have a better opportunity to write you.

Nathanael Greene to George Washington

Camp near the Iron works
10 Miles from Guilford Court House

Sir   March 18th 1781

My letter to Congress a copy of which I inclose your Excellency will inform you of an unsuccessful action with Lord Cornwallis on the 15th. Our prospects were flattering; and had the North Carolinia Militia seconded the endeavors of their officers, victory was certain. But they left the most advantageous position I ever saw without scarcely firing a gun. None fird more than twice and very few more than once, and near one half not at all. The Virginia Militia behaved with great gallantry, and the success of the day seemed to be doubtful for a long time. The action was long and severe.

In my former letters I inclosed your Excellency the probable strength of the british Army, since which they have been constantly declining. Our force as you will see by the returns were respectable, and the probability of not being able to keep it long in the field, and the difficulty of subsisting Men in this exhausted Country, together with the great advantages which would result from the action, if we were victorious, and the little injury if we were otherwise, determin'd me to bring on an action as soon as possible. When both parties are agreed in a matter, all obstacles are soon removed. I thought the determination warranted by the soundest principles of good policy, and I hope event will prove it so, tho we were unfortunate. I regret nothing so much as the loss of my Artillery, tho it was of little use to us, nor can it be in this great wilderness. However as the enemy have it we must *also*.

Lord Cornwallis will not give up this Country without being soundly beaten. I wish our force was more competent to the business. But I am in hopes by little and little to reduce him in time. His troops are good, well found and fight with great obstinacy.

I am very happy to hear the Marquis de la Fyette is coming

to Virginia, tho I am afraid from a hint in one of Baron Stubens letters, he will think himself injurd in being superceded in the command. Could the Marquis join us at this moment, we should have a glorious campaign. It would put Lord Cornwallis and his whole army into our hands.

I am also happy to hear that the Pennsylvania line are coming to the Southward. The mutiny in that line was a very extraordinary one. It is reported here, to have proceeded from the great cruelty of the officers. A member of Congress writes this; but I believe it to be so far from the truth, that I am perswaded it originated rather through indulgence than from any other cause.

Virginia has given me every support I could wish or expect since Lord Cornwallis has been in North Carolinia, and nothing has contributed more to this than the prejudices of the people in favor of your Excellency, which has been extended to me from the friendship you have been pleasd to honor me with.

The service here is extreme severe, and the Officers and Soldiers bears it with a degree of patience, that does them the highest honor. I have never taken off my cloaths since I left the Pedee. I was taken with a fainting last night, owing I imagine to excessive fatigue, and constant watching. I am better to day, but far from being well.

I have little prospect of acquiring much reputation, while I labour under so many disadvantages. I hope my friends will make such allowances, and as for vulgar opinion I regard it not. Time nor health will not permit me to write your Excellency upon many matters which are upon my Mind.

I beg my best respects to Mrs Washington. With esteem & regard I am your Excel most Obedt humble Sr

Nathanael Greene to Thomas Jefferson

April 28, 1781

Sir

Since I wrote your Excellency in answer to the resolutions of your Assembly relative to the conduct of the Cavalry Officers, and the measures pointed out to supply this Army in future with Horses, I have been considering more fully the tendency and consequences that would attend it.

It is to be lamented that Officers will not exercise more discretion and prudence when entrusted with the execution of an order which seems to invade the rights of a Citizen not perfectly conformable to the Laws and constitution of the Land. And it is equally to be lamented that a Legislature should from a resentment for the misconduct of a few individuals, bring upon an Army employed in their service inevitable ruin, and upon the community disgrace and distress.

I was very particular in giving my orders to guard against the evils complained of, a copy of which is inclosed; and I have no wish to screen a single Officer who has wantonly invaded the property of the People, or offered any insult to the Inhabitants; but I wish the improper conduct of a few Officers may not be made to operate as a punishment upon the whole Army. Particular situations and particular circumstances often make measures necessary that have the specious shew of oppression, because they carry with them consequences pointed and distressing to individuals. It is to be lamented that this is the case, but pressing emergencies make it political and sometimes unavoidable.

When we retired over the Dan our force was too small to stop the progress of the Enemy, or mark the limits of their approach. We appealed to the only means left us to save your Country, and prevent the destruction of a virtuous little Army. Men were called for, they turned out with a spirit that did honor to themselves and their Country; Horses were wanted to mount our Dragoons, they could not be procured but by virtue of impress Warrants. You was convinced of this fact and therefore furnished me with the Warrants for the purpose. I took the most adviseable, and as I thought the most effectual means to have the business conducted with propriety; and I cannot but think the Gentlemen generally who were entrusted with the execution of my orders, were governed entirely by a principle of public good. Some mistakes and several abuses appear to have happened in impressing Studd Horses instead of geldings, but those mistakes arose from the necessity of mounting our Dragoons in such a manner as to give us an immediate superiority over the Enemy, as well in the quality of the Horses as their number. The People complained, I was willing to redress their grievances; some of the most valuable covering Horses were returned, and I shall direct some others to be restored notwithstanding the great inconvenience which must inevitably attend this Army by it.

The Assembly of your State appear to have taken up the matter from a principle tho' acknowledged to be virtuous, yet from its tendency, must be allowed to be impolitic. The rights of Individuals are as dear to me as to any Man, but the safety of a community I have ever considered as an object more valuable. In politics as well as every thing else a received and established axiom is, that greater evils should in every instance give way to lesser misfortunes. In War it is often impossible to conform to all the ceremonies of Law and equal justice; and to attempt it would be productive of greater misfortunes to the public from the delay than all the inconveniencies which individuals may suffer.

Your Excellency must be sensible of the innumerable inconveniencies I had to labor under at the time, and the variety of difficulties that still surround us. Nothing but light Horse can enable us, with the little Army we have, to appear in the field; and nothing but a superiority in Cavalry can prevent the Enemy from cutting to pieces every detachment coming to join the Army or employed in collecting supplies. From the open State of this Country their services are particularly necessary, and unless we can keep up the Corps of Cavalry and constantly support a superiority it will be out of our power to act or to prevent the Enemy from overruning the Country, and commanding all its resources.

The Assembly I fear by their resolves have destroyed my hopes and expectations on this head. Under the Law as it at present stands it is certain nothing can be done. By limitting Dragoon Horses to the narrow price of five thousand Pounds it amounts only to a prohibition, and cuts off the prospect of any future supplies. At this moment the Enemy are greatly superior to us, and unless Virginia will spring immediately to the most generous exertions they will indubitably continue so. It is in vain to expect protection from an Army which is not supported, or make feeble efforts upon narrow principles of prudence or economy; they only serve to procrastinate the War, and tire out the patience of the People. Already have we experienced in many instances, the ill consequences of neglecting the Army when surrounded with difficulties and threatened with ruin. Great expence of blood and treasure have attended this policy and to redress the grievances of a few Individuals when it will entail calamity upon the Community, will be neither political or just.

If Horses are dearer to the Inhabitants than the lives of Subjects or the liberties of the People there will be no doubt of the Assembly persevering in their late resolution, otherwise I hope they will reconsider the matter and not oblige me to take a measure which cannot fail to bring ruin upon the Army, and fresh misfortunes upon the Country.

Ebenezer Denny: Journal, May 1–15, 1781

CARLISLE, *May 1st, 1781.* — The Pennsylvania Line, after the revolt and discharge of the men, last winter, were reduced to six regiments; the officers ordered to different towns within the State to recruit. An appointment of ensign in the 7th had been obtained for me in August last; the 7th and 4th were incorporated, and under command of Lt.-Col. Comt. William Butler, rendezvoused at this place — companies now about half full. The effective men were formed into four companies, and marched to Little York; I was arranged to one of the marching companies, Samuel Montgomery, captain, and George Bluer, lieutenant. All the recruits fit for service, from the different stations, were brought to York, formed into two regiments of eight companies each, destined for the State of Virginia. A few days spent in equipping, &c., and for the trial of soldiers charged with mutiny, General Anthony Wayne, the commanding officer, influenced, no doubt, by experience of the revolt last winter, expresses a determination to punish, with the utmost rigor, every case of mutiny or disobedience. A general court martial continued sitting several days; twenty odd prisoners brought before them; seven were sentenced to die. The regiments paraded in the evening earlier than usual; orders passed to the officers along the line to put to death instantly any man who stirred from his rank. In front of the parade the ground rose and descended again, and at the distance of about three hundred yards over this rising ground, the prisoners were escorted by a captain's guard; heard the fire of one platoon and immediately a smaller one, when the regiments wheeled by companies and marched round by the place of execution. This was an awful exhibition. The seven objects were seen by the troops just as they had sunk or fell under the fire. The sight must have made an impression on the men; it was designed with that view.

YORK, *May 15th.* — Provision for transporting baggage, &c., and other necessary preparation. Commenced our march for

Virginia; the weather pleasant and roads tolerably good. Passed through Frederick Town (Maryland), where were some British prisoners quartered; they turned out to see us. Next day reached the Potomac; here we were detained for want of craft — boats few and in bad condition. The artillery passed over first (a battalion of artillery accompanied the brigade). The second flat-boat had left the shore about forty yards, when the whole sunk. Several women were on board; but as hundreds of men were on the bank, relief soon reached them; none were lost — got all over. Proceeded a few miles and encamped. Struck our tents every morning before day. About eight or nine o'clock, as we found water, a short halt was made, the water-call beat; parties, six or eight from each company, conducted by a non-commissioned officer, with canteens, fetched water. Seldom allowed to eat until twelve o'clock, when the arms were stacked, knapsacks taken off, and water sent for by parties as before. Officers of a company generally messed together, sometimes more; one of their servants carried cooked provisions for the day; no cooking until night. Not acquainted with the country on our route, but understood that we were marching much about — very circuitous — keeping off the Blue Ridge close on our right. This to avoid the enemy and secure our junction with the Marquis Lafayette.

Thomas Browne to David Ramsay

Sir: — The publication of an extract from your History of the Revolution of South Carolina, highly injurious to my reputation as an officer and a man of humanity, induces me to address this letter to you.

Having professed yourself "an advocate for truth, uninfluenced by passion, prejudice, or party spirit," you declare that, embracing every opportunity of obtaining genuine information, you "have asserted nothing but what you believed to be fact."

If I am to credit these professions, I must believe, sir, that no party motive would tempt you to defame the reputation of an individual, or advance the reputation of your country at the expense of your own.

The scandalous imputations, therefore, thrown upon my humanity, must be imputed to the malignity of some wretch as devoid of honour as of truth, who attempts to acquire fame by ruining that of others. Conscious of the rectitude of my intentions, although I may have erred in judgment, the censure or praise of an unprincipled person, who has wilfully misrepresented facts, and wantonly departed from truth, ought to be indifferent to me; yet the duty I owe to the officers and men serving under me, and a reverence for the opinion of the world, which often judges from caprice or common report, prompt me to state to you an account of the material transactions on which these charges are founded, lest my silence might be imputed to a consciousness of merited reproach. A civil war being one of the greatest evils incident to human society, the history of every contest presents us with instances of wanton cruelty and barbarity. Men whose passions are inflamed by mutual injuries, exasperated with personal animosity against each other, and eager to gratify revenge, often violate the laws of war and principles of humanity.

The American war exhibits many dreadful examples of wanton outrages, committed by both parties, disgraceful to human nature. From the commencement of the war, in the limited sphere in which I acted, it was my duty, and the first wish of my heart, to carry it on agreeably to the rules which humanity formed to alleviate its attendant calamities. The criminal excesses of individuals were never warranted by authority, nor ever obtained the sanction of my approbation.

Could violations of humanity be justified by example, the cruelties exercised on my person by a lawless Committee, in the wanton abuse of power, might have justified the severest vengeance; but, esteeming it more honourable to forgive than to revenge an injury to those men who had treated me with the most merciless cruelty, I granted protection and safeguards to such as desired them. In the discharge of the duties of my profession, I can say with truth, I never deviated from the line of conduct the laws of war and humanity prescribed. In your History of the Revolution of South Carolina, you have been pleased to form a different judgment. From what source you have obtained your information relative to the circumstances of General Screven's death, I cannot pretend to determine; but give me leave to say, not from "an advocate for truth, uninfluenced by passion, prejudice, or party spirit." So malicious a representation requires a brief detail of the truth. The frontier of East Florida being exposed to the incursions of the Georgia Militia, a party from the districts of Newport and Medway entered the Province, plundered and destroyed every house and plantation on St. Mary's River, and carried off all the inhabitants prisoners, without distinction of age or sex. The garrison of St. Augustine being reduced to great difficulties by an extreme scarcity of provisions, General Prevost was under the necessity of detaching Colonel Prevost, with a party of light troops, to collect cattle in the settlements of Medway and Newport. With this detachment I had the honour of serving. To enable this light corps to forage with greater effect and security, a party was ordered by the inland navigation, under the command of Colonel Fuser, to present itself before Sunbury, to divert the attention of the Americans from us to its security.

After various skirmishes with the Americans near Medway, our spies brought intelligence that their army, said to consist of nine hundred men, under the command of General

Screven and Colonel White, was on its march to attack us. Colonel Fuser ordered me to reconnoitre the position and movements of the Americans, and if possible to harass them on their march. The country being full of swamps and difficult passes, I selected thirty-two men from the regiment I commanded, to whose spirit and activity I could trust. About a mile in front of our camp, the ground being particularly favourable to my purpose, an ambuscade was formed in a thicket. General Screven and Colonel White harangued their men to prepare for action. After finishing their harangue, I ordered my party to fire. General Screven and a Captain Struthers fell. The Americans, I presume, mistaking this for our whole force, instantly retreated. The General (Screven) being grievously wounded, was treated with tenderness and humanity. He had the character of a brave, worthy man. I sincerely felt for his misfortune, and ordered him to be conveyed to our camp, where every attention was paid to him by Colonel Prevost, and every assistance given to him by our surgeons. (Vol. ii., page 2.)

With respect to the devastations you complain of, I shall decline the ungrateful task of justifying the loyalists on St. Mary's River retaliating on the property of such of the militia of Newport and Medway as had previously destroyed theirs, and dragged their families into captivity. I only wish to call to your remembrance the generous invitation of the Governor and Council of Georgia, by the proclamation, "to all the friends of liberty and independence in and throughout the United States of America," to come and partake of the plunder of East Florida; for which purpose, they had nothing to do but to repair to the camp in Burke County, where provisions and ammunition would be supplied gratis, and from thence march, under the command of the Governor of the State, by whom every encouragement would be given, and all captures free plunder.

The account you have obtained relative to the death and sufferings of McCoy and his confederates, in Carolina, is equally delusive. After the reduction of Charleston by Sir Henry Clinton, I was detached by Brigadier-General Clarke to Augusta. On our march, the Carolinians of the districts near Savannah River voluntarily took the oaths of allegiance, and received protection. Among the number, one McCoy, a young man of a character notoriously infamous, applied for protection.

His mother, from a knowledge of the character he bore, accompanied him, and promised she would be responsible for his future conduct; he received protection, and was told if he persisted in plundering and destroying the peaceable inhabitants, he would receive no favour. About twelve months subsequent to this period, numbers of Carolinians who had received protection, formed themselves into plundering parties, under the command of a Captain McCoy, robbed and murdered many of his Majesty's peaceable and loyal subjects, and attacked the guards of the public boats navigating the Savannah River, with provisions, ammunition, and clothing, for the garrisons of Ninety-six and Augusta. Having received intelligence that the King's stores had been intercepted, I dispatched Lieutenant Kemp, of the King's Rangers, from Augusta, with ten soldiers and twenty militia, to pursue the plunderers.

He engaged one Willie as a guide, a man who had taken the oath of allegiance, and received protection; this traitor conveyed information to McCoy of Kemp's force, design, and intended route, and led him into an ambuscade previously formed. The militia under the command of Kemp fled upon the first fire; he and the soldiers, unable to resist a very superior force, surrendered themselves prisoners. Captain McCoy asked Kemp to join his party. On his refusal, he stripped and shot him. The same question was put to the soldiers; nine out of the ten refused, and shared the same fate. The other joined them to save his life, and in a few days afterwards made his escape, and brought me intelligence of the murder of Kemp and his men, and that Willie and young McCoy were the most active in putting them to death; that the inhabitants in general had converted their written protections into cockades, and had joined a Colonel Harden; that the King's stores taken from the boats were distributed among the plunderers, and secreted in or near their houses. Apprehending a general revolt in that quarter of the country, I immediately marched from Augusta with one hundred and seventy Indians, and was joined by four hundred militia. About thirty miles from Black

Swamp, Colonel Harden, about midnight, attacked our camp, and was repulsed. The militia under my command during the action deserted to a man, joined Colonel Harden, who, thus reinforced, at ten in the morning renewed the attack, but his men being totally without discipline, were defeated with considerable loss. Among the prisoners, Willie and young McCoy, and eleven of Kemp's murderers, were taken. The identity of their persons, and the fact being proved and confirmed by their own confession, they (Willie excepted) suffered on the gallows; and the houses of the plunderers where the King's stores were secreted, were ordered to be burnt. Although I lamented the necessity of having recourse to these extremities, a necessity created by themselves, I am persuaded, on a similar occasion, Dr. Ramsey would have done the same. Willie, Kemp's guide, experienced a different fate. An Indian chief, a friend of Kemp, on learning from the soldiers that Willie was the man who had betrayed and murdered his friend, immediately killed him with his tomahawk. This is the only outrage, if it ought to be called one, ever committed by any Indians under my command, and of which you have been pleased to give so truly a tragical and melancholy narrative. After so pathetic a display of your descriptive talents, how ample a field for your fertile genius, without a flight into the regions of fiction, will the Indian expedition of General Pickens afford you — such a scene of devastation and horror! Thirteen villages destroyed! Men, women, and children thrown into the flames, impaled alive, or butchered in cold blood! How different the conduct of those you style savages! Not an outrage was committed on the reduction of Fort Howe, in Georgia; on that service three-fourths of that detachment consisted of Indians, and the fort was carried by assault; half of the officers with me killed or wounded; yet the Indians, less savage than their adversaries, [   ]

The account you have obtained of the events at Augusta is, I must confess, as well adapted to the prejudices of the weak, as the credulity of the ignorant. Your very honourable and genuine informer, with a truly patriotic spirit, disdains to charge his memory with transactions that might stain the reputation of your arms; or it was not convenient to his purpose to remember the shameful violation of the capitulation of Augusta, the horrid cruelties exercised on the prisoners, the barbarous murder of Colonel Grierson, and others, with the bloody achievements of Colonels Dun,* Burnett, and Dooly, previous to the siege. In either case, it will not be amiss to refresh his memory with the following narrative: — The port of Augusta being invested and besieged near three months, was surrendered by capitulation. From Colonel Lee, who commanded the Continental Legion, a gentleman of the most honourable and liberal sentiments, and from his officers, the King's troops experienced every security and attention; from the militia, under a General Pickens, every species of abuse and insult. Colonel Lee and his officers exerted themselves in an uncommon degree, and took every possible precaution to protect the prisoners from violence. The King's Rangers were paroled, and quartered at a gentleman's house, with a guard of Continental dragoons, under the command of Captain Armstrong. The militia prisoners were confined to a stockade fort, where General Pickens and his militia were quartered. After Colonel Lee marched from Augusta, Colonel Grierson, who had rendered himself peculiarly obnoxious to the enemy by his spirited and unwearied exertions in the cause of his country, was under the custody of the main guard, about ten paces from General Pickens' quarters. His spirit and unshaken loyalty in every change of fortune, marked him out as a proper victim to sacrifice to their savage resentment. One of General Pickens' men, named James Alexander, entered the room where he was confined with his three children, shot him through the body, and returned unmolested by the sentinel posted at the door, or the main guard. He was afterwards stripped, and his clothes divided among the soldiers, who, having exercised upon his dead body all the rage of the most horrid brutality, threw it into a ditch without the fort. Thus fell the brave, unfortunate Colonel Grierson, a man high in the estimation of his country, valued by his acquaintances, beloved by his friends — not by the shot of *an unseen marksman*, but under the eye of General Pickens, by the hand of a

---

*Sixty peaceable loyalists on the ceded lands were murdered in their own houses in the course of a week by these execrable ruffians.

bloody, sanctioned, and protected villain, in shameful violation of a solemn capitulation.

After the murder of Colonel Grierson, another execrable villain named Shields, (an unseen marksman,) the same day, in the same fort, under the eye of General Pickens, in the presence of his officers, without interruption from the sentries or guards, called Major Williams, of the Georgia Militia, to the door of the prison, and shot him through the body. These outrages served only as a prelude to a concerted plan for murdering all the prisoners. To execute this diabolical design, a hundred of General Pickens' *unseen marksmen*, accompanied by three colonels, marched with drawn swords to the quarters of the King's Rangers. Captain Armstrong being informed of their intention, threatened, and ordered his guards to oppose them if they advanced. Then, addressing himself to the King's Rangers, he told them, that if attacked, to consider themselves released from their paroles, and defend themselves. The determined spirit of Captain Armstrong and Major Washington, who were present, struck such a terror into these ruffians, that, apprehending an obstinate resistance, they instantly retired.

Enraged at the repetition of such abominable outrages by this band of assassins, not yet satiated with blood, I wrote to General Pickens, reproaching him with a violation of the articles of capitulation, in defiance of every principle of honour and good faith, and informed him, that the officers and men, having acted by my orders, ought to be exempted from violence; and if it was his determination that I should share the fate of Colonel Grierson, he would at least find that a man, conscious of having faithfully discharged his duty to his king and country, would meet his fate with indifference.

The prisoners shortly afterwards embarked for Savannah, under the charge of Major Washington, who, apprehending the commission of further outrages, distributed the guards among the different boats. By this precaution, the different detachments from General Pickens' camp, who had taken post on the banks of the river, were prevented, after repeated attempts, from firing into the boats.

Your account of a skirmish between General Wayne's army and a party of militia and dragoons, consisting of fifty men, who composed the advance of a small detachment I had the honour to command, I presume is taken from General Wayne's hyperbolical report to the Congress. As this buckram feat is altogether a fancy piece, it does not merit a comment.

I have the honour to be, Sir,

Your most obedient, humble servant,

NASSAU, BAHAMAS, *Dec. 25, 1786.*

Josiah Atkins: Diary, June 5–July 7, 1781

Tuesday. June 5th.   we came to Bladenburg in Virginia. This is considerable of a little town & is thirty miles from Baltimore. We crost Patowmac ferry into Alexandria standing on Virginia side. This river is very large: will let up large ships; and is the boundary between the states of Maryland & Virginia. Alexandria is not every extensive; but is pleasantly situated on the river.

The 6th.   we left this place. How vastly different is this part of the world from the ideas I used to have of it! Instead of a plain clear'd country (as I used think it), I find it cover'd with vast, lonely woods. Sometimes 'tis ten, 15 or 20 miles between houses; & they say we have a place to pass that is thirty. This day we pass gen Washington's plantation, which is of large extent. (Some men in these parts, they tell me, own 30,000 acres of land for their *patrimony*; & many have two or 300 Negroes to work on it as slaves. Alas! That persons who pretend to stand for the *rights of mankind* for the *liberties of society*, can delight in oppression, & that even of the worst kind! These poor creatures are enslav'd: not only so, but likewise deprived of that which nature affords even to the beasts. Many are almost without provision, having very little for support of nature; & many are as naked as they came into the world. What pray is this but the strikingly inconsistent character pointed out by the apostle, *While they promise them liberty, they themselves are the servants of corruption!* But when I speak of *oppression* it readily suggests to my mind my own troubles & afflictions. Am not I oppressed, as being oblig'd to leave my own state of peace & happiness, friends & relation, wife & Children, shop & tools, & customers, against my mind & expectation, & come these hundreds of miles distance in the capacity of a soldier carrying the cruel & unwelcome instruments of war. Alas! my heart is full! but I forbid my pen. Oh! that I were as great as my grief, or less than my name! Oh! that I might forget what I have been, or not remember what I must now become! But my weeping eyes cannot ease my pain.)

We pass his Excellency's *house*; & 'tis said, we march ten miles on his land. — We also went into a beautiful Church & saw his *pew*. We came to Colchester; & pass'd the ferry, where the river will let up a large ship. The name of the river is Obion — the town is small situated on the bank of it — & is 18 miles from Alexandria.

The country here, (& in Pensilvania) abounds with cotten, growing on a small bush, planted every year in May, & plow'd & hoed like corn.

The 7th. we press'd a Negro waggoner, belonging to a widow who has 900 slaves. And, what is remarkable, she, according to this Negro, keeps them all victual'd & cloth'd. This, I think, worthy to be noted, where almost all their slaves of both sexes go naked.

The 8th. we continued our march in a great wilderness; & dined on the ground gen-Wane left in the morning. We expect soon to join the Marquess, who is pursuing the enemy. (O Lord be merciful to us in this land according to thy tender mercy.)

The 9th. we lodg'd on the ground the Marquess marched from yesterday; & which gen. Wane left to day noon. We are all in pursuit after the British enemy, which we expect, providence favoring, soon to overtake.

The 10th. we came up with the baggage belonging to the Marquess, who has a days march the start of us. . . . This is a long & tedious road, thro' a wilderness, where *no water* is to allay ones parching thirst: But there is a greater drought with respect to hearing the word of the Lord, the everlasting gospel dispens'd (Is not this the holy Sabbath? Yet where am I? & what am I about? O Lord, forgive my sins: For tho' I am here, yet my heart is at home with thy worshipping people.) We still direct our course thro' this lonsome desert. We march'd not far from 40 miles without finding above one or 2 houses, & as little water; finding none unless some swamps or mud-holes. At night we past gen. Wane — & joined the Infantry at 8 o'clock on the morning of the 11th, after a long & tedious march of more than 600 miles (perhaps 700) which cost us near a month's time, together with much fatigue & great hardship. We left three of our party sick on the road . . . gen Wane join'd soon after, & the militia are coming on. We have *orders* to march at 2 o'clock this day. We expect to come up with the enemy in a day or two. (This encampment is upwards of 100 miles from Alexandria) Our Infantry, this day, (except those who came with me) had dealt out to them one Holland shirt, one linning one, one frock, and two pair of over-alls. At revelee-beating we march'd off the ground & past along a solitary desert, where we were in great strait for drink Which is but too common in these parts; houses being as seldom as colleges in Connecticut, & wells as scarce as virtuous pools). This day we had one months pay in hard money. We are still in the woods, 15 miles from our last camp.

The 13th. We lay under marching orders; but did not move till the 14th. at the sun. We march'd 12 or 15 miles before we halted. And tho the last night was so severely cold that we cou'd not lie warm with all the cloths we had; yet after the sun rose the heat increas'd to that degree, together with the dust & want of water, as to render the air almost suffocating. We found not a drop of water all the way. We came near famishing all, & some fainted, while others drop'd with weary legs by the way. This was our fore-noons march. What then may we expect (rather, what may we not expect) in the afternoon! & O Lord, what must be our fate thro' the summer!

The 15th. We lay, 'tis said within 4 miles of the enemy. Tis said too our men took a spy to day, who has followed us for several days. The enemy, we hear, retreated all the night of the 14th. & got some start of us. This morning we began our route at break of day, & encamp'd in the woods, about 50 miles from Richmond (Virginia). From what we can gather the enemy retreat with great precipitation, leaving behind them horses, waggons & baggage . . . This evening we had our generals applause for our fortitude to bear hardships with patience, especially the want of provision, meat being out, & our bread but poor (Our bread was made chiefly of coarse Indian meal, which we wet & bake on barks, on stones. This is what people live on chiefly in these parts, & what they call Hoo-cakes) However, we not being used to such bread, nor such a country; the day being intensely hot, & the night as cold, (we having no tents to cover us) our march long, water unwholesom & rum not very plenty; & the great & unexpected distance from home; all these together make my trials almost insupportable. They are too heavy, especially for one disappointed every way, & unaccustomed to the service.

The 16th. In the morning we march'd five miles & encamp'd, in order to clean our arms & lining. Among the many insects that trouble us, *wood-ticks* are not the least: They are exceeding many, & exceeding troublesome . . . There is also a most venomous *spider*, but none have been as yet hurt by them. — Beside; there is a small creature that afflicts us far worse than *wood-ticks*, yea, tho' they are the smallest living things I ever saw. Indeed I think they wou'd hardly be discerned were it not for their colour, which is scarlet red. They go thro one's clothes, creep into the pores of the skin, where they cause it to swell to the degree of a bee sting, & are exceeding itching smarting: & sometimes dangerous. They have a shell like a tortoise; the inhabitants call them gigar & they comparatively, are as thick as the dust of the earth.

The 17th. This morning we march'd about daybreak towards Richmond, went about 15 or 20 miles, & encamp'd in about five miles of where the enemy had their head-quarters a day or 2 before. They are now in Rich-mond. (O Lord God, our fatigue & troubles are so great, that one can scarcely attend even so much as to think on thy holy day! Yea, we can scarcely attend to our necessary food. But may we sooner forget what to eat, than the Sabbath of the Lord. My desires are drawn forth towards thy worshiping assemblys, tho' I am far from any) There was a *duel* fought this day between a militia officer, & Lieut. Wheaton (of the Connecticut line) in which encounter the latter was kill'd or at least mortally wounded. He was our brigade quarter master, or waggon master general. — This night we doubled our guards & pickets.

The 18th. We lay still; sent out scouts; & took some prisoners belonging to Tarlton's light horse; who came out within   miles of our lines (When we march'd after Tarlton's light horse, we went without our pieces being loaded, & with our flints taken out: This, all may see, was that no one might fire a gun. Gen Wane, whom they call mad anthony, & sword-in-hand, intended to have put them all to the bayonet.) About dusk, the Marquess stole a march on the enemy (which is no new thing with him) but without success. We had a fatigueing march all night & arriv'd at their camp before sun-rise next morning; but are found them just gone (perhaps well for them)

The 19th. We retir'd six miles & encamp'd. The next day we had orders to clean our arms & cloths, to cook our provisions, & be ready to parade at 5 o'clock.

The 21. We march'd at 4 o'clock P.M. & reach'd 8 miles. The next morning we set out at one o'clock A.M. march'd upwards of 20 miles, & encamp'd. We past Richmond 4 miles. (This a considerable town situated on each side James river.) In Richmond the enemy had large stores of various kinds of private property many thousand hogsheads of tobacco, rope works, & so on. . . . Our marching is truly fatigueing! We halt scarcely time eno' for cooking something to put in our mouths. We seldom can catch more than 2 hours sleep in 24.

June 23d. We march'd at 2 o'clock A.M. in pursuit of the enemy; who have gotten one days start of us. This day I was expos'd again to the terrible distemper, the small pox & if I have not taken it, I can impute it to nothing but to the kind hand of my watchful guardian & Preserver, but shou'd I have catch'd it, I have nothing to look to unless the same hand, to raise myself again to health or to receive my departing spirit to himself. O Lord, may I be sincerely & truly resign'd to thy will! At 11 o'clock A.M. we halted for some refreshment. But I must shut my book for the present: the drum beats for parading; the news, the enemy are upon us. On this we form'd a *solid column*, in order to receive their horse which were approaching with their *infantry*, whom they preceded. They came in sight, but durst not give us battle. They retreated precipitately; by which we soon understood they were a rearguard, sent back to cause us to make a hault, that our foes might slip away with their main body & baggage . . . After this alarm we march'd as far as Botoms bridge, about 16 miles from Richmond, where we encamp'd. . . .

The 24th. Thanks be to thy name, O Lord, that thou hast added another favor to the many receiv'd! Thou hast brought me to the returns of another of thy Sabbaths! O may I never forget from whom all blessings flow! May I this day have some realizing sense of my obligation to be thine! & may I devote some of these hours to thee this day tho' encompass'd with so many evils & inconveniences. This day we had orders to clean our arms & linnings & lay still thro' this holy day. — Here I must take notice of some vilany. Within these days past, I have marched by 18 or 20 Negroes that lay dead by the way-side, putrifying with the *small pox*. How such a thing came about, appears to be thus: The Negroes here being much disaffected (arising from their harsh treatment), flock'd in great numbers to Cornwallis, as soon as he came into these parts. This artful general takes a number of them, (several hundreds) innoculates them, & just as they all are growing sick, he sends them out into the country where our troops had to pass & repass. These poor creatures, having no care taken of them, many crawl'd into the bushes about & died, where they lie infecting the air around with intolerable stench & great danger. This is a piece of Cornwallisean cruelty. He is not backward to own that he has inoculated 4 or 500 in order to spread *smallpox* thro' the country, & sent them out for that purpose: Which is another piece of his conduct that wants a name. But there is a King superior to the British King, & a Lord far above their lords. He is Lord of all. May he prevent any sad fatal consequences from this conduct, take care of us (I have no tho'ts that I have not taken the infection! but were there no more than myself, it cou'd not be much but what when thousands & thousands are expos'd! May the Lord take care of us, & may the mischief return upon the authors own fate; for Gods sake . .

At even, there was a man executed for desertion. He belong'd to the Pensylvania line; was taken up near the enemy lines. This is no less than the seventh which has been shot since we left W-point. But the first since I join'd the infantry in this quarter. Defecters are continually coming in to us from the enemy; & now & then some of them are taken.

The 25th. We again began our march at break of day when we had not proceeded above two miles before there was a small alarm, by means of several pieces being discharg'd in front, at I know not what. We march'd till night, & then encamp'd in about 5 miles of Williamsburg. This day we pass'd by Kent court house; & truly it was an odd disagreeable spectacle, A court in a wilderness, where was no house, great or small, within two miles of it! However the court house was answerable to the place. Wheat harvest begins to come on in this State: & it is good.—Indian corn too is very promising; but as their slaves are gone, they apprehend a famine because they see not how to gather their harvest.

The 26th. We began our march at sun rise in pursuit of our unnatural foes, who are not far distant. We expect an action & it will not be amiss to take some notice how our forces on each side stand. Their army, according to all counts, consists of about 5000. Ours, I suppose may amount to 2,500 regulars, 300 volunteer light-horse, 300 rifles on horse back, & 300 foot besides, from what I can gather, 3 or 4,000 militia: doubtless these are 3,000 & these constantly reinforcing, Which will make our force about 6,400. This day a party of our horse & riflemen had a scurmish with the enemy, in which we lost several in kill'd & wounded; & they, 'tis said, lost 200. Our men oblig'd them to retreat to the main body.

The 27th. Last evening, near midnight, we took an unexpected rout, retreating about 3 miles. This was, perhaps, because our forces lay too much scatter'd to venture an action, or the enemy's falling on us. Our Commanders are sensible, that the state & situation of our troops are not hidden from the *tories* in the least; & they constantly give information to Cornwallis, as well as all their assistance possible. But our army is a little better collected this day, & in better readiness to meet the enemy shou'd they not decline it.—This day is warm, & exceeding bad for marching. At night we turn'd our route back & encamp'd. Our army lies now together. Our *park* of artilery, which was left behind, is come on. Our army is constantly reinforcing, & becomes formidable.

The 28th. We be still at present; but expect every moment to move, we know not where, the enemy appearing on the point of something new.

The 29th. We march'd again at 2 o'clock, & went 14 miles, even within 6 miles of Williamsburg. There we lay all day, & sent out scouting parties, but came across none of the enemy, they retreating before us with precipitation. At even

we came back again 8 miles, & encamp'd about 10 o'clock.
(Wheat harvest comes on apace: apples begin to be fit for eating (where there is any: but little or no fruit in these parts this
year)

The 30th.   we lay still all day & rested . . .

July the 1st.   With the dawning light of this day I arose in
healthful circumstances! Blessed be my kind Benefactor! O
Lord, with the morning light of this thy day, lift on me the
light of thy glorious reconcil'd countenance, & help me to rejoice in God, that I am brought to the beginning of another
day, of another week, & of another month! O that this day
may be as the beginning of days to my soul O Lord, grant,
that I this day may have some unfeigned holy desires; some
unfeigned tears of repentance; some unfeigned devotion; &
some unfeigned joy & rejoising in the Lord!

This morning we set out at 4 o'clock A.M. & marched'd
8 or 10 miles, & encamp'd. This is the pleasantest march,
I think that I have had since I left any dwelling, even tho'
thro' a wood: It is pleasant, because, as it has not been much
frequented by the enemy in their tours; so it is not troubled
with the loathsome & dangerous stench of putrifying
Negroes. . . . Our camp lieth on the river Pamunsky ((or
York-river)) Williamsburg, they say, lieth about 20 miles below, at the meeting of this & the James river, & little York 20
miles below that on the same stream.) Here we had orders to
wash our clothes & bodies. A sad accident happen'd while we
were washing: one man was drown'd; another taken up for
dead, but recovered. At nine o'clock we mov'd, & march'd all
night to the enemy's lines, in the morning, where we shou'd
have taken 2, or 3,00, of them, had it not been for the discharge of a piece, which alarm'd them & they made their escape. A few minutes more wou'd have been sufficient, as we
had almost surround'd them before they were alarm'd. We retreated 10 miles.

The 3rd.   We mov'd to a new encampment, 5 miles distant
from the last.

The 4th.   Last night we had a very heavy & tremendous
thunder storm, which lasted thro' the night. Truly, it seem'd
as tho' the God of war & terrors had taken arms, & risen in
his own defense. But suprisingly awful! to see helpless mortals

stand & insult the insens'd Jehovah! Who has (at least to appearance) already descended to take vengeance on his adversaries. How he manifests his displeasure in flashes of fire! How he manifests his indignation with tremendous peals of thunder, that causes all nature around to tremble! This terrible voice strikes as awe of the divine Majesty on every creature but man! Man, who has all reason to fear, can stand stupid & secure, & even mock the direful voice! — Have they not reason to expect, that he who is able to dash in pieces ten thousand works in a moment, will mock when their fear cometh. At 2 oclock, we had a *feu-de-joy* on account of the *anniversary* of American independance, being the entrance of the 6th year. . . . 3. o'clock. The thunder begins to roar, & we may expect another terrible night to us, who have no tent to shelter us.

The 5th. we march'd ten miles towards *Wm*sburg & halted, about sunset, at a place call'd Birdshoner; There we tho't to encamp; but at dark we had orders, to proceed toward *Wm*sburg. . . .

The 6th. We continued our route till we (somewhat unexpectedly) came upon a large body of the enemy, all paraded in a line of battle ready to receive us. This was sudden business, because the inhabitants had continually declar'd to us, That there was no enemy within six miles of our troops. It appear'd unexpected to our general: He hardly dream'd of finding such a formidable body of the enemy so near him. We too, were hardly prepar'd for so severe an action, our men being very much scattered. However, our officers & soldiers, like brave heroes, begun the attack with (at first) but an *handful of men*: The other regiments came on with all possible speed. The attack began about 5, & lasted till dark: The rifle men, tis said, some of them stay'd & scirmish'd with the enemy in the woods all night, & all day, that they have not found time nor opportunity to pick up their dead. . . . Our party consisted only of the brigade of infantry & one brigade of Pensylvanians (& these not more than half of them engag'd) & a few rifle-men. The enemy were more than 6 times our number. This not withstanding, our troops behaved well, fighting with great spirit & bravery. The infantry were oft broke; but as oft rallied & form'd at a word: While the

Pensylvanians, when broken cou'd not be form'd again for action: by which they lost their *field-piece* & we the ground. Our loss of men cannot be yet ascertain'd, tho' I wou'd hope it is inconsiderable.—The enemy gain'd the ground, but have no cause to glory, their dead from all appearance, being many.—(Tho' this was a severe action for us, yet the loss of our regiment is trifling: gen Wanes considerable) We retir'd five miles that night to rest, & get some refreshment, of which we stood in much need, having had neither victuals, rum, nor water; & all we then had, was one gill of vinegar to 4 men. (How great was thy mercy, O Lord, in our deliverance! The like was hardly ever heard of! Six hundred men have attack'd & stood, the fire, sword, & bayonet, of the force of an army of 5,000, yea, of the whole army under Lord Cornwallis. When we were often broke, often form'd; several times almost surrounded; & yet all, as I may say, in comparison of what might have been expected: came off again in heart! Wonderful Providence!)

The 7th. Our missing are continually coming in. I had forgot, Our general, the Marquess, had 2 horses shot under him; yet he is not daunted; He is collecting his army, & designes to have another action immediately, if the enemy will.

Ebenezer Denny:
Journal, June 18–July 7, 1781

June 18th. — Joined the troops under command of Lafayette. The Marquis had marched two or three days to meet us. His men look as if they were fit for business. They are chiefly all light infantry, dressed in frocks and over-alls of linen. One day spent in washing and refreshing — in fixing arms, carriages, &c., and served out ammunition. Move toward Richmond, where Lord Cornwallis with the British army lay. Heard that his lordship was employed burning and destroying ware-houses of tobacco, all the public store-houses, &c. Passed through Richmond toward Williamsburg after the enemy — joined by Baron Steuben with some new levies. Near Bacon's Bridge the British turned upon us; our advance pressed them too close. The army was formed for a fight — they did not come on. General Wayne very anxious to do something. Colonel Simcoe, who commands the British legion (horse and mounted infantry), is constantly committing some depre-dation abroad, and foraging for their army. Wayne hears of him — our brigade leave their tents and baggage, march at dark, with piece of white paper in each man's hat — flints taken out. At day-light reach place called the Bowling Green, where Simcoe had been the evening before. This was a severe march for me — found myself asleep more than once on the route. Returned and met the baggage. A detachment from the brigade put under command of Colonel Richard Butler. After a variety of marching and counter-marching, Butler at length intercepts Simcoe; a smart skirmish takes place; Wayne supports Butler, and Simcoe retreats. Here for the first time saw wounded men; feelings not very agreeable; endeavor to conquer this disposition or weakness; the sight sickened me. This little engagement within six miles of Williamsburg, where the enemy were encamped. Pennsylvania troops retreat — advance again. See the Marquis' light troops but seldom — know they are not far off. Kept constantly on the move. Hear that the enemy have decamped and preparing to cross James river at Jamestown. Our brigade move down; lay on arms all night about nine miles from the enemy. At daylight move on; middle of the afternoon of the 6th of July firing ahead. Our advance drove in the enemy's pickets, marching at this time by companies, in open order. My captain (Montgomery) fell behind his company where my place was, talked with me; gives me a lesson useful to me. When perhaps within one hundred and fifty yards of the enemy, we closed column and displayed; advanced in battalion until the firing commenced, and ran along the whole line. A regiment or more of the light infantry and three pieces of artillery were in the line. Saw the British light infantry, distinctly, advancing at arm's-length distance, and their second line in close order, with shouldered musket, just in front of their camp — their infantry only engaged. The main body were discovered filing off to the right and left, when orders were given us to retreat. My captain, Montgomery, received a shot in his foot and had hopped back in the rear; Lieutenant Bluer being absent, the charge of the company devolved on me; young and inexperienced, exhausted with hunger and fatigue, had like to have disgraced myself — had eat nothing all day but a few blackberries — was faint, and with difficulty kept my place; once or twice was about to throw away my arms (a very heavy espontoon). The company were almost all old soldiers. Kept compact and close to our leading company, and continued running until out of reach of the fire. The enemy advanced no farther than to the ground we left. We could not have been engaged longer than about three or four minutes, but at the distance of sixty yards only. Our loss is said to be upward of one hundred killed and wounded; among the latter twelve officers, one of whom, Lieutenant Herbert, taken prisoner; a few of the wounded not able to get off, were also taken. The artillery horses all killed; two pieces were lost. Retreated two miles to very commanding ground, where we met the Marquis with our main body; halted and had some Indian meal served out, the wounded dressed, &c., and before day changed our ground and encamped about five miles from the field.

July 7th.—An officer, surgeon, and a few men, sent with flag to bury the dead, &c. This was done in company with an equal number of the enemy. Our wounded who were prisoners, had been properly treated. The British moved from Jamestown. About a fortnight after the action, visited the field; could trace plainly the ground occupied by both, from the tops of the cartridges which lay in a line; the distance between about sixty paces. The army marched and crossed James river at Westover, the seat of Colonel Bird, said to have been once the most wealthy planter in the State; the improvements superb, saw nothing like them before. Kept at a respectful distance from the enemy; rather between them and the route to North Carolina. Some idea of their design to return to the southward. Report going of a French fleet below. This news confirmed — great joy — army on the alert.

James Robertson to William Knox

Near New York, 12th July 1781.

Dear Sir,

Before you get thro' this, I doubt you will repent your wish to have from me the present stage of things here, tho' knowing how much better you are usually employed, I will respect your time, and try to be short tho' I should fail in being clear —

It has been known for some weeks by intercepted letters and otherwise that Washington in forming a plan for the Campaign with the french Generals proposed to relieve Virginia by a direct move to the Chesapeak, with all the french land and naval force, that Rochambault opposed this, because he judged the french sea force inferior to ours, and the season destructive to any troops that attempts to operate in Virginia in the hot months. Washington then proposed to relieve Virginia by attacking this place with all the french and rebel force, and hoped greatly to encrease the last by holding out the lure of the plunder of this wealthy City. This was agreed to, and least these moves should not effect the relief of Virginia by inducing us to call away our troops, the french Commander said he would represent the state of that country to Monsr. de Grasse Commanding the french fleet at Martinico, from whom he might with confidence expect effectual aid —

It appeared to Sir Henry Clinton that Marquis de Fayette had with him remaining in Virginia about eight out of the twelve hundred Continentals he took from hence — that Wayne was endeavoring to goad on about twelve hundred of the Pennsylvania line to join La Fayette, by whose letters the Militia were said to be few, unwarlike, and unarmed. He Sir Henry judged that Lord Cornwallis however rapid his motions might be would never be able to overtake La Fayette, and tho' he might destroy Magazines of the enemy's would ruin what is of more value to us, our troops, proposed, If his

Lordship did not think it advisable to turn his arms towards Baltimore, and the Head of Elk, where our friends call for our aid, that he would cease operating in Virginia in the hot months, and content himself with occupying and fortifying the important post at York, where our fleet might and no where else find security against a superior fleet — to keep with him a sufficient number for this service, and for occasional excursions by water only, which Sir Henry reckoned between four and five thousand men — and to send out of the way of disease to this more healthy region the remainder of his army between two and three thousand men — transports were sent to bring these hither —

Apprized of all this, I represented to the Commander in Chief, that since the abolition of paper-money, the rebels have formed a bank, and appointed a Financier whose sole hope of getting Specie and Credit is by a trade with the Havanah from the Delaware, this has by our fleets being necessarily otherwise employed, succeeded beyond belief, and the river is full of Ships and the city of Philadelphia full of Stores, and is only protected by the Militia of the Country — with secrecy and dispatch I am well informed that three thousand men could destroy all these. I proposed that in place of coming here the troops bound from Virginia should stop off but out of sight of the Delaware, where Admiral Graves after taking on board here a thousand men under the pretence of strengthening his Squadron against the french fleet should meet them, and while he secured the mouth of the river with his large Ships, I should proceed up to Chester with the frigates and troops and execute a plan of which I gave a detail for taking and destroying all that could be useful to the rebels, I proposed saving the town, as a valuable part of the King's dominions, and not to have brought away any thing, that our sea and land men might have no room to squabble about the division of plunder — Any preparations here would have pointed out the object, and that Washington could have rendered the attempt impracticable by a march of six days — orders were sent by the Orpheus to make all these in the Chesapeak. This ship was to return as soon as she could fix the day of sailing with the Officer Commanding in Chesapeak — we have not heard of this ships arrival, but by letters from Lord Cornwallis just received it appears, That his Lordship does not approve of remaining on the defensive in Virginia, that he was preparing to repass James river La Fayette and Wayne close on his rear — His Lordship offers however unpleasant it may be to return to Charlestown — this would leave no post in Virginia ours, but Portsmouth — which cannot cover a fleet, and has lost the reputation of being a desirable situation.

Sir Henry after consulting with the Admiral has by an express told his Lordship — that it is of the utmost moment he take and keep the post he recommends in Virginia, York or Point Comfort — that if every man with him be necessary for this purpose he is to keep them all — and least any are put to Sea — the Captain of the man of war carries them orders to return till they receive further directions from Lord Cornwallis — who has notice by the same advice that he can expect no succours from hence, where our force is only eleven thousand men. As Washington's army cannot collect in force nor the expected french fleet arrive before the tenth of August, I saw that the attempt on Philadelphia might without risque have been made before that time, and however useful this desultory expedition might have been, it was not offered with a view of taking any troops from Virginia, but of employing those usefully who were ordered hither — I have too fondly dwelt too long on a project I begin to fear will not take place —

Washington and Rochambault are with their armies on the White plains, they have a great apparatus of Artillery, some of their guns and mortars heavy. The Romulus and two french frigates three days ago came up the Sound, and drove all our small Craft into Huntington Bay, our Admiral has ordered two frigates into the Sound by Hell gate — before their appearance the french were gone away, they did little damage. I suspect they covered some heavy stores which the enemy found it difficult to carry by land — by one I trust, I have reason to believe the french who form on the left, are about 5,000, and the rebels about eight — most of the last raw soldiers — New England men, raised for a few months —

The return of the Royal Oak from Halifax where she went to heave down, and the junction of two fifty gun ships, gives our fleet a decisive superiority over the french — Admiral

Graves lyes at anchor with all his line of battle ships three leagues without the Hook — The french fleet which without the assistance of troops they dont reckon fit for sea service, it is said by orders from De Grasse lyes quiet in Rhode Island till further orders —

Our Militia are armed and ready to take care of the city and leave the whole of the King's troops at liberty to attack the enemy should they attempt to possess any situation from whence this place may be annoyed, even the hope of plunder does not induce the country to rise in proportion to Washington's expectations and the Congress resolves, and from the ground they have taken and the precautions they use, they seem determined to wait at a post from which we probably wont endeavor to make them fall back, in expectation of further aid, than with a view to any present enterprise —

Let me now talk to the Secretary of the Province of New York —

Bayard's letter will tell you of the importance of the Books the Asia carryed home, and of the disappointment of our expectations in what we only have received —

The part of the Army under Arnold took many Vessels and much Tobacco, etc., in James's river and on its banks fifty miles higher than any of our men o'war went — As these Vessels with this sort of lading was proceeding down the river with military prize masters on board a man o'war met them took out the prize masters and put in their own and proceeded with them to New York to libel them as prizes to the Navy — On this and no other occasion Sir Henry Clinton begged me to assume the powers of a Civil Governor and to direct the Advocate General to libel all these as prizes to the King — The Advocate who derives great wealth from the Navy wished to decline doing this, but finally complied. Soon after the Candidates, uncertain how the King might bestow the produce came to a sort of compromise — and wished me to countermand the directions given to the Advocate General — this could not be gone into as proceedings had been held in the Admiralty Court —

Care is taken to examine all letters that come from the Country occupied by the rebels, some of these contain bills payable to good subjects here or in England for debts due to them in the rebel Countrys—all such are permitted to take their course. But one drawn by the Financier of Congress in favor of a house not inimical to Congress, and seeming to have a tendency to give a Credit and Circulation to Congress bills, I have thought proper to enclose to you, and to beg that by your means, the matter may be subjected to the judgment of Lord George Germain, so that the bill may be forwarded to the owner or perhaps used to produce discoverys or prevent the growth of Congress Credit—

I have the honor to be, Sir, etc.

Otho Holland Williams:
Narrative of the Battle of Eutaw Springs

At 4 o'clock in the morning, the American army moved in four columns from its bivouac, in the following order: The South Carolina State Troops and Lee's Legion, formed the advance, under command of Col. Henderson. The militia, both of North and South Carolina, under Marion, moved next. Then followed the regulars, under Gen. Sumner; and the rear was closed by Washington's Cavalry and Kirkwood's Delawares, under Col. Washington. The Artillery moved between the columns. The troops were thus arranged in reference to the order of battle, in which they were to be formed on the field.

It is an admitted fact, that on the evening of the 7th, Stewart was unapprized of the approach of the American army. He supposed them to be still posted at Laurens', and the apology which he makes for it is—"that the Americans had way-laid the swamps and passes in such a manner, as to cut off every avenue to intelligence." He would have found a better apology in the fact, that the only patrol which appears to have been dispatched up the Congaree road, had been entrapped and captured by Col. Lee, during the night. So entirely secure had he felt himself in his position, that an unarmed party, under a small escort, had been advanced up the river for the purpose of collecting the sweet potatoe, (very generally cultivated in this State) to contribute to the subsistence of his army. This party, commonly called a rooting party, consisting of about one hundred, after advancing about three miles, had pursued a road to their right, which led to the plantations on the river.

The first intelligence, that Greene had approached within seven miles of his position, was communicated to Stewart by two of the North Carolina conscripts, who had deserted early in the night. And Captain Coffin, at the head of his Cavalry, was advanced, as well to recall the rooting party, as to reconnoitre the American position, and ascertain their views.

The American advance had already passed the road pursued by the rooting party, when they were encountered by Coffin; who immediately charged with a confidence which betrayed his ignorance of its strength, and of the near approach of the main army. It required little effort to meet and repulse the British Cavalry; but, the probability that their main army was near at hand to support the detachment forbade the measure of a protracted pursuit. The firing at this point drew the rooting party out of the woods, and the whole fell into the hands of the Americans.

In the mean time, Col. Stewart had pushed forward a detachment of Infantry to a mile distant from the Eutaws, with orders to engage and detain the American troops, while he formed his men and prepared for battle. But, Greene, persuaded by the audacity of Coffin, that the enemy was at hand, and wishing to have time for his raw troops to form with coolness and recollection, halted his columns, and after distributing the contents of his rum casks, ordered his men to form in the order for battle.

The column of militia, when deployed, formed the first line; the South Carolinians, in equal divisions, on the right and left, and the North Carolinians in the centre; Gen. Marion commanded the right, Gen. Pickens the left, and Col. Malmady, (who held a commission under North Carolina) commanded the centre. Col. Henderson, with the State troops, including Sumter's Brigade, covered the left of this line, and Col. Lee, with his Legion, the right.

The column of regulars also deployed into one line; the North Carolinians under Gen. Sumner, occupied the right, divided into three Battalions, commanded by Col. Ash, and Majors Armstrong and Blunt; the Marylanders, under Col. Williams, on the left, divided into two Battalions, commanded by Col. Howard and Major Hardman; the Virginians, in the centre, under command of Col. Campbell, were also divided into two Battalions, led by Major Sneed and Captain Edmonds. The two three-pounders, under Capt. Lieut. Gaines, moved in the road with the first line, which was equally distributed to the right and left of it; and the two six-pounders, under Capt. Brown, attended the second line, in the same order. Col. Washington still moved in the rear in column, with orders to keep under cover of the woods, and hold himself in reserve. The relative numbers of the corps that formed the American second line, were nearly as follows: The North Carolina line, 350; the Virginians, 350; the Marylanders, 250. Those of the militia have been already mentioned. The troops of the two covering parties, and the reserve, make up the total of the regulars before stated.

In this order the troops moved forward. The whole country on both sides of the road, being in woods, the lines could not move with much expedition consistently with preserving their order. The woods were not thick, nor the face of the country irregular; it undulated gently, presenting no obstacles to the march, although producing occasional derangements in the connection of the lines.

When the first American line reached the ground on which it encountered Stewart's advanced parties it was ordered to move on in order, driving the enemy before it. And in this manner it advanced firing, while the enemy retreated, and fell into their own line.

At about two hundred yards west of the Eutaw Springs, Stewart had drawn up his troops in one line, extending from the Eutaw Creek beyond the main Congaree road. The Eutaw Creek effectually covered his right, and his left, which was in the military language, in air, was supported by Coffin's Cavalry, and a respectable detachment of Infantry, held in reserve at a convenient distance in the rear of the left, under cover of the wood.

The ground on which the British army was drawn up, was altogether in wood; but, at a small distance in the rear of this line, was a cleared field, extending west, south and east from the dwelling house, and bounded north by the creek formed by the Eutaw Springs, which is bold, and has a high bank thickly bordered with brush and low wood. From the house to this bank, extended a garden enclosed with palisadoes, and the windows of the house, which was two-stories high, with garret rooms, commanded the whole circumjacent fields. The house was of brick, and abundantly strong to resist small arms, and surrounded with various offices of wood; one particularly, a barn of some size, lay to the southeast, a small distance from the principal building. In the open ground, to the south and west of the house, was the British encampment, the tents of which were left standing.

The American approach was from the west; and at a short distance from the house, in that direction, the road forks, the right hand leading to Charleston, by the way of Monk's Corner, the left running along the front of the house by the plantation of Mr. Patrick Roche, and therefore called, by the British officers, Roche's road; being that which leads down the river, and through the parishes of St. Johns and St. Stephens.

The superiority of his enemy in Cavalry, made it necessary that Col. Stewart should cast his eye to the Eutaw house for retreat and support. To that, therefore, he directed the attention of Major Sheridan, with orders, upon the first symptoms of misfortune, to throw himself into it, and cover the army from the upper windows. On his right also, he had made a similar provision against the possibility of his lines being compelled to give ground. In the thickets which border the creek, Major Majoribanks, with three hundred of his best troops, was posted, with instructions to watch the flank of the enemy, if ever it should be open to attack. This command had assumed a position having some obliquity to the main line, forming with an obtuse angle.

The Artillery of the enemy was also posted in the main road.

As soon as the skirmishing parties were cleared away from between the two armies, a steady and desperate conflict ensued. That between the Artillery of the first line, and that of the enemy, was bloody and obstinate in the extreme; nor did the American Artillery relax for a moment from firing or advancing, until both pieces were dismounted and disabled. One of the enemy's four pounders had shared the same fate, and the carnage on both sides had been equal and severe.

Nor had the militia been wanting in gallantry and perseverance. It was with equal astonishment, that both the second line and the enemy, contemplated these men, steadily, and without faltering, advance with shouts and exhortations into the hottest of the enemy's fire, unaffected by the continual fall of their comrades around them. Gen. Greene, to express his admiration of the firmness exhibited on this occasion by the militia, says of them, in a letter to Steuben, "such conduct would have graced the veterans of the great king of Prussia." But it was impossible that this could endure long, for these men were, all this time, receiving the fire of double their number; their Artillery was demolished, and that of the enemy still vomiting destruction on their ranks. They at length began to hesitate.

Governor Rutledge, who was anxiously attending the event of this battle, a few miles in the rear, wrote to the South Carolina delegates, that the militia fired seventeen rounds before they retired. That distrust of their own immediate commanders, which militia are too apt to be affected with, never produced an emotion where Marion and Pickens commanded.

Gen. Sumner was then ordered to support them. This was done with the utmost promptness, and the battle again raged with redoubled fury. In speaking of General Sumner's command, Gen. Greene observes, "that he was at a loss which most to admire, the gallantry of the officers or the good conduct of the men."

On the advance of Gen. Sumner's command, Col. Stewart had brought up the Infantry of his reserve into line on his left, and the struggle was obstinately maintained between fresh troops on both sides.

From the first commencement of the action, the Infantry of the American covering parties, on the right and left, had been steadily engaged. The Cavalry of the Legion, by being on the American right, had been enabled to withdraw into the woods and attend on its Infantry, without being at all exposed to the enemy's fire. But the State Troops under Henderson had been in the most exposed situation on the field. The American right, with the addition of the Legion Infantry, had extended beyond the British left. But the American left fell far short of the British right; and the consequence was that the State Troops were exposed to the oblique fire of a large proportion of the British right, and particularly of the Battalion commanded by Majoribanks. Never was the constancy of a party of men more severely tried. Henderson solicited permission to charge them, and extricate himself from their galling fire, but his protection could not be spared from the Artillery or the militia. At length he received a wound which disabled him from keeping his horse, and a momentary hesitation in his troops was produced by the shock. The exertions of Col. Wade Hampton, who succeeded to the command, aided by those of Col. Polk and Middleton, proved successful in restoring them to confidence and order, and they resumed their station in perfect tranquility.

In the mean time things were assuming important changes along the front line. Sumner's Brigade, after sustaining for some time, a fire superior to their own in the ratio of the greater numbers opposed to them, at length yielded, and fell back. The British left, elated at the prospect, sprang forward as to certain conquest, and their line became deranged. This was exactly the incident for which the American commander was anxiously watching, and the next moment produced the movement for availing himself of it. Col. Williams now remained in command of the second line. "Let Williams advance and sweep the field with his bayonets," was the order delivered to a gentleman of medical staff, who acted the surgeon, the aid, and the soldier, indifferently, as occasion required.

Never was order obeyed with more alacrity; the two Brigades received it with a shout; emulous to wipe away the recollections of Hobkirk's Hill, they advanced with a spirit expressive of the impatience with which they had hitherto been passive spectators of the action. When approached within forty yards of the enemy, the Virginians delivered a destructive fire, and the whole second line, with trailed arms, and an animated pace, advanced to the charge. Until this period their progress had been in the midst of showers of grape, and under a stream of fire from the line opposed to them. But eye-witnesses have asserted, that the roll of the drum, and the shouts which followed it, drew every eye upon them alone; and a momentary pause in the action, a suspension by mutual consent, appeared to withdraw both armies from a sense of personal danger, to fix their attention upon this impending conflict. It may well be supposed with what breathless expectation the Southern commander hung upon a movement on

which all his hopes depended. Had it failed, he must have retired under cover of his Cavalry.

Under the approach of the second line, the advanced left of
the British army had commenced a retrograde movement, in
some disorder. This was confirmed by the good conduct of
Col. Lee. The Legion Infantry had steadily maintained its order in its position on the extreme right; and the advance of
the British left having exposed its flank, the Legion Infantry
were promptly wheeled, and poured in upon them a destructive enfilading fire; then joining in the charge, the British left
wing was thrown into irretrievable disorder. But their centre
and right still remained; greatly outnumbering the assailing
party, and awaiting the impending charge with unshaken constancy.

If the two lines on this occasion, did not actually come to
the mutual thrust of the bayonet, it must be acknowledged,
that no troops ever came nearer. They are said to have been
so near, that their bayonets clashed and the officers sprang at
each other with their swords, before the enemy actually broke
away.

But, the scales of victory, fortunately for man, are never
long in equipoise on these occasions.

In this instance, the left of the British centre appear to have
been pressed upon, and forced back by their own fugitives,
and began to give way from left to right. At that moment, the
Marylanders delivered their fire, and along their whole front
the enemy yielded.

The shouts of victory resounded through the American
line, affording a gleam of consolation to many a brave man,
bleeding and expiring on the field. Among these was the gallant Campbell, who received a ball in the breast during this
onset.

The victory was now deemed certain; but, many joined in
the shouts of victory who were still destined to bleed. The
carnage among the Americans had but commenced; it was in
the effort to prevent the enemy from rallying, and to cut him
off from the brick house, which was all that remained to compel the army to surrender, that their great loss was sustained.

A pursuing army is always impeded by the effort that
is necessary to maintain its own order; while, whether from

terror, for safety, or for rallying the speed of the fugitive, is unrestrained. Hence, Cavalry are the military means for rendering disorder irretrievable. It is obvious, that at this point of time, the Legion Cavalry might have been turned upon the British left with very great effect. Their position was highly favorable to such a movement, and their Infantry was close up with the enemy to afford support. Why this was was not done, has never been explained; we can only conjecture, that it was prevented by one or both of two causes known to have existed on that day. Col. Lee was generally absent from it during the action, and bestowing his attention upon the progress of his Infantry; and Captain Coffin was in that quarter, attending on the retreat of the British left. Coffin's force was, probably, superior to that of Lee in Cavalry; whether so superior as to justify the latter's not attempting the charge in the presence of the British Cavalry, although supported by that of his own Infantry, could only have been decided by the attempt.

At this stage of the battle, Majoribanks still stood firm in the thickets that covered him; and, as the British line extended considerably beyond the American left, their extreme right still manifested a reluctance to retire; and as their left had first given way, and yielded now without resistance, the two armies performed together a half wheel, which brought them into the open ground towards the front of the house.

Gen. Greene now saw that Majoribanks must be dislodged, or the Maryland flank would soon be exposed to his fire, and the conflict in that quarter renewed under his protection. Therefore, orders were dispatched to Washington, to pass the American left and charge the enemy's right. The order was promptly obeyed, and galloping through the woods, Washington was soon in action. Had he had the good fortune to have taken on Kirkwood's Infantry behind his men, all would have gone well; to have been detained by their march, would have been inconsistent with his general feeling.

Col. Hampton, at the same time, received orders to co-operate with Col. Washington; and the rapid movement which he made to the creek, in order to fall in upon Washington's left, probably hastened the forward movement of the latter. On reaching the front of Majoribanks, and before Hampton had joined him, Washington attempted a charge, but it was impossible for his Cavalry to penetrate the thicket. He then discovered that there was an interval between the British right and the creek, by which he was in hopes to succeed in gaining their rear. With this view, he ordered his troop to wheel by sections to the left, and thus, brought nearly all his officers next to the enemy, while he attempted to pass their front. A deadly and well directed fire, delivered at that instant, wounded or brought to the ground many of his men and horses, and every officer except two.

The field of battle was, at this instant, rich in the dreadful scenery which disfigures such a picture. On the left, Washington's Cavalry, routed and flying, horses plunging as they died, or coursing the field without their riders, while the enemy with poised bayonet, issued from the thicket, upon the wounded or unhorsed rider. In the fore-ground, Hampton covering and collecting the scattered Cavalry, while Kirkwood, with his bayonets, rushed furiously to revenge their fall, and a road strewed with the bodies of men and horses, and the fragments of dismounted Artillery. Beyond these, a scene of indescribable confusion, viewed over the whole American line advancing rapidly, and in order: And, on the right, Henderson borne off in the arms of his soldiers, and Campbell sustained in his saddle by a brave son, who had sought glory at his father's side.

Nothing could exceed the consternation spread at this time through the British ground of encampment. Every thing was given up for lost, the commissaries destroyed their stores, the numerous retainers of the army, mostly loyalists and deserters, who dreaded falling into the hands of the Americans, leaping on the first horse they could command, crowded the roads and spread alarm to the very gates of Charleston. The stores on the road were set fire to, and the road itself obstructed by the felling of trees, for miles, across it.

Lieut. Gordon, and Cornet Simmons, were the only two of Washington's officers who could return into action. The Colonel himself had his horse shot under him, and his life saved by the interposition of a British officer. The melancholy group of wounded men and officers, who soon presented themselves to the General's view, convinced him of the severity of his misfortune; but, he had not yet been made acquainted with the full extent of it.

The survivors of Washington's command being rallied, united themselves to Hampton's, and were again led up to the charge upon Majoribanks, but without success. That officer was then retiring before Kirkwood, still holding to the thickets, and making for a new position, with his rear to the creek, and his left resting on the palisadoed garden. By this time Sheridan had thrown himself into the house, and some of the routed companies from the left had made good their retreat into the picketted garden; from the intervals of which, they could direct their fire with security and effect. The whole British line was now flying before the American bayonet. The latter pressed closely upon their heels, made many prisoners, and might have cut off the retreat of the rest, or entered pell-mell with them into the house, but for one of these occurrences, which have often snatched victory from the grasp of a pursuing enemy.

The retreat of the British army lay directly through their encampment, where the tents were all standing, and presented many objects to tempt a thirsty, naked and fatigued soldiery to acts of insubordination. Nor was the concealment afforded by the tents at this time a trivial consideration, for the fire from the windows of the house was galling and destructive, and no cover from it was anywhere to be found except among the tents, or behind the building to the left of the front of the house.

Here it was that the American line got into irretrievable confusion. When their officers had proceeded beyond the encampment, they found themselves nearly abandoned by their soldiers, and the sole marks for the party who now poured their fire from the windows of the house.

From the baneful effects of passing through the encampment, only a few corps escaped. Of this number, the Legion Infantry appears to have been one. Being far on the American right, it directed its movements with a view to securing the advantage of being covered by the barn; and the narrow escape of the British army, is sufficiently attested by the fact, that this corps was very near entering the house pell-mell with the fugitives. It was only by closing the door in the face of some of their own officers and men, that it was prevented; and in retiring from the fire of the house, the prisoners taken at the door, were interposed as a shield to the life of their captors.

Everything now combined to blast the prospects of the American Commander. The fire from the house showered down destruction upon the American officers; and the men, unconscious or unmindful of consequences, perhaps thinking the victory secure, and bent on the immediate fruition of its advantages, dispersing among the tents, fastened upon the liquors and refreshments they afforded, and became utterly unmanageable.

Majoribanks and Coffin, watchful of every advantage, now made simultaneous movements; the former from his thicket on the left, and the latter from the wood on the right of the American line. Gen. Greene soon perceived the evil that threatened him, and not doubting but his Infantry, whose disorderly conduct he was not yet made acquainted with, would immediately dispose of Majoribanks, dispatched Capt. Pendleton with orders for the Legion Cavalry to fall upon Coffin and repulse him.

We will give the result in Captain Pendleton's own language: "When Coffin's Cavalry came out, Gen. Greene sent me to Col. Lee, with orders to attack him. When I went to the corps Lee was not there, and the order was delivered to Major Egleston, the next in command, who made the attack without success." "The truth is, Col. Lee was very little, if at all, with his own corps after the enemy fled. He took some dragoons with him, as I was informed, and rode about the field, giving orders and directions, in a manner the General did not approve of. Gen. Greene was, apparently, disappointed when I informed him Col. Lee was not with his Cavalry, and that I had delivered the order to Major Egleston."

By this time Gen. Greene, being made acquainted with the extent of his misfortune, ordered a retreat.

Coffin, who certainly proved himself a brave and active officer on this day, had no sooner repulsed the Legion Cavalry, than he hastened on to charge the rear of the Americans, now dispersed among the tents. Col. Hampton had been ordered up to the road to cover the retreat, at the same time the order was issued to effect it, and now charged upon Coffin with a vigour that was not to be resisted. Coffin met him with firmness, and a sharp conflict, hand to hand, was for a while maintained. But Coffin was obliged to retire, and in the ardour of pursuit, the American Cavalry approached so near Majoribanks, and the picketted garden, as to receive from them a fatally destructive fire. Col. Polk, who commanded Hampton's left, and was, of consequence, directly under its influence, describes it by declaring "that he thought every man killed but himself." Col. Hampton then rallied his scattered Cavalry, and resumed his station in the border of the wood. But before this could be effected, Majoribanks had taken advantage of the opening made by his fire, to perform another gallant action, which was decisive of the fortune of the day.

The Artillery of the second line had followed on, as rapidly as it could, upon the track of the pursuit, and, together with two six-pounders abandoned by the enemy in their flight, had been brought up to batter the house. Unfortunately, in the ardour to discharge a pressing duty, the pieces had been run into the open field, so near as to be commanded by the fire from the house. The pieces had scarcely opened their fire, when the pressing danger which threatened the party in the house, and, consequently the whole army, drew all the fire from the windows upon the Artillerists, and it very soon killed or disabled nearly the whole of them. And Majoribanks who no sooner disembarrassed of Hampton's Cavalry, than he sallied into the field, seized the pieces, and hurried them under the cover of the house. Then being re-inforced by parties from the garden and the house, he charged among the Americans, now dispersed among the tents, and drove them before him. The American army, however, soon rallied, after reaching the cover of the wood, and their enemy was too much crippled to venture beyond the cover of the house.

Gen. Greene halted on the ground only long enough to collect his wounded; all of whom, except those who had fallen under cover of the fire from the house, he brought off; and having made arrangements for burying the dead, and left a strong picket, under Col. Hampton, on the field, he withdrew his army to Burdell's, seven miles distant. At no nearer point could water be found adequate to the comforts of the army.

Both parties claimed, on this occasion a complete victory; but there is no difficulty in deciding the question between them, upon the plainest principles. The British army was chased from the field at the point of the bayonet, and took refuge in a fortress; the Americans were repulsed from that fortress. And, but for the demoralizing effect of possessing themselves of the British tents, the cover of the barn presented the means of forcing or firing the house with certainty, and reducing the whole to submission.

But if further evidence of victory than driving the enemy from the field, occupying his position, and plundering his camp, be required, it is found in the events of the succeeding day.

M'Arthur was called up from Fairlawn to cover Gen. Stewart's retreat; and leaving seventy of his wounded to his enemy, and many of his dead unburied; breaking the stocks of one thousand of arms, and casting them into the spring; destroying his stores, and then moving off precipitately, he fell back, and retreated to Fairlawn. The possession of the American Artillery, was the strong ground on which the British founded their claim to victory. But in this the trophies were divided, for one of the enemy's pieces, the four pounder that was disabled on the field, was carried off by the Americans, and the two others were fairly in their hands, and would have been secured, had they not been brought up, through the officious zeal of some of the staff of the army, to attack their prior owners.

On the other hand, the enemy took no prisoners, except about forty wounded, whilst the Americans made five hundred prisoners, including the seventy who were abandoned when the enemy retreated.

But the best criterion of victory is to be found in consequences; and here the evidence is altogether on the American side. For the enemy abandoned his position, relinquished the country it commanded, and although largely re-enforced, still retired, when the Americans advanced within five miles of him, to Ferguson's Swamp, where he had first halted.

It was Gen. Greene's intention to have renewed the action the next day; and in hopes to prevent a junction with M'Arthur, Lee and Marion had been detached to watch the line of communication between the Eutaws and Fairlawn. By the simultaneous movements of the two corps, so as to meet at mid-distance and out number Marion, their junction and retreat was effectually secured. This was the evening of the day after the battle. Gen. Greene pressed the pursuit on the road to Charleston, during the whole of one day; but, finding that Col. Stewart still retired before him, and being now left at liberty to watch the movements of Lord Cornwallis, and his wounded and prisoners requiring attention, he resolved to retire again to the High Hills of Santee.

Ebenezer Denny:
Journal, September 1–November 1, 1781

Sept. 1st. — Army encamped on the bank of James river — part of French fleet, with troops on board, in view. Recrossed James river and encamped at Williamsburg. Army in high spirits — reinforcements coming on.

14th. — General Washington arrived; our brigade was paraded to receive him; he rode along the line — quarters in Williamsburg.

15th. — Officers all pay their respects to the Commander-in-chief; go in a body; those who are not personally known, their names given by General Hand and General Wayne. He stands in the door, takes every man by the hand — the officers all pass in, receiving his salute and shake. This the first time I had seen the General. We have an elegant encampment close to town, behind William and Mary College. This building occupied as an hospital. Williamsburg a very handsome place, not so populous as Richmond, but situate on evenly, pretty ground; streets and lots spacious — does not appear to be a place of much business, rather the residence of gentlemen of fortune; formerly it was the seat of government and Dunmore's late residence. A neat public building, called the capitol, fronts the principal street; upon the first floor is a handsome marble statue of William Pitt.

The presence of so many general officers, and the arrival of new corps, seem to give additional life to everything; discipline the order of the day. In all directions troops seen exercising and manœuvring. Baron Steuben, our great military oracle. The guards attend the grand parade at an early hour, where the Baron is always found waiting with one or two aids on horseback. These men are exercised and put through various evolutions and military experiments for two hours — many officers and spectators present; excellent school, this. At length the duty of the parade comes on. The guards are told off; officers take their posts, wheel by platoons to the right; fine corps of music detailed for this duty, which strikes up; the whole march off, saluting the Baron and field officer of the day, as they pass. Pennsylvania brigade almost all old soldiers, and well disciplined when compared with those of Maryland and Virginia. But the troops from the eastward far superior to either.

25th. — Joined by the last of the troops from the eastward. French encamped a few miles on the right; busy in getting cannon and military stores from on board the vessels.

28th. — The whole army moved in three divisions toward the enemy, who were strongly posted at York, about twelve miles distant. Their pickets and light troops retire. We encamped about three miles off — change ground and take a position within one mile of York; rising ground (covered with tall handsome pines) called Pigeon Hill, separates us from a view of the town. Enemy keep possession of Pigeon Hill. York on a high, sandy plain, on a deep navigable river of same name. Americans on the right; French on the left, extending on both sides of the river; preparations for a siege. One-third of the army on fatigue every day, engaged in various duties, making gabions, fascines, saucissons, &c., and great exertions and labor in getting on the heavy artillery. Strong covering parties (whole regiments) moved from camp as soon as dark, and lay all night upon their arms between us and the enemy. Our regiment, when on this duty, were under cover, and secured from the shot by Pigeon Hill; now and then a heavy shot from the enemy's works reached our camp. Our patrols, and those of the British, met occasionally in the dark, sometimes a few shot were exchanged — would generally retire. Colonel Schamel, adjutant-general to the army, with two or three attendants, on a party of observation, ventured rather close; they were seen and intercepted by a few smart horsemen from the British. Schamel forced his way through, and got back to camp, but received a wound, of which he died next day. His death was lamented, and noticed by the Commander-in-chief in his orders. Possession taken of Pigeon Hill, and temporary work erected. Generals and engineers, in viewing and surveying the ground, are always fired upon and sometimes pursued. Escorts and covering parties stationed at convenient distances under cover of wood, rising ground, &c., afford support. This business reminds me of a play among the boys, called Prison-base.

At length, everything in readiness, a division of the army broke ground on the night of the 6th of October, and opened the first parallel about six hundred yards from the works of the enemy. Every exertion to annoy our men, who were necessarily obliged to be exposed about the works; however, the business went on, and on the 9th our cannon and mortars began to play. The scene viewed from the camp now was grand, particularly after dark — a number of shells from the works of both parties passing high in the air, and descending in a curve, each with a long train of fire, exhibited a brilliant spectacle. Troops in three divisions manned the lines alternately. We were two nights in camp and one in the lines; relieved about ten o'clock. Passed and repassed by a covert way leading to the parallel.

Oct. 11th. — Second parallel thrown up within three hundred yards of the main works of the enemy; new batteries erected, and additional number of cannon brought forward — some twenty-four pounders and heavy mortars and howitzers. A tremendous fire now opened from all the new works, French and American. The heavy cannon directed against the embrasures and guns of the enemy. Their pieces were soon silenced, broke and dismantled. Shells from behind their works still kept up. Two redoubts advanced of their lines, and within rifle shot of our second parallel, much in the way. These forts or redoubts were well secured by a ditch and picket, sufficiently high parapet, and within were divisions made by rows of casks ranged upon end and filled with earth and sand. On tops of parapet were ranged bags filled with sand — a deep narrow ditch communicating with their main lines. On the night of the 14th, shortly after dark, these redoubts were taken by storm; the one on our right, by the Marquis, with part of his light infantry — the other, more to our left, but partly opposite the centre of the British lines, by the French. Our batteries had kept a constant fire upon the redoubts through the day. Belonged this evening to a command detailed for the purpose of supporting the Marquis. The night was dark and favorable. Our batteries had ceased —

there appeared to be a dead calm; we followed the infantry and halted about half way—kept a few minutes in suspense, when we were ordered to advance. The business was over, not a gun was fired by the assailants; the bayonet only was used; ten or twelve of the infantry were killed. French had to contend with a post of more force—their loss was considerable. Colonel Hamilton led the Marquis' advance; the British sentries hailed them—no answer made. They also hailed the French, "Who comes there?" were answered, "French grenadiers." Colonel Walter Stewart commanded the regiment of reserve which accompanied the Marquis; they were immediately employed in connecting, by a ditch and parapet, the two redoubts, and completing and connecting the same with our second parallel. The British were soon alarmed; some from each of the redoubts made their escape. The whole enemy were under arms—much firing round all their lines, but particularly toward our regiment, where the men were at work; the shot passed over. In about three quarters of an hour we were under cover. Easy digging; light sandy ground.

15th.—Heavy fire from our batteries all day. A shell from one of the French mortars set fire to a British frigate; she burnt to the water's edge, and blew up—made the earth shake. Shot and shell raked the town in every direction. Bomb-proofs the only place of safety.

16th.—Just before day the enemy made a sortie, spiked the guns in two batteries and retired. Our troops in the parallel scarcely knew of their approach until they were off; the thing was done silently and in an instant. The batteries stood in advance of the lines, and none within but artillery. This day, the 16th, our division manned the lines—firing continued without intermission. Pretty strong detachments posted in each battery over night.

17th.—In the morning, before relief came, had the pleasure of seeing a drummer mount the enemy's parapet, and beat a parley, and immediately an officer, holding up a white handkerchief, made his appearance outside their works; the drummer accompanied him, beating. Our batteries ceased. An officer from our lines ran and met the other, and tied the handkerchief over his eyes. The drummer sent back, and the

British officer conducted to a house in rear of our lines. Firing ceased totally.

18th. — Several flags pass and repass now even without the drum. Had we not seen the drummer in his red coat when he first mounted, he might have beat away till doomsday. The constant firing was too much for the sound of a single drum; but when the firing ceased, I thought I never heard a drum equal to it — the most delightful music to us all.

19th. — Our division man the lines again. All is quiet. Articles of capitulation signed; detachments of French and Americans take possession of British forts. Major Hamilton commanded a battalion which took possession of a fort immediately opposite our right and on the bank of York river. I carried the standard of our regiment on this occasion. On entering the fort, Baron Steuben, who accompanied us, took the standard from me and planted it himself. The British army parade and march out with their colors furled; drums beat as if they did not care how. Grounded their arms and returned to town. Much confusion and riot among the British through the day; many of the soldiers were intoxicated; several attempts in course of the night to break open stores; an American sentinel killed by a British soldier with a bayonet; our patrols kept busy. Glad to be relieved from this disagreeable station. Negroes lie about, sick and dying, in every stage of the small pox. Never was in so filthy a place — some handsome houses, but prodigiously shattered. Vast heaps of shot and shells lying about in every quarter, which came from our works. The shells did not burst, as was expected. Returns of British soldiers, prisoners six thousand, and seamen about one thousand. Lord Cornwallis excused himself from marching out with the troops; they were conducted by General O'Hara. Our loss said to be about three hundred; that of the enemy said not more than five hundred and fifty. Fine supply of stores and merchandise had; articles suitable for clothing were taken for the use of the army. A portion furnished each officer to the amount of sixty dollars.

20th. — Joined by a new raised regiment from Pennsylvania. Officers hastened to partake of the siege, but were too late. British troops march into the interior — to Winchester and other places. Visit Gloucester, small village opposite York;

nothing seen there. Some of our officers return to Pennsylvania, others take their place. Visit Williamsburg in company with young gentlemen of the country, on horseback; spend a few days very agreeably. Militia employed leveling the lines. Our brigade prepare for a long march.

Nov. 1st. — Three regiments of Pennsylvania, a detachment of artillery, and Maryland troops, commence their march for South Carolina — General St. Clair, the commanding officer. Easy, regular marching; roads generally good, through sandy country. Pass through Richmond and Guilford, in North Carolina, where General Green and the British had a hard fight; also Camden, where Gates was defeated. Halted at least one day in the week for purpose of washing and refreshing.

St. George Tucker:
Journal, September 28–October 20, 1781

Friday September 28th, 1781. This Morning at five OClock the whole Army marchd from Williamsburg, Mulenburg's Brigade of Infantry Lewis's Corps of Riflemen & the Light Dragoons forming the advanced Guard — The continental & French Troops march'd by the ordinary Road of Burwells Mill; after passing the half way house the former filed off to the Right & falling into the White Marsh road were joined By Nelson's Division of Militia who had march'd down the Warwick Road from Williamsburg passing over Harwoods Mill — The french Troops continuing their March on the ordinary Road took post on the left & part of the rear of York Town — The continentals having march'd to Secretary Nelson's quarter on the Mulberry Island road, discovered Tarlitons Legion posted at their Ordinary Quarters about a mile below York at the forks of the Hampton & Warwick roads (at one Hudson Allens I think). At the Appearance of our Troops Tarliton paraded his horse & came down within three hundred yards of a Meadow which lay between him & our reconnoitring party — 4 field pieces were brot. down to the Brow of the Hill to drive him off, & cover some Pioneers who were sent to repair Munfords Bridge where the Army were to cross — the second shot produced the desired Effect — The Bridge being mended Genl. Mulenburg passed over & occupied the Ground on the opposite side of the Meadow. A few more Shot were fired but I believe without Execution.

Sat. 29. This morning about eight o Clock the Enemy fired a few shot from their advanced Redoubts, our Right wing having now passed over Munford's Bridge. About nine or ten the Riflemen & Yagers exchanged a few shot across Moores Mill pond at the Dam of which the British had a redoubt — a few shot were fired at different times in the Day and about sunset from the Enemy's Redoubts — we had five or six men wounded; one mortally & two others by the same Ball. The Execution was much more than might have been expected from the Distance, the dispersed situation of our Men and the few shot fired.

Sunday 30th. This morning it being discovered that the Enemy had abandoned all their advanced Redoubts on the South & East Ends of the Town a party of French Troops between seven & eight OClock took possession of two Redoubts on penny's Hill or Pigeon Quarter, an eminence which it is said commands the whole Town — About ten a smart firing was heard on the upper End of the Town, accompanied by some Guns from the Ships — Being at this time in one of the Redoubts at penny's Hill I saw some of the British retreating or rather running very hastily across the sandy Beach into the Town; soon after which the firing ceas'd & a very considerable smoke (on the upper side of the town across the Creek) indicated the Destruction of their advanced Redoubt on that Quarter by the French Troops; and this I take to be really the Case; but if it should prove otherwise I shall mention it in the sequel — A party under Major Reid having advanced pretty near to their Works on our right, were obliged by a few well directed shot from them to retire. It is now conjectured by many that it is Lord Cornwallis's Intention to attempt a retreat up York river by West point, there being no Ships yet above the Town to prevent such a Measure. This morning Coll. Scammel of the Lt. Infantry reconnoitring the Enemies Works rather too near was wounded & taken prisoner.*

The conflict at the upper End of York was between a party of French who attack'd a Redoubt of the British at Nelson's Farm — The officer comg. the party was mortally wounded, two Men slightly wounded — The Redoubt was evacuated & burnt.†

Monday, Octr. 1st 1781. Last night our Works were set on Foot at the Redoubts which had been abandoned by the

---

*Coll. Scammel was taken prisoner by two Officers who permitted a Dragoon to ride up & shoot him after he surrendered — He is since dead of his wounds.

†This account is erronerous — the redoubt was not evacuated untill the surrender.

Enemy yesterday—Several Cannon were fired from the Enemy's Works during the night—In the Morning twelve hundred Militia comprehending the whole of Lawson's & part of Steven's Brigade were ordered on a Fatigue—One Militia man was killd at the Redoubt on the right of Pigeon Hill—A Waiter was killd in the Fields at some distance from the rear of those Redoubts—I have not heard of any other injury, altho' the firing has been continued with small Intermissions during the whole Day—The Shot, however which were well directed gave great Interruption to the Soldiers employ'd in carrying on the works—

Tuesday Octr. 2d. The Firing from the Enemies works was continued during the whole night at the distance of fifteen or twenty Minutes between every Shot—By these means our works were interrupted altho' no Execution was done—Since Sunrise this Morning the firing has been much more frequent the Intermissions seldom exceeding five Minutes and often not more than one or two Minutes—Our Men are so well covered by their Works that I have not heard of any Execution done to day. This Forenoon I rode down to the mouth of Wormeley's Creek but could not descry any of the French Ships in the River—As the Wind has been perfectly favourable yesterday & to day I am apt to conclude it is not intended that they shall cooperate with the Army in the Siege—but whether this is really the Case or not I can not hear—The British Ships are stretch'd across the Channel of the River between York & Gloster point—It is said five of them are fire ships chaind to each other. But of this Circumstance I have not been inform'd from good Authority. This Afternoon from Mr. Moores I cou'd discover two of the French Ships which were conceald by a point of Land from Wormeley's Creek—I discovered by the Assistance of a Glass from seventy to an hundred horses dead on the shore of York or floating about in the River—This seems to indicate a Want of Forage & no Intention of pushing a March. I could also discover that the British had sunk several square rigged Vessels near the Shore and at the distance of one hundred and fifty, or two hundred Yards from it—Whether this was meant as a precaution against the French landing from their Ships in Case of a general Assault I can not determine.

Wednesday 3d. Last night the Enemy continued their Fire on our Works as usual; but without Execution except in the Instance of one Ball which kill'd 4 men belonging to the covering party — I find that a new work, on the right of the Enemies Redoubts which they had constructed on pigeon Hill, has been set on Foot, and those two Redoubts appear to remain without any additional Work. At Sun rise this morning the firing ceasd and has not yet been renewed. Our works still go on.

Thursday 4th. The Enemy fired a few shot after ten OClock and during the Night of yesterday — but without Effect.*

We are Told that Tarliton made an Excursion yesterday with two hundred Horse into Gloster; it is also said a Firing was heard on that side & that Tarliton was repulsed but we have not yet heard any particulars of the affair — the number of dead horses seen yesterday by some Gentlemen amounted to near four hundred — A few shot fired during the Course of the Day — This Evening it was mentioned in Gen. Orders that the Duke de Lozun's Legion with Mercers Corps of Grenadier Militia (about 150) repuls'd Tarliton yesterday & drove him back to the Enemy's Lines — Our loss was three Hussars Kill'd, eleven and an officer wounded — the Enemy lost fifty Men in kill'd and wounded — The Officer commanding the Infantry was kill'd, & Tarliton himself badly wounded† — It is said his own men rode over him in the precipitancy of their Retreat — About three Days ago about nineteen hundred French Troops were landed from the Fleet in Gloster — Our Force there amounts to near four thousand men at present *I am told.* 2300. only.

Fryday, 5th Our patroling parties & the Enemy's meeting last night between the Lines occasioned a little skirmishing in which we lost one Man — As soon as the Enemy's Patroles retired within their Works a general Discharge of Cannon and Musketry in platoons took place along their whole Lines — Some Deserters who came out yesterday say that the Besieged lie on their Arms every night apprehending a general Assault & Storm. A good deal of our Ordnance being

---

*Two Frenchmen and one American deserted this night
†Tarliton is not wounded.

now brought up we may expect that some of it will be mounted in a few days.

Saturday 6th. Last night a discharge of Musketry was heard on the Enemys Lines succeeded by Cannon rather more frequent than in the Day — the cause was probably the same as the night before. Yesterday we had one Man mortally wounded at our Works by a Cannon Ball which carried off part of his Hips — The Enemy have for some days had recourse to an Expedient for interrupting our Men at work without wasting their Ammunition, by flashing a small Quantity of Powder near the Muzzles of their Cannons, which is frequently mistaken for the fusing at the Touch-hole. It is worth Observation that a Man was kill'd by a Cannon Ball a day or two past without any visible Wound — He was lying with his Knapsack under his head which was knock'd away by the Ball, without touching his Head — A Sentry was yesterday kill'd on his post —

Sunday 7th. Last night we begun to run our first paralel on our Right — The French Army on the left I believe commenced their operations in like Manner — About nine O Clock a very smart cannonade begun from the Enemy on our left — A Rocket was fired from their Works — The Cannonade after some time begun on our Right & continued with very little Intermission the whole night — I have not yet heard the result of the operations of the night. The French lost fourteen men killd & wounded — A Hessian Hussar deserted from them & gave the Information of their Intentions of opening the Trenches — The night being very dark & favourable for our operations it was very late before the operations on our right were discovered — probably those of the French would not have been discovered but for the Deserter's Information — We lost not a single Man — Our Trenches were carried on with spirit all this Day, the Enemy firing but few Cannon and doing no Execution at all by their Fire.

Monday 8th. This Morning the Major of the Regmt. of deux ponts had his Arm shot off as he entered the Trenches — There was a smart Cannonade during a small part of the night, in which the French had seven men kill'd & wounded — I was on Duty in the Trenches to day & sent out a small patrolling party at night under John Hughes who meeting with the Enemys patroles exchanged a few shot with them & was wounded in the Knee. A number of Shot were fired into the Battery during the Evening and between eleven & three at night but without Effect — I now had an opportunity of observing our Works; on the right on the Bank of the River they are engaged in constructing a Battery for twelve heavy Cannon — on the left of these at intermediate Spaces are two Redoubts — opposite the South East End of Secretary Nelsons house we are constructing a Battery for five Cannon — I had not an opportunity of reconnoitering the works further on the left except a single Redoubt which the French are constructing nearly in Front of the Secretary's, at the distance of five hundred yards (as I concieve at most) — We had one Man kill'd & one wounded in the continental Line during the Day & night. The Battery on the right will be finishd before Noon to morrow. One french Soldier was killd sitting down in the Trenches —

Tuesday 9th. Nothing remarkable happened last night or to day untill five O Clock unless the passage of a Flag from ours to the Enemy's Lines during which they continued firing on our Works be worthy remembrance. At five this Evening the continental Standard was hoisted at our Battery on the Right — a discharge of Cannon instantly ensued — One or two shells were discharged from eight Inch Howitzs without effect falling many yards short of the Enemy's Works. Our Cannon were so well directed that the first shot after the general Discharge struck within a foot of the Embrasure of the Enemys works on the right. Several succeeding Shot were lodged in their Works further to the left — A few Minutes after sun-set I left the Lines and have not yet heard the Events of the night. Coll. Meriwether who reliev'd me to day had three Men wounded this forenoon.

Wednesday 10th. Last night & this Morning a very smart Cannonade & Bombardment has been kept up from our Batteries & those of the French — Several Bombs have been thrown into the Enemy's works, where they have bursted, apparently with some Effect. The Enemy last night shut up the Embrasures of their Battery opposite to ours on the right, & their next Battery is entirely silent the Cannon being drawn in from the Embrasures. Some Shells were thrown at the

Shipping this morning but I have not heard with what Effect. A smart firing of Musketry was heard to day at Gloster.— Since writing the above I have rode out—The French have a Battery on the Hampton road about six hundred Yards below the Secry Nelson's House opposite the South West Angle, consisting of four twenty four pounders and six other Cannon which appear to be somewhat smaller, two eight inch Howitz, two twelve Inch Mortars and six eight Inch ones—these have been employ'd incessantly the whole Day—A number of Shells have been thrown into the Enemy's Works, & the shot so well directed in general that many of the Embrasures of the Enemies are wholly rendered incapable of offensive Operations—there are but two Cannon now to be seen in their Embrasures—the large Shells were generally directed for the shipping—I am told the Enemy have sunk twenty or thirty of their Vessels to day in shallow Water. On the left of the above Battery is another not yet finishd constructed for four Guns—Another still further on the left (about two hundred Yards from the principal Battery) for the like number.— On the Margin of the river over the Creek on the upper End of York is a considerable Redoubt or Battery of the British— The French have also a redoubt in that Quarter which commands both the Enemy's Works on our right & the River, but as I have not seen it I can not precisely determine the Spot where it is—Secry Nelson this Day came out of York I am told he is not restricted by a Parole—I shall insert whatever Information he brings which may hereafter come to my Knowledge.

Thursday 11th. Last Evening and during the night the Cannonade & Bombardment from ours & the french Batteries were kept up with very little Intermission. Red hot Balls being fired at the Shipping from the french Battery over the Creek, the Charon a forty four Gun ship and another ship were set fire to & burnt during the night & a Brig in the morning met with the same Fate—Our Batteries have continued an incessant Firing during the whole Day—This Evening I walk'd down to the Trenches—The Enemy threw a few shells from five mortars which appear to be in the Battery in front of Secry Nelson's House, at the French Battery near the Clay Hill (a small distance from Pigeon Hill).

Most of these burst in the Air at a considerable Height nor do I know whether any one of them fell into, or near the Battery. After this their shells were directed apparently towards the place where we this Evening begun to open our second para-lel — One half of them at least burst in the Air; I do not know what Effect the remainder had — A few shot at the Interval of twenty or thirty minutes were all the Annoyance we recieved from their works during the Evening, except the Shells — I this day dined in Company with the Secretary. He says our Bombardment produced great Effects in annoying the Enemy & destroying their Works — Two Officers were killed & one wounded by a Bomb the Evening we opened — Lord Shuten's Cane was struck out of his Hand by a Cannon Ball — Lord Cornwallis has built a kind of Grotto at the foot of the secretary's Garden where he lives under Ground — A negroe of the Secretary's was kill'd in his House — It seems to be his Opinion that the British are a good deal dispirited altho' he says they affect to say they have no Apprehendsions of the Garrison's falling — An immense number of Negroes have died, in the most miserable Manner in York. A Whale Boat from New York arrived at York the morning the Secry came out, with two British Major's on board — He could not hear any news from N.Y. except that it was probable that Admiral Digby with his Squadron would shortly make a push at the Count de Grasse however inferior he may be to him in Strength. We may therefore expect some important news from the Fleet soon —

Fryday 12th. Last night our second parallel was begun — It is within two hundred yards in some points of the Enemies Works — During the Course of this Day the Enemy have kept up a more considerable Fire than for some Days past, chiefly shells — they have kill'd & wounded five or six Men to day — A pretty constant Cannonade & Bombardment has been kept up from our Batteries during the Day & the last night — I have not yet been in the new Trenches and am not inform'd what new works we are erecting on our second Line.

Saturday 13th. The works on our second parallel were car-ried on last night with great Spirit. We lost some Men from the Enemies Fire which was rather encreased than diminish'd during the Night. The Enemy have drawn off most of their Ships across the Channel to the Gloster Shore —

Sunday 14th. Last night I was on Duty again. The party under my Comand was employ'd in erecting a Battery opposite the South East End of Secry Nelsons house, at the distance of about two hundred Yards from one of the Enemies Batteries and a Redoubt from which they discharged Shells — The French at the same time were constructing two considerable Batteries further on the left — the furthest is about one hundred & fifty Yards in front of the Enemies Battery in Front of Secry Nelson's house. The other about one hundred and seventy Yards on the Flank of the same Work — between our Battery and these is a Redoubt which I apprehend is intended as a Bomb Battery — The Enemy kept up an extremely hot fire during night but with no other Injury in the Battery where I was employd than the wounding two men by the bursting of a shell — As soon as it was so light as for them to discover our situation (for the work was begun after Dark) they annoyd us excessively with round and Grape Shot as well as Shells of all which there was an incessant Fire untill twelve OClock when I was relieved — We lost one Man killd & eight wounded after day Light — the Continental Troops had an Officer & nine or ten Men killd or wounded in the same Battery — As we march'd out of the Trenches a Shell fell in among the first plattoon of my Men, and wounded three men very badly & Several others slightly — tho' within ten Foot of it I was happy enough to escape without Injury as I did from five others which burst within that or near the same Distance in the Course of the Morning — The Enemy have continued a very galling Fire from their Works the whole Day. In the morning several Yagers or Rifle men fired at us for some time — A few rifle men being posted to return their Fire soon silenc'd it.

Monday 15th. Last Night the French Troops, at a Quarter before seven, under command of Baron Viominit attack'd the Enemy's Redoubt on York River at the upper End of the Town across the Creek and carried it — at half after seven the continental Troops under Marquis la Fayette attack'd the Redoubt from which we had been so much annoy'd in the Morning with Shells — at the same time another party under

Mulenburg attack'd the Redoubt on the River which form'd the left of the Enemy's whole Works, being opposite our Battery on the Right of the first parallel. The latter was carried in four Minutes, the former in seven — the French succeeded in about ten if I may judge from the Firing — Being overwhelm'd for want of Sleep I left the Trenches where I was a spectator of the Scene as soon as it was known that we had succeeded, and it being now early in the Morning I know nothing of the particulars of the several Actions, of which I shall make Enquiries after Breakfast. —

I have above given a very unjust Account of the proceedings of last night; a proof how difficult it is to gain accurate Intelligence in Camp — What I have represented as an Attack on the Enemies Redoubt on their Right, was but a Feint made by the French in that Quarter under the Comand of the Marquis de St Simon to draw their Attention from their Left where the real Attack was made on the two Redoubts I have described, with this difference, that the Americans attackt the Redoubt next the River and the French the other. The Success was as before represented — We lost about thirty Men kill'd and wounded — the French thirty one — The British had eighteen Men killd in the Redoubt attack'd by the French but I can not learn how many in the other — Our second Parallel is now compleated running across from the Batteries we were erecting near the Secry's House to the two Redoubts which were taken last night — A Line of Communication parallel to the River is drawn between the Lines running from the left of our Principal Battery on the first Line to the Redoubt on the River on the second — This Redoubt appears to me of great Importance as it seems to comand the Communications from York to Gloster point — It also appears to command some of their Works — The other Redt. being an hundred & eighty yards distant only from one of the Enemies Batteries appears likewise to be of very great Consequence. It is said some of our Batteries on the second parallel will open this Evening; I think this probable as I observed all the platforms in the French Batteries in the first Line are taken up — Coll. Gimat, Coll. Barber and Major Barber were wounded in the Attack last night, tho' but slightly — the latter reciev'd a Contusion on his left Side. Not a single Gun was fired either by the French or Americans during the Attack — Major Campbell of the seventy first, 5 other commisioned officers & sixty four 64 privates made Prisoners — many of the British in these Redoubts made their Escape, some sliding down the steep, or rather perpendicular Bank to the river shore. 1 Majr. 3. Capt. 2 Subs. Prisoners

Tuesday 16. Just at Daybreak this Morning the Enemy made a Sally & attack'd the Redoubt which the French had taken the night before — Skipwith with one hundred Men was in the Redoubt; their Arms were deposited in the Trenches behind — As soon as the Enemy were discovered he march'd his Men out of the Redoubt to take their Arms — by this time the Enemy had gained the parapet but the French Troops who formed the covering party rushing in immediately, soon repulsed them. At the same time the Enemy attackd another Redoubt further on our left and scaling the Works with great Alacrity Spiked up eight pieces of Cannon which were intended for a Battery on which we were at that time employ'd. They were immediately after repulsed — The Cannon were cleared again before the Battery was in readiness to mount them, So that they effected no good purpose by the Sally & lost some Men; six or eight were killed in the Redoubt where Skipwith was stationed. This Afternoon one of our Batteries on the second parallel was opened — All those on the first I believe are dismantled — At least the two principal ones are. As the Genl. Orders of to day prohibit any officer from entering the Trenches I must write by Guess hereafter except when I go upon Duty.

Wednesday 17th An officer's Baggage by some means or other fell into our hands by the running on shore of a Boat destin'd for N. York. A Journal of the Siege to yesterday was found — In it this remarkable Conclusion — Our provisions are now nearly exhausted & our Ammunition totally. The Marquis de St Simon recieved a slight wound on his Ankle & Genl Knox a similar one on the Ear last Evening from the bursting of a Bomb.

Wednesday 17. As we have heard a very smart or rather incessant Cannonade last night and this Morning I take it for granted that all or the greater part of our Batteries are opened by this time. This Forenoon a Flag from York brought a Letter couch'd nearly in the following Terms —

Sir, I propose a Cessation of Hostilities for twenty four
Hours, and that two Officers be appointed from both
sides to meet at Mr. Moores, and agree on Terms for
the surrender of the posts of York & Gloucester — I
have the Honor to be your Excellency's most obedt. &
most hble Servant — Cornwallis
Directed
    To his Excellency
General Washington, Comdr. in Chief of the combined
Forces of France & America.

The Answer was to the following purport. "Sir, I have recieved your Favor of this Morning. Regard to humanity induces me to agree to a suspension of hostilities for two hours
that your Lordship may propose the Terms on which you
choose to surrender," &ca

I am now ordered on Duty, & with more Sanguine hopes
than ever filld the Mind of Man I now set out for the
Trenches.

Thursday 18th. Lord Cornwallis being allow'd but two
hours sent out another Flag to request further time to digest
his proposals — It has been granted and Hostilities have
ceased ever since five OClock. It was pleasing to contrast the
last night with the preceeding — A solemn stillness prevaild —
the night was remarkably clear & the sky decorated with ten
thousand stars — numberless Meteors gleaming thro' the
Atmosphere afforded a pleasing resemblance to the Bombs
which had exhibited a noble Firework the night before, but
happily divested of all their Horror. At dawn of day the
British gave us a serenade with the Bag pipe, I believe, &
were answered by the French with the Band of the Regiment
of deux ponts. As Soon as the Sun rose one of the most striking pictures of War was display'd that Imagination can paint
— From the point of Rock Battery on one side our Lines
compleatly mann'd and our Works crowded with soldiers
were exhibited to view — opposite these at the Distance of
two hundred yards you were presented with a sight of the
British Works; their parapets crowded with officers looking at
those who were assembled at the top of our Works — the
Secretary's house with one of the Corners broke off, & many

large holes thro the Roof & Walls part of which seem'd tottering with their Weight afforded a striking Instance of the Destruction occasioned by War — Many other houses in the vicinity contributed to accomplish the Scene — On the Beach of York directly under the Eye hundreds of busy people might be seen moving to & fro — At a small distance from the Shore were seen ships sunk down to the Waters Edge — further out in the Channel the Masts, Yards & even the top gallant Masts of some might be seen, without any vestige of the hulls. On the opposite of the river the remainder of the shipping drawn off as to a place of security. Even here the Guadaloupe sunk to the Waters Edge shew'd how vain the hope of such a place. On Gloster point the Fortifications and Encampment of the Enemy added a further Variety to the scene which was compleated by the distant View of the french Ships of War, two of which were at that time under sail — A painter need not to have wish'd for a more compleat subject to imploy his pencil without any expence of Genius.

This was the Scene which ushered in the Day when the pride of Britain was to be humbled in a greater Degree than it had ever been before, unless at the Surrender of Burgoyne — It is remarkable that the proposals for a surrender of Lord Cornwallis's Army were made on the Anniversary of that important Event — At two o Clock the Surrender was agreed on & Commissioners appointed to draw up the Articles of Capitulation — They are now employed on that Business —

The Guadaloupe or some other Frigate was sunk two night ago — we know not whether by Design or Accident —

I can not omit one Anecdote which happened during the Siege — Baron Viominit at the Attack on the Enemy's redoubts on Monday Evening observing two Sargeants distinguish themselves by their Intrepidity, sent for them to dine with him the next Day & placed them at his right hand where he treated them with the highest Respect and Attention —

Fryday — This Morning at nine oClock the Articles of Capitulation were signed and exchanged — At retreat beating last night the British play'd the Tune of "Welcome Brother Debtor" — to their conquerors the tune was by no means dissagreeable —

Fryday 19th. At two OClock to day a Detachmt. of American Light Infantry and French Grenadiers took possession of the horn-work on the East End of York town — Our Army was drawn up in a Line on each side of the road extending from our front parallel to the Forks of the Road at Hudson Allen's the Americans on the right, the French on the left. Thro' these Lines the whole British Army march'd their Drums in Front beating a slow March. Their Colours furl'd and Cased. I am told they were restricted by the capitulation from beating a French or American march. General Lincoln with his Aids conducted them — Having passed thro' our whole Army they grounded their Arms & march'd back again thro' the Army a second Time into the Town — The sight was too pleasing to an American to admit of Description —

I have not yet been happy enough to see, or hear of the particular's of the capitulation.

Three thousand two hundred & seventy three Men march'd out & grounded their Arms on the York side of the River — Including the non commission'd Officers the Garrison in York amounted to five thousand five hundred and sixty four Men, and two hundred & fifty four commission'd Officers, including thirty two Surgeons with their Mates — Lord Cornwallis and General O Hara are not included — I have not yet heard the strength of the post at Gloucester — It is about a thousand Men I believe — At York there were taken sixty five pieces of Brass Ordnance, and twenty two Standards —

York Garison

Col.	2	Sarjeants	295
Lt. Col.	8	Dr. & Fifes	121
Majors	11	R & F	3273
Capt.	52	Fit for	3943 Duty
Lts.	89	Sarjn.	90
Ens.	36	Dr. & F.	44
Chaplns.	2	R. & F.	1741
Adjutn.	12	Sick &	1875 woundd.
Qr. Mrs.	10		3943
Surgeons	10	Total	5818
Surg. M	22	The Garrison at Gloster not	
Comd.	254 Offrs.	included in the above—	

Saturday 20. I went into York to day with Genl. Lawson who waited on Lord Cornwallis on some Business relative to the prisoners which he was appointed to conduct to Winchester — His Lordship in the course of conversation told us that he had meditated a transition over the river on the night of Tuesday but was prevented by his Boats being blown away from the Shore in a very severe squall — A thousand Men had actually cross'd — Their Intention was to have suprised our Camp in Gloster & endeavoured to push their Way thro' the Country.

The total number of prisoners including commissioned Officers at both posts amounts to six thousand eight hundred & odd Men — The present return of ordnance is one hundred and forty Iron, and seventy four Brass — seven thousand three hundred & twenty stand of Arms and Accoutrements are also return'd. It is said this return is by no means exact. No account yet of the quantity of military Stores, or number of horses that I have heard.

James Robertson to Lord Amherst

New York, 17th Octr. 1781.

My Lord,

You have with this a duplicate of my last — Since that date, several dispatches have been sent to and some received from Lord Cornwallis, in one he was told we should sail to relieve him on the fifth, in another he had notice, that we probably might not get over the bar till the 12th, Ideas were offered but submitted to his correction for the best mode of giving him aid — Signals to convey different meanings were sent by this occasion, which Major Cochran took charge of. The Cutter is returned, with a letter from his Lordship dated the 11th — On the 30th of September the enemy broke ground at eleven hundred yards distance, on the 6th their works were advanced within 600 yards — places of arms were established, and batteries of heavy Cannon and Mortars mostly of 16 inches diameter were raised — they play incessantly. My Lord says in the beginning of his letter that they had killed 70 men, before he closes, he says 30 more were killed — he says he cannot hold out long, and that no Move but one directly to York and a Naval Victory can *save him* —

Our fleet consisting of 25 Ships of the line two fiftys and several frigates with four fire ships are now getting under way, they take on board Sir Henry Clinton, Generals Leslie, Paterson, Lord Lincoln, with nearly seven thousand of our choice troops, while I dread their coming too late, and can turn my thoughts to no other subject — I will only mention what at any other time I should set forth at large — I have taken pains in all Councils of War to represent the decisive influence this event would have on His Majesty's affairs — that not only America, but the importance of Britain hung upon it — that every thing was to be risqued, and nothing to be feared by delay, which would operate as fatally as defeat — Sir Samuel Hood possest the same Ideas, and with a commanding steadyness urged the Council, he is all a fire, and thinks no moment to be lost, it is principally owing to him, that the risque of encountering 37 french ships is overlooked — Every hand every thing in this place has been offered for expediting the fleet — The Merchants at my desire exerted themselves in getting Volunteers to man it, they subscribed very generously to encourage this — 240 went on board, and I pressed yesterday morning all whom this encouragement had not had effect on — The fleet is finely manned —

After being promised leave to share in the expedition with Sir Samuel Hood, I am ordered to remain — We have seven or eight thousand men here — I wish four-fifths of them were going to the Chesapeak — but the men o'war can hold no more, and transports are judged improper — Should our Armies join at York and beat the rebels and french, we stand prepared to improve the advantage, by an attack on Philadelphia — I write only to You, there would perhaps be an impropriety in my writing to Lord George Germain — if there be any matter in mine, he is not better informed of, I am sure You will have the goodness to present me favorably to him — I ever am,

My Lord, etc.

Colonel Goreham who has had some hardships will give You this — Had General Amherst been alive he would have been his Advocate to Your Lordship —

A Captain Lamb of the 35th, a good Officer, and an intelligent young man, who was prisoner in the french army, begs me to give him an introduction to You —

Lord Cornwallis to Henry Clinton

York Town, Virginia, October 20, 1781.

Sir, I have the mortification to inform your Excellency that I have been forced to give up the posts of York and Gloucester, and to surrender the troops under my command, by capitulation on the 19th inst. as prisoners of war to the combined forces of America and France.

I never saw this post in a very favourable light, but when I found I was to be attacked in it in so unprepared a state, by so powerful an army and artillery, nothing but the hopes of relief would have induced me to attempt its defence; for I would either have endeavoured to escape to New-York, by rapid marches from the Gloucester side, immediately on the arrival of General Washington's troops at Williamsburgh, or I would notwithstanding the disparity of numbers have attacked them in the open field, where it might have been just possible that fortune would have favoured the gallantry of the handful of troops under my command: but being assured by your Excellency's letters, that every possible means would be tried by the navy and army to relieve us, I could not think myself at liberty to venture upon either of those desperate attempts; therefore, after remaining for two days in a strong position in front of this place, in hopes of being attacked, upon observing that the enemy were taking measures, which could not fail of turning my left flank in a short time, and receiving on the second evening your letter of the 24th of September, informing that the relief would sail about the 5th of October, I withdrew within the works on the night of the 29th of September, hoping by the labour and firmness of the soldiers, to protract the defence until you could arrive. Every thing was to be expected from the spirit of the troops, but every disadvantage attended their labour, as the works were to be continued under the enemy's fire, and our stock of intrenching tools, which did not much exceed four hundred, when we began to work in the latter end of August, was now much diminished.

The enemy broke ground on the night of the 30th, and constructed on that night, and the two following days and nights, two redoubts, which, with some works that had belonged to our outward position, occupied a gorge between two creeks or ravines, which come from the river on each side of the town. On the night of the 6th of October they made their first parallel, extending from its right on the river to a deep ravine on the left, nearly opposite to the center of this place, and embracing our whole left at the distance of six hundred yards. Having perfected this parallel, their batteries opened on the evening of the 9th, against our left, and other batteries fired at the same time against a redoubt, advanced over the Creek upon our right, and defended by about one hundred and twenty men of the 23d regiment and marines, who maintained that post with uncommon gallantry. The fire continued incessant from heavy cannon and from mortars and howitzes, throwing shells from eight to sixteen inches, until all our guns on the left were silenced, our work much damaged, and our loss of men considerable. On the night of the 11th they began their second parallel, about three hundred yards nearer to us; the troops being much weakened by sickness as well as by the fire of the besiegers, and observing that the enemy had not only secured their flanks, but proceeded in every respect with the utmost regularity and caution, I could not venture so large sorties, as to hope from them any considerable effect; but otherwise, I did every thing in my power to interrupt this work, by opening new embrazures for guns, and keeping up a constant fire with all the howitzes and small mortars that we could man. On the evening of the 14th, they assaulted and carried two redoubts that had been advanced about three hundred yards for the purpose of delaying their approaches, and covering our left flank, and during the night included them in their second parallel, on which they continued to work with the utmost exertion. Being perfectly sensible that our works could not stand many hours after the opening of the batteries of that parallel, we not only continued a constant fire with all our mortars, and every gun that could be brought to bear upon it, but a little before day break on the morning of the 16th, I ordered a sortie of about three hundred and fifty men under the direction of

Lieutenant-colonel Abercrombie to attack two batteries, which appeared to be in the greatest forwardness, and to spike the guns. A detachment of guards with the eightieth company of Grenadiers, under the command of Lieutenant-colonel Lake attacked the one, and one of Light Infantry under the command of Major Armstrong attacked the other, and both succeeded by forcing the redoubts that covered them, spiking eleven guns, and killing or wounding about one hundred of the French troops, who had the guard of that part of the trenches, and with little loss on our side. This action, though extremely honourable to the officers and soldiers who executed it, proved of little public advantage, for the cannon having been spiked in a hurry, were soon rendered fit for service again, and before dark the whole parallel and batteries appeared to be nearly complete. At this time we knew that there was no part of the whole front attacked, on which we could show a single gun, and our shells were nearly expended; I therefore had only to chuse between preparing to surrender next day, or endeavouring to get off with the greatest part of the troops, and I determined to attempt the latter, reflecting that though it should prove unsuccessful in its immediate object, it might at least delay the enemy in the prosecution of further enterprizes: sixteen large boats were prepared, and upon other pretexts were ordered to be in readiness to receive troops precisely at ten o'clock. With these I hoped to pass the infantry during the night, abandoning our baggage, and leaving a detachment to capitulate for the town's people, and the sick and wounded; on which subject a letter was ready to be delivered to General Washington. After making my arrangements with the utmost secrecy, the Light Infantry, greatest part of the Guards, and part of the twenty-third regiment landed at Gloucester; but at this critical moment, the weather from being moderate and calm, changed to a most violent storm of wind and rain, and drove all the boats, some of which had troops on board, down the river. It was soon evident that the intended passage was impracticable, and the absence of the boats rendered it equally impossible to bring back the troops that had passed; which I had ordered about two in the morning. In this situation, with my little force divided, the enemy's batteries opened at day break; the passage between this place and Gloucester was much exposed, but the boats having now returned, they were ordered to bring back the troops that had passed during the night, and they joined us in the forenoon without much loss. Our works in the mean time were going to ruin, and not having been able to strengthen them by abbatis, nor in any other manner but by a slight fraizing which the enemy's artillery were demolishing wherever they fired, my opinion entirely coincided with that of the engineer and principal officers of the army, that they were in many places assailable in the forenoon, and that by the continuence of the same fire for a few hours longer, they would be in such a state as to render it desperate with our numbers to attempt to maintain them. We at that time could not fire a single gun, only one eight-inch and little more than an hundred cohorn shells remained; a diversion by the French ships of war that lay at the mouth of York-river, was to be expected. Our numbers had been diminished by the enemy's fire, but particularly by sickness, and the strength and spirits of those in the works were much exhausted by the fatigue of constant watching and unremitting duty. Under all these circumstances, I thought it would have been wanton and inhuman to the last degree to sacrifice the lives of this small body of gallant soldiers, who had ever behaved with so much fidelity and courage, by exposing them to an assault, which from the numbers and precautions of the enemy could not fail to succeed. I therefore proposed to capitulate, and I have the honour to inclose to your Excellency the copy of the correspondence between General Washington and me on that subject, and the terms of capitulation agreed upon. I sincerely lament that better could not be obtained, but I have neglected nothing in my power to alleviate the misfortune and distress of both officers and soldiers. The men are well cloathed and provided with necessaries, and I trust will be regularly supplied by the means of the officers that are permitted to remain with them. The treatment, in general, that we have received from the enemy since our surrender, has been perfectly good and proper; but the kindness and attention that has been shewn to us by the French officers in particular, their delicate sensibility of our situation, their generous and pressing offer of money both public and private, to any amount, has really gone beyond what I can possibly describe, and will, I hope, make an impression on the breast of every British officer, whenever the fortune of war should put any of them into our power.

Although the event has been so unfortunate, the patience of the soldiers in bearing the greatest fatigues, and their firmness and intrepidity under a persevering fire of shot and shells, that I believe has not often been exceeded, deserved the highest admiration and praise. A successful defence, however, in our situation was perhaps impossible, for the place could only be reckoned an intrenched camp, subject in most places to enfilade, and the ground in general so disadvantageous, that nothing but the necessity of fortifying it as a post to protect the navy, could have induced any person to erect works upon it. Our force diminished daily by sickness and other losses, and was reduced when we offered to capitulate on this side to little more than three thousand two hundred rank and file fit for duty, including officers, servants, and artificers; and at Gloucester about six hundred, including cavalry. The enemy's army consisted of upwards of eight thousand French, nearly as many continentals, and five thousand militia. They brought an immense train of heavy artillery, most amply furnished with ammunition, and perfectly well manned.

The constant and universal chearfulness and spirit of the officers in all hardships and danger, deserve my warmest acknowledgments; and I have been particularly indebted to Brigadier-general O'Hara, and to Lieutenant-colonel Abercrombie, the former commanding on the right and the latter on the left, for their attention and exertion on every occasion. The detachment of the twenty-third regiment of Marines in the redoubt on the right, commanded by Captain Apthorpe, and the subsequent detachments commanded by Lieutenant-colonel Johnson, deserve particular commendation. Captain Rochfort who commanded the artillery, and indeed every officer and soldier of that distinguished corps; and Lieutenant Sutherland the commanding Engineer have merited in every respect my highest approbation; and I cannot sufficiently acknowledge my obligations to Captain Symonds, who commanded his Majesty's ships, and to the other officers and seamen of the navy for their active and zealous co-operation.

I transmit returns of our killed and wounded the loss of seamen and townspeople was likewise considerable.

I trust that your Excellency will please to hasten the return of the Bonetta, after landing her passengers, in compliance with the article of capitulation.

Lieutenant-colonel Abercrombie will have the honour to deliver this dispatch, and is well qualified to explain to your Excellency every particular relating to our past and present situation.

I have the honour to be, &c.

Anna Rawle: Diary, October 25, 1781

October 25. — Fifth day. I suppose, dear Mammy, thee would not have imagined this house to be illuminated last night, but it was. A mob surrounded it, broke the shutters and the glass of the windows, and were coming in, none but forlorn women here. We for a time listened for their attacks in fear and trembling till, finding them grow more loud and violent, not knowing what to do, we ran into the yard. Warm Whigs of one side, and Hartley's of the other (who were treated even worse than we), rendered it impossible for us to escape that way. We had not been there many minutes before we were drove back by the sight of two men climbing the fence. We thought the mob were coming in thro' there, but it proved to be Coburn and Bob. Shewell, who called to us not to be frightened, and fixed lights up at the windows, which pacified the mob, and after three huzzas they moved off. A number of men came in afterwards to see us. French and J. B. nailed boards up at the broken pannels, or it would not have been safe to have gone to bed. Coburn and Shewell were really very kind; had it not been for them I really believe the house would have been pulled down. Even the firm Uncle Fisher was obliged to submit to have his windows illuminated, for they had pickaxes and iron bars with which they had done considerable injury to his house, and would soon have demolished it had not some of the Hodges and other people got in back and acted as they pleased. All Uncle's sons were out, but Sammy, and if they had been at home it was in vain to oppose them. In short it was the most alarming scene I ever remember. For two hours we had the disagreeable noise of stones banging about, glass crashing, and the tumultuous voices of a large body of men, as they were a long time at the different houses in the neighbourhood. At last they were victorious, and it was one general illumination throughout the town. As we had not the pleasure of seeing any of the gentlemen in the house, nor the furniture cut up, and goods stolen, nor been beat, nor pistols pointed at our breasts, we may count our sufferings slight compared to many others. Mr. Gibbs was obliged to make his escape over a fence, and while his wife was endeavouring to shield him from the rage of one of the men, she received a violent bruise in the breast, and a blow in the face which made her nose bleed. Ben. Shoemaker was here this morning; tho' exceedingly threatened he says he came off with the loss of four panes of glass. Some Whig friends put candles in the windows which made his peace with the mob, and they retired. John Drinker has lost half the goods out of his shop and been beat by them; in short the sufferings of those they pleased to style Tories would fill a volume and shake the credulity of those who were not here on that memorable night, and to-day Philadelphia makes an uncommon appearance, which ought to cover the Whigs with eternal confusion. A neighbour of ours had the effrontery to tell Mrs. G. that he was sorry for her furniture, but not for her windows — a ridiculous distinction that many of them make. J. Head has nothing left whole in his parlour. Uncle Penington lost a good deal of window-glass. Aunt Burge preserved hers thro' the care of some of her neighbours. The Drinkers and Walns make heavy complaints of the Carolinians in their neighbourhood. Walns' pickles were thrown about the streets and barrells of sugar stolen. Grandmammy was the most composed of anybody here. Was I not sure, my dearest Mother, that you would have very exaggerated accounts of this affair from others, and would probably be uneasy for the fate of our friends, I would be entirely silent about it, but as you will hear it from some one or another, not mentioning it will seem as if we had suffered exceedingly, and I hope I may depend on the safety of this opportunity.

People did nothing to-day but condole and enquire into each others honourable losses. Amongst a great variety who were here was Aunt Rawle; next to her sisters this was the family, she said, whom she felt most interested for; her visit was quite unexpected. Uncle and Aunt Howell went from here to Edgely this morning. Aunt Betsy to tea. Becky Fisher and her brother in the evening.

Robert Gray:
Observations on the War in Carolina

THE conquest of Charlestown was attended with the conquest of the back country because all the Continental troops in the Southern department were taken in that place except the party under Col Beaufort which was soon after cut to pieces at the Wexaws by Col. Tarlton. The people at that time not much accustomed to arms & finding no troops to support them submitted when they saw the Kings troops in possession of the back country. Posts were established at Augusta, Ninety-Six, Camden,* Cheraw Hill & Georgetown. The conquest of the Province was complete. The loyal part of the inhabitants being in a number about one third of the whole & these by no means the wealthest, readily took up arms to maintain the British government, the others also enrolled themselves in the Militia party because they believed the war to be at an end in the Southern provinces & partly to ingratiate themselves with the conquerors, they also fondly hoped that they would enjoy a respite from the Calamities of war — and that the restoration of the Kings Government would restore to them the happiness they enjoyed before the war began, with these views on both sides, the Whigs & Tories seemed to vie with each other in giving proof of the sincerity of their submission & a most profound calm succeeded. This was not confined only to the Country within the new established posts. The panic of the Whigs & the exultation of the Tories produced the same consequences in the back Country beyond the reach of the posts, the people in many places coming in from the distance of fifty miles to take the Oath of Allegiance or to surrender themselves prisoners on parole. All the inhabitants seemed intent upon cultivating their farms & making money great quantities of produce were

---

*This post was withdrawn before the battle of Camden & never afterwards reestablished.

sent to Charlestown & great numbers of wagons even from the mountains crowded the roads travelling in every direction.

This tranquility was of short duration, the abuses of the Army in taking the peoples Horses, Cattle & provisions in many cases without paying for them, abuses perhaps inseperable from a Millitary Government disgusted the inhabitants, but this was by no means the principal cause of the disorders which followed, they flowed from another source, the disaffection of the Whigs. the establishment of the Kings government naturally & unavoidably occasioned an entire change of Civil & Millitary officers throughout the province. A new set of men were elevated into power & place, whilst their predecessors in office were stripped of their consequence & sent to cultivate their plantations. the pangs of disappointed ambition soon made these men view all our transactions with jaundiced eyes, and as Genl Gates approach put an end to the hopes of tranquillity they had at first expected to enjoy, they were in general, especially the Millitia officers determined to avail themselves of that opportunity to reestablish themselves in power, never doubting of Genl Gates being able to effect it, as, like other men they easily believed what they eagerly wished for. Lord Cornwallis with great sagacity foresaw what followed. he instantly ordered all the leadings Whigs who had been paroled to their plantations, to repair to Johns & James Island.

A great number obeyed while others went off & met Genl Gates. the approach of the army seemed to be a signal for a general revolt in the disaffected parts of the back Country, but the speedy & successful issue of the action at Camden put an end to it immediately, and restored tranquillity to the Country.

Lord Cornwallis made some severe examples of the Revolters, a measure which was become absolutely necessary to deter others from the same conduct, as many of those who had taken up arms again had never had the smallest cause of Complaint, but had been treated with every mark of attention & respect by the Kings officers. A universal panic seized the rebels after the battle of Camden and had Lord Cornwallis had a sufficient army to have marched into North Carolina & to have established posts in his rear at convenient places to preserve his communication with South Carolina & to prevent the rebels from assembling in arms after he had passed along North Carolina would have fallen without a struggle, but the smallness of his numbers soon turned the tide against him. He marched from Camden to Charlotte with the army & at the same time directed Major Fergusson with the Ninety Six Militia to advance into North Carolina, betwixt his left flank & the Mountains. The rebels dispairing of being able to effect anything against his Lordship, resolved to make a grand effort against Major Fergusson, who, although he knew his danger & was ordered to join the army, yet after retreating 60 miles he loitered away two days most unaccountably at Kings Mountain & thereby gave time to the rebel Militia under the command of Genl Williams to come up with him, the rebels were greatly superior to him in number

He had about 600 Militia & 60 regulars, an action ensued in which our Militia behaved with a degree of steadiness & spirit that would not have disgraced any regular troops. & the rebels were repulsed three times, but having changed their mode of attack & made an attempt on a small party of North Carolinians on our left flank who were not so well diciplined as the South Carolinians succeeded in breaking them, they soon communicated the disorder to the others & at this critical moment Major Fergusson fell. A total rout ensued.

This unfortunate affair gave a new turn to the War. All the country on Lord Cornwallis' rear was laid open to the incursions of the enemy, who, if they had made a proper use of their victory might have taken both Ninety Six & Augusta, nevertheless the consequences were very important. Lord Cornwallis was obliged to retreat & take a position at Winsburg in the fork of Santee between the Wateree & Congaree Rivers, that he might be at hand to succor Camden & Ninety Six & to cover the country within these posts.

This gave new spirits to the rebel Militia on the Western & Northern frontiers, who began to turn out in great numbers & with more confidence. they were led by Sumpter & Marion who had both been field officers in the South Carolina State troops. the former commanded on the Western frontier beyond Camden & Ninety Six & the latter on the Northern betwixt Santee & peedee.

Both these countries were highly disaffected to us and the people wanted only leaders. It was therefore those people who formed & supported Sumpter & Marion & not any superiority of genius in those officers that formed & called for the Militia in those parts Sumpter was bold & rash, and run many risks from which his good fortune always extricated him. Marion was timid & cautious & would risk nothing, yet both succeeded in their attempts. During all this time the Continental troops in general kept a cautious distance & chiefly made use of Sumpter & Marion, who began to grow extremely troublesom & established a decided superiority in the Militia line — Major Fergussons' loss was now severely felt. The officers of Royal Militia being possessed themselves nor were able to inspire their followers with the confidence necessary for soldiers. While almost every British officer regarded with contempt and indifference the establishment of a militia among a people differing so much in customs & manners from themselves. Had Major Fergusson lived, the Militia would have been completely formed. He possessed all the talents & ambition necessary to accomplish that purpose & set out exactly in that line, he therefore would have achieved with the inhabitants of the country what the other British officers can only effect with important soldiers. the want of a man of his genius was soon severely felt & if ever another is found to supply his place he will go great lengths towards turning the scale of the war in our favor.

The want of paying sufficient attention to our Militia produced daily at this time the most disagreeable consequences. In the first place, when the Rebel Militia were made prisoners, they were immediately delivered up to the Regular Officers, who, being entirely ignorant of the dispositions & manners of the people treated them with the utmost lenity & sent them home to their plantations upon parole & in short they were treated in every respect as foreign enemies. the general consequences of this was, that they no sooner got out of our hands than they broke their paroles, took up arms, and made it a point to murder every Militia man of ours who had any concern in making them prisoners, on the other hand when ever a Militia Man of ours was made a prisoner he was delivered not to the Continentals but to the Rebel Militia, who looked upon him as a State prisoner, as a man who deserved a halter, & therefore treated him with the greatest cruelty.

If he was not assassinated after being made a prisoner, he was instantly hurried into Virginia or North Carolina where he was kept a prisoner without friends, money, credit, or perhaps hopes of exchange. This line being once drawn betwixt their militia & ours, it was no longer safe to be a loyalist in the frontiers. These last being overwhelmed with dismay became dejected & timid while the others increasing in boldness & enterprise made constant inrodes in small parties & murdered every loyalist they found whether in arms or at home. Their irruptions answered the descriptions we have of those made by the Goths & Vandals.

Whilst the inhabitants of Charles Town were amusing themselves with the aspect of the war in the different quarters of the globe, the unfortunate loyalists on the frontiers found the fury of the whole war let loose upon him. He was no longer safe to sleep in his house. He hid himself in the swamps. It was perfectly in vain to take a prisoner, he was either liberated upon parole to commit fresh murders & depredations, or if his character was very notorious, he was sent in irons to Charles Town, where after some months confinement, the witnesses against him not appearing, being deterred by the distance & uncertain of the time at which he would be brought to trial, he pestered the principal officers here with petitions until he was turned loose again, irritated with his confinement, to murder more loyalists. The effect of all this was that the loyalist, if he did not choose to retire within the posts, a ruined Refugee either joined them openly or gave them private intelligence of the movements of our parties for which he enjoyed real protection & was safe to go to sleep without danger of having his throat cut before morning. Had our militia been certain of being treated as prisoners of war by the enemy, many more would have sided with the royal Standard.

It may be said that bad treatment will make them desperate. It has at length had that effect, but for a long time it produced a very contrary one as they did not care to expose themselves in situations pregnant with every danger — & where they fought under peculiar disadvantages. The case of the regulars was very different. When made prisoners they met with the mildest treatment & were always sent to Charles Town upon parole until exchanged.

This mismanagement of the King's officers proceeded from their want of knowledge of the manners of the people. They sometimes interposed in behalf of the Militia, & hanged notorious murderers, but these efforts were not sufficiently frequent to produce any effect. Nothing will ever be able here to put our Militia here on a proper footing, but giving up to them all the rebel Militia when prisoners to be dealt with according to the laws of retaliation, subject however to the control of the commander in chief in the Southern department.

The regulars altho' they take perfect care of their own interests in war, will never take the same care of the militia. It is against all experience. No class of men will consider the interests of another class so attentively as they do their own.

About this time Lord Cornwallis being reinforced by General Lesly marched into North Carolina, but before the subsequent transactions are mentioned it will be proper to take notice of the situation of our affairs in South Carolina at this period.

Lord Rawdon was left commanding officer on the frontiers. His Head Quarters was Camden where he had about 800 men, a body sufficient to afford a detachment superior to the united force of Sumpter & Marion, especially when to that were added about five hundred men under command of Colonel Watson who lay at Wright's Bluff. Besides the other posts at Ninety Six & Augusta, a new one was added at Friday's Ferry on the Congaree river betwixt the former of these places & Camden. These covered the western frontier. A chain of small posts were erected from Camden along the Santee to Monks Corner, to preserve the communication to Charlestown. The first from Camden was the Fort at Mottes house upon the South side of the Congaree river about three miles from the fork of Santee & about a mile from McCords Ferry. The second was Fort Watson at Wright's Bluff on the North side of Santee about 30 miles down the river. The third was at Nelson's ferry on the South side of Santee about 40 miles below McCords ferry, & 20 from Monks Corner, which last was on Cooper river & 30 from Charles Town.

The stores for the army at Camden were sent by water from Charles Town to Monks Corner, from thence waggoned to a landing on Santee near Nelson's ferry where they were embarked in boats for Camden. There was no post to the Northward of Charles Town except Georgetown. The rebel Militia under Sumpter & Marion were now highly elated, & made no dowbt of Lord Cornwallis & his army being *burgoyned* if he should attempt to follow Genl Greene into North Carolina, while they reckoned themselves able to cope with Lord Rawdon. This will not appear surprising when it is known that they were so grossly ignorant that at the distance of forty miles from Camden they were continuously made to believe that Genl Wayne or some other officer had invested Camden, that Lord Rawdon had not more than 300 men & Lord Cornwallis not more than 800 & that General Lesly had been driven out of Virginia with great loss, by a vast army there which was the cause of his coming to South Carolina.

Full of these ideas & confident of being on the strongest side, they were ready for any enterprise; accordingly they were daily joined by many men of influence who had been a few months before admitted to become British subjects, after they had earnestly petitioned for that purpose, which however they only did to prevent their estates from being sequestered whilst their political sentiments remained unaltered, in the same manner as many of our friends go into the country at present & submit to the rebels to save their estates from confiscation.

Daily inroads were now made across the Santee & scarce a public waggons escaped to Nelson's ferry. Almost all the public boats on the Santee were destroyed & the communication with Camden was almost at an end.

All the loyal inhabitants at Ninety-Six district being about one half & living partly betwixt Broad & Saluda rivers, commonly called the Dutch Fork, & in other places of that district, all the inhabitants of Orangeburg District from a few miles to the Southward of Santee to the Saltketchers, being almost unanimous in favor of Government were the friendly parts of this province on the South side of Santee, the rest were enemies while Sumpter & Marion gave great uneasiness to our posts in their reach. one McKay another partisan about

Savannah river, & Col. Clark of the cedeed lands in Georgia harrassed the Country near Augusta. The rebel militia were now bold & elated, their partisans had hitherto escaped every attempt made to crush them & they were all become familiar with danger.

A few months before this when any party of troops marched into their country they were so alarmed that they retired back for 50 or 60 miles or hid themselves in the swamps, but now when in a similar situation, if unable to oppose the troops in the field they kept hovering round them in small parties, picked up stragglers & fired upon them from every swamp. The troops were obliged to act with caution & to keep within their pickets. The loyal inhabitants were still dejected & not sufficiently used to arms. On the frontiers they were continually harassed with small murdering parties of rebels, but in Orangeburg they were in profound peace; upon the whole however they could not in general be trusted upon any expedition by themselves. While the rebel Militia were every day growing more troublesome, the loyal inhabitants of Little Pedee had become in their turn extremely troublesome to Marion and his brigade. They inhabit the country betwixt the North Side of Pedee & North Carolina in one Direction & from the Cheraw Hill to Waccomaw Lake in the other. Their numbers are about 500 men fit for war. They had arms put into their hands when the post was established at the Cheraw Hill before Genl Gates' arrival. When that Post was withdrawn to Camden at his approach they were the only people on the North side of Santee who did not join in the general revolt. The inhabitants of Williamsburg "Township" not yet headed by Marion made an unsuccessful attempt to crush them & they have ever since stood their ground.

They carried on a continual predatory war against the rebels & sometimes surprised them at their musters. In short, they carried on the war against the rebels precisely as they had set the example & as the post at George Town supplied them with arms & ammunition they overawed & harrassed Marion's brigade so much that he was obliged to leave the inhabitants of the Cheraw District at home to protect their properties while he could only call out the people of Williamsburgh Township & the neighborhood of George

Town; when a small party of the rebels ventured among them they were cut to pieces — when a large body invaded them, which they found they could not withstand they hung in small parties upon their skirts, harrassed them with false alarms, killed their sentries, drove in their pickets, & soon compelled them to leave the Country. It may not be improper to observe here that the Rebel Militia did not at all times turn out voluntarily under their leaders, for when they were averse to an expedition they compelled them on pain of death, & there have been often severe examples made of them. On the other hand the Little Pedee men only defended their own country & never went upon a more distant expedition than to Georgetown. The Rebel Militia from Bladen country in North Carolina at times also harassed the loyal inhabitants of Little Pedee, but with little effect.

Lord Cornwallis had now marched into North Carolina, & Major Craig took post at Wilmington. If I have time I shall mention in general terms the subsequent transactions of the militia in that Province where about one half of the inhabitants are our friends.

Lord Rawdon had no sooner taken the command than he found employment from Genl Sumpter.

That Partisan called a general muster of his people & told them that Ld Cornwallis has gone into N. Car — to seek a grave for himself & his army, that Ld Rawdon had only 300 men at Camden & could not detach a man, that by making a sudden march to the Congaree they would surprise the Fort where they would get a quantity of stores & clothing — that by proceeding down the South side of Santee river they would be joined by McKay from Augusta, by Marion from Williamsburgh Township, that a general revolt would ensue, that all communication being cut off betwixt Camden & Charles Town, Ld Rawdon would be compelled to evacuate that place & leave the back country, which would put an end to the war, & might be effected in a fortnight's time, after which they might return & plant their crops in peace forever after. This seemed so plausible that they set out in the highest spirits being about 300 men. They failed in surprising the Congaree Fort, but invested it closely, not dreaming that Ld

Rawdon could attempt its relief. In the third day they learnt that Col. Doyle with the volunteers of Ireland was crossing the river at a ford about 8 miles above. They were obliged to raise the seige & marched down the South side of the river expecting to be joined by Marion who was to cross the Santee, & not expecting that the troops would follow them any distance from Camden. After they had proceeded about 20 miles they got a fresh alarm, they learnt that Major M'Intosh with the 64th Regiment, the cavalry of the N. York volunteers & a field piece was upon the march from Camden to McCords ferry after them, & that a detachment of troops & Militia from Ninety Six was approaching from that quarter, to add to their misfortune a party they had sent down the Congaree river to secure all the flats, canoes & boats there & on Santee for the purpose of crossing the river & making a junction with Marion, this party was surprised by some Militia & Regulars they had made prisoners, & all the boats &c carried to our post at Wright's Bluff. Sumpter's ruin seemed inevitable. He was left in an enemy's country with a large deep river before him, which he must cross to effect a retreat. In this dilemma Major M'Intosh's advance guard came in sight of his rear about 5 miles below Motte's house. To the astonishment of the whole province Maj. McIntosh instantly retreated above him on their way home to the Waxaws, certain that having got two small canoes carried his men & swam his horses across Santee unmolested, altho' it took up two days to effect it. Having crossed Santee they thought themselves safe, but they now found out that Col. Watson & 500 men were just at hand. By a rapid march they got clear of him when they found that Ld Rawdon with his own regiment was hurrying over from Camden after them. Being all mounted they gave his Lordship the slip & got about 4 miles, where he lay looking on while Sumpter all danger was over. In this they were again disappointed. Ld Rawdon finding they had out marched him sent for Major Frazer of the South Carolina Regiment to march with it & intercept them at Lynch's Creek. They had just crossed the creek when Maj. Frazer came up with them who attacked them & routed their whole body in a few minutes. They were now exceedingly dejected; instead of 300 men under Ld Rawdon's command they had seen so many different detachments of troops superior to their whole force that they despaired of success & notwithstanding Sumpter who had carried off a number of negroes, offered one to every person who would enlist for ten months as a dragoon to form a body of State cavalry, he could hardly procure a single recruit & he began to grow extremely unpopular. They raised so great a clamor against him for deceiving them with regard to Ld Rawdon's strength that he was obliged at a muster to enter into a long vindication of his conduct. All this however was ineffectual, & Marions followers began also to lose all hopes. In short So. Car. seemed to be on the eve of peace. The transactions that succeeded I shall pass over only observing that Ld Rawdon adopted the plan of giving up all the Rebel Militia who were not prisoners of war to be tried by our Militia. This plan ought to have extended to all the rebel Militia without exception. At this period Genl Green invaded this province what followed is publicly known. The more Lord Rawdons conduct is investigated the more blameless he will appear. We soon lost great part of the back country, the cruelty exercised by the rebels on our Militia exceed all belief. Lord Rawdon finding he could not bring Green to action embarked for England on account of his health.

The battle of the Eutaws quickly followed and our army lay in the neighborhood of Monks Corner within 37 miles of Charlestown and abandoned the back country. The rebels determined that no Tories should live among them, ordered them & their families within the British lines or in other words to Charlestown. At this time, or rather just after Lord Rawdon sailed the loyalists seemed to have acquired a new character, their situation & sufferings had made them desperate, they became familiar with danger & acquired the use of arms. According to the usual theory of this war, it might have been expected that all the country above our army would have revolted and turned their arms against us & I make no doubt that almost all the inhabitants of Charlestown who wrote to England at this time represented the whole country as in the enemies hands, as they are in general perfectly ignorant of the back country the mistake may be natural but this was so far from being the case that from this place to what is

called the Ridge betwixt Saluda & Edisto Rivers on the road
to Ninety Six on one hand & from a few miles to the
Southward of Santee to the Saltcatcher on the other, the inhabitants refused to submit to the rebels although left by the
army & surrounded at most every hand the enemy who were
in possession of Ninety Six district & the disaffected inhabitants of the Forks of Santee the country betwixt Saltketcher &
Savannah river & all the Rice lands from thence to Ashley
river having revolted gave the enemy possession of the country, in short, the whole province resembled a piece of patch
work, the inhabitants of every settlement, when united in sentiment being in arms for the side they liked best & making
continual inroads into one anothers settlements. The country
betwixt Cooper river & Santee as far up as Monks Corner
seemed to be in dispute, the inhabitants at the greatest distance from the garrison taking up arms & the others who
were more in reach although friends in their hearts to the
rebels, yet not being used to arms refused to turn out when
called upon by Marion, & compounded the matter by paying
fifty silver dollars in lieu of a years service. This was in Sept.
when Genl Green lay at the high hills of Santee. When our
army came to the Quarter House & Genl Green crossed
Santee, the rebels made them turn out to a man, without regard to the contributions they had paid, the district of Ninety
Six being all this while much divided in sentiment suffered severely. the tories in many places would neither submit nor go
to Charlestown, they hid themselves in the swamp, from
whence they made frequent incursions upon their enemies.
when opposed by a superior force they dispersed, when the
storm blew over they embodied again & recommenced their
operation. A petty partizan startel up in every settlement &
headed the Whigs or Tories, both parties equally afraid of the
other dared not sleep in their Houses, but concealed themselves in swamps, this is called lying out. Both parties were in
this condition in general all over Ninety Six District & every
other part of the province wherever it was checquered by this
intersection of Whig & Tory settlements.

Ninety Six district also suffered severely by the incursions of
the loyal refugees, from the mountains on the one hand &
from Charlestown on the other. As it had no great River or

other natural boundary to defend it, nothing could prevent these incursions in a country covered with woods and "penetrable in every part." The cruelties the Whigs exercised upon the Tories, which seemed to be carried to their utmost excess under the auspices of Genl Green when he invaded the province, were now returned upon them with interest, and both parties in this petty, but sanguinary war displayed prodigies of military skill & address & seemed to breathe the extirpation of their enemies. In a large Rebel settlement at a distance from a Tory country, the people were at peace except upon the alarm of a Tory invasion, & the center of Orangeburg District being in the heart of an extensive friendly country, was also at peace the people sleeping safely in their houses, nay they enjoyed so much tranquillity that many of the loyal refugees who came from Ninety-Six as late as August & Sept stopped in that country at the distance of 100 miles from Charles Town & leased plantations. The inhabitants there used to say that if our army kept off Genl Green's they could defend themselves. In Nov. Genl Green crossed the Santee & our army retreated to the Quarter House, giving up the whole country. Greene sent Genl Sumpter with a detachment of 400 men to take post at Orangeburg & to reduce that Country. He pubd a general pardon to all who would submit except two. Our friends there did not upon this determine to submit. Maj. Giessandanoer, the commanding officer there sent an express to Genl Lesly requesting assistance, & in the mean time kept Sumpter pretty much within his pickets, but unfortunately no assistance could be given them. After a few weeks the people disheartened by being unsupported, gradually made a submission to the enemy, but the war was now too far advanced & both parties too much irritated against each other to coalesce easily. It was no uncommon thing for a party to submit & in a few days to turn their arms against their new master. The swamps were filled with loyalists, the rebels durst not sleep in their houses, & Sumpter irritated by the hostility of the Country, got the Catawba Indians to track the loyalists from the swamps, wh were at the same time traversed by large parties of armed rebels to kill or take the tories. Giessandanner was made a prisoner & without the least regard to the established cartel, he was thrown into the common jail, stripped to his shirt & breeches & threatened to have his two sons, boys abt 10 or 12 yrs old carried off & made drummers to a continental regiment. He was therefore under the necessity of submitting to them. Our friends from thence & the other parts of the country are daily taking refuge in this place & it is certain that such as have submitted are more irritated than ever & eagerly disposed to revolt, while the rebels themselves disgusted with the abuses of Genl Greene's army & their own government find in many places that they have not changed masters for the better. The loyalists on Little Pedee, alarmed at the evacuation of George Town last June entered into a truce for three months with Marion who gladly embraced the opportunity of disarming a hardy & intrepid race of men whom he had never been able to crush & which would enable him to call the inhabitants of Big Pedee & the Cheraws District from the defence of their properties to augment his brigade, besides they were so powerfully backed by the extensive loyal country in North Carolina & countenanced by the post at Wilmington that he had nothing to hope from force, therefore agreeing to the truce was removing a most troublesome thorn from his own side — at the end of three months the truce was renewed for nine more wh expired the 17th of June next. When the truce was first made the inhabitants of the Northern parts of that country furtherest removed from Marion's adherents, refused to accede to it — looking upon it as a timid & ignominious measure, & blamed Capt Ganey the officer who made it with Marion. They accordingly put themselves under Maj. Craigs command at Wilmington & continued in arms; but upon the evacuation of that post they found it their interest to accede to it. That country is the only place in these two provinces, except Charles Town & James Island where the British government is at present established. They muster regularly once a month agreeable to our militia law & have a general muster once in three months. At their particular request Lt Col. Balfour commandant of this place has lately appointed Justices of peace among them, a regulation highly necessary to enable them to ascertain disputed property. They often come to this place in boats & the commandant always loads them back with salt gratis & supplies them with ammunition. Marion has behaved with great good faith towards them & ordered his people when they stop any of their boats to suffer them to pass unmolested unless they find ammunition aboard.

The country comprehended in the truce has furnished a safe asylum for the loyal refugees from N. Ca. who are suffered to settle among them upon promising to observe conditions of the truce.

This has given great umbrage to the N. Car. rebels. Genl Rutherford who commands the Militia Brigade from Mecklenburg & Salisbury is a perfect savage & bears the most rancorous hatred to Tories. He has lately made a peremptory demand that all the N. Ca. refugees shall be delivered up. This requisition our officers there with great spirit have refused to comply with, declaring that no peacable man who applies to them for protection and observes the conditions of the truce shall be delivered up. I expect shortly to hear that hostilities have ensued. In the mean time our friends there are in great spirits, being much elated with the Kings' Speech & with the check Marion recd lately from Col. Thomson.

Upon hearing of this last affair they had public rejoicing for three days. At present they seem determined to repel force by force, but being totally unsupported they are unequal to the contest. When they fall they will give but a small accession of strength to the enemy as they never will be able to get them to do any duty which is at present an indispensable preliminary with all who join them. Want of room prevents me from saying anything with regard to N. Ca. where one half of the people are our friends & where with only the countenance of 300 Brit. troops in Wilmington the loyalists had like to have over turned the rebel govt. A sufficient proof of the fallacy of that kind of reasoning which in a war of this nature, where every man is a soldier, estimates the strength of a country from the number of regular troops of wh an army is composed, without regarding the dispositions of the inhabn of the country wh is the seat of war. By attending to this we shall be able to acct for the success of the royal cause in N. Ca. & in some measure the misfortunes that attended it here.

In the above remarks I have only mentioned such circumstances of the ill fortune that attended our exertions, exclusive of Cornwallis's fall. The want of a sufficient concurrence on the part of the people compelled Ld Rawdon to leave the back country after having missed of crushing Green's army. To that & to Genl Greene invading the province when we had not a sufficient force to meet him in the field & at the same time to preserve our outposts, we are to attribute the loss of the country. Had Ld Cornwallis followed Gen. Greene to the Southward or had the reinforcements from Ireland arrived a month sooner, in either of these cases, we should have had an army in the field superior to Greene's & all our posts would have been safe, wh would have soon crushed any internal insurrection that took place; & we should have been in the same situation as we were before Ld Cornwallis marched into N. Car—when he lay at Winnsboro & obliged Green to keep a respectful distance at the Waexaws. But not having a sufficient army in the field, enabled Greene to reduce our outposts especially as Ld Rawdon had not sufficient warning of Ld Cornwallis' going into Virginia, wh prevented him from withdrawing his posts in time to form a sufficient army—but even if he could have effected this issue the measure would have been ruinous because removing the posts would have laid open the whole country to the enemy.

The re-inforcements not having arrived until the posts were broke up rendered their re-establishment impossible without crushing the enemys army.

Should offensive measures be attempted here with a view to reduce this country the enemies army must be destroyed or driven away, posts must be established & an army kept on the frontiers to prevent any attempts from the Northward, & the militia must be embodied. I am aware that the general opinion of the merchants in Charles Town is that every person must be disarmed & the protection of the country left to the troops only. If I had time I could demonstrate this to be impossible. Every man must take a side if he submits to our govt, if he is averse to personal service let him find a substitute or pay a stipulated sum in money. This is the method the rebels have adopted. Let these men serve six months properly regimented & in the meantime let the militia who stay at home do patrol duty to preserve internal peace. Whenever this Militia is formed, the life of a Militia man when a prisoner must be considered to be as sacred as that of a regular soldier. The rebel Militia when prisoners must be at the disposal in the first instance of the royal Militia with the approbation of the Commander in Chief. Before the reduction of Charlestown, the loyalists promised I suppose great assistance in wh they were sincere — but men cannot be taken from the plough & made veterans in a short time. This is only to be acquired by hard service & long experience. The loyalists in this Province, as well as the S. parts of N. Car — have now reached that point. If ever our army take the field they will give a powerful assistance. Ninety-Six & Orangeburg Districts would be recovered by their own inhabitants & they would not be easily dispossessed again. Indeed whatever the issue of the campaign might be, it would be the most calamitous period that ever this Province saw, for the loyal refugees inflamed with the loss of their properties & relations, & loyalists who have now submitted irritated with the indignities & abuses of a govt they hate would make severe retaliations. Every man exclusive of his attachment to the Common Cause would have a number of private injuries to revenge. The same appearances would take place in N. Car., but on a much larger scale as the loyalists there are so much more numerous.

The above observations have fallen far short of the idea I wished to convey but before I conclude I cannot avoid remarking that all our friends who come in at present from the country are prodigiously irritated against the enemy.

After staying sometime in town they become often dissatisfied & disgusted & many of them go out & submit.

But they have no sooner submitted in a fit of pique than they return to their former principles from the insults & indignities they suffer from the enemy — every man of whom if he has lost any property by any part of the British army in which the other served, compels him in pain of death to make restitution, so that many of them are wholly ruined besides many after receiving pardon are killed by those who have them in bondage.

William Feilding to the Earl of Denbigh

New York August ye. 10th. 1782

My Lord

I wrote to your Lordship the 2d. instant by the Ship *Sr. Guy Carleton* acquainting your Lordship that the French Fleet was on the American coast, and that the Hook was secured from their coming in, by Transports to be sunk on the Bar, and the Men of War to cover them. They have not as yet made their Appearance off the Hook, therefore it is imagined they are either gone to the Chesapeake or Boston, dreading the Approach of the Fleet from Jamaica. On the Arrival of the Packet Sr. Guy Carleton & Admiral Digby acquainted General Washington & Congress that Independence would be granted to America. The Inhabitants of York & Loyall Refugees are very much hurt at this sudden change of Affairs, saying that their Loyalty to their King and Mother Country, has sold them, & made them worse than slaves, that great Britain has convinced the world she was superior to her Enemies by sea, & had lately gained a compleat Victory of over the Fleet of France, that the American Army was reduced very low, and their Trade wholly destroy'd, & that the French & Dutch had lost all their possessions in the East: And that in the very Hour of prosperity, & triumph over all her Enemies, grants Independence to the undutiful Americans, & sues for Peace with all the other Powers at war with her. Nothing but long faces & dejected Countenances to be seen. Washington's whole force including the French (I am told) does not exceed 5,000, and was decreasing daily; while that of the British is 14,000, besides what is at Charleston & Halifax. I have sent your Lordship the particulars of the *St. Margaretta*'s Action with the French Frigate *L'Amazon*, and of the chase the *Warwick, Astraea* & *Carysfort* had after *L'Eville* French 64. I have just heard from New York, that the Inhabitants hearing Independence was to be granted to America waited on Sr. G: Carleton to know weither such report was true, who desired,

they would meet him the next day at Head Quarters for an
Answer, when Mr. Morgan (the General's Secretary) read to
several Thousands the inclos'd Letter, which infused Melancholy in the Face of every Spectator, and the whole dispersed very much displeased, and immediately sent Word to
the General that they would do no more Duty in Town (The
Militia of York then doing Garrison Duty and the Army was
in Camp) as they were not to be protected: on which some of
the Troops were immediately order'd to Town to relieve the
Guards & Posts. Many very respectable Characters & Friends
to old England are ruined, and are sure to meet no Mercy
from Congress. A paper has been stuck up at the Coffee-
House saying if Sr. G: Carleton and Prince William will open
the Campaigne, the whole of the Inhabitants &c. &c. will
join the Army and sacrifice their Lives rather than live under
the American Government. The *Assurance* & *Adamant* are
just arrived with the Troops from Savannah that place being
evacuated and not an Inhabitant left behind.

Ebenezer Denny:
Journal, January 4–December 13, 1782

Jan. 4th, 1782. — Joined the troops under General Green at Round O, in the State of South Carolina. Moved to Pond-Pond; here we lay some time. Rice farms around this neighborhood — the fields almost all under water; immense quantities of ducks; excellent sport at times. Planters return to their homes — live in style. Army change their ground; march to Ashley. Was on picket the night before we reached Ashley; got exceedingly wet — it rained all night. Marched next morning in wet clothes twelve miles, to Ashley, exposed to very hot sun; laid up with fever — carried to hospital; as soon as able, returned to camp. Hospital very disagreeable place — all sick, and some continually dying. Attendance good; surgeons very kind; furnished with some stores, sugar, tea and molasses. Continued weak and unfit for duty for some weeks. Ashley a very good position — ground high and dry; but it is now midsummer and sickly season. Men die very fast; lost several valuable officers. Ashley river low; full of alligators.

August. — Camp continued on bank of Ashley river, eighteen or twenty miles above Charleston. Enemy confine themselves to city. Their light troops and horse advanced five miles, at place called Quarter House. Armies both seem disposed to be quiet; ours in no condition for doing much. Some talk of peace, and of the enemy evacuating Charleston. Detailed for command. Joined a captain of the Maryland line; marched with two sergeants, two corporals, and thirty men, for Georgetown, about sixty miles distant, coast-wise. Escorted a brigade of wagons loaded with rum for the army. Country appears deserted; the few people we saw looked bad enough, poor and dejected; they fled from us, and in some instances hid themselves. Farms on this route have been neglected; exposed to the incursions of the British. Negroes and stock either removed or taken. Fell in with an alligator, twelve feet in length, in the middle of the road; supposed that his pond had dried up, and that he was in search of another; soldier shot him.

September. — Our camp very thin; not more than three relieves of officers and men for the ordinary duties. Hospitals crowded, and great many sick in camp; deaths so frequent, the funeral ceremony dispensed with. Provisions scarce and very indifferent; the beef brought from the back counties of North Carolina, by the time they reach the camp, poor indeed, and must be unwholesome. Commissary's yard and slaughter place commonly short distance from camp. Soldier going there in morning about killing time, met his comrade returning in; asked how was the beef this morning? other replied, that it took two men to hold up the creature until the butcher knocked it down. Says the other, And why didn't he knock it down as it lay? Flour a rare article. Troops have lived chiefly upon rice, now and then a small allowance of Indian meal served out — rice very good for the sick, but rather washy for duty men. Governor Hamilton, of this State, himself and family, quarter at a pleasant seat, two miles in rear of camp — General Green not quite so far; each has a subaltern's guard. Very fond of getting one or other of these guards better fare than we have in camp. Officer considered and treated as one of the family.

October. — Camp at Ashley Hill. Ranks thinned very much; deaths not so frequent. Our situation as to ground, a handsome one, and, as far as I can judge, eligible, but assuredly the climate is severe upon northern constitutions. Gentlemen who can afford it, reside during summer in the city and spend the winter in the country. An unpleasant week's command. At a bridge over Ashley, six or seven miles from camp, where the great road from Charleston to the upper country crosses, a subaltern and thirty men have been stationed. It became my turn. Orders were to suffer no people to pass or repass without proper permit. It was now pretty well known that the enemy would soon evacuate the city. Many poor devils had taken protection and followed the British in; provisions scarce in town, and those people sick of their situation — they were anxious to get back to their old places of abode in the country. Some very miserable objects came out — whole families, battered and starving. Was sure, upon my representation, leave would be given to let them pass. Stated the business in writing, and dispatched a sergeant. No — ordered not to let them pass; thought this an unnecessary cruelty.

Dec. 13th. — Had been expecting, every day for a month past, to hear of the intended evacuation of Charleston. The Governor's guard was an object at this time, as the officer commanding would, of course, accompany or escort him into the city. I was so fortunate as to have the guard this day, when advice was received that the British would embark next morning. A few hours for the Governor to get ready, we set out in the evening with one tumbrel, containing books, papers, &c., and reached the city early next day. Saw the last of the enemy embark in their boats and put off to the shipping. An immense fleet lay in sight all day; found the city very quiet — houses all shut up. A detachment from the army had marched the day before to take possession as soon as the English would be off. Guards stationed at proper places, and small parties, conducted by an officer, patrolled the streets. Charleston a handsome town, situate on neck of land between the confluence of Ashley and Cooper rivers; Cooper river, however, appears to be the only harbor. Town here fronts the east; business all done on this side. Second and third day people began to open their houses and show themselves, and some shops opened. Stayed a week, and returned to our old encampment.

John Armstrong: The Newburgh Address

To the Officers of the Army.

GENTLEMEN,— A fellow soldier, whose interest and affections bind him strongly to you, whose past sufferings have been as great, and whose future fortune may be as desperate as yours — would beg leave to address you.

Age has its claims, and rank is not without its pretensions to advise: but, though unsupported by both, he flatters himself, that the plain language of sincerity and experience will neither be unheard nor unregarded.

Like many of you, he loved private life, and left it with regret. He left it, determined to retire from the field, with the necessity that called him to it, and not till then — not till the enemies of his country, the slaves of power, and the hirelings of injustice, were compelled to abandon their schemes, and acknowledge America as terrible in arms as she had been humble in remonstrance. With this object in view, he has long shared in your toils and mingled in your dangers. He has felt the cold hand of poverty without a murmur, and has seen the insolence of wealth without a sigh. But, too much under the direction of his wishes, and sometimes weak enough to mistake desire for opinion, he has till lately — very lately — believed in the justice of his country. He hoped that, as the clouds of adversity scattered, and as the sunshine of peace and better fortune broke in upon us, the coldness and severity of government would relax, and that, more than justice, that gratitude would blaze forth upon those hands, which had upheld her, in the darkest stages of her passage, from impending servitude to acknowledged independence. But faith has its limits as well as temper, and there are points beyond which neither can be stretched, without sinking into cowardice or plunging into credulity. — This, my friends, I conceive to be your situation — Hurried to the very verge of both, another step would ruin you forever. — To be tame and unprovoked when injuries press hard upon you, is more than weakness;

774

but to look up for kinder usage, without one manly effort of your own, would fix your character, and show the world how richly you deserve those chains you broke. To guard against this evil, let us take a review of the ground upon which we now stand, and from thence carry our thoughts forward for a moment, into the unexplored field of expedient.

After a pursuit of seven long years, the object for which we set out is at length brought within our reach. Yes, my friends, that suffering courage of yours was active once — it has conducted the United States of America through a doubtful and a bloody war. It has placed her in the chair of independency, and peace returns again to bless — whom? A country willing to redress your wrongs, cherish your worth and reward your services, a country courting your return to private life, with tears of gratitude and smiles of admiration, longing to divide with you that independency which your gallantry has given, and those riches which your wounds have preserved? Is this the case? Or is it rather a country that tramples upon your rights, disdains your cries and insults your distresses? Have you not, more than once, suggested your wishes, and made known your wants to Congress? Wants and wishes which gratitude and policy should have anticipated, rather than evaded. And have you not lately, in the meek language of entreating memorials, begged from their justice, what you would no longer expect from their favour? How have you been answered? Let the letter which you are called to consider tomorrow make reply.

If this, then, be your treatment, while the swords you wear are necessary for the defence of America, what have you to expect from peace, when your voice shall sink, and your strength dissipate by division? When those very swords, the instruments and companions of your glory, shall be taken from your sides, and no remaining mark of military distinction left but your wants, infirmities and scars? Can you then consent to be the only sufferers by this revolution, and retiring from the field, grow old in poverty, wretchedness and contempt? Can you consent to wade through the vile mire of dependency, and owe the miserable remnant of that life to charity, which has hitherto been spent in honor? If you can — GO — and carry with you the jest of tories and scorn of whigs — the ridicule, and what is worse, the pity of the world. Go, starve, and be forgotten! But, if your spirit should revolt at this; if you have sense enough to discover, and spirit enough to oppose tyranny under whatever garb it may assume; whether it be the plain coat of republicanism, or the splendid robe of royalty; if you have yet learned to discriminate between a people and a cause, between men and principles — awake; attend to your situation and redress yourselves. If the present moment be lost, every future effort is in vain; and your threats then, will be as empty as your entreaties now.

I would advise you, therefore, to come to some final opinion upon what you can bear, and what you will suffer. If your determination be in any proportion to your wrongs, carry your appeal from the justice to the fears of government. Change the milk-and-water style of your last memorial; assume a bolder tone — decent, but lively, spirited and determined, and suspect the man who would advise to more moderation and longer forbearance. Let two or three men, who can feel as well as write, be appointed to draw up your last remonstrance; for, I would no longer give it the sueing, soft, unsuccessful epithet of memorial. Let it be represented in language that will neither dishonor you by its rudeness, nor betray you by its fears, what has been promised by Congress, and what has been performed, how long and how patiently you have suffered, how little you have asked, and how much of that little has been denied. Tell them that, though you were the first, and would wish to be the last to encounter danger: though despair itself can never drive you into dishonor, it may drive you from the field: that the wound often irritated, and never healed, may at length become incurable; and that the slightest mark of indignity from Congress now, must operate like the grave, and part you forever: that in any political event, the army has its alternative. If peace, that nothing shall separate them from your arms but death: if war, that courting the auspices, and inviting the direction of your illustrious leader, you will retire to some unsettled country, smile in your turn, and "mock when their fear cometh on." But let it represent also, that should they comply with the request of your late memorial, it would make you more happy and them more respectable. That while war should continue, you would follow their standard into the field, and when it came to an end, you would withdraw into the shade of private life, and give the world another subject of wonder and applause; an army victorious over its enemies — victorious over itself.

George Washington to Joseph Jones

Newburgh, March 12, 1783.
Dear Sir: I have received your letter of the 27th. Ulto., and thank you for the information and freedom of your communications.

My Official Letter to Congress of this date will inform you of what has happened in this Quarter, in addition to which, it may be necessary it should be known to you, and to such others as you may think proper, that the temper of the Army, tho. very irritable on acct. of their long-protracted sufferings has been apparently extremely quiet while their business was depending before Congress untill four days past. In the mean time, it should seem reports have been propagated in Philadelphia that dangerous combinations were forming in the Army; and this at a time when there was not a syllable of the kind in agitation in Camp.

It also appears, that upon the arrival of a certain Gentleman from Phila. in Camp, whose name, I do not, at present, incline to mention such sentiments as these were immediately and industriously circulated. That it was universally expected the Army would not disband untill they had obtained Justice. That the public creditors looked up to them for redress of their Grievances, would afford them every aid, and even join them in the Field, if necessary. That some Members of Congress wished the Measure might take effect, in order to compel the Public, particularly the delinquent States, to do justice. With many other suggestions of a Similar Nature; from whence, and a variety of other considerations it is generally believ'd the Scheme was not only planned, but also digested and matured in Philadelphia; and that some people have been playing a double game; spreading at the Camp and in Philadelphia Reports and raising jealousies equally void of Foundation untill called into being by their vile Artifices; for as soon as the Minds of the Army were thought to be prepared for the transaction, anonymous invitations were circulated, requesting a general Meeting of the Officers next day; at the same instant many Copies of the Address to the Officers of the Army was scattered in every State line of it.

So soon as I obtained knowledge of these things, I issued the order of the 11th. (transmitted to Congress;) in order to rescue the foot, that stood wavering on the precipice of despair, from taking those steps which would have lead to the abyss of misery while the passions were inflamed, and the mind trimblingly alive with the recollection of past sufferings, and their present feelings. I did this upon the principle that it is easier to divert from a wrong to a right path, than it is to recall the hasty and fatal steps which have been already taken.

It is commonly supposed, if the Officers had met agreeable to the anonymous Summons, resolutions might have been formed, the consequences of which may be more easily conceived than expressed. Now, they will have leisure to view the matter more calmly and seriously. It is to be hoped they will be induced to adopt more rational measures, and wait a while longer for the settlemts. of their Accts.; the postponing of which gives more uneasiness in the Army than any other thing. there is not a man in it, who will not acknowledge that Congress have not the means of payment; but why not say they, one and all, liquidate the Accts. and certifie our dues? are we to be disbanded and sent home without this? Are we, afterwards, to make individual applications for such settlements at Philadelphia, or any Auditing Office in our respective states; to be shifted perhaps from one board to another; dancing attendence at all, and finally perhaps be postponed till we loose the substance in pursuit of the shadow. While they are agitated by these considerations there are not wanting insiduous characters who tell them, it is neither the wish nor the intention of the public to settle your accounts; but to delay this business under one pretext or another till Peace wch. we are upon the eve of, and a seperation of the Army takes place when it is well known a generl settlement never can be effected and that individual loss, in this instance, becomes a public gain.

However derogatory these ideas are with the dignity, honor, and justice of government yet in a matter so interesting to the Army, and at the same time so easy to be effected by the Public, as that of liquidating the Accounts, is delayed without any apparent, or obvious necessity, they will have their place in a mind that is soured and irritated. Let me entreat you therefore my good Sir to push this matter to an issue, and if there are Delegates among you, who are really opposed to doing justice to the Army, scruple not to tell them, if matters should come to extremity, that they must be answerable for all the ineffable horrors which may be occasioned thereby. I am etc.

George Washington: Speech to the Officers

Head Quarters, Newburgh, March 15, 1783.
Gentlemen: By an anonymous summons, an attempt has been made to convene you together; how inconsistent with the rules of propriety! how unmilitary! and how subversive of all order and discipline, let the good sense of the Army decide.

In the moment of this Summons, another anonymous production was sent into circulation, addressed more to the feelings and passions, than to the reason and judgment of the Army. The author of the piece, is entitled to much credit for the goodness of his Pen and I could wish he had as much credit for the rectitude of his Heart, for, as Men see thro' different Optics, and are induced by the reflecting faculties of the Mind, to use different means, to attain the same end, the Author of the Address, should have had more charity, than to mark for Suspicion, the Man who should recommend moderation and longer forbearance, or, in other words, who should not think as he thinks, and act as he advises. But he had another plan in view, in which candor and liberality of Sentiment, regard to justice, and love of Country, have no part; and he was right, to insinuate the darkest suspicion, to effect the blackest designs.

That the Address is drawn with great Art, and is designed to answer the most insidious purposes. That it is calculated to impress the Mind, with an idea of premeditated injustice in the Sovereign power of the United States, and rouse all those resentments which must unavoidably flow from such a belief. That the secret mover of this Scheme (whoever he may be) intended to take advantage of the passions, while they were warmed by the recollection of past distresses, without giving time for cool, deliberative thinking, and that composure of Mind which is so necessary to give dignity and stability to measures is rendered too obvious, by the mode of conducting the business, to need other proof than a reference to the proceeding.

Thus much, Gentlemen, I have thought it incumbent on me to observe to you, to shew upon what principles I opposed the irregular and hasty meeting which was proposed to have been held on Tuesday last: and not because I wanted a disposition to give you every oppertunity consistent with your own honor, and the dignity of the Army, to make known your grievances. If my conduct heretofore, has not evinced to you, that I have been a faithful friend to the Army, my declaration of it at this time wd. be equally unavailing and improper. But as I was among the first who embarked in the cause of our common Country. As I have never left your side one moment, but when called from you on public duty. As I have been the constant companion and witness of your Distresses, and not among the last to feel, and acknowledge your Merits. As I have ever considered my own Military reputation as inseperably connected with that of the Army. As my Heart has ever expanded with joy, when I have heard its praises, and my indignation has arisen, when the mouth of detraction has been opened against it, it can *scarcely be supposed*, at this late stage of the War, that I am indifferent to its interests. But, how are they to be promoted? The way is plain, says the anonymous Addresser. If War continues, remove into the unsettled Country; there establish yourselves, and leave an ungrateful Country to defend itself. But who are they to defend? Our Wives, our Children, our Farms, and other property which we leave behind us. or, in this state of hostile seperation, are we to take the two first (the latter cannot be removed), to perish in a Wilderness, with hunger, cold and nakedness? If Peace takes place, never sheath your Swords Says he untill you have obtained full and ample justice; this dreadful alternative, of either deserting our Country in the extremest hour of her distress, or turning our Arms against it, (which is the apparent object, unless Congress can be compelled into instant compliance) has something so shocking in it, that humanity revolts at the idea. My God! what can this writer have in view, by recommending such measures? Can he be a friend to the Army? Can he be a friend to this Country? Rather, is he not an insidious Foe? Some Emissary, perhaps, from New York, plotting the ruin of both, by sowing the seeds of discord and seperation between the Civil and Military powers of the Continent? And what a Compliment does he pay to our Understandings, when he recommends measures in either alternative, impracticable in their Nature?

But here, Gentlemen, I will drop the curtain, because it wd. be as imprudent in me to assign my reasons for this opinion, as it would be insulting to your conception, to suppose you stood in need of them. A moment's reflection will convince every dispassionate Mind of the physical impossibility of carrying either proposal into execution.

There might, Gentlemen, be an impropriety in my taking notice, in this Address to you, of an anonymous production, but the manner in which that performance has been introduced to the Army, the effect it was intended to have, together with some other circumstances, will amply justify my observations on the tendency of that Writing. With respect to the advice given by the Author, to suspect the Man, who shall recommend moderate measures and longer forbearance, I spurn it, as every Man, who regards that liberty, and reveres that justice for which we contend, undoubtedly must; for if Men are to be precluded from offering their Sentiments on a matter, which may involve the most serious and alarming consequences, that can invite the consideration of Mankind, reason is of no use to us; the freedom of Speech may be taken away, and, dumb and silent we may be led, like sheep, to the Slaughter.

I cannot, in justice to my own belief, and what I have great reason to conceive is the intention of Congress, conclude this Address, without giving it as my decided opinion, that that Honble Body, entertain exalted sentiments of the Services of the Army; and, from a full conviction of its merits and sufferings, will do it compleat justice. That their endeavors, to discover and establish funds for this purpose, have been unwearied, and will not cease, till they have succeeded, I have not a doubt. But, like all other large Bodies, where there is a variety of different Interests to reconcile, their deliberations are slow. Why then should we distrust them? and, in consequence of that distrust, adopt measures, which may cast a shade over that glory which, has been so justly acquired; and tarnish the reputation of an Army which is celebrated thro' all Europe, for its fortitude and Patriotism? and for what is this done? to bring the object we seek nearer? No! most certainly, in my opinion, it will cast it at a greater distance.

For myself (and I take no merit in giving the assurance, being induced to it from principles of gratitude, veracity and justice), a grateful sence of the confidence you have ever placed in me, a recollection of the chearful assistance, and prompt obedience I have experienced from you, under every vicissitude of Fortune, and the sincere affection I feel for an Army, I have so long had the honor to Command, will oblige me to declare, in this public and solemn manner, that, in the attainment of compleat justice for all your toils and dangers, and in the gratification of every wish, so far as may be done consistently with the great duty I owe my Country, and those powers we are bound to respect, you may freely command my Services to the utmost of my abilities.

While I give you these assurances, and pledge myself in the most unequivocal manner, to exert whatever ability I am possessed of, in your favor, let me entreat you, Gentlemen, on your part, not to take any measures, which, viewed in the calm light of reason, will lessen the dignity, and sully the glory you have hitherto maintained; let me request you to rely on the plighted faith of your Country, and place a full confidence in the purity of the intentions of Congress; that, previous to your dissolution as an Army they will cause all your Accts. to be fairly liquidated, as directed in their resolutions, which were published to you two days ago, and that they will adopt the most effectual measures in their power, to render ample justice to you, for your faithful and meritorious Services. And let me conjure you, in the name of our common Country, as you value your own sacred honor, as you respect the rights of humanity, and as you regard the Military and National character of America, to express your utmost horror and detestation of the Man who wishes, under any specious pretences, to overturn the liberties of our Country, and who wickedly attempts to open the flood Gates of Civil discord, and deluge our rising Empire in Blood. By thus determining, and thus acting, you will pursue the plain and direct road to the attainment of your wishes. You will defeat the insidious designs of our Enemies, who are compelled to resort from open force to secret Artifice. You will give one more distinguished proof of unexampled patriotism and patient virtue, rising superior to the pressure of the most complicated sufferings; And you will, by the dignity of your Conduct, afford occasion for Posterity to say, when speaking of the glorious example you have exhibited to Mankind, "had this day been wanting, the World had never seen the last stage of perfection to which human nature is capable of attaining."

Samuel Shaw to the Rev. Eliot

THESE will give you a pretty good idea of our proceedings; and that you may not want any information on the subject, I shall take the liberty of adding a few particulars, by way of narrative.

The accumulated hardships under which the army had so long labored made their situation intolerable, and called aloud for immediate redress. An application to the supreme authority of America was thought a salutary measure, and the improbability of obtaining relief from the States individually, after the treatment the Massachusetts line had experienced from their State, rendered it absolutely indispensable.

With this view, a delegation from the several regiments composing the Massachusetts line, having conferred together, came to a determination of taking the sense of the army at large; and on the 16th of November appointed a committee of seven, who should assemble on the 24th of the same month, and, in conjunction with the delegates from those lines who might see fit to send any, agree and determine upon such measures as should be found best calculated to promote the desirable purposes for which the convention was called.

Agreeably to this proposal there was a full representation of the whole army, when "it was unanimously agreed that Major-General Knox, Brigadier-General Huntington, Colonel Crane, Colonel Courtlandt, and Doctor Eustis, be a committee to draft an address and petition to Congress, in behalf of the army, and lay the same before this assembly for consideration at their meeting on the 1st of December."

At the meeting on the 1st of December, "the draft of the address and petition to Congress was read, and voted to be laid before the several lines of the army for consideration," and it was determined, "that the army at large choose a general officer, and each line send a field-officer, any two of whom, as a majority of them should agree, should, in conjunction with the said general officer, form a committee to wait on Congress and execute the business of said address." Instructions were also directed to be prepared for the conduct of said committee, and the necessary sum of money raised for their expenses.

On opening the ballots the 5th of December, Major-General McDougall, Colonel Ogden, and Colonel Brooks were chosen to proceed to Congress with the address and petition, which was signed on the 7th, and delivered to the committee, — after which the meeting adjourned without day.

The delegation from the army to Congress set out on their mission the 21st of December. On the address and petition being read in Congress, a grand committee, consisting of a member from each State, was chosen to confer with our commissioners. The result of this conference was certain resolves of Congress, passed on the 25th of January, the purport whereof was, that the army should receive one month's pay, and that their accounts should be settled as soon as possible, for discharging the balances of which Congress would endeavour to provide adequate funds. The matter respecting a commutation of the half-pay was recommitted. These resolutions at large were transmitted by our commissioners, in a letter of the 8th of February, to General Knox, which was immediately communicated to the respective lines of the army.

This report, though far from being satisfactory, joined to the certainty that we were on the eve of a general peace, kept the army quiet. In this state of patient expectation, the anonymous address to the officers made its appearance. Immediately on this, the Commander-in-chief, by an order of the 11th of March, directed the officers to assemble on the 15th, which produced the second anonymous address.

The meeting of the officers was in itself exceedingly respectable, the matters they were called to deliberate upon were of the most serious nature, and the unexpected attendance of the Commander-in-chief heightened the solemnity of the scene. Every eye was fixed upon the illustrious man, and attention to their beloved General held the assembly mute. He opened the meeting by apologizing for his appearance there, which was by no means his intention when he published the order which directed them to assemble. But the diligence used in circulating the anonymous pieces rendered it necessary that he should give his sentiments to the army on the nature and tendency of them, and determined him to avail himself of the present opportunity; and, in order to do it with greater perspicuity, he had committed his thoughts to writing, which, with the indulgence of his brother officers, he would take the liberty of reading to them. It is needless for me to say any thing of this production; *it speaks for itself.* After he had concluded his address, he said, that, as a corroborating testimony of the good disposition in Congress towards the army, he would communicate to them a letter received from a worthy member of that body, and one who on all occasions had ever approved himself their fast friend. This was an exceedingly sensible letter; and, while it pointed out the difficulties and embarrassments of Congress, it held up very forcibly the idea that the army should, at all events, be generously dealt with. One circumstance in reading this letter must not be omitted. His Excellency, after reading the first paragraph, made a short pause, took out his spectacles, and begged the indulgence of his audience while he put them on, observing at the same time, that he had grown gray in their service, and now found himself growing blind. There was something so natural, so unaffected, in this appeal, as rendered it superior to the most studied oratory; it forced its way to the heart, and you might see sensibility moisten every eye. The General, having finished, took leave of the assembly, and the business of the day was conducted in the manner which is related in the account of the proceedings.

I cannot dismiss this subject without observing, that it is happy for America that she has a *patriot army*, and equally so that a *Washington* is its leader. I rejoice in the opportunities I have had of seeing this great man in a variety of situations; — calm and intrepid where the battle raged, patient and persevering under the pressure of misfortune, moderate and possessing himself in the full career of victory. Great as these qualifications deservedly render him, he never appeared to me more truly so, than at the assembly we have been speaking of. On other occasions he has been supported by the exertions of an army and the countenance of his friends; but in this he stood single and alone. There was no saying where the passions of an army, which were not a little inflamed, might lead; but it was generally allowed that longer forbearance was dangerous, and moderation had ceased to be a virtue. Under these circumstances he appeared, not at the head of his troops, but as it were in opposition to them; and for a dreadful moment the interests of the army and its General seemed to be in competition! He spoke, — every doubt was dispelled, and the tide of patriotism rolled again in its wonted course. Illustrious man! what he says of the army may with equal justice be applied to his own character. "Had this day been wanting, the world had never seen the last stage of perfection to which human nature is capable of attaining."

A New York Loyalist to Lord Hardwicke

THE Rebels breathe the most rancorous and malignant Spirit everywhere. Committees and Associations are formed in every Colony and Resolves passed that no Refugees shall return nor have their Estates restored. The Congress and Assemblies look on tamely and want either the Will or the Power to check those Proceedings. In short, the Mob now reigns as fully and uncontrolled as in the Beginning of our Troubles and America is as hostile to Great Britain at this Hour as she was at any Period during the War. From all this many people conclude that the Army will not be withdrawn from hence this Year, that the British Troops at least will keep Possession of New York, as it will be very difficult, if possible, to send off any more than the Foreign Troops, and as it would be highly imprudent to abandon this Place in the present Posture of Affairs. Certain it is that, if the whole Army goes away this Year, very few Refugees or Inhabitants within the British Lines will be able to stay behind. Besides those gone to Europe and Canada, upwards of eleven thousand persons have already removed to Nova Scotia and twelve thousand more have given in their Names to be carried to Nova Scotia and other Places. Almost all the principal people here are gone or going; not the tenth part of the Inhabitants will be able to remain if the Army goes this year.

Without the Lines every thing is equally gloomy. Confusion and Discontent prevail. The Load of Taxes is intolerable. Farms in general pay a Tax which is greater than the Rents they paid formerly. Every other Species of Property is proportionably taxed. This, joined to the Insolence of the new Rulers, the unsettled State of Government, and the want of Security for the Persons and Property of Individuals induce Multitudes to wish for a removal and accordingly have applied to Sir G. Carleton for the purpose. I am told that upwards of One hundred thousand people without the Lines have already applied to be transported to Nova Scotia and Canada. At the same time the cool and dispassionate Adherents to Congress are of Opinion that their present System of Government cannot hold long and that the Powers of Congress are utterly inadequate to the Government of this Country. A very sensible Man from without the Lines told me lately that the judicious people among them did not expect their present Form of Government could last longer than four or five Years, if so long; and, on asking him what Form would be adopted in its Place, he answered, Monarchy.

In the several Assemblies there are some liberal Persons who are for recalling all the Loyalists, or for excluding none but a few that are most obnoxious hitherto. However, there has been a Majority against such Motions in each Assembly and the Leaders of the Mob will not listen to anything of that Kind. The purchasers of confiscated Estates and all who have risen from Obscurity to Power and Eminence are violent against the Loyalists and the Return of Refugees, the former least they should lose the Estates which they purchased for a Trifle, the latter least they should again sink into their Original Obscurity; and it unfortunately happens that those two Descriptions are not only numerous, but also include many of the most active Men and such as have most Influence.

The Congress have disbanded most of their Army — all that were enlisted during the War. None remain but those that were enlisted for three Years and amount, as I am told, to about 4000. Congress have also stated their public Debt, the whole of which, Foreign and Domestic, as far as it could be ascertained, amounts, according to their Statement, to forty-two million of Spanish Dollars. It is supposed that it must be much more, as many Domestic Debts could not be ascertained and the Debts of particular Colonies which cannot be less than a fourth part of this Sum are not included. But supposing the Debt to be no more, it is absolutely impossible for America in its present exhausted State to pay either the Interest or Principal; and indeed many declare without Hesitation that the Americans neither can nor will pay either. Moral Principles, I do assure you, are at a very low Ebb in America at present, and I should not be surprized to hear of an explicit Refusal to pay any part of this Money.

The only good Tidings I have to send you is that Sir G. Carleton is not leaving us. While he stays I think myself safe; and were he left intirely to himself to manage Affairs as he pleased, with the Army he has, I have not the least Doubt but he would yet bring everything in America to a happy Conclusion. He sees Things in a just Light, has Judgment and Penetration to manage Affairs properly, and will neither be frightened, cajoled, nor diverted by Congress or their Adherents in any Measure he undertakes. He has an Altercation with those People at present about Negroes. An Article of the *wise* provisional Treaty obliges us to give up all Negroes and, accordingly, the Rebels have claimed all that came within the Lines. But many Negroes came in Consequence of Royal Proclamations promising them Protection and Liberty. Sir G. thinks that no minister can by a Treaty disannull those Proclamations; and indeed it would be inhuman to the last Degree and a base Violation of Public Faith to send those Negroes back to their Masters who would beat them with the utmost Cruelty. Accordingly, such Negroes as came in by Virtue of those Proclamations are permitted to go wherever they please. If they chuse to go to their Masters, it is well; if not, they are transported to Nova Scotia or else where as they desire. Sir Guy Carleton in this, as in every thing else, has acted with Openness and Candor. Before any Negroes went off, he desired M^r. Washington to appoint Commissioners to inspect all Embarkations. The Commissioners accordingly came and take Account of all Negroes that go away. The Rebels bluster about this Matter and declare it a Violation of the Provisional Treaty, but Sir Guy goes on deliberately and steadily and refers the Business to future Discussion, that Compensation may be made to the Masters of the Negroes if judged necessary. No Man can be a warmer Friend to the Loyalists than Sir Guy and perhaps no Man has it so much in his Power to serve them.

George Washington and Thomas Mifflin: Speeches in the Continental Congress

December 23, 1783

According to order, his Excellency the Commander in Chief was admitted to a public audience, and being seated, the President, after a pause, informed him, that the United States in Congress assembled, were prepared to receive his communications; Whereupon, he arose and addressed Congress as follows:

MR. PRESIDENT: The great events on which my resignation depended, having at length taken place, I have now the honor of offering my sincere congratulations to Congress, and of presenting myself before them, to surrender into their hands the trust committed to me, and to claim the indulgence of retiring from the service of my country.

Happy in the confirmation of our independence and sovereignty, and pleased with the opportunity afforded the United States, of becoming a respectable nation, I resign with satisfaction the appointment I accepted with diffidence; a diffidence in my abilities to accomplish so arduous a task; which however was superseded by a confidence in the rectitude of our cause, the support of the supreme power of the Union, and the patronage of Heaven.

The successful termination of the war has verified the most sanguine expectations; and my gratitude for the interposition of Providence, and the assistance I have received from my countrymen, increases with every review of the momentous contest.

While I repeat my obligations to the army in general, I should do injustice to my own feelings not to acknowledge, in this place, the peculiar services and distinguished merits of the gentlemen who have been attached to my person during the war. It was impossible the choice of confidential officers to compose my family should have been more fortunate. Permit me, sir, to recommend in particular, those who have continued in the service to the present moment, as worthy of the favorable notice and patronage of Congress.

I consider it an indispensable duty to close this last act of my official life by commending the interests of our dearest country to the protection of Almighty God, and those who have the superintendence of them to his holy keeping.

Having now finished the work assigned me, I retire from the great theatre of action, and bidding an affectionate farewell to this august body, under whose orders I have so long acted, I here offer my commission, and take my leave of all the employments of public life.

He then advanced and delivered to the President his commission, with a copy of his address, and having resumed his place, the President returned him the following answer:

Sir, The United States in Congress assembled receive with emotions, too affecting for utterance, the solemn resignation of the authorities under which you have led their troops with success through a perilous and a doubtful war. Called upon by your country to defend its invaded rights, you accepted the sacred charge, before it had formed alliances, and whilst it was without funds or a government to support you. You have conducted the great military contest with wisdom and fortitude, invariably regarding the rights of the civil power through all disasters and changes. You have, by the love and confidence of your fellow-citizens, enabled them to display their martial genius, and transmit their fame to posterity. You have persevered, till these United States, aided by a magnanimous king and nation, have been enabled, under a just Providence, to close the war in freedom, safety and independence; on which happy event we sincerely join you in congratulations.

Having defended the standard of liberty in this new world: having taught a lesson useful to those who inflict and to those who feel oppression, you retire from the great theatre of action, with the blessings of your fellow-citizens, but the glory of your virtues will not terminate with your military command, it will continue to animate remotest ages.

We feel with you our obligations to the army in general; and will particularly charge ourselves with the interests of those confidential officers, who have attended your person to this affecting moment.

We join you in commending the interests of our dearest country to the protection of Almighty God, beseeching him to dispose the hearts and minds of its citizens, to improve the opportunity afforded them, of becoming a happy and respectable nation. And for you we address to him our earnest prayers, that a life so beloved may be fostered with all his care; that your days may be happy as they have been illustrious; and that he will finally give you that reward which this world cannot give.

James McHenry to Margaret Caldwell

December 23, 1783

HAD I been obliged to count the sands as they fall from an hour glass, since last Friday, I could not have done it with more exactness than I have counted the minutes of each day. It is, my dear Peggy, impossible for me to tell or you to feel the solicitudes and suspenses I have experienced. I am now become reasonable and do not think you are sick: but this does not relieve me. I do not think you have neglected me; but this does not place me at rest. I suppose that some sufficient cause must have intervened to prevent me getting your letter, as clouds intervene and prevent the sight of the sun. But I will say no more on this subject, for I do not wish to communicate any distress this incident has caused me to my affectionate Peggy.

To day my love the General at a public audience made a deposit of his commission and in a very pathetic manner took leave of Congress. It was a solemn and affecting spectacle; such an one as history does not present. The spectators all wept, and there was hardly a member of Congress who did not drop tears. The General's hand which held the address shook as he read it. When he spoke of the officers who had composed his family, and recommended those who had continued in it to the present moment to the favorable notice of Congress he was obliged to support the paper with both hands. But when he commended the interests of his dearest country to almighty God, and those who had the superintendence of them to his holy keeping, his voice faultered and sunk, and the whole house felt his agitations. After the pause which was necessary for him to recover himself, he proceeded to say in the most penetrating manner, 'Having now finished the work assigned me I retire from the great theatre of action, and bidding an affectionate farewell to this august body under whose orders I have so long acted I here offer my commission and take my leave of all the employments of public life.' So saying he drew out from his bosom his commission and delivered it up to the president of Congress. He then returned to his station, when the president read the reply that had been prepared—but I thought without any shew of feeling, tho' with much dignity.

This is only a sketch of the scene. But, were I to write you a long letter I could not convey to you the whole. So many circumstances crowded into view and gave rise to so many affecting emotions. The events of the revolution just accomplished—the new situation into which it had thrown the affairs of the world—the great man who had borne so conspicuous a figure in it, in the act of relinquishing all public employments to return to private life—the past—the present—the future—the manner—the occasion—all conspired to render it a spectacle inexpressibly solemn and affecting.

But I have written enough. Good night my love, my amiable friend good night.

Chronology, 1774–1783

1774 British Parliament passes Boston Port Act, signed by George III on March 31. Act closes Boston harbor until obedience to the law is restored in the town and its people pay for the tea destroyed in the Boston Tea Party of December 16, 1773. General Thomas Gage, commander in chief of the British army in North America, is commissioned as royal governor of Massachusetts and arrives in Boston on May 13 to enforce closing of the harbor. Parliament also passes: the Massachusetts Government Act, signed May 20, abrogating the 1691 royal charter for the province; the Administration of Justice Act, also signed May 20, allowing royal officials accused of capital crimes in Massachusetts to be tried outside the colony; the Quartering Act, signed June 2, allowing quartering of troops in occupied dwellings throughout the 13 colonies; and the Quebec Act, signed June 22, which extends borders of the province of Quebec to the Mississippi and Ohio rivers. British troops begin landing in Boston in June.

Delegates to an intercolonial congress called in response to the passage of the Boston Port Act are chosen in every colony except Georgia, June 15–August 25. Widespread disobedience and mob action in Massachusetts prevents Gage from enforcing the laws outside of Boston, and on September 5 he begins to fortify the city. First Continental Congress meets in Philadelphia on September 5. Gage dissolves Massachusetts House of Representatives, but its members meet on October 7 and establish a Provincial Congress. Continental Congress approves resolution on October 14 denouncing the recent acts of Parliament (widely known in the colonies as the Intolerable Acts) and on October 18 adopts agreement for the colonies to cease importing British goods after December 1, 1774, and to cease exports to Britain and the West Indies after September 10, 1775. Continental Congress adjourns October 26. Massachusetts Provincial Congress assumes government of the colony, including control of the militia.

1775 Ministry led by Lord North decides on January 25 to order Gage to arrest the leaders of the Massachusetts Provincial Congress and to restore British authority in the colony by force. Parliament declares Massachusetts to be in rebellion on

February 9. Gage receives instructions on April 14 and on night of April 18 sends detachment of 700 soldiers from Boston to destroy military supplies stored at Concord. Confrontation between British advance guard and small party of Massachusetts militia at Lexington on morning of April 19 leads to outbreak of firing in which eight Americans are killed and one British soldier is wounded. British encounter resistance from militia at North Bridge in Concord and retreat under fire to Lexington, where they meet relief force sent by Gage from Boston. Skirmishing continues until British reach Charlestown at nightfall; 73 British soldiers and 49 Americans are killed during the fighting. Massachusetts militia begin siege of Boston, and on April 23 the Massachusetts Provincial Congress votes to raise an army of 13,600 men. Gage strengthens fortifications around city and awaits reinforcements. American forces led by Benedict Arnold and Ethan Allen capture Fort Ticonderoga in northeastern New York on May 10 and occupy nearby Crown Point, May 12, gaining control of the southern end of Lake Champlain.

Second Continental Congress meets in Philadelphia on May 10 with delegates present from every colony except Georgia (delegates from Georgia will join Congress on September 12). Lord Dunmore, royal governor of Virginia, flees to warship in the York River on June 8 as British authority collapses throughout the colonies. (British troops along the Atlantic seaboard are concentrated at Boston and Halifax, Nova Scotia, leaving royal officials elsewhere without significant military support.) Congress votes on June 14 to create a Continental army. Massachusetts delegate John Adams nominates George Washington, a Virginia delegate and colonel in the Virginia militia, to be commander in chief. Washington receives unanimous vote of Congress on June 15.

Reinforcements increase British strength at Boston from 4,000 to 6,500, while combined Massachusetts, New Hampshire, Rhode Island, and Connecticut forces outside city total about 15,000. On the night of June 16 New England troops move onto the Charlestown peninsula opposite Boston and begin fortifying Breed's Hill and Bunker Hill. British land 2,200 men on the peninsula and succeed in capturing American positions on June 17 while losing more than 1,000 men killed or wounded; losses cause British commanders not to make further attacks on American positions outside Boston. Congress authorizes military action against British forces in Canada on June 27. Washington takes command at Cambridge on July 3 and works to equip, train, and reorganize army; becomes dismayed by lack of discipline among New England troops and inability of their elected officers to exercise authority.

Congress approves the Olive Branch Petition, a conciliatory message to George III, on July 5 and on July 6 adopts the Declaration of the Causes and Necessity of Taking Up Arms. North ministry rejects Olive Branch Petition and George III proclaims all 13 colonies to be in rebellion on August 23. American force of 1,200 men led by General Richard Montgomery leaves Fort Ticonderoga August 28 and begins invasion of Canada by way of Lake Champlain. Washington organizes second invasion force of 1,100 men under command of Benedict Arnold; it begins advance up Kennebec River in Maine on September 25. General William Howe succeeds Gage as British commander in chief in the 13 colonies, October 10. Congress authorizes fitting out of two warships, October 13. (American naval ships and privateers will capture British merchant vessels throughout war, but are unable to oppose operations by the Royal Navy along the American coast.) Lord Dunmore proclaims martial law in Virginia, November 7; begins to enlist Loyalists, and promises freedom to slaves who fight with the British. Arnold and about 700 men reach St. Lawrence River opposite Quebec, November 9. Montgomery occupies Montreal November 13 after General Guy Carleton, commander of British forces in Canada, retreats to Quebec.

Lord George Germain succeeds Lord Dartmouth as Secretary of State for the American Colonies on November 15 and becomes the principal minister directing the war. Congress appoints Committee of Correspondence to establish contact with foreign powers on November 29. Montgomery and 300 men join Arnold outside Quebec on December 2. Virginia militia defeat force of British troops, Loyalists, and escaped slaves in skirmish at Great Bridge on December 9 and occupy Norfolk on December 13 after Lord Dunmore withdraws his men to ships in the harbor. George III signs Prohibitory Act on December 23, closing off commerce with the 13 colonies and making American ships and crews subject to seizure by the Royal Navy. Enlistments of New England soldiers besieging Boston expire in December, but by the end of 1775 almost 10,000 men enlist in the Continental army for one year. (In 1776 Congress authorizes three-year enlistments in the Continental army; during the remainder of the war, American forces in the field are generally made up of both Continental soldiers and state militia.) Attack on Quebec, December 31, results in defeat in which Montgomery is killed and more than 400 Americans are captured.

1776   Dunmore burns much of Norfolk on January 1; attack helps discredit Loyalist cause in Virginia. (Dunmore retreats to Chesapeake Bay, then returns to England in summer 1776.) Americans continue siege of Quebec. Germain approves plan by Howe to capture New York City, gain control of the Hudson Valley, and isolate New England from the other colonies. Unable to recruit sufficient men in Britain and Ireland, ministry hires 18,000 mercenaries from Hesse-Kassel, Brunswick, and other German states (German mercenaries become generally known in America as Hessians).

Common Sense, pamphlet by Thomas Paine denouncing monarchical rule and advocating an independent American republic, is published in Philadelphia on January 10; it sells tens of thousands of copies throughout the colonies. North Carolina militia defeat force of 1,700 Loyalists at Moores Creek, about 20 miles north of Wilmington, on February 27, and capture 850 prisoners the following day, ending Loyalist resistance in the colony. Washington moves artillery brought overland from Fort Ticonderoga onto Dorchester Heights overlooking Boston harbor, March 4. British garrison evacuates Boston on March 17 and sails to Halifax, Nova Scotia. Washington moves army to New York in April in anticipation of British attack. Louis XVI authorizes clandestine support for the Americans on May 2 at the urging of his foreign minister, the Comte de Vergennes, who works with Pierre-Augustin Caron de Beaumarchais to arrange covert shipments of arms, supplies, and money to America. (Spain joins France in funding shipments in August 1776.) Americans abandon siege of Quebec and retreat toward Montreal after British garrison is reinforced on May 6.

Congress recommends on May 10 that each of the colonies form a government and on May 15 calls for the complete suppression of royal authority in the colonies. (Eleven states adopt constitutions between 1776 and 1783, while Connecticut and Rhode Island revise their existing charters.) Virginia delegate Richard Henry Lee submits resolution in Congress on June 7 calling for independence and urging the formation of foreign alliances. Proposal for immediate declaration of independence meets with opposition, and Congress postpones decision. British troops advancing from Quebec defeat Americans at Trois Rivières, June 8. Americans evacuate Montreal, June 9, and begin retreating from Canada. Attack on Charleston,

South Carolina, fails on June 28 when British ships are repulsed by artillery fire from fortifications on Sullivan's Island. British fleet anchors off New York on June 29 and Howe begins landing troops on Staten Island on July 2.

Congress votes on July 2 to sever all political ties with Great Britain and on July 4 adopts revised version of Declaration of Independence drafted by Thomas Jefferson. Silas Deane, agent appointed by Congress to purchase military supplies in Europe, arrives in Paris on July 7 and begins working with Beaumarchais on clandestine arms shipments. American troops retreating from Canada reach Fort Ticonderoga in early July as Carleton begins building boats to transport his army south on Lake Champlain. Congress begins debating Articles of Confederation and Perpetual Union drafted by John Dickinson, July 22. British troops on Staten Island total 32,000 by mid-August, including 8,000 Hessians, facing 19,000 Continental soldiers and state militia. Howe begins landing troops at Gravesend Bay on eastern end of Long Island, August 22, and orders attack on American lines on August 27. Americans lose 1,400 men killed or captured in the battle of Long Island (fought in present-day Brooklyn) and are forced to retreat behind their fortified lines on Brooklyn Heights. Washington withdraws 9,000 men from Brooklyn Heights to Manhattan on night of August 29–30. British successfully land at Kips Bay on east side of Manhattan on September 15, but fail to block northward retreat of 5,000 Americans along the west side of the island. Americans take up positions on Harlem Heights in northern Manhattan as British occupy New York City.

Congress appoints Benjamin Franklin, Silas Deane, and Thomas Jefferson as commissioners to negotiate treaties with European powers on September 26 (Jefferson declines position and is replaced by Arthur Lee). British destroy most of the American flotilla defending Lake Champlain, October 11–12, and occupy Crown Point, but then return to Canada when Carleton decides it is too close to winter to launch an attack on Fort Ticonderoga. British land troops at Pell's Point on Long Island Sound on October 18, forcing Washington to evacuate Harlem Heights and move army to White Plains. British attack American lines at White Plains, October 28, forcing American withdrawal to North Castle on November 1. Washington divides army between New Jersey and New York banks of Hudson River, placing 6,000 men at North Castle, 3,000 at Peekskill, and over 5,000 in northeastern New Jersey, while continuing to hold Fort Washington, the last remaining American outpost in Manhattan.

British capture Fort Washington and take 2,800 prisoners and large amounts of weapons and supplies on November 16, then cross Hudson on November 20 and force evacuation of Fort Lee. Washington leads retreat across New Jersey and crosses Delaware River into Pennsylvania on December 8. British force commanded by General Henry Clinton occupies Newport, Rhode Island, on December 8. Continental army is seriously weakened by desertions and expired enlistments, and Washington fears it will dissolve when enlistments of most soldiers expire at end of year. Howe abandons plans for immediate capture of Philadelphia and disperses much of his army into garrisons across central New Jersey. Washington leads 2,400 men across the Delaware on night of December 25 and defeats Hessian garrison at Trenton, New Jersey, on morning of December 26, capturing more than 900 prisoners.

1777 Washington leads successful attack against British troops at Princeton, New Jersey, on January 3, then moves army into winter quarters at Morristown, New Jersey, on January 6. Howe withdraws British troops in New Jersey north to New Brunswick and Amboy. Germain approves plan by Howe to use the army at New York for attack on Philadelphia instead of an advance up the Hudson Valley to Albany, while also approving plan by General John Burgoyne for advance south from Canada toward Albany. By late May army at Morristown numbers 9,000 men, many of them equipped with French arms (Royal Navy lacks sufficient ships to effectively blockade American ports).

Washington moves army south to Middlebrook, New Jersey, on May 29. Howe begins series of maneuvers in northern New Jersey on June 12, intending to bring the Continental army into battle. Burgoyne leaves southern Canada with more than 7,000 British and Hessian troops and begins moving south toward Fort Ticonderoga. Howe removes troops from New Jersey on June 30 and prepares to move army by sea. Americans evacuate Fort Ticonderoga on July 5 after British place cannon on hill overlooking their positions. Howe sails from New York on July 23 with 18,000 men. Colonel Barry St. Leger leaves Oswego, New York, on July 26 with force of 2,000 British regulars, Hessians, Loyalists, and Iroquois, and begins advance along the Mohawk Valley toward Albany in support of Burgoyne's invasion. Americans evacuate Fort Edward on the upper Hudson, July 29, as advance of Burgoyne's army is slowed by difficult terrain and obstacles created by retreating Americans. St. Leger begins siege of Fort Stanwix (now Rome, New York) on August 2. American militia attempting to relieve the fort are ambushed by Iroquois and Loyalists at Oriskany, August 6, but are able to retreat after both sides suffer heavy casualties. Force of 2,000 New England militia defeat 1,400 mostly Hessian troops attempting to raid supply stores at Bennington, Vermont, on August 16, killing or capturing 900 men. St. Leger abandons siege of Fort Stanwix, August 22, and retreats to Montreal.

Howe begins landing troops at Head of Elk, Maryland, on August 25 as Washington moves to defend Philadelphia with army of 11,000 men. American army of 7,000 men commanded by General Horatio Gates fortifies Bemis Heights along the Hudson, 25 miles north of Albany. Howe defeats Americans at Brandywine Creek, Pennsylvania, on September 11; Washington retreats to Chester after losing 700 men killed or captured. Burgoyne unsuccessfully attacks American positions at Bemis Heights, September 19, losing 600 men killed, wounded, or captured in battle of Freeman's Farm. Howe occupies Philadelphia September 26 and begins operations against American forts along the Delaware below the city. Washington attacks detachment of 9,000 British troops at Germantown, Pennsylvania, on October 4 but is forced to retreat after initial success and loses more than 1,000 men killed, wounded, or captured. Second British attack on Bemis Heights is defeated on October 7, and Burgoyne retreats toward Saratoga as Gates is reinforced by several thousand militia. Burgoyne surrenders army of 5,000 men on October 17.

Congress submits revised Articles of Confederation to states for ratification, November 15. British occupy Fort Mercer, the last American post on the lower Delaware, November 20. After learning of American victory at Saratoga, French officials tell Franklin that France will recognize American independence and sign treaty of alliance. Washington takes army into winter quarters at Valley Forge, Pennsylvania, on December 21.

1778   Army at Valley Forge suffers from cold and hunger, caused in part by depreciation of Continental currency and ineffectiveness of supply service. (Congress lacks power to levy taxes and must finance war by issuing paper money and by making requisitions on the states for funds and supplies; requisitions frequently go unfulfilled.) France and the United States sign treaties of alliance and commerce in Paris on February 6; under their terms, France recognizes the independence of the United States and pledges to fight until American independence is won if the treaties lead to war between France and Britain. Conditions at Valley Forge improve after General Nathanael Greene is appointed quartermaster general on February 25. Washington has troops trained and drilled by Friedrich von Steuben, a former Prussian officer.

In anticipation of outbreak of war with France, North ministry orders Henry Clinton, the new British commander in chief, to withdraw army from Philadelphia to New York and remain on the defensive while sending 8,000 troops to the West Indies and Florida. Clinton succeeds Howe on May 8. Britain declares war on France, June 14. Congress rejects British peace proposal that fails to recognize American independence, June 17. Clinton evacuates Philadelphia on June 18 and begins withdrawing army across New Jersey. Continental troops leave Valley Forge, June 19, and Washington orders attack on British at Monmouth Court House, New Jersey, on June 28. Battle is inconclusive, and British continue their withdrawal, reaching Sandy Hook on June 30. Loyalists and Iroquois kill more than 200 American militiamen in Wyoming Valley of northeastern Pennsylvania, July 3, beginning series of raids on frontier settlements in Pennsylvania and New York. (British also support series of raids by Loyalists and Indians on settlements in the Ohio Valley.)

French fleet and expeditionary force of 4,000 men under the Comte d'Estaing arrives off Delaware Bay on July 8. Washington moves army to White Plains, New York, on July 30. Combined French and American attack on Newport, Rhode Island, August 5–31, fails, in part due to poor coordination between d'Estaing and General John Sullivan, the American commander; failure causes mistrust between new allies. British begin series of coastal raids in New England and New Jersey. Washington deploys army to the north and west of New York City. French fleet sails for West Indies on November 4. British expeditionary force sails from New York on November 27 and captures Savannah, Georgia, on December 29, beginning campaign intended to rally Loyalists and restore royal authority in the southern states.

1779   British occupy Augusta, Georgia, January 29. Virginia forces led by George Rogers Clark capture British post at Vincennes on February 25, giving Americans control of the Illinois territory (fighting continues in the Ohio Valley until 1782). British defeat Americans at Briar Creek, Georgia, March 3, and advance into South Carolina, threatening Charleston, May 11–12, before withdrawing to Georgia. Clinton begins advance up the Hudson with 6,000 men on May 30 and captures Stony Point, June 1. Spain declares war on Great Britain on June 21 but does not recognize American independence. Washington orders night attack on Stony Point, July 16, that captures 500 prisoners, halting British attempts to occupy the Hudson Highlands. British restore royal government in Georgia on July 20. Washington orders Sullivan to mount punitive expedition into Iroquois territory in central New York; Americans destroy Iroquois orchards and crops and burn 40 villages, August 22–September 30. French fleet arrives off Georgia in early September, and on September 23 d'Estaing and General Benjamin Lincoln begin siege of Savannah with 3,500 French and 1,500 American troops. Assault on British lines at Savannah is defeated, October 9; French and Americans lose 800 men killed, wounded, or captured. British evacuate Newport on October 11. D'Estaing abandons siege of Savannah and sails for West Indies on October 20 as Americans retreat to Charleston. Washington takes army into winter quarters at Morristown, New Jersey, on December 1. Leaving garrison of 10,000 men to hold New York City, Clinton sails for South Carolina with army of 8,500 on December 26.

1780 Army at Morristown suffers from severe cold and hunger as Continental currency rapidly depreciates. Clinton begins landing troops in South Carolina on February 11 and lays siege to Charleston on April 1. Lincoln surrenders Charleston garrison of 2,500 Continental soldiers and as many as 3,000 militia on May 12. Strength of Continental army at Morristown falls to 4,000 men as enlistments expire and desertions increase. British victory at Waxhaws Creek, May 29, ends organized American resistance in South Carolina. Clinton returns to New York, June 8, leaving Lord Charles Cornwallis in command of 8,000 men to continue southern campaign. Bitter conflict begins in South Carolina between American partisans and British forces, which include both local Loyalist militias and Loyalist regiments recruited in the North. Partisan raids force Cornwallis to garrison numerous posts in South Carolina and Georgia, reducing the number of men available for offensive operations. Congress appoints Horatio Gates to replace Lincoln as commander of the Southern Department on June 13.

French expeditionary force of 5,500 men under the Comte
de Rochambeau lands at Newport on July 11. British force of
2,000 men commanded by Cornwallis routs American army of
4,000 men under Gates at Camden, South Carolina, on August 16; Americans retreat to Hillsborough, North Carolina.
Cornwallis begins advance into North Carolina on September 8. General Benedict Arnold escapes to British lines on
September 25 after discovery of his plot to betray key Hudson
River post at West Point. Carolina militia defeat Loyalists at
Kings Mountain, South Carolina, on October 7, killing or cap-
turing more than 800 men. Washington appoints Nathanael
Greene to replace Gates as commander of the Southern De-
partment, October 14. Following defeat at Kings Mountain,
Cornwallis retreats to Winnsboro, South Carolina, on Octo-
ber 29. Greene takes command at Charlotte, North Carolina, on
December 3. Seeking to close off Dutch trade with the United
States, Britain declares war on the Netherlands, December 20.

1781   Pennsylvania Continental regiments at Morristown mutiny on
January 1 and begin marching on Philadelphia. Benedict
Arnold, now a general in the British army, raids Richmond,
Virginia, on January 5, then establishes base at Portsmouth.
Pennsylvania mutiny ends January 8 after Congress makes
concessions regarding pay and enlistments (further mutinies
by Continental troops in January and May are forcibly suppressed, and several mutineers are shot). Cornwallis leaves
Winnsboro, January 8, and begins advance into North Carolina. Americans win battle at Cowpens, South Carolina, on
January 17, killing or capturing more than 900 British and
Loyalist soldiers. Greene retreats across Dan River into Virginia on February 14; lack of supplies and boats forces Cornwallis to abandon pursuit of American army, and British
withdraw to Hillsborough.

      Ratification of Articles of Confederation is completed on
March 1. Greene returns to North Carolina with army of
4,000 men and is attacked by Cornwallis at Guilford Courthouse on March 15. British force Americans to retreat, but
lose 500 men killed and wounded out of force of 2,000. Cornwallis withdraws to Wilmington, North Carolina, while
Greene moves into South Carolina and joins partisans in successful operations against British posts. Cornwallis leaves
Wilmington on April 25, beginning campaign in Virginia intended to deprive American forces in the Carolinas of supplies
and reinforcements. Robert Morris takes office as superinten-

dent of finance on May 14 and begins to ease financial crisis with help of French loans and subsidies (Continental currency ceases to circulate early in 1781). Cornwallis reaches Petersburg, Virginia, on May 20, and joins forces commanded by Arnold. Washington and Rochambeau meet at Wethersfield, Connecticut, May 21–22, to plan operations against British at New York. After receiving reinforcements, Cornwallis begins Virginia campaign with army of 7,000 men, opposed by smaller force of Continental soldiers and militia led by the Marquis de Lafayette. Clinton orders Cornwallis to establish base on Chesapeake Bay, and Cornwallis occupies Yorktown, Virginia, on August 2.

After learning on August 14 that large French fleet under the Comte de Grasse is sailing from the West Indies to Chesapeake Bay, Washington orders American and French armies outside of New York City to march to Virginia. French victory in the naval battle of the Chesapeake Capes on September 5 prevents British at Yorktown from being reinforced or evacuated by sea. Greene attacks British at Eutaw Springs, South Carolina, on September 8, but withdraws after battle in which both sides suffer heavy casualties. British retreat to Charleston and abandon attempts to hold other posts in South Carolina. Washington begins siege of Yorktown on September 28, commanding army of 9,000 American and 7,000 French soldiers. Cornwallis surrenders more than 7,000 men on October 19, ending major fighting in the Revolutionary War. British evacuate Wilmington, North Carolina, on November 18, leaving Savannah, Charleston, and New York as their only remaining garrisons along the American seaboard.

1782 House of Commons votes against continuing the war in America on February 27 and Lord North resigns, March 20. New ministry led by Lord Rockingham opens peace negotiations with Franklin in Paris on April 12. Carleton succeeds Clinton as commander in chief in America on May 9. Rockingham dies July 1 and is succeeded by Lord Shelburne, who continues negotiations. British evacuate Savannah on July 11. Franklin, John Jay, John Adams, and Henry Laurens sign preliminary peace treaty with Britain in Paris on November 30. Its terms provide for a cessation of hostilities; the evacuation of British forces from American territory; British recognition of an independent United States with borders extending north to the Great Lakes, west to the Mississippi, and south to the 31st parallel; the honoring of debts owed to British and American

creditors; the recognition of American fishing rights off
Canada; and a pledge that Congress recommend to the state
legislatures the restoration of the rights and properties of Loyalists. British evacuate Charleston, December 14.

1783   Britain, France, and Spain sign preliminary peace agreement
on January 20, and Britain proclaims an end to hostilities on
February 4. Anonymous addresses are circulated among Continental officers camped at Newburgh, New York, March
10–12, denouncing failure of Congress to pay them and incit-
ing the army to rebellion if its demands are not met. Washington condemns the addresses at an assembly held on March 15
and calls upon his officers to express their loyalty to Congress;
officers adopt a resolution declaring their obedience to civil
authority. Congress ratifies the preliminary peace treaty on
April 15, and cessation of hostilities is announced on April 19.
Continental troops who enlisted for the duration of the war
are furloughed on May 26. Final peace treaty between Great
Britain and the United States of America is signed in Paris,
September 3. British evacuate New York City on November 25,
accompanied by several thousand Loyalists (at least 50,000
Loyalists emigrate to Canada, Europe, and the West Indies
during and after the war). Washington leads his troops into
the city later in the day. After farewell meeting with his officers
on December 4, Washington goes to Annapolis, Maryland,
where he addresses Congress on December 23 before returning the commission given him in 1775.

Biographical Notes

ABIGAIL ADAMS (November 11, 1744–October 28, 1818) Born Abigail Smith in Weymouth, Massachusetts, the daughter of a Congregational minister. Educated at home. Married John Adams in 1764. Moved to farm in Braintree (later Quincy), Massachusetts. Managed farm while John Adams served as a delegate to the Continental Congress and as diplomatic envoy in Europe. Friend and correspondent of Mercy Otis Warren. Traveled to Paris in 1784 to join husband, then moved the following year to London, where John Adams served as first American minister to Great Britain. Returned to farm in Quincy, Massachusetts, in 1788. After John Adams was inaugurated as president in 1797, moved to Philadelphia, then to Washington, D.C., when it became the capital in 1800. Returned in 1801 to Quincy farm, where she died.

JOHN ADAMS (October 30, 1735–July 4, 1826) Born Braintree, Massachusetts, the son of a farmer. Graduated from Harvard College in 1755 and was admitted to the Massachusetts bar in 1758. Married Abigail Smith in 1764. Served in First Continental Congress, 1774, and in the Second Continental Congress, 1775–78. Went to France as a diplomatic commissioner in 1778 and returned in 1779. Served in Europe as a peace commissioner and as an envoy to Holland, 1780–84. Appointed by Congress as the first American minister to Great Britain in 1785 and served until 1788. Returned to the United States and became vice president in the Washington administration, 1789–97. Elected president as a Federalist in 1796, defeating Thomas Jefferson. Served one term, 1797–1801; defeated for reelection by Jefferson. Retired to his farm in Quincy, Massachusetts, where he died.

ANTHONY ALLAIRE (February 22, 1755–1839) Born New Rochelle, New York. Commissioned on April 22, 1777, as lieutenant in the Loyal American Regiment, which was recruited from among New York Loyalists. Sailed for Georgia in December 1779 and saw action during the Charleston campaign. Captured at Kings Mountain on October 7, 1780, but escaped and made his way to Charleston. Charged with murder for the killing of another Loyalist officer during a quarrel in Charleston in March 1781, but was acquitted at court martial. Immigrated to Canada and settled in New Brunswick after the war.

ETHAN ALLEN (January 21, 1738–February 11, 1789) Born Litchfield, Connecticut. Fought in French and Indian War. Settled by 1770 in the New Hampshire Grants (present-day Vermont), territory disputed by New York and New Hampshire. Became commander of the Green Mountain Boys, militia formed by settlers opposed to New York claims on the territory. Led Green Mountain Boys in capture of Fort Ticonderoga on May 10, 1775. Taken prisoner during attack on Montreal in September 1775 and imprisoned in England and New York City before being exchanged in May 1778. Unsuccessfully petitioned Congress in 1778 to have Vermont recognized as a state. Returned to Vermont and began correspondence in 1780 with General Frederick Haldimand, British commander at Quebec, discussing the possibility of making Vermont a British province. Withdrew from politics in 1784 and published a controversial deistic treatise, *Reason the Only Oracle of Man*. Settled on farm in Burlington, where he died.

JOHN ANDRÉ (May 2, 1750–October 2, 1780) Born in London, the son of a Swiss merchant. Purchased commission in British army in 1771. Studied military engineering at the University of Göttingen before joining his regiment in Canada in 1774. Captured by Americans at St. Johns, near Montreal, in November 1775; exchanged at the end of 1776. Promoted to captain and appointed as aide to General Charles Grey. Served during Philadelphia campaign at Brandywine, Paoli, Germantown, and Whitemarsh. Fought at Monmouth and became aide to Sir Henry Clinton after British withdrawal to New York City. Appointed deputy adjutant general with rank of major on October 23, 1779. Accompanied Clinton on expedition against Charleston in 1780, then returned to New York. Conducted secret correspondence with Benedict Arnold, beginning in May 1779, and met with Arnold on September 21, 1780, to arrange surrender of West Point. Captured by New York militia on September 23 while attempting to return to British lines in civilian disguise. Condemned as a spy by military tribunal on September 29 and hanged at Tappan, New York.

JOHN ARMSTRONG (November 25, 1758–April 1, 1843) Born in Carlisle, Pennsylvania, the son of a surveyor and Pennsylvania militia officer. Left College of New Jersey (now Princeton) in 1776 to join the Continental army and became an aide to General Hugh Mercer. Fought at Trenton and Princeton. Became aide to General Horatio Gates in 1777 with rank of major. Served in Saratoga campaign. Anonymously wrote Newburgh Addresses in 1783. Served as secretary to the Pennsylvania supreme executive council, 1783–87. Moved to New York in 1789. Served in U.S. Senate, November 1800–February 1802 and November 1803–June 1804. Appointed minister to France by Thomas Jefferson in 1804 and held position until 1810. Named secretary of war by James Madison on January 13, 1813. Forced to resign on August 30, 1814, after the British burned Washington, D.C. Died in Red Hook, New York.

BENEDICT ARNOLD (January 14, 1741–June 14, 1801) Born in Norwich, Connecticut. Apprenticed to druggist. Served with militia during French and Indian War, 1758–59 and 1760. Moved in 1762 to New Haven, where he sold books and drugs; later became merchant trading with Canada and the West Indies. Elected captain in Connecticut militia in 1774. Shared command with Ethan Allen of expedition that captured Fort Ticonderoga on May 10, 1775. Commanded expedition that invaded Canada through Maine wilderness, September–November 1775. Wounded in failed attack on Quebec, December 31, 1775. Appointed brigadier general in the Continental army in January 1776. Retreated from Canada in June 1776. Organized and commanded boat flotilla that delayed British advance on Lake Champlain in October 1776. Commanded Connecticut militia during British raid on Danbury in April 1777.

Promoted to major general on May 2, 1777, but almost left the army in dispute over seniority. Served in Saratoga campaign and fought at Freeman's Farm and Bemis Heights, where he was again wounded. Appointed military commander of Philadelphia on June 19, 1778. Began secret correspondence with British in May 1779 after Congress ordered him court-martialed on charges of financial misconduct. Found guilty in January 1780 and reprimanded by George Washington. Became commander of garrison at West Point, New York, on August 3, 1780. Agreed to betray West Point to British for £20,000. Fled to British lines on September 25, 1780, after plot was uncovered. Commissioned as brigadier general by British. Led British and Loyalist troops in series of raids in Virginia, December 1780–May 1781, and in attack on New London, Connecticut, on September 6, 1781. Sailed for England in December 1781. Lived in Canada, 1785–91. Died in London.

JOSIAH ATKINS (d. 1781) Lived in Waterbury, Connecticut, where he may have worked as a blacksmith. Enlisted in Continental army in January 1781. Joined his regiment in New York State in April 1781 and then marched to Virginia. Fought in battle of Green Spring on July 6. Began working as doctor's assistant in army hospitals on August 24. Fell ill with fever; his last diary entry was made in a hospital in Hanover, Virginia, on October 15, 1781.

ROBERT AUCHMUTY (1725–December 11, 1788) Born in Boston, the son of a lawyer. Educated at Boston Latin School, then began legal practice in Boston. Appointed judge of the vice-admiralty court for Massachusetts and New Hampshire in 1767 and served until the beginning of the Revolution. Immigrated to England in 1776; his estate in Roxbury was confiscated in 1779. Died in London.

ISAAC BANGS (December 11, 1752–September 12, 1780) Born in Harwich, Massachusetts. Graduated from Harvard in 1771. Began medical practice in Harwich. Joined Massachusetts militia regiment in January 1776 and was elected a second lieutenant. Served in siege of Boston. Joined Continental army in April 1776 and was sent with his regiment to New York City; kept diary from April 1 to July 29, 1776. Left Continental army when enlistment expired on December 31, 1776. Joined crew of frigate *Boston* as doctor's mate on March 8, 1779.

WILLIAM BARTON (d. April 1802) Served in New Jersey regiments of the Continental army as an ensign, November 1776–February 1777; second lieutenant, February–October 1777; first lieutenant, November 1777–December 1781; and captain, December 1781–April 1783.

JOHN BOWATER Commissioned as captain in the Royal Marines in 1760. Arrived in Boston in January 1776 and served in New York campaign later that year. Captured by French in 1778 while returning to England on leave. Exchanged in 1779 and promoted to major. Eventually achieved rank of colonel. Died at age 71.

THOMAS BROWN (May 27, 1750–August 3, 1825) Born Whitby, Yorkshire, the son of a shipowner. Immigrated to Georgia in 1774 and established plantation near Augusta. Badly beaten, tarred, and feathered by Sons of Liberty on

August 2, 1775, after he refused to declare allegiance to the Continental Congress. Went to East Florida in 1776, where he was commissioned as a lieutenant colonel by the royal governor and given command of the East Florida Rangers. Led Loyalists and Indians in series of raids and skirmishes along the Florida-Georgia frontier, 1777–78. Joined British invasion of Georgia in 1779. Became commander of King's Carolina Rangers and fought at Savannah in October 1779. Returned to Augusta in June 1780 and defeated American attack in September 1780. Surrendered to besieging force on June 5, 1781; exchanged later in the year. Returned to East Florida in 1782, immigrated to the Bahamas in 1785, then returned to England in 1802. Established plantation on St. Vincent in 1806–8. Convicted of forgery in London in 1812 and served two years in prison. Returned in 1817 to St. Vincent, where he died.

JOHN BURGOYNE (1722–June 4, 1792) Son of an army captain. Educated at Westminster School. Entered army in 1740. Fought during the Seven Years' War in France, 1758–59, and in Portugal, 1762. Elected to Parliament in 1761. Promoted to major general in 1772. Wrote play *Maid of the Oaks* in 1774. Arrived in Boston in May 1775 and witnessed battle of Bunker Hill. Returned to England in December 1775 and was sent to Canada with reinforcements. Reached Quebec in May 1776 and served as second in command to Guy Carleton. Returned to England in December 1776 and won approval for his plan to attack the upper Hudson Valley by way of Lake Champlain. Arrived in Canada in May 1777 and began invasion in June. After defeats at Bennington, Freeman's Farm, and Bemis Heights, surrendered his army to Horatio Gates at Saratoga on October 17, 1775. Returned to England on parole in May 1778 and defended himself against criticism in Parliament and the press. Wrote libretto for comic opera *The Lord of the Manor* (1780). Served as commander in chief in Ireland, 1782–83. Wrote successful comedy *The Heiress* (1786). Died in London.

ROBERT CAMPBELL (d. December 27, 1781) Served as ensign in the Virginia militia in 1780.

LANDON CARTER (August 18, 1710–December 22, 1778) Son of Robert "King" Carter, a wealthy Virginia landowner. Educated in England. Inherited several plantations on death of father in 1732. Served as justice of the peace, 1734–78. Built large mansion at Sabine Hall, his plantation in Richmond County. Served in Virginia assembly, 1752–68. Opposed Stamp Act and wrote numerous newspaper articles in defense of American rights. Elected to American Philosophical Society in 1769. Kept diary from 1752 to 1778.

GEORGE ROGERS CLARK (November 19, 1752–February 13, 1818) Born near Charlottesville, Virginia, the son of a farmer; older brother of West explorer William Clark. Made surveys in Ohio and Kentucky valleys. Served as captain in Virginia militia in Dunmore's War against the Shawnee, 1774. Settled in Kentucky. Promoted to major in 1776 and lieutenant colonel in 1778. Helped defend Kentucky settlements against Indian raids and in 1777 persuaded Virginia authorities to mount expedition into the Illinois territory. Captured British posts at Kaskaskia, Cahokia, and Vincennes in July 1778. After the British recaptured Vincennes in December 1778, Clark led expedition from

Kaskaskia to Vincennes in February 1779 and regained the post, securing American control over the territory. Continued to serve in the Northwest for the remainder of the war, and commanded expeditions that burned several Shawnee villages in Ohio in 1780 and 1782. Lost support of Virginia authorities after unsuccessful expedition against Wabash Indians in 1786. Became involved in French plans to seize Louisiana from the Spanish in 1793 and 1798. Suffered stroke in 1809 and went to live with sister in Locust Grove, Kentucky, where he died.

CHARLES CORNWALLIS (December 31, 1738–October 5, 1805) Born in London, the eldest son of the first Earl Cornwallis. Entered army in 1757, and served in Germany during the Seven Years' War. Became second Earl Cornwallis in 1762 and was promoted to major general in 1775. Arrived in America in 1776 and commanded troops at Long Island, Kips Bay, the capture of Fort Washington, the New Jersey campaign, Brandywine, Germantown, and Monmouth. Commanded British forces in the South from June 1780 until his surrender at Yorktown on October 19, 1781. Served as governor general of India from 1786 to 1793. Defeated Tipu Sultan in 1792. Made Marquis Cornwall in 1792. Served as viceroy of Ireland, 1798 to 1801; defeated French invasion and Irish uprising in 1798, then resigned when George III refused Roman Catholic emancipation. Negotiated peace of Amiens with French, 1801–2. Returned to India in 1805, where he died at Ghazipore.

NICHOLAS CRESSWELL (December 1750–July 14, 1804) Born in Derbyshire, England, the son of a landowner and sheep farmer. Arrived in Virginia in May 1774 intending to buy western land. Wrote letters in March 1775 condemning American resistance to British authority that were intercepted and given to the Alexandria Committee of Safety. Threatened with imprisonment in October 1775 but was released when a friend posted bond. Went to New York City in early September 1776 but was unable to reach British forces. Returned to Virginia and remained free on parole. Along with a Scottish friend, seized boat at pistol point in May 1777 and escaped to a British warship in Chesapeake Bay. Reached England in August 1777 and returned to Derbyshire. Died at Wickworth.

J. HECTOR ST. JOHN CRÈVECOEUR (January 31, 1735–November 12, 1813) Born Michel Guillaume Jean de Crèvecoeur in Caen, France. Immigrated to Canada in 1755. Served as an officer and mapmaker with the French army under Montcalm during the French and Indian War, exploring the Ohio River and Great Lakes region. Immigrated to New York in 1759 and became a British subject in 1765. Settled on farm near Goshen, New York, in 1769. Sympathized with Loyalists during Revolution. Went to New York City in 1779, where he was imprisoned for two months by the British as a suspected American spy. Returned to Europe in 1780. Published collection of essays *Letters from an American Farmer* in London in 1782. Returned to New York in November 1783 and learned that his house had been burned, his wife was dead, and his two younger children were living in Boston. Served as French consul for New York, New Jersey, and Connecticut, 1783–90. Returned to France in 1790. Died at Sarcelles.

OLIVER DE LANCEY (1749–1822) Born in New York City, the son of Oliver
De Lancey, a wealthy merchant, and brother of Stephen De Lancey. Educated in England. Entered British army in 1766. Promoted to captain in 1773.
Served in siege of Boston and fought at Long Island, White Plains, and Monmouth. Promoted to major in 1778, and served as deputy quartermaster
general during the Charleston campaign in 1780. Succeeded John André as
adjutant general to Sir Henry Clinton in fall of 1780 and directed British secret service efforts during the 1781 mutiny of the Pennsylvania Continental
regiments. Promoted to lieutenant colonel in 1781. Went to England after the
war and served in Parliament, 1796–1802. Promoted to general in 1812. Died
in Edinburgh.

STEPHEN DE LANCEY (1748–1798) Son of the elder Oliver De Lancey, a
wealthy merchant in New York City, and brother of the younger Oliver De
Lancey. Educated in Europe. Practiced law in New York. Commissioned as
lieutenant colonel in 1776 and appointed commander of battalion in De
Lancey's Brigade, Loyalist formation raised by his father. Went to Georgia
with British expedition in December 1778 and served there until 1781, when
he returned to New York. Commanded battalion of New Jersey Loyalists on
Long Island. Immigrated to Nova Scotia in 1783 and became member of its
assembly. Appointed chief justice of the Bahamas in 1789 and governor of
Tobago in 1796. Died in Portsmouth, New Hampshire, after falling ill while
at sea.

EBENEZER DENNY (1761–1822) Born in Carlisle, Pennsylvania. Commissioned
as ensign in Pennsylvania Continental regiment in 1781. Fought at Green
Spring, July 6, and in siege of Yorktown. Remained in army after the war and
served in the Northwest Territory as aide to Josiah Harmar and Arthur St.
Clair. Survived defeat of St. Clair expedition on November 4, 1791, and carried news of the disaster to President Washington. Resigned from the army
in 1794 and settled near Pittsburgh. Elected the first mayor of Pittsburgh
when the town was incorporated in 1816.

JOHN DICKINSON (November 8, 1732–February 14, 1808) Born on family estate in Talbot County, Maryland. Family moved to Kent County, Delaware,
in 1740. Studied law in London, 1753–57, and was admitted to Pennsylvania
bar in 1760. Served in Delaware assembly, 1760–61, and Pennsylvania assembly, 1762–65 and 1770–76. Delegate to Stamp Act Congress, 1765. Published
Letters from a Farmer in Pennsylvania (1767–68), a defense of colonial rights.
Delegate to First Continental Congress, 1774, and Second Continental Congress, 1775–76. Voted against declaring independence; drafted Articles of
Confederation in 1776. Delegate to Congress from Delaware, 1779–80. Served
as president of Delaware, 1781–82, and as president of the Pennsylvania
supreme executive council, 1782–85. Delegate from Delaware to the Constitutional Convention in 1787. Died in Wilmington, Delaware.

WILLIAM DIGBY Entered British army as ensign in 1770. Promoted to lieutenant in 1773. Landed in Canada on June 1, 1776. Fought at Trois Rivières,
June 8, 1776, and served in advance on Crown Point in October 1776. Spent
winter in Canada before moving south with Burgoyne expedition in June

1777. Surrendered with Burgoyne's army at Saratoga on October 17, 1777. Retired from army in 1786.

ELIPHALET DYER (September 14, 1721–May 13, 1807) Born Windham, Connecticut, the son of an army officer. Graduated from Yale College in 1740 and was admitted to the bar in 1746. Served as delegate to the general assembly, 1747–62, and on governor's council, 1762–84. Delegate to the Stamp Act Congress, 1765. Appointed associate judge of the superior court of Connecticut in 1766 and served until 1789, when he was named chief judge. Served as delegate to Continental Congress, 1774–79 and 1782–83. Retired from superior court in 1793 to farm in Windham, where he died.

WILLIAM FEILDING (d. January 11, 1789) Son of a Royal Navy officer. Fought at Bunker Hill as lieutenant in the Royal Marines and remained in Boston until the British evacuation in March 1776. Promoted to captain in 1776. Served on board several warships and in New York City, June 1781–August 1783. Died at Portsmouth, Hampshire, England.

JABEZ FITCH (1737–1812) Born in Norwich, Connecticut. Served in French and Indian War. Joined the Sons of Liberty in 1766. Appointed first lieutenant in Connecticut militia in June 1775 and later joined Continental army. Served in siege of Boston. Captured at battle of Long Island on August 27, 1776. Exchanged in December 1777. Served as militia captain in 1779, but saw no further action during the war. Kept diary for over 50 years. Died in Vermont.

PHILIP VICKERS FITHIAN (1747–October 8, 1776) Born in Greenwich, New Jersey. Graduated from College of New Jersey (now Princeton) in 1772. Worked as tutor to children of wealthy Virginia planter Robert Carter, 1773–74. Received A.M. degree from College of New Jersey in 1775 and was ordained as a Presbyterian minister. Appointed in June 1776 as chaplain to the New Jersey militia serving with the Continental army. Died of dysentery in New York.

BENJAMIN FRANKLIN (January 17, 1706–April 17, 1790) Born in Boston, the son of a candle and soap maker. Learned printing trade in Boston and London. Settled in Philadelphia in 1726 and bought *The Pennsylvania Gazette* in 1729. Published *Poor Richard's Almanack*, 1732–57. Founded American Philosophical Society in 1743. Member of the Pennsylvania assembly, 1751–64. Proposed plan for colonial union in 1754. Elected to the Royal Society in 1756 after conducting series of experiments with electricity. Represented Pennsylvania assembly in London, 1757–62. Went to London as Pennsylvania agent in 1764, and by 1770 was also representing Georgia, New Jersey, and Massachusetts. Returned to Philadelphia on May 5, 1775. Served as delegate to the Second Continental Congress, 1775–76. Appointed diplomatic commissioner by Congress on September 26, 1776, and arrived in France on December 3, 1776. Negotiated treaty of alliance with France, 1778, and peace treaty with Britain, 1782. Returned to United States in September 1785. Served as president of the Pennsylvania supreme executive council, 1785–88. Delegate to the Constitutional Convention, 1788. Died in Philadelphia.

THOMAS GAGE (1721–April 2, 1787) Born Firle, Sussex, England, son of an Irish peer. Commissioned as a lieutenant in 1741. Served in Flanders, 1747–48. Sent to America in 1754, where he fought in French and Indian War and served with George Washington. Wounded during Braddock's defeat on the Monongahela in 1755, then saw action at Oswego, Fort Ticonderoga, and Montreal. Served as military governor of Montreal, 1760–63. Promoted to major general in 1761. Moved to New York after his appointment as commander in chief of North America in 1763. Traveled to England on leave in 1773, then returned in May 1774 after he was named governor of Massachusetts. Sent troops to seize supplies at Concord on April 19, 1775, precipitating outbreak of war. Succeeded as commander in chief by William Howe on October 10, 1775. Returned to England in November 1775. Died at Portland, Dorset.

JOHN GLOVER (November 5, 1732–January 30, 1797) Born in Salem, Massachusetts. Moved to Marblehead, where he worked as a shoemaker, fishmonger, and merchant. Commissioned as colonel by Massachusetts provincial congress on May 19, 1775, and made commander of regiment of Marblehead boatmen. Equipped and led flotilla of small vessels during siege of Boston. Commanded boats that evacuated Continental army from Brooklyn Heights on August 29–30, 1776. Fought at Pell's Point and White Plains, October 1776, then commanded boats that transported Continental army across the Delaware on December 25, 1776, for attack on Trenton. Promoted to brigadier general in February 1777 and served in the Saratoga campaign, in the unsuccessful attack on Newport, Rhode Island, in 1778, and in the Hudson Highlands of New York from 1779 until 1782. Retired from the army in 1782 due to poor health. Member of the Massachusetts ratifying convention, 1788, and the Massachusetts legislature, 1788–89. Died in Marblehead.

ROBERT GRAY A South Carolina Loyalist, Gray was commissioned as a colonel in the provincial (Loyalist) forces following the British occupation of the state in 1780. He settled in Nova Scotia after the war.

NATHANAEL GREENE (August 7, 1742–June 19, 1786) Born in Warwick, Rhode Island. Worked in family iron foundry and operated a forge. Appointed brigadier general of Rhode Island militia in May 1775, he became a brigadier general in the Continental army on June 22, 1775, and a major general on August 9, 1776. Commanded troops at the siege of Boston, the New York and New Jersey campaigns, Brandywine, Germantown, Monmouth, and Newport. Served as quartermaster general of the Continental army, February 1778–August 1780. Appointed by George Washington as commander of the Southern Department on October 14, 1780, Greene successfully led American forces in the Carolinas during the 1781 campaign and remained in South Carolina until after the British evacuation of Charleston in December 1782. Returned to Rhode Island in 1783, then moved to an estate outside of Savannah, Georgia, where he died.

ALEXANDER HAMILTON (January 11, 1755–July 12, 1804) Born on Nevis, in the West Indies. Moved to St. Croix in 1765 and worked as clerk for trading firm, 1766–72. Immigrated to America in 1772 and entered King's College (now

Columbia) in 1773. Appointed captain of artillery by New York provincial congress in March 1776. Fought at Long Island, Harlem Heights, White Plains, Trenton, and Princeton. Became aide to George Washington on March 1, 1777, and served on his staff with rank of lieutenant colonel until April 1781. Commanded light infantry battalion at Yorktown. Admitted to New York bar in 1782. Served as delegate to the Continental Congress, 1782–83, and in New York assembly, 1786–87. Delegate to the Constitutional Convention, 1787, and the New York ratifying convention, 1788; wrote most of the *Federalist* essays advocating ratification of the Constitution, 1787–88. Appointed secretary of the treasury by George Washington in September 1789 and served until January 1795; continued to advise Washington after returning to law practice in New York City. Appointed major general and inspector general of the army in July 1798 during Franco-American crisis and served until June 1800. Mortally wounded in duel with Vice President Aaron Burr. Died in New York City.

JOSEPH HODGKINS (1743–1829) Born Ipswich, Massachusetts. Worked as a shoemaker. Elected lieutenant in Massachusetts militia in January 1775. Fought at Bunker Hill and served throughout the siege of Boston. Joined Continental army in January 1776. Fought at Long Island, Harlem Heights, and in the Trenton campaign. Reenlisted in 1777 and became captain in brigade commanded by John Glover. Fought in the Saratoga campaign and served at Valley Forge and in the unsuccessful attack on Newport in 1778. Resigned his commission in June 1779. Served in Massachusetts legislature, 1810–16.

SARAH HODGKINS (1750–March 13, 1803) Born Sarah Perkins. Married Joseph Hodgkins on December 3, 1772. Stayed in Ipswich, Massachusetts, with her children and her stepdaughter during the war.

THOMAS JEFFERSON (April 13, 1743–July 4, 1826) Born in Goochland (now Albemarle) County, Virginia, son of a landowner and surveyor. Educated at College of William and Mary. Admitted to the Virginia bar in 1767. Served in Virginia assembly, 1769–74. Published *A Summary View of the Rights of British America* in 1774. Delegate to the Continental Congress, 1775–76; drafted the Declaration of Independence. Served in Virginia assembly, 1776–79, and as governor of Virginia, 1779–81. Delegate to the Continental Congress, 1783–84. Served as American minister to France, 1785–89. Appointed secretary of state by George Washington and held office from March 1790 until December 1793. Vice President of the United States, 1797–1801. President of the United States, 1801–9. Founded University of Virginia. Died at Monticello, his estate near Charlottesville.

JOHN PAUL JONES (July 6, 1747–July 18, 1792) Born John Paul in Kirkcudbrightshire, Scotland, the son of a gardener. Apprenticed to shipowner at age 12. Served on merchant ships and slavers before becoming commander of merchant ships in the West Indian trade in 1769. Fled to Fredericksburg, Virginia, in 1773 after killing the leader of a mutiny on board his ship and added "Jones" to his name. Commissioned a lieutenant in the Continental navy in December 1775. Served on the *Alfred* before being promoted to captain and given command of the *Providence* in August 1776. Made successful cruises against British merchant shipping in the West Indies and off Nova Scotia. Given command of the sloop *Ranger* in June 1777 and sailed for France in November 1777. Raided English and Scottish coastal towns and captured first warship ever to surrender to an American vessel during cruise made from France, April–May 1778. Sailed from France on the *Bonhomme Richard* on August 14, 1779, and captured British frigate *Serapis* in the North Sea before reaching Holland on October 3. Returned to France in February 1780 and to the United States in February 1781. Held no further command at sea for remainder of war. Went to France and Denmark after the war to secure prize money owed to the United States. Served as rear admiral in Russian navy, 1788–89, during war against Turkey. Died in Paris.

HENRY LAURENS (March 6, 1724–December 8, 1792) Born in Charleston, South Carolina, the son of a saddler. Became successful Charleston merchant and landowner. Served in South Carolina assembly, 1757–64 and 1765–74, and in the South Carolina provincial congress, 1775–76. Helped organize defense of Charleston against British attack in 1776. Delegate to the Continental Congress, 1777–80, and served as its president from November 1777 to December 1778. Appointed American minister to Holland, but was captured at sea en route to Europe in September 1780 and imprisoned in the Tower of London until December 1781. Exchanged for Lord Cornwallis in April 1782. Signed preliminary treaty of peace with Britain on November 30, 1782. Returned to United States in 1784. Died on his plantation near Charleston.

JOHN LAURENS (October 28, 1754–August 27, 1782) Born in Charleston, South Carolina, the son of Henry Laurens. Began study of law in London in 1772. Returned to America in 1777 and became volunteer aide to George Washington. Served at Brandywine and was wounded at Germantown and Monmouth. Challenged and wounded Major General Charles Lee in a duel fought on December 23, 1778, after Lee insulted George Washington. Commissioned as a lieutenant colonel in the Continental army in March 1779. Went to South Carolina after the British invaded the state and fought at Savannah in October 1779. Taken prisoner in the surrender at Charleston in May 1780, but was paroled and exchanged. Went to France with Thomas Paine in 1781 on successful mission to secure additional French aid. Returned to the United States and fought at Yorktown. Killed in skirmish at Combahee Ferry, South Carolina.

JAMES MCHENRY (November 16, 1753–May 3, 1816) Born in Ballymena, Country Antrim, Ireland. Educated in Dublin. Immigrated in 1771 to Philadelphia, where he studied medicine under Benjamin Rush. Joined medical staff of military hospital in Cambridge, Massachusetts, in January 1776. Appointed surgeon of Pennsylvania Continental regiment in August 1776. Captured at Fort Washington on November 16, 1776. Paroled in January 1777 and exchanged in March 1778. Appointed secretary to George Washington in May 1778. Joined staff of the Marquis de Lafayette in August 1780. Served in Maryland senate, 1781–86, and in Congress, 1783–86. Delegate to the Constitutional Convention, 1787, and to the Maryland ratifying convention, 1788. Served in Maryland assembly, 1788–91, and in the Maryland senate, 1791–96.

Appointed secretary of war by Washington in January 1796. Retained post during the administration of John Adams until May 1800, when Adams demanded his resignation. Retired to his estate near Baltimore, where he died.

FREDERICK MACKENZIE (d. 1824) Son of a Dublin merchant. Arrived in Boston in 1774 as lieutenant in British army. Promoted to captain in fall of 1775 and to major in August 1780. Served in siege of Boston, New York campaign, and expedition against Newport, Rhode Island, in December 1776. Volumes of his diary record his service in Rhode Island, 1777–78, and New York City, 1781. Promoted to lieutenant colonel in 1787. Died in Teignmouth, Devonshire, England.

THOMAS MIFFLIN (January 10, 1744–January 20, 1800) Born in Philadelphia, the son of a merchant. Graduated from College of Philadelphia (now University of Pennsylvania) in 1760. Became a successful merchant in partnership with his brother. Served in Pennsylvania assembly, 1772–75, and in the First and Second Continental Congress, 1774–75. Commissioned as major in Continental army in May 1775. Appointed as aide to George Washington on June 23, 1775, and as quartermaster general on August 14, 1775. Promoted to colonel, December 22, 1775; brigadier general, May 16, 1776; and major general, February 19, 1777. Resigned as quartermaster general on November 7, 1777. Served on Board of War from November 18, 1777, to April 18, 1778. Supported replacing George Washington with Horatio Gates as commander in chief. Resigned from army on August 17, 1778 (accepted February 25, 1779). Served in Pennsylvania assembly, 1778–79, and in Congress, 1782–84; president of Congress from December 1783 to June 1784. Member of Constitutional Convention in 1787. Served three terms as governor of Pennsylvania, 1790–99. Fled Philadelphia in 1799 to escape a creditor. Died in Lancaster, Pennsylvania.

DANIEL MORGAN (1736–July 6, 1802) Born in Hunterdon County, New Jersey, the son of an ironworker. Moved to Shenandoah Valley of Virginia at age 17. Served as civilian teamster during French and Indian War, participating in Braddock's expedition. Became officer in Virginia militia in 1758. Began farming near Winchester in 1762. Fought Indians as militia officer during Pontiac's Rebellion, 1763–64, and Dunmore's War, 1774. Commissioned as captain in June 1775 and led company of Virginia riflemen to Boston. Served under Benedict Arnold in the invasion of Canada and was captured during the attack on Quebec on December 31, 1775. Exchanged in autumn of 1776 and commissioned as colonel in the Continental army. Commanded corps of riflemen in battles of Freeman's Farm and Bemis Heights during the Saratoga campaign. Resigned his commission in July 1779; returned to service as brigadier general in North Carolina in October 1780. Defeated British in battle of Cowpens, South Carolina, on January 17, 1781. Resigned for reasons of health in February 1781. Commanded Virginia militia during the Whiskey Rebellion in 1794. Served one term in the House of Representatives as a Federalist, 1797–99. Died in Winchester.

ROBERT MORTON (1760–August 17, 1786) The son of a Quaker merchant, Morton remained in Philadelphia during the British occupation of 1777–78.

WILLIAM MOULTRIE (December 4, 1730–September 27, 1805) Born in
Charleston, South Carolina, the son of a physician. Served almost continuously in provincial assembly between 1752 and 1771. Fought in Cherokee War
as militia captain. Elected colonel of a South Carolina regiment on June 17,
1775. Built fort made of palmetto logs and sand on Sullivan's Island in
Charleston harbor, and successfully defended it against naval attack on June
28, 1776, ending British attempt to invade South Carolina. Appointed
brigadier general in Continental army in September 1776. Defeated British at
Beaufort, South Carolina, on February 3, 1779. Captured when Charleston
garrison surrendered on May 12, 1780. Exchanged in February 1782 and promoted to major general in October 1782. Served as governor, 1785–87 and
1794–96, in the state senate, and in the South Carolina ratifying convention,
1788. Died in Charleston.

PETER OLIVER (March 26, 1713–October 1791) Born Boston, Massachusetts.
Graduated from Harvard in 1730. Served as justice of the common pleas
court of Plymouth County, 1747–56, and as justice of the Massachusetts superior court, 1756–71. Presided over trial of British soldiers charged in the
Boston Massacre. Served as chief justice of the superior court, 1771–75; was
threatened with impeachment by the legislature for accepting grants from the
crown in addition to his salary. Moved with family in 1774 to Middleborough,
Massachusetts, where he established an iron works. Stayed in Boston during
the siege of 1775–76 and sailed to Halifax with the British army in March 1776.
Settled in Birmingham, England. House in Middleborough was burned in
1782. Published *A Scripture Lexicon* in 1787. Died in Birmingham.

THOMAS PAINE (January 29, 1737–June 8, 1809) Born in Thetford, Norfolk,
England, the son of a corsetmaker. Worked in the excise service, 1762–65 and
1768–74. Immigrated to Philadelphia in November 1774 and began writing for
newspapers and magazines. Published widely read pamphlet *Common Sense*,
advocating independence from Britain and republican government, on January 10, 1776. Served with Pennsylvania militia in New Jersey, July–December
1776. Published pamphlet *The American Crisis, Number I* on December 19,
1776. Wrote a further 12 numbers of *The Crisis*, 1777–83, along with many
other political articles and pamphlets. Went to France with John Laurens in
1781 on mission to secure additional French aid. Returned to England in 1787
to work on his design for a wrought-iron bridge. Published *The Rights of
Man* (1791–92), a defense of the French Revolution. Served as a member of
the French National Convention, 1792–93. Arrested by the Jacobins and imprisoned in Paris, December 1793–November 1794. Published *The Age of
Reason* (1794–95), a deistic attack on Biblical religion. Returned to the
United States in 1802 and continued to write for the press until his death in
New York City.

JOHN PEEBLES (September 11, 1739–1823) Born Irvine, Ayrshire, Scotland.
Served as surgeon's mate with British army in North America, 1758–63. Commissioned as ensign in 1763 and promoted to lieutenant in 1770. Returned to
America; fought at White Plains, Fort Washington, Brandywine, Germantown, Monmouth, Newport, and in the Hudson Highlands. Promoted to

captain in 1779. Served in Charleston campaign in 1780, then returned to New York. Sold his commission in 1782 and returned to Scotland, where he later became surveyor of customs at Irvine.

FRANCIS RAWDON (December 9, 1754–November 28, 1826) Son of an Irish aristocrat. Educated at Harrow. Entered the army in 1771 and was sent to America in 1773. Fought at Bunker Hill, Long Island, White Plains, Fort Washington, and the assault on Fort Clinton in the Hudson Highlands in October 1777. Raised Loyalist regiment. Promoted to lieutenant colonel, June 15, 1778, and named adjutant general to Sir Henry Clinton. Fought at Monmouth. Resigned as adjutant general in September 1779. Went to South Carolina in April 1780 and served in siege of Charleston. Fought at Camden and assumed command of British forces in South Carolina and Georgia in April 1781. Defeated Americans under Nathanael Greene at Hobkirk's Hill, on April 25, 1781, but was forced to evacuate several posts in South Carolina. Resigned command due to ill health and sailed for England in July 1781. Added "Hastings" to his name in 1790. Promoted to general in 1803. Served as governor general of India, 1813–22, and governor of Malta, 1822–24. Died at sea off Naples.

ANNA RAWLE (October 30, 1757–July 1828) Born in Philadelphia to a Quaker family. Educated at Quaker girls' school run by Anthony Benezet, where her friends included Sarah Wister. Stepfather Samuel Shoemaker became a well-known Philadelphia Loyalist during the Revolution. Married John Clifford, a Philadelphia merchant, on September 16, 1783.

JOSEPH REED (August 27, 1741–March 5, 1785) Born Trenton, New Jersey, son of a successful merchant. Graduated from the College of New Jersey (now Princeton) in 1757 and was admitted to the bar in 1763. Continued legal studies for two years in London, then established legal practice in Philadelphia in 1770. Served as secretary to George Washington, July 1775–May 1776, with rank of lieutenant colonel. Appointed adjutant general of the Continental army in June 1776 and promoted to colonel. Resigned from army in January 1777, but served as volunteer aide to George Washington at Brandywine, Germantown, and Monmouth. Delegate to the Continental Congress, 1777–78. Declined and exposed offer of £10,000 bribe from British peace commissioner in 1778. Served as president of the Pennsylvania supreme executive council, 1778–81. Died in Philadelphia.

ENOS REEVES (d. 1807) Enlisted in Continental army as private. Commissioned ensign in 1777 and promoted to lieutenant in 1778; served in Pennsylvania Continental regiments. Moved to South Carolina after the war.

PAUL REVERE (January 1, 1735–May 10, 1818). Born Boston, Massachusetts, the son of a metalsmith. Apprenticed at father's shop. Served for six months as lieutenant of artillery in 1756 during French and Indian War, then returned to Boston. Worked as metalsmith, engraver, and dentist. Joined Sons of Liberty. Engraved political drawings, including a widely circulated print of the Boston Massacre. Helped plan and participated in Boston Tea Party in December 1773. Served as courier for Boston Committee of Correspondence and the Massachusetts Committee of Safety. Warned of British troops marching toward Concord on night of April 18, 1775. Commissioned to design seals and money for the colonies. Supervised the manufacture of gunpowder at a mill in Canton, Massachusetts. Opened foundry in 1788 and established first sheet-copper mill in America in 1801. Retired in 1811; died in Boston.

JAMES ROBERTSON (June 29, 1717–March 4, 1788) Born in Fifeshire, Scotland, the son of a landowner. Commissioned as second lieutenant in the Royal Marines in 1739. Served in the Caribbean, 1740–42, and in the Scottish Highlands during the Jacobite uprising, 1745–46. Purchased captain's commission in the British army in 1749. Became deputy quartermaster general of British forces in North America in 1756 and held that position through the French and Indian War. Served as barrackmaster general for North America from 1765 to June 1776. Commanded brigade that landed on Staten Island in July 1776 and later fought on Long Island. Appointed military commander of New York City on September 16, 1776. Went to England on leave in November 1778. Commissioned as civil governor of New York on May 11, 1779, but did not return and take office until March 21, 1780. Gave up office and sailed for England in April 1783. Died in London.

THOMAS RODNEY (June 4, 1744–January 2, 1811) Born on family plantation in Kent County, Delaware. Became farm manager for older brother Caesar in 1762. Appointed justice of the peace in 1770. Kept shop in Philadelphia, 1772–74. Elected to assembly and appointed as captain of militia in 1775. Served with militia during Trenton campaign and at Princeton, December 1776–January 1777, then returned to Delaware. Delegate to the Continental Congress, 1781–83 and 1785–87. Appointed associate justice of the Delaware supreme court in 1802. Resigned in 1803 when Thomas Jefferson named him United States judge for Mississippi Territory. Died in Natchez.

ISAAC SENTER (1753–1799) Born in New Hampshire. Moved to Newport, Rhode Island, and studied medicine. Volunteered as surgeon for Benedict Arnold's expedition to Quebec in 1775. Appointed surgeon general of Rhode Island militia in 1779. Established practice in Pawtucket, then moved to Newport, where he died.

AMBROSE SERLE (August 30, 1742–August 1, 1812) Served as under secretary to Lord Dartmouth, secretary of state for the American colonies, 1772–75. Published pamphlet *Americans against Liberty* in 1775. Appointed solicitor and clerk of reports for the Board of Trade in January 1776. Arrived at New York on July 12, 1776, to serve as private secretary to Admiral Lord Howe, who had been appointed as a peace commissioner for the colonies. Wrote articles for Loyalist *New-York Gazette* from September 1776 to July 1777, and became acquainted with prominent Loyalists in New York and Philadelphia. Returned to England on July 22, 1778. Published several works on Christian theology. Appointed a commissioner for the care and exchange of prisoners of war in 1795, and was reappointed in 1803 and 1809.

SAMUEL SHAW (October 2, 1754–May 30, 1794) Born in Boston, Massachusetts, the son of a successful merchant. Joined Continental army artillery as second lieutenant in 1775. Served in the siege of Boston, then fought at Trenton, Princeton, Brandywine, Germantown, and Monmouth. Promoted to first lieutenant on January 1, 1777, and to captain on April 12, 1780. Served as aide to Major General Henry Knox from June 1782 to November 1783. Assumed post of supercargo on the first American vessel to sail to Canton, the *Empress of China*, February 1784 to May 1785. Appointed by Congress as consul to China in 1786. Returned to Canton, and continued to travel between the United States and Asia. Contracted a liver disease in Bombay and died near the Cape of Good Hope.

HENRY STRACHEY (May 23, 1736–January 1, 1810) Born in Edinburgh. Worked as a clerk in the War Office before becoming private secretary to Robert Clive, governor of Bengal, in 1764. Returned to England in 1768 and was elected to the House of Commons, where he served until 1807. Appointed secretary in 1776 to the Howe Commission for restoring peace in the American colonies. Returned to England in 1778. Helped negotiate peace treaty between Great Britain and the United States in 1782. Made a baronet in 1801. Died in London.

BENJAMIN TRUMBULL (December 19, 1735–February 2, 1820) Born Hebron, Connecticut. Graduated Yale College in 1759. Became pastor of the Congregational Church of North Haven, Connecticut, in 1760 and held the position until his death. Served as chaplain of Connecticut militia brigade, June 24–December 25, 1776. Published numerous books on political, historical, and theological subjects, including *A General History of the United States of America* (1810) and the two-volume *A Complete History of Connecticut . . . to the Year 1764* (1818).

ST. GEORGE TUCKER (July 10, 1752–November 10, 1827) Born in Port Royal, Bermuda, the son of a plantation owner and trader. Went to Virginia in 1771 and graduated from College of William and Mary in 1772. Studied law with George Wythe and was admitted to Virginia bar in 1774. Returned to Bermuda in 1775 and helped smuggle gunpowder to America, then returned to Virginia in 1777. Joined Virginia militia in 1779; with rank of colonel, fought in 1781 at Guilford Courthouse and in the siege of Yorktown. Appointed judge of the Virginia general court in 1788. Succeeded Wythe as professor of law at College of William and Mary. Published pamphlet *A Dissertation on Slavery: With a Proposal for the Gradual Abolition of It, in the State of Virginia* in 1796 and a five-volume annotated edition of Blackstone's *Commentaries* in 1803; also wrote poetry. Resigned from college in 1804 after his appointment to the Virginia court of appeals. Named U.S. district judge for Virginia by James Madison in 1813. Retired in 1825. Died in Warminster, Virginia.

ALBIGENCE WALDO (February 27, 1750–January 29, 1794) Born in Pomfret, Connecticut. Apprenticed to surgeon in Canterbury. Served as surgeon with Connecticut militia, July–September 1775. Appointed surgeon of Connecticut Continental regiment in January 1777 and served until October 1779, when he resigned because of ill health. Settled in Windham County, Connecticut, where he died.

GEORGE WASHINGTON (February 22, 1732–December 14, 1799) Born on family plantation in Westmoreland County, Virginia. Worked as surveyor in western Virginia. Appointed major in Virginia militia in 1752 and traveled to Ohio in 1753 to deliver British ultimatum to the French. Commanded Virginia militia in first skirmish of the French and Indian War, May 28, 1754. Served as aide to General Edward Braddock during British expedition against Fort Duquesne at the Forks of the Ohio in 1755 and helped command retreat after Braddock's defeat near the Monongahela River. Commissioned as colonel and commander of Virginia militia in August 1755. Served with successful expedition against Fort Duquesne in 1758, then resigned his commission. Elected to Virginia assembly in 1758 and served until 1774. Inherited Mount Vernon estate in 1761. Delegate to First Continental Congress, 1774, and Second Continental Congress. Chosen by Congress to be general and commander in chief of the Continental army on June 15, 1775, and served until December 23, 1783, when he resigned his commission and returned to Mount Vernon. Attended Constitutional Convention in 1787 and was unanimously elected as its president. Elected first president of the United States in 1789 and served until 1797, twice receiving the unanimous vote of the electors. Commissioned lieutenant general and commander in chief of the army on July 4, 1798, during crisis in relations with France. Died at Mount Vernon.

MARTHA WASHINGTON (June 2, 1731–May 22, 1802) Born Martha Dandridge in New Kent County, Virginia, on a plantation near Williamsburg. Married wealthy planter Daniel Parke Custis in 1749 and moved to estate on the Pamunkey River in New Kent County. Widowed in July 1757. Married George Washington on January 6, 1759, and moved with her two children to Washington's Mount Vernon estate. Spent winters with Continental army at Cambridge, Morristown, Valley Forge, and Newburgh. Lived in New York and then Philadelphia during Washington's presidency. Died at Mount Vernon.

SAMUEL BLACHEY WEBB (December 13, 1753–December 3, 1807) Born Wethersfield, Connecticut, son of a merchant; after father's death in 1761, mother married Silas Deane. Became supercargo in West Indies trade in 1774. Commissioned as lieutenant in Connecticut militia on May 1, 1775. Fought at Bunker Hill. Promoted to major July 22, 1775, and appointed aide to Major General Israel Putnam. Became aide to George Washington on June 21, 1776, with rank of lieutenant colonel. Served at Long Island and Princeton, and was wounded at White Plains and Trenton. Promoted to colonel in January 1777 and given command of a Continental regiment. Captured during raid on Long Island, December 10, 1777; exchanged a year later. Commanded regiment until 1783. Moved in 1787 to Claverack, New York, where he died.

OTHO HOLLAND WILLIAMS (March 1749–July 15, 1794) Born in Prince Georges County, Maryland, son of Welsh immigrants. Worked in Baltimore county clerk's office, 1767–74. Commissioned as first lieutenant in June 1775; promoted to major in June 1776. Wounded and captured at Fort Washington on November 16, 1776. Exchanged in January 1778. Commanded a Maryland Continental regiment during Monmouth campaign. Became assistant adjutant general to Horatio Gates in summer of 1780. Fought at Camden. Made adjutant general by Nathanael Greene and commanded a brigade at Guilford Courthouse and Eutaw Springs. Promoted to brigadier general in May 1782.

Retired from army in 1783 and subsequently served as collector of customs at Baltimore. Died at Miller's Town, Virginia.

SARAH WISTER (July 20, 1761–April 21, 1804) Born in Philadelphia, the daughter of a Quaker wine merchant. Educated at Quaker girls' school run by Anthony Benezet, where her friends included Anna Rawle. Lived with family at Foulke mansion in Gwynedd, Pennsylvania, from fall of 1776 until July 1778, when they returned to Philadelphia; kept journal from September 20, 1777, to June 20, 1778. Moved to family house in Germantown, Pennsylvania, in 1787, where she cared for her mother and wrote religious poems and a devotional journal. Died in Germantown.

WILLIAM WOODFORD (October 6, 1734–November 13, 1780) Born in Caroline County, Virginia, son of an army officer. Served as Virginia militia officer during French and Indian War. Appointed colonel in Virginia militia in August 1775. Successfully defended Hampton, Virginia, against British raid on October 25, 1775, and defeated British and Loyalist troops at Great Bridge, Virginia, on December 9, 1775, causing Lord Dunmore to evacuate Norfolk. Commissioned as a colonel in the Continental army in February 1776 and promoted to brigadier general in February 1777. Fought at Brandywine, Germantown, and Monmouth. Ordered to South Carolina in December 1779 and reached Charleston with Virginia brigade in April 1780. Captured in surrender of Charleston garrison on May 12, 1780, and sent as prisoner of war to New York City, where he died.

Note on the Texts

This volume collects 18th-century writing about the American Revolution, bringing together letters, narratives, memoranda, addresses, proclamations, newspaper articles, journal and diary entries, and excerpts from memoirs written by British and American participants and observers and dealing with events in the period between April 1775 and December 1783. Most of these documents were not written for publication, and most of them existed only in manuscript form during the lifetimes of the persons who wrote them. The texts presented in this volume are taken from the best printed sources available. In cases where there is only one printed source for a document, the text offered here comes from that source. Where there is more than one printed source for a document, the text printed in this volume is taken from the source that contains the fewest editorial alterations in the spelling, capitalization, paragraphing, and punctuation of the document.

This volume prints texts as they appear in the sources listed below, but with a few alterations in editorial procedure. The bracketed conjectural readings of editors, in cases where original manuscripts or printed texts were damaged or difficult to read, are accepted without brackets in this volume when those readings seem to be the only possible ones; but when they do not, or when the editor made no conjecture, the missing word or words are indicated by a bracketed two–em space, i.e., [   ]. In cases where an obvious misspelling was marked by earlier editors with "[*sic*]," the present volume omits the "[*sic*]" and corrects the slip of the pen. In some cases, obvious errors were not marked by earlier editors with "[*sic*]" but were printed and then followed by a bracketed correction; in these instances, this volume removes the brackets and accepts the editorial emendation. Bracketed editorial insertions used in the source texts to identify persons or places have been deleted in this volume. In cases where the source text printed superseded wordings from an earlier draft of a document within brackets, this volume deletes the bracketed material and presents the final text of the document. In instances where canceled, but still legible, words were printed in the source texts with lines through the deleted material, this volume omits the canceled words. If the source text used marks to indicate interlineated material in the original manuscript, this volume prints the interlineated material but deletes the indicative marks.

The following is a list of the documents included in this volume, in the order of their appearance, giving the source of each text.

Paul Revere: Memorandum on Events of April 18, 1775. Eldridge Henry Goss, *The Life of Colonel Paul Revere*, vol. 1 (Boston: J.G. Cupples, 1891), 213–29.

Frederick MacKenzie: Diary, April 18–21, 1775. *Diary of Frederick MacKenzie: Giving a Daily Narrative of his Military Service as an Officer in the Regiment of Royal Welch Fusiliers During the Years 1775–1781 in Massachusetts Rhode Island and New York*, vol. 1, ed. Allen French (Cambridge: Harvard University Press, 1930), 17–29. © 1930, 1958 by the President and Fellows of Harvard College. Reprinted by permission of Harvard University Press.

Thomas Gage to the Earl of Dartmouth, April 22, 1775. *The Correspondence of General Thomas Gage*, vol. 1, ed. Clarence Edwin Carter (New Haven: Yale University Press, 1931), 396–97. © 1931 by Yale University Press.

John Dickinson to Arthur Lee, April 29, 1775. Richard Henry Lee, *Life of Arthur Lee, LL.D.*, vol. 2 (Boston: Wells and Lilly, 1829), 307–11.

Peter Oliver: from "The Origin & Progress of the American Rebellion." *Peter Oliver's Origin & Progress of the American Rebellion: A Tory View*, ed. Douglass Adair and John A. Schutz (Stanford, California: Stanford University Press, 1967), 118–23. © 1961 by the Henry E. Huntington Library and Art Gallery. Reprinted with the permission of the Henry E. Huntington Library.

George Washington: Address to the Continental Congress, June 16, 1775. *George Washington: Writings*, ed. John Rhodehamel (New York: The Library of America, 1997), 167. Reprinted with permission of the University Press of Virginia.

John Adams to Abigail Adams, June 17, 1775. *The Book of Abigail and John: Selected Letters of the Adams Family, 1762–1784*, ed. L. H. Butterfield, Marc Friedlaender, and Mary–Jo Kline (Cambridge: Harvard University Press, 1975), 89–90. © 1963 by The Massachusetts Historical Society. Reprinted by permission of Harvard University Press.

Eliphalet Dyer to Joseph Trumbull, June 17, 1775. *Letters of Delegates to Congress, 1774–1789*, vol. 1, ed. Paul H. Smith (Washington: Government Printing Office, 1976), 499–500.

Samuel Blachley Webb to Joseph Webb, June 19, 1775. *Correspondence and Journals of Samuel Blachley Webb*, vol. 1, ed. Worthington C. Ford (New York: 1893), 64–65.

George Washington to Burwell Bassett, June 19, 1775. *George Washington: Writings*, ed. John Rhodehamel (New York: The Library of America, 1997), 169–70. Reprinted with permission of the University Press of Virginia.

John Adams to Abigail Adams, June 23, 1775. *The Book of Abigail and John: Selected Letters of the Adams Family, 1762–1784*, ed. L. H. Butterfield, Marc Friedlaender, and Mary–Jo Kline (Cambridge: Harvard University Press, 1975), 91–92. © 1963 by The Massachusetts Historical Society. Reprinted by permission of Harvard University Press.

Peter Oliver: from "The Origin & Progress of the American Rebellion." *Peter Oliver's Origin & Progress of the American Rebellion: A Tory View*, ed. Douglass Adair and John A. Schutz (Stanford, California: Stanford University Press, 1967), 123–32. © 1961 by the Henry E. Huntington Library and Art Gallery. Reprinted with the permission of the Henry E. Huntington Library.

Benjamin Franklin to William Strahan, July 5, 1775. *Benjamin Franklin: Writings*, ed. J. A. Leo Lemay (New York: The Library of America, 1987), 904.

The Continental Congress: Address to the Six Nations, July 13, 1775. *Journals of the Continental Congress 1774–1789*, vol. 2, ed. Worthington C. Ford (Washington: Government Printing Office, 1905), 178–83.

Abigail Adams to John Adams, July 16, 1775. *The Book of Abigail and John: Selected Letters of the Adams Family, 1762–1784*, ed. L. H. Butterfield, Marc Friedlaender, and Mary-Jo Kline (Cambridge: Harvard University Press, 1975), 99–104. © 1963 by The Massachusetts Historical Society. Reprinted by permission of Harvard University Press.

Lord Rawdon to the Earl of Huntingdon, August 3, 1775. *Report on the Manuscripts of the Late Reginald Rawdon Hastings, Esq.*, vol. 3, ed. Francis Bickley (London: His Majesty's Stationery Office, 1934), 154–59.

Ethan Allen: from "A narrative of Col. Ethan Allen's captivity." Ethan Allen, *A Narrative of Colonel Ethan Allen's Captivity, From the Time of his Being Taken by the British, near Montreal, on the 25th day of September, in the year 1775, to the Time of his Exchange, on the 6th Day of May, 1778* (Boston: Draper and Folsom, 1779), 3–9.

To the *Virginia Gazette*, November 24, 1775. *Virginia Gazette*, November 24, 1775.

William Woodford to Edmund Pendleton, December 5, 1775. *Richmond College Historical Papers*, vol. 1 (Richmond, Va.: 1915), 110–13.

Martha Washington to Elizabeth Ramsay, December 30, 1775. *"Worthy Partner": The Papers of Martha Washington*, ed. Joseph E. Fields (Westport, Connecticut: Greenwood Press, 1994), 164–65.

Isaac Senter: Journal, November 1–December 31, 1775. *March to Quebec: Journals of the Members of Arnold's Expedition*, ed. Kenneth Roberts (New York: Doubleday, Doran & Company, Inc., 1938), 218–35. Reprinted with permission of the Estate of Kenneth Roberts.

Sarah Hodgkins and Joseph Hodgkins, February 1–20, 1776. Herbert T. Wade and Robert A. Lively, *This Glorious Cause: The Adventures of Two Company Officers in Washington's Army* (Princeton, N.J.: Princeton University Press, 1958), 190–94. Copyright © 1958 by Princeton University Press. Reprinted by permission of Princeton University Press.

John Bowater to the Earl of Denbigh, March 25, 1776. *The Lost War: Letters from British officers during the American Revolution*, ed. Marion Balderston and David Syrett (New York: Horizon Press, 1975), 70–72.

Abigail Adams to John Adams, March 31, 1776. *The Book of Abigail and John: Selected Letters of the Adams Family, 1762–1784*, ed. L. H. Butterfield, Marc Friedlaender, and Mary-Jo Kline (Cambridge: Harvard University Press, 1975), 120–21. © 1963 by The Massachusetts Historical Society. Reprinted by permission of Harvard University Press.

Peter Oliver: from "The Origin & Progress of the American Rebellion." *Peter Oliver's Origin & Progress of the American Rebellion: A Tory View*, ed. Douglass Adair and John A. Schutz (Stanford: Stanford University Press, 1967), 140–44. © 1961 by the Henry E. Huntington Library and Art Gallery. Reprinted with the permission of the Huntington Library.

John Adams to Abigail Adams, July 3, 1776. *The Book of Abigail and John: Selected Letters of the Adams Family, 1762–1784*, ed. L. H. Butterfield, Marc Friedlaender, and Mary-Jo Kline (Cambridge: Harvard University Press, 1975), 138–42. © 1963 by The Massachusetts Historical Society. Reprinted by permission of Harvard University Press.

The Declaration of Independence, July 4, 1776. *The Papers of Thomas Jefferson*, vol. 1, ed. Julian P. Boyd (Princeton: Princeton University Press, 1950), 429–32. Copyright © 1950 renewed 1978 by Princeton University Press. Reprinted by permission of Princeton University Press.

Isaac Bangs: Journal, July 10, 1776. *Proceeding of the New Jersey Historical Society, 1856–1859*, vol. 8 (Newark, N.J.: 1859), 125.

Landon Carter: Diary, June 26–July 16, 1776. *The Diary of Colonel Landon Carter of Sabine Hall, 1752–1778*, vol. 2, ed. Jack P. Greene (Charlottesville: University Press of Virginia, 1965), 1051–59. Courtesy Special Collections Department, University of Virginia Library (MSS 2658).

Ambrose Serle: Journal, July 12–23, 1776. *The American Journal of Ambrose Serle, Secretary to Lord Howe 1776–1778*, ed. Edward H. Tatum Jr. (San Marino, California: Huntington Library, 1940), 28–40. Copyright © 1940 by the Henry E. Huntington Library and Art Gallery.

Joseph Reed: Memorandum on Meeting Between George Washington and James Paterson, July 20, 1776. *The Papers of George Washington: Revolutionary War Series*, vol. 5, ed. Philander D. Chase (Charlottesville: University Press of Virginia, 1993), 398–401. Reprinted with permission of the University Press of Virginia.

Benjamin Franklin to Lord Howe, July 20, 1776. *Benjamin Franklin: Writings*, ed. J. A. Leo Lemay (New York: The Library of America, 1987), 992–94. *The Papers of Benjamin Franklin*, Vol. xxii, Leonard Larabee et al., (New Haven: Yale University Press) 519–21.

Henry Laurens to John Laurens, August 14, 1776. *The Papers of Henry Laurens*, vol. 11, ed. David R. Chesnutt (Columbia: University of South Carolina Press, 1988), 222–35. © 1988 by University of South Carolina Press. Reprinted with permission.

Philip Vickers Fithian: Journal, August 11–30, 1776. *Philip Vickers Fithian: Journal, 1775–1776, Written on the Virginia-Pennsylvania Frontier and in the Army around New York*, ed. Robert Greenhalgh Albion and Leonidas Dodson (Princeton: Princeton University Press, 1934), 207–21.

Jabez Fitch: Diary, August 27–28, 1776. *The New-York Diary of Lieutenant Jabez Fitch of the 17th (Connecticut) Regiment from August 2, 1776 to December 15, 1777*, ed. W.H.W. Sabine (New York: Colburn & Tegg, 1954), 30–34.

Henry Strachey: Memorandum on Meeting Between Lord Howe and the American Commissioners, September 11, 1776. Paul Leicester Ford, "Lord Howe's Commission to Pacify the Colonies," *Atlantic Monthly*, vol. 77 (June 1896), 758–66.

Ambrose Serle: Journal, August 22–September 15, 1776. *The American Journal of Ambrose Serle, Secretary to Lord Howe 1776–1778*, ed. Edward H. Tatum Jr. (San Marino, California: Huntington Library, 1940), 71–105. Copyright © 1940 by the Henry E. Huntington Library and Art Gallery.

Philip Vickers Fithian: Journal, September 15, 1776. *Philip Vickers Fithian: Journal, 1775–1776, Written on the Virginia-Pennsylvania Frontier and in the Army around New York*, ed. Robert Greenhalgh Albion and Leonidas Dodson (Princeton: Princeton University Press, 1934), 232–35.

Benjamin Trumbull: Journal, September 15–16, 1776. *Collections of the Connecticut Historical Society*, vol. 7 (Hartford: Connecticut Historical Society, 1899), 193–96.

Frederick MacKenzie: Diary, September 20–22, 1776. *Diary of Frederick MacKenzie: Giving a Daily Narrative of his Military Service as an Officer in the Regiment of Royal Welch Fusiliers During the Years 1775–1781 in Massachusetts Rhode Island and New York*, vol. 1, ed. Allen French (Cambridge: Harvard University Press, 1930), 58–62. © 1930, 1958 by the President and Fellows of Harvard College. Reprinted by permission of Harvard University Press.

Robert Auchmuty to the Earl of Huntingdon, January 8, 1777. *Report on the Manuscripts of the Late Reginald Rawdon Hastings, Esq.*, vol. 3, ed. Francis Bickley (London: His Majesty's Stationery Office, 1934), 189–92.

George Washington to Lund Washington, December 10 and 17, 1776. *George Washington: Writings*, ed. John Rhodehamel (New York: The Library of America, 1997), 258–62. Reprinted with permission of the University Press of Virginia.

Thomas Paine: The American Crisis, Number I, December 19, 1776. *Thomas Paine: Collected Writings*, ed. Eric Foner (New York: The Library of America, 1995), 91–99.

Thomas Rodney: Diary, December 18–25, 1776. *Diary of Captain Thomas Rodney, 1776–1777*, ed. Cæsar A. Rodney (Wilmington: The Historical Society of Delaware, 1888), 14–23.

George Washington to John Hancock, December 27, 1776. *George Washington: Writings*, ed. John Rhodehamel (New York: The Library of America, 1997), 262–64. Reprinted with permission of the University Press of Virginia.

Thomas Rodney: Diary, January 2–4, 1777. *Diary of Captain Thomas Rodney, 1776–1777*, ed. Cæsar A. Rodney (Wilmington: The Historical Society of Delaware, 1888), 30–39.

Nicholas Cresswell: Journal, January 5–17, 1777. *The Journal of Nicholas Cresswell, 1774–1777* (New York: The Dial Press, 1924), 179–81.

Jabez Fitch: Narrative. *The New-York Diary of Lieutenant Jabez Fitch of the 17th (Connecticut) Regiment from August 22, 1776 to December 15, 1777*, edited by W.H.W. Sabine (New York: Colburn & Tegg, 1954), 136–58.

John Peebles: Diary, February 13–24, 1777. *John Pebbles' American War: the Diary of a Scottish Grenadier, 1776–1782*, ed. Ira D. Gruber (Mechanicsburg, Pennsylvania: Stackpole Books, 1998), 92–98. Reprinted by permission of Sutton Publishing, Ltd.

Abigail Adams to John Adams, March 8, 1777. *The Book of Abigail and John:*

Selected Letters of the Adams Family, 1762–1784, ed. L. H. Butterfield, Marc Friedlaender, and Mary-Jo Kline (Cambridge: Harvard University Press, 1975), 168–69. © 1963 by The Massachusetts Historical Society. Reprinted by permission of Harvard University Press.

John Burgoyne: Proclamation, June 23, 1777. *Proceedings of the Massachusetts Historical Society: 1871–1873* (Boston: Massachusetts Historical Society, 1873), 189–90.

William Digby: Journal, July 24–October 13, 1777. James Phinney Baxter, *The British Invasion from the North* (Albany: Joel Munsell's Sons, 1887), 233–305.

John André: Journal, August 31–October 4, 1777. *Major André's Journal: Operations of the British Army under Lieutenant Generals Sir William Howe and Sir Henry Clinton, June 1777 to November 1778* (Tarrytown, N.Y.: William Abbatt, 1930), 41–57. Reprinted by permission of Ayer Co. Publishers.

John Glover to Jonathan Glover and Azor Orne, September 21 and 29, 1777. *Historical Collections of the Essex Institute*, vol. 5. (Salem, Massachusetts: G.M. Whipple & A.A. Smith, 1863), 101–3.

John Adams to Abigail Adams, September 30, 1777. *The Book of Abigail and John: Selected Letters of the Adams Family, 1762–1784*, ed. L. H. Butterfield, Marc Friedlaender, and Mary-Jo Kline (Cambridge: Harvard University Press, 1975), 193–94. © 1963 by The Massachusetts Historical Society. Reprinted by permission of Harvard University Press.

Samuel Shaw to Francis Shaw, September 30, October 3, 13, and 15, 1777. Josiah Quincy, *The Journals of Major Samuel Shaw, the first American Consul at Canton, with a Life of the Author* (Boston: Wm. Crosby and H.P. Nichols, 1847), 37–43.

Robert Morton: Diary, September 16–December 14, 1777. *Pennsylvania Magazine of History and Biography*, vol. 1 (Philadelphia: Historical Society of Pennsylvania, 1877), 2–37.

Sarah Wister: Journal, October 19–December 12, 1777. *The Journal and Occasional Writings of Sarah Wister*, ed. by Kathryn Zabelle Derounian (Rutherford, N.J.: Fairleigh Dickinson University Press, 1987), 44–56. Reprinted with permission of Associated University Presses.

George Washington: General Orders, December 17, 1777. *George Washington: Writings*, ed. John Rhodehamel (New York: The Library of America, 1997), 280–81.

Albigence Waldo: Diary, December 11–29, 1777. *Pennsylvania Magazine of History and Biography*, vol. 21 (Philadelphia: Historical Society of Pennsylvania, 1897), 305–15.

John Laurens to Henry Laurens, January 14 and February 2, 1778. *The Papers of Henry Laurens*, vol. 12, ed. David R. Chesnutt (Columbia: University of South Carolina Press, 1990), 305, 390–92. © 1990 by University of South Carolina Press. Reprinted with permission.

John Laurens to Henry Laurens, May 7, 1778. *The Papers of Henry Laurens*, vol. 13, ed. David R. Chesnutt (Columbia: University of South Carolina Press, 1992), 264–66. © 1992 by University of South Carolina Press. Reprinted with permission.

Ambrose Serle: Journal, March 9–June 19, 1778. *The American Journal of Ambrose Serle, Secretary to Lord Howe 1776–1778*, ed. Edward H. Tatum Jr. (San Marino, California: Huntington Library, 1940), 278–313. Copyright © 1940 by the Henry E. Huntington Library and Art Gallery.

The Continental Congress: Response to British Peace Proposals, June 13–17, 1778. *The Annual Register, or a View of the History, Politics, and Literature for the Year 1778* (London: J. Dodsley, 1779), 327–30.

Henry Laurens to Horatio Gates, June 17, 1778. *The Papers of Henry Laurens*, vol. 13, ed. David R. Chesnutt (Columbia: University of South Carolina Press, 1992), 472–73. © 1992 by University of South Carolina Press. Reprinted with permission.

John André: Journal, June 16–July 5, 1778. *Major André's Journal: Operations of the British Army under Lieutenant Generals Sir William Howe and Sir Henry Clinton, June 1777 to November 1778* (Tarrytown, N.Y.: William Abbatt, 1930), 74–82. Reprinted by permission of Ayer Co. Publishers.

James McHenry: Journal, June 18–July 23, 1778. *Journal of a March, a Battle, and a Waterfall, being the version elaborated by James McHenry from his Diary of the Year 1778, Begun at Valley Forge, & containing accounts of the British, the Indians, and the Battle of Monmouth*, ed. Helen Flynt and Henry Flynt (Greenwich, Connecticut: privately printed, 1945), 1–11.

John Laurens to Henry Laurens, June 30 and July 2, 1778. *The Papers of Henry Laurens*, vol. 13, ed. David R. Chesnutt (Columbia: University of South Carolina Press, 1992), 532–37, 543–46. © 1992 by University of South Carolina Press. Reprinted with permission.

J. Hector St. John Crèvecoeur: Narrative of the Wyoming Massacre. St. John de Crèvecœur, *Sketches of Eighteenth Century America: More "Letters from an American Farmer,"* ed. Henri L. Bourdini, Ralph H. Gabriel, and Stanley T. Williams (New Haven: Yale University Press, 1925), 192–206. © 1925 by Yale University Press.

Peter Oliver: from "The Origin & Progress of the American Rebellion." *Peter Oliver's Origin & Progress of the American Rebellion: A Tory View*, ed. Douglass Adair and John A. Schutz (Stanford, California: Stanford University Press, 1967), 132–34. © 1961 by the Henry E. Huntington Library and Art Gallery. Reprinted with the permission of the Henry E. Huntington Library.

George Washington to Henry Laurens, November 14, 1778. *George Washington: Writings*, ed. John Rhodehamel (New York: The Library of America, 1997), 327–30.

George Washington to Benjamin Harrison, December 18, 1778. *George Washington: Writings*, ed. John Rhodehamel (New York: The Library of America, 1997), 330–34.

Stephen De Lancey to Cornelia Barclay De Lancey, January 14, 1779. Catherine S. Crary, *The Price of Loyalty: Tory Writings from the Revolutionary Era* (New York: McGraw-Hill, 1973), 271–74. Reprinted by permission.

George Rogers Clark: Narrative of the March to Vincennes. William Hayden English, *Conquest of the Country Northwest of the River Ohio, 1778–1783*; *and*

Life of Gen. George Rogers Clark, vol. 1 (Indianapolis: Bowen–Merrill Company, 1896), 520–42

Alexander Hamilton to John Jay, March 14, 1779. *The Papers of Alexander Hamilton*, vol. 2, ed. Harold C. Syrett (New York: Columbia University Press, 1961), 17–18. © 1961 Columbia University Press. Reprinted by permission of the publisher.

George Washington to Henry Laurens, March 20, 1779. *George Washington: Writings*, ed. John Rhodehamel (New York: The Library of America, 1997), 337–38.

Samuel Shaw to Francis and Sarah Shaw, June 28, 1779. Josiah Quincy, *The Journals of Major Samuel Shaw, the first American Consul at Canton, with a Life of the Author* (Boston: Wm. Crosby and H.P. Nichols, 1847), 58–60.

"A Whig": To the Public, July 30, 1779. *Pennsylvania Packet*, August 5, 1779.

William Barton: Journal, August 27–September 14, 1779. *Proceedings of the New Jersey Historical Society, 1846–1847*, vol. 2 (Newark, N.J.: 1848), 29–37.

John Paul Jones to Benjamin Franklin, October 3, 1779. *The Papers of Benjamin Franklin*, vol. 30, ed. Leonard Larabee et al. (New Haven: Yale University Press, 1993), 444–62.

William Moultrie: Journal, April 2–May 12, 1780. William Moultrie, *Memoirs of the American Revolution, So Far As It Related to the States of North and South-Carolina, and Georgia*, vol. 2 (New York: David Longworth, 1802), 66–85, 108–12.

The Sentiments of a Lady in New-Jersey, July 12, 1780. *New-Jersey Gazette*, July 12, 1780.

Otho Holland Williams: Narrative of the Battle of Camden. William Johnson, *Sketches of the Life and Correspondence of Nathanael Greene, Major General of the Armies of the United States, in the War of the Revolution*, vol. 1 (Charleston, S.C.: A.E. Miller, 1822), 492–98.

Royal Gazette: "Strayed . . . a Whole Army," September 16, 1780. *Royal Gazette*, September 16, 1780.

Benedict Arnold: To the Inhabitants of America, October 7, 1780. Isaac N. Arnold, *The Life of Benedict Arnold* (Chicago: Jansen, McClurg & Company, 1880), 330–32.

Benedict Arnold to Lord Germain, October 7, 1780. *Winnowings in American History: Revolutionary Narratives, No. V*, ed. Paul Leicester Ford (Brooklyn, N.Y.: Historical Printing Club, 1891), 5–7, 9–17.

Alexander Hamilton to John Laurens, October 11, 1780. *The Papers of Alexander Hamilton*, vol. 2, ed. Harold C. Syrett (New York: Columbia University Press, 1961), 460–70. © 1961 Columbia University Press. Reprinted by permission of the publisher.

Robert Campbell: Narrative of the Battle of King's Mountain. Lyman C. Draper, *King's Mountain and its Heroes: History of the Battle of King's Mountain, October 7th, 1780, and the events which led to it* (Cincinnati: P.G. Thomson, 1881), 537–40.

George Washington: Circular to the State Governments, October 18, 1780. *George Washington: Writings*, ed. John Rhodehamel (New York: The Library of America, 1997), 393–400.

Anthony Allaire: Diary, October 7–November 25, 1780. Lyman C. Draper, *King's Mountain and its Heroes: History of the Battle of King's Mountain, October 7th, 1780, and the events which led to it* (Cincinnati: P.G. Thomson, 1881), 510–15.

Enos Reeves: Letterbook Extracts, January 2–17, 1781, *Pennsylvania Magazine of History and Biography* (Philadelphia: Historical Society of Pennsylvania, 1897), 72–80.

Oliver De Lancey: Journal, January 3–21, 1781. Carl Van Doren, *Mutiny in January* (New York: The Viking Press, 1943), 243–49. Copyright © 1943 by Carl Van Doren; renewed 1970 by Margaret Van Doren Bevans. Used by permission of Viking Penguin, a division of Penguin Putnam Inc.

George Washington to Philip Schuyler, January 10, 1781. *The Writings of George Washington from the Original Manuscript Sources, 1745–1799*, vol. 21, ed. John C. Fitzpatrick (Washington: United States Government Printing Office, 1937), 79–80.

Nathanael Greene to Alexander Hamilton, January 10, 1781. *The Papers of General Nathanael Greene*, vol. 7, ed. Dennis M. Conrad and Richard K. Showman (Chapel Hill: University of North Carolina Press, 1994), 87–91. Copyright © 1994 by the University of North Carolina Press. Used by permission of the publisher.

Nathanael Greene to Catherine Greene, January 12, 1781. *The Papers of General Nathanael Greene*, vol. 7, ed. Dennis M. Conrad and Richard K. Showman (Chapel Hill: University of North Carolina Press, 1994), 102–3. Copyright © 1994 by the University of North Carolina Press. Used by permission of the publisher.

Thomas Jefferson: Narrative of Arnold's Raid, January 13, 1781. *The Papers of Thomas Jefferson*, vol. 4, ed. Julian P. Boyd (Princeton: Princeton University Press, 1951), 269–70. Copyright © 1951 renewed 1979 by Princeton University Press. Reprinted by permission of Princeton University Press.

Daniel Morgan to Nathanael Greene, January 19, 1781. *The Papers of General Nathanael Greene*, vol. 7, ed. Dennis M. Conrad and Richard K. Showman (Chapel Hill: University of North Carolina Press, 1994), 152–55. Copyright © 1994 by the University of North Carolina Press. Used by permission of the publisher.

George Washington to Robert Howe, January 22, 1781. *The Writings of George Washington from the Original Manuscript Sources, 1745–1799*, vol. 21, ed. John C. Fitzpatrick (Washington: United States Government Printing Office, 1937), 128–29.

Royal Gazette: "Our Last Will and Testament," January 31, 1781. *Royal Gazette*, January 31, 1781.

Nathanael Greene to George Washington, February 9, 1781. *The Papers of General Nathanael Greene*, vol. 7, ed. Dennis M. Conrad and Richard K. Showman (Chapel Hill: University of North Carolina Press, 1994), 267–69. Copyright © 1994 by the University of North Carolina Press. Used by permission of the publisher.

Nathanael Greene to Joseph Reed, March 18, 1781. *The Papers of General Nathanael Greene*, vol. 7, ed. Dennis M. Conrad and Richard K. Showman

(Chapel Hill: University of North Carolina Press, 1994), 448–51. Copyright © 1994 by the University of North Carolina Press. Used by permission of the publisher.

Nathanael Greene to George Washington, March 18, 1781. *The Papers of General Nathanael Greene*, vol. 7, ed. Dennis M. Conrad and Richard K. Showman (Chapel Hill: University of North Carolina Press, 1994), 451–52. Copyright © 1994 by the University of North Carolina Press. Used by permission of the publisher.

Nathanael Greene to Thomas Jefferson, April 28, 1781. *The Papers of General Nathanael Greene*, vol. 8, ed. Dennis M. Conrad (Chapel Hill: University of North Carolina Press, 1995), 165–67. Copyright © 1995 by the University of North Carolina Press. Used by permission of the publisher.

Ebenezer Denny: Journal, May 1–15, 1781. *Military Journal of Major Ebenezer Denny, an Officer in the Revolutionary and Indian Wars* (Philadelphia: Historical Society of Pennsylvania, 1859), 33–35.

Thomas Brown to David Ramsay, December 25, 1786. George White, *Historical Collections of Georgia* (New York: Pudney & Russell, 1854), 614–19.

Josiah Atkins: Diary, June 6–July 7, 1781. *The Diary of Josiah Atkins*, ed. Steven E. Kagle (New York: Arno, 1975), 24–39. Reprinted by permission of Ayer Co. Publishers.

Ebenezer Denny: Journal, June 18–July 7, 1781. *Military Journal of Major Ebenezer Denny, an Officer in the Revolutionary and Indian Wars* (Philadelphia: Historical Society of Pennsylvania, 1859), 35–38.

James Robertson to William Knox, July 12, 1781. *The Twilight of British Rule in Revolutionary America: The New York Letter Book of General James Robertson, 1780–1783*, ed. Milton M. Klein and Ronald W. Howard (Cooperstown: The New York State Historical Association, 1983), 209–12. Reproduced courtesy of the New York State Historical Association, Cooperstown, New York.

Otho Holland Williams, Narrative of the Battle of Eutaw Springs. R. W. Gibbes, ed., *Documentary History of the American Revolution . . . Chiefly in South Carolina, in 1781 and 1782*, vol. 3 (New York: D. Appleton & Co., 1857), 144–57.

Ebenezer Denny: Journal, September 1–November 1, 1781. *Military Journal of Major Ebenezer Denny, an Officer in the Revolutionary and Indian Wars* (Philadelphia: Historical Society of Pennsylvania, 1859), 38–46.

St. George Tucker: Journal, September 28–October 20, 1781. Edward M. Riley, "St. George Tucker's Journal of the Siege of Yorktown," *William and Mary Quarterly*, 3rd series, vol. 5 (1948), 380–94.

James Robertson to Lord Amherst, October 17, 1781. *The Twilight of British Rule in Revolutionary America: The New York Letter Book of General James Robertson, 1780–1783*, ed. Milton M. Klein and Ronald W. Howard (Cooperstown: The New York State Historical Association, 1983), 220–22. Reproduced courtesy of the New York State Historical Association, Cooperstown, New York.

Lord Cornwallis to Henry Clinton, October 20, 1781. Theodore Thayer, *Yorktown: Campaign of Strategic Options* (Philadelphia: Lippincott, 1975), 127–30.

Anna Rawle: Diary, October 25, 1781. *Pennsylvania Magazine of History and Biography*, vol. 16 (Philadelphia: Historical Society of Pennsylvania, 1892), 104–7.

Robert Gray: Observations on the War in Carolina. *South Carolina Historical and Genealogical Magazine*, vol. 11 (1910), 140–59.

William Feilding to the Earl of Denbigh, August 10, 1782. *The Lost War: Letters from British officers during the American Revolution*, ed. Marion Balderston and David Syrett (New York: Horizon Press, 1975), 218–20.

Ebenezer Denny: Journal, January 4–December 13, 1782. *Military Journal of Major Ebenezer Denny, an Officer in the Revolutionary and Indian Wars* (Philadelphia: Historical Society of Pennsylvania, 1859), 46–49.

John Armstrong: The Newburgh Address, c. March 10, 1783. *Journals of the Continental Congress 1774–1789*, vol. 24, ed. Gaillard Hunt (Washington: Government Printing Office, 1922), 295–97.

George Washington to Joseph Jones, March 12, 1783. *George Washington: Writings*, ed. John Rhodehamel (New York: The Library of America, 1997), 493–95.

George Washington: Speech to the Officers, March 15, 1783. *George Washington: Writings*, ed. John Rhodehamel (New York: The Library of America, 1997), 496–500.

Samuel Shaw to the Rev. Eliot, April 1783. Josiah Quincy, *The Journals of Major Samuel Shaw, the first American Consul at Canton, with a Life of the Author* (Boston: Wm. Crosby and H.P. Nichols, 1847), 99–105.

A New York Loyalist to Lord Hardwicke, c. Summer 1783. Catherine S. Crary, *The Price of Loyalty: Tory Writings from the Revolutionary Era* (New York: McGraw–Hill, 1973), 360–62. Reprinted by permission.

George Washington and Thomas Mifflin: Speeches in the Continental Congress, December 23, 1783. *Journals of the Continental Congress 1774–1789*, vol. 25, ed. Gaillard Hunt (Washington: Government Printing Office, 1922), 837–39.

James McHenry to Margaret Caldwell, December 23, 1783. *Letters of Delegates to Congress, 1774–1789*, vol. 21, ed. Paul H. Smith (Washington: Government Printing Office, 1994), 221–22.

This volume presents the texts of the printings chosen as sources here but does not attempt to reproduce features of their typographic design, or to reproduce features of 18th-century typography such as the long "s." The use of quotation marks in 18th-century texts has been modernized; only beginning and ending quotation marks are provided here, instead of placing a quotation mark at the beginning of every line of a quoted passage. Letters printed as superscript at the end of abbreviations in the source texts have been printed on the line in this volume. Names of letter writers, addresses, and endorsements by recipients appearing at the end of letters have been omitted, except in the case of the exchange of letters between Sarah Hodgkins and Joseph Hodgkins (pp. 109–12 in this volume). The texts are printed without alteration except for the changes previously discussed and for the correction of typographical errors. Spelling, punctuation, and capitalization are often expressive features, and they are not altered, even when inconsistent or irregular. The following is a list of typographical errors corrected, cited by page and line number: 55.37, there; 75.27, Lapraier; 81.17, enterained; 89.22, as; 183.18, Order d; 183.25, Scatter d; 274.23, fo; 339.3, 17st; 461.17, calvary; 463.37, calvary; 463.38, calvary; 532.15, seing; 533.5, lentiy; 534.29, radid; 542.9, of; 578.8, quare r–master's; 581.8, substitue; 689.25, a naked; 708.13, meantime time; 720.13, af; 754.6, Forgusson.

Notes

In the notes below, the reference numbers denote page and line of this volume (the line count includes headings). No note is made for material included in standard desk-reference books such as Webster's *Collegiate*, *Biographical*, and *Geographical* dictionaries. Biblical references are keyed to the King James Version. Quotations from Shakespeare are keyed to *The Riverside Shakespeare*, ed. G. Blakemore Evans (Boston: Houghton, Mifflin, 1974). Footnotes and bracketed editorial notes within the text were in the originals. For historical background, see Chronology in this volume. For further historical background and references to other studies, see Robert Middlekauff, *The Glorious Cause: The American Revolution, 1763–1789* (New York: Oxford University Press, 1982) and Mark M. Boatner III, *Encyclopedia of the American Revolution* (3rd edition; Mechanicsburg, PA: Stackpole Books, 1994).

1.2   *Paul Revere: Memorandum*]   This account was first printed in 1891 in *The Life of Colonel Paul Revere* by Elbridge Henry Goss, who wrote that it was "evidently written in the year 1783."

1.10   Light . . . Grenadiers]   British infantry regiments in 1775 were organized into eight line companies and two flank companies, one of light infantry and one of grenadiers. Light infantry were used for scouting and skirmishing, while grenadier companies were made up of the tallest and strongest men in the regiment (by the time of the Revolutionary War, grenadiers no longer carried hand grenades). British commanders often detached light infantry and grenadier companies from their regiments for use in special missions, and sometimes used them to form light infantry and grenadier battalions.

4.15   further saith not.]   Revere's manuscript ended at this point.

5.6   Commander in Chief's]   General Thomas Gage was commander in chief of the British army in North America.

5.7   suspension . . . Walcott]   A court martial had found Walcott guilty of striking Patrick in front of his regiment on March 23, 1775, and sentenced him to be reprimanded and suspended for three months.

6.27   Six pounders]   Cannon capable of firing six-pound solid shot.

7.25   the flank Companies]   The detached light infantry and grenadier companies; see note 1.10.

12.5–6   the opposite page]   See page 11 in this volume.

19.3   *Earl of Dartmouth*]   William Legge, second Earl of Dartmouth, was secretary of state for the colonies from August 1772 until November 1775.

19.8–10   Address . . . February]   Parliament had voted to declare Massachusetts to be in a state of rebellion.

21.5   '*immedicabile vulnus*']   Incurable wound.

23.5–6   St. James or St. Stephens]   St. James's Palace in Westminster was the official London residence of George III. The House of Commons met in St. Stephen's Chapel in the Palace of Westminster from 1547 to 1834.

25.3–4   "*The Origin . . . Rebellion*"]   Oliver wrote "The Origin & Progress of the American Rebellion" while in exile in England. The manuscript, dated 1781, was first published in 1961.

25.15   *Suffolk* Resolves]   Drafted by Joseph Warren, the resolves were adopted on September 9, 1774, by delegates from Boston and other towns in Suffolk County, Massachusetts. The resolves denounced the Intolerable Acts as unconstitutional and called for the nonpayment of taxes, the nonimportation of British goods, the formation of a provincial congress, and weekly musters of the provincial militia. Paul Revere carried a copy of the resolves to Philadelphia, and the First Continental Congress endorsed them on September 17, 1774.

26.13–15   Battle of . . . *that Day*]   Cf. the English ballad "Chevy Chase," in which Earl Percy causes a bloody battle by leading a hunting expedition across the border into Scotland.

27.21   *the wicked . . . pursueth*]   Proverbs 28:1.

28.1–2   Variety . . . cloy]   Cf. "The Turtle and the Sparrow" by Matthew Prior (1664–1721).

28.18–19   *qui . . . decipiatur*]   Who wishes to be deceived will be deceived.

28.22   famous Mr. *Putnam*]   Israel Putnam (1718–90).

31.5   THE President]   John Hancock, who served as president of the Continental Congress from May 24, 1775, to October 29, 1777.

34.2   *Joseph Trumbull*]   Trumbull (1737–78) was named commissary general of the Connecticut troops outside of Boston in April 1775, and on July 19, 1775, was appointed commissary general of the Continental army. He resigned in the summer of 1777.

35.11–12   Genlls How & Burgoyne]   Major generals William Howe and John Burgoyne arrived in Boston on May 25, 1775.

36.6–33   The Horrors . . . 2 & 2.]   This portion of the letter was written by Captain John Chester.

40.20 Capt. General] Artemas Ward (1727–1800) was named comman-der in chief of the Massachusetts provincial army on May 19, 1775, and led the troops besieging Boston until George Washington assumed command of the Continental army on July 3, 1775. Ward then served as a major general in the Continental army until March 1777, when he resigned his commission.

41.3 *Burwell Bassett*] Bassett (1734–93) was the husband of Martha Washington's sister Anna Maria Dandridge.

45.37 the Admiral] Samuel Graves (1713–87), commander of the Royal Navy in North America, 1774–76.

47.13 *in terrorem*] As a warning.

47.18 Succours] Reinforcements.

48.31–32 *Massianello . . . rapid*] Tommaso Aniello (1620–47), known as Masaniello, was a fisherman who led an uprising in 1647 against the nobility who ruled Naples under Spanish viceroyship. The uprising began on July 7, and Massianello was assassinated on July 16.

49.15 *Fabius*] Quintus Fabius Maximus (d. 203 BCE), Roman general whose strategy of attrition and delay helped defeat Hannibal's invasion of Italy during the Second Punic War.

49.22 Projector] Promoter; speculator.

49.24 *Caput Mortuum*] Worthless residue (literally, "dead head").

50.16–17 *Samaritan . . . Oil & Wine*] See Luke 10:33–34.

51.13 *felix quem faciunt*] Cf. *Felix quem faciunt aliena pericula cautum,* "Happy is he whom others' experiences make cautious."

51.17 *Dr. Busby*] Richard Busby (1606–95), headmaster of Westminster School, 1638–95.

52.2 Ordnance Ship] The *Nancy* was captured off the Massachusetts coast on November 28, 1775.

52.19–20 The Pulpit, . . . Stick] From *Hudibras*, Part I (1663), by Samuel Butler (1613–80).

53.2–3 *Franklin . . . Strahan*] Franklin did not send this letter. William Strahan (1715–85) was a successful printer in London.

54.5–6 *Mohawks . . . Senekas*] In 1777 the Mohawks, Onondagas, Cayu-gas, and Senecas became active British allies, while the Oneidas and Tuscaro-ras either remained neutral or began to aid the American cause.

63.30 Long Island] In Boston Harbor.

63.36 Simple Sapling] Name given to Massachusetts Loyalist Nathaniel Ray Thomas by Mercy Otis Warren in her satirical play *The Group* (1775).

65.17   Mr. Trot]   George Trott, the husband of a cousin of John Adams, who had fled Boston.

65.29–32   Be not . . . increase.]   Cf. Joel 2:22.

66.31   Portia]   Portia (or Porcia) was the daughter of Cato the Younger and wife of Brutus, the leader of the conspiracy against Julius Caesar.

71.15–16   Green Mountain Boys]   Militia formed in Vermont in 1770 by settlers who held land grants from New Hampshire and opposed attempts by New York to extend its jurisdiction over the region.

72.11   fusee]   A light flintlock musket.

73.6   swivels]   Swivel guns, small cannon mounted on swivels.

74.14–15   lost the command . . . Burgoyne]   See Chronology, July–October 1777.

77.3   Gen. Carlton]   Guy Carleton (1724–1808) was governor of Quebec and commander of British forces in Canada, 1775–78. He later served as commander in chief of British forces in America, 1782–83.

80.20   Tyburn]   Gallows used for public executions in London until 1783, located on the site of present-day Marble Arch at the northeast corner of Hyde Park.

81.7   lord Dunmore's]   John Murray, Earl of Dunmore (1732–1809), was appointed governor of Virginia in 1771. Fearing for his safety, he had taken refuge on board a British warship on June 1, 1775. After the defeat of his forces at Great Bridge on December 9, 1775, Dunmore burned much of Norfolk on January 1, 1776, then established a base on Gwynn Island in Chesapeake Bay. In the summer of 1776 he returned to England by way of New York.

87.28–29   your Honble. Boddy]   The fourth Virginia Convention. Five conventions were held in Virginia between 1774, when Governor Dunmore dissolved the colonial assembly, and 1776, when the fifth convention adopted the first state constitution.

91.3   *Elizabeth Ramsay*]   A friend of the Washingtons who lived in Alexandria, Virginia.

93.28   the river]   The Chaudière, in southern Quebec.

94.31   the Colonel]   Benedict Arnold.

95.37   one Portuguese]   Probably the widely circulated Portuguese half johannes gold coin, worth about eight dollars.

102.27   *brodel*]   Brothel.

106.30   Pharsalia]   Battlefield in Greece where Julius Caesar defeated Pompey in 48 BCE.

108.35–36   "Oh, Liberty! . . . country!"] From *Cato*, IV, i (1713), by Joseph Addison.

109.26   Prospect Hill] The hill, northeast of Cambridge, was part of the American siege lines around Boston.

109.30   our Children] Sarah, born 1773, and Joseph, born 1775. Joseph Hodgkins' daughter by his first marriage, Joanna, born 1765, also lived with the family in Ipswich.

113.3   *Earl of Denbigh*] Basil Feilding, the sixth Earl of Denbigh, was a politically influential landowner and friend of Lord Sandwich, the first lord of the admiralty.

119.23   Lieut. Governor *Oliver*] Thomas Oliver (1734–1815), who became lieutenant governor of Massachusetts in 1774, was not related to Peter Oliver.

122.19   *Castle William*] The fortress was built on Castle Island in Boston Harbor.

125.22   Argument . . . Assistance] Writs of assistance were general warrants issued to customs officers authorizing them to search any ship or building they suspected contained contraband goods. Attorney James Otis argued before the Massachusetts superior court in February 1761 that general search warrants were contrary to the principles of Magna Carta and English common law and therefore should be considered void, even if authorized by an act of Parliament. In November 1761 the court rejected his argument and ruled that writs of assistance were lawful.

133.18–23   {Col. Carter . . . Col. Carter}] The selection from the diary of Landon Carter printed here is taken from *The Diary of Colonel Landon Carter of Sabine Hall, 1752–1778*, edited by Jack P. Greene (1965). While preparing this edition, Greene discovered that portions of the manuscript of the diary were missing, including the entries for June 26–July 16, 1776. For these entries, Greene used an earlier text, edited by Lyon G. Tyler and printed in the *William and Mary Quarterly* in 1908, and placed within braces "all those sections that seemed to be editorial summaries by Tyler."

133.35   King and Queen] King and Queen County.

135.3   Eden] Robert Eden (1741–84) became the royal governor of Maryland in 1769. He was asked to leave the province in May 1776 by the Maryland Council of Safety and sailed from Annapolis on June 26, 1776.

135.39–136.1   Gen. Thomas . . . the cedars] Major General John Thomas (1724–76) assumed command of the American army in Canada on May 1, 1776, and died of smallpox on June 2. The British captured 400 prisoners at The Cedars, a post 30 miles west of Montreal, on May 16, 1776, and another 100 in an American relief expedition on May 20.

136.9   the N. Y. conspiracy]   Thomas Hickey, a Continental soldier and member of George Washington's guard, was convicted of mutiny and sedition by a court-martial on June 26, 1776, and hanged on June 28. David Mathews, the mayor of New York City, and 12 other men were arrested for their alleged participation in a Loyalist conspiracy involving Hickey, but all of them either escaped from custody or were released before being tried.

142.25   Admiral Shuldham]   Molyneux Shuldham (1717?–98), commander of the Royal Navy in North America, January–July 1776.

143.5–6   the Admiral]   Viscount Richard Howe (1726–99), commander of the Royal Navy in North America, 1776–78, and older brother of General William Howe.

144.17–18   Objects . . . Declaration]   The declaration announced that the Howe brothers had been appointed as peace commissioners and given the power to grant pardons and restore the king's protection to regions of the colonies that had ceased to be in rebellion.

146.23–24   Highlanders . . . Boston]   Four British troop transports were captured off the Massachusetts coast between June 10 and June 19, 1776. They had sailed from Scotland in late April, unaware that the British had evacuated Boston in March 1776.

148.25–26   famous Major Rogers]   Robert Rogers (1731–95), the commander of Rogers' Rangers during the French and Indian War, led the Queen's Rangers, a Loyalist regiment, from 1776 to 1777. He immigrated to England in 1780.

149.26   Adams's Pamphlet . . . Sense."]   The authorship of *Common Sense*, published anonymously by Thomas Paine on January 10, 1776, was attributed to both John Adams and Samuel Adams.

152.5   *James Paterson*]   Paterson served as adjutant general to General William Howe, 1776–78.

153.17   Genl Prescott]   Richard Prescott (1725–88) was captured in Canada on November 17, 1775, and exchanged for General John Sullivan in September 1776.

153.25–26   Case of Col. Allen]   Prescott was accused of harshly treating Ethan Allen after Allen was captured at Montreal in September 1775.

154.27–28   Govr Skene . . . Lovel]   Philip Skene (1725–1810), a retired British army officer and the lieutenant governor of Ticonderoga and Crown Point, was arrested in Philadelphia in June 1775. James Lovell (1737–1814), a Boston schoolteacher, was arrested as a spy in 1775 and taken to Halifax when the British evacuated the city in March 1776. The exchange was made in October 1776.

154.35   blinding]   Blindfolding.

157.34 Sister's in London] Franklin and Lord Howe met on December 25, 1774, at Caroline Howe's house, where Howe told Franklin that some members of the North ministry "were extremely well disposed to any reasonable accommodation" between the British government and the American colonists. At a subsequent meeting on December 28, Howe rejected the terms Franklin had outlined in a memorandum written on December 5, 1774. Further conversations between the two men before Franklin's departure from London on March 21, 1775, failed to make progress toward resolving the crisis in Anglo-American relations.

159.15 Govr.—Wright] James Wright (1716–85), royal governor of Georgia, 1762–76.

162.25 President] John Rutledge (1739–1800) was president of the South Carolina general assembly from 1776 to 1778 (during this period, South Carolina had no governor).

163.6 Sullivant's] Sullivan's Island.

163.26 James Grant] Grant (1720–1806) served as governor of East Florida from 1764 until 1771. In a speech in Parliament on February 2, 1775, Grant predicted that the Americans would not fight and "would never dare to face an English army." He commanded troops in America, 1776–78, then fought the French in the West Indies, 1778–79.

174.33 Powles Hook] Paulus Hook, New Jersey, now part of Jersey City.

175.19 Daemon *Wallace*] Captain James Wallace (1731–1803), commander of the *Rose*.

178.25 "sub-jove."] Beneath the open sky.

180.10 General Lord Sterling] William Alexander (1726–83), born in New York City to a Scottish father, had unsuccessfully claimed the earldom of Stirling while living in England between 1756 and 1762 and continued to use the title Lord Stirling after returning to America. He was commissioned as a brigadier general in the Continental army in March 1776. Captured in the battle of Long Island, Alexander was exchanged in October 1776 and promoted to major general in 1777. He served with the Continental army until his death from illness.

186.3–4 *Meeting . . . Commissioners*] Lord Howe met with General John Sullivan after he was captured in the battle of Long Island and told him of his willingness to open peace negotiations with members of the Continental Congress. Sullivan was then paroled and permitted to go to Philadelphia, where he conveyed Howe's message. On September 6, 1776, Congress appointed Benjamin Franklin, John Adams, and Edward Rutledge to meet with Howe. The conference was held on Staten Island on September 11.

186.19–21 Massachusetts . . . eldest Brother] George Augustus Howe (1724–58), a brigadier general in the British army, was killed near Fort

Ticonderoga during the French and Indian War. The Massachusetts legislature appropriated £250 for a memorial tablet in Westminster Abbey in his honor.

187.2   Petition to the King]   The Olive Branch Petition, adopted by the Continental Congress on July 5, 1775.

187.7–8   Address to the People]   The Declaration of the Causes and Necessity of Taking Up Arms, adopted by the Continental Congress July 6, 1775.

189.35   Prohibitory Act]   See Chronology, December 1775.

198.27   *Quos . . . dementat.*]   Whom God wishes to destroy, he first drives mad.

200.6   M. Rollin]   French historian Charles Rollin (1661–1741).

200.32–33   Nutting Island]   Also known as Governors Island.

203.7–8   *in . . . otas*]   Time will bring to light.

203.24–32   O who shall . . . them]   Cf. Shakespeare, *2 Henry IV*, IV, ii, 22–30.

205.1   King's bridge]   Bridge across the Harlem River at the northern end of Manhattan Island.

206.29   Oliverian]   An adherent of Oliver Cromwell.

212.8–9   Observation of the Poet]   Horace, *Epistles*, I, xi, 27: "They change their sky, not their soul, who run across the sea."

212.9   *Et coelum . . . mutaverunt*]   Their sky and their soul indeed changed.

214.39   Lp's]   Lordship's.

215.23   Thraso]   A soldier in *Eunuchus*, a comedy by the Roman dramatist Terence (d. 159 BCE).

216.24   *bona terra, mala gens*]   Good land, bad people (this phrase does not appear in the original passage in Mather's book).

226.2   C S S C D P]   Captains, subalterns, sergeants, corporals, drummers, privates.

229.10   Nathaniel Hales]   Nathan Hale.

230.4–5   The following account]   The writer of the account forwarded by Auchmuty has not been identified.

230.16   Knephausen]   General Wilhelm von Knyphausen (1716–1800) arrived in New York on October 18, 1776, with 4,000 Hessian troops. He became the senior Hessian officer in America in 1777.

234.3   *Lund Washington*] Lund Washington (1737–96) was a distant cousin to George Washington. He managed Mount Vernon during the Revolutionary War.

234.13   Political Deaths] Expired terms of enlistment.

234.20–21   saild . . . Clinton] See Chronology, December 1776.

238.16–17   declared, . . . WHATSOEVER,"] The Declaratory Act of 1766, passed after the repeal of the Stamp Act, reasserted Parliament's legislative authority over the American colonies.

245.1–2   "*a peace . . . understanding*"] Cf. Philippians 4:7.

267.7   New Lots] Village on Long Island, now a neighborhood in Brooklyn.

273.9   French] French Canadian.

274.9   Snow] A two-masted sailing vessel resembling a brig.

275.38   Dehighster] Leopold Philip von Heister (1707–77) was the senior Hessian general in America, 1776–77.

284.27   Governor Scheene] Philip Skene; see note 154.27–28.

286.21   Col: Allen] Ethan Allen.

288.30   Prophet Hugh Gaine] Hugh Gaine (1727–1807) was the printer of the *New-York Gazette*, and the *Weekly Mercury*. Gaine left New York in September 1776 and published his newspaper in Newark, New Jersey, from September 21 to November 2, writing in support of the American cause. He then returned to the city and on November 11, 1776, began publishing the *New-York Gazette* as a Loyalist newspaper.

290.6–7   Gracious Proclamation . . . Run out] The Howe brothers issued a proclamation on November 30, 1776, offering pardons and papers of protection to colonists who would swear an oath of allegiance to the king within 60 days.

291.5–6   "from . . . dealeth falsely"] Jeremiah 6:13, 8:10.

298.38   plattoon] Volley.

300.19   Drrs.] Drummers.

301.23–28   "But tis . . . of ages?"] Cf. *The American Crisis, Number II* by Thomas Paine, published as a pamphlet in Philadelphia on January 17, 1777.

305.9   River BONGRETT] The Boquet River flows into the western side of Lake Champlain about 40 miles north of Fort Ticonderoga.

306.5   Skeensborough] Now Whitehall, New York.

306.18   the 8th,]   July 8, 1777.

307.12   Lord George Germaine]   Lord George Germain (1716–85) was secretary of state for the colonies from November 1775 to February 1782.

315.4   provincial]   Loyalist.

335.17   Chasseurs]   Literally, "hunters"; riflemen.

343.15   Major Washington]   George Washington.

346.33   Jägers]   Literally, "hunters"; German riflemen.

355.17   * * *]   The text of this letter is taken from Josiah Quincy, *The Journals of Major Samuel Shaw, the first American Consul at Canton, with a Life of the Author* (1847). Quincy writes that the letter of September 30, 1777, is "given nearly entire."

357.19   "The ways . . . intricate,"]   Joseph Addison.

358.14   forts . . . North River]   Forts Clinton and Montgomery, on the western bank of the Hudson about 40 miles north of New York City, were captured by the British on October 6, 1777. The British abandoned the forts and withdrew from the Hudson Highlands later in the month.

359.8–9   Friends . . . Virginia]   The Pennsylvania executive council arrested 17 Quakers from Philadelphia, including Robert Morton's stepfather, James Pemberton, in September 1777 on suspicion of disloyalty. The men were exiled to Winchester, Virginia, after they refused to affirm allegiance to the state, but were permitted to return to Pennsylvania in the spring of 1778.

360.19   I. P.]   Israel Pemberton, a brother of James Pemberton.

362.5   T. Willing]   Thomas Willing (1731–1821) was a prominent merchant and lawyer in Philadelphia who had served as a justice of the Pennsylvania supreme court, 1767–77, and as a delegate to the Continental Congress, 1775–76.

362.13   Galloway . . . Allen]   Joseph Galloway (c. 1731–1803) was speaker of the Pennsylvania assembly, 1766–75, and a delegate to the First Continental Congress in 1774. A public opponent of American independence, Galloway crossed over to the British lines in 1776. Andrew Allen (1740–1825) was attorney general of Pennsylvania, 1769–76, and a delegate to the Second Continental Congress, 1775–76. Allen voted against declaring independence and in December 1776 crossed over to the British lines with his brothers, John and William, and accepted a pardon. William Allen had resigned his commission as a lieutenant colonel in the Continental army after the Declaration of Independence. He became the commander of a regiment of Pennsylvania Loyalists late in 1777 and served until 1782, when he went into exile. The Allen brothers were the sons of William Allen (1704–80), the chief justice of Pennsylvania from 1750 to 1774.

362.30   "Esto Perpetua."] Let it be everlasting.

368.29   Governor McKinley] John McKinley (1721–96) was elected president of Delaware in February 1777. Captured by the British in September 1777, he was paroled in August 1778 and later exchanged for William Franklin, the former royal governor of New Jersey.

369.4   J. P.] John Pemberton, brother of James Pemberton.

373.12   Esopus] Kingston, New York.

383.5   seconday] Sunday.

383.8   see you] Wister addressed her journal to her friend Deborah Norris (1761–1839).

383.8   Liddy] Lydia Foulke (b. 1756). Wister was staying in the Foulke mansion in Gwynedd, Pennsylvania.

384.25   somnus] Sleep; the Roman god of sleep.

385.14   Major of brigade] Senior staff officer of the brigade.

389.3–4   On her . . . adore] Cf. "The Rape of the Lock" (1712), canto II, lines 7–8, by Alexander Pope (1688–1744).

403.22   * * *] Asterisks were used by the editors of the *Pennsylvania Magazine of History and Biography* to indicate a hiatus in the manuscript.

406.21   Linctus] Medicine licked with the tongue.

415.11   York] York, Pennsylvania, where Congress met from September 30, 1777, to June 27, 1778.

416.8   the Town] Newport, Rhode Island, where Serle arrived with Lord Howe on January 2, 1778.

420.13–14 Declaration . . . Taxation] As part of the conciliation plan proposed by Lord North on February 17, 1778, Parliament declared its willingness to repeal the tax on tea and to renounce the power to levy revenue taxes on the colonies.

420.16   certain . . . Parliament] North's conciliation plan called for the repeal of the Coercive (Intolerable) Acts of 1774 and the possible suspension of other colonial acts passed by Parliament since 1763.

421.21   Nebuchadnezzar's Image] See Daniel 2:31–45.

423.15   Mr. Galloway] Joseph Galloway; see note 362.13.

425.8   famous Dr. Smith] William Smith (1727–1803) was provost of the College of Philadelphia, 1755–79.

429.2   Skinner] Cortlandt Skinner (1728–99), former attorney general of New Jersey and commander of the Loyalist New Jersey Volunteers.

431.28 Sign Man.] Sign manual; signature.

437.6 Lee] Charles Lee was exchanged in April 1778 and rejoined the Continental army on May 20.

439.19 *Parturiit . . . mus*] The mountains are in labor, and will bring forth a mouse.

442.12 Lord D.] Lord Dartmouth.

442.15 two Principals] Lord Germain, secretary of state for the colonies, and John Montagu, Earl of Sandwich (1718–92), the first lord of the admiralty, 1771–83.

449.9 *July 17*] June 17.

451.14 foolish Virgins] See Matthew 25:1–10.

457.28 31st] The British completed their withdrawal to New York on July 5, 1778.

473.35 Lee . . . misconduct] A court martial convened on July 2 to try Lee for disobeying orders, misbehavior before the enemy, and showing disrespect to the commander in chief in two letters he wrote to Washington after the battle. On August 12, 1778, Lee was found guilty of all three charges and sentenced to be suspended from command for 12 months. Congress approved the sentence on December 5, 1778, and dismissed Lee from the army on January 10, 1780.

476.4 *Narrative . . . Massacre*] Crèvecoeur appears to have written this account sometime between 1778 and 1781. It was first published in 1925.

476.9–11 dispute . . . their own] Royal charters granted to Connecticut colonists in 1662 and to William Penn in 1681 resulted in conflicting claims to jurisdiction over the Susquehanna Valley. In 1769 Connecticut settlers began moving into the valley, and in 1774–75 the Connecticut colonial government organized the region as a township, and then as a separate county, in Connecticut. A commission appointed by Congress awarded jurisdiction to Pennsylvania in 1782.

489.5–6 *Saratoga* Convention] Under the terms of the agreement signed at Saratoga by John Burgoyne and Horatio Gates on October 16, 1777, Burgoyne's troops would be permitted to return to Britain on the condition that they not serve again in North America during the war. Critics of the convention believed that the return of Burgoyne's army would allow the British to send an equal number of other soldiers to America, and Congress refused to honor it, citing a series of alleged British violations of its terms. Most of the "Convention army" remained in the United States as prisoners until the end of the war.

492.22 the Marquis] The Marquis de Lafayette.

502.4 *Narrative . . . Vincennes*] The selection printed in this volume is taken from a memoir Clark is believed to have written around 1791. The memoir was first published in full in 1896.

512.34 Captain Helm] Captain Leonard Helm had occupied Vincennes in August 1778 during Clark's initial campaign in the Illinois territory. He was taken prisoner when the British recaptured the town on December 17, 1778.

523.3 *John Jay*] Jay (1745–1829) was president of Congress from December 1778 to September 1779.

523.14 recommended by Congress] On March 29, 1779, Congress recommended that Georgia and South Carolina recruit 3,000 slaves to serve under white officers in separate battalions. Slaveowners would receive up to $1,000 for each slave who enlisted; at the end of the war, the slaves would be freed and paid $50 for their service. The government of South Carolina rejected the proposal in May 1779.

528.14 *thirty for one.*] The ratio at which Continental currency traded for specie.

531.14–15 hewers . . . water] Joshua 9:23.

532.2 villain Matthews] See note 136.9.

536.19 * * *] This excerpt from Barton's journal is taken from *Proceedings of the New Jersey Historical Society, 1846–1847* (1848). Its editors wrote that they printed the manuscript of Barton's journal from June 8 to October 9, 1779, "excepting some unimportant or uninteresting details."

540.7 Powles Hook] Continental troops led by Major Henry Lee raided the British outpost at Paulus Hook, New Jersey (see note 174.33) on August 19, 1779, and captured 150 prisoners.

543.22 Isle of Groa] Île de Groix, off the southern coast of Brittany near Lorient.

560.26 K. B.] Knight of the Bath.

561.32 redan] A V-shaped earthwork fortification, with its point projecting toward the enemy.

561.38 carcasses] Incendiary shells.

562.5 matrosses] Assistant gunners; the rank was equivalent to a private in the infantry.

563.7–8 royals and Cohorns] Small mortars.

563.39 Monk's-corner] The engagement at Monck's Corner, South Carolina, was fought on April 14, 1780.

567.12 Captain Moultrie] Thomas Moultrie, brother of William Moultrie.

575.36–576.2 Charlestown . . . Falmouth] Charlestown, Massachusetts, was burned by the British during the battle of Bunker Hill on June 17, 1775. Lord Dunmore burned much of Norfolk, Virginia, on January 1, 1776. Falmouth, Massachusetts (now Portland, Maine) was burned during a raid by the Royal Navy on October 18, 1775.

576.6 fate of Mrs. Caldwell] Hannah Caldwell was shot to death by a British soldier in her house in Connecticut Farms (now Union), New Jersey, on June 7, 1780, during a raid by British and Hessian troops on Springfield, New Jersey. Her husband, the Rev. James Caldwell, was a Presbyterian minister known for his support of the Revolutionary cause.

576.16 Ladies of Philadelphia] Esther De Berdt Reed (1746–80), the wife of Joseph Reed, published a broadside, "Sentiments of an American Woman," in Philadelphia on June 10, 1780, in which she called for women to donate money to support the Continental army. By early July the Ladies' Association organized by Reed and 35 other Philadelphia women had raised more than $300,000 in Continental currency, then worth about $7,500 in specie. The funds were eventually used to make 2,000 linen shirts for soldiers.

577.11–12 battle . . . Thrasymene] In 217 BCE Carthaginians led by Hannibal ambushed and destroyed a Roman army at Lake Trasimene in central Italy. The story of the two mothers is told by Livy in Book XXII of *The History of Rome*.

579.33 deputy adjutant general] Otho Holland Williams.

583.35 displaying] Deploying.

600.17 Col. Robinson] Beverley Robinson (1721–92), a Loyalist officer who had owned an estate on the Hudson across from West Point.

607.8–9 choice in the mode] André asked to be executed by firing squad, which was considered a more honorable form of execution than death by hanging.

612.11 nothing but their rifles] The rifles used during the Revolutionary War lacked bayonet mounts and had a slower rate of fire than smoothbore muskets.

613.27 Field Officers] Officers above the rank of captain and below the rank of general.

629.7 the Legion] The British Legion, a Loyalist formation of cavalry and light infantry troops commanded by a British officer, Lieutenant Colonel Banastre Tarleton (1754–1833).

631.10 Mount Kemble] An encampment used by Pennsylvania troops outside of Morristown, New Jersey.

632.12   Espontoon] A short pike.

651.37–38   halted . . . eighty miles] Gates reached Hillsborough, North Carolina, 160 miles from Camden, on August 19, 1780, three days after the battle.

656.3   *Narrative of Arnold's Raid*] Jefferson's narrative was published in the *Virginia Gazette* on January 13, 1781.

663.3   *Robert Howe*] Howe (1732–86) was a major general in the Continental army.

663.15–16   execute . . . leaders] Howe reached Pompton, New Jersey, on January 27, 1781, and suppressed the mutiny; two of its leaders were then immediately court-martialed and shot.

665.1   armed Neutrality] Russia, Sweden, and Denmark formed a league of armed neutrality in 1780 designed to protect their merchant ships carrying timber and other naval supplies to France and Spain against seizure by the Royal Navy.

671.8–9   Lees . . . Haw] Cavalry commanded by Henry Lee defeated a Loyalist force at Haw River, North Carolina, on February 25, 1781, after the Loyalists mistook the approaching troops of Lee's Legion for men of the British Legion (see note 629.7); both formations wore green coats as part of their uniforms.

681.4–5   History . . . Carolina] *The History of the Revolution of South-Carolina, from a British Province to an Independent State* (1785), by David Ramsay (1749–1815).

682.19   General Screven's death] James Screven, a brigadier general in the Georgia militia, was killed in November 1778.

682.30–31   General Prevost . . . Colonel Prevost] Augustine Prevost (1723–86), commander of British forces in East Florida, and his younger brother, Marc Prevost.

683.19   (Vol. ii., page 2.)] The reference is to Ramsay's *The History of the Revolution of South-Carolina*.

685.24–25   Indians . . . Pickens] In March 1782 Brigadier General Andrew Pickens (1739–1817) of the South Carolina militia led an expedition against the Cherokee in northwestern South Carolina.

686.1–2   capitulation of Augusta] Brown surrendered the garrison at Augusta on June 5, 1781, to American forces commanded by Pickens and Lieutenant Colonel Henry Lee.

686.3   Colonel Grierson] James Grierson, a Georgia Loyalist.

689.27–28   *While . . . corruption*] 2 Peter 2:19.

702.3   *William Knox*] Knox (1732–1810) was undersecretary of state for the colonies, 1770–82, and also served as secretary of the province of New York.

703.15   bank . . . Financier] Congress appointed Robert Morris (1734–1806), a leading Philadelphia merchant, superintendent of finance on February 20, 1781, and on May 26 approved his proposed charter for the Bank of North America.

704.11   Point Comfort] The end of the peninsula between the York and James rivers, where Hampton Roads flows into Chesapeake Bay.

705.18   the Books] Public records removed from New York by Governor William Tryon in 1775. Some of the documents were returned in July 1781.

712.26   Hobkirk's Hill] Maryland and Virginia Continental troops had broken and fled during the American defeat at Hobkirk's Hill, South Carolina, on April 25, 1781.

722.22   saucissons] Large fascines.

724.7   Colonel Hamilton] Alexander Hamilton.

727.16–17 Secretary Nelson's] Thomas Nelson (1715–87), former secretary of the Virginia council and uncle of Thomas Nelson (1738–89), who served as governor of Virginia from June to November 1781.

743.23   General Amherst] Lieutenant General William Amherst, a younger brother of Lord Amherst, who had died in May 1781.

750.4   dear Mammy] Rawle addressed her diary to her mother, who had gone to New York City with her stepfather Samuel Shoemaker, a prominent Philadelphia Loyalist.

750.5   illuminated] In honor of the American victory at Yorktown.

761.2   volunteers of Ireland] A Loyalist regiment mainly recruited from among Irish deserters from the Continental army.

766.19–20 the King's Speech] In his speech at the opening of Parliament on November 27, 1781, George III pledged to continue the war in America despite the surrender at Yorktown.

767.9–10 reinforcements . . . sooner] Three infantry regiments arrived in Charleston, South Carolina, on June 3, 1781.

769.3   *Feilding . . . Denbigh*] Feilding was a distant relative of Basil Feilding, the sixth Earl of Denbigh.

769.15–16 Independence . . . America.] The letter from Carleton and Digby, dated August 2, 1782, formally notified Washington that Britain had opened peace negotiations with the American commissioners in Paris.

769.21–22   Victory . . . France]   In the battle of the Saints, fought in the West Indies between Guadeloupe and Dominica on April 12, 1782.

774.3   *Newburgh Address*]   The address was anonymously circulated among Continental army officers camped at Newburgh, New York, on March 10, 1783.

775.23–24   entreating memorials]   A delegation of officers from the Continental army presented a memorial to Congress on January 6, 1783, protesting its failure to pay them and asking that officers receive several years' full pay in lieu of the lifetime pensions at half pay granted them in 1780.

776.37   "mock . . . on."]   Cf. Proverbs 1:26.

778.3   *Joseph Jones*]   Jones (1727–1805) served as a Virginia delegate to Congress, 1777–78 and 1780–83.

778.19   a certain Gentleman]   Colonel Walter Stewart (c. 1756–96), a colonel of the Pennsylvania Line and former aide to Horatio Gates.

779.5   order of the 11th.]   In his order of March 11 Washington convened a meeting of officers at Newburgh on March 15, 1783, while expressing his disapproval of the call for a meeting on March 11 that was circulated along with the Newburgh Address.

786.4   THESE will give you]   Shaw included with his letter copies of the memorial submitted to Congress by the officers, the Newburgh Address, the proceedings of the meeting held on March 15, 1783, and Washington's address to the officers.

787.31   second anonymous address]   The second address, also written by John Armstrong and circulated on March 12, 1783, asserted that Washington's order on March 11 demonstrated sympathy with the aims and methods of the disaffected officers at Newburgh.

788.12   a worthy member]   Joseph Jones.

788.27   business of the day]   After Washington left the meeting, major generals Henry Knox and Israel Putnam introduced and carried a resolution strongly repudiating the anonymous address of March 10 and pledging the army's obedience to civil authority.

794.16   *President . . . answer*]   Mifflin's remarks were drafted by Thomas Jefferson.

796.3   *Margaret Caldwell*]   Caldwell was engaged to McHenry; they married on January 8, 1784.

Index

Library of Congress Cataloging-in-Publication Data

The American Revolution : writings from the War of Independence.
p. cm — (The Library of America ; 123)
Includes bibliographical references and index.
ISBN 1-883011-91-4 (alk. paper)
1. United States—History—Revolution, 1775–1783—Sources. 2. United
States—History—Revolution, 1775–1783—Personal narratives. I. Series.

E203 .A579 2001
973.3—dc21

00-045373

THE LIBRARY OF AMERICA SERIES

The Library of America helps to preserve our nation's literary heritage by publishing, and keeping permanently in print, authoritative editions of America's best and most significant writing. An independent nonprofit organization, it was founded in 1979 with seed money from the National Endowment for the Humanities and the Ford Foundation.

This book is set in 10 point Linotron Galliard,
a face designed for photocomposition by Matthew Carter
and based on the sixteenth-century face Granjon. The paper is
acid-free Ecusta Nyalite and meets the requirements for permanence
of the American National Standards Institute. The binding
material is Brillianta, a woven rayon cloth made by
Van Heek-Scholco Textielfabrieken, Holland.
The composition is by The Clarinda
Company. Printing and binding by
R.R.Donnelley & Sons Company.
Designed by Bruce Campbell.

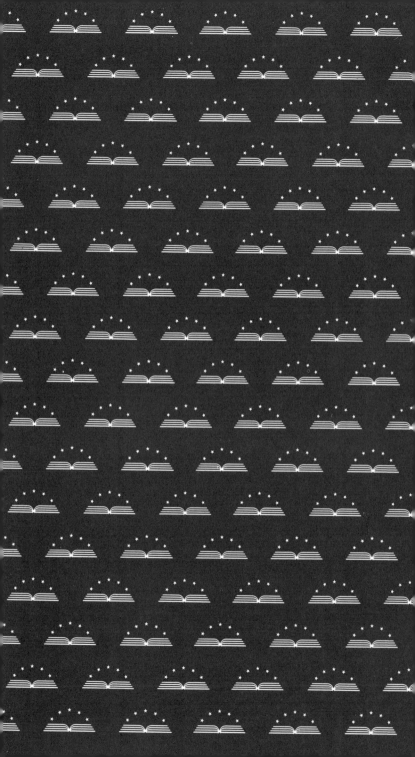